LIBRARY
St. Michael's College Prep H.S.
19292 El Toro Rd., Silverado, CA 92676

P9-EDF-045

10174

55 *Victorian Prose Writers Before 1867*, edited by William B. Thesing (1987)

56 *German Fiction Writers, 1914-1945*, edited by James Hardin (1987)

57 *Victorian Prose Writers After 1867*, edited by William B. Thesing (1987)

58 *Jacobean and Caroline Dramatists*, edited by Fredson Bowers (1987)

59 *American Literary Critics and Scholars, 1800-1850*, edited by John W. Rathbun and Monica M. Grecu (1987)

60 *Canadian Writers Since 1960, Second Series*, edited by W. H. New (1987)

61 *American Writers for Children Since 1960: Poets, Illustrators, and Nonfiction Authors*, edited by Glenn E. Estes (1987)

62 *Elizabethan Dramatists*, edited by Fredson Bowers (1987)

63 *Modern American Critics, 1920-1955*, edited by Gregory S. Jay (1988)

64 *American Literary Critics and Scholars, 1850-1880*, edited by John W. Rathbun and Monica M. Grecu (1988)

65 *French Novelists, 1900-1930*, edited by Catharine Savage Brosman (1988)

66 *German Fiction Writers, 1885-1913*, 2 parts, edited by James Hardin (1988)

67 *Modern American Critics Since 1955*, edited by Gregory S. Jay (1988)

68 *Canadian Writers, 1920-1959, First Series*, edited by W. H. New (1988)

69 *Contemporary German Fiction Writers, First Series*, edited by Wolfgang D. Elfe and James Hardin (1988)

70 *British Mystery Writers, 1860-1919*, edited by Bernard Benstock and Thomas F. Staley (1988)

71 *American Literary Critics and Scholars, 1880-1900*, edited by John W. Rathbun and Monica M. Grecu (1988)

72 *French Novelists, 1930-1960*, edited by Catharine Savage Brosman (1988)

73 *American Magazine Journalists, 1741-1850*, edited by Sam G. Riley (1988)

74 *American Short-Story Writers Before 1880*, edited by Bobby Ellen Kimbel, with the assistance of William E. Grant (1988)

75 *Contemporary German Fiction Writers, Second Series*, edited by Wolfgang D. Elfe and James Hardin (1988)

76 *Afro-American Writers, 1940-1955*, edited by Trudier Harris (1988)

77 *British Mystery Writers, 1920-1939*, edited by Bernard Benstock and Thomas F. Staley (1988)

78 *American Short-Story Writers, 1880-1910*, edited by Bobby Ellen Kimbel, with the assistance of William E. Grant (1988)

79 *American Magazine Journalists, 1850-1900*, edited by Sam G. Riley (1988)

80 *Restoration and Eighteenth-Century Dramatists, First Series*, edited by Paula R. Backscheider (1989)

81 *Austrian Fiction Writers, 1875-1913*, edited by James Hardin and Donald G. Daviau (1989)

82 *Chicano Writers, First Series*, edited by Francisco A. Lomelí and Carl R. Shirley (1989)

83 *French Novelists Since 1960*, edited by Catharine Savage Brosman (1989)

84 *Restoration and Eighteenth-Century Dramatists, Second Series*, edited by Paula R. Backscheider (1989)

85 *Austrian Fiction Writers After 1914*, edited by James Hardin and Donald G. Daviau (1989)

86 *American Short-Story Writers, 1910-1945, First Series*, edited by Bobby Ellen Kimbel (1989)

87 *British Mystery and Thriller Writers Since 1940, First Series*, edited by Bernard Benstock and Thomas F. Staley (1989)

88 *Canadian Writers, 1920-1959, Second Series*, edited by W. H. New (1989)

89 *Restoration and Eighteenth-Century Dramatists, Third Series*, edited by Paula R. Backscheider (1989)

90 *German Writers in the Age of Goethe, 1789-1832*, edited by James Hardin and Christoph E. Schweitzer (1989)

91 *American Magazine Journalists, 1900-1960, First Series*, edited by Sam G. Riley (1990)

92 *Canadian Writers, 1890-1920*, edited by W. H. New (1990)

93 *British Romantic Poets, 1789-1832, First Series*, edited by John R. Greenfield (1990)

94 *German Writers in the Age of Goethe: Sturm und Drang to Classicism*, edited by James Hardin and Christoph E. Schweitzer (1990)

95 *Eighteenth-Century British Poets, First Series*, edited by John Sitter (1990)

96 *British Romantic Poets, 1789-1832, Second Series*, edited by John R. Greenfield (1990)

97 *German Writers from the Enlightenment to Sturm und Drang, 1720-1764*, edited by James Hardin and Christoph E. Schweitzer (1990)

98 *Modern British Essayists, First Series*, edited by Robert Beum (1990)

99 *Canadian Writers Before 1890*, edited by W. H. New (1990)

100 *Modern British Essayists, Second Series*, edited by Robert Beum (1990)

101 *British Prose Writers, 1660-1800, First Series*, edited by Donald T. Siebert (1991)

102 *American Short-Story Writers, 1910-1945, Second Series*, edited by Bobby Ellen Kimbel (1991)

103 *American Literary Biographers, First Series*, edited by Steven Serafin (1991)

104 *British Prose Writers, 1660-1800, Second Series*, edited by Donald T. Siebert (1991)

105 *American Poets Since World War II, Second Series*, edited by R. S. Gwynn (1991)

106 *British Literary Publishing Houses, 1820-1880*, edited by Patricia J. Anderson and Jonathan Rose (1991)

107 *British Romantic Prose Writers, 1789-1832, First Series*, edited by John R. Greenfield (1991)

108 *Twentieth-Century Spanish Poets, First Series*, edited by Michael L. Perna (1991)

109 *Eighteenth-Century British Poets, Second Series*, edited by John Sitter (1991)

110 *British Romantic Prose Writers, 1789-1832, Second Series*, edited by John R. Greenfield (1991)

111 *American Literary Biographers, Second Series*, edited by Steven Serafin (1991)

112 *British Literary Publishing Houses, 1881-1965*, edited by Jonathan Rose and Patricia J. Anderson (1991)

113 *Modern Latin-American Fiction Writers, First Series*, edited by William Luis (1992)

114 *Twentieth-Century Italian Poets, First Series*, edited by Giovanna Wedel De Stasio, Glauco Cambon, and Antonio Illiano (1992)

115 *Medieval Philosophers*, edited by Jeremiah Hackett (1992)

116 *British Romantic Novelists, 1789-1832*, edited by Bradford K. Mudge (1992)

(Continued on back endsheets)

Dictionary of Literary Biography®
Yearbook: 1994

Dictionary of Literary Biography®
Yearbook: 1994

Edited by
James W. Hipp

George Garrett, Consulting Editor

A Bruccoli Clark Layman Book
Gale Research Inc.
Detroit, London

Printed in the United States of America

Published simultaneously in the United Kingdom
by Gale Research International Limited
(An affiliated company of Gale Research Inc.)

The paper used in this publication meets the minimum requirements
of American National Standard for Information Sciences–Permanence
Paper for Printed Library Materials, ANSI Z39.48-1984. ∞ ™

Library of Congress Catalog Card Number 94–075218

ISBN 0-8103-5705-4

The trademark **ITP** is used under license.

10 9 8 7 6 5 4 3 2 1

Contents

Plan of the Series...vii

Foreword xi

Acknowledgments ....

The 1994 Nobel Prize in Literature Kenzaburo Oe 3
Kiyohiko Tsuboi and Nobuko Tsuboi

The Year in Poetry, 1993 14
Robert McPhillips

The Year in Poetry, 1994 48
David R. Slavitt

The Year in Fiction 72
George Garrett

The Year in Literary Biography 95
William Foltz

The Year in Drama 121
Howard Kissel

The Year In Children's Books 131
Caroline C. Hunt

Book Reviewing in America VIII 150
George Garrett

Writers and their Copyright Holders: the WATCH project 176
Cathy Henderson and David Sutton

Letter from Japan 179
Kiyohiko Tsuboi and Nobuko Tsuboi

Building the New British Library at St Pancras 181
Charles Egleston

The University of South Carolina Press 186
Joyce Harrison

Conversations with Rare Book Dealers II: An Interview with Ralph Sipper 193

Conversations with Publishers II: An Interview with Charles Scribner III 200

Who Runs American Literature? 206
George Garrett

The Practice of Biography VIII: An Interview with Joan Mellen 224

Cleanth Brooks 236
    Mark Royden Winchell
    Tributes from Judith Farr and Hugh Kenner

Paxton Davis 253
    R. H. W. Dillard
    Tributes from George Garrett and William Hoffman

Ralph Waldo Ellison 261
    Leonard J. Deutsch

Seymour Lawrence 266
    Darren Harris-Fain
    Tributes from Thomas McGuane, Susan Minot, and Jayne Anne Phillips

Peter Taylor 272
    Mark Trainer
    Tributes from Richard Bausch, Madison Smartt Bell, Fred Chappell, George Garrett
        and Daniel O'Neill

Helen Wolff 281
    Darren Harris-Fain
    Tributes from Günter Grass and Amos Oz

Literary Awards and Honors Announced in 1994 287

Checklist: Contributions to Literary History and Biography 297
Necrology 299
Contributors 301
Index 305

Plan of the Series

. . . Almost the most prodigious asset of a country, and perhaps its most precious possession, is its native literary product — when that product is fine and noble and enduring.

Mark Twain*

The advisory board, the editors, and the publisher of the *Dictionary of Literary Biography* are joined in endorsing Mark Twain's declaration. The literature of a nation provides an inexhaustible resource of permanent worth. We intend to make literature and its creators better understood and more accessible to students and the reading public, while satisfying the standards of teachers and scholars.

To meet these requirements, *literary biography* has been construed in terms of the author's achievement. The most important thing about a writer is his writing. Accordingly, the entries in *DLB* are career biographies, tracing the development of the author's canon and the evolution of his reputation.

The purpose of *DLB* is not only to provide reliable information in a convenient format but also to place the figures in the larger perspective of literary history and to offer appraisals of their accomplishments by qualified scholars.

The publication plan for *DLB* resulted from two years of preparation. The project was proposed to Bruccoli Clark by Frederick C. Ruffner, president of the Gale Research Company, in November 1975. After specimen entries were prepared and typeset, an advisory board was formed to refine the entry format and develop the series rationale. In meetings held during 1976, the publisher, series editors, and advisory board approved the scheme for a comprehensive biographical dictionary of persons who contributed to North American literature. Editorial work on the first volume began in January 1977, and it was published in 1978. In order to make *DLB* more than a reference tool and to compile volumes that individually have claim to status as literary history, it was decided to organize vol-

*From an unpublished section of Mark Twain's autobiography, copyright by the Mark Twain Company

umes by topic, period, or genre. Each of these freestanding volumes provides a biographical-bibliographical guide and overview for a particular area of literature. We are convinced that this organization — as opposed to a single alphabet method — constitutes a valuable innovation in the presentation of reference material. The volume plan necessarily requires many decisions for the placement and treatment of authors who might properly be included in two or three volumes. In some instances a major figure will be included in separate volumes, but with different entries emphasizing the aspect of his career appropriate to each volume. Ernest Hemingway, for example, is represented in *American Writers in Paris, 1920–1939* by an entry focusing on his expatriate apprenticeship; he is also in *American Novelists, 1910–1945* with an entry surveying his entire career. Each volume includes a cumulative index of the subject authors and articles. Comprehensive indexes to the entire series are planned.

With volume ten in 1982 it was decided to enlarge the scope of *DLB*. By the end of 1986 twenty-one volumes treating British literature had been published, and volumes for Commonwealth and Modern European literature were in progress. The series has been further augmented by the *DLB Yearbooks* (since 1981) which update published entries and add new entries to keep the *DLB* current with contemporary activity. There have also been *DLB Documentary Series* volumes which provide biographical and critical source materials for figures whose work is judged to have particular interest for students. One of these companion volumes is entirely devoted to Tennessee Williams.

We define literature as the *intellectual commerce of a nation:* not merely as belles lettres but as that ample and complex process by which ideas are generated, shaped, and transmitted. *DLB* entries are not limited to "creative writers" but extend to other figures who in their time and in their way influenced the mind of a people. Thus the series encompasses historians, journalists, publishers, and screenwriters. By this means readers of *DLB* may be aided to perceive literature not as cult scripture in the keeping of intellectual high priests but firmly positioned at the center of a nation's life.

DLB includes the major writers appropriate to each volume and those standing in the ranks immediately behind them. Scholarly and critical counsel has been sought in deciding which minor figures to include and how full their entries should be. Wherever possible, useful references are made to figures who do not warrant separate entries.

Each *DLB* volume has a volume editor responsible for planning the volume, selecting the figures for inclusion, and assigning the entries. Volume editors are also responsible for preparing, where appropriate, appendices surveying the major periodicals and literary and intellectual movements for their volumes, as well as lists of further readings. Work on the series as a whole is coordinated at the Bruccoli Clark Layman editorial center in Columbia, South Carolina, where the editorial staff is responsible for accuracy of the published volumes.

One feature that distinguishes *DLB* is the illustration policy – its concern with the iconography of literature. Just as an author is influenced by his surroundings, so is the reader's understanding of the author enhanced by a knowledge of his environment. Therefore *DLB* volumes include not only drawings, paintings, and photographs of authors, often depicting them at various stages in their careers, but also illustrations of their families and places where they lived. Title pages are regularly reproduced in facsimile along with dust jackets for modern authors. The dust jackets are a special feature of *DLB* because they often document better than anything else the way in which an author's work was perceived in its own time. Specimens of the writers' manuscripts are included when feasible.

Samuel Johnson rightly decreed that "The chief glory of every people arises from its authors." The purpose of the *Dictionary of Literary Biography* is to compile literary history in the surest way available to us – by accurate and comprehensive treatment of the lives and work of those who contributed to it.

The *DLB* Advisory Board

Foreword

The *Dictionary of Literary Biography Yearbook* is guided by the same principles that have provided the basic rationale for the entire *DLB* series: 1) the literature of a nation represents an inexhaustible resource of permanent worth; 2) the surest way to trace the outlines of literary history is by a comprehensive treatment of the lives and works of those who contributed to it; and 3) the greatest service the series can provide is to make literary achievement better understood and more accessible to students and the literate public, while serving the needs of scholars. In keeping with those principles, the *Yearbook* has been planned to augment *DLB* by reflecting the vitality of contemporary literature and summarizing current literary activity. The librarian, scholar, or student attempting to stay informed of literary developments is faced with an endless task. The purpose of *DLB Yearbook* is to serve those readers while at the same time enlarging the scope of *DLB*.

The *Yearbook* is divided into two sections: articles about the past year's literary events or topics; and obituaries and tributes. The updates and new author entries previously included as supplements to published *DLB* volumes are no longer included. (These essays will appear in future *DLB* volumes.) Among the pieces included in the articles section are a report on the New British Library at St Pancras; an article on the WATCH Copyright Project; a letter from Japan; an article on the University of South Carolina Press; an inquiry into who runs American

literature; interviews with publisher Charles Scribner III, rare-book dealer Ralph Sipper, and biographer Joan Mellen; and extended discussions of the year's work in fiction, drama, children's books, poetry, and literary biography. Because poetry was not included in last year's *Yearbook,* the poetry segment this year has been expanded to include work from both 1993 and 1994. The *Yearbook* continues a survey begun in 1987, an in-depth examination of the practice of book reviewing in America. In addition, the *Yearbook* features the Nobel speeches of the winner of the 1994 Nobel Prize in literature, Kenzaburo Oe.

The death of a literary figure prompts an assessment of his achievements and reputation. The obituaries section marks the passing of Cleanth Brooks, Paxton Davis, Ralph Ellison, Seymour Lawrence, Peter Taylor, and Helen Wolff.

Each *Yearbook* includes a list of literary prizes and awards, a necrology, and a checklist of literary histories and biographies published during the year.

This *Yearbook* continues the *Dictionary of Literary Biography Yearbook* Awards for novel, first novel, volume of short stories, poetry, and literary biography.

From the outset, the *DLB* series has undertaken to compile literary history as it is revealed in the lives and works of authors. The *Yearbook* supports that commitment, providing a useful and necessary current record.

Dictionary of Literary Biography®
Yearbook: 1994

The 1994 Nobel Prize in Literature
Kenzaburo Oe
(31 January 1935 –)

Kiyohiko Tsuboi
Okayama University

and

Nobuko Tsuboi
Toyo University

The Japanese titles of books by Oe have been transliterated into English.

SELECTED BOOKS: *Lavish are the Dead* (Tokyo: Bungei-shunju-sha, 1958);

Nipping in the Bud, Shooting the Young (Tokyo: Kodan-sha, 1958);

Jump Before Look (Tokyo: Shincho-sha, 1958);

Our Age (Tokyo: Chuokoron-sha, 1959);

Night, Walk Slow, (Tokyo: Chuokoron-sha, 1959);

Holidays of a Lonely Boy (Tokyo: Shincho-sha, 1960);

Disgrace of a Youth (Tokyo: Bungei-shunju-sha, 1960);

The Voice of Europe, the Voice of Ours (Tokyo: Mainichi Newspaper Press, 1962);

The Youth Who Came Late (Tokyo: Shincho-sha, 1962);

A Sexual Being (Tokyo: Shincho-sha, 1963);

The Adventures in the Daily Life (Tokyo: Bungei-shunju-sha, 1964);

A Personal Matter (Tokyo: Shincho-sha, 1964; English translation by John Nathan, New York: Grove, 1968);

Tight Rope (Tokyo: Bungei-shunju-sha, 1965);

Hiroshima Notes (Tokyo: Iwanami-shoten, 1965);

The Silent Cry (Tokyo: Kodan-sha, 1967; English translation by John Bester, Tokyo: Kodansha International, 1974);

Enduring Will (Tokyo: Shincho-sha, 1968);

Teach Us to Outgrow Our Madness (Tokyo: Shincho-sha, 1969; English translation by John Nathan, New York: Grove, 1977);

Fragile Human Beings (Tokyo: Kodan-sha, 1970);

The Imaginative Power in the Atomic Age (Tokyo: Shincho-sha, 1970);

Okinawa Notes (Tokyo: Iwanami-shotent, 1970);

The Day When Whales Shall Perish (Tokyo: Shincho-sha, 1972);

The Day He Himself Shall Wipe My Tears (Tokyo: Kodan-sha, 1972);

The Deluge Flooded into My Soul (Tokyo: Shincho-sha, 1973);

Our Post-War Days (Tokyo: Kodan-sha, 1973);

Situation (Tokyo: Iwanami-shoten, 1974);

Literary Notes (Tokyo: Shincho-sha, 1974);

By Words (Tokyo: Shincho-sha, 1976);

The Pinch Runner Memorandum (Tokyo: Shincho-sha, 1976; English translation by Michiko Wilson and Michael K. Wilson, Armonk, New York: M.E. Sharpe, 1994);

The Craft of the Novel (Tokyo: Iwanami-shoten, 1978);

One Who Wishes to Express Himself (Tokyo: Shincho-sha, 1978);

Games in Our Age (Tokyo: Shincho-sha, 1979);

The Women Who Listen to the Rain Tree (Tokyo: Shincho-sha, 1983);

Wake Up, the New Generation (Tokyo: Kodan-sho, 1983);

Kenzaburo Oe (photograph © The Nobel Foundation)

Reading a Japanese Humanist, Prof. Kazuo Watanabe
  Tokyo: Iwanami-shoten, 1984);
To Kill a Tree (Tokyo: Bungei-shunju-sha, 1984);
The Definition of Life or on Situation Again (Tokyo:
  Iwanami-shoten, 1985);
The Tricks of the Novel and Intellectual Pleasure (Tokyo:
  Shincho-sha, 1985);
A Man Who Was Bitten by a Hippo (Tokyo: Bungei-
  shunju-sha, 1985);
M/T and a Mysterious Story of the Woods (Tokyo:
  Iwanami-shoten, 1986);
A Letter to the Good Old Days (Tokyo: Kodan-sha,
  1987);
The Quilp Army Corps (Tokyo: Iwanami-shoten,
  1988);
Toward the New Literature (Tokyo: Iwanami-shoten,
  1988);
The Last Novel (Tokyo: Kodan-sha, 1988);
Relatives of My Life (Tokyo: Sincho-sha, 1989);
The Asylum Tower (Tokyo: Iwanami-shoten, 1990);
The Quiet Life (Tokyo: Kodan-sha, 1990);
A Planet Asylum (Tokyo: Iwanami-shoten, 1991);

A Flaming Tree: Part I, When the Savior Was Beaten
  (Tokyo: Sincho-sha, 1993);
A Flaming Tree: Part II, Vacillation (Tokyo: Sincho-
  sha, 1994);
The Complete Works of Kenzaburo Oe, 12 volumes
  (Tokyo: Sincho-sha, 1994).

OTHER: *The Crazy Iris and other stories of the atomic af-
  termath,* edited, with an introduction, by Oe
  (Tokyo: Sincho-sha, 1984; New York: Grove
  Press, 1985).

Kenzaburo Oe became the second Japanese writer to win the Nobel Prize in literature when the award was announced on 13 October 1994. As a writer and philosopher, Oe has lived through and contributed to the drastic changes in Japanese culture and society brought about by the experiences of World War II. The unconditional surrender of the Japanese Imperial Empire to the United States and other Allied nations marked not only the most devastating defeat in her history, but also the beginning of a colossal change in the philosophy of the country and the Japanese people. Many Japanese people, especially young men of Oe's generation, were greatly affected and influenced by the American occupation and the resulting influx of American and other Western cultures and ideas. The philosophies of the European Enlightenment tradition began to compete and take the place of the traditional thought of Buddhism and Confucianism. Oe's generation found it impossible to produce traditional literature like that of Yasunari Kawabata (1899–1972), the first Japanese winner of the Nobel Prize in literature (1968), known for his subtle, exotic Japanese sensibility, but instead produced more radical, indelicate, rude, and modern writers such as Oe, Takashi Kaiko, and Shintaro Ishihara.

When compared to that of his predecessors, Oe's style is somewhat uncouth and impenetrable unless readers follow his writings logically and painstakingly. The difficulty arises from Oe's attachment to French and other Western writers and the allegorical and metaphoric treatment of his subjects. His works are also challenging because their fictional world is a filthy, tortured, ugly place.

Oe was born on 31 January 1935 in a remote mountain village in Ehime Prefecture on Shikoku Island, the smallest of the four main Japanese islands. After graduating from a local high school, Oe studied at the University of Tokyo, where he wrote stories published in the student newspaper and little magazines. He also wrote plays that were performed by a university theatrical group.

In 1957 he published the short story "A Strange Job" in the university newspaper and was awarded the Satsuki Prize. The story recounts the experience of a college student who is hired for the "strange job" of killing dogs at a hospital. Despite the almost absurd cruelty, he tries to accomplish the job along with other students, but they find themselves unpaid for their work. The job ends as only a waste of labor. Masato Ara, a noted critic and a judge for the prize, praised the story for its portrayal of the nihilistic and absurdist tendencies of contemporary Japanese youth.

The same year he published the story "Lavish are the Dead" in *Bungakukai,* one of leading literary magazines in Japan. The narrator, as in "A Strange Job," is a university student in need of a job. He is hired at the medical school to transport dead bodies for an anatomy class from one location to another. His coworker is a female student who is working to raise money for an abortion. The man in charge of the mortuary is proud of his work, although his cynical motto is "the more births, the more deaths." In this ironic framework of life and death, Oe depicts the impotent and weary life of youth during the postwar period.

In 1958 he published "The Catch" in *Bungakukai* and won the Akutagawa Prize. A World War II story of a Japanese boy and a captured black American pilot, "The Catch" is a strange story of bonding between the boy and the pilot. Held as a prisoner in a remote village, the American pilot reacts to his impending execution by taking the boy as a hostage. The boy's father finally kills the pilot and frees the boy, but only after the boy has experienced life in a closed situation and the stark reality of death. The Akutagawa Prize propelled Oe into being regarded as the most important young Japanese writer.

In 1959 Oe graduated from the University of Tokyo with a degree in French literature, writing his senior paper on Jean-Paul Sartre. His concentration on French thought reinforced his reputation as an existentialist with a Japanese sensibility.

In *Our Age* (1959) a university student majoring in French is living in a despairing relationship with a prostitute. He writes a paper to escape from his closed situation and wins a scholarship to study in France for three years. An Arabian friend tells him that the French publisher who sponsors the scholarships is extremely conservative, and therefore to accept the scholarship will help the cause of the conservative power establishment. Meanwhile, his brother is a member of a band called The Unlucky Young Men, which unsuccessfully attempts to attack "the Quiet Man" (the emperor) through its music. The student eventually loses the scholarship and again falls into the closed situation. This story was criticized for its description of degraded morality. In the book Oe makes use of sex as a tool to understand society. He divides men into two groups: the sexual men and the political men. The former align themselves with the establishment, while the latter confront the status quo. By describing a sexual man, Oe was attempting to describe and change his contemporaries, who were meekly assenting to the U.S.-Japan Security Treaty establishment. Generally, in Oe's fiction sex and politics are treated as two opposed ideas, and his protagonists tend to grow from sexual men into political men.

In 1960 he aggressively opposed the U.S.-Japan Security Treaty and emphasized his beliefs in "Sovereignty in people" and "Renunciation of war," two principles written in the Japanese constitution. In 1961 he wrote two stories, "Seventeen" and "The Death of a Political Youth." Both are based on the incident of the fatal stabbing of Mr. Asanuma, chairman of the Japan Socialist Party, by an ultra-conservative boy. For these stories Oe was severely challenged by the conservative Right, and even in the 1990s the latter story is not printed in any of his collections.

After his son, Hikari, was born in 1963 with a congenitally malformed skull, Oe visited Hiroshima. There he was deeply impressed by a conversation with a doctor who had treated the victims of the bomb. The talk led Oe to live on courageously with his disabled son, whom doctors had advised Oe and his wife to let die. *A Personal Matter* (1964) is the fictional rendering of his struggle to come to terms with his son's disability. The protagonist, a young man nicknamed "Bird," is a failed graduate student in English at a national university graduate school who has married a daughter of one of his professors. He finds a job teaching at a preparatory school through the help of his father-in-law but always dreams of escaping from his miserable reality to Africa. When the couple's first child is born with a malformed skull, as was Oe's own son, Bird suffers through many things and finally comes to the decision to spend the rest of his life together with his son. This too-optimistic and moralistic ending was controversial. Yukio Mishima praised the novel in general but said that he was disappointed in the ending. The short story "Aghwee the Sky Monster," published half a year before the novel and which covers much of the same material, ends in a very different manner. A composer called "D" kills his son (who has a malformed skull) by feeding him

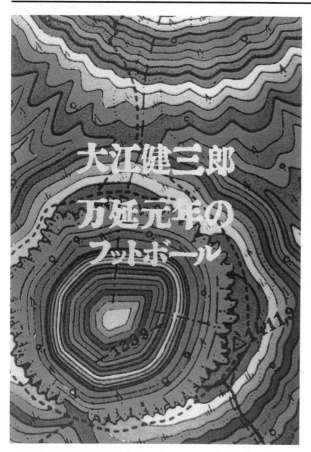

Slipcover for Oe's The Silent Cry, *an allegorical novel about the decline of tradition within a rural family*

only sweetened water instead of milk. After the child's death, the composer begins to see an illusionary baby, whom he calls Agwhee, clad in white and descending from the sky. The composer is killed in a traffic accident, and the story does not make it clear whether the composer brought about his own death or met with an accident in trying to help the nonexistent baby. Some studies, most of them unconvincing, have been made contrasting John Updike's *Rabbit, Run* (1960) with *A Personal Matter,* discussing the common elements between the two novels.

In 1965 he visited Harvard University to attend a literary seminar, his first visit to the United States. After *A Personal Matter* Oe changed his writing style drastically and published a highly metaphoric and allegorical novel, *The Silent Cry,* in 1967. The novel is set in a remote mountain village, as are many of his stories and novels, and the story covers the years from the farmers' riot in 1890 to the U.S.-Japan Security Treaty in 1960, criticizing the quasi-modernization of Japan. One of the protagonists, Mitsuzaburo Negoro, a descendant of an old family,

is making a living by translating foreign books while living with an alcoholic wife and a disabled son. His brother Takashi, who had been in the United States working in the theater, comes back to Japan. The two brothers travel home to Shikoku, the remote mountain village, in order to agitate the villagers to attack a Korean entrepreneur and to liberate the village from his oppressive grasp. Their attempt fails. Takashi commits suicide because of his guilt over his incestuous relationship with his retarded sister. Mitsu determines to go to Africa to start his new life with his wife and son. This story of the deteriorated old family in a fictitious mountain village, full of mythic allusions and fantastic symbolism, is reminiscent of William Faulkner's Yoknapatawpha stories and of such old families as the Satoris and the Compsons.

In 1968 Oe traveled to Australia and the United States, and back in Japan he visited Okinawa, where the last land battle of the Pacific theater in World War II was fought, and he wrote *Okinawa Notes* (1970). In this book Oe's anti-atomic bomb and antiwar beliefs become more distinctive and solid. In November 1968 the malformed skull of his son was operated on successfully. Oe redetermined to live with his son and his faith in democracy.

In *Deluge Flooded into My Soul* (1973) a man named Isana (meaning "whale") Oki lives in the atomic-bomb shelter with his mentally handicapped son, Jin, who can discriminate among fifty different birdcalls. They are to survive the coming doomsday by relying on the woods and the whales. Then a group of armed young men calling themselves the Liberty Fleet comes and persuades them to join the group in sailing out to sea and facing the end of the world. They live in a kind of commune, but as a result of the betrayal of some members of the group, they are seized by the police. Jin, who once refused to survive, now grows powerful enough to be the leader of the group and leaves his father behind. Isana stays in the shelter awaiting the end of the world. In this allegorical novel Oe presents the nuclear age, where the fate of the human race is to perish.

In 1973 Oe visited the Soviet Union to attend a writers' conference. In 1974 he signed the statement requesting the liberation of Soviet writer Aleksandr Solzhenitzyn. In 1975 he staged a hunger strike for Kim Jiha, a Korean poet, demanding his release from government custody. Such political activities were sometimes severely criticized as subjective, ineffectual, and irresponsible gestures of an intellectual.

In 1976 he was invited to El Colegio de Mexico to lecture on postwar trends in Japanese thought. From this experience was born *Games in Our Age* (1979), which consists of six letters to the narrator's twin sister. Through these letters the narrator tells of the myth and history of his so-called age=nation=microcosms. He is the son of a Shinto priest and is destined to write for posterity, while his sister is to be the necromancer for the destroyer who had built a village at the end of the feudal age. The destroyer survives through death and rebirth to the present days, having invented a census-registration system for taxation and fighting imperial Japan. In this highly allegorical novel, and elsewhere in his works, Oe has made use of Gothic letters to emphasize protagonists as Faulkner used italics (since Japanese is usually written lengthways from top to bottom, it is not possible to use italics). This has been criticized as a lengthy, boring story and a highly intellectual, anthropological puzzle. Thus Oe wrote *M/T and a Mysterious Story of the Woods* (1986), in which the same story was again told in language easy enough for children to understand. The child narrator tells the myth and history of the village, which his grandmother had told him (*M* stands for *matriarch,* and *T* stands for *trickster*).

In 1983 Oe wrote *The Women Who Listen to the Rain Tree,* a collection of stories using the rain tree as a metaphor. The narrator, who participates in a seminar at the East-West Center at the University of Hawaii, meets an old college classmate and his girlfriend. The rain tree in the garden of the seminar house symbolizes the grief of the narrator. In *Wake Up, the New Generation* (1983) he wrote about his handicapped son and his growth.

A Man Who Was Bitten by a Hippo (1985) is a collection of short stories based on an incident caused by the ultraradical leftist student group called the United Red Army. This group is again used in *The Quilp Army Corps* (1988), *The Deluge Flooded into my Soul* (1973), and *The Pinch Runner Memorandum* (1976). In *The Quilp Army Corps* the narrator, a high-school student, becomes involved in an in-group fight between radical leftists and witnesses an accidental murder. With the help of his father and his handicapped brother, the strongly disturbed narrator survives the impact of the violence and grows into manhood.

The chief motifs of Oe's recent works, and indeed throughout his entire career, are his faith in democracy without war and the saving of human souls through the perspectives of the handicapped and of the people involved with them. In a sense he has been writing and rewriting one book all his life.

In an interview given after he was awarded the Nobel Prize, Oe said that he has just finished writing *A Flaming Green Tree,* the last novel in a trilogy; he called this book the last novel he would write and said that he must find some other artistic form or genre by which to express himself.

When the Japanese government offered Oe the Culture Medal, he turned it down, saying that Japan is still a monarchy under the emperor and that he could not accept the medal from a government that supports such an establishment.

References:

Masaki Enomoto, *Kenzaburo Oe – Theme and Motif of 1980s* (Tokyo: Shinbi-sha, 1989);

Takao Ichijo, *The World of Kenzaburo Oe* (Tokyo: Izumi-Shoin, 1985);

Izuo Kuroko, *A Study of Kenzaburo Oe / Philosophy of Woods and Principles of Living* (Tokyo: Sairyu-sha, 1989);

Susan J. Napier, *Escape from the Wasteland: Romaticism and Realism in the Fiction of Mishima Yukio and Oe Kenzaburo* (Cambridge, Mass.: Harvard University Press, 1991);

Shigeru Shinohara, *Dictionary of Kenzaburo Oe's Literature* (Tokyo: Studio VI, 1984);

David Streitfeld, "Japanese Writer Wins Nobel," *Washington Post,* 14 October 1994, pp. F1–F4;

Samuel Yokoji Yoshiko, Yoshio Iwamoto, and Katsuhiko Takeda, eds., *The Literature of Kenzaburo Oe: Evaluations Abroad* (Tokyo: Sorin-sha, 1987).

NOBEL BANQUET STATEMENT

Kenzaburo Oe

I am a strange Japanese who spent his infancy and boyhood under the overwhelming influence of Nils Holgersson. So great was Nils' influence on me that there was a time I could name Sweden's beautiful locales better than those of my own country.

Nils' ponderous weight extended to my literary predilections. I turned a cold shoulder to "The Tale of Genji." I felt closer to Selma Lagerlöf and respected her more than Lady Murasaki, the author of this celebrated work. However, thanks again to Nils and his friends, I have rediscovered the attraction to "The Tale of Genji." Nils' winged comrades carried me there.

Genji, the protagonist of the classic tale, bids a flock of geese he sees in flight to search for his wife's departed soul which has failed to appear even in his dreams.

The destination of the soul: this is what I, led on by Nils Holgersson, came to seek in the literature of Western Europe. I fervently hope that my pursuit, as a Japanese, of literature and culture will, in some small measure, repay Western Europe for the light it has shed upon the human condition. Perhaps my winning the Prize has availed me of one such opportunity. Still, so many gifts of thought and insight keep coming, and I have hardly begun to do anything in return. This banquet, too, is another gift which I accept with deep gratitude. I thank you.

NOBEL LECTURE 1994

Kenzaburo Oe

Japan, the Ambiguous, and Myself

During the last catastrophic World War, I was a little boy and lived in a remote wooded valley on Shikoku Island in the Japanese Archipelago, thousands of miles away from here. At that time there were two books by which I was really fascinated: *The Adventures of Huckleberry Finn* and *The Wonderful Adventures of Nils*. The whole world was then engulfed by waves of horror. By reading *Huckleberry Finn* I felt I was able to justify my act of going into the mountain forest at night and sleeping among the trees with a sense of security which I could never find indoors. The protagonist of *The Adventures of Nils* is transformed into a little creature, understands birds' language and makes an adventurous journey. I derived from the story sensuous pleasures of various kinds. Firstly, living as I was in a deep wood on the Island of Shikoku just as my ancestors had done long ago, I had a revelation that this world and this way of life there were truly liberating. Secondly, I felt sympathetic and identified myself with Nils, a naughty little boy, who, while traversing Sweden, collaborating with and fighting for the wild geese, transforms himself into a boy, still innocent, yet full of confidence as well as modesty. On coming home at last, Nils speaks to his parents. I think that the pleasure I derived from the story at its highest level lies in the language, because I felt purified and uplifted by speaking along with Nils. His words run as follows (in French and English translation): "Maman, Papa! Je suis grand, je suis de nouveau un homme!" cria-t-il. "Mother and father!" he cried. "I'm a big boy. I'm a human being again!"

I was fascinated by the phrase "je suis de nouveau un homme!" in particular. As I grew up, I was continually to suffer hardships in different realms of life – in my family, in my relationship to Japanese society and in my way of living at large in the latter half of the twentieth century. I have survived by representing these sufferings of mine in the form of the novel. In that process I have found myself repeating, almost sighing, "je suis de nouveau un homme!" Speaking like this as regards myself is perhaps inappropriate to this place and to this occasion. However, please allow me to say that the fundamental style of my writing has been to start from my personal matters and then to link it up with society, the state and the world. I hope you will forgive me for talking about my personal matters a little further.

Half a century ago, while living in the depth of that forest, I read *The Adventures of Nils* and felt within it two prophecies. One was that I might one day become able to understand the language of birds. The other was that I might one day fly off with my beloved wild geese – preferably to Scandinavia.

After I got married, the first child born to us was mentally handicapped. We named him *Hikari*, meaning "Light" in Japanese. As a baby he responded only to the chirps of wild birds and never to human voices. One summer when he was six years old we were staying at our country cottage. He heard a pair of water rails (*Rallus aquaticus*) warbling from the lake beyond a grove, and he said with the voice of a commentator on a recording of wild birds: "They are water rails." This was the first moment my son ever uttered human words. It was from then on that my wife and I began having verbal communication with our son.

Hikari now works at a vocational training centre for the handicapped, an institution based on ideas we learnt from Sweden. In the meantime he has been composing works of music. Birds were the originators that occasioned and mediated his composition of human music. On my behalf *Hikari* has thus accomplished the prophecy that I might one day understand the language of birds. I must say also that my life would have been impossible but for my wife with her abundant female force and wisdom. She has been the very incarnation of Akka, the leader of Nils's wild geese. Together with her I have flown to Stockholm and the second of the prophecies has also, to my utmost delight, now been realised.

Kawabata Yasunari, the first Japanese writer who stood on this platform as a winner of the Nobel Prize for Literature, delivered a lecture entitled *Japan, the Beautiful, and Myself*. It was at once very beautiful and *vague*. I have used the English word *vague* as an equivalent of that word in Japanese *aimaina*. This Japanese adjective could have several alternatives for its English translation. The kind of vagueness that Kawabata adopted deliberately is implied in the title itself of his lecture. It can be transliterated as "myself *of* beautiful Japan." The vagueness of the whole title derives from the Japanese particle "no" (literally "of ") linking "Myself" and "Beautiful Japan."

The vagueness of the title leaves room for various interpretations of its implications. It can imply "myself as a part of beautiful Japan," the particle "no" indicating the relationship of the noun following it to the noun preceding it as one of possession, belonging or attachment. It can also imply "beautiful Japan and myself," the particle in this case linking the two nouns in apposition, as indeed they are in the English title of Kawabata's lecture translated by one of the most eminent American specialists of Japanese literature. He translates "Japan, the beautiful *and* myself." In this expert translation the *traduttore* (translator) is not in the least a *traditore* (betrayer).

Under that title Kawabata talked about a unique kind of mysticism which is found not only in Japanese thought but also more widely Oriental thought. By "unique" I mean here a tendency towards Zen Buddhism. Even as a twentieth-century writer Kawabata depicts his state of mind in terms of the poems written by medieval Zen monks. Most of these poems are concerned with the linguistic impossibility of telling truth. According to such poems words are confined within their closed shells. The readers can not expect that words will ever come out of these poems and get through to us. One can never understand or feel sympathetic towards these Zen poems except by giving oneself up and willingly penetrating into the closed shells of those words.

Why did Kawabata boldly decide to read those extremely esoteric poems in Japanese before the audience in Stockholm? I look back almost with nostalgia upon the straightforward bravery which he attained towards the end of his distinguished career and with which he made such a confession of his faith. Kawabata had been an artistic pilgrim for decades during which he produced a host of masterpieces. After those years of his pilgrimage, only by making a confession as to how he was fascinated by

Front cover for the U.S. paperback edition of Oe's autobiographical novel about a young composer's struggle to come to terms with his disabled son

such inaccessible Japanese poems that baffle any attempt fully to understand them, was he able to talk about "Japan, the Beautiful, and Myself," that is, about the world in which he lived and the literature which he created.

It is noteworthy, furthermore, that Kawabata concluded his lecture as follows:

> My works have been described as works of emptiness, but it is not to be taken for the nihilism of the West. The spiritual foundation would seem to be quite different. Dogen entitled his poem about the seasons "Innate Reality," and even as he sang of the beauty of the seasons he was deeply immersed in Zen. (Translation by Edward Seidensticker)

Here also I detect a brave and straightforward self-assertion. On the one hand Kawabata identifies himself as belonging essentially to the tradition of Zen philosophy and æsthetic sensibilities pervading the classical literature of the Orient. Yet on the other he goes out of his way to differentiate emptiness as an attribute of his works from the nihilism of the West. By doing so he was whole-heartedly addressing the coming generations of mankind with whom Alfred Nobel entrusted his hope and faith.

To tell you the truth, rather than with Kawabata my compatriot who stood here twenty-six years ago, I feel more spiritual affinity with the Irish poet William Butler Yeats, who was awarded a Nobel Prize for Literature seventy-one years ago when he was at about the same age as me. Of course I would not presume to rank myself with the poetic genius Yeats. I am merely a humble follower living in a country far removed from his. As William Blake, whose work Yeats revalued and restored to the high place it holds in this century, once wrote: "Across Europe & Asia to China & Japan like lightnings."

During the last few years I have been engaged in writing a trilogy which I wish to be the culmination of my literary activities. So far the first two parts have been published and I have recently finished writing the third and final part. It is entitled in Japanese *A Flaming Green Tree*. I am indebted for this title to a stanza from Yeats' poem "Vacillation":

A tree there is that from its topmost bough
Is half all glittering flame and half all green
Abounding foliage moistened with the dew . . .
                    (W. B. Yeats, "Vacillation," 11–13)

In fact my trilogy is soaked in the overflowing influence of Yeats's poems as a whole. On the occasion of Yeats's winning the Nobel Prize the Irish Senate proposed a motion to congratulate him, which contained the following sentences:

> . . . the recognition which the nation has gained, as a prominent contributor to the world's culture, through his success.
> . . . a race that hitherto had not been accepted into the comity of nations.
> . . . Our civilisation will be assessed on the name of Senator Yeats.
> . . . there will always be the danger that there may be a stampeding of people who are sufficiently removed from insanity in enthusiasm for destruction. (The Nobel Prize: Congratulations to Senator Yeats)

Yeats is the writer in whose wake I would like to follow. I would like to do so for the sake of another nation that has now been "accepted into the comity of nations' but rather on account of the technology in electrical engineering and its manufacture of au-

tomobiles. Also I would like to do so as a citizen of such a nation which was stampeded into "insanity in enthusiasm for destruction' both on its own soil and on that of the neighbouring nations.

As someone living in the present world such as this one and sharing bitter memories of the past imprinted on my mind, I cannot utter in unison with Kawabata the phrase "Japan, the Beautiful, and Myself." A moment ago I touched upon the "vagueness" of the title and content of Kawabata's lecture. In the rest of my lecture I would like to use the word "ambiguous" in accordance with the distinction made by the eminent British poet Kathleen Raine; she once said of William Blake that he was not so much vague as ambiguous. I cannot talk about myself otherwise than by saying "Japan, the Ambiguous, and Myself."

My observation is that after one hundred and twenty years of its modernisation since the opening of the country, present-day Japan is split between two opposite poles of ambiguity. I too am living as a writer with this polarisation imprinted on me like a deep scar.

This ambiguity which is so powerful and penetrating that it splits both the state and its people is evident in various ways. The modernisation of Japan has been orientated toward learning from and imitating the West. Yet Japan is situated in Asia and has firmly maintained its traditional culture. The ambiguous orientation of Japan drove the country into the position of an invader in Asia. On the other hand, the culture of modern Japan, which implied being thoroughly open to the West, long remained something obscure that was forever inscrutable to the West or at least that impeded understanding by the West. What was more, Japan was driven into isolation from other Asian countries, not only politically but also socially and culturally.

In the history of modern Japanese literature the writers most sincere and aware of their mission were those "post-war writers" who came onto the literary scene immediately after the last War, deeply wounded by the catastrophe yet full of hope for a rebirth. They tried with great pains to make up for the inhuman atrocities committed by Japanese military forces in Asian countries, as well as to bridge the profound gaps that existed not only between the developed countries of the West and Japan but also between African and Latin American countries and Japan. Only by doing so did they think that they could seek with some humility reconciliation with the rest of the world. It has always been my aspiration to cling to the very end of the line of that literary tradition inherited from those writers.

The contemporary state of Japan and its people in their post-modern phase cannot but be ambivalent. Right in the middle of the history of Japan's modernisation came the Second World War, a war which was brought about by the very aberration of the modernisation itself. The defeat in this War fifty years ago occasioned an opportunity for Japan and the Japanese as the very agent of the War to attempt a rebirth out of the great misery and sufferings that were depicted by the "Post-war School" of Japanese writers. The moral props for Japanese aspiring to such a rebirth were the idea of democracy and their determination never to wage a war again. Paradoxically, the people and state of Japan living on such moral props were not innocent but had been stained by their own past history of invading other Asian countries. Those moral props mattered also to the deceased victims of the nuclear weapons that were used for the first time in Hiroshima and Nagasaki, and for the survivors and their off-spring affected by radioactivity (including tens of thousands of those whose mother tongue is Korean).

In the recent years there have been criticisms levelled against Japan suggesting that she should offer more military forces to the United Nations forces and thereby play a more active role in the keeping and restoration of peace in various parts of the world. Our heart sinks whenever we hear these criticisms. After the end of the Second World War it was a categorical imperative for us to declare that we renounced war forever in a central article of the new Constitution. The Japanese chose the principle of eternal peace as the basis of morality for our rebirth after the War.

I trust that the principle can best be understood in the West with its long tradition of tolerance for conscientious rejection of military service. In Japan itself there have all along been attempts by some to obliterate the article about renunciation of war from the Constitution and for this purpose they have taken every opportunity to make use of pressures from abroad. But to obliterate from the Constitution the principle of eternal peace will be nothing but an act of betrayal against the peoples of Asia and the victims of the Atom Bombs in Hiroshima and Nagasaki. It is not difficult for me as a writer to imagine what would be the outcome of that betrayal.

The pre-war Japanese Constitution that posited an absolute power transcending the principle of democracy had sustained some support from the populace. Even though we now have the half-

Front cover for the 1994 English translation of Oe's 1976 novel, a story of a father and his retarded son

century-old new Constitution, there is a popular sentiment of support for the old one that lives on in reality in some quarters. If Japan were to institutionalize a principle other than the one to which we have adhered for the last fifty years, the determination we made in the post-war ruins of our collapsed effort at modernisation – that determination of ours to establish the concept of universal humanity would come to nothing. This is the spectre that rises before me, speaking as an ordinary individual.

What I call Japan's "ambiguity" in my lecture is a kind of chronic disease that has been prevalent throughout the modern age. Japan's economic prosperity is not free from it either, accompanied as it is by all kinds of potential dangers in the light of the structure of world economy and environmental conservation. The "ambiguity" in this respect seems to be accelerating. It may be more obvious to the critical eyes of the world at large than to us within the country. At the nadir of the post-war economic poverty we found a resilience to endure it, never losing our hope for recovery. It may sound curious to say so, but we seem to have no less resilience to endure our anxiety about the ominous consequence emerging out of the present prosperity. From another point of view, a new situation now seems to be arising in which Japan's prosperity is going to be incorporated into the expanding potential power of both production and consumption in Asia at large.

I am one of the writers who wish to create serious works of literature which dissociate themselves from those novels which are mere reflections of the vast consumer cultures of Tokyo and the subcultures of the world at large. What kind of identity as a Japanese should I seek? W. H. Auden once defined the novelist as follows:

> . . . , among the Just
> Be just, among the Filthy filthy too,
> And in his own weak person, if he can,
> Must suffer dully all the wrongs of Man.
> ("The Novelist," 11–14)

This is what has become my "habit of life" (in Flannery O'Connor's words) through being a writer as my profession.

To define a desirable Japanese identity I would like to pick out the word "decent" which is among the adjectives that George Orwell often used, along with words like "humane," "sane" and "comely," for the character types that he favoured. This deceptively simple epithet may starkly set off and contrast with the word "ambiguous" used for my identification in "Japan, the Ambiguous, and Myself." There is a wide and ironical discrepancy between what the Japanese seem like when viewed from outside and what they wish to look like.

I hope Orwell would not raise an objection if I used the word "decent" as a synonym of "humanist" or "*humaniste*" in French, because both words share in common qualities such as tolerance and humanity. Among our ancestors were some pioneers who made painstaking efforts to build up the Japanese identity as "decent" or "humanist."

One such person was the late Professor Kazuo Watanabe, a scholar of French Renaissance literature and thought. Surrounded by the insane ardour of patriotism on the eve and in the middle of the Second World War, Watanabe had a lonely dream of grafting the humanist view of man on to the traditional Japanese sense of beauty and sensitivity to Nature, which fortunately had not been entirely eradicated. I must hasten to add that Professor Watanabe had a conception of beauty and Nature different from that conceived of by Kawabata in his "Japan, the Beautiful, and Myself."

The way Japan had tried to build up a modern state modelled on the West was cataclysmic. In ways different from, yet partly corresponding to, that process Japanese intellectuals had tried to bridge the gap between the West and their own country at its deepest level. It must have been a laborious task or *travail* but it was also one that brimmed with joy. Professor Watanabe's study of François Rabelais was thus one of the most distinguished and rewarding scholarly achievements of the Japanese intellectual world.

Watanabe studied in Paris before the Second World War. When he told his academic supervisor about his ambition to translate Rabelais into Japanese, the eminent elderly French scholar answered the aspiring young Japanese student with the phrase: "L'entreprise inouïe de la traduction de l'intraduisible Rabelais" (the unprecedented enterprise of translating into Japanese untranslatable Rabelais). Another French scholar answered with blunt astonishment: "Belle entreprise Pantagruélique" (an admirably Pantagruel-like enterprise). In spite of all this not only did Watanabe accomplish his great enterprise in a poverty-stricken environment during the War and the American Occupation, but he also did his best to transplant into the confused and disorientated Japan of that time the life and thought of those French humanists who were the forerunners, contemporaries and followers of François Rabelais.

In both my life and writing I have been a pupil of Professor Watanabe's. I was influenced by him in two crucial ways. One was in my method of writing novels. I learnt concretely from his translation of Rabelais what Mikhail Bakhtin formulated as "the image system of grotesque realism or the culture of popular laughter"; the importance of material and physical principles; the correspondence between the cosmic, social and physical elements; the overlapping of death and passions for rebirth; and the laughter that subverts hierarchical relationships.

The image system made it possible to seek literary methods of attaining the universal for someone like me born and brought up in a peripheral, marginal, off-centre region of the peripheral, marginal, off-centre country, Japan. Starting from such a background I do not represent Asia as a new economic power but an Asia impregnated with everlasting poverty and a mixed-up fertility. By sharing old, familiar yet living metaphors I align myself with writers like Kim Ji-ha of Korea, Chon I and Mu Jen, both of China. For me the brotherhood of world literature consists in such relationships in concrete terms. I once took part in a hunger strike for the political freedom of a gifted Korean poet. I am now deeply worried about the destiny of those gifted Chinese novelists who have been deprived of their freedom since the Tienanmen Square incident.

Another way in which Professor Watanabe has influenced me is in his idea of humanism. I take it to be the quintessence of Europe as a living totality. It is an idea which is also perceptible in Milan Kundera's definition of the spirit of the novel. Based on his accurate reading of historical sources Watanabe wrote critical biographies, with Rabelais at their centre, of people from Erasmus to Sébastien Castellion, and of women connected with Henri IV from Queen Marguerite to Gabrielle Destré. By doing so Watanabe intended to teach the Japanese about humanism, about the importance of tolerance, about man's vulnerability to his preconceptions or machines of his own making. His sincerity led him to quote the remark by the Danish philologist Kristoffer Nyrop: "Those who do not protest against war are accomplices of war." In his attempt to transplant into Japan humanism as the very basis of Western thought Watanabe was bravely venturing on both "l'entreprise inouïe" and the "belle entreprise Pantagruélique."

As someone influenced by Watanabe's humanism I wish my task as a novelist to enable both those who express themselves with words and their readers to recover from their own sufferings and the sufferings of their time, and to cure their souls of the wounds. I have said I am split between the opposite poles of ambiguity characteristic of the Japanese. I have been making efforts to be cured of and restored from those pains and wounds by means of literature. I have made my efforts also to pray for the cure and recovery of my fellow Japanese.

If you will allow me to mention him again, my mentally handicapped son Hikari was awakened by the voices of birds to the music of Bach and Mozart, eventually composing his own works. The little pieces that he first composed were full of fresh splendor and delight. They seemed like dew glittering on grass leaves. The word *innocence* is composed of *in* – "not" and *nocere* – "hurt," that is, "not to hurt." Hikari's music was in this sense a natural effusion of the composer's own innocence.

As Hikari went on to compose more works, I could not but hear in his music also "the voice of a crying and dark soul." Mentally handicapped as he was, his strenuous effort furnished his act of composing or his "habit of life" with the growth of compositional techniques and a deepening of his conception. That in turn enabled him to discover in the depth of his heart a mass of dark sorrow which he had hitherto been unable to identify with words.

"The voice of a crying and dark soul" is beautiful, and his act of expressing it in music cures him of his dark sorrow in an act of recovery. Furthermore, his music has been accepted as one that cures and restores his contemporary listeners as well. Herein I find the grounds for believing in the exquisite healing power of art.

This belief of mine has not been fully proved. "Weak person" though I am, with the aid of this unverifiable belief, I would like to "suffer dully all the wrongs" accumulated throughout the twentieth century as a result of the monstrous development of technology and transport. As one with a peripheral, marginal and off-centre existence in the world I would like to seek how – with what I hope is a modest descent and humanist contribution – I can be of some use in a cure and reconciliation of mankind.

The Year in Poetry, 1993

Robert McPhillips
Iona College

Among the most notable events in American poetry in 1993 was the publication of two major historical surveys – *The Columbia History of American Poetry* (Columbia University Press), edited by Jay Parini with the assistance of Brett C. Millier, and *American Poetry: The Nineteenth Century* (*Volume One: Philip Freneau to Walt Whitman; Volume Two: Herman Melville to Trumball Strickney; American Indian Poetry; Folk Songs and Spirituals* [Library of America]), edited by John Hollander. These volumes invite viewing the year's new poetry within a broader historical context, an invitation reinforced by the publication of two volumes of "new" poems by Emily Dickinson – "poems," that is, "found" within the prose of Dickinson's letters – along with a volume of Walt Whitman's poems allegedly expurgated from the Library of America's purportedly "complete" 1982 edition of Whitman's poetry and prose. These historical reminders of American poetry's public dimension in a year in poetry which could have said to have been initiated – as noted in my 1992 roundup – with the reading of a poem by an African American woman poet, Maya Angelou (subsequently published as the best-selling *On the Pulse of the Morning* [Random House] as well as released as a recording which won a Grammy Award). Rita Dove was chosen as the first African American poet laureate of the United States as well as the youngest. In 1994 her term as poet laureate was extended another year.

Running to almost nine hundred pages, Parini and Millier's *The Columbia History of American Poetry* is an ambitious but highly uneven and incomplete enterprise. Many of the essays are perfunctory, including those by Francis Murphy on Anne Bradstreet and Edward Taylor, and Carolivia Herron's study of early African American poetry, the latter of which, unfortunately, reads like a poorly annotated shopping list. If Ann Charters's discussion of Beat poetry is serviceable, Diane Wood Middlebrook's discussion of the confessionals, given the compassion and insight of her recent biography of Anne Sexton, is disappointingly narrow in focus. Her vi-

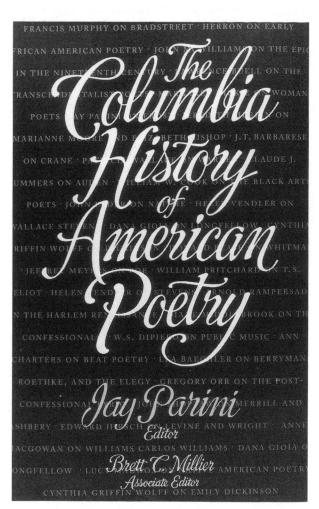

Dust jacket for Jay Parini and Brett Millier's "ambitious but highly uneven and incomplete" history of American poetry

sion of confessional poetry – despite the obvious continuation of the tradition among such young living poets as Sharon Olds – is limited to four poets: W. D. Snodgrass, Robert Lowell, Sylvia Plath, and Sexton. Snodgrass is included because of the influence of *Heart's Needle* (1959) on Lowell's *Life Studies* (1959), while Plath and Sexton qualify as students of Lowell's poetry workshop at Boston University. (John Berryman is discussed in conjunction with Theodore Roethke as an elegist in an essay by Lea Baechler.)

Among the more predictably solid entries are those by Lawrence Buell on the transcendentalists, William Pritchard on T. S. Eliot, and Helen Vendler on Wallace Stevens. The most stimulating essay in the book is Dana Gioia's imaginative reevaluation of the significance of Henry Wadsworth Longfellow, the most popular of America's nineteenth-century poets but one who has long suffered, because of his accessibility and frequent sentimentality, from critical derision and, perhaps more damning, critical neglect. On the other hand, John McWilliams's discussion of the nineteenth-century epic, which quickly dismisses (with reason) such disasters as Joel Barlow's *The Columbiad,* focuses upon such prose works as William Prescott's *The History of the Conquest of Mexico* and Herman Melville's *Moby Dick,* claiming that there is no acceptable extant distinction between poetry and prose. (This is the kind of downright stupidity which is often confused with brilliance in contemporary academia). Certainly a case can be made for the novel as an epic form; *The Columbia History of American Poetry* is not the appropriate forum for it, however, especially since the volume lacks essays on several important nineteenth-century American poets such as William Cullen Bryant, James Russell Lowell, John Greenleaf Whittier, and others.

The closer *The Columbia History of American Poetry* gets to the present, the more problematic it becomes. While John Ashbery and James Merrill deserve the serious attention they get, it is nonetheless disturbing that such poets of arguably equal (and, in some cases, superior) talent and significance as Robert Bly, John Haines, Donald Hall, Anthony Hecht, Donald Justice, Adrienne Rich, Louis Simpson, and Mona Van Duyn – among others – receive little or no attention. (Parini apologizes only to Rich for the oversight in his introduction.) While no book could be expected to discuss all of these poets adequately, surely a volume that ignores them all yet finds room to devote an entire chapter to Philip Levine and Charles Wright – considerably more minor talents, in my estimation – deserves faint applause at best. Also vexing is that, with the exception of a few mentions of African American and Native American poets such as Dove and Louise Erdrich, the book mentions virtually no poets born after 1940.

With a few notable exceptions, then, this history is marred at once by mediocrity and by obligatory political correctness – the latter without really radically challenging one's received opinions of the American poetic canon. A new history of American poetry is sorely needed; it is lamentable, then, that *The Columbia History of American Poetry* is both so incomplete and inadequate.

Among the charges leveled by Sam Abrams in his rather poorly written and overstated introduction to his *The Neglected Walt Whitman: Vital Texts* (Four Walls Eight Windows) against Justin Kaplan's Library of America one-volume Whitman is that Kaplan fails to include such antidemocratic poems as "Respondez!" and that he attempts to tone down the full range of Whitman's homoeroticism (or what the publicity release calls – despite Whitman's own lifelong, if albeit not entirely credible, denial of it – "the poet's openly gay sexuality"), even though, in addition to publishing the original 1855 edition of *Leaves of Grass,* Kaplan follows the very deletions that Whitman made in his final version of the *Leaves of Grass,* the authorized 1891–1892 "deathbed" edition. Much of the rhetorical thunder that Abrams generates here is quietly undermined, however, by the Whitman that emerges in John Hollander's generous and well-selected group of 240 pages of Whitman's poetry which concludes the first volume of *American Poetry: The Nineteenth Century.* For one thing, Hollander includes such poems as "Respondez!" (certainly, despite Abrams's extravagant claims for the poem's political significance, one of Whitman's most conspicuous artistic failures) that were absent from Kaplan's volume. For another, with Hollander's decision to include the 1855 version of *Leaves of Grass* as well as *Calamus,* Whitman's sequence of love poems to men celebrating "the dear love of comrades," in their entirety (albeit with the deletions from *Calamus* that Whitman made over the years), never has the radical nature of Whitman's homoeroticism been so powerfully evident. In "Whoever You Are Holding Me Now in Hand," for instance, Whitman boldly asserts: "I give you fair warning before you attempt me further, / I am not what you supposed, but far different" and goes on to address his imagined ideal readers:

Or possibly with you sailing at sea, or on the beach of
    the sea or some quiet island,
Here to put your lips upon mine I permit you,
With the comrade's long-dwelling kiss or the new
    husband's kiss,
For I am the new husband and I am the comrade.

Or if you will, thrusting me beneath your clothing,
Where I may feel the throbs of your heart or rest upon
    your hip,
Carry me when you go forth over the land or sea;
For thus merely touching you is enough, is best,

And thus touching you would I silently sleep and be carried
eternally.

For Whitman, his book is his body. As complete as
this sequence seems as presented here, Abrams's
volume does contain one "fallen leaf" (as he refers
to the poems Whitman dropped from his book)
from *Calamus,* "Calamus 9," (from the numbering of
the original edition, the table of contents of which
Abrams includes in an appendix), an extremely
moving poem about lost love:

> Hours of my torment – I wonder if other men ever
> have the like, out of the like feelings?
> Is there even one other like me – distracted – his
> friend, his lover, lost to him?
> Is he too as I am now? Does he still rise in the morning,
> dejected, thinking who is lost to him? and at night
> awaking, think who is lost?
> Does he too harbor his friendship silent and endless?
> harbor his anguish and passion?
> Does some stray reminder, or the casual mention of a
> name, bring the fit back upon him, taciturn and
> deprest?
> Does he see himself reflected in me? In these hours, does he
> see the face of his hours reflected?

As a sequence, *Calamus* equals more than the sum of
its parts; it is perhaps the finest sequence of love
poems written by an American poet, and it is indeed
far more convincing than Whitman's sequence of
love poems addressed to women, *Children of Adam,*
from which Hollander only reprints three poems,
including "As Adam Early in the Morning." With
few exceptions the poems in this sequence seem to
be perfunctory "democratic" posing on Whitman's
part.

It would be misleading, however, to suggest
that Hollander presents a one-sided, politically correct version of Whitman here. The individual
poems which make up the backbone of Whitman's
corpus are all here: "Crossing Brooklyn Ferry"
(perhaps Whitman's greatest, most prophetic, and
most influential poem), "As I Ebb'd with the Ocean
of Life," "Drum Taps," "The Wound Dresser,"
"When Lilacs Last in the Dooryard Bloom'd," and
"Passage to India." Whitman remains America's
greatest poet of the body and the body politic, and it
must be admitted that he towers above all of the
three dozen or so poets who precede him in this volume.

This is not, to be sure, purely a one-man
show. Still, I must admit that some of my favorite
American poets from the nineteenth century do not
quite live up to my memories. With the exception,
for instance, of such obvious poems as "To Helen,"

"Lenore," "The Raven," "The Bells," "For Annie,"
and "Annabel Lee," Edgar Allan Poe's gothic imagination comes off far better in his tales than in his
poems; and even this handful of his best is more
likely to appeal to the fervidly romantic imagination
of adolescence than to the somberness of maturity.
Similarly, despite the strong case Dana Gioia has
made for him, Longfellow too, with the exception of
a few lyrics like "Mezzo Camin," "The Evening
Star," "Snow-Flakes," and "Divina Commedia," is
likely to appeal to an even younger audience,
though clearly the failure to include any of his
book-length poems such as *Evangeline* or *The Song of
Hiawatha* fails to do a poet of Longfellow's storytelling abilities full justice. Despite a large selection
of Ralph Waldo Emerson's poetry, the essay remains Emerson's claim to fame, just as prose is
more suitable to his transcendental protégé, Henry
David Thoreau. On the other hand, I had never
read the sonnets of fellow transcendentalist Jones
Very and was glad finally to have done so. And, in
a different vein, amid the coldest and snowiest winter in the Northeast since my childhood, I was glad
to discover that Whittier's "Snow-Bound" had not
lost its atmospheric or narrative appeal.

As powerfully as Whitman dominates the first
volume of Hollander's *American Poetry: The Nineteenth
Century,* so too does Emily Dickinson eclipse the talent of any of the other poets included in the second
volume. Indeed, Dickinson comes across, in the
more than ninety pages (and more than twice as
many poems) given over to her, as one of the purest
lyric poets ever to have written, rivaled, but I think
not equaled, in America only – in terms of lyric purity – by Wallace Stevens. Dickinson, of course, is
in most ways the opposite of Whitman: neither a
celebrator nor a promoter of herself, this self-
defined "Queen of Calvary" was a withdrawn imagination who meticulously examined the inner work-
ings of the soul, finding her metaphors, astonish-
ingly enough, in the New England landscape in and
around Amherst, Massachusetts, in domestic details, and in her wide reading – it would seem – of
the Bible, poetry, philosophy, and probably even
fiction. A minor quibble about Hollander's editing
of Dickinson's poems is that he does not number
them following the pattern set in the definitive
Thomas H. Johnson edition of the poems; his selection, however, is impeccable. It is difficult to
do justice to a poet of Dickinson's idiosyncratic
profundity, a poet whose goal it is "To tell all the
Truth but tell it slant," in such limited space, but
my favorite of Dickinson's poems remains the following:

After great pain, a formal feeling comes –
The Nerves sit ceremonious, like Tombs –
The stiff Heart questions was it He, that bore,
And Yesterday, or Centuries before?

The Feet, mechanical, go round –
Of Ground, or Air, or Ought –
A Wooden way
Regardless grown,
A Quartz contentment, like a stone –

This is the Hour of Lead –
Remembered, if outlived,
As freezing persons, recollect the Snow –
First – Chill – then Stupor – then the letting go –

As in all of her best poems, Dickinson's metaphors here are stunningly etched, but perhaps the poem's real psychological hook is contained in her devastating, seemingly casually dropped line, "Remembered, if outlived," a line that reminds us how close to the edge Dickinson ventured in the exploration of her "Soul *at the White Heat?*" (to quote from another memorable first line). But one is always discovering something new when rereading Dickinson, and among the most powerful stanzas I came across reading Hollander's selection is this final one from "I would not paint – a picture – ":

Nor would I be a Poet –
It's finer – own the Ear –
Enamored – impotent – content –
The License to revere,
A privilege so awful
What would the Dower be,
Had I the Art to stun myself
With Bolts of Melody!

Needless to say, Dickinson is a poet with such power.

A related volume of questionable scholarly value but undeniable interest, *Emily Dickinson: Woman of Letters* (State University of New York Press), contains critical essays, primarily from a feminist perspective. The most provocative essay is by Ellen Louise Hart arguing that Dickinson's lesbian attachment to her sister-in-law, Susan Huntington Gilbert Dickinson, lasted far longer than most critics have claimed, from their adolescence through Dickinson's death at fifty-six, and is the underlying subject of many of Dickinson's poems. But the primary raison d'être of this volume is clearly the sequence of "Poems and Centos from Lines in Emily Dickinson's Letters" by its editor, Lewis Turco. This sequence, "A Sampler of Hours," which contains poems derived from Dickinson's letters but also amplified by lines from Turco, includes a poem, "Poetry," drawn entirely from Dickinson's

statements on poetry in her letters. Dickinson's views on poetry, fame, and Whitman are poeticized by Turco thus:

Two editors of journals came and asked me
    for my mind. When I asked them, "Why?" they
    said I was penurious – they'd use it
for the world. I could not weigh my self myself –
my size felt small to me One hears of Mister

Whitman – I never read his book, but was told
    he is disgraceful. To my thought, "To
    publish" is foreign as firmament
to fin. My barefoot rank is better. If fame
belonged to me, I could not escape her – if

she did not, the longest day would pass me on
    the chase.
                    There seems a spectral power
    in thought that walks alone. I find
ecstasy in living – the mere sense of life
is joy enough. The chestnut hit my notice

suddenly, and I thought the skies in blossom!

I should mention that while this is one of the best two poems in the Turco/Dickinson sequence (the other is "A Dream of Roses"), its primary "value" is its bringing together of Dickinson's aperçus; it lacks the rhythmic excitement of Dickinson's typical three- and four-beat off-rhymed quatrains. Another volume, *New Poems of Emily Dickinson* (University of North Carolina Press), edited by William H. Shurr with Anna Dunlop and Emily Grey Shurr, is a more straightforwardly scholarly attempt to retrieve poems largely from the prose of Dickinson's letters (some are poems in letters overlooked by Johnson in his definitive edition of the poems) following Johnson's own rationale that Dickinson often did not make clear delineations between poetry and prose in her letters. Shurr comes up with some good material, particularly in his section of epigraphs reprinted as fourteeners, a poetic form (an iambic tetrameter line followed by an iambic trimeter one) favored by Dickinson. This volume is marred, however, by Shurr's editorial inconsistency in presenting his 498 "new" poems. He argues that wrenching them from their context in Dickinson's letters enables us to experience them from a fresh perspective; yet a good number of the poems (each numbered) are presented in their entirety within the introduction to each of the volume's six chapters.

In addition to Dickinson, the second volume of Hollander's anthology of nineteenth-century American poetry includes generous selections from the poetry of Melville, Sidney Lanier, Ambrose

Bierce, George Washington Cable, Edward Arlington Robinson, Stephen Crane, Paul Laurence Dunbar, and Trumbull Stickney, as well as briefer selections from, among others, Stephen Foster, Helen Hunt Jackson, Bret Harte, Emma Lazarus, James Whitcomb Riley (those not content with the four poems included by Hollander will be pleased to know that Indiana University Press has published *The Complete Poetical Works of James Whitcomb Riley,* a hefty double-columned tome of almost nine hundred pages), George Santayana, and William Vaughn Moody. But, in addition to the poems of Dickinson, what is most welcome in this second volume is Hollander's inclusion of almost two hundred pages of "19th-Century Versions of American Indian Poetry" and "Folk Songs and Spirituals," expanding the "official" canon of American poetry to include the voices of Native American and African American writers beyond the relatively few of the latter who, previous to the twentieth century, published poetry under their own names as opposed to passing it on through oral and musical traditions.

Last year I found some things to praise in series editor David Lehman's annual *The Best American Poetry* series edited by Charles Simic. But as admirable as Lehman's intentions have been, as insistently as he believes in the vitality of contemporary American poetry, as successful as he has even been in its marketing (it is now available through the Quality Paperback Book Club), the series has largely been an artistic disappointment. This aesthetic failure is evident in the exceedingly unrewarding pages of *The Best American Poetry 1993* (Scribners), edited by Louise Glück, whose *The Wild Iris* (Ecco) perhaps not surprisingly but certainly undeservingly won the 1993 Pulitzer Prize for poetry. Glück's introduction spins together a strand of observations on poetry that are stunningly banal and unilluminating, such as this: "Poems *are* autobiography, but divested of the trappings of chronology and comment, the metronomic alternation of anecdote and response." (What?) Or this:

As for the poet: mere unease, mere doubting of received ideas is never enough: the poem must, on whatever scale, dislodge assumption, not by simply opposing it, but by dismantling the systemic proof on which its inevitability depends. In other words: not "C is wrong" but "who says A has to lead to B?" High seriousness, in its common disguise as tedious sobriety, is one of intelligence's readiest targets.

Or this equally nebulous formulation: "Poetic intelligence lacks, I think, such focused investment in conclusion, being naturally wary of its own assump-

tions. It derives its final energy from a willingness to discard conclusions in the face of evidence, its willingness, in fact to discard anything." (Such a definition of energy at least helps to explain why Glück's own poetry is so linguistically anemic.) Glück even questions the whole notion of editing an anthology because of the implied critical judgments it entails:

Finally, I think poets are not served by the existence of another mechanism of ranking, however sweet recognition may seem. Hierarchy dissolves passionate friendship into bitter watchfulness – those who aren't vulnerable are usually those who are regularly honored. What is essential is that we sustain our readiness to learn from each other, a readiness that, by definition, requires from each of us the best work possible. We must, I think, fear whatever erodes the generosity on which exacting criticism depends.

Glück naively assumes that poetry is created by and for poets only, poets who should be "passionate friends," and equally ludicrous is the notion that "exacting criticism" is a function of "generosity" rather than of scrupulous honesty. Glück's view of poetry, then, is that of a never-never land where no common reader of poetry exists. Such a reader, with the exception of a few poems which hardly conform to Glück's aesthetics of vagueness, such as those here by Thom Gunn, Donald Hall, Donald Justice, Jane Kenyon, Susan Mitchell, Adrienne Rich, Gjertrud Schnackenberg, Louis Simpson, and John Updike, will find most of this volume forbidding or just plain tedious, including the longer sequences (or excerpts therefrom) for which Glück shows a particular fondness, including those by A. R. Ammons, Allen Grossman, and Mark Strand.

Just as Random House honored Maya Angelou's inaugural poem by its publication, so too was Rita Dove's elevation to the position of poet laureate marked by the publication of her *Selected Poems* (Pantheon/Vintage) – something of a misnomer as it is actually a reprint of Dove's first three books (all originally published by the University of Pittsburgh Press) in their entirety, including her Pulitzer Prize–winning 1986 volume, *Tom and Beulah,* her book-length sequence on the lives of her grandparents. *Selected Poems,* along with her fourth individual volume, *Grace Notes* (1989), shows Dove to be a poet of great intelligence, genuine skill, and a wide range of interests, from her African American heritage to European culture (Dove has studied in Germany and is married to a German) to sexuality and motherhood. Dove's early prominence, however, should not obscure the talent of other equally gifted Afri-

can American poets. Audre Lorde, who was named
New York State poet in 1991 and died from breast
cancer in 1992, was nominated for the National Book
Critics Circle Award for Poetry in 1993 for her strong
posthumous collection, *The Marvelous Arithmetics of Distances: Poems 1987–1992* (Norton). The poems in this
volume range from the political to the personal. Stylistically, they are conspicuous for their infrequent punctuation, as if Lorde were simultaneously contemplating openness, death, continuity, and eternity. In
"Party Time" Lorde juxtaposes the freedom of African dance with oppressive politics in South Africa,
racism in South Africa with the shooting death of Eleanor Bumpers, a black woman, by the police in the
Bronx, and Bumpers's death with the poet's impending one, which is itself finally juxtaposed against celebratory dance. "Prism" is a meditation on Soweto,
while "Thanks to Jesse Jackson" concludes with this
rather prosaically factual observation:

> By the year 2000
> the 20 largest cities in the world
> will have two things in common
> none of them will be in Europe
> and none in the United States.

Even here, however, Lorde is speaking in the voice
of a prophet. She is a bit heavy-handed, however, in
"Jesse Helms," an obscene put-down of the senator
in response to his campaign against "obscenity" in
art. Helms deserves the censure, but he is a rather
easy target. Indeed, while Lorde's political poems,
commenting not only on racial politics but on global
politics as well, are central to her work, some of the
finest poems in this collection are personal lyrics.
These include "Inheritance – His," about her Caribbean father, as well as some particularly impressive
poems at the end of the volume, perhaps the foremost of them being "The Night-blooming Jasmine."
This flower becomes a moving image of the poet's
vitality even in the late throes of cancer:

> I still patrol that line
> sword drawn
> lightening red-glazed candles of petition
> along the scar
> the surest way of knowing
> death is a fractured border
> through the center of my days.
>
> Bees seek their need
> until flowers beckon
> beyond the limit of their wings
> then they drop where they fly
> pollen baskets laden
> the sweet work done.

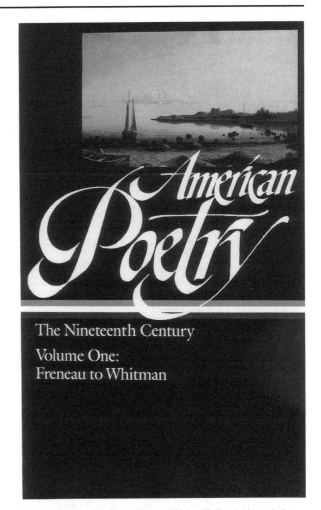

*Dust jacket for the first volume of John Hollander's anthology
of nineteenth-century American poetry*

Similarly moving are a number of elegiac late love
poems such as "Girlfriend," "Lunar Eclipse," and
"Change." The volume's penultimate poem,
"Today is Not the Day," both defies and accepts the
imminence of death, of love's simultaneous transience and permanence, without what should have
been an understandable self-pity and bathos. It is a
poignant conclusion to an important and, sadly, too
brief career.

Lucille Clifton is another seasoned African
American poet to publish a new volume in 1993.
The Book of Light (Copper Canyon Press) begins
with "Light," in a sense a found poem created from
the synonyms for light found in *Roget's Thesaurus,*
which she somehow makes "luminous," to use one
of those synonyms, followed by what seems to be
her own reimagining of the biblical tale of Jacob's
ladder, "climbing." Both of these poems announce

Clifton's search for religious radiance within mundane experience. Some of the more successful poems here have an unlikely addressee: Clark Kent. Others draw upon the myth of Leda and the Swan, retold from a feminist perspective, while still others draw, like "climbing," upon the Bible. (And, like Lorde, she also includes a poem critical of Jesse Helms.) She is at her characteristic best, however, in passages such as this, section 7 from her poem "far memory," *"gloria mundi"*:

> so knowing
> what is known?
> that we carry our baggage
> in our cupped hands
> when we burst through
> the waters of our mother.
> that some are born
> and some are brought
> to the glory of this world.
> that is more difficult
> than faith
> to serve only one calling
> one commitment
> one devotion
> in one life.

The pleasure to be derived from *The Book of Light* is somewhat diminished by the seemingly knee-jerk political correctness of both the Helms and some of the Leda poems, as well as by Clifton's insistence upon writing all of her poems in lowercase letters, an avant-garde technique that, in the 1990s, seems downright anachronistic. The seriousness of her spiritual quest, however, shines through.

Yusef Komunyakaa is a younger African American poet whose poems on his experience as a reporter covering the Vietnam War have earned him considerable praise. For his most recent collection, *Neon Vernacular: New and Selected Poems* (Wesleyan University Press / University Press of New England), which contains a brief sampling of new work along with excerpts from seven of his previous books – all excepting *Magical City* (1992), Komunyakaa received the Pulitzer Prize for poetry. The influence of jazz on Komunyakaa's work is on clearest display in *Copacetic* (1984), which contains several powerfully erotic love poems such as "More Girl Than Boy" and "Safe Subjects," as well as poems to such jazz legends as Leadbelly, Thelonius Monk, and Charles Mingus, the latter in this segment from "Copacetic Mingus":

> I listen to *Pithecanthropus*
> *Erectus:* Up & down, under
> & over, every which way –

> thump, thump, dada – ah, yes.
> Wood heavy with tenderness,
> Mingus fingers the loom
> gone on Segovia,
> dogging the raw strings
> unwaxed with rosin.
> Hyperbolic bass line. Oh, no!
> Hard love, it's hard love.

His most successful book so far is *Dien Cai Dau* (1988), drawn from Komunyakaa's experience in Vietnam and in the aftermath of the war. If *Copacetic* resonates with jazz, then rock and soul music – Ray Charles, Tina Turner, Jimi Hendrix – inform the aesthetic of this volume as strongly as in Francis Ford Coppola's *Apocalypse Now* (1979). In the final poem from this volume, "Facing It," Komunyakaa presents a black vet facing the Vietnam Veterans Memorial, attempting to come to terms with a war many of whose casualties were black men. Here is his final vision:

> I go down the 58,022 names,
> half-expecting to find
> my own in letters like smoke.
> I touch the name Andrew Johnson;
> I see the booby trap's white flash.
> Names shimmer on woman's blouse
> but when she walks away
> the names stay on the wall.
> Brushstrokes flash, a red bird's
> wings cutting across my stare.
> The sky. A plane in the sky.
> A white vet's image floats
> closer to me, then his pale eyes
> look through mine. I'm a window.
> He's lost his right arm
> inside the stone. In the black mirror
> a woman's trying to erase names:
> No, she's brushing a boy's hair.

On a quite different aesthetic plane from Komunyakaa, and in many ways from his first volume, *My Father's Geography* (1992), is Michael S. Weaver's *Stations in a Dream* (Dolphin-Moon Press and Lite Circle Books). Weaver's focus here is not upon African American experience but is instead a meditation on Marc Chagall's paintings of eastern European Jewry. The volume is characterized by a dreamy voluptuousness in such poems as "The Violinist," "Red Nude Sitting Up," "Lovers under Lilies," and the typically beautiful "The Dream":

> I am numb and naked from ecstasy.
> My legs are parted and hung round
> the neck of some obedient phantasm,
> where they burn at the apex,
> as my pelvis has been set aflame

by this journey to heaven, lovemaking
that removes me from earth
and sets me on the tiny clamor
of angels examining my nudity and dazed splendor.
Walking on stars, the earth hangs
its trees and patterned fields in my eyes;
moving mouths utter conversations minute
and inaudible, as I dream that
I can illumine the world with
my body naked and empowered by sex,
joining the moon in its white casting of light.

Weaver demonstrates, I think, in this passage, how much more resonant language can be when freed from the outmoded minimalist poetics that places severe aesthetic limitations on a poet like Lucille Clifton and imitated, in their own ways, by the likes of Wanda Coleman (*Hand Dance* [Black Sparrow]) and Ruth Forman (*We Are The Young Magicians* [Beacon]), whatever their own genuine achievements. Weaver refuses to be imprisoned either by the techniques or the subject matter that came to fruition among black poets in the 1960s and 1970s.

In many ways 1993 was as significant a year for Asian and Asian American culture as it was for African American literature. Two of the most widely acclaimed films – and to my mind, the two best films – of 1993 were directed by Chinese directors who studied at the film school of New York University: Chen Kaige's *Farewell My Concubine* and Ang Lee's *The Wedding Banquet*. But the achievement of Asians and Asian Americans was not limited to film. No fewer than three important volumes of translations from Chinese poetry crossed my desk this year – *Three Chinese Poets* (HarperCollins), translated by Vikram Seth; *The Selected Poems of T'ao Ch'ien* (Copper Canyon Press), translated by David Hinton; and *Out of the Howling Storm: The New Chinese Poetry* (Wesleyan University Press / University Press of New England). Similarly at least three major anthologies devoted to Asian American experiences were published – *Growing Up Asian-American* (Morrow), a collection of autobiographical essays edited by Maria Hong; *Charlie Chan Is Dead* (Penguin), an anthology of Asian American fiction edited by Jessica Hagedorn; and *The Open Boat: Poems from Asian America* (Anchor/Doubleday), edited and introduced by Garrett Hongo. And, finally, individual volumes by poets included in Hongo's anthology were published as well.

The real gem among these volumes is the slenderest, *Three Chinese Poets,* Seth's translation of selected lyrics of Wang Wei, Li Bai (also known as Li Po), and Du Fu (also known as Tu Fu), all poets of the T'ang dynasty. The delicate scale of these

translations is in striking contrast to Seth's more attention-getting publication of 1993, his massive novel on the mores of modern-day India, *A Suitable Boy* (HarperCollins). As in his own lyrics, what typifies the strength of these translations is Seth's supple use of rhyme and meter. This is seen in these lines from "Lament for Yin Yao," reflecting Wang Wei's "typical mood . . . of aloneness, quiet, a retreat into nature, and Buddhism":

Clouds float into a great expanse.
Birds fly but do not sing in flight.
How lonely are travellers.
Even the sun shines cold and white.

Alas, when you still lived, and asked
To study non-rebirth with me,
My exhortations were delayed –
And so the end came fruitlessly.

All your old friends have brought you gifts
But for your life these are too late.
I failed you in more ways than one.
Weeping, I walk back to my gate.

By contrast, according to Seth, Li Bai, a Taoist, "made a great impression on his contemporaries as a paradigm of the intoxicated and the impulsive with his flashing eyes and great iconoclastic energy," which is evident in such poems as "Drinking Alone with the Moon" and "Bring in the Wine," as well as in "Parting at a Wineshop at Nanjing":

Breeze bearing willow-cotton fills the shop with scent.
A Wu girl, pouring wine, exhorts us to drink up.
We Nanjing friends are here to see each other off.
Those who must go, and those who don't, each drains
    his cup.
Go ask the Yangtze, which of these two sooner ends:
Its waters flowing eat – the love of parting friends.

Du Fu, by contrast, was "a man bred in Confucian traditions [for whom] unselfish service to the emperor, to the state and to the people was what gave life meaning." His poems thus reflect a concern with the public world of history and politics, as does "Thoughts on an Ancient Site: The Temple of Zhu-ge Liang":

The name of Zhu-ge Liang resounds through time.
The statesman's likeness awes: revered, sublime.
The empire, split in three, curbed his great aim
But not the soaring feather of his fame.
He equalled Yi and Lü; if he'd gained power
Great names like Cao and Xiao would have ranked lower –

But time would not restore the Han again.
He died, devoid of hope, his plans all vain.

Seth's introduction provides a useful overview of the three poets, of Chinese poetical forms, and an argument that "[m]uch of the pleasure of rhymed and metred poetry depends, obviously enough, on rhyme and metre; and these are intrinsic to the enjoyment of classical Chinese verse." He also pointedly criticizes "[t]the famous translations of Ezra Pound, compounded as they are by ignorance of Chinese and valiant self-indulgence" as "a warning of what to shun." With this slim, unpretentiously scholarly and delightfully accessible volume of translations, Seth both enhances the contemporary English-speaking audience's appreciation of the tradition of Chinese poetry and his own reputation as one of the finest younger English-language poets writing today.

David Hinton's *The Selected Poems of T'ao Ch'ien,* his first volume of translation, brings a larger number of poems from this earlier Chinese poet from the Eastern Chin dynasty centered in present-day Nanjing effectively into English than does Seth's selection from three poets whom, as Hinton claims as the first modern Chinese poet speaking in a distinctly individual voice, distinctly influenced all of these late poets. And indeed, T'ao Ch'ien's range extends to include nature, drinking, religion, philosophy (he is influenced by both Taoism and Confucianism), and politics, most of which can be found in a poem like "Early Spring, *Kuei* Year of the Hare, Thinking of Ancient Farmers" and many in the briefer "Untitled":

I couldn't want another life. This is my
true calling, working fields and mulberries

with my own two hands. I've never failed it,
and still, against hunger and cold, there's

only hull and chaff. I'm not asking for more
than a full stomach. All I want is enough

common rice, heavy clothes for winter and
open-weaves for the summer heat – nothing

more. But I haven't even managed that. O,
it can leave you stricken so with grief.

And character is fate. If you're simple-
minded in life, its ways elude you. That's

how it is. Nothing can change it. But then,
I'll delight in even a single cup of wine.

This is a welcome addition to Copper Canyon's series of translations of Asian poets. (Another notable volume in translation from Copper Canyon's Latin American series is Eliot Weinberger's translation of Xavier Villaurrutia's *Nostalgia for Death,* published in the same volume with Octavio Paz's study of this poet, who has been described as a Mexican Cavafy, *Heiroglyphs of Desire,* translated by Esther Allen.)

Out of the Howling Storm: The New Chinese Poetry, edited by Tony Barnstone, provides a useful introduction to fourteen contemporary Chinese poets belonging to two generational schools – the Misty Poets and the younger generation of Post-Misty Poets – united in their rejection of the social realism imposed on earlier twentieth-century Chinese poets by the Communist government. Both these schools flourished between the spring of 1979, when Mao's Cultural Revolution came to an end, and the spring of 1989 with the government massacre of pro-democratic students at Tiananmen Square. Bei Dao, one of the most prominent of the Misty Poets, wrote these lines on the latter siege in "Requiem":

Not gods but the children
amid the clashing helmets
say their prayers
mothers breed light
darkness breeds mothers
the stone rolls, the clock runs backwards
the eclipse of the sun has taken place

Not your bodies but your souls
shall share a common birthday every year
You are all the same age
love has founded for the dead
an everlasting alliance
you embrace each other closely
in the massive register of deaths[.]

In making available the work of Bei Dao and other such notable poets as Duo Duo, Mang Ke, and such younger poets (many of whom have lived abroad – many in the United States – since Tiananmen Square) as Chou Ping and Ha Jin (both of whom compose in English) and Bei Ling and Zhang Zhen, Barnstone makes clear that the cultural ferment in contemporary China is not limited to the extraordinary accomplishments of the latest generation of film directors whose presence has been felt in the country for the past several years.

The emergence of Asian American writers into the mainstream of American literature probably began with the publication of Maxine Hong Kingston's *The Woman Warrior* in 1977 and has accelerated in recent years with the publication of the immensely popular novels of Amy Tan, *The Joy Luck Club* (1989) and *The Kitchen God's Wife* (1991), as well as other works of fiction by Bharati

Mukherjee, Gish Jen, Cynthia Kohadata, Gus Lee, Jessica Hagedorn, David Wong Louie, and Fae Myenne Ng. No Asian American poet has yet attained the prominence of this plethora of prose writers, though perhaps the one to have come the closest is Garrett Hongo, the editor of *The Open Boat: Poems from Asian America,* a book that one would hope to redress this imbalance. If, like most anthologies of contemporary poetry, this one is decidedly uneven, there are probably as many good poets here to balance off the truly bad ones.

Of the thirty-one poets included in *The Open Boat,* the best known, in addition to Hongo (and Kingston and Hagedorn, whose reputations are based on their prose), are Ai, Mei-mei Berssenbrugge, Lawson Fusao Inada (the first Asian American to publish a collection of poems in the United States – *Before the War* [Morrow, 1971]), Li-Young Lee, Cathy Song, and John Yau. Hongo, a poet of Japanese descent who grew up in Volcano, Hawaii, writes autobiographical narrative poems, five of which are published here, including the title poem from his first volume, *Yellow Light* (Wesleyan University Press, 1982) and "The Unreal Dwelling: My Years in Volcano." Hongo's free-verse poems are written largely in the prosy style of Philip Levine's realistic poems on factory workers in Detroit and the like and so are of primary interest for their details on growing up in Hawaii and the various J-towns of California. Song, who also grew up in Hawaii and is of Chinese and Korean descent, provides a more lyrical vision of growing up in Honolulu in poems such as "Easter: Wahiawa, 1959," about searching for Easter eggs at her grandparents' house:

> When Grandfather was a young boy
> in Korea,
> it was a long walk
> to the riverbank,
> where, if he were lucky,
> a quail egg or two
> would gleam from the mud
> like gigantic pearls.
> He could never eat enough
> of them.

> It was another long walk
> through the sugarcane fields
> of Hawaii,
> where he worked for eighteen years,
> cutting the sweet stalks
> with a machete. His right arm
> grew disproportionally large
> to the rest of his body.
> He could hold three
> grandchildren in that arm.

Inada, whose *Legends from Camp* (Coffee House Press) was published this year, a volume of more historic than artistic interest, I am sad to report, for his eyewitness account of spending time during his youth during World War II in detention camps for Japanese Americans, is here represented by two poems on his other great poetic interest (besides Japanese American life), jazz.

By contrast, Mei-mei Berssenbrugge, John Yau, and Jessica Hagedorn are more experimental. Both Beijing-born Berssenbrugge and Yau are part of a younger generation of poets, sometimes aligned with the L*A*N*G*U*A*G*E poets, influenced (particularly Yau) by John Ashbery. For me, Berssenbrugge's poetry is fatally crippled by its reliance on the rhetoric of Lacanian psychoanalysis, as such terms as "mirror stage" and "the imaginary" in this passage from the long-lined "The Swan" attest:

> A flock of birds flying up acquires the shape of her
> arcs across the ice, a mirror stage,
> echoing our first misrecognition or the imaginary, to
> look again and then look,
> so that if he says or she says, my dream about you is
> older than my knowing you,
> does that mean the dream was dreamed before your
> meeting him or her?

Yau is here represented by the sequence "Radiant Silhouette I–V," as well as "Postcard from Trakl," poems whose surrealistic aesthetic might appeal to his mentor Ashbery but strike me as pretentious and deliberately incoherent.

Jessica Hagedorn, of Philippine American descent who, in addition to being a poet, is also a member of a rock band, a performance artist, and a fiction writer, derives not from the heady L*A*N*G*U*A*G*E school but from the Beat poets of San Francisco and Manhattan's Lower East Side. Largely, I suspect, due to the attention garnered by her novel, *Dogeaters,* Penguin Books has brought out *Danger and Beauty,* a collection of Hagedorn's poetry, stories, and autobiographical essays previously published by small presses, as well as a selection of more-recent short work, primarily poetry, written since 1982. Hagedorn's strong point is narrative, on its best display in the first third of *Dogeaters,* a brilliant piece of writing about growing up in the surreal Manila of the Ferdinand Marcos era, and in her novella in *Danger and Beauty,* "Pet Food," a seemingly autobiographical piece about a young Filipino woman, who has immigrated to San Francisco with her mother, growing up in the 1960s, an often obscene chronicle of the underground art, poetry, and "sex, drugs, and rock 'n' roll" scene. Her poetry is

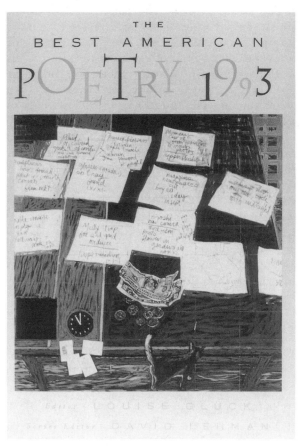

Dust jacket for the 1993 volume, edited by Louise Glück, of the series edited by David Lehman

influenced by and often concerned with the rock music of Elvis Presley, Smokey Robinson, Otis Redding, and Jimi Hendrix. She is at her most characteristic in the autobiographical poem included in both *Danger and Beauty* and *The Open Boat,* "Yolanda Meets the Wild Boys," set amidst the punk-rock scene in Amsterdam, which, derived from Allen Ginsberg, William S. Burroughs, and the name-dropping, "I do this – I do that" poems of Frank O'Hara is likely to appeal to a younger audience still enamored with the glamour of the Beats and the 1960s and 1970s rock scenes and to offend readers with more traditional tastes.

Ai, a poet of mixed ethnic background – part Japanese, part African American, part Choctaw, part Irish – writes public, political poems, usually dramatic monologues which infrequently draw upon Asian American experience – never, as it turns out, in the two poems of hers included in *The Open Boat* or in her 1993 collection, *Greed* (Norton). Like Hagedorn's, Ai's poetry at its most successful has a strong narrative drive and even stronger subject matter; indeed, in a blurb on *Greed,* David Ig-

natow calls her "[t]he hardest-hitting poet of her generation." The book is dedicated to Ai's "loyal fans," and I am afraid that on the basis of reading it, I hardly fit into that group. The book is too topical, offering immediate, politically correct commentary on such current events as the Rodney King riots in Los Angeles, the conviction of the African American former, now again, mayor of Washington, D.C., for cocaine possession and use, and the recent allegation that the late FBI director J. Edgar Hoover was not only homosexual but also a cross-dresser. In "Life Story," a poem dedicated to "Father Ritter and other priests accused of sexual abuse," she tackles pedophilia performed by a priest who "explains" that his actions – as has become the defense strategy of the 1990s in such cases as the trial of the Menendez brothers – were prompted by his own abuse by a priest, a trusted family friend, when he was a child. As the summary of subject matter of *Greed* might suggest, it is the most lurid and ludicrous book of poetry of the year, perhaps the most sordid work of "mainstream" literature I have ever read, the poetry of tabloid journalism.

Among the lesser-known and younger poets included in *The Open Boat,* the most impressive are James Masao Mitsui, David Mura, Li-Young Lee, David Woo, and Indran Amirthanayagam. Masao's poems deal, in far more touching detail than those of Inada, with photographs of Japanese Americans on their way to or in concentration camps during World War II. Mura, a *Sansei,* or third-generation Japanese American, is, among other things, the author of one book of poetry, *We Lost Our Way* (Dutton, 1989), and of the memoir *Turning Japanese: Memoirs of a Sansei* (Atlantic Monthly Press, 1991). Though he was himself born after World War II in 1952, Mura writes convincingly about Japanese survivors of the atomic bomb in "The *Hibakusha's* Letter (1955)":

> Like them we had no warning. Flames filled kimonos
>
> With limbs of ash, and I wandered past
> Smoldering trolleys away from the city.
> Of course you're right. We can't even play beauty
> Or taste of steel quickens our mouths.
>
> I can't conceive, and though Matsuo says
> It doesn't matter, my empty belly haunts me:
> Why call myself a woman, him a man,
> If on our island only ghosts can gather?

In a more recent poem Mura writes well about the role of husband and father in the seven-part "Gardens We Have Left," a poem which opens out into a broader examination of the poet's life and the experience of Japanese Americans in the United States to become (like his daughter) "my hymn to America."

Still in his thirties and with two volumes to his credit – *Rose* (BOA Editions, 1986) and *The City In Which I Love You* (BOA Editions, 1990) – Li-Young Lee, who was born in Jakarta and is of Chinese descent, has already earned a reputation as one of the finest young poets in America. Lee is represented by four poems in *The Open Boat,* one on each of his parents, and another, "The Room and Everything in It," a fine love poem to his wife. But the most impressive poem here is the longest and most ambitious, "The Cleaving," a meditation on an older butcher "in the Hon Kee Grocery" with "Such a sorrowful Chinese face, / nomad, Gobi, Northern / in his boniness," a man who "gossips like my grandmother," who "could be my grandfather," and in whom the poet sees his own face. As such, Lee sees his own life reflected in that of the butcher, making astonishing analogies between butchering and making love (a tender and profound analogy rather than a grotesque and gratuitous one), butchering and poetry, all acts of cleaving:

> What I thought were the arms
> aching *cleave,* were the knees trembling *leave.*
> What I thought were the muscles
> insisting *resist, persist, exist,*
> were the pores
> hissing *mist* and *waste.*
> What I thought was the body humming *reside, reside,*
> O, the murderous deletions, the keening
> down to nothing, the cleaving,
> All of the body's revisions end
> in death.
> All of the body's revisions end.

The poem itself ends, like Mura's "my hymn to America," in a vision of the poet's democratic identity:

> What then may I do
> but cleave to what cleaves me.
> I kiss the blade and eat my meat.
> I thank the wielder and receive,
> while terror spirits
> my change, sorrow also.
> The terror the butcher
> scripts in the unhealed
> air, the sorrow of his Shang
> dynasty face,
> African face with slit eyes. He is
> my sister, this
> beautiful Bedouin, this Shulamite,
> keeper of sabbaths, diviner

> of holy texts, this dark
> dancer, this Jew, this Asian, this one
> with the Cambodian face, Vietnamese face, this Chinese
> I daily face,
> this immigrant,
> this man with my own face.

David Woo, born in 1959 and two years younger than Lee, has yet to publish his first book, but he establishes himself as a poet of genuine promise here. In "Eden," which first appeared in *The New Yorker,* Woo meditates on the similarity between his parents, who immigrated to Arizona from China, and himself, who travels from city to city to escape Arizona, leading him to conclude:

> . . . I feel the desert heat
> and see the beautiful shudders of the palms in the
>   yard
> and wonder why I despised this place so,
>
> why I moved from city to temperate city, anywhere
> without palms and cactus trees.
> I found no paradise, as my parents know,
>
> but neither did they, with their eager sprinklers
> and scrawny desert plants pumped to artificial
>   splendor,
> and their lives sighing way, exhaling slowly,
>
> the man and woman
> who teach me now as they could not before
> to prefer real hell to any imaginary paradise.

"Grandfather's Rockery" is equally impressive. In addition to his appearance in *The Open Boat,* Indran Amirthanayagam, born in Sri Lanka and currently residing in Brooklyn, also published an impressive first volume in 1993, *The Elephants of Reckoning* (Hanging Loose Press). Many of the poems here, drawing upon the folklore of Ceylon, have the feel of magic realism, like the volume's title poem. He also meditates upon the nightmarish violence in his native Sri Lanka while trying to imagine a future rebirth, as in these two stanzas from "Star Over Jaffna."

All in all, it must be said that Asian American poetry has already established itself in the mainstream of contemporary American poetry. The challenge for an even younger generation of poets than that represented by Mura, Lee, Woo, and Amirthanayagam will be how to grapple with the issue of dual versus single identity, otherness, and assimilation.

One of the most prestigious awards to go to an unpublished first manuscript is the Walt Whitman

Award of the American Academy of Poets. The judge for the 1992 award (the book itself was not published in 1993) was Richard Howard, and the winner was Stephen Yenser for *The Fire in All Things* (Louisiana State University Press). Yenser, a professor of English at UCLA and the author of book-length critical studies of Robert Lowell and James Merrill, is an academic in the worst sense of the word. His poems are the musings of a man more interested in his own perceptions than any reader – presumably other than Howard or Merrill or a younger poet with a similar sensibility, J. D. McClatchy – is likely to be. There is a mistaken assumption in certain types of contemporary poetry that careful description and judicious allusion have an a priori claim on the reader's attention. The vitality of a real poem, however, depends on an imaginative or emotional impulse that the reader can share. One has the feeling that so tangibly human an entrée seems slightly vulgar to a writer of so overtly sophisticated and refined a sensibility as Yenser.

By contrast, Andrea Hollander Budy is a poet animated by accessible imaginative and emotional impulses in *House Without a Dreamer* (Story Line Press), a book which well deserves the recognition it received as the winner of the 1993 Nicholas Roerich Poetry Prize for a first volume. Budy establishes herself as a poet with a remarkable ear in the first poem of her book, "When She Named Fire":

> When she named the sun, she didn't think
> of fire at first. *Sun,* she claimed,
> because it was huge and unexplainable,
> a oneness that she loved
> for its ability to command
> the whole sky and the earth too;
> and because it was the warmest thing
> she knew, and she sang
> its tunes and missed it every night.

Here, Budy not only demonstrates the subtle facility with internal rhyme, tying lines musically together without the obviousness of end rhyme ("all" and "unexplainable"; "too" and "knew"). She also manifests her belief in the ability of poetic language to name the most nebulous yet crucial of human emotions – an embodied belief that sets her apart from such deconstructionist poets as Ashbery and Jorie Graham, as well as the philosophically related L*A*N*G*U*A*G*E poets. While much of this book is focused on Budy's life in rural Arkansas and on her reimagining of fairy tales, she is at her strongest as a love poet. "Black" is a memorable meditation on passion:

> . . . Passion
>
> travels in the dark – the animal
> we do not truly know, the one
> we never pet, the one so foreign
> to our lives we do not have a sense
> of what it eats or where it sleeps, and only know
> its death. I meant
>
> to watch the hills instead, the greens
> reduced, the reds so dominant
> the rest pull back.
> My mother told me don't wear black until
> you're grown. Back then I thought
> of widow's clothes. The kind
>
> of passion I have known
> at first is wet and thunderous and new as grass
> that's greener after rain, then briefly blazes red,
> then is black and thunderous and wet – and then
> the nakedness, the nakedness again.

Budy's is a quietly impressive and melodic debut.

Another worthy award-winning first volume is William C. Bowie's *The Conservator's Song* (University of Arkansas Press), chosen by Donald Justice for the 1992 Arkansas Poetry Prize. Justice praises what he sees to be the "oddly reassuring . . . basic *reality* of this poem," the kind of reality which Dana Gioia specifies in the book's other blurb when he comments, "[h]ad Philip Larkin lived in Baltimore, I suspect he would have written just like Bowie." And indeed there is something Larkinesque, something distinctly British, dourly humorous, about these poems whose American settings are decidedly middle-class. For one thing, Bowie is unpretentious enough to take light verse seriously, as few contemporary American poets do, feeling no need for ersatz profundity. Many of Bowie's poems are about drinking – "Waking and Drinking," "Court Street Pub," "The Drinker," "Back at the Bar." The final two stanzas of "The Drinker" demonstrate the poet's humorous distance from his subject, a distance emphasized by the intricate formal pattern of the poem; and yet, there is a kind of imaginative sympathy in evidence here as well:

> He wakes or thinks he wakes.
> The television's on. It must be late –
> *GE*'s jingle
> "We bring good things to life" ushers in
> tonight's *Nightline* debate.
>
> Abortion. He turns it off.
> A face folds in an origami of light
> to a single point
> and flies into space to take its place
> among the other stars.

Bowie is a also drawn to the light epigraph as is evidenced by "An Epic (Couplet)." In "Letter to the Office of the Alumni" the persona amusingly explains why he does not wish to attend a college reunion. The book's strongest section is a four-part sequence, "The Thomas Family," based on a "Decorator's House" brochure. Once again, Bowie's approach is satiric and epigrammatic, as in the third poem, "Joseph's Room," comprised of a single quatrain prefaced by this excerpt from the brochure: "*One wonders how such a 'with-it' kid really functions . . . but then, that's the challenge*":

> My dad droning about
> "Get in touch with how you feel,
> Joseph, and work through it yourself."
> I think, like, try 1-900-GET REAL.

Bowie can move beyond satire in a poem such as "Headed Toward Forty," in which he imagines the possibility of having an affair with a young woman who, as a freshman in college twenty or more years ago, inscribed her name in the secondhand copy of *Tender Is the Night* he bought and periodically takes off the shelf to leaf through. Indeed, there is a nostalgia close to sentimentality here – quite in distinction to "Letter to the Office of the Alumni." But once again, Bowie's use of fixed form serves as a guard against sloppy emotion. Bowie's first offering is deliberately modest but at once entertaining and assured.

Tory Dent, a woman in her mid thirties with AIDS, has written a harrowingly powerful debut with *What Silence Equals* (Persea Books). (The title alludes, of course, to the AIDS activist slogan "Silence = Death.") The book is filled with powerful rhetorical strategies; gruesome (and often obscene) images of life and sex in the shadow of death are balanced by a willful optimism and philosophical passages on the language of poetry which will be most accessible to those familiar with the basic tenets of literary theory, though probably not too forbidding to those who are not. These qualities justify David Shapiro's comparison of Dent to Sylvia Plath.

Dent is most powerful in flashes of savage brilliance, verbal as well as imagistic; in fact, she is, at this point, more effective as a writer of poetic passages than of fully developed individual poems. The volume as a whole gains coherence and strength by the repetition of imagery among numerous poems. Yet in the book's final poem, "Poem for a Poem," Dent achieves the organic unity that eludes her elsewhere, drawing to this profound conclusion:

> Now riddle me permanently, bodily, a body tattoo,
> internally ruinous, a virus not just deadly
> but deadening to all other poems and men.
> Everything breaks down to the denomination of you,
> everything I write simply to the dissemination of you,
> replicating in my body. O my molecule.

The molecule that Dent seems to be Whitmanically singing – or addressing with ambivalence – is the HIV virus, death. And it is understandable, then, that Dent's poetry is at once obscene and spiritual, aesthetic yet deeply religious, open-ended and yet meticulously structured. All seems an extension of her simultaneous understanding that her life is like "giving head to a loaded gun" (from "A Two-Way Mirror"), facing imminent death, where the permanent and the provisional, eternity and death, are in such profound conjunction. "Let," for instance, concludes with this powerful plea:

> O let, o let, let, let, o let, please, let that happen
> let me rise up into that pleasure with all its
>   gradations
> so blue and green and white and pink and brilliantly
>   textured
> as water, medicinal and base,
> let love be an element and let me be amongst it,
> let me be in it, a pine tree in a pine forest.
> Let me, let me, let me, let me, let me, please, at
>   least be its metaphor
> and fulfill no less soberingly the destiny of a spore.
> Let my silly life break swiftly, fail-safe as a Timex
> scatter its parts, hither and thither, on the
>   egalitarian landscape
> leveled at last (as if in an afterlife) with the
>   pinecone and its mulch
> no less graceful than the pinecone, no less purposeful
>   than its mulch.

One is ultimately left with the impression that the immense promise contained within these poems, the profound potential that seems poised to explode into greatness, might instead be destroyed by the very disease which to so large an extent propels them. As such, fragmentary as the book's success and luminosity might be, in the context of the subject matter the book addresses – the ravages of AIDS – the very existence of the book itself represents a triumph of art over both silence and death. One yearns for this talent, hope against hope, to survive and for a cure for the disease which generates Dent's devastatingly incomplete art.

In a much quieter but nonetheless pleasing poetic debut, Greg Johnson also addresses the subject of AIDS in his more traditionally crafted *Aid and Comfort* (University Press of Florida). The volume is divided into two sections, "Unacceptable Losses" and "The Burning House," the former devoted to poems on AIDS and its impact on contemporary society. Many of these poems deal with the difficulty of attempting to comfort friends who are dying of what, in the title of one of his poems Johnson calls this "Disease Without a Name," a "[. . .] Clever acronym that denies / just what it spells! – grisly flesh / eater, with nothing but whites in your eyes." The book's epigraph is drawn from a letter by Walt Whitman describing his ministering to wounded soldiers in the Civil War which leads him to lament that "[t]o see such things & not be able to help them is awful – I feel almost ashamed of being so well & whole." Johnson echoes this feeling in the book's title poem:

> But these men, like Whitman's in a far
> more shameful war, can seldom resist
> a complicitous wink, or a bearded kiss
> or some stray hint of whoever we are
>
> from a stranger's patient but steady breath.
> When the wound-dresser wrote, "Little he knew, poor
> death-stricken boy, the heart of the stranger
> that hover'd near," he held to some faith
>
> in "the simple matter of Personal Presence,"
> and claimed, at last, "I was never so beloved."
> So the racked, and the merely discomforted,
> in their dismal but lovely alliance
>
> muddle through, knowing "The real war
> will never get in the books," however our poems
> may try, however our help lately seems
> the saddest naiveté, the emptiest gesture,
>
> the waste of still-yearning health and breath
> in these already desolate years.
> If so, still we live, and so here's
> yet another song to you, oh death.

"A Death That Dare Not Speak . . . " recounts the poet's witnessing of a friend's death, gathered at the hospital with his family, while "Elegy for a Marine" records the death of another friend who died while the poet was on an airplane en route to a final visit. This section also contains a few irregularly rhymed sonnets – "Withholding the Last Word," "Spinster," and "A Resting Case." (An argument perhaps could be made that "Disease Without a Name" is a thirteen-line sonnet whose missing line emphasizes that AIDS is a disease of absence – of T-cells, an immune system – and its concluding couplets that it is fatal.) "Safe Sex" examines the impact of AIDS on the heterosexual community, while one of the most imaginative of the sequence's poems, "Words for St. Veronica," is at once a reminder of the poet's

Catholic upbringing explored in Johnson's first novel, *Pagan Babies* (Dutton, 1993), and an ingenious reimagining of Saint Veronica, "a sort of Biblical groupie and righteous dame" with "a passion for the first celeb, the king of the hill," as a "ghost from everywhere" who haunts the hospitals nationwide with AIDS patients,

> " [. . .] a good witch, I guess, in flowered dress
>   and blue hair,
>
> not a spare aunt or mother, but just a reminder
> for them, a conscience for the rest, a friendly thorn
> in the doctor's side. I'm anyone who takes the forlorn
> last look from the boy – so handsome! – in Intensive
>   Care,
>
> or whoever enfolds despair in a long embrace,
> or whoever will look, long and hard, into the quick
> of anguish – and I'm the one who must glimpse, as I
>   pull back
> the sweat-stained cloth from his face, my own humble
>   face."

In the book's second section Johnson touches on many subjects, ranging from the "Bad Ends" of three writers – Nietzsche, Virginia Woolf, and Anne Sexton – to more extreme forms of deviant behavior – the torturing of animals ("Somewhere in Georgia"), the sexual abuse of children ("Tabloid") – that emphasize Johnson's affinity to southern gothic, to the conventional nature lyric ("Forecast"). All in all, this is a well-crafted first volume eloquent enough to receive a blurb from James Merrill even as it remains strongly rooted in a concern for significant human drama.

Another elegantly written first collection is Fred Dings's *After the Solstice* (Orchises), a quietly elegiac volume of poems distinguished by a sensitive eye, primarily for natural landscapes – mountains, woods, lakes, streams, the hills of Italy, redwinged blackbirds, aspens, sycamores, crabs – and an exceptionally fine ear, most notable in his subtle use on internal rhyme. Both of these strengths can be seen in these lines from "Sycamores":

> As a child I was enchanted by their white branches,
> Their cool lightning veining dark wood along streams,
> but soon was disappointed they were not *pure* white
> and here and there were blotched gray-green.
> I see them in a different light now, here in Assisi,
>
> the sun splashing everywhere, swallows sickling the
>   air,
> as a girl unshuttered her window and waters the
>   geraniums
> you see flaming the sills eternally in Italy.

*Dust jacket for the edition of Rita Dove's poems published in
honor of her selection as the poet laureate of the United States*

While one arm pours and the other tends the soil,
her skin is clearly unmarred as it brindles

with the alive shadows of the rich green leaves.

Dings's most obvious influences here are William
Wordsworth and Robert Frost (as opposed to Whitman and James Wright, both cited by Richard Howard in his typically baffling and breathless blurb),
and it should be noted that the poem's concluding
four lines resound with the kind of philosophical
wisdom associated with these poets. In other poems
in this carefully constructed book, Dings turns his
attention to various forms of art — opera and classical music, the piano, pottery — which allow him to
reflect on craft, as in "The Potter":

> . . . She Listens
> to the first faint strains of that voice
> in the mind's winds and blood's tides
> which begins whispering *give form to clay*
> as God itself must have first heard it

before turning us on the years of experience
to impress us with what we call loss,
Its invisible hands forming gloves of matter
to fit the accuracy of love. So it is love
she brings to her bowl-making, making nearly
any unusual shape so long as the bowlness
holds what needs to be held. . . .

No empty exercise this. Absence, pain, and death
animate the volume's most powerful poems, most
notably "The Concession," about a trapped, dying
beaver, and three particularly moving elegies to a
lost love or spouse, the prayerlike "A Last Request"; "Primal Sun, Primal Moon"; and "Paper
Bridge." In these musical poems Dings attains rare,
genuine eloquence.

Matthew Brennan is a poet in his late thirties
whose poems I have long admired for their dignified humanity and solid craft. It is good finally to
see his first collection, *Seeing in the Dark* (Hawkhead
Press), in print. Brennan, who was raised in Saint
Louis, educated at Grinnell College in Iowa and at

the University of Minnesota in Minneapolis, and currently teaches at Indiana State University in Terre Haute, is very much a midwestern poet in the tradition of Wright, Ted Kooser, and Jared Carter. His primary subjects are family life, love, art, and mortality. Brennan writes on the illness and deaths of parents and other relatives; on conjugal and parental love and on the painful disintegration of a first marriage; on the midwestern landscape; on baseball, Breughel, and Keats. In "Sky Lights," a poem on the death of his grandmother, Brennan's unpretentious directness of approach is at its strongest:

> When my grandmother died, sky –
> white as if embalmed – buried
> roads and parking lots with snow.
> The next day, though, as we drove
> to her grave in north St. Louis
> the sun penetrated ice like light
> pulsing through glass tubes.
>
> I remembered then a hot June night,
> months before: late, I'd walked
> by a huge house lit from rathskeller
> to rafters, Mozart thundering
> through its open door, while above
> stars splinted like bones withdrawing
> into the cold folds of earth.

In two brief stanzas characterized by a Wordsworthian juxtaposition of two physical and psychic landscapes, Brennan demonstrates both his economy and his unobtrusive music, characterized here by off rhyme, both internal ("though . . . drove"; "cold folds") and end ("sky" / "light"; "snow" / "drove"), as well as assonance and consonance. "Anniversary of the End of a Honeymoon" at once commemorates even as it anticipates the end of "a fair-weather marriage," one whose demise is presented in the bitterly confessional "A Divorcee's Revenge":

> Hearing your poisoned voice again today
> Makes me think of the great Christian martyrs
> Like Agatha who, when ripped from sackcloth
> And sandals like leftovers from Glad Wrap,
> Then raped, raped again, and finally rolled
> Over forty feet of burning coals and gravel,
> Never once lost her smile – not until blisters
> Blurred what had been her lips. And I as well
> Won't budge: you hate my "Goddamned guts" for
>   what
> I've got and won't give up – our kids, my neck.
> But now I've cut the wires, to keep my cool,
> And love all the wide world that is not you.

(The cut wires here recall an image from one of Brennan's other more emotionally extreme, confessional poems, " The Vasectomy," in which " . . . the surgeon's pulled black thread / like drawstring through your sack.") Brennan speaks with open emotion and gentle music, transmogrifying the quotidian details which anchor his vision into the more elevated realm of verse.

Bruce Bawer is known primarily as a literary critic of great acumen, a man whose literary essays appeared regularly for ten years in the *New Criterion,* as well as in other prestigious literary journals. These essays, collected in three volumes, have established Bawer as the closest thing we have in this country to a young Edmund Wilson. His first volume of poetry, *Coast to Coast* (Story Line Press), is divided into four sections, and the best poems in the first are two sequences, "Poems for Brian" and "Long Island Poems," and a longer autobiographical narrative, "Jeremy." Brian is the poet's younger nephew, and the two poems devoted to him, "Beach," set at the ocean in Rockaway, Queens, and "Thirteen," present touching glimpses of a young boy growing into manhood – with grace in the former and awkwardness in the latter. "Beach" presents the poet playing an improvised game with a tennis ball with his nephew, a physical activity which could have "been / choreographed for us by Fred Astaire" and which brings them into a momentary state of "a rare communion." In "Thirteen" "Brian is troubled," and the poet, faced with a cousin "Handsome now, not beautiful, / [looking] less like a child, more like a teen," comes to the realization that "there's nothing I can say" to help Brian overcome his adolescent problems. The three "Long Island Poems" delineate the movement from friendship to love to loss and the desire, in "Letter to Cambridge," to salvage something from the failed relationship:

> From the moment that a moment
>   enters the memory, it begins
> to feed on fantasy and fear.
>   Memory mixes with desire, never
> to be divorced. The past cannot
>   move into the present uncorrupted.
>
> That is why I reach out to you now,
>   not as a beloved, myth-laced memory
> but as a friend, estranged, in Cambridge.
> Please do not think me tiresome
>   for troubling you with memory. I ask
>   nothing of you but a moment's thought.

"Jeremy" presents a comic vision of a southern cousin, frequently inebriated, who moves to Manhattan and assumes the role of a young Truman Capote, albeit one with no discernible talent.

The second and briefest section of *Coast to Coast* is set in California, opening with a sonnet, "The View from an Airplane at Night, Over California," and closing with another lengthy and intricately structured autobiographical narrative, "California," in which the poet juxtaposes the stories of his parents' courtship, marriage, and tentative separation with that of a love affair of his own, begun in Manhattan in 1976 during the Democratic National Convention and moving on to California, the home of the speaker's lover. If the fate of both the marriage and the romance remain open-ended, the poem nevertheless comes to an effective conclusion with the poet attending a college reunion of his father with him.

It is in the final section of *Coast to Coast* that Bawer truly comes into his own as a poet in a series of love poems — especially the sequence "Sixty-Fifth Street Poems" — in which eros is accompanied by a sense of spiritual renewal and religious conversion. The eight "Sixty-Fifth Street Poems," dedicated to Bawer's companion Christopher, limn the unexpected joy that arises from the growth of their mutual love. If, as Molly Peacock observes, this sequence "crowns" the volume, then it is the sixth of these extraordinary love poems that is the jewel in this particular crown. "Confirmation," written to commemorate Christopher's being confirmed in the Episcopal Church on 5 November 1989, also celebrates the "grace" that animates their relationship:

> How is it that an old devotion calls
> across the years, and in a different key,
> discovering you in this far, foreign place,
> heart harnessed to and bedstead shared with me?
> How to discern the turnings of a grace
> that waits long years to raise a soul that falls
> out of its palm — and, in another land
> finding it, lifts with a different hand?

If Bruce Bawer is a New Formalist, then this certainly ranks as one of the finest lyrics to have come out of that movement.

But there are other exceptional poems in the third section of *Coast to Coast* as well. One of these is the first, "Grand Central Station, 20 December 1987," an elegy to a child who died in infancy. The others are the volume's final poems, "Poems for Chip," "Art and Worship," and "Devotions." In "Ferry," one of the two "Poems for Chip," Bawer writes of a sermon given by the former Episcopal bishop of New York, Paul Moore, where he embraces all forms of human love as sacred:

> The bishop recalled his own
> road to Damascus: year after year,
> he'd denied his vocation. Came the war,
> and he nursed battle-blasted men,
>
> their bodies repulsive, shattered.
> Only afterwards did he realize
> that when he stared into their eyes
> he'd seen the eyes of the Lord.
>
> For, he told us, that's where God
> resides: in the flesh,
> in the corrupt, imperfect flesh
> "in the flesh of everybody
>
> around you — your closest friend,
> the homeless man on the curb,
> your lover." Yes, that was the word
> he used: *lover.* And when I turned
>
> to you, your blue eyes burning red,
> your face wet with tears,
> as if all your twenty-three years
> had been comprehended in what he said.

In "Devotions," the book's final poem, the poet equates his own spiritual rebirth with the birth of his love for his companion:

> Years passed. Then, on a spring night
> no different from any other, a benign face
> appeared before him, and two radiant eyes.
> Falling in love he fell . . . or so he thought,
>
> till one day in almost-winter it struck
> like thunder in his breast: not only his flesh
> was taking long-sought nourishment from flesh.
> Quietly, too, his soul had been partaking.
>
> Flesh had come accompanied by grace; the light
> in his love's eyes was the love of God.
> It was that which filled him, night after night,
> in his love's warm arms. And so he prayed.

In *Coast to Coast* Bruce Bawer has written the finest first volume of poetry of the year.

Among the most honored collections of poetry of 1993 is Mark Doty's third collection, *My Alexandria* (University of Illinois Press), chosen (and glowingly praised) by Philip Levine, nominated for the National Book Award for poetry, and winner of both the National Book Critics Circle Award and *The Los Angeles Times* Book Award for Poetry for 1993. It deserves its honors. Doty's title refers, of course, to the Egyptian city memorialized by the twentieth-century Greek poet, C. P. Cavafy, whose poems juxtapose a concern with classical history and mythology with a frank presentation of casual homosexual encounters in the environs of his contemporary turn-of-the-century Alexandria. Cavafy would seem to be a particularly resonant model for Doty to emulate in a volume of poems which examines, among other subjects, the AIDS epidemic amidst the relics and ruins of American history and culture. The homoerotic, contemporary side of Cavafy is evident in Doty's "The Days of 1981," a poem about an evanescent homosexual affair begun at a Cambridge, Massachusetts, tea dance at the end of the disco era effectively brought to a close by the evolving awareness of the AIDS crisis. The poem also reflects the title of numerous Cavafy poems also imitated by James Merrill in his ongoing series Days of . . . poems. Doty's poem is an elegy to an epoch as well as to a failed love:

> If I knew where he was, even his last name,
> (something French?) I might call again
> to apologize for my naive
>
> persistence, my lack of etiquette,
> my ignorance of the austere code of tricks.
> I didn't know then how to make love like that.
>
> I thought of course we'd go on learning
> the fit of chest to chest, curve to curve.
> I didn't understand the ethos, the drama
>
> of the search . . .[.]

"Chanteuse," a meditation on Boston (one of two things identified in this poem as "my Alexandria"), which he sees embodied in the song as a black drag queen, is another direct homage to Cavafy, whom he quotes directly here (in the Keeley and Sherard translation), identifying Cavafy as a poet "of regret and desire" who "had no other theme / than memory's erotics, his ashen atmosphere." Doty adapts this theme as his own by the conclusion of "Chanteuse":

> That is how I would describe her voice,
>
> her lyric that becomes, now, my city:
> torch, invitation, accomplishment. *My romance*
> *doesn't need a blue lagoon standing by . . .*
>
> As she invented herself, memory revises
> and restores her, and the moment
> she sang. I think we were perfected,
>
> when we became her audience,
> and maybe from that moment on
> it didn't matter so much exactly
>
> what would become of us.
> I would say she *was* memory,
> and we were restored by

> the radiance of her illusion,
> her consummate attention to detail,
>   — *name the colors* — her song: my Alexandria,
>
> my romance, my magnolia
> distilling lamplight, my backlit glory
> of the wigshop, my haze
>
> and glow, my torch, my skyrocket,
> my city, my false,
> my splendid chanteuse.

(By poem's end, then, not only Boston but the drag queen chanteuse and her song also are identified by Doty as "my Alexandria.")

Among the volume's other poems concerned with AIDS are "Fog" and "The Wings," both perhaps too derivative of both Wallace Stevens and his "necessary angel" (as angel imagery figures strongly in the latter) and of Merrill's ouija board imagery so central to his epic *The Changing Light at Sandover* that most contemporary poets would, it seems to me, be reluctant to try to touch the subject. More successful and original is "With Animals," which concludes with the powerfully moving image of a dog, shot in the head, but nonetheless struggling to say alive, clearly an image for Doty of the struggle of those in the final stages of AIDS:

> . . . Something cleaves to form
>   until the last minute, past it,
>
> and though the vet's needle was an act
>   of mercy, the life needed to continue,
>
> the life was larger than cruelty,
>   the life denied the obliterating gesture
>
> where only kindness had been expected.
>   Even with one eye shot away and the brain spasming
>
> the life takes it in and says *more,*
>   just as it takes in the quick jab of the needle
>
> and the flooding darkness. The life doesn't care.
>   The life only wants, the fugitive life.

Powerful as well is the volume's final poem, "Lament-Heaven," which at once presents an image of poetry, art, and music as transcending mortality against AIDS, though the poem's final lines present both the image of art as transcendent and a lament for imminent death:

> *Oh why aren't I what I wanted to be,*
>
> *exempt from history?*
>   The music mounts up,
>   assembles its architecture

> larger than any of us
> and doesn't need you to continue.
> Do you understand me?
>
> I heard it, the music
> that could not go on without us,
> and I was inconsolable.

Many readers will find consolation in Doty's finely written book.

Donald Hall's latest collection of poems, *The Museum of Clear Ideas* (Ticknor and Fields), is another book which received much deserved attention, being nominated for both the National Book Award and the National Book Critics Circle Award for Poetry. I, for one, would have predicted him to be the winner of both of these awards, though a recent book of his, *The One Day,* did win the NBCC Award in 1988. Anyone who has read *The One Day* and *Old and New Poems* (Ticknor and Fields, 1990) knows that Hall is not only one of our best poets, he is also one of our wisest. (This wisdom comes through as clearly in Hall's wonderfully pellucid prose, as was evident last year in his revised collection of memoirs of poets, *Their Ancient Glittering Eyes* [Ticknor and Fields] as it is in his other volumes of memoirs — including this year's *Life Work* [Beacon] — and in his short stories.) In these works, which combine to seem a seamless whole, we have followed Hall's life, from his childhood in suburban North Haven, Connecticut, just north of the New Haven city limit, to his summers spent on his grandparents' farm in New Hampshire (where Hall retired with his wife, poet Jane Kenyon, after years of teaching at the University of Michigan, in 1975), through marriages and child rearing and bouts with drinking and, most recently, with grave illness, we have come to know and value Hall as if he were a good friend to whom we would turn to advice for that most difficult of questions: How to live?

Though all three books can and do stand on their own, it is most rewarding to read *The Museum of Clear Ideas* in conjunction with *Life Work* and Kenyon's book of poems *Constance. Life Work* is a meditation on work begun before Hall was diagnosed with cancer of the liver, a cancer that was a metastisization of the colon cancer for which he had been operated on two years previously, and continued after a successful operation for it. *Constance* (Graywolf) was written during the same time period and reflects on both her own battles with manic-depression and mortal illness as well as on Hall's health problems. It would be tempting to dismiss *The Museum of Clear Ideas* as pleasing light verse: after all, the first of the volume's four sec-

tions, "Another Elegy," is a mock elegy to an imaginary representative poet of Hall's generation; the second and fourth, "Baseball" and "Extra Innings," are meditations on baseball by a speaker named K. C.; and the third, the title sequence, is an imitation of the first book of Horace's *Odes* spoken in the voice of a minor Disney cartoon character (as Hall points out in the book's "Notes"), Horace Horsecollar. But treating it as merely light verse would be a serious mistake. If "Another Elegy," with all of its pointed allusions to John Milton's "Lycidas," is primarily a comic tour de force, it is also a deadly satire on all of the foibles — the drinking, the drugs, the failed marriages, the found religions, the trips to the detox centers, the maniacal artistic ambitions — which Eileen Simpson deals with seriously and with exquisite restraint in *Poets in Their Youth,* her memoir of her first husband, John Berryman, and his various literary friends — Robert Lowell, Delmore Schwartz, Jean Stafford, R. P. Blackmur, and others. How many contemporary poets can we say have done the same?

Despite the comic pseudonym based on Muddville's legendary "Casey at the Bat," Hall's meditations on baseball — which he is trying to explain to Kurt Schwitters, an imaginary, dead "Merzpoet and artist" — are in fact philosophical meditations on living an organized, productive, and happy life in the face of inescapable human suffering and mortality and the pleasures of sex. (This is the same territory covered in *Life Work.*) As if to emphasize the serious play that underlies both baseball and poetry, he has had fun with poetic form in both "Baseball" and in "Extra Innings": the former is written in nine parts, one corresponding to each inning of a regulation-length game, each of which itself is divided into nine sections each containing nine lines; in his three extra innings, Hall adjusts the lengths of each section and the number of lines in each accordingly. Never, however, does Hall's clever artifice interfere with the sage if playful philosophic voice which runs throughout. In the final three sections of "The Third Inning" of "Baseball," we can see the kind of connections he makes between baseball, life, and poetry throughout these poems:

> 7. All winter aged ballplayers try
> rehearsing their young manhood, running
> and throwing in Florida's sunshine;
> they remain old. In my sixtieth
> year I wake fretting over some new
> failure. Meeting an old friend's new wife,
> I panicked and was rude. Or I ache
> mildly, feeling some careless anger
> with my son I cannot push away.

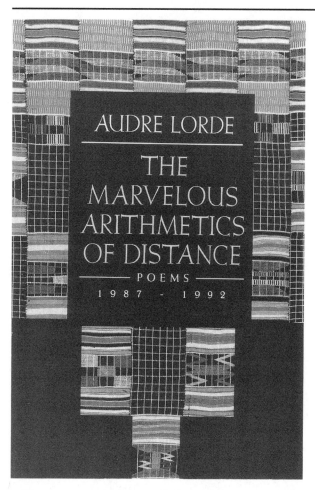

Dust jacket for Audre Lorde's last collection of poems. She died of breast cancer in 1993.

8. The bodies of major league baseball
players are young. We age past the field
so quickly; we diminish, watching
over decades, observing the young
as they dodder. The old cat hisses
at the kitten and pokes the new dog;
her life is ruined and she declines
bitterly toward death. At night she purrs
briefly, lying restored on our bed.

9. The leg is the dancer and the mouth
the sculptor. The tongue models vowels
or chisels consonants. Pause, pitch, pace,
length, and volume patine a surface
of shapes that the mouth closes over.
Behind our listening lips, working
the throat's silent machine, one muscle
shuts on/off/on/off: the motionless
leg of the word that leaps into the world.

"The Museum of Clear Ideas," based on the
Horatian odes, is by contrast exuberantly erotic and
wildly comic rather than quietly wise and playfully
mediative. One example will have to suffice, though

numerous passages beg to be quoted. Here is
"Don't let It bother":

Don't let it bother you, Flaccus, that Kimberly
dumped you for a younger chap — but stop this whin-
    ing;
this blubbering cacophony is repulsive
                            and self-pity requires stran-
    gling.

You say she promised? Drusilla complains of Marve,
who in his turn laments over Fidelia, who
will enter his sheets as soon as hollyhocks per-
                    form sexual intercourse
    with

horses. Aphrodite, provoking erectile
tissue, enjoys the consternation she contrives
by engendering unreciprocal desires.
                        We become friezes of pur-
suit.

Even Horsecollar, in his youthful days sometimes
sought after, developed erotic ambition
toward Bubbles the Body — as when the glass village
                    lusted for Hurricane Venus.

This is a delightful performance from beginning to
end. One hopes that Donald Hall has many more
extra innings in him left to play.

In *Constance,* her fourth volume of poems (she
has also published a translation of Anna Akhmatova), Jane Kenyon covers the same years in her
marriage with Hall as he does in his two 1993 volumes. But, despite their shared experience and frequently shared subject matter, Kenyon's voice is
distinctly her own, and the experience of reading
this fine volume of lyrics is a unique pleasure. In
one passage from his Horatian imitations in *The Museum of Clear Ideas,* Hall writes:

Or say: Mania like despair
is doubtless useful to poets
but grossly unreliable as
an index to reality.

Kenyon, like so many creative artists (Hall, it would
seem, included) is a manic-depressive; unlike Lowell and his generation, however, Kenyon has access
to numerous drugs — lithium being the first and
probably still most widely used — which can, to
greater and lesser extents, control the violent mood
swings that accompany this affliction. Still, the aid
provided by these drugs is not always a panacea, as
Kenyon demonstrates in her powerfully varied sequence, "Having it Out with Melancholy." Part 2 of

this poem, "Bottles," presents a catalogue of these pills:

> Elavil, Ludiomil, Doxepin,
> Nopramin, Prozac, Lithium, Xanax,
> Wellbutrin, Parnate, Nardil, Zoloft.
> The coated ones smell sweet or have
> no smell; the powdery ones smell
> like the chemistry lab at school
> that made me hold my breath.

Part 4, "Often," shows how, despite this battery of available pills, the poet still is prey to depression:

> Often I go to bed as soon after dinner
> as seems adult
> (I mean I wait for dark)
> in order to push away
> from the massive pain in sleep's
> frail wicker coracle.

Part 8, "Credo," includes this quatrain:

> Pharmaceutical wonders are at work
> but I believe only in this moment
> of well-being. Unholy ghost,
> you are certain to come again.

And yet the poem's ninth and final section, "Wood Thrush," ends in exultation not unconnected to pharmaceutical wonders":

> High on Nardil and June light
> I wake at four,
> waiting greedily for the first
> note of the wood thrush. Easeful air
> presses through the screen
> with the wild, complex song
> of the bird, and I am overcome
>
> by ordinary contentment.
> What hurt me so terribly
> all my life until this moment?
> How I love the small, swiftly
> beating heart of the bird
> singing in the great maples;
> its bright, unequivocal eye.

Rarely has a poet delineated the pain and exhilaration associated with manic-depression with such an "unequivocal eye."

Among the other successful poems in *Constance* are "The Stroller," providing a compressed autobiographical sketch of the poet from 1949 to 1991. "Chrysanthemums" poignantly records Kenyon's emotional response to the test results following one of her husband's cancer operations, while "Fear of Death Awakens Me" is a brief prose poem on the general anxiety deriving from an environment filled with grave illness. And, in the volume's penultimate poem, "Otherwise," Kenyon celebrates her life with Hall after one of his recoveries, even as she recognizes the precariousness of her happiness:

> At noon I lay down
> with my mate. It might
> have been otherwise.
> We ate dinner together
> at a table with silver
> candlesticks. It might
> have been otherwise.
> I slept in a bed
> in a room with paintings
> on the walls, and
> planned another day
> just like this day.
> But one day, I know,
> it will be otherwise.

Kenyon is a subtle celebrator of "ordinary contentment."

A. R. Ammons won the 1993 National Book Award for Poetry for his book-length poem *Garbage* (Norton). I am an admirer of Ammons at his best when he writes about nature in the philosophic manner of a current-day Wordsworth, as in such lyrics as "Corson's Inlet" and such book-length meditations as *Sphere*. Unlike Harold Bloom – the critic primarily responsible for creating Ammons's reputation as a poet to be contended with in the 1970s – who praises the book as "strong Ammons: wise, eloquent, exuberantly argumentative, imbued with the continued inventiveness of a maker who would have delighted Whitman and Emerson," I do not consider *Garbage* to be anywhere near Ammons at his best. At the opening of this eighteen-part meditation on America at the end of the twentieth century inspired by the sighting of a dump of garbage along I-95 in Florida, Ammons makes rather large claims for himself (even as his mocking tone seemingly lets him off the hook, should he fail in his ambition):

> Creepy little creepers insinuatingly
> curling up my spine (bringing the message)
>
> aging, Boy!, are you writing the great poem
> the world's waiting for: don't you know you
>
> have an unaccomplished mission unaccomplished;
> someone somewhere may be at this very moment
>
> dying for the lack of what W. C. Williams says
> you could (or someone could) be giving: yeah?

so these little messengers say, what do you
mean teaching school (teaching *poetry* and

poetry writing and wasting time painting
sober little organic, meaningful pictures)

when values thought lost (but only scrambled into
disengagement) lie around demolished

and centerless because you (that's me, boy)
haven't elaborated everything in everybody's

face, yet:

To me, it should be apparent from the sloppy language here ("unaccomplished mission unaccomplished"), the frequency and tediousness of Ammons's asides (and we have not gotten beyond the book's first page), and Ammons's lazily meandering style, that, though apparently he thinks it possible, seemingly spontaneous writing is not going to be enough to organize itself into an "elaborated everything" to give order to our seemingly chaotic age. (Apparently the National Book Award judges thought otherwise.)

While nonnarrative long poems are usually replete with yawning passages – if no one wished *Paradise Lost* longer, certainly this would, if possible, be more emphatically true of *The Prelude* or "Song of Myself" or "An Ordinary Evening in New Haven" – they are usually redeemed by eloquent moments of epiphany or what Wordsworth called "spots of time." Instead of achieving such moments (although he alludes to them), Ammons frequently achieves moments of embarrassingly, sloppily, and abstractly written passages of pseudoprofundity such as this:

and limits we can play through emergences free
of complexes of Big Meaning, but is there

really any meaninglessness, isn't meaninglessness
a funny category, meaninglessness missing

meaning, vacancy still empty, not any sort of
disordering, or miscasting or fraudulence of

irrealities' shows, just a place not meaning
yet – perhaps, of course, and appropriately,

never to mean:

There is, as we discover, a method behind Ammons's sloppiness, we discover toward the end of this book when he offers some theories of poetry which, if not new – they reflect the ideas of William Carlos Williams, Charles Olson, and other purvey-

ors of "open form" – but it is decidedly not Wordsworthian. Wordsworth wrote that a poem should prevent "strong emotion recollected in tranquility." For Wordsworth such recollection led to what he called the "philosophic mind," a condition to which not only the poet but all people should aspire. Not so does Ammons, who declares "but life is not first / for being remembered but for being lived!" This leads him to the inevitable conclusion that

                              . . . poetry
    is not logic
or knowledge or philosophy; it is action and

action's pleasure, but where does action end
and pleasure end, short of logic altogether,

not a dabble in theology, so airy and delightful:
you take even my old history teacher, his

commanding command of vocabulary was just part
of the trouble he couldn't stop talking, now

he's sitting in ward so and so, muttering: so,
put a period here and there, come around to a

closure, give somebody else the word: shut up
reticence's fullness in emptiness

should I go on

I don't think that Ammons is being at all self-parodic here in his description of "old history teacher," but any seasoned poet whose own "commanding command of vocabulary" admits such frequent, self-consciously repetitive phrases as "commanding command" might pause to consider his own advice to "shut up." To Ammons's question (posed, as usual here, without a question mark) "should I go on," I can only speak for myself by saying that I wish he had not. I think it can be safely said that people are not dying for lack of what Ammons has to offer in *Garbage.*

Linda Hogan was nominated for the National Book Critics Circle Award for *The Book of Medicines* (Coffee House Press). It is somewhat difficult to describe the eerie, elemental power of Hogan's poetry. Though its vision derives from the songs of her "grandmothers [who] were my tribal gods," the book that *The Book of Medicines* most resembles is Ted Hughes's *Crow,* despite the fact that, as the book's title suggests, Hogan's outlook is ultimately more benign than Hughes's. Yet if for Hogan poetry song, derived from the primitive form of chanting, is a form of "medicine," it is medicine that arises from the harshness of nature, from the various forms of "Hunger" described throughout the volume's three sections, particularly the second, which bears that title. But it would perhaps be more accurate to describe this book as a contemporary *Metamorphoses* as Hogan sees a continuity among all forms of nature – mineral, vegetable, animal, and human. Her poems are at their magical best when she seizes upon astonishing images that symbolize that interconnectedness, as that of a fetal whale described in "Crossings," perhaps the most successful poem in the volume:

> There is a place at the center of the earth
> where one ocean dissolves inside the other
> in a black and holy love;
> It's why the whales of one sea
> know songs of the other,
> why one thing becomes something else
> and sand falls down the hourglass
> into another time.
>
> Once I saw a fetal whale
> on a block of shining ice.
> Not yet whale, it still wore the shadow
> of a human face, and fingers
> that had grown before the taking
> back and turning into fin.
> It was a child from the curving world
> of water turned square,
> odd, small.
>
> Sometimes the longing in me
> comes from when I remember
> the terrain of crossed beginnings
> when whales lived on land
> and we stepped out of water
> to enter our lives in air.

Within this mythopoeic conception of "crossed beginnings" Hogan not only sees interconnections among herself and bears, mountain lions, buffalo, and bamboo, but between the material out of which poems are created as well – words. This can be seen most powerfully in "Tear," a poem about tear dresses, which a note describes as "traditional Chickasaw women's clothing":

> Tear dresses they were called
> because settler cotton was torn
> in straight lines
> like the roads we had to follow
> to Oklahoma.
>
> But when the cloth was torn,
> it was like tears,
> impossible to hold back,
> and so they were called

by this other name,
for our weeping.

Here Hogan weaves as well the actual history of Native American oppression directly into her poem, establishing it as one of the many wounds this magical "book of medicines" hopes miraculously to cure through contemplation, synthesis, and transformation.

Another Coffee House book nominated for the NBCC Award is Jack Marshall's *Sesame*. Marshall is of Arabic and Jewish descent. Central to this volume is its long, multipartite title poem emanating from the death of the poet's Lebanese grandmother whose gifts to him included not only sesame cookies and baklava but – despite her illiteracy in both written Arabic and English – language itself. One such gift is derived from Arabic:

> her never asking
> "What's on your mind?"
> but *"Ish fee elbak?"* Arabic for
> "What's in your belly?"

Another is in her confused English: "Mimicking Pop's 'Don't give me a lecture,' / with 'Don't give me a rupture.'" Clearly the folk-wisdom-like language of this Arabic grandmother is a significant source of the linguistic punning and play characteristic of this volume's best moments. Among the better poems here besides "Sesame," which goes on to examine the conflicts engendered by Marshall's mixed Islamic-Jewish background, are "G-D," about his Jewish heritage; "Crane," on his childhood in Elizabeth, New Jersey, as well as on Stephen Crane's death (his grave is in Elizabeth), and Hart Crane's, whose poetry proved more influential. In "Cross Street" Marshall presents a lively view of San Francisco street life:

> On Mission Street's sizzling McMeat rack,
> past a punk blond with spiked hair tufts
> speaking Queen's English; yakking
> through a bullhorn's snout in an apostolic fit for the
>   sheer
> thumping hell of it, zeal-crazed, hormone-hit, a teenage
>   kid
> brandishing a black Bible beats the air
> over pedestrians' heads. Soon as gawking
> girls stop to stare, his hoarse voice cracks; no less
> than everyone dropping in their tracks, on their knees
> at his feet, penitential sobs, mass conversion will do
> in full view of the born-again street. . . .

More serious are "Radio Tehran" and "The Home-Front," an Arab American perspective on "the air war on Baghdad, concrete-and-steel / rosette of a Babylonian garden" during the Gulf War.

Most prominent among the distinguished books of poetry lamentably overlooked by awards committees is Jared Carter's largely and inexplicably ignored *After the Rain* (Cleveland State University Press.) Carter deservedly won the Walt Whitman Award for his first collection of poems, *Work, for the Night is Coming* (Macmillan, 1981), in which he first introduced the midwestern landscape of the Mississinewa Valley, which he continues to explore in his second, extraordinary volume of mostly narrative poems, though it opens and closes with lyrics, with others effectively placed elsewhere in the volume. In "After the Rain," the lyric which serves as the prelude to the volume, Carter describes his poetic intention: to excavate the history and culture of his patch of midwestern land with the clarity which, in the aftermath of a rainstorm, allows a man to see arrowheads which have been churned to the surface of the earth by a plow:

> Still, even these are hard to see —
> at first they look like any other stone.
> The trick to finding them is not to be
> too sure about what's known;
>
> conviction's liable to say straight off
> this one's a leaf, or that one's merely clay,
> and miss the point: after the rain, soft
> furrows show one way
>
> across the field, but what is hidden here
> requires a different view – the glance on one
> not looking straight ahead, who in the clear
> light of the morning sun
>
> simply keeps wandering across the rows,
> letting his own perspective change.
> After the rain, perhaps something will show,
> glittering and strange.

One of the "glittering and strange" motifs that unifies *After the Rain* is the tale of the destruction of an entire town in the Mississinewa Valley, or rather, its evacuation and flooding with water to create a reservoir, the town itself remaining submerged. The first section of the book is concerned with antediluvian tales of life in the old town. The most effective of these narrative poems is "The Gleaning," about a man killed in a farming accident who is shaved by the town barber, an old friend, at the end of the day's farm chores in order to prepare his body for burial. His careful ministrations seem an act of love, the only way the barber knows how to express it:

> In the parlor
> the barber throws back the curtains
> and talks to this man, whom he has known
> all his life, since they were boys
> together. As he works up a lather
> and brushes it onto his cheeks,
> be tells him the latest joke. He strops
> the razor, tests it against his thumb,
> and scolds him for not being more careful.
> Then with darkness coming over the room
> he lights a lamp, and begins to scrape
> at the curve of the throat, tilting the head
> this way and that, stretching the skin,
> flinging the soap into basin, gradually
> leaving the face glistening and smooth.
>
> And as though his friend had fallen asleep
> and it were time now for him to stand up
> and stretch his arms, and look at his face
> in the mirror, and feel the closeness
> of the shave, and marvel at his dreaming –
> the barber trims the lamp, and leans down,
> and says, for the last time, his name.

The first section of the book closes with an extremely powerful short narrative, "The Purpose of Poetry," which tells of how an old man responds to being told his town will be flooded and he had best move to Florida with his daughter:

> Evenings by the barn he could hear the dogs
> talking to each other as they brought in
> the herd; and the cows answering them.
> It was the clearest thing he knew. That night
> he shot both dogs and then himself.
> The purpose of poetry is to tell us about life.

Carter tells us about life in all its complexity in poems too numerous to discuss in the detail they deserve. These include "Mississinewa Reservoir at Winter Pool," in which former residents return to look at their flooded town from the shore of the reservoir created there; "Panorama," about the uses made over the years in a rural farm out of strips from panoramic murals lost in the woods by a circus in the nineteenth century, strips which add a touch of wonder and beauty to the drabness of farm life; and four other poems concerning art – "Drawing the Antique," "Configuration," "Moire," and "Double Jacquard Coverlet." The volume's longest poem, "Barn Siding," is a narrative tour de force, a tale of love, betrayal, cruelty, retribution, and salvation, all narrated by a man injured when a house he is gathering wood from collapses around him. Among the volume's strongest lyrics are "Cicadas," "Head of the God of the Number Zero," "Frieze," "Cecropia Moth," "For Starr Atkinson, Who Designed Books," "Seed Storm," and "Mourning

Doves." And finally, the book closes with a moving evocation of another lost civilization, the Shaker community in Pleasant Hill, Kentucky, its only remnants being the buildings left behind. It is difficult to comprehend how the work of such a fine poet as Jared Carter could be so overlooked by the poetic establishment. *After the Rain* is a collection to read and savor, one which, in "This is Not a Poem," a meditation of the atomic bombing of Japan fulfills the other definition of poetry Carter gives in this volume:

> This is not a poem. It is brave reporting; it invites
>   you
> to think about the task before us even after The Bomb
>   is dismantled,
> after we have taken it apart and beaten it into
>   plowshares.
>
> It asks how we shall live, even then.
>   A poem asks how we shall live
> now.

Perhaps the finest individual volume of lyric poetry published in 1993 is Kelly Cherry's *God's Loud Hand* (Louisiana State University Press). Cherry, who was the first recipient of the James G. Hanes Poetry Prize of the recently established Fellowship of Southern Writers, is the author of three previous books of poetry, five works of fiction, and a memoir, *The Exiled Heart: A Meditative Autobiography,* recounting an affair with a Russian musician who was not allowed to immigrate to the United States by the Soviet Union. *God's Loud Hand* is divided into four sections. The first, "Common Prayers," contains largely devotional poems on New Testament subjects, while the latter three – "Songs for a Soviet Composer," "Plainsongs," and "A Joyful Noise" – all deal primarily with her love for the Soviet composer. These move from despair to joy and comment on the historical forces which tragically conspired to keep them apart.

Cherry's ability to move so facilely among religion, erotic love, and politics is nothing short of astonishing. In some of the poems – "Galilee," "The Radical," "Gethsemane," "Golgotha," "In the Garden by the Sea" – Cherry recounts Christ's ministry on earth, his Passion, death, and Resurrection. "Galilee" – one of many extremely effective sonnets in the volume – concludes with this sestet:

> You on the shore! Can you imagine how
> you would have felt, knowing that here was a god
> at sea, one who had already gotten
> his feet wet, one who, though he was not in
> over his head, was drifting even then
> toward the nakedness of eternity?

Dust jacket for Donald Hall's book of poems about living happily and productively in the face of inescapable human suffering

In "Signs" Cherry seamlessy combines the religious and the erotic:

> The way a man says *Can I go in you again,*
> *I want to swim up you forever,*
> The way his hands move over your body
> Like a fish, or like water moving
> Over the skin of a fish,
> The way he gives himself to you, sinking
> Into you,
> Signs that say
> *If there could be fish on the moon*
> *They would gleam with a silvery light*
> *Like his sides, they would glide*
> *Through the blue watery heavens*
> *Like small sleek gods,*
> *Each carrying in its mouth*
> *The image of*
> *Him.*

In "Songs for a Soviet Composer: A Text for a Musical Cycle" Cherry alternates between hope and despair as she recalls her lost love. Despair combines both emotions in "Approggiatura":

> Lover, beloved, hoped-for one, listen:
> Away from you, I'm as pale as the moon by day, a winter afternoon.
> Antlers glisten in the dying light – deer draw near. I curl up like a snail,
> or like drying leaves, lying on the riverbank, my ear to the earth, eavesdropping.
> Rock's heart beats, gravity sighs; my breath knocks against cold clay; I hear death
> keeping time until at last the land lies mute. There's sand in my eyes, salt in my tears.
> I make shale my pillow, sleeping, having hanged my harp upon the willow, weeping.

Yet the sequence concludes with hope in "Song Prophesying Happiness":

> He'll kiss my hands,
> and when I touch his forehead, the torment there will take wing.
> Then we'll sing.

The poems in "Plainsongs" are primarily political and historical, though her view of both is tempered by her politically interrupted affair; Cherry views history – in a sonnet bearing that title – as "this monumental subject being / The decline and fall of almost everything." By contrast the poems in the book's final section, "A Joyful Noise," as its title suggests, are celebratory. Among the many fine poems here celebrating love – "Love," "Grace," "Redemption," "Waiting for the End of Time," and "Prayer" – perhaps the most witty and appealing is Cherry's linguistic meditation in "*Grammaire Générale:* A Review" on language itself:

> Love is a verb, bringing one object to bear
> Upon another. It modifies fear.
> Lord, we are brave and gerundive, giving
> Ourselves to each other. Language is for the living;
> Love is a diphthong.
> (I could have parsed you all night long.)

> Ten years later, I remember your mouth
> On mine, its sweetness inflected with the South.
> Fluent in love, you affixed your root to my prefix.
> (We used adverbs for kicks.)
> That night we taught each other what we'd known all along.
> (And I could have parsed you all night long.)

God's Loud Hand is that rare volume of lyrics so animated by linguistic and musical grace its words seem to float off the page.

Several well-known poets published disappointing books in 1993, among them W. D. Snodgrass and Frederick Seidel. Snodgrass's first two collections of poems, *Heart's Needle* (1959) and *After Experience* (1968), are among the best books connected with the confessional poets, but his more recent work has been decidedly more uneven; that is certainly the case with his latest collection, *Each in His Season* (BOA Editions). The volume's first sequence, "Birds Caught, Birds Flying," opens with an embarrassingly banal love poem, "Anniversary Verses for My Oldest Life," a poem that in and of itself could give rhyme a bad name, as in its penultimate quatrain:

> Through ten years you've endured
> Me older than all others;
> Since aging hasn't cured
> Your tastes, stay thou my druthers.

"Stay thou my druthers?" "An Old Flame," on the other hand, is an effective love poem; there are several other effective lyrics, such as "Birds Caught, Birds Flying," "Pretexts," the comic "In Memory of Lost Brain Cells," and "An Envoi, Post-TURP." "A Teen-Ager," by contrast, is tasteless, while his "The Ballad of Jesse Helms" is as self-congratulatory as most such exercises encountered this year. The volume's other four sequences alternate between two containing fairly effective nature poems and two which grew out of a collaboration with painter DeLoss McGraw. This collaboration has resulted in overwhelmingly puerile poems featuring two of Snodgrass's most obnoxious creations, the characters W. D. and Cock Robin. I think it is time he laid these to rest. Frederick Seidel's *My Tokyo* (Farrar, Straus and Giroux) is at once slight and pretentious. Its slightness (the book runs only to fifty pages) is apparent in the one-lined "The": "The poem is a human torch. I burn. Burns out." Both weaknesses are apparent in "The Hour" (page 6) and "The New Woman" (page 25): they are virtually the same poem, with one change in punctuation and one different phrase between them. Seidel shows similar economy in recycling "The Last Poem in the Book," from his most recent previous volume, *These Days* (Knopf, 1989), as "The Death of Meta Burden in an Avalanche" in *My Tokyo*.

One distinguished older poet, albeit one less well known than Snodgrass and Seidel, who did not disappoint in 1993 is David Ferry, whose *Dwelling Places* (The University of Chicago) is a minor but genuine success. Ferry's title comes from 1 Cor. 4:11: "Even unto this present hour we hunger, and thirst, and are naked, and are buffeted, and have no certain dwelling place." His main theme, then, is the difficulty human beings have attaining psychic, spiritual, and physical security in the world. In "Dives" he deals with homelessness, while both homelessness and madness are both covered in "The Guest Ellen at the Supper for the Street People":

> It speaks itself over and over again in her voice,
> cursing maybe or not a familiar obscene event
> or only the pure event of original enchantment
> from the birth of the river waters, the pure unclean
> rising from the source of things, in a figure of torment
> seeking out Ellen, finding its home in her poor body.
>
> Her body witness is, so also is her voice,
> of torment coming from unknown event;
> unclean is the nature and name of the enchantment.

Two of Ferry's best poems, "Epigraph" and "Of Rhyme," meditate on poetry itself as being a dwelling place to inhabit, as can be seen in the latter:

> The task is the discovering of a rhyme
> whose consequence is just though unforeknown
> either in its completion having been
> prepared for though in secret all the time
>
> or in the way each step of the way brings in
> to play with one another in the game
> considerations hitherto unknown,
> new differences discovering the same.
>
> The discovering is an ordering in time
> such that one seems to chance upon one's own
> birth name strangely engraved upon a stone
> its consequence of the completion of the rhyme.

Many of Ferry's poems here are translations from Johann Wolfgang von Goethe, Jorge Guillén, Charles Baudelaire, and others, but the strongest poem here is a sequence, "Mary in Old Age," influenced by Wordsworth, about whom Ferry, the Sophie Chantal Hart Professor of English at Wellesley College, has published a critical work. In this six-part sketch of an old woman in a nursing home, reminiscent of Wordsworth's poems on peasants, all of Ferry's thematic concerns – with home, language, madness, isolation, and salvation – come together. As a visitor at Mary's nursing home, Ferry tries to make sense of her "babble":

> *"I don't want to stay here. I want to stop it."*
> Was "here the nursing home? Was it the chair?
>
> The condition she was in? Her life? Life? The body?
> Which of these things was it she wanted to stop?

> Was she imprisoned in a world whose meanings
> she was so familiar with that she needed to make
>
> no translations at all, and no translation would be
> anything fatuous? Thus "Life" seems melodramatic,
>
> too large and general to fit the case.
> But "the chair" seems too small. And "the nursing home"
>
> too obviously the right answer to be so.

But Mary achieves no salvation, no release from "the unclean spirit" who inhabits her, so that, by poem's end, "it is worse / for her, much worse, than it had earlier been." There is little verbal flash in *Dwelling Places;* merely a sober, compassionate attention paid to the precariousness of the human predicament.

Three younger poets published impressive second collections in 1993 – Rosanna Warren, Richard Foerster, and Michael Donaghy. In *Stained Glass* (Norton) Warren, whose frequent and deft use of meter, rhyme, and fixed forms (especially the sonnet) clearly aligns her with the New Formalist movement of poets now primarily in their forties, goes a long way toward establishing herself as one of her generation's more accomplished poets. Hers is, by and large, a quiet, refined sensibility, albeit one of admirable range. In many of her lyrics on the New England landscape – "Season Due"; the sonnets "Noon" and "Farm"; "His Long Home" (dedicated to her late father, Robert Penn Warren); "From New Hampshire"; "Mountain View"; and others – Warren writes in the tradition of Robert Frost. (Indeed, many of these poems were written while Warren was in residence at the Robert Frost Farm in Franconia, New Hampshire.) Her interests extend, however, to classical Greece and French life and civilization in general; the Angmagssalikmiut Eskimos of eastern Greenland; religion; pornography; and the surrealist poems of Max Jacob and Pierre Reverdry, translations of which are included here. In "Noon" Warren demonstrates her quirky way with the fixed form of the sonnet and her rootedness in the landscape of New England:

> High summer. Plenitude. The granite knoll
> thrusts through gray soil at the hill crest. Drought:
> spring is fulfilled. I crouch on the warm skull
> of New Hampshire. Spikes of patched grass jut
> through the anthill at my feet, and the whole field
> grates with small oracles of cicadas
> scrape between thigh and wing. What do I hold
> at bay? The idea of harvest, days that ooze . . .
> From the valley rises the Interstate's purr,
> the whine of outboards from the lake, a child's voice
> quarreling. Someone's hammer raps the air,

duet with its own knocked echo. Here is the precise dead heart of the living day, the hollow core, the pit around which light thickens, and we eat.

In the volume's final poem, "The Twelfth Day," a meditation on *The Iliad,* Warren demonstrates both her familiarity with the classics and her skill with open forms as well:

> So what if everything
> echoes the Father *let go let*
> *go* This is Ancient
>
> Poetry It's supposed
> to repeat
> The living mangle the dead
>
> after they mangle the living
> It's formulaic
> That's how we love It's called
>
> compulsion Poetry can't
> help itself
> And no one has ever
>
> explained how
> light stabbed
> the hero how he saw
>
> in dawn salt mist
> his Mother's face (she who
> Was before words she
>
> who would lose him)
> Saw her but heard
> words *Let him let*
>
> *go* Saw her and let
> his fingers loosen
> from that
>
> suspended decay and
> quietly
> too quietly
>
> turned away.

Warren's career is progressing nicely.

Last year I all too briefly discussed *Sudden Harbor* (Orchises), Richard Foerster's first collection of poetry. I am happy to report that his second, *Patterns of Descent* (Orchises), is even stronger. In many ways Foerster has abandoned the Bronx of his childhood, which figured so strongly in many of the autobiographical poems in his first volume, both to inhabit the rural landscape of coastal Maine, where the poet now resides, and into the heady world of art and culture, which Foerster happily handles far better than Stephen Yenser. (The book *does* have an

epigraph by James Merrill.) The title of the book comes from the poem "Covenant," an elegy to the son of a friend who died in a hang-gliding accident:

> A hawk is soaring in tightening loops.
> Its pinions splay for banking. It stalls
> an instant. Turns like a parasol.
> Tilts left, then right, then dizzyingly stoops.
>
> Such patterns of descent – and then the aborted
> squeal of field prey. But we're taught "It's nature,"
> oiled like a fine machine, and the creature's
> done, swept through the zero of vortex.
>
> And yet, watching the predatory fall,
> I can't forget the ordered world,
> this stingy solace, when a parent's hurled
> in grief's inhabitable hell.
>
> This side the barbwire field, unable
> to see the object in the claws,
> I think of the sons *I* never saw,
> the too rash boy in Ovid's fable,
>
> and yours aloft in that jerry-built plane,
> so full of the April day, raw joy
> riding the sky, the machine his toy
> turned mangling raptor in Berwick, Maine.

Foerster also draws well on myth in "Actaeon" and "Arachne," and on Dante in "Canto XIII." His interest in fixed form is on good display in "Terzanelle," and he has written an impressive prayer-cycle, "The Hours" (which was published in a limited edition by Red Hydra Press). And, in the book's final section, Foerster writes far more boldly (and well) about gay sex than he dared in his first book in poems such as "Victoria Station," "Gay Head," and "Life Drawing," which concludes with this description of a model "with hard Euclidean curves":

> The taut musculature of his abdomen and
> thighs,
> the languid sex and gaze – all the im-
> pediments
>
> of time – he bares before the world, as if they were mir-
> acles
> intended to disrupt this moment's purity
> and the paper's immaculate void.

In many ways Foerster is developing into a genuine heir of James Merrill, who, as Yenser and so many others prove, is no easy act to follow.

The reasons a poet of Michael Donaghy's stature has remained so little known in America are not hard to discover. This Bronx-born Irish American poet immigrated to England a decade ago, and though his two collections have gained him a considerable reputation in the United Kingdom, his books have not been reviewed in his native land. (His first collection, *Shibboleth,* was first published by Oxford University Press in England in 1988 and won both the Whitbread Poetry Category and the Geoffrey Faber Memorial Prize.) This neglect is especially unfortunate in light of his excellent second volume, *Errata* (Oxford University Press). The poems in this collection are exceedingly well crafted, wide-ranging, witty, imaginative, and often deeply moving.

A performer with a group of traditional Irish musicians, Donaghy's interest in the roots of folk music forms the core of "O'Ryan's Belt," the second of the book's three sections. In these five poems Donaghy writes of the influx, early in the twentieth century, of gramophone records and Victrolas into Ireland from the United States, either with returning immigrants or with their corpses ("The Hunter's Post"); the poet's recording of Irish folk songs sung upon request by the bartender, dying of cancer, in a Blarney Stone bar in the South Bronx in 1971, a neighborhood whose ethnic makeup was shifting from Irish to Puerto Rican ("A Repertoire"); and a similar type of oral tradition in Chicago ("Reprieve" and "The Classics"). The blues are the focus of "Down," while "Theodora, Theodora" focuses on the folk music heard in a Greek taverna. There are three impressive narrative poems in the volume. "The Incense Contest" is told in an opium-induced trance by an eleventh-century Japanese courtesan formerly married to a prince; "The Commission" reads like a Browningesque tale of intrigue and revenge against the setting of Pope Clement's reign in Renaissance Italy; and "True" recounts the fatal journey of a Victorian sea captain, with allusions to Alfred Tennyson's "Ulysses," and passages derived from travel narratives and a folk ballad. "Glass" is notable at once as a successful rendering of a shaped poem even as it is a delicately rendered love lyric. "Alas, Alice" is one of the most engaging brief prose poems I have read because Donaghy's prose here is metrical.

Donaghy's technical skill is on display in the cleverly structured "A Discourse on Optics," a two-part poem whose unifying metaphor is a mirror, as well as in the delicate love lyric that opens the book, "Held":

Not in the sense that this snapshot, a girl in a garden,
Is named for its subject, or saves her from ageing,

Not as this amniotic changed like a sinner to minerals
Heavy and cold on my palm is immortal,
But as we stopped for the sound of the lakefront one
    morning
Before the dawn chorus of sprinklers and starlings.

Not as this hieroglyph chiselled by Hittites in lazuli,
Spiral and faint, is a word for 'unending',
Nor as the hands, crown, and heart in the emblem of
    Claddagh,
Pewter and plain on that ring mean forever,
But as we stood at the window together, in silence,
Precisely twelve minutes by candlelight waiting for thun-
    der.

And finally, for all his cosmopolitan polish, no other American poet from his generation whose work I am aware of has written as poignantly as Donaghy on growing up Irish American, not only in "A Repertoire" but also in several lyrics at the close of the book, especially "Fraction" and "Erratum," both concerned with error and with the bridge – and the connection – between the poet and his mother. Here is "Fraction":

The fourteenth time my mother told the story
Of her cousins dismembered by a British bomb,
I turned on her, her Irish son. 'I'm American.
I was born here.' She went to pieces.

And would not be solaced. I had her eyes,
The aunt's, that is, who, the story goes,
Was brought to the jail to sort the bits in tubs.
Toes. I meant to renounce such grotesque pity.

I was thirteen. I didn't know who I was. She knew.
As I held her wrists, reassuring,
Repeating, that I was her Irish son,
I was the man who'd clicked the toggle switch

Bracing himself between two branches,
Between the flash and the report.

Errata is an unusually strong and entertaining second collection of poems, one which firmly establishes Donaghy as one of a handful of the finest American poets of his generation. I hope that his work will win the American audience it so richly deserves.

Cynthia Zarin, on the staff at *The New Yorker,* also published a second volume of poems, *Fire Lyric* (Knopf), which marks a happy advance of her rather lifeless debut volume, *The Swordfish Tooth* (Knopf, 1989). Like Brad Leithauser, Zarin remains perhaps too much influenced by Marianne Moore, particularly in the nature lyrics in the volume's first section, "Terra Anima." Elizabeth Bishop is another strong influence she is still working through. And yet the book's final poem, "Song," seemingly about an infant in her womb, is one of the most beautiful lyrics I read in 1993:

> My heart, my dove, my snail, my sail, my
>   milktooth, shadow, sparrow, fingernail,
>   flower-cat and blossom-hedge, mandrake
>
> root now put to bed, moonshell, sea-swell,
>   manatee, emerald shining back at me,
>   nutmeg, quince, tea leaf and bone, zither,
>
> cymbal, xylophone; paper, scissors, then
>   there's stone – Who doesn't come through the door
>   to get home?

"Song" shows Zarin's potential to break through into a voice more fully her own.

Anne Stevenson, born in 1933, is another American poet who has long been a resident of England and is probably best known in her native United States as the official biographer of Sylvia Plath. Stevenson received unusual attention for that role this year in a lengthy article on the art of contemporary biography by Janet Malcolm that took up virtually the entire 23 and 30 August 1993 double issue of *The New Yorker*. In addition to much else, Malcolm, who knew Stevenson as an undergraduate at the University of Michigan in the 1950s, is to be congratulated for her astute critical judgment of Stevenson as an important poet – one who – like Donaghy, one hopes – finds the American audience her poetry deserves with the publication of her latest volume, *Four and a Half Dancing Men* (Oxford University Press).

Stevenson's poetry has some things in common with that of her younger expatriate poet, Donaghy: a concern with meter and craft; an ironic sense of distance between herself and her subject matter, whether or not her focus is on the lyric eye; and intellectual curiosity combined with keen wit. (These qualities, needless to say, are rare among most contemporary American poets.) But Stevenson has lived in England longer than Donaghy, and her subject matter and diction are almost exclusively British. She is particularly drawn to the flora of the English and Welsh landscapes and to the Welsh language, which she often uses, with a Hopkinsesque effectiveness, as in "May Bluebells, Coed Aber Artro" and "Binoculars in Ardudwy":

> Look now, the sun's reached out,
> painting turf over ice-smoothed stone.
> A green much younger than that
> praises *Twllnant* and *Pen-isa'r-cwm*.

> All this through the lens of a noose
> I hold to my focusing eyes,
> hauling hill, yard, barn, man, house
> and a line of blown washing across
>
> a mile of diluvian marsh.

Stevenson is as effective at sketching portraits of people as she is of describing nature. In "The Professor's Tale (New England)" Stevenson etches with brilliant economy the life of a woman obsessed with ritual, art, and order who is humiliated by her inability to control the lives of her children. In her sequence "Visits to the Cemetery of the Long Alive" she brings to life, with a grim humaneness, a series of inhabitants in a nursing home, most of whom would prefer to be dead; it reads like a poetic condensation of Barbara Pym's excellent novel on the elderly, *Quartet in Autumn*. The most successful poem in this sequence is "A Sepia Garden," which sketches in the entire life of a woman who believes *"I won't last the night,"* in effect creating a social history of mid- to late-twentieth-century Cambridge and Oxford, even as it distinguishes between British and American theories of the self. In "Politesse" Stevens vividly recalls a desired affair in the 1950s with a young man – "Your hair was gods' gold, curled, / and your cricketer's body / tanned" – with whom she is touring Italy, an affair which remained unconsummated because of what Stevenson wittily shows to be the young man's inappropriate sense of politesse:

> If I weren't *virgo intacta,*
>   you told me sternly,
> you'd take me like a cat in heat
>   and never respect me.
> That was something I thought about
>   constantly, deeply,
>
> in the summer of '54, when I
>   fell completely
> for a Milanese I only met once
>   while tangoing, tipsy,
> on an outdoor moon-lit dance-floor.
>   I swear you lost me
> when he laid light fingers on my lips
>   and then, cat-like, kissed me.

Stevenson's gift for witty, concise characterization is most succinctly and amusingly on display in "A Quest":

> Precocious, in the news at nine or ten,
> She hero-worshipped creamy Englishmen,
> Doe-eyed like Rupert Brooke, with downy chin,
> A type that dies in youth and likes to swim.

An Alpha graduate at twenty-one,
She picked them macho and American,
Big Michelin shoulders with a greasy tan,
Sliced pie from hunk to hips like Superman.

She hit the acid road at thirty, when
Her analyst unearthed a psychic yen
To crumple under hairy, beery men.
Her Id was rampant and bohemian,

But still she married Mr IBM
Whose cash came handy when she scuppered him
And went to Cambridge where she lived in sin
With deconstructed Cath'lic Marxism.

At fifty, menopausal, nervous, thin,
She joined a women's group and studied Zen.
Her latest book, *The Happy Lesbian,*
Is recommended reading for gay men.

With *Four and a Half Dancing Men,* Stevenson makes it patently clear that she is more than just a biographer of Sylvia Plath; she is among the wisest, wittiest, and most accomplished of contemporary poets in the language.

One of the most purely entertaining volumes of poetry to appear in 1993 is John Updike's *Collected Poems, 1953–1993* (Knopf). Updike is a genuine man of letters and one of the few living novelists who is a first-rate poet as well, though his poetry has not – because it is often light (and frequently erotic) – gotten the general attention it would have received had he not been so successful a creator of Rabbit Angstrom, Henry Bech, the Maples, and other notable fictional characters. Among other treasures contained in the volume is Updike's illustrated autobiographical narrative sequence, "Midpoint," originally published in 1969. Here is one of Updike's most notorious (yet certainly touching) erotic poems, "Fellatio":

How beautiful to think
that each of these clean secretaries
at night, to please her lover, takes
a fountain into her mouth
and lets her insides, drenched in seed,
flower into landscapes:
meadows sprinkled with baby's breath,
hoarse twiggy woods, birds dipping, a multitude
of skies containing clouds, plowed earth stinking
of its upturned humus, and small farms each
with a silver silo.

And here is one of his witty epigraphs, "Déjà, Indeed": "I sometimes fear that I shall never view / A French film lacking Gérard Depardieu." Fred Chappell, another contemporary master of both fiction and poetry, published this entertaining book of one

hundred of his epigraphs, *C* (Louisiana State University Press).

Finally, the most welcome volume of collected poems published in 1993 is John Haines's *The Owl in the Mask of the Dreamer: Collected Poems* (Graywolf). This volume provides a welcome occasion to reevaluate the work of one of America's finest senior poets. John Haines's literary career would be unusual in any era, but it is absolutely singular in the age of workshop-oriented professor poets. After serving in the navy in World War II and spending several years studying art, Haines moved to Alaska, where he homesteaded in the remote north for over twenty years, living mostly alone and supporting himself off the land, largely by hunting, fishing, and trapping. Haines came to slow maturity as a writer in a sort of intense solitude more reminiscent of early Christian or Buddhist mystics than of contemporary poets. It is not surprising, therefore, that Haines's poetry is primarily existential in its concerns. His subject matter – the insignificance of human life against the panorama of nature, the inevitability of death, the grace afforded by the imagination's encounter with reality and great art – might seem shockingly old-fashioned to a thoroughly postmodernist reader. He makes no attempts to be contemporary, so absolutely sure is he of the authenticity of his vision.

His allegiances, in fact, lie with the great early modernists – T. S. Eliot, Rainer Maria Rilke, Armando Vallejo, Hermann Broch, and Robinson Jeffers. He is, perhaps, the last American poet writing convincingly in this high modernist mode. His work is dense, difficult, and highly charged. Haines first came into prominence at the height of the deep image school and his early work possibly constitutes the strongest argument in favor of that short-lived movement that quickly became more of a clichéd technique than a genuine vision. His best poems from that early period include "If the Owl Calls Again," "The Mole," "Horns," "South Wind," "The End of Summer," "Into the Glacier," "The Stone Harp," "The Lemmings," "The Snowbound City," and "Wolves," which is representative:

Last night I heard wolves howling,
their voices coming from afar
over the wind-polished ice – so much
brave solitude in that sound.

They are death's snowbound sailors;
they know only a continual
drifting between moonlit islands,
their tongues licking the stars.

But they sing as good seamen should,
and tomorrow the sun will find them,
yawning and blinking
the snow from their eyelashes.

Their voices range through the frozen
water of my human sleep,
blown by the night wind
with the moon for an icy sail.

Haines's work is more ambitious with each succeeding volume. His most recent book previous to this one, *New Poems, 1980-88* (Story Line Press, 1990), contained long sequences quite distinct from his earlier brief lyrics, some of them long meditations on art, including "Days of Edward Hopper," "Of Michelangelo, His Question," and "On a Certain Field in Auvers," the latter a fine re-creation of the mind of Vincent Van Gogh:

I, who never for one hour
forgot how the light seizes
both field and striding sower;
who held my hand steady
in the solar flame, and drank
for my thirst the fiery
mineral spirit of the earth.

Who remembered always, even
in the blistering south,
a cellar in the north
where a handful of stunted
people peeled their substance

day by day, and all their
dumb and patient misery
steeped in a cold green light.

This volume earned renewed respect in the form of a nomination for the National Book Critics Circle Award for Poetry and the Lenore Marshall Poetry Prize. In the new and uncollected poems contained in *The Owl in the Mask of the Dreamer,* Haines continues to mine the subject of art in poems on Heironymus Bosch, Francisco Goya, Auguste Rodin, Pablo Picasso, Marsden Hartley, and David Smith. Haines is increasingly concerned with spirituality and death, as in his meditation on Michelangelo's painting of *Night* in the Medici Chapel in Florence. "Night," as well as the volume, concludes thus:

So I in this quiet sleep of stone
can say to you: Leave to me
this one sustaining solace —

my night that has more night
to come. To the sun that set,
whose dawn I cannot see . . .

Mute in my transformation,
and do not wake me.

Graywolf is to be congratulated for publishing this volume of such austere but "sustaining solace."

Dictionary of Literary Biography Yearbook Award for a Distinguished Volume of Poetry Published in 1993

Jared Carter won the Walt Whitman Award for his first book of poems, *Work, for the Night Is Coming* (Macmillan, 1981), a collection of largely narrative poems set in the mythical midwestern landscape of the Mississinewa Valley. In the twelve years between this fine first volume and his even more extraordinary second one, Carter's poems were largely disseminated through slender limited editions, a process that engendered a small, enthusiastic readership, but not the kind of national reputation that other, less significant poets of his generation have earned. With *After the Rain* (Cleveland State University Press) that unfortunate situation deserves to change. From the exquisite opening lyric, "After the Rain," through the powerfully rendered narratives ranging from the midlength "The Gleaning" to the longer and expertly paced "Barn Siding," Carter has created a poetic universe as memorable as Sherwood Anderson's Winesburg, Ohio, or Edgar Lee Masters's Spoon River. He has made the nonautobiographical narrative a vital contemporary poetic form being mined by such younger poets as Robert McDowell, Mark Jarman, Dana Gioia, David Mason, and Paul Lake. Well crafted, philosophically profound, and eminently readable, *After the Rain* is the finest, most varied, and most rewarding volume of poetry published in 1993.

– *Robert McPhillips*

Dust jacket for Jared Carter's volume of poems set in the mythical landscape of the Mississinewa Valley

The Year in Poetry, 1994

David R. Slavitt
University of Pennsylvania

What we have, it appears, is poetry in a vacuum, which is even worse than poetry in a salad shooter or a hot-air corn popper. There is no consensus about the culture and therefore no common ground on which poets, critics, scholars, students, and even readers (are there any left?) can share assumptions and discuss with some coherence the great questions of Dichtung and Wahrheit.

To suggest this tohubohu in a manner that may be unfair but is quick, efficient, and vivid, let me cite a few blurbs from the pile of books on the table (see key below):

"[A's book] offers . . . the sense of a writer maturing into a deeper idiom, reaching the full length of his stride. . . . [A] may be one of the poets on whom the future of the genre depends."

"The striking classical severity and concision of [B's] poems convey something by turns histrionic, Romantic, vertiginous, savage. Clarity and maelstrom at the same moment. Or eerie poise."

"Love and anxiety, memories and mysteries — [C]'s woven them all into a rich verse fabric, thrown like a flowered shawl over her shoulders as she stands out under the chilling night sky, no other soul around but (for that haunting moment) the reader's own."

"There is only so much the English language can do. [D] . . . tries to make it do more. The very effort results in marvelous uniquities, extending and dogged."

"[E] breaks through the ring of fire and captures his Muse. The voice is now uncannily his own; uncanny because we believe we have heard it before, yet the accents are unearthly and utterly fresh."

"This is [F's] finest book yet, with its knife sharp, poignant erotic comedy, its low life and high meters. These are poems that go down like aged brandy, burning the throat, easing the heart."

A brief portion of this article appeared in *The New York Times Book Review*, 12 February 1995. ©copyright David R. Slavitt.

And to conclude, a twofer, with one blurbist proclaiming that "[G's] poetry goes straight to the elastic, infinite core of time," while another says, enthusiastically if not entirely coherently, "[G] makes elegy like pilgrimage, like epistle, like quest; elegy paradoxically filled like a cornucopia, for abundance and loss are the terms."

One could go on, but you get the idea. There are no standards, no rules, nothing to appeal to except excess. The illusion of assertion (or, say, the energetic declaration of nothing in particular) carries weight because of the name at the end of the weird remark. We are not actually supposed to think much about these recommendations, asking odd questions about "uniquities," wondering why the endorser of E has conflated Brunhilde and Thalia, or trying to imagine whether the recommender of F has ever once tasted aged brandy (desirable and worth its greater price precisely because it does *not* burn the throat). We are not expected to pause to wonder whether there is anything like a "core of time," elastic, infinite, or otherwise.

A cheap trick, you think? Well, it would be if these weren't all by and for major poets — which is to say poets whose commercial viability or intellectual prestige is great enough to keep the trade publishers dabbling from time to time in poetry. (Or, no, sorry — D's book is from a university press, but the curious encomium is by a poet whose work appears in all the anthologies these days.)

Nobody knows what poetry is, and so it has become a breach of manners to propose any norma-

Key to Blurbs
A=Sven Birkets on Thomas Lux
B=Frank Bidart on Michael Fried
C=J. D. McClatchy on Eavan Boland
D=Gwendolyn Brooks on Stephen Todd Booker
E=Harold Bloom on Edward Hirsch
F=Alicia Ostriker on Marilyn Hacker
G=John Ashberry and Rachel Blau DuPlessis on Ann Lauterbach

tive standards. An elitist trick, even – for if there are no judgments to be made about quality, then the prizes, writer-in-residence jobs, fellowships, and honors can be apportioned in politically equitable ways among all the various *Untermenschen* groups (except, perhaps, straight white males). Having been confronted in schools and colleges by difficult poems that could serve as occasions for smart exegetical exercises, some readers have learned to expect of poetry that it make no immediate sense. A certain kind of poet caters to this bizarre conditioning, flouting sense and even syntax, in neurasthenic displays of distraction and dislocation to which we are supposed to respond with a clinician's attention, figuring that such ravings must be the product of an exquisite sensibility in all but unspeakable suffering. Figure, then, that these blurbs are endorsements of the aesthetic qualities of the ravings of a bunch of loonies and . . . you begin to admire their inventiveness.

My reading of the poems themselves was somewhat less chaotic. There were the books from those with large reputations in which I looked for justification of so many honors, awards, and emoluments, sometimes finding it and sometimes not. There were books by writers I have known and liked before, at which I looked with special interest and even fondness. (One has one's poets, Pablo Picasso said, the same way one has one's preferred tobacco, wine, and dog.) And there were books by those writers with whom I had no familiarity and no particular expectations, a few of them delightful or interesting and many others much less so.

Three of the most interesting books of the year were from transplanted Brits – Geoffrey Hill, Thom Gunn, and Paul Muldoon. Hill, who teaches at Boston University, is a religious poet, and his *New and Collected Poems – 1952–1992* (Houghton Mifflin) is wracked with a dramatic struggle of faith and doubt, an almost unbearable mixture of yearning and loathing. His poetry is concentrated, even difficult, which is likely to put off some readers. But there is no exam. What we do with difficult poetry is sidle up to it, attracted in the first instance maybe by a review – or even a jacket blurb ("Christopher Ricks, writing in *The New York Times Book Review,* has called Geoffrey Hill 'the best poet now writing in England . . . ' "). But then as we read, we may be hooked by some lines that resound in our own depths whether we understand them entirely or not – as I was by these, from the second part of the double sonnet he calls "Annunciations," which hit me when I came across them some years ago:

Geoffrey Hill, whose New and Collected Poems – 1952–1992 *was published in 1994*

O Love, subject of the mere diurnal grind,
Forever being pledged to be redeemed,
Exposed yourself for charity; be assured
The body is but husk and excrement.
Enter these deaths according to the law,
O visited women, possessed sons. Foreign lusts
infringe our restraints; the changeable
Soldiery have their goings-out and comings-in
Dying in abundance. Choicest beasts
Suffuse the gutters with their colorful blood.
Our God scatters corruption. Priests, martyrs,
Parade to this imperious theme: 'O Love,
You know what pains succeed; be vigilant; strive
to recognize the damned among your friends.'

I was not crystal clear about what this means and do not claim now to have worked out every nuance, but, as Tommy Lee Jones calls out to Harrison Ford in *The Fugitive* (1993), "I don't care!" The subject is Love, clearly, or Christian charity. *Caritas.* And it is clear that the suggestion that "Our God scatters corruption," which hangs there in the mind, means both that God defies and destroys corruption, scattering it as a victorious general scatters fleeing soldiers of his adversary, but also in the sense of strewing, inviting corruption in order that, by *caritas* (by faith and hope, too, but mainly by *caritas*) we might transcend the corruption. There is the same doubleness in the first line, for "subject" can mean the topic and therefore the point of the "mere diurnal grind," or it can mean that the diurnal grind is sovereign, in which case Love is subject *to* it. In any event, for those priests and martyrs who do succeed – whatever that means – the rewards are paradoxical, for they have to recognize the damned among their friends, the ones they loved, the ones they would have liked to have saved.

Novels are long; collections of poems are mostly short. But the density of the poetry, which is what makes it difficult, invites us to reread and then rewards us, because we have developed a relationship with the work, an intimacy, one might say, of the kind that long marriages can occasion. There are code words and phrases that suggest whole worlds of experience. It is not merely that we have come to know the poet, although that happens too, but we have discovered new territory in our own sensibilities and souls, hidden vistas we would not have found otherwise.

Hill, born in 1932 and educated at Oxford, has taught, first in England then, since 1988, at Boston University. One of his previous books was the hundred-quatrain poem – included in this volume – *The Mystery of the Charity of Charles Péguy* (1993), one of the finest long poems of this century. The odd title is an adaptation of Péguy's own little-known verse drama, *Le Mystère de la Charité de Jeanne d'Arc,* and what the Hill piece does is to take the life of Péguy and mythologize it. Péguy was a French poet who wrote a tract that may have prompted an assassin to kill the French Socialist Jean Jaurès, and who – fairly deliberately – got himself killed on the first day of the Battle of the Marne. Péguy, a right-winger and a Catholic, is an ideal figure with which Hill can torment himself, for his abiding concern is, as he has put it, his "heretic's dream of salvation expressed in the images of the orthodoxy from which he is excommunicate."

A poem of such scope is too long to quote, too long even to attempt to describe. (There are, in any event, a number of books that explicate Hill's work, providing an easy introduction and a reliable guide – the best of these being Henry Hart's *The Poetry of Geoffrey Hill* (Southern Illinois University Press, 1986). But I can present at least the opening, which is what any reader starts with:

> Crack of a starting-pistol. Jean Jaurès
> dies in a wine-puddle. Who or what stares
> through the café-window crêped in powder-smoke?
> The bill for the new farce reads *Sleepers Awake.*

History commands the stage wielding a toy gun, rehearsing another scene. It has raged so before, countless times; and will do, countless times more, in the guise of supreme clown, dire tragedian.

> In Brutus' name martyr and mountebank
> ghost Caesar's ghost, his wounds of air and ink
> painlessly spouting. Jaurès' blood lies stiff
> on menu-card, shirt-front and handkerchief.

> Did Péguy kill Jaurès? Did he incite
> the assassin? Men stand by what they write
> as by their camp-beds or their weaponry
> or shell-shocked comrades while they sag and cry?

> Would Péguy answer – stubbornly on guard
> among the *Cahiers,* with his army cape
> and steely pince-nez and his hermit's beard
> brooding on conscience and embattled hope?

Metrically and formally this is a bit *arrière garde,* as Bach was too, for that matter, but then Hill's intellectual and theological nostalgia would express in just such clipped, tight-lipped stanzas the passions of his that are all the more attractive for his mannerly restraint.

Thom Gunn's *Collected Poems* (Farrar, Straus and Giroux) is also formally restrained, which is what gives the poems their power. I had, I confess, lost interest in Gunn, writing him off as one of those leather-clad fellows in San Francisco gay bars in whose concerns and perceptions I was unlikely to be interested. I was absolutely wrong, for all this time Gunn was writing away, writing right on. One starts wherever one is, but the discipline of the art is such that, when there's a talented practitioner doing the magic, the spells work, reaching across continents, across differences of background and gender. Gunn's statement of his methodology comes in "Transients and Residents," in which he remarks

>   Starting outside,
> Thus by the seen the unseen is implied.
> *I like loud music, bars and boisterous men.*
> You may from this conclude I like the things
> That help me if not lose then leave behind,
> What else, the self.

The leaving behind of the self, through technical and rhetorical dexterity, is nothing short of miraculous. How it transforms both the speaker and the listener is one of the great mysteries. Gunn is able to reach out to us with verses that are elegantly measured, in every sense of that word. Here is his poem "To Isherwood Dying," which is as fine a farewell as any in the language:

It could be, Christopher, from your leafed-in house
In Santa Monica where you lie and wait
    You hear outside a sound resume
      Fitful, anonymous,
    Of Berlin fifty years ago
      As autumn days got late –
The whistling to their girls from young men who
    Stood in the deep dim street, below
Dingy façades which crumbled like a cliff,
    Behind which in a rented room
      You listened, wondering if
By chance one might be whistling up for you,
    Adding unsentimentally
      'It could not possibly be.'
Now it's a stricter vigil that you hold
And from the canyon's palms and crumbled gold
    It could be possibly
    You hear a single whistle call
      Come out
    Come out into the cold.
Courting insistent and impersonal.

The efficiency of that made me think first of W. H. Auden, but also of John Dryden, for the aplomb, the tact, the poise of the speaker on a high wire, balancing grief and affection on one side with restraint on the other, as one would have to do, addressing a dying person.

Paul Muldoon's poetry is less congenial to me, but, just as there are wines that take longer to mature, there are poets whose work requires more aging, as one gets used to its turns and tropes. (I was less comfortable with Hill years ago when I first encountered his work.) Muldoon, an Irishman who now lives in the United States, is also a craftsman of dense, even clotted poetry, whose fondness for low-frequency words is almost defiant. He once called one of his volumes *Quoof* – and the word, meaning a bed warmer, recurs in his new book *The Annals of Chile* (Farrar, Straus and Giroux). When he deigns to be intelligible, however, he can be most persuasive, gritty, and powerful, as in "The Sonogram," where he writes

Only a few weeks ago the sonogram of Jean's womb
resembled nothing so much
as a satellite-map of Ireland:

now the image
is so well-defined we can make out not only a hand
but a thumb;

on the road to Spiddal, a woman hitching a ride;
a gladiator in his net, passing judgement on the crowd.

Even when he is more opaque, as he sometimes gets in "Yarrow," the long poem that takes up most of the volume, one has a general sense of what he's

Thom Gunn, a British poet living in San Francisco, whose Collected Poems *was published in 1994*

doing, and there can be no question of his sprightly energy. One of the sections of this poem about the coming-into-being of the poet's imagination reads as following:

Only yesterday I heard the cry go up, '*Vene sancti
   Spiritu,*'
as our old crate
overshot the runway at Halifax,

Nova Scotia: again I heard Oglalagalagool's
cackackle-Kiowas
as blood gushed from every orifice;

an ampoule of Lustau's port; a photograph of Godfrey
   Evans
who used to keep wicket – perhaps even went to bat –
for the noble and true-hearted Kent.

It's agreeably boyish, at the very least.

Auden, to whom I made reference a moment ago, is also represented by a new book, *Juvenilia: Poems, 1922–1928,* edited by Katherine Bucknell and published by Princeton University Press in their series that will bring forth the complete works of Auden. The book is typographically and editorially beetling, as if in an effort to make up in scholarly earnestness for the slightness and playfulness of some of these youthful poems. Still, for those interested in Auden's gradual development of that voice we all can recognize, building it from elements of Edward Thomas, Walter de la Mare, and Thomas Hardy and making it his own, this is a fascinating volume. And there are passages – not whole poems, necessarily, but lines and stanzas here and there – surely worth reading and rereading. "Inn Song" of 1924, when Auden was seventeen, begins with remarkable poise:

> Traveller, stay
> On your long way;
> Dusk falls on day,
> Dark grows the hour.
> Here is good ale
> That will not fail;
> Tell us your tale
> By the bright fire.

It does not maintain at that level, but to have reached it at all was no small accomplishment. In hindsight one tries to sort out the truly Audenesque from the general intellectual and artistic weather of the 1920s. Auden writes in "Before":

> Unkempt and furtive the wind crawls
> Round houses stupid in the rain;
> The drops unwinding down the glass inspect
> Clouds spawning in a nasty sky.

We perhaps do not need Bucknell's forty-four-line-long gloss on the poem that lets us have such insights as, "The ghost of early Eliot haunts numerous lines in 'Before.'"

But having run that string, what remains is a more or less chaotic pile of books that can be categorized only very roughly. My notion, faute de mieux, is to begin with big names, those poets laureate who published books in 1994, and winners of the Pulitzer and Bollingen Prizes. These distinctions don't mean much, being the results of committee decisions (and the intelligence of any committee is just slightly lower than the meanest intelligence of its constituent members). Still, there is a kind of crude truth these honors have, if only as self-fulfilling prophecies.

So we begin with the present occupant of the office, Rita Dove, a Pulitzer Prize winner in 1987, whose verse play, *The Darker Face of the Earth,* appeared from Story Line Press. For a young woman – she is only in her early forties – the weight of these laurels is not inconsiderable, and evidently she now has the sense, as she picks up the pen, that she is about to write something important. Importance, like beauty, is what we may stumble on but ought not pursue directly. In this version of the Oedipus story set on an antebellum South Carolina plantation, we get slaves and masters, miscegenation and murder, in declamations of all but mind-numbing pomposity:

> A man should be able to kill
> when he has to.
> Love is as good a reason
> as any other, don't you agree?

We get another strain when the chorus of slaves comes on to do minstrel-show routines:

> Oh Deat' him is a little man,
> And him goes from do' to do',
> Him kill some souls and him cripple up,
> and him lef' some souls to pray.
>
> Do Lord, remember me,
> Do Lord, remember me,
> I cry to the Lord as de year roll aroun',
> Lord, remember me.

Among other questions this raises, there is that of the inconsistency of the dialect ("the Lord" but "de year"), but one does not want to niggle.

Mona Van Duyn, who preceded Dove, had two books out during the year, a thickish volume, *If It Be Not I: Collected Poems 1959–1982,* and a thinner one of new work, *Firefall,* both from Knopf. Van Duyn, who was the laureate in 1992–1993, also won the Pulitzer Prize, the Bollingen Prize, and the National Book Award. She is an elegant performer, and her tatting and crocheting with language makes Marianne Moore look like a stevedore. Many of the poems are presentations for other poets, especially for Howard Nemerov, who was a neighbor in Saint Louis. Ordinarily I do not mind this kind of showing off, but somewhere along under the frothy head there ought to be some honest beer. She is sometimes so twee that she forgets the actual word, as in "Christmas Present for a Poet," which comes with the strange epigraph "The shirt you gave me made me look like a hornet! And the only word I can think of that rhymes with 'hornet' is 'hairnet.'"

Well, obviously, that's not a rhyme at all (as *cornet* or *torn it* would be), but an odder game she is willing to play:

That Henley I sent you was certainly never meant
to disguise a loving heart as a hate-filled hornet!
Your friend can only offer her old excuse
for sending a black with yellow stripes – it's hernit-
wit bargain buying. But seeing golden bars
as restraints on dark might strike a sweeter, highernote
of appreciation: golden bars of a form
in poetry, for example, that, like a hairnet,
holds flyaway passion and pain: appearances,
manners that keep the poor, keep even the whoreneat.
Or hope lighting *any* black. No knitted bargain,
of course comes near the shirt I might like to hireknit
out of the delicate yarns of dearness and dream.
But the war between world and word goes on, and
    how'reneut-
rals to find a shop that is still stocked with goods? . . .

It goes on this way, like the racket of change ringers at their carillons, beyond the point where admiration has given way to a kind of stupefaction. *Howornate* is one of the slant rhymes, and *horrornaught* is another, and neither, I think, is un-self-referential. She also has sonnets in monometer and dimeter in a series of experiments that is unlikely to find imitators. Still, if one were to have to choose between the sins of overearnestness and frivolity, I think the latter is the lesser and, therefore, the direction in which to err.

Mark Strand was the poet laureate in 1990–1991, and his *Dark Harbor* (Knopf) is a book-length poem in tercets about . . . well, if not the *aesthetique du mal,* then the malaise of aesthetic. With assurance and deftness he makes odd and unsettling connections that turn out to be nevertheless unimpeachable:

Still, it is possible to say this has been
An amazing century for fashion if for nothing else,
The way brave models held back their tears

When thinking of the millions of Jews and Serbs
That Hitler killed, and how the photographer
Steadied his hand when he considered

The Muzhiks that Stalin took care of.
The way skirts went up and down; how breasts
Were in, then out; and the long and the short of hair.

But the road that winds through the canyon
Is covered with snow, and the river flows
Under the ice. Cross-country skiers are moving

Like secrets between the trees of the glassed-in forest.
The day has made a fabulous cage of cold around

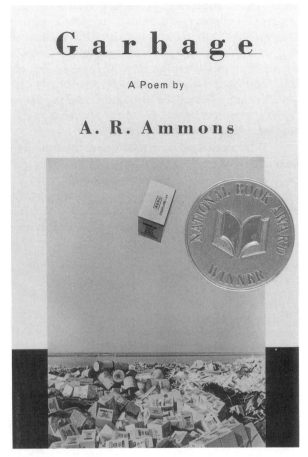

Garbage

A Poem by

A. R. Ammons

Dust jacket for A. R. Ammons's long poem about garbage, love, creation and renewal, and the place of humanity in the world

My face. Whenever I take a breath I hear cracking.

He makes a remarkable music that may be unequal to the great disasters of our time but at least admits that inadequacy and carries on with an honesty and precision in which we cannot help but find at least a little reassurance. This is a fine book by a truly accomplished poet.

There were four Pulitzer Prize winners to publish in 1994 – John Ashberry, Galway Kinnell, W. S. Merwin, and James Tate. And the fact that they won the prize ought to earn them some notice, although even that rule doesn't seem to work reliably anymore. Karl Shapiro had a book out in 1992, not his best book maybe, but an interesting and quirky volume with some fine pieces in it, *The Old Horsefly,* from Northern Lights in Orono, Maine, and I think I saw one review, a couple of years later, a churlish piece in the *American Book Review.*

I am frank to confess that I do not understand Ashberry's poems. I have read essays that presume to explain them, but I still have the sense that this is an enormous practical joke being played on us by a small band of perverse pranksters in New York City who are also selling baboon spatterings as abstract art. Ashberry isn't supposed to make sense, evidently, but only whet the appetite for meaning and then endlessly frustrate that expectation. Words like *then* and *after* signal a passage of time so that we try to invent narratives, but these are random dots that were never meant to connect.

Whether as poet or prankster, though, Ashberry had a busy year with two books, the paperback edition of *Hotel Lautréamont* (Knopf) and the hardback *And the Stars Were Shining* (Farrar, Straus and Giroux). I quote at random, which is the only way to demonstrate what seems to have been written at random:

> After ten years, my lamp
> expired. At first I thought
> there wasn't going to be any more of this.
> In the convenience store of spring
>
> I met someone who knew someone I loved
> by the dairy case. All ribbons parted
> on a veil of musicks, wherein
> unwitting orangutans gambled for socks,
> and the tasseled enemy was routed.

The nutsy specificity of the bizarre word *musicks* gives us an urgent signal that this is not just casual raving, but what is a "veil of musicks," and why are unwitting orangutans gambling for socks inside it? Connect the dots and you see a clown face that looks more like your own than Ashberry's. I think that is the game, at any rate. But to play it for a whole book, for book after book, and to make a career of it seems to me very strange indeed.

The title poem of *Hotel Lautréamont* is a series of pantoums, and I have always believed that the trick of that form is to seem to approximate linear thought in a kind of versification that all but defies the poet's effort. If randomness and incoherence are the objects, however, then pantoums are so easy as to be uninteresting. Here are a couple of stanzas of the first one:

> Research has shown that ballads were produced by all
>   of society
> working as a team. They didn't just happen. There was
>   no guesswork.
> The people, then, knew what they wanted and how to
>   get it.
> We see the results in works as diverse as "Windsor
>   Forest" and "The
>   Wife of Usher's Well."

> Working as a team, they didn't just happen. There was
>   no guesswork.
> The horns of elfland swing past, and in a few seconds
> We see the results in works as diverse as "Windsor
>   Forest" and "The
>   Wife of Usher's Well,"
> or, on a more modern note, in the finale of the Sibelius
>   violin
>   concerto.

The demonstration that these line-repetition forms can sound dopey is not startling. Indeed, for a while it can even seem cute. But it soon gets tiresome. This is not, as I have already admitted, my idea of poetry. Ashberry has bet his life one way, and I understand this, but I have bet mine another. Time will no doubt clarify the issue.

Galway Kinnell is a much easier case. He has a kind of countrified earnestness we see on the faces of those models in commercials who wake up early and walk their dogs and then come home and consume vast quantities of oat bran. When this posture is convincing, as it often is in *Imperfect Thirst* (Houghton Mifflin), he can be very effective. But when he goes off, pushing too far or indulging himself only a little, he goes way off. This passage, which appears on the back of the dust jacket, is Kinnell at his best and then, I think, Kinnell losing it:

> How much do I have left of the loyalty to earth,
> which human shame, and dislike of our own lives,
> and others' deaths that take part of us with them,
> wear out of us as we go toward that moment
> when we find out how we die: clinging and pleading,
> or secretly relieved that it is all over,
> or despising ourselves, knowing that death
> is a punishment we deserve, or like an old dog
> off his feed, who suddenly is ravenous,
> and eats the bowl clean, and the next day is a carcass.

Up to there it is just splendid. But Kinnell seems more interested in the vatic resonance of his voice than in the poetry, for he allows himself to continue:

> There is an unfillableness in us – in some of us,
> a longing for that blue-shaded black night
> where the beloved dead, and all those others
> who suffered and sang and were not defeated –
> the one who hushed them by singing "Going Home"
> when they lynched him on Bald Mountain,
> the klezmer violinists who pressed bows
> across strings until eyes, by near-starvation
> enlarged, grew wet and sparkled – have gone.

It is a question, I guess of taste, which is what keeps talent from going haywire, ruining itself, and alienating readers who got the point already with that nice bit about the dog, after which the awful abstraction of "unfillableness" is more a betrayal than an explication. Kinnell enjoys the vertiginous tottering at the brink of foolishness, finds it exhilarating perhaps, and even manages to persuade us to follow him most of the time. Who else could write, without arousing gales of derisive giggles, "The biting insects don't like the blood of people who dread dying. / They prefer the blood of people who can imagine themselves entering other life-forms . . ."?

W. S. Merwin's *Travels* (Knopf) is also earnest and countrified, but Merwin's lapses are less catastrophic. He is, at his worst, just a bit boring because he is more than a little mannered, but that does not happen often. And at his best he does with great stylishness exactly what he proposes in "Cover Note":

> . . . reader I do
> not know that anyone
> else is waiting for these
> words that I hoped might seem
> as though they had occurred
> to you and you would take
> them with you as your own

He looks at nature, as many poets do, but also at naturalists, whom he proposes as heroes of looking. One of his finest pieces, in this book and in his long and distinguished career, is "The Lost Camelia of the Bartrams," in which he tells us about those botanists and arboriculturalists, father and son, whose gardens are perhaps a mile from my house in Philadelphia. They find, as the poem's title suggests, a camelia, a particularly splendid one, deep in some southern swamp, and

> never
> the son said did we find
> that tree growing
>
> wild anywhere else
> so it was fortunate
> that he gathered seed and cuttings and took them
>
> away to bring on
>
> in gardens for
>
> by the time he was fifty
> it had vanished from
>
> its own place altogether
> only surviving here and there
> as a cultivated
> foreigner

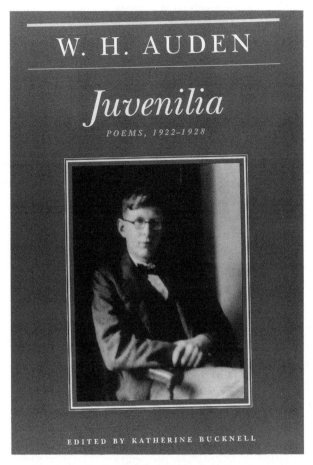

Dust jacket for the edition of W. H. Auden's early poems

The economy of that series of gestures is remarkable. Merwin does not condescend to lecture us about that sense we have that most religions invoke of having been banished from a paradisaical state. The words *garden* and *exile* are enough, if we are paying attention – as it of course behooves cultivated foreigners to do.

Finally, among the winners of Pulitzer Prizes there is James Tate, whose *The Worshipful Company of Fletchers* came out in 1994 and won the National Book Award. Tate teaches at the University of Massachusetts, Amherst. His work is not easy to characterize – something between surrealism and a series of *Saturday Night Live* routines. You take an absolutely demented premise – assume, for instance, that there is some confusion between the words *poodle* and *pope,* and then you do riffs, such as

> Popes are very intelligent.
> There are three different sizes.
> The largest are called standard Popes.
> The medium-sized ones are called miniature Popes.
> I could go on like this, I could say:

"He is a squarely built Pope, neat,
well-proportioned, with an alert stance
and an expression of bright curiosity,"
but I won't. After a poodle dies
all the cardinals flock to the nearest 7-Eleven.
They drink Slurpies until one of them throws up
and then he's the new Pope.

John Belushi's line in which an immigrant is being taught useful phrases in English and he is either teaching or learning "I will feed your fingertips to the wolverines!" is at least as good as most of Tate's, and it is the same game, exactly. But where is the knack of it, the trick, the charm? What is interesting about the language? One of my quick tests for undergraduate poetry is to check to see whether all the line endings are at punctuational and syntactic occasions, which is a pretty reliable indication that what I am looking at is chopped-up prose. That is what I'm looking at here.

How then do I explain his prizes and honors? I do not even try. But a possible view is that Tate has learned to play to an audience that hates poetry, enjoys these travesties and games, and takes a certain reassurance from his debunking, which is one of the suggestions of his obvious meaninglessness. How much "meaning" could there have been in all those knotty poems by John Milton and John Donne and William Blake they had to read back in school? No more than the dumbest of them could glean, dragging his eyes across the lines of unjustified type and wishing that he could feed the poet's fingertips to the wolverines. . . .

Casting the net only a little more widely so as to include winners of the Bollingen Prize, we get A. R. Ammons's book *Garbage* (Norton). The paperback came out in 1994, which counts, but I include it mostly because I admire it. Ammons's long poem about – well – garbage is, among other things, an expression of *nostalgie de la boue:*

garbage has to be the poem of our time because
garbage is spiritual, believable enough

to get our attention, getting in the way, piling
up, stinking, turning brooks brownish and

creamy white: what else deflects us from the
errors of our illusionary ways, not a temptation

to trashlessness, that is too far off, and,
anyway, unimaginable, unrealistic: I'm a

hole puncher or hole plugger: stick a finger
in the dame (*dam,* damn, dike), hold back the issue

of creativity's flood, the forthcoming, futuristic,
the origins feeding trash: down by I-95 in

Florida where flatland's ocean- and gulf-flat,
mounds of disposal rise . . .

It is hard to imagine anything much more relaxed, where a typo "dame" turns into a joke, "dam," "damn", which then has a topper on it, "dike." We are obviously in an unbuttoned and informal mood with such hard enjambments as in the third couplet, where the break comes between an article and its noun. And yet, in a hypnotic, wacky, discursive way, Ammons manages to extend his attention and ours to the great subjects, including those of destruction and renewal, love, the creation of the world, and our uncertain place in its haphazard scheme. These are hardly cozy questions, but with a disarming modesty (false, of course, as all modesty must be, or it would not be modesty) he can set us up for what we only later realize was an authentic and moving lyric flight.

And now where? I suppose I could begin with the Compulsory Figures of *The New York Times* list of the best books of the year. (The phrase gets the majuscule because of Henry Taylor's elegant use of it some years back as a title for a book of criticism.) From the list we might as well begin with Amy Clampitt, who died only a few months after her *A Silence Opens* was published by Knopf. Looking at her work, not just in this book but in an oeuvre of five volumes, we tend to concentrate on the masterpieces, but it is in the ordinary, journeyman poems that we get a clearer idea of how she managed the moves:

To more than give names
to these random arrivals –
teeterings and dawdlings
of dunlin and turnstone,
black bellied or golden
plover, all bound for

what may be construed as
a kind of avian Althing
out on the Thingstead,
the unroofed synagogue
of the tundra – is already
to have begun to go wrong.

This is how she begins "Shorebird-Watching," a routine performance. The split infinitive of the first line is, for so precise and punctilious a practitioner, an act of girlish sass. Its studied negligence suggests that perhaps she is not looking up in some arcane ornithological tome the dunlin, the turnstone, and the different kinds of plovers. The mock Norse "Althing out on the Thingstead" is fun, but the "unroofed synagogue of the tundra" is maybe funnier than I think she thought it was.

Still, these are the same mannerisms that, when they work, give us her best work, with an intimacy and authority that were hers alone. Her poem about "The Horned Rampion" is one such piece, up there, I think, on the same meadow with Wordsworth's daffodils, which is high country indeed:

Daily, out of that unfamiliar,
entrancingly perpendicular
terrain, some new
and, on minute
inspection, marvelous
thing would be opening –

yet another savory-
flowery permutation of selene or salvia,
of scabious, of rockrose,
of evening primrose, of
bellflower such as the one

I'd never before laid eyes
on the like of: spurred,
spirily airy, a sort of
stemborne baldachin,
a lone, poised,
hovering rarity, hued

midway between the clear
azure of the rosemary
and the aquilegia's
somberer purple,
that turned out to be
named the horned rampion.

Next day it was no longer
singular but several;
the day after many.
Within a week it was
everywhere, had become
the mere horned rampion,

I had grown so familiar
I forgot it, had not
thought of it since,
it seems, until the moment
a volume of the Encyclopedia
Britannica, pulled down

for some purpose, fell open
at random, and there was
the horned rampion, named
and depicted, astonishing
in memory as old love
reopened, still quivering.

Rita Dove, the poet laureate of the United States, published The Darker Face of the Earth, *a version of the Oedipus story set on an antebellum South Carolina plantation.*

The peripety of the poem is its leap from botany to the anatomy of love. The two come together (as it were) in that elegant and sexy last line which is about the flower, the speaker, and the way life sometimes is. Like that rampion's root, it is good enough to eat. This is what Clampitt could do – and did fairly often – which is reason for gratitude, celebration, and a sense of loss.

Along with *A Silence Opens, The New York Times* mentioned the books of Ammons, Ashberry, and Gunn that I have already discussed, as well as six others. *Breakdown Lane,* by Robert Phillips (Johns Hopkins University Press), veers between the spleen and sentiment, but one learns to admire the veering, as if the two extremes were the balancing pole of a high-wire performer. I cite the last section of "Flower Fires" in which he talks about Muriel Ruckeyser:

There are many Monet *Waterlilies.*
I have been surrounded by them
in the Musée de l'Orangerie.
But that is the one I miss,

waterlilies in Manhattan
of my young manhood, just as I miss
fiery Muriel, who first wrote
of the phenomenon of waterlily fire.
Before she died her ample body dwindled,
a flame gasping in the crosscurrent,
going, going, gone. Ashes on a hearth,
ashes in an urn. Her poems still burn.

These are elegant and graceful moves that make me wish, as I only do occasionally these days, that I'd written that. *Crossroads,* by David R. Slavitt (Louisiana State University Press), I did write. This is my book, and, while I do not want to appear to be blowing my own horn, neither am I willing to hide my light under a bushel. I list it because they did. Selah.

Earthly Measures (Knopf) is by Edward Hirsch, who, like Robert Philips, is on the faculty of the University of Houston. He writes aggressively bookish poems, about Paul Celan or Simone Weil in Assisi or Henry James in Rome or Hugo von Hofmannsthal in Athens, but that is because he likes narrative, which is not surprising because he is good at it. The less bristly poems, though, are the ones I find most appealing. He begins "Summer Surprised Us" thus:

These first days of summer are like the pail
of blueberries that we poured out together
into the iron sink in the basement —

a brightness unleashed and spilling over
with tiny bell-shaped flowers, the windows
opened and the shrubs overwhelming the house

like the memory of a forgotten country, Nature,
with its wandering migrations and changing borders,
its thickets, woodlands, bee-humming meadows. . . .

Curiously, such demonstrations give a kind of authority to the more elaborately footnoted poems if only because they show how well he can operate without all that apparatus.

Hinge and Sign: Poems 1968–1993, by Heather McHugh (Wesleyan University/University Press of New England), is a frantic, almost hysterical book with poems of an astonishing intensity. They do not always work and sometimes go on for too long, but here that does not seem to matter so much. McHugh's basic unit is not the single poem anyway, but the sequence, the arch of the rhetorician's performance over dizzying chasms the psyche has proposed. Her usual pattern is some extravagance that is then reined in for a moment of stasis, which is a

practice she does not try to keep secret. As she explains in "What Poems are For,"

They aren't for everything.
I better swallow this, or else
wind up shut up by openness so utter.
Nip and tuck, poems are for

a bit, a patch, a mended
hem, carnation's cage – and then
the heart may bloom, the sex may roar, the moment
widen to be the well the child

fell in forever – yes – but not until
I've checked the pinafore
and laced the meat,
puttied the stones, and pinched

the flowers back. I can't give you
a word to hold the dead. I can't give you a name
to hold a god, a big enough denomination. Find yourself

a church instead, where roofs are all allusions
to the sky, and words are all
incorrigible. Timelessness, and time,

they are not mine to give. I have
a spoon, a bed,
a pen, a hat.
The poem
is for something,
and the world is small.
I'll give you that.

The incorrigibility of her words at play – what she does, in that third line, for instance, with *utter* – isn't like anyone else's. She is willing to risk occasional ridiculousness, and the successes, which are frequent, make us willing to overlook them, too.

Out of Danger, by James Fenton (Farrar, Straus and Giroux), is not my cup of tea. Veddy British, tight-lipped, assertively coy . . . Stevie Smith in pants, perhaps. Fenton was elected professor of Poetry at Oxford last year, and what he does in light verse and pastiche is fancy-dress stuff that makes fun of itself before any of us can venture to criticize. A fair sample is called "An Indistinct Inscription Near Kom Ombo," which pretends to be a translation from the "Meroitic Cursive":

I was born to a kiss and a smile
I was born to the hopes of a prince.
I dipped my pen in the Nile
And it hasn't functioned since.

He can manage a reasonable impersonation of A. E. Housman, maybe, and throw in some middle- and far-Eastern fragments in the spirit of Rudyard Kip-

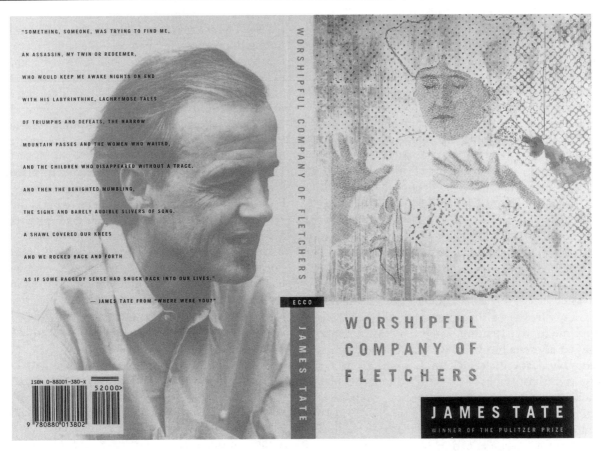

Dust jacket for James Tate's poems that exist somewhere "between surrealism and a series of Saturday Night Live *routines"*

ling ("There's a mynah bird a-squawking / In the ipil-ipil tree . . ."), but it never goes much beyond the cuteness of after-dinner country-house parlor games.

when new time folds Up, by Kathleen Fraser (Chax Press), is not my kind of thing either. My suspicion is that *The New York Times* put it on the list in order to show that they are not unaware of small presses and can deal with the theoretically aggressive modernism — or I guess it's postmodernism — of some of the fringier practitioners. (If they really cared, they might not have gotten the title screwed up, omitting the second word.) Fraser's twelfth book, it is made up of four suites, "Etruscan Pages," "Frammenti Romani," "Giotto: Arena," and the eponymous one. I cite one of the sections of the Giotto piece, because I admire the Scrovegni chapel and because Proust wrote about it, too:

Nothing's sad
nor appears

to be thought
of devotional

sediment. No
thing

required but
firmness

to draw
difference of

wrong or right
in line's this power

shone by accuracy's
disdaining errorr

fFretwork

in fretwork's
stone
  error
even
smallest
incident
suggesting   error
departure   even

Well, I see that *error* is misspelled once, which is a self-actualization of some sort, and that later it is indented an em, but what that has to do with the price of linguine, I cannot begin to imagine. In her review in the *The New York Times* Carol Muske said that "Error 'pops up,' . . .; history revises itself and evolves through mistakes, missed connections, misspelled messages, as well as through organized systems of thought. Poems, like human beings, are products of creative misunderstandings as often as they are results of premeditated effort."

I suspect it because it is too intellectual, or else not intellectual enough. It just does not do anything for me. Chax of Minneapolis, O Books of Oakland, Sun and Moon of Los Angeles, and other chapels of true believers worship their strange literary gods in these prayer books they publish that do not seem to parse. God knows what they mean and may even be interested in this *fFretwork;* I, a mere mortal, am not.

This leaves us the optional books, the ones that came to my attention, caught my interest, and engaged my sensibility one way or another, which is all an honest critic can claim. Looking around at these tumuli of books, I do notice one trend with which I can commence my conspectus. Poets seem to be more and more interested in the book-length poem, the extended performance that is in part enabled by the marginalization of the entire art. If there are no commercial considerations playing any role in the decisions of editors and publishers and therefore of practicing poets, then why not do long poems? The downside risk is negligible. Those magazine editors who think they are performing such cultural good deeds as accumulating points for themselves in heaven by using poems as aids to lay out (they are cheaper than cartoons) don't count anymore. They don't pay all that much, and there aren't enough of them to have any real clout. The main use of poetry in our culture is to provide material for explication in English classes, and that market, too, much prefers short poems.

The few trade presses and those university presses who are in the game of doing books of poetry are content – or anyway reconciled – to having sales in the upper three figures. Any poetry title that sells more than fifteen hundred copies is a runaway smash hit – "Socko in Chi," "Boffo in Cleve," and all those other catchy descriptions of economic robustitude I remember from the days when I used to read *Variety* headlines. In those ranges the difference between a huge success and a modest disaster is a few hundred copies, which is not enough for a gentleman to worry about. Therefore, understanding that we are all amateurs, we can mount our hobbyhorses and ride off in whatever directions we please. There are risks of course. As with novels, a wrong beginning can be impossible to retrieve. But there is, even beyond the fascination with what is difficult and the charm of the unfashionable, a kind of attraction in exploring such subjects as take time to yield themselves. Long poems can delve and delight in complicated areas where sustained attention to a subject is the best or maybe even the only way of understanding it.

Of the books I have discussed already, Strand's *Dark Harbor* and Ammons's *Garbage* are book-length poems. Donald Finkel's remarkable *Beyond Despair* (Garlic Press), which I am pleased to recognize as the winner of the *Dictionary of Literary Biography* Award For A Distinguished Volume of Poetry of 1994, is a book-length poem. And Mark Rudman's *Rider* (Wesleyan/New England) is nothing less than a bildungsroman with the boring parts left out, an account of Rudman's boyhood as a Jewish Gentile in Salt Lake City – where anyone who isn't a Mormon is a "gentile."

A rich, complicated, thoroughly satisfying book-length poem, *Rider* is evidence, among other things, of Rudman's interest in exploring that marshland territory between verse and prose. How prosy can one be and still be writing poetry? How much can one rely on narrative? How factual and novelistic can one be, without having it seem that the unjustified right-hand margins are just pretentiousness?

I offer a small sample, which depends, of course, on the ironic twist of its admission at the end. Young Mark has been falsely accused of throwing a ball through a schoolroom window, and the principal is interviewing him:

>   And yet the principal, perhaps because I came
> from the middle-class, never considered
> that I might be innocent and spent the day
>
> trying to get me to confess.
> The light scalded the venetian blinds
> and heated the room intolerably,
>
> while this hairy hulk, whose 5 o'clock shadow
> already heightened the whiteness of his shirt at 9,
> turned his tannish jacket – silver lined – inside out;
>
> laid it over the back of his chair
> and rolled up his sleeves.
> He snarled like a pit bull about to decimate a stick.
>
> He flexed his hands again and again
> as if to practice wringing my neck.
> He sweated. He shouted. He harangued. He shook

me by the shoulders. Threatened
me with expulsion.
Expulsion! I thought that was reserved

for my classmates, hard-core delinquents,
true sociopaths on the fast track to reform school,
12 and 13 year olds repeating 4th grade

for the 3rd or 4th time.
For the first hour, I cried like a normal child
when wronged, and begged to be let go,

but the more the room heated up,
the more hirsute and sweaty he became,
the more his triceps bulked and his body swelled,

the more I clung to a stony silence, a steely-eyed
glare broken by occasional nervous laughter
which, I quickly discovered, worked

the miracle of getting his goat more than my naive
straightforward request to be believed. . . .

With the two of us closeted together in that hotbox he
    began
to wilt, to sag, to breathe

stertorously. The room lay in shadow now
and I had the sense that, one on one, I could break
    him.
I began to sense the power

of innocence – a thrill of illicit pleasure
when my cold grin brought the blood to his face so fast
he gasped and for the first time that day I felt
guilty. Not as charged, but guilty.

A long, brooding elegy about his stepfather, the tippling rabbi, the poem arises from a consideration of Rembrandt's *The Polish Rider* in the Frick collection and R. B. Kitaj's painting of the schlumpy *Jewish Rider*. With this lively, sometimes funny, sometimes moving book, Rudman, who teaches at Columbia and New York Universities, confirms his reputation as one of the most interesting young American poets now at work.

Other poets, though, whether through choice or necessity, find themselves focused throughout whole books and producing, therefore, instead of the usual collections, a sustained suite. Some of these I found less congenial or appealing than others, but I note them because they are evidence for what seems to me an interesting development. Andrew Hudgins's *The Glass Hammer* (Houghton Mifflin) is a little folksy and flat-footed but is an interesting, vigorous account of "A Southern Childhood" – or, more accurately, a Southern boyhood and adolescence. James McMichael's *Each in a Place Apart*

Dust jacket for May Sarton's volume of poems about aging

(University of Chicago Press) is fundamentally a novel about the breakup of a marriage and then the second marriage and its collapse, and it offers at its best a pathologist's nutsy fascination with how things can go wrong. My impression is that it does not quite sustain itself, but then the fault may have been in my reading: I was plowing through a great number of books in an absurdly short period of time, after all. McMichael is surely a poet of considerable talents and impressive resources. And it may be that the desired result of his excursus was the communication of the very distaste I began to experience. *Magnificat,* by Marilyn Nelson Waniek (Louisiana State University Press), is a wacky thing, a book largely about a woman in love with a Benedictine monk. This is not a relationship with a lot going for it, but the strange merging of the theological and the erotic at the boundaries of pleasure and pain make for a series of poems that is not easy to forget. Tom Andrews's *The Hemophiliac's Motorcycle* (University of Iowa Press) is also strange, being about exactly what the title suggests. Counterphobic, some hemophiliacs do go in for motorcross adventures, and Andrews has done this. Evidently, he also made the *Guinness Book of World Records* when he was eleven for continuous clapping (fourteen hours and thirty-one minutes). The writing of poetry is not just the third string to his bow. He has in this volume one of the few really honest accounts I have read of the nature of illness. The title poem, a Christopher Smart-ass riff, begins from a line from *Jubilate Agno,* "For the sin against the HOLY GHOST is INGRATITUDE," and goes on from there:

> May the Lord Jesus Christ Bless the hemophiliac's motorcycle, the
> smell of knobby tires,
>
> Bell-Ray oil mixed with gasoline, new brake and clutch cables and
> handlebar grips,
>
> the whole bike smothered in WD40 (to prevent rust, and to make
> the bike shine),
>
> may He divine that the complex smell that simplified my life was
> performing the work of the spirit. . . .

It is an irresistible beginning from which Andrews goes on building through "Codeine Diary," an account of his thoughts, feelings, spiritual state, and hallucinations during the infusion of the narcotic and factor VIII that addresses in a remarkably intelligent and inventive way the great and dreadful questions: What is life about? and How can we bear it?

George Keithley's *Earth's Eye* (Story Line Press) is a novelistic series of poems exploring the aftermath of a crime of passion. One can read these pieces independently, and they are perfectly acceptable that way, even adept and impressive, but the shadow of the violence at the opening of the book gives a slightly different texture of shadow and quality of light to whatever Keithley considers. He has a great ear, a keen instinct for just the right image, and the good sense to know when to leave an accomplished gesture alone to let it resonate and reveal itself.

Maurice Kilwein Guevara – he uses both names, I am told – has a book called *Postmortem* (University of Georgia Press), which is maybe a book and maybe a joke. Or maybe a jokebook, because it has lots of jokes, many of them fine. There is a character, *el joven bestia,* "the Young Beast," who keeps recurring and provides a kind of organiza-

tion. But his interests and Kilwein Guevara's are never far apart. He can be a breathtaking parodist:

> All poets
> are L*A*N*G*U*A*G*E
> poets
> like an ear the size of Utah
> in which there are
> many fleas laughing Ha Ha

But he can turn serious, or the wit can turn angry, or . . . anything can happen. He is as fast as any stand-up comic and yet curiously moving, as some comics can be.

Suzanne Gardinier's *The New World* (University of Pittsburgh Press) is defiantly a book, by which I mean that there are twenty titles that she lays out four times, as if she were dealing some elaborate solitaire. Exactly what these titles or topics have to do with one another isn't clear to me, but they go around and around – "To the City of Fire," "Admirals," "The Ghost of Santo Domingo," "To Peace," "Our American Way of Life," and so on – and her authority is such that the cumulative effect is irresistible. The early exploration of North America, the first smashing of the atom, the heritage of slavery, smatterings of military history, odd arpeggios about love or work, and other disparate ingredients come together somehow to make an impressive collage about how we live and what we think. Her technique goes back to Ezra Pound, I suppose, but with the refinement of one of the neo-Poundians – Basil Bunting, maybe. Her book is weird and mannered, but I kept going back to it, even to – or especially to – the weirdest parts, as for instance:

> Leviathan scarify and scour
> Leviathan leave barren dirt
> Leviathan bend you to the diggin
> Leviathan stipple lungs with chasms
> Leviathan sow fevers and thirst
> Leviathan lash-boss the first ones
> Leviathan big bellies and flies
> Leviathan broadcast sprays of shrapnel
> Leviathan spavin all the smallers
> Leviathan call it Civilize
> Leviathan bill you for the pillage
> Leviathan leave you stonybroke
> Leviathan counterfeit the bargains
> Leviathan oversee the strongbox
> Leviathan lock it paper yoke. . . .

Finally, there is Rosellen Brown's odd production, *Cora Fry's Pillow Book* (Farrar, Straus and Giroux), which is essentially a verse novel about life in rural New Hampshire. This volume includes the earlier longish poem, *Cora Fry,* and its sequel and is just a little soap-operatic for my taste. Still, I admire Brown's novels, and there were moments here when, in a down-to-earth flowery-housedress way, she catches an undeniable sense of things up there in Pepperidge Farm land:

> I swear, the deeper into the muck and muddle of our
>   particulars —
> the insulin shots, the weddings, wills,
> douches and rhododendrons, the pills and potato bugs,
>   the
>   bankruptcies
> and valedictorians and drop-outs, the picnics and tea-
>   pots and wakes —
> the farther away we get.
>
>   No, the higher up. I feel like a pilot
> flying over the tiny, separate plots of our lives,
> I see how the shapes we've worked so hard at carving
>   out and
>   cultivating
> to look like no one else's begin to resemble each other.

It is not great by any means, but it's not trying to be. And I suppose I have to approve of poetry that sets out only to be competent, to be okay, if it succeeds as well as this does.

Now we are left with a pile of books that have nothing whatever in common except merit, or, to be even less assertive about it, I will say that they all, in one way or another, appealed to me. Alphabetically, by author, they are as follows.

*Kim Addonizio's *The Philosopher's Club* (BOA Editions) is earnest, almost artless, a "woman's book," albeit a step and a half down the social ladder from where such books mostly arise. On the other hand, that often gives her a kind of arresting novelty:

> All over the city
> something gets into people.
> Women tucking in their kids
> close their eyes, think of men
> they should have followed off buses.
> Girls rouge their cheeks with lipstick,
> their bodies telling lies
> to anyone who'll listen.
> Cars with their lights off glide
> under the trees, heading for the ocean . . .

The poem is called "Full Moon," and where it gets to is

> Desire is a cold drink
> that scalds the heart.
> Somewhere women are standing
> at their windows! like lit candles,
> and boys in Army boots

> go dancing through the streets,
> singing, and shoot
> at anything that moves.

So long as it is not in my neighborhood, it is okay with me.

*Doug Anderson's *The Moon Reflected Fire* (Alice James Books) is a studied exercise of putting the new wine of the Vietnam experience into old bottles of the Western tradition and, in particular, Homer. The nuggets of fresh horror give an immediacy to the section he calls "Raids on Homer," just as those old stories suggest, in some teasing way, that this is how things have always been and we ought to toughen up. It is an impossible moral imperative, perhaps, but it gives us wonderful poems. Anderson's piece about Paris and Helen is unforgettable. It ends as follows:

> . . . Aphrodite sits by the bronze lamp and trem-
>   bles,
> watches the soft roundness of flesh shift and clutch,
> lock and shudder, the mist of sweat
> catching the flame's flicker
> and Helen looks at Paris, breathing hard, *I hate you,*
> and Paris says, *I hate you too,* the sound of the fighting
> beyond the walls like drunken cooks,
> their bronze pots falling down the stairs.

His is surely one of the most impressive debut collections of the year.

*Eavan Boland's *In a Time of Violence* (Norton) has had quite a success, measuring that by what books of poems usually do. Boland has published widely in magazines and been busy on the university reading and lecturing circuit. I am not astonished to find that she has an easy, accessible voice, is all but overwhelmingly earnest, and plays the Irish card for all it is worth (we can differ about art, but suffering is there, in your face, and difficult to dismiss). Undergraduates are inevitably impressed by such lines as

> I am sure
> The body of an aging woman
> Is a memory
> And to find a language for it
> Is as hard
> As weeping and requiring
> These birds to cry out as if they could
> Recognize their element
> Remembered and diminished in
> A single tear.

The birds are gulls at the mouth of the Liffey and have been properly introduced before, but it still seems breathy to me and excessively end-stopped.

Pattiann Rogers, whose Firekeeper: New and Selected Poems *was published in 1994*

Still, there are passages where even a crank like myself is won over. Her poem to her daughter ends:

> Our children are our legends.
> You are mine. You have my name.
> My hair was once like yours.
>
> And the world
> is less bitter to me
> because you will retell the story.

Nothing wrong with that at all, at all.

*R. H. W. Dillard's *Just Here, Just Now* (Louisiana State University Press) is unabashedly brilliant. Dillard's great gift, I think, is his boldness in exploring that odd territory where the moving and the profound border on silliness. It takes considerable aplomb to be able to operate in these tricky places, and Dillard's rhetorical and spiritual abilities are mutually enabling. "Winter Letter to Bluefield," the poem with the phrase on which he plays for his title, concludes:

> It is true we lose the things we hold dearest
>   But equally true that because we hold them dear
> We find ourselves which we otherwise had lost,
>   Find ourselves whole – just now, just here.

To know what's valuable and what isn't, to recognize the preciousness of the everyday and the exquisite singularity of the ordinary is to risk looking and sounding like a fool, but Dillard's folly is only wisdom disguising itself with southern good manners. "A Dream of Uncles" begins:

> I have been blessed with uncles
> Who took me hunting for squirrel
> And for crows, who shoveled
> The stiff hound into the hole
> I helped dig, who rode with me
> In the bed of the truck, tilted
> In a cane-bottom chair, showed
> Me the rhythm of words on a page,
> Let me ramble the bookshelves,
> Palmed a silver dollar into my hand
> for no reason other than I was there.

Dillard won the O. B. Hardison, Jr., Poetry Prize from the Folger Shakespeare Library this year.

*Irving Feldman's *Life and Letters* (University of Chicago Press) is a hearty, even bearish, book, sometimes clumsy but so full of wisecracks and mostly good-natured *shpritzing* as to be endearing:

> Introduced to me, his next-to-unknown
> and near-anonymous host, Gregory [Corso] exclaimed,

"'Irving Feldman?' 'Irving *Feldman?*' '*Oiving* Feldman?'
— what kind of name is that for a poet?"

There is not space enough here to explain how it comes out, but it is with the right combination of generosity, rue, and amusement that thirty years and a successful career can enable — and that passage of time and change of circumstance is Feldman's subject, here and elsewhere. He takes chances and sometimes falls on his keester, but when he wins, as he does often, he wins big.

*Carol Frost's *Pure* (Triquarterly Books/ Northwestern University Press) is purely splendid. A sample poem, "Sexual Jealousy," reads in its entirety:

The queen mole, who is unequivocal,
exudes a scent to keep the other females neuter
and brings forth the colony's only babies, hairless and
    pink in the dark
of her tunneled chamber. She may chew a pale some-
    thing, a root,
find it tasteless, drop it for dreary others to take away,
    then demand
more; she must suckle the young. Of course
they all hate her and are jealous of the attention given
    her
by her six bedmates. In their mutual dream she is dead
    and her urine
no longer arrests their maturing. As irises infallibly un-
    fold,
one of their own will feel her sex grow quickest and
    greatest. As they
        dig
together, their snouts full of soil, they hope this and
    are ruthless in
        their waiting.

She is a wonderful nature poet, which I don't mean as any kind of diminution. Indeed, she's up there with Brendan Galvin, Maxine Kumin, and a few others.

*Jack Gilbert's is a voice that only occasionally deigns to speak. He made his debut as a Yale Younger Poet more than thirty years ago, and *The Great Fires* (Knopf) is only his third book. The verse, too, is tight-lipped, as if overcoming great reluctance. This elicits in the reader a heightened attention, to which he plays most skillfully. Here is a whole poem, "The Edge of the World":

I light the lamp and look at my watch.
Four-thirty. Tap out my shoes
because of the scorpions, and go out
into the field. Such a sweet night.
No moon, but urgent stars. Go back inside
and make hot chocolate on my butane burner.
I search around with the radio through

the skirl of the Levant. "Tea for Two"
in German. Finally, Cleveland playing
the Rams in the rain. It makes me feel
acutely here and everybody somewhere else.

It has that air of easy negligence of one of Beau Brummel's carefully executed cravats.

*Debora Greger's *Off-Season at the Edge of the World* (University of Illinois Press) is a civilized, richly allusive, and entirely coherent collection of poems. Greger can put Ovid onto the Outer Cape and have both of them seem all the more persuasive for her rearrangement. Her assiduous attention to tiny details is what sustains her in the most ambitious grands jetés, as here, in "The Later Archaic Wing":

One Venus tries to loosen her marble sandal;
another disrobes as if in the next room

a bath of rock were being drawn. Without a blush,
they bare the flesh made perfect, made of stone.

Still, a Dionysus turns his sculpted back,
his the only head preserved.

Her arms missing, and her nose,
a caryatid elevates the motes and beams of dust

into the art of aging ravage by ravage.
How beautiful the old gods in their idleness....

*Linda Gregg's *Chosen by the Lion* (Graywolf) is attractive in similar ways, offering us a passionate voice that is restrained or, I should say, supported, by a comfortable range of cultivated allusion. Any writer of earthy "women's poetry" who starts out with a consideration of Virgil's *Georgics* has, at the very least, my attention. And when I see such moves as this in the first poem in the volume, I am irretrievably hooked:

. . . The gods instruct us to cut
the throats of eight beasts, throw in poppies,
kill the jet-black ewe in the beautiful Italian
light so the bees, who have been the real business
all along, will swarm out again under the pliant boughs.

This is performance at a high level, which she maintains, seeing the other sides of things, the way what the world presents to us can be only the off note from which the jazz saxophonist ascends to the true tone he intended all along:

. . . The delicate blue of an iris,
almost white, blooming under the tall fir tree
in silence, in a shade that was a kind of sunlight.

It is a series of small but significant accomplishments that add up to an important book.

*Jane Hirshfield demonstrates in *The October Palace* (HarperCollins) that she can do a series of modest, graceful, even memorable gestures and can often combine them to make an altogether satisfactory and achieved poem. "The Thief" is such. It begins with an elegant conceit:

> Every fire is stolen.
> And so lovers,
> after, their arms or thighs touching
> lightly, find themselves
> even in daylight speaking in whispers.
> Not to escape the passionate,
> vanquished gods, who, the Greeks told us,
> hated our happiness with an inexplicable heat,
> but because their tenderness raises
> its clear, wild sap in artesian tongues of desire
> wedded wholly to jealous time.

This is most agreeable, especially in the slight shyness of "after" and in the wit of the not-this-but-that construction that is the preparation for the poem's main move. Hirshfield is uneven (are not we all?) and now and then displays a beamish, alfalfa-sprout consciousness that may seem a little less silly in Marin County than it does in the rest of the world, but she is a woman of real talent who may do better with readers less curmudgeonly than myself.

*Brigit Pegeen Kelly's *Song* (BOA Editions) was the winner of the 1994 Lamont Poetry Selection, an award now given to second books, on the theory, I imagine, that first books have novelty going for them and third books are by poets who ought by then to be at least partially established. Kelly's voice is strong, assured enough to allow her to push toward the mythic without seeming ridiculous or pompous. It is difficult to give a fair sample of her voice in a short excerpt, but here is just the beginning of "Pipistrelles":

> In the damp dusk
> The bats playing spies and counterspies by the river's
> Bankrupt water station
>
> Look like the flung hands of deaf boys, restlessly
> Signing the dark. Deaf boys
> Who all night and into the half lit hours
>
> When the trees step from their shadows
> And the shadows go to grass
> Whistle those high-pitched tunes that, though unheard hurt
>
> Our thoughts. Pipistrelles, little pipes, little
> Night pipes, the peculiar
> Lost fluting of the outcast heart. Poor heart.

To get away with that last quoted line, as I think she does, is a demonstration of real resourcefulness. I can look at the passage, see how the play with "Pipistrelles" and "little / Night pipes" and "fluting" enables that concluding coup, but having figured it out, I only admire it all the more. Her book is full of such surprises and lessons.

*Ted Kooser's *Weather Central* (University of Pittsburgh Press) is a series of quirky pieces, expressions of a sensibility that wins us by its small accuracies and then takes us for surprising flights. "Skywalk" is a short, but fairly representative, poem:

> It bridges the busy street, building to building
> like an enormous cocoon, spun out
> between one nowhere and the next, and in it
> tight knots of teenaged boys in leather skins
> press out against its walls, working their
> mandibles, breathing the stream of air,
> their faces tight and impatient and sore,
> each waiting for his stiff black shell to split
> and his beautiful wings to unfold.

*Dorianne Laux is one of those poets who seems to eschew artifice, relying on accuracy of perception and honesty of emotion. Her first book, *What We Carry* (BOA Editions) is mostly about sex and loss and the small redeeming moments of pleasure of working-class lives, about which she writes with authority and economy. She is sly, though, and can work a perfectly ordinary donnée into a conclusion that is altogether surprising. She is pumping gas, for instance, in "Fast Gas," and with a sudden backsplash she gets the fuel all over herself. Then:

> I was twenty. In a few weeks I would fall,
> for the first time, in love, that man waiting
> patiently in my future like a red leaf
> on the sidewalk, the kind of beauty
> that asks to be noticed. How was I to know
> it would begin this way: every cell of my body
> burning with a dangerous beauty, the air around me
> a nimbus of light that would carry me
> through the days, how when he found me,
> weeks later, he would find me like that,
> an ordinary woman who could rise
> in flame, all he would have to do
> is come close and touch me.

That has the kind of liveliness we remember from films noir but without that hamminess and cheap music.

*Philip Levine is also a poet of feigned simplicity, and his new book, *The Simple Truth* (Knopf), is more or less what we'd expect from a well-known old hand we've learned to admire. His *What Work Is* won the National Book Award for Poetry in 1991, and his new volume is just as accomplished. I think he is wrongheaded about some things, but that does not keep me from reading him with great admiration, as I do here in the title piece:

> Some things
> you know all your life. They are so simple and true
> they must be said without elegance, meter and rhyme,
> they must be laid on the table beside the salt shaker,
> the glass of water, the absence of light gathering
> in the shadows of picture frames, they must be
> naked and alone, they must stand for themselves.
> My friend Henri and I arrived at this together in 1965
> before I went away, before he began to kill himself,
> and the two of us to betray our lives. Can you taste
> what I'm saying? It is onions or potatoes, a pinch
> of simple salt, the wealth of melting butter, it is obvi-
> ous,
> it stays in the back of your throat like truth
> you never uttered because the time was always wrong,
> it stays there for the rest of your life, unspoken,
> made of that dirt we call earth, the metal we call salt,
> in a form we have no words for, and you live on it.

Do the elegance of meter and rhyme necessarily betray a thing? For that matter, is salt a metal? (Sodium is, but salt?) On the other hand, there is no possible nitpicking with the "truth / you never uttered because the time was always wrong." If the choice is between abandoning my aesthetic prejudices and missing out on work of this caliber, I have no problem. My principles go out the window every time.

    *Richard Moore's *Bottom Is Back* (Orchises Press) is a title that makes no sense unless you understand that it is a sequel to *No More Bottom* of 1991, which had in it the memorable epigram, "A Place to Stand":

> All falls away; skies frown;
> the dawn's dim, the grass brown.
> Drips, drips . . . the leaky gutter.
> Soon now my love will utter
> the dreary ultimatum:
> marriage – or no more bottom.

The misanthropic, misogynist master of mordancy is back with more epigrams, mutterings, grumblings, and fragments he has shored against his ruin and everyone else's. Among the many that I liked in this new collection, there was "What's in a Name? or Stanley's Misunderstanding: A Tale of Marital Guilt":

> In her talk – sense
> current events,
> and such – occurred
> the striking word

Dabney Stuart, editor of Shenandoah *and author of* Light Years: New and Selected Poems

> *Uzbekistan.*
> Replied her man,
> "I can't say, Liz,
> who Becky is."

Moore's work is known to a small coterie. The danger of his popularity growing, his life improving, and his voice mellowing out is . . . negligible, but it is not altogether without trepidation that I proclaim his virtues here.

    *Patiann Rogers's work first came to my attention some years ago when she came to do a reading at a nearby campus. I thought she was terrific, got hold of the poems, and confirmed in private that my judgment was not just of her performance at the podium but on the page, too. Or on the page, first. Her book *Firekeeper: New and Selected Poems* (Milkweed) is a generous selection from earlier volumes and a clutch of new work. Its 260 pages ought to be on the shelves of all serious readers of poetry. Here's a small snippet of the end of "Till My Teeth Rattle," one of the new poems:

Whoever said *the ordinary, the mundane,*
the commonplace? Show them to me.
Wait a minute – a hummingbird moth
so deep now inside a rose petunia
that its petals flutter too, like wings.

There's no remedy, I suppose – this body
just made from the beginning to be shocked,
constantly surprised, perpetually stunned,
poked and prodded, shaken awake,
shaken again and again, roughly rudely,
then left, even more bewildered,
even more amazed.

*Natasha Sajé makes her debut with considerable panache in *Red under the Skin* (Pittsburgh), and she is a lot of fun, arch, but with a conspiratorial chumminess that can be most winning. "Dress Code" ends:

I think of the Countess de Ribes's
bon mot: "only the bourgeois need real jewels."
My skin's that of a middle manager's
daughter, whose family toiled
its way up the ladder: slipping
down is just a spot of grease away.

She is worth keeping an eye on, and my guess is that we won't have to try too hard.

*May Sarton's *Coming into Eighty* (Norton) is, not surprisingly, about aging. One's impulse, out of good manners if nothing else, is to list her book. But then one rebels against such promptings. Let the book stand or fall on its merits, as it should. As it does, with great eloquence. "The Teacher" goes:

I used to think
Pain was the great teacher
But after two years
Of trying to learn
Its lessons
I am hoping my teacher
Will go away
She bores me almost to death,
She is so repetitive.

The pain I meant
Is the pain of separation
The end of a love.
That lesson is never learned
And is never boring.
Only a kind of
Desolation
Like a crow cawing
In the depth of winter.
Memory is merciless.

I think of the late poems of Robert Penn Warren or John Hall Wheelock, poems for which we are particularly grateful. Vivat!

*Stephen Sandy's *Thanksgiving Over the Water* (Knopf) came out in 1992, but the paperback was published in 1994, which allows me to mention it if I really want to. And I do, not only because he and I were at school together, but because he is a poet of amazing delicacy. Compared to Sandy, a lot of Wallace Stevens seems crude and burly. I can not think of anyone else who could write such lines as these, from "Those Sky Days":

The field was like an endpaper stroked with pen trials
Of a book about to be sacred
Written in
With patience
Along the scored guidelines of the frost.

*Marc J. Straus is a physician-poet, which is quite a different thing from being a poet-physician. What I mean to say is that he is strikingly good, only rarely melodramatic, never overbearing or pompous. I think of Dannie Abse or John Stone or even William Carlos Williams when I look through the impressive pieces of *One Word* (Triquarterly Books). "What I Heard on the Radio Today" is a remarkable piece in which the speaker is listening to a Horowitz recording of some Schumann piece, a live recording from a recital in 1928 on which there is "a persistant cough from the audience, / loud, in two parts, both exhaled sounds, / (B flat, then c-sharp) the second / higher and more forceful. It sounds like / a man's cough, a mature man, in his forties or fifties . . ."

The connoisseur's knowledge of the music moves seamlessly into his knowledge of coughs, and the deformities of that move – on the part of the cougher, the speaker, and the world at large – are Straus's general subject. The cough is not an annoyance or a distraction but all that remains of the probably tubercular concertgoer who doubtless died in the early 1930s. Straus's basic move is an abrupt shift in context, but I think of Stravinsky's line about Vivaldi, who "had only one trick, but a very good one." In the "Size of the Lesion" Straus sets us up by talking about those things that are better left unsaid, out of politeness or kindness or cowardice or some combination of these:

It's this way more
as time goes on. A daughter comes in late
and you don't say exactly what you feel
and her vague answer is probably

all you want to hear. Patients are proficient
at this. You tell them the X ray showed
little change, knowing they won't ask
if the lesion's a little smaller or larger.

*Dabney Stuart is about to step down as editor
of *Shenandoah,* which I mention because, given the
ratio of rejections to acceptances, the editorship of a
journal is a sure way of creating resentments and
making fervent enemies. It is no doubt because of
his work as an editor that he has been less highly
valued as a poet than he deserves. *Light Years: New
& Selected Poems* (Louisiana State University Press)
may help these witty and abruptly rueful poems get
more attention. He is really most engaging, as in the
start of "This Is No Dream, This Is My Life":

I am Humphrey Bogart.

I can do
anything.

I can take the wheel.

I can ride
the wild lust of a flame-haired woman

morning to morning,

smoke two packs
of nonfiltered cigarettes
a day,
fly.

I can
not give a damn.

I can go into my private
room, sit on the bed
and put my feet in my ears . . .

What's impressive about this, and the rest of the
poem, too, isn't its madness but its sanity.
*Michael Van Walleghen's *Tall Birds Stalking*
(University of Pittsburgh Press) is his fourth collection, and he is developing a distinctive hard-bitten
kind of speech, a little countrified but all the more
persuasive. In "Crawlspace" there's a twenty-one-
foot-long python that the police and zookeepers
have pulled out from under someone's porch:

There's even a picture of it
in the paper: *Long Lost Pet*

Found at Last . . . but nervous
and with an appetite for dogs.

Then it's time to have a drink
and consider citrus canker

or mothlike flakes of snow
that kill oranges overnight.

We're all like kids down here . . .
our fathers, our lovely mothers

having all gone off somewhere
leaving us alone and listening

to something awful moving
in the leaves beneath the house.

*Theodore Weiss is professor emeritus of En-
glish and creative writing at Princeton, and coedi-
tor, with his wife, Renée, of the *Quarterly Review of
Literature.* His new book is *A Sum of Destructions* (Louisiana State University Press), and the ill-advised
flap-copy reveals perhaps too much when it tells us
that Weiss has been "a member of the National
Book Award jury for poetry and the Bollingen
Committee . . . ," which are credits more of poi-
gnance than distinction. Still, he trudges on in a
hopeful way, and the songs he mutters and sometimes sings are often effective. "Satisfied" begins as
follows:

Why should it ever be satisfied,
the mind? Changing every instant
as the instant changes, it knows
without knowing only by going
it remains.
                So this wave on wave
erasing each other, ruffled shift
cast off, another and another
for the body twisting
                        underneath,
but never caught . . . .

*Rachel Wetzsteon, on the other hand, is just
starting out. *The Other Stars* (Penguin) was picked by
John Hollander as one of the National Poetry series
publications. She is still in her middle twenties, and,
as a Yalie, probably studied with Professor Hollander, who teaches there. But as Cornelius Nepos
figured out, such connections need not always be
disqualifications. I looked hard at her poems and
had to admit that she is pretty good, and sometimes
better than pretty good, as in "Making Scenes," a bit
of which goes like this:

Each view is threefold. There is the topmost
layer of things unequivocally seen: the man
in loud pants, the forlorn sidewalk café, and the
ever-present pigeon who gnaws a wrapper.
There is, beneath these things but glaring

as black at a wedding, a list of what they are not:
not a loved one spotted, not the locus
of a tryst, not a rare, significant seabird.
And onto these two pictures clamps a troublesome
third, through whose distorting surface
birds are half swan, half sparrow, and slumming kings
and their well dressed subjects eat lunch together.
This last layer, a patchwork of givens and
engineering, shakes the first two until nothing is solid.

It seems admirably solid to me.

    *David Wojahn's *Late Empire* (University of Pittsburgh Press) is his fourth book, and it is accomplished and assured. Wojahn can write political poetry — or, at any rate, can include politics in his poetry — without getting strident or partisan. He has a suite, "Homage to Ryszard Kapuscinski," that suggests how he is interested in the batty aesthetics of horror and cruelty. Or, to put it another way, he is not asking the dull question: What then is to be done? but the much smarter and tougher one: Considering that there is nothing to be done, how are we to proceed? I was attracted immediately to his poem about Tomis, curious as to what new he could find to say about Ovid's exile, and it turns out to be a brilliant and devastating narrative piece about Elena, who lives in Chicago and drives every week

> to Tomis, Indiana.
> Spanish for grades 10–12, ninety five miles one way
>   to the Loop, and six
>
> thousand more to Buenos Aires, where spring's begun,
>   her mother
>   planting squash in the backyard
> garden plot. At Tomis, Ovid ate red seaweed all one
>   winter,
>   and took years to learn
> the native's guttural tongue. . . .

It goes on like that, having made the connection, and it performs as well as any poem I've read this month, which is many.

    Too many. I feel like a taster at the Godiva chocolate plant. That diet of red seaweed begins to seem attractive.

Dictionary of Literary Biography Yearbook Award for a Distinguished Volume of Poetry Published in 1994

Donald Finkel's *Beyond Despair* (Garlic Press) is one of the great American poems. A piece of just over thirty pages, it sings of the River des Peres, (River of the Fathers), that runs through the city of Saint Louis to empty into the Mississippi. Named for the settlement of Jesuit fathers along its banks about two hundred years ago – the first white settlement west of the Mississippi – it is mostly buried now and, as the River des Peres Sewerage and Drainage Works, was designated in 1988 as a National Historic Civil Engineering Landmark. Who could make up such stuff?

Neither of his neighbor laureates – Howard Nemerov and Mona Van Duyn – deigned to notice this sorry sluiceway. But Finkel has written a moving, funny, outrageous, and altogether brilliant piece about this ruin of a river near where he lives.

> Despair – that's what the locals call her –
> a moniker, like Old Trollop, or Granny Goat,
> but who knows what names the Father of Rivers
> mutters each morning as she ambles to greet him
> in her slush peignor, slovenly, pensive, wanted,
> cleansed of hope?

Poetry as musing, as repentance, as celebration, as a way of holding on to important pieces of our shreddy heritage and facing what we have been and done. This is serious undertaking indeed, and I can think of few pieces like it. *Paterson,* let us admit, does go on for too long, makes its point but then forgets what it was and perseverates. (And compared to Despair, the Passaic is the Blue goddamn Danube.)

I assumed that this was a small chapbook appearance of a poem too good to hold onto until Knopf, Finkel's usual publisher, got around to doing his next collection. Such assumptions are dangerous though. I am informed that Harry Ford rejected this back at Atheneum, rejected it again at Knopf, and . . . just hated it.

But what does he know?

The famous Harry of Mark Strand's "Lunch at Lutèce," he is one of the movers and shakers of our poetry establishment – but the last time I ate there, I did not see any *corbeau roti.* I guess he must order off the menu.

Dust jacket for Donald Finkel's poems about the environmental degradation of the River Des Peres in Missouri

Finkel fretted for several years, then gave up and turned the poem over to Garlic Press – the only outfit by that name that does not publish cookbooks. Their address, which I offer, both for believers and skeptics, is 606 Rosewood, Saint Louis, Missouri 63122.

– David R. Slavitt

The Year in Fiction

George Garrett
University of Virginia

Every work of fiction exists just to remind us of what isn't there – as when we prospect for gold (or buy a lottery ticket) – every small success only serves to remind us of everything that still eludes our grasp.

–Jim Krusoe, "What Can't be Written,"
Los Angeles Times Book Review, 25 December 1994.

At first glance the year 1994 in fiction does not seem to be a prosperous or propitious one. It seems to have been a year (in the newspapers and magazines and, as well, in the independent bookstores and the chains) devoted to nonfiction, to biographies, histories, political and social issues, popular science, editions of letters, personal essays, confessions, manifestos, everything from D day to O. J., without much interest in or space for novels and short stories. The real numbers are not in yet and, in a book business which by design runs as much as six months behind the present situation, are not likely to be until much later in 1995. Nevertheless, there are signs and portents, bits and pieces of strong anecdotal evidence. For example, one kind of measure of the place of new fiction in the scheme of things is the number of front-cover reviews devoted by the leading newspapers to works of fiction. I can make no claim here to more than casual accuracy; but, according to my count, *The New York Times Book Review* featured fiction on its front cover roughly, and at most, about one in five times; the *Los Angeles Times Book Review* did one in ten; the *Washington Post Book World,* one in fifteen. Of course all three reviewed plenty of new fiction in their pages, but it does seem that nonfiction predominated. To be sure, the situation is made more complex by the increasing separation – you could call it an actual divorce – of the blockbusters and best-sellers in fiction from what is now simply defined and described as "literary fiction." From time to time during the year literary fiction earned a slot on *The New York Times* best-seller list. For instance, a midyear check (3 July) revealed Cormac McCarthy's *The Crossing* (Knopf), Caleb Carr's *The Alienist*

Wendell Berry, author of Watch With Me, *a collection of interrelated stories about Ptolemy Proudfoot, a Kentucky farmer*

(Random House), and E. L. Doctorow's *The Waterworks* (Random House) up there in the top fifteen. The list in the *Washington Post Book World* for the same date, limited to ten and strictly local in its view, has the same three plus Walter Mosley's *Black Betty* (Norton), a genre crossover. The *Los Angeles Times Book Review* list, also limited to ten and to "Southern California ranking," has exactly the same list as the *Washington Post Book World.* Coming toward year's end and allowing for the wildly successful oddity – *Politically Correct Bedtime Stories* (Macmillan), by James Finn Garner – the supreme *shlockmeisters* (Danielle Steele, Tom Clancy, Stephen King, Mary Higgins Clark, Dean Koontz, Robert James Waller, Anne Rice, Sidney Sheldon, John Grisham, and others) were back in charge of the hardcover lists. Oddly, the *Los Angeles Times* listed Tim O'Brien and his *In the Lake of the Woods* at number ten. Add to all the above observations one more wrinkle of complexity: by and large, the major reviewing publications do not trouble themselves to review the blockbusters, estimating, with good reason, that these books found in mounds and pyramids in most of the bookstores are beyond their power to add or detract. The major reviewers of fiction are concerned with literary fiction, though mainly they give space to reasonably well known and established literary authors who are being actively promoted by their publishers and who stand some real chance of achieving and enjoying a breakthrough to successful popularity if not to actual blockbuster status. Also factored in to the space and attention equation are earlier and significant successes and prizes. Thus, for example, the cover reviews of new fiction in *The New York Times* were (among a few others): Doctorow's *The Waterworks,* Alice Munro's *Open Secrets* (Knopf), Joseph Heller's *Closing Time* (Simon and Schuster), John Irving's *A Son of the Circus* (Random House), and O'Brien's *In the Lake of the Woods* (Houghton Mifflin).

When the numbers are all in and the year really behind us, 1994 may well prove to have been, as it seems, a slow year for literary fiction; but there were a great many novels and collections of short fiction published and many of them outstanding work (and why not, with such urgent competition?) – some of them noticed, widely received, and honored, and some of them, equally excellent, not. There is the evidence of the lists. "Editor's Choice" (*The New York Times Book Review,* 4 December) of the best books names four works of fiction among the eleven selections – *A Frolic of His Own* (Poseidon), by William Gaddis; *In the Lake of the Woods,* by O'Brien; *Open Secrets,* by Alice Munro; and *A Way in the World* (Knopf), by V. S. Naipaul. (This last, a mixture of fact and fiction, is classified by *The New York Times* as nonfiction, though its author calls it a novel). In the larger context of "Notable Books of the Year," *The New York Times* lists one hundred titles, not including genre fiction. The December list of recommendations for awards by *The National Book Critics Circle Journal* included forty-seven fiction titles, among them several which were not noticed by *The New York Times.* "PW's Best Books '94," in *Publishers Weekly* (7 November), chose twenty-six titles under "Fiction." Significantly, seven of these do not appear on the "Notable" list of *The New York Times: Tales From Two Pockets* (Catbird), by Karel Caper; *The Illustrious House of Ramires* (New Directions), by Eca de Quieros; *The End of Vandalism* (Houghton Mifflin), by Tom Drury; *The Folding Star* (Pantheon), by Alan Hollinghurst; *Mother Tongue* (Coach House), by Emine Seugi Ozdamar; *The Grass Dancer* (Putnam), by Susan Power; and *The Cares of the Day* (Fiction Collective Two), by Ivan

Webster. Even allowing for aggressive multiculturism in *Publishers Weekly* and (perhaps) its general guilt about ignoring the products of small presses, this list is another clear indication that there were many good books of fiction published in 1994 and that the variety was wide.

In a season and context of lists, perhaps the *DLB* annual report on fiction can begin that way, with a brief list of this reviewer's special favorites from the year's harvest. It needs to be understood that I do have a certain modest bias toward good works which did not (in my opinion) receive notice or attention commensurate with their quality. But it is also true, as I believe the list will demonstrate, that I am at least sometimes ready, willing, and able to acknowledge that a good book can, in spite of everything, be recognized and successful and that even well-known and well-regarded writers can rise to new occasions.

Before presenting the list, however, I pause to identify the three books I have chosen for *Dictionary of Literary Biography* awards for 1994. (For more detail see the award citations at the end of this essay).

Novel: *Merry Men* (Harcourt Brace), by Carolyn Chute. Her largest (695 pages), most extravagant, ambitious, and daring exploration of her own special territory – the hard world of Egypt, Maine. Intensely imagined and energetically written, *Merry Men,* as its title implies, summons up the tale/myth of Robin Hood and surrounds it with a multitude of characters rich and (mostly) poor. Her best work so far. A major contribution to our literature.

First novel: *Hero* (Steerforth Press), by Frederick G. Dillen. A bright new talent introduced by a bright new press. A down and out waiter, "Hero," in a Manhattan steak house, with a motley international crew of colleagues and cohorts – Castro the Cuban, the Bolivian, Hussein, Frankenstein, Andy – is the center of attention. Except for the briefest of excursions we never really are allowed to leave the tight, tough world of the kitchen and the dining room, a world where love and death and victory and defeat are played out for keeps. This intense little book is an experience and becomes a memory. André Dubus is dead right when he calls it (on the jacket) "an enrapturing dance beautifully choreographed and performed by Frederick G. Dillen."

Short fiction: *Rare & Endangered Species: A Novella & Stories* (Houghton Mifflin), by Richard Bausch. There is a certain earned bravado, after six first-rate novels and two earlier, highly regarded collections of stories, in Bausch's "Author's Note," wherein he asserts that "all resemblances to actual persons – that is, to recognizable, complicated human beings caught in their time and place — are exactly, wholly, lovingly intended, even though I have imagined them all." Eight stories, various but alike in voice and mastery, together with a powerful novella, allow Bausch to summon up unforgettable characters whose joys and suffering matter much. Nobody else is quite as good at what he does here so well, so effortlessly.

The DLB Roll of Honor

As is the case with any list, be it ever so arrogant or humble, there are good things (books) not on this limited list. Maybe we missed them completely. Maybe, for one reason or another, we did not like them or did not like them enough or, anyway, failed to appreciate them fully. What is more certain is that the books on the honor roll are, in our opinion and best judgment, excellent and are here strongly recommended.

In his latest novel (his ninth novel and twelfth book) — *Once Upon a Time: A Floating Opera* (Little, Brown) — John Barth writes, "What's more, for readers and writers alike, I've always thought the first and final narrative question is not 'What Happened?' but 'Who am I?'" *Once Upon a Time,* for the third time, sends its narrator, this time Barth, sailing down the Chesapeake Bay toward the open sea. It takes the outward form of an opera and, as he indicates early in his "Program Note," of a "memoir bottled in a novel." Barth's work is never simply what it seems to be or even what it claims to be, but this latest is his finest. As R. H. W. Dillard wrote in *The New York Times Book Review* (3 July): "*Once Upon a Time* is, then, its own complex and complete self, but it is also the satisfying last chapter and tying up of a much larger twelve-volume work, the remarkable and altogether noteworthy opera and virtual voyages of Barth."

Wendell Berry, one of the three living American writers to have been awarded the T. S. Eliot Prize by the Ingersoll Foundation and this year's winner of the ten-thousand-dollar Aiken-Taylor poetry award, brought out *Watch With Me* (Pantheon), seven interrelated short stories, all of them dealing with Ptolemy (Tol) Proudfoot, a farmer from (where else?) Port William, Kentucky. These stories are set there between 1908 and 1941. Poet and essayist of distinction as well as a fiction writer, Berry has developed a perfect touch to clothe his character, clean and clear and direct, but never without a gentle irony: "A little later, having eaten a good breakfast and hitched his team to the wagon, Tol experienced a transformation that he had expe-

Frederick G. Dillen, author of Hero, *the recipient of the* DLB Yearbook *Award for a Distinguished First Novel (photograph by Jack Parsons Photo)*

rienced many times before. He passed through all his thoughts and dreads about the day, emerging at last into the day itself, and he liked it."

After a brief period of silence (too long for her faithful readers) Doris Betts returned to the scene with her seventh work of fiction, the novel *Souls Raised From the Dead* (Knopf). At the center of the story is the teenager Mary Grace Thompson, who is being raised by her divorced father, Frank, a North Carolina state trooper. Mary Grace is, in due course, diagnosed with an incurable disease and finally dies of it. The story line is of her struggle and the effect of her example on a crew of characters. Betts handles this without any easy sentimentality, and the result is a moving and affirmative story. A host of North Carolina writers rallied around *Souls Raised From the Dead* with advance praise, from Louis D. Rubin, Jr., to Reynolds Price; but perhaps Clyde Egerton's comment best describes her magical powers: "Doris Betts is the only writer I know of, besides James Agee, who can make me feel as though I am touching what she is describing."

T. Coraghessan Boyle, *Without a Hero* (Viking). Boyle, author of five popular novels and four collections of stories, including this one, is an acquired taste. Unlike most of his contemporaries he is an "idea" man. His stories are mostly tales of "what if?" and depend as much on plot and subject as anything else. Precious little fine writing and/or delicate perceptions. More cute than clever. And funny. What is he doing here? What he does, he does well. And in passing, working out the little jump-rope tricks of his plot, he tells a lot of things about the shiny surfaces of contemporary America that better and deeper writers often miss. His natural mode is satiric. His natural rhythm is high energy. And the fifteen stories of *Without a Hero,* each a separate entity, add up to a funny and scathing documentary on how a whole lot of us are living in this day and age.

Irvin Faust's seventh novel, and his first one in fourteen years, is *Jim Dandy* (Carroll and Graf). Set in a splendidly evoked and entirely credible 1936, *Jim Dandy* is the fast-moving story of a fast-moving protagonist, Hollis Cleveland, called Jim Dandy. Dandy, a black man and a successful numbers runner in Harlem (until he gets too cute with the man who runs the numbers), is off and running on an adventure which takes him as far as Ethiopia, in those days trying to fight off Benito Mussolini. The story ends back in New York with the second Schmelling fight in 1938. It is all wonderfully imagined and re-created, told in Faust's trademark high-energy jolts of prose. This is an important book by one of our best writers, a book that somehow failed to catch the fancy of the critics and reviewers. More is the pity for them. We pause to praise *Jim Dandy* here and now.

Key West Tales (Knopf) is John Hersey's second collection of short stories in twenty-five books. All of these stories, fifteen in all, are set in Key West, historically and in the present. Short factual pieces act as interchapters between the more purely fictional short stories, and, from time to time, "real" historical figures appear – Harry Truman, John James Audubon, Jefferson Davis, and others. Writing in the *Washington Post,* Alan Ryan describes the book precisely: "*Key West Tales* has all the marks of a master who knows what readers want: a good story; characters who, but for the grace of God, might be us; writing as bright and clear as ice."

Benita Kane Jaro's first novel, *The Key* (1988), moved critic Doris Grumbach to write, "If there is to be a worthy successor to Mary Renault or to Marguerite Yourcenar it may be Benita Kane Jaro." Her latest, *The Door in the Wall* (Permanent Press), is set in the

---

IRVING FAUST ON *Jim Dandy*

Jim Dandy was conceived fifteen years ago at the confluence of intensive and extensive research, personal history, and empathic imagination. The novel is chiefly preoccupied with a black numbers runner, Hollis Cleveland (Jim Dandy), who is surely no angel; he can be ruthless and quixotic and sometimes is forced to be both in the world of the 1930s, but he is fundamentally a person of substance and qualitative weight. His worth, however, is not perceived on its own merits by his American contemporaries except in perverse ways. It is *because* of a perverse circumstance that he is forced out of his milieu, and *then* he is responded to by others, good, bad, and even certifiable, all of whom project their hopes, fears, ambitions, and aspirations onto him; he, in turn, responds, not always with expected behaviors, but at least with behaviors that tap into his humanity, his *reality.*

There is a story line in the novel, but it is not a traditional one. Often, as in life, it is exasperating. The book darts ahead of itself, loops back, and dances in place like a hummingbird. The action is propelled by narration, of course, but also through dreams, myth, interpolations, newspaper accounts, minstrel-show commentary, and the career and fights of Joe Louis. It has many voices; sometimes, like a Robert Altman movie, they speak at the same time.

Its publishing history has been a strange one. *Jim Dandy* was turned down by a least ten publishers (I have lost count). But it bothered many of them, which I found most encouraging. One editor sent a four-page letter that I had to read over and over before I figured out he was saying no. But then Carroll and Graf said yes.

A happy ending? Perhaps. I am more inclined to think, as Churchill said about the victories in North Africa, that it is the end of the beginning. . . .

---

times of Julius Caesar and narrated in the form of a report being prepared by one Marcus Caelius Rufus (82–48 B.C.), a young military commander, formerly a student of Cicero and protégé of Caesar. This is a vivid and powerful re-creation of a complex time. As historian Allen Ward has written, "Benita Kane Jaro recreates the major characters and events in the waning Roman Republic with a solid command of the ancient sources and the kind of disciplined imagination that brings history alive."

Dust jacket for Joyce Carol Oates's novel about real-estate developer Jerome ("Corky") Corcoran and his life and times

One of these days the greatly gifted Albanian novelist Ismail Kadare is going to be awarded the Nobel Prize in literature. Meanwhile, we have five of his novels in English, including this latest and, in a sense, most ambitious – *The Concert* (Morrow). Since World War II Albania had defined itself and its identity by its breaks with other Communist nations. In 1948 Albania ended its alliance with Yugoslavia. The Soviet Union was dismissed in 1961. And in 1978 came the break with China, leaving Albania all alone, a small enclave of communistic purity and poverty. *The Concert* deals with the effects of the break with China, and the story switches back and forth between Albania and Mao's China. Something of the spirit of Albania is represented by old Aunt Hasiye, who says, late in the story: "I listen to the radio, but I can't understand a word these modern politicians say. Who was it, now, that they were insulting on the radio yesterday? The Turks?"

"No, Aunt Hasiye – the Chinese."

In the Arms of Our Elders (Carolina Wren Press), by William Henry Lewis. Winner of the Sonja H. Stone Fiction Contest, this first book is a collection of nine short stories by a young African American writer that comes with the highest praise of writers Ann Beattie, Peter Matthiessen, and Marita Golden. It is a virtuoso performance of points of view, ways of telling, variety of characters, times, and places. Not surprising, perhaps, because Lewis, now a teacher himself at Denison University, is a college graduate and holds an M.F.A. in creative writing as well. In a real sense he is representative of the newest generation of writers whose competence can be taken for granted and whose potential is great. The stories in *In the Arms of Our Elders* offer, from a variety of different angles, fresh views of African American life in our times.

Thomas Mallon, fiction editor for *GQ*, has turned to history for *Henry and Clara* (Ticknor and Fields), telling the "true" story of Clara Harris and Maj. Henry Rathbone, the young couple who shared box number eight with President and Mrs. Lincoln at Ford's Theater on Good Friday, 14 April 1865. Young Rathbone, already a wounded war hero, was savagely knifed by John Wilkes Booth and came close to death himself. This is Rathbone's story, a story that gradually builds to murder and madness early in our own century. The powerful story is superbly told, in a sequence of dramatic scenes, by a narrative voice which is appropriately and consistently stylish and plausibly different from our present written or spoken vernacular. The writing about the Civil War itself, in Washington and on the battlefields, is outstanding. This is a first-rate historical novel.

D. J. Meador's *His Father's House* (Pelican) is technically a first novel, though its author, the James Monroe Professor of Law at the University of Virginia, has written numerous books on legal subjects. Here Meador tells the tale of an American and a southerner, Robert Trepnitz Kirkman, who in the 1970s goes to East and West Germany to solve a family mystery and to make contact with relatives there. It is a generational tale of politics, religion, history, romance, and mystery moving in time across the two world wars and the American Civil War. It touches on the unique kinship between defeated Germany and the American South. The writing is clear and strong and straightforward. The characters are memorable; the story line is fully satisfying.

Stephen Millhauser has earned a reputation as a master of "writerly fiction" with six complex, clever, and brilliantly executed books since *Edwin Mullhouse: The Life and Death of an American Writer*

(1972). His latest, *Little Kingdoms* (Poseidon), is made up of three distinctly separate novellas, radically different in ways and means and arranged in a challenging sequence, which are kin to each other in their concern with the making of art from "reality" and the high price that is paid for it. Brilliantly written, deftly intricate, these gifted fabulations are lighthearted without being lightweight and can be wonderfully funny. There are plenty of jokes in the worlds created, then exploited by Millhauser, but his work is no joke. He is a daring and successful adventurer who knows what he is about.

Poet Robert Morgan's *The Hinterlands: A Mountain Tale in Three Parts* (Algonquin) is his first novel and second book of fiction (he published a collection of stories, *The Blue Valleys,* in 1989). *The Hinterlands* consists of two novellas and one long story, separate but linked together in interesting ways: all deal with the same family, the Richards, from 1772 to the present; all are told in first person, and in each case it is a grandparent telling the story to grandchildren. Morgan's language is lovely and accessible; his intelligent characters are passionate and active people. Three generations of road builders relate their wild and woolly adventures in the gradual taming of the Appalachian wilderness. It is all worth listening to with closest attention.

Open Secrets (Knopf), by Alice Munro. Eight new stories by the Canadian who is one of the best story writers in the language. Seven of them first appeared in *The New Yorker,* the other in the *Paris Review*. Munro has written one novel and six previous collections of stories. Women are the central characters, the makers and movers, of these stories, set mostly in Canada, but also Australia and even ("The Albanian Virgin") in Albania. There is nothing fancy about the way Munro tells a story; they are straightforward and direct, mostly relaxed and cumulative in their effects. Yet they are quite different in shape and feel from each other, and all are characterized by a magical authority. The reader enters into the story and believes it: "Lucille was a thin, fair-haired girl, with a finicky stomach, irregular periods, and a sensitive skin. The vagaries of her body fascinated her and she treated it as if it was a troublesome, but valuable pet."

A Way in the World (Knopf), by V. S. Naipaul, is set in the same general autobiographical mode that Naipaul explored and exploited in *The Enigma of Arrival* (1987). Here, however, he cuts between fact and fiction, history and memory, finished event and what he calls "unwritten story." We are given elements of his own life story, juxtaposed against historical figures such as Sir Walter Ralegh aboard

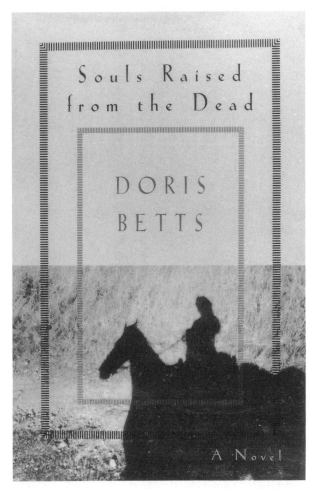

Dust jacket for Doris Betts's novel about a terminally ill teenage girl and the effect of her illness and death on her friends and family

the *Destiny* in 1618 and Francisco Mirandor, nineteenth century Venezuelan revolutionary. The great pleasure of this book and its highly unusual, if not unique, strategy is the way in which all these things somehow come together in the consciousness of Naipaul the author so as to make that, his inner life, the unifying force. It is more than autobiography, then, and in a real sense a new form of fiction wherein the maker is the central and essential character. It may be the best literary novel, about the literary gift and life, of our age.

Much, maybe too much, has been made of how prolific author Joyce Carol Oates has proved to be; and, indeed, this is not her only book of 1994. But *What I Lived For* (Dutton) is a large novel, 608 pages, and is described by her publisher as her masterpiece. Set, except for the December 1959 prologue, over Memorial Day weekend of 1992, the story follows the life and times, the fate, of Jerome ("Corky") Corcoran, real-estate developer and all-

Dust jacket for Irving Faust's novel about a black numbers runner in Harlem in the middle 1930s

the more the land seemed to dip and puddle, the more lush, sunken and secretive the roadside woods grew.

His characters, of all ages and classes, are fully dimensional, and the stories he tells about them are credible and authentic. On the jacket Lee Smith calls Parker "a major writer." He's getting there.

Joanna Scott, *Various Antidotes: Stories* (Holt). Scott has published three highly original and celebrated novels, but this is her first story collection. The eleven stories gathered here are no less original in form and content. Each deals, one way or another, with aspects of science and medicine. "Real" as well as wholly imaginary figures appear. Among the former are the Dutch lens grinder Antonie van Leeuwenhoek of Delft, who invented a microscope; Dorothea Dix; Charlotte Corday; and William Burke, hanged for murder in Edinburgh in 1829. Each of these tales has a different (and appropriate) style and is told in a different way. All involve obsessions and the potential and danger of the imagination. The appreciative Guy Davenport writes that "Joanna Scott's imagination is purest magic." Scott herself, writing about Francis Huber in "Bees, Bees, Bees," inadvertently perhaps, describes her own great gift: "With such sensitivity to sensation, it was natural that he cultivated the parallel faculty: imagination. With remarkable accuracy he could imagine the experiences of others; he had watched attentively for fifteen years, and with a few sensory clues he could follow people in his mind almost as though he *were* them."

David R. Slavitt's new novel (and his fiftieth book so far), *The Cliff* (Louisiana State University Press), takes an almost-down-and-out John Smith, something of a fraud and a con man as well as a loser, for a residency, under false pretenses, at the fabulous artists' colony on Lake Como – Villa Sfrondata (read, only diaphonously disguised, the Rockefeller Foundation's Villa Serbelloni). There is some marvelously funny satire of the pretensions of the literary life, and of the literati here, a certain amount of name-dropping and name-guessing and a great deal of fun and games as fact and fiction collide and ricochet. But this is also a serious, if seriously camouflaged, novel about one unreliable man's "cloudy afternoon of the soul" and how he manages to amend his life and even to revive his abandoned literary career. One of the finest "literary" novels since Slavitt's own *Anagrams* (1970).

Peter Taylor died not long after his fourteenth book, *In the Tennessee Country* (Knopf), was published. The new novel received mixed notices but is a superb example of Taylor's singular art, a large

around hustler, a marvelously realized character who carries everything, including the dazzled reader, with him. What she has achieved (with the help of Corky) may well be her masterpiece. Critic Alan Cheuse, writing in the *Los Angeles Times* (18 December), had this to say: "She's pushed art to the limits here and shown us, to paraphrase old Hemingway, that she can go a few rounds with the champion of us all."

Michael Parker, *The Geographical Cure* (Scribners). Having won both attention and praise for his first novel, *Hello Down There* (1993), Parker here presents three novellas and three stories, all set in Parker's native eastern North Carolina. The sense of place, as in his novel, is powerful and fits the separate stories together:

> All day long they drove east, past tobacco farms and hogs rooting through cornfields, past cows standing in muddy ponds which came only to their knees, through funneled passages where dusty-leafed trees dripped shadows over the highway. The further east they drove

story told easily in a small space (225 pages), an urgent story, in its own way, told in a leisurely, even subdued manner. The central character and narrator, Nathan Longfort, is one of Taylor's gentle, well-mannered, soft-spoken, and deeply conflicted protagonists, measuring his life, sad in general if not in details, against the imagined life of a vanished cousin, Aubrey, and judging his own success as an art historian against that of his youngest son, Braxton, who is something else – a real artist. Taylor, too, was a real artist and we shall miss his voice, so well represented by this rich, ambiguous novel.

Slow year in fiction or not, there were plenty of books published by major players in the literary fiction scene, some of them good enough to make any list of outstanding fiction for any given year. Alphabetically, here is a list of this reviewer's favorites:

• Kingsley Amis, *The Russian Girl* (Viking). Things are jumping at the London School of Slavonic Studies when forty-six-year-old Dr. Richard Vaisey has an adulterous affair with Russian poet Anna Danilova. Things are made more complicated by the fact that the good Dr. Vaisey hates her poetry.

• Paul Auster, *Mr. Vertigo* (Viking). Auster sets this flight of fancy in the Midwest during the 1920s and 1930s. Walter Rawley, following an apprenticeship with Master Yehudi and Mother Sue (a Sioux) and Aesop, an Ethiopian boy, masters the art of levitation and becomes "Walt the Wonder Boy."

• Pat Barker, *The Eye in the Door* (Dutton). Pat Barker, author of *Regeneration* (1992), continues that story and the story of Siegfried Sassoon and Dr. William Rivers, though this novel centers mainly on Lt. Billy Prior.

• John Calvin Batchelor, *Father's Day* (Holt). Set in 2003, this is an elaborately plotted and smoothly developed account of a plot by the vice-president (T. E. Garland of Texas) to depose or to kill the new president – Theodore G. Jay of Michigan.

• Louis Begley, *As Max Saw It* (Knopf). This, Begley's third novel, is told in the first person by the eminently civilized Maximillian Hafter (Max) Strong, Harvard law professor, and mostly concerns his larger-than-life friend, architect Charlie Swan, and Swan's teenage acolyte and lover, Toby. It begins in August 1974 on the day of Nixon's resignation and covers sixteen years, during which, among other events, Toby dies of AIDS.

• Thomas Berger, *Robert Crews* (Morrow). Though Berger has written nineteen novels, including this one, he seems doomed to be always identi-

Alice Munro, whose story collection Open Secrets *was published in 1994 (photograph by Marion Ettlinger)*

fied by his publishers on book jackets as "author of *Little Big Man*." This one is an homage and updated revision of Robinson Crusoe (Friday here is a woman on the run from an abusive husband). Crews, a man of our times, has a tougher time keeping alive than in the original and has to learn a few things and does – and so do we, his readers. Berger is a master and one of the funniest writers we have on the scene.

• Harold Brodkey, *Profane Friendship* (Farrar Straus Giroux). This is a book mostly set in Venice that was commissioned by the Consorzo Venezie Nuova. It follows the relationship, from boyhood into their sixties, of Niles ("Nino") O'Hara and Giangiacomo ("Onni") Gallieni. Nino becomes a screenwriter and Onni an actor. The narrator is Nino, whose chief ambition is "to make the world as much a matter of one's own vocabulary of memory and experience as a dream is."

• Charles Bukowski, *Pulp* (Black Sparrow). Told in the Bukowskiesque voice of private eye Nicky Belane, this is a parody of the hard-boiled detective novel. It is described by *The New Yorker* (15 August) as a mixture of "Groucho Marx and Samuel Beckett."

• Caleb Carr, *The Alienist* (Little, Brown). A highly and widely praised first novel. Set in a vividly imagined New York City of 1896, it follows the search for a serial killer by Lazlo Kreizler, an alienist. "Real" characters appear and are involved, among them Theodore Roosevelt.

• J. M. Coetzee, *The Master of Petersburg* (Viking). Told in the first person by Fyodor Dostoyevsky, it is set in 1869 as the author tries to solve and to understand the mystery of the death of his stepson Pavel Isaev. Throughout he is building toward the writing of *The Demons* (1871), and we see how characters and experiences are transformed into fiction. His own view of the creative process? "I write perversions of the truth. I choose the crooked road and take children into dark places. I follow the dance of the pen."

• Dennis Cooper, *Try* (Grove). Described thus by Catherine Texier in *The New York Times Book Review:* "Once again, he looks at the world of super-hard-core pornography, sado-masochism, pedophilia and necrophilia."

• E. L. Doctorow, *The Waterworks* (Random House). One of the most widely reviewed books (of any kind) during 1994. Set in New York in 1871, told from the point of view of McIlvaine, editor of the *Telegram,* it is a picture of unbridled capitalism at its worst. The reviews were mixed. Here is Malcolm Jones, Jr., in *Newsweek* (27 June): "This is a sci-fi horror movie masquerading as a novel with every wisp of fog, every plot twist in place."

• John Gregory Dunne, *Playland* (Random House). Another widely reviewed novel which opened to mixed reviews. Story of Jack Broderick (who was also the protagonist of Dunne's *The Red White and Blue*) and his search for former child star Blue Tyler and *her* true story. Dunne's tenth book and fifth novel.

• Brett Easton Ellis, *The Informers* (Knopf). Speaking of bad reviews, Ellis's latest (his usual raw materials, angst and anomie among the California young) was swarmed by negative words. In *The New York Times* Michiko Kakutani called it (2 August) "a novel that is as shallow and stupid as the people it depicts." Said *The New Yorker* (26 September, "*The Informers* is a Jackie Collins novel plus literary devices but minus fun — not everyone's cup of tea, to be sure, but, in its own slipshod way, true to its meta-lack of a nonpoint about the place, time, and class it concerns: emptiness is as emptiness does." Diligent search missions uncovered a few kind words by Phil Baker in the *Times Literary Supplement* (28 October). "The characters may be dumb but the book is emphatically not. It is a well-observed and bleakly funny indictment of a culture saturated with money, cars, and drugs, where the nearest things to spiritual values are health food and good luck."

• William Gaddis, *A Frolic of His Own* (Poseidon). Gaddis won his second National Book Award (the first was for *J. R.*, 1975) for this one, a large and emphatically long-winded satiric novel on the theme stated in the story's first line: "Justice — You get justice in the next world, in this world you have the law." There are people suing each other, deposing, testifying, litigating — high energy stuff that, according to the jacket blurb by Louis Auchincloss, "confirms Gaddis's reputation as our most wittily observant, devastating and profound novelist of manners." Joseph Heller calls the novel "consistently original, authentic, comic, and bold." How can Gaddis lose?

• Gail Godwin, *The Good Husband* (Ballantine). An academic setting, if not an academic novel: Magda Danvers, a scholar of visionary experience, and Francis Lake, her good husband, together with novelist Hugo Henry and his wife Alice are the four points of view at the imaginary upstate New York Aurelia College. Magda, sixty-eight, is dying of cancer: "Well, I was always a good student; now I must see what I can learn from my final teacher."

• Nadine Gordimer, *None to Accompany Me* (Farrar Straus Giroux). Like Godwin's, this novel is about two interconnected couples — Vera and Ben Stark, well-to-do, good liberals; and their black friends Didymus and Sally Maqoma. It is set in the changing South Africa of the early 1990s, beset by new forms of violence and greed.

• William Goyen, *Half a Look of Cain* (TriQuarterly Books). This brief novel (136 pages) was written in the early 1950s but never published until now. Goyen, who died in 1983, was, in his own way, a major American writer, and anything by him is worth the effort. Described by critic Bruce Bawer (*The New York Times Book Review,* 17 July) as an "aggressively unrealistic Chinese box of a book," the novel tells stories of Curren, the lighthouse keeper, an aerialist named Marvello, and famous flagpole sitter Shipwreck Kelly. Its basic theme? "The destiny of the world and of the race is in the human body, in the flesh and in the spirit of the human body."

• Shirley Ann Grau, *Roadwalkers* (Knopf). Her ninth work of fiction and her first novel in eighteen years (she won a Pulitzer Prize for *The Keepers of the House,* 1964), *Roadwalkers* is mostly concerned with a black child named Baby (who becomes Mary Woods) in the Great Depression. Some of the novel, which earned mixed reviews, is derived from an earlier short story, "The Beginning."

• Jane Hamilton, *A Map of the World* (Doubleday). In some ways Job had an easier time of it than

Alice Goodwin, Hamilton's protagonist. Writing in the *Philadelphia Inquirer* (17 July), Karen Heller noted: "Jane Hamilton's second novel is one of the most relentlessly forlorn books in memory."

• Mark Harris, *The Tale Maker* (Donald J. Fine). The thirteenth novel by Harris, this one set, more or less, in academe in the late 1950s and early 1960s, is all about Rimrose the writer and the conniving critic Kakapick. What is there to say? It is not *Wake Up, Stupid* (1959), and it sure is not *Bang the Drum Slowly* (1956), but the presence of a book by Harris is far better than the absence of same.

• Joseph Heller, *Closing Time* (Simon and Schuster). Nobody but Heller would dare what he has done by writing a sequel to *Catch-22* (1961). Some of the old guys are back – Yossarian, to be sure, Milo Minderbender (now an arms merchant), Chaplain Shipman (now called Tappman), Sammy Singer (a name at last for the tail gunner of the earlier novel). There are new people like Lew Rabinowitz, an old infantryman who ended up in Dresden with Kurt Vonnegut. And there are *other* people who maybe do not belong here – Truman Capote, Dr. Strangelove, a good soldier named Schweik, and a poor nerd named Joseph Kaye. There are thirty-four chapters in thirteen "books." There is a wedding at the Port Authority terminal. It, like other books by Heller (even his biggest hit), will take some time to assimilate. It has the potential to grow on its readers. It has the potential to prove (down the road) to have been the best novel of 1994.

• John Irving, *A Son of the Circus* (Random House). Huge (633 pages), Irving's three-ring enterprise is set in Bombay, India (dedicated "to Salman"), and its central character in a cast of at least hundreds is orthopedic surgeon Dr. Farokh Daruwalla. There is a murder mystery, and there are wheels within wheels running the plot. And there is lots of laughing and scratching, high jinks and low comedy. Not everybody loved it to death. Wrote Walter Kirn in *New York* (29 August): "Much of the humor in *A Son of the Circus* is reminiscent of bad clowning, the kind that revolted and disturbed generations of trusting kiddies with its flatfooted, dorky, faintly cruel perversity."

• Ward Just, *Ambition & Love* (Houghton Mifflin). This novel, Just's sixteenth book, opens in the grand old expatriate fashion: "When the weather cleared I left my apartment, with no destination in mind. I wanted only fresh air and the mild morning commotion of a city street, and you could find that anywhere in Paris. I bought a newspaper and read it while I drank a coffee at the cafe around the cor-

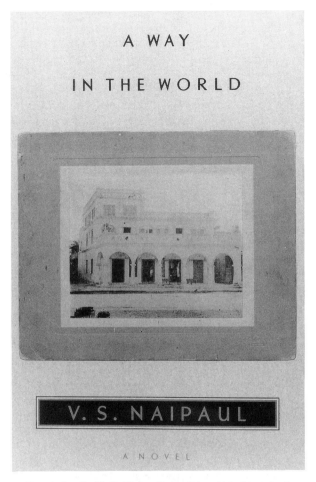

Dust jacket for V. S. Naipaul's novel in which the author's inner life is the unifying force

ner." This story, told by Harry Forrest, a middle-aged writer of crime novels, concerns the life and art of Georgia Whyte, an American painter in Paris, beginning in Winnetka in tumultuous 1968 and continuing to the present.

• Cormac McCarthy, *The Crossing* (Knopf). It is safe to say that no literary novel, not even *The Waterworks*, earned as much national attention as this one, the second novel of a trilogy by McCarthy. The story begins in the winter of 1939, ending 16 July 1945, and tells the story of Billy Parham (age sixteen), his younger brother Boyd, and their parents, who are murdered. The setting is the family ranch near Cloverdale in Hidalgo County, New Mexico. Plenty happens, including several (three) extended adventures in Mexico. It is at once lyrical and elegiac. Critic Gail Caldwell (*Boston Globe*, 19 June) noted, "The novel is signature McCarthy: no quotation marks around its terse dialogue, laconic speech interjected among crescendo descriptive prose."

• Larry McMurtry and Diana Ossana, *Pretty Boy Floyd* (Simon and Schuster). Another view of the American West; this one a novel derived from an unproduced screenplay about the "Robin Hood" of the Southwest in the 1920s and 1930s, Charles Arthur ("Pretty Boy") Floyd. Together with his partner, George Birdwell, he cuts a swath as he robs the rich and shares with the poor. Other significant characters are his wife Ruby, his son Dempsey, Ma Ash, and Beulah Baird. Anything McMurtry touches shines whether it turns to gold or not.

• Lorrie Moore, *Who Will Run the Frog Hospital?* (Knopf). Berie, visiting Paris with her husband, Daniel Hiawatha Bergman, thinks back and forth to and from the time she was fifteen years old (1972) in the upstate New York town of Horsehearts. Her story is about herself and her best friend at the time, the beautiful Silsby ("Sil") Chaussee, who plays the role of Cinderella in a local theme park called "Storyland." This coming-of-age novel earned widespread and respectful attention for its bittersweet, funny-sad ambience. Moore is a favorite of reviewers coast to coast. How readers really feel remains to be seen.

• Howard Norman, *The Bird Artist* (Farrar Straus Giroux). Set in Witless Bay, Newfoundland, this is the story of Fabian Vas, who works at the dry dock and is, as well, a bird artist. It is a story of adultery, murder, loneliness, and quiet oppression. Fabian's art teacher (Isaac Sprague of Nova Scotia) sets the tone for the art of this novel: "Bird art must derive its power from emotion, naturally, but emotions have to be tempered and forged by sheer discipline, all for the sake of posterity." *The Bird Artist* was described by Anne Whitehouse in the *Boston Globe* (24 July) as "a completely original and compelling book about people in extremity."

• Edna O'Brien, *House of Splendid Isolation* (Farrar Straus Giroux). Edna O'Brien's twentieth work of fiction centers on the interaction of a bedridden widow and an IRA terrorist in hiding who holds her hostage. Book editor Gail Caldwell of the *Boston Globe* (10 July): "Full of the bloody poetry and violence of Ireland, this is an oddly, achingly *sweet* novel." The narrator describes the situation clearly enough: "Trust had gone out of the land and out of the people, the old wars, the old atrocities had been replaced with crookeder and bitterer ones, and brother no longer gasped at the bloodshed of brother."

• Tim O'Brien, *In the Lake of the Woods* (Houghton Mifflin). It is the complex story of John Wade, who runs for the Senate and is trounced after it is discovered that he was one of the soldiers of the American division at My Lai and had covered this up. He and his wife Kathy take a vacation in Minnesota's north woods on a lake. Kathy disappears. An amateur magician, Wade, who was nicknamed "Sorcerer" in Vietnam, appears. The novel received mixed reviews, some critics objecting to certain distancing narrative devices – epigraphs, footnotes, and active participation and speculation by the narrator. But these devices are economical in this context, and the counterpoint of fact and fiction, narrative and exposition, works to give the story some of the ragged edges of truth. As the narrator says in a footnote near the end: "Nothing is fixed, nothing is solved. The facts, such as they are, finally spin off into the void of things missing, the inconclusiveness of conclusion. Mystery finally claims us."

• Jayne Anne Phillips, *Shelter* (Houghton Mifflin). Set in West Virginia, Phillips's first novel since *Machine Dreams* (1984) chiefly involves some teenage girls at summer camp, Camp Shelter. It is aptly described by Michiko Kakutani in her 30 August review in *The New York Times*: "Ms. Phillips is concerned here with the disillusionments of adolescence and the passing of childhoods with the initiation into the mysteries of love and death experienced by two teenage girls one hot summer week in the early 60s." It was given a lot of respectful attention and earned mixed praise. Here is critic Richard Eden of the *Los Angeles Times* (4 September): "*Shelter* moves, sometimes bewilderingly, between a lyrically perceptive psychological realism and a gothic primal savagery."

• Will Self, *My Idea of Fun* (Grove/Atlantic). Self is a cult figure in Great Britain. This book is based on sadomasochistic fantasies and takes off from an epigraph of Isaac Bashevis Singer: "I have told myself a thousand times not to be shocked, but every time I am shocked again by what people will do to have fun, for reasons they cannot explain."

• Isaac Bashevis Singer, *Meshugah* (Farrar Straus Giroux). This novel was published serially in 1981–1983, then, evidently, forgotten and rediscovered. It tells the stories of refugee survivors of the Holocaust in New York and, briefly, in Israel, during the early 1950s. The narrator is Aaron Greidinger, a writer for the *Forward*. The heart of the story, however, is the mystery of Miriam, a survivor, who is simultaneously in love with an old and a middle-aged man. Singer is quoted on the jacket as allowing that it is "a strange situation, with lots of promise."

• D. M. Thomas, *Pictures at an Exhibition* (Scribners). In this, his tenth novel, Thomas mixes personal experiences with factual history. Organized in nine sections, each with the title of an Edvard Munch painting, the story moves between the here and now of the 1990s and the then and there of the Holocaust camps. Fiction is placed cheek by jowl with documentary excerpts. Oddly, success or failure of Thomas's method depends on credibility which is sometimes tested to the quick. Some critics were offended by the book.

　• John Updike, *Brazil* (Knopf). This novel appeared in the early spring and was out in mass-market paperback (Fawcett) before the end of the year. It is a complex and highly ambitious retelling of the myth of Tristan and Iseult set in contemporary Brazil. It has magic – for example, the young couple change color in the midst of the story, he (Tristao) from black to white, she (Isabel) vice versa. There is, not surprisingly, brilliant writing, but critical reaction was mixed. Wrote John Bayley in *The New York Review of Books* (12 May): "Updike in this world is about as naturally at home as Mark Twain would have been in the Berkeley Square high life of Disraeli and Trollope." Bayley calls it "a gallant try." Like *The Coup* (1987), however, this one may age well. Certainly it is an elegant display of the moves of magic realism.

　• Theodore Weesner, *Novemberfest* (Knopf). Weesner, author of *The Car Thief* (1972) and *The True Detective* (1987), has both Glen Cady as his protagonist and a before-and-after story line. We see Cady as a young soldier in postwar Germany who falls in love and has an affair with an older married woman. And we see him as an assistant professor of German having another affair (he is married now) with a young student. At the end he returns to Germany and witnesses the breakup of the Berlin Wall. Wessner is a good, realistic writer who has suffered a string of bad luck. He may have turned the corner with *Novemberfest,* which received a starred review in *Publishers Weekly.*

　Some other literary novels which received serious attention and certainly deserve to be mentioned here include *The Mortician's Apprentice* (Norton), by Rick DeMarinis; *The American Woman in the Chinese Hat* (Dalkey Archive), by Carole Maso; *White Man's Grave* (Farrar Straus Giroux), by Richard Dooling; *Thank You For Smoking* (Random House), by Christopher Buckley; *The Longings of Women* (Fawcett), by Marge Piercy; *Stones From the River* (Poseidon), by Ursula Hegi; *Ancestral Truths* (Holt), by Sara Maitland; *Tunnel of Love* (Harper-Collins), by Hilma Wolitzer; *Half Asleep in Frog Pajamas* (Bantam), by Tom Robbins; *The Partisan* (Atheneum), by Benjamin Cheever; *Life Estates* (Knopf),

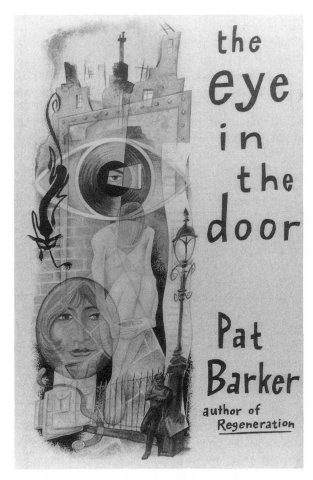

Dust jacket for Pat Barker's novel about World War I

by Shelby Hearon; *Shear* (Grove), by Tim Parks; *Called Out* (Doubleday), by A. G. Mojtabai; *The Game of Thirty* (Houghton Mifflin), by William Kotzwinkle; and *The Book of Dreams* (Ticknor and Fields), by Craig Nova.

　At least a brief mention is in order for the continuing gradual blurring of the lines between genre and literary fiction. For example, many writers of thrillers found their work respectfully treated in the review pages. Among these were Donald E. Westlake, *Baby, Would I Lie?* (Mysterious); Lawrence Block, *A Long Line of Dead Men* (Morrow); Dick Francis, *Wild Horses* (Putnam); and James W. Hall, *Mean High Tide* (Delacorte). Robert B. Parker's *All Our Yesterdays* (Delacorte) is not a thriller but a literary novel of three generations of Boston Irish. But he has already escaped the genre ghetto. African American writer Walter Mosley made his breakthrough with *Black Betty* (Norton), the fourth novel in his series about Ezekiel ("Easy") Rawlins. Called by reviewers his bleakest novel yet, this one is set in Los Angeles in the 1950s and early 1960s and is rich with allusions and homage to Raymond Chandler. Mosley was warmly praised for the creation of the fluent voice of Easy Rawlins.

In good times and bad, first novels continue to be written and somehow published. *Publishers Weekly* devoted a whole section to first novels of the fall season, featuring both forthcoming hardcover and trade paperback originals – "First Fiction: New Writers to Bet on This Fall" (5 September). Judging by the announced print orders, ranging (with two modest exceptions) from 15,000 to 250,000 copies, by announced author tours and promotional activities, first novels must be thriving like kudzu. Most of these, however, vanished without more than a trace or two in the papers and, more important, in the bookstores. Still, there were moderately successful first novels and others which, vanished or not, fully deserve mention.

Playwright David Mamet's *The Village* (Little, Brown), set in an unnamed but classical New England village, was highly praised for the characteristics it shares with his popular drama and for its language, described by Michiko Kakutani (*The New York Times,* 4 October) as "an almost musical idiom made up of silences and short-cuts, innuendos, ellipses and repetitions." Mamet's book (whose jacket features his name in huge letters looming over the modest title) is built around a half-dozen major characters and takes place in twelve chapters and a year's time. In the *Times Literary Supplement* (14 October) Bharat Tandon gave the book a rave review, noting: "Mamet writes with decency and integrity of a place where everyone has a story, even if they can't tell it out loud; of people both united and lonely."

Some other first novels started their lives with an asset of respect. John Dufresne, who had already received praise for an earlier collection of stories, *The Way That Water Enters Stone* (1991), earned more of that precious commodity with *Louisiana Power & Light* (Norton), a first-person *plural* accounting of the Fontana family of Monroe, Ouachita Parish, Louisiana, a family "with bad water in the gene pool." It is all over the lot (Ron Carlson calls it "*Tristram Shandy* with bayous") but chiefly focuses on the last of the Fontanas, young Billy Wayne.

Pinckney Benedict had two well-received collections of stories to his credit before he published *Dogs of God* (Doubleday). He keeps to his native West Virginia turf and puts his protagonist, Goody, against a mighty drug lord named Tannhauser. Describing the ambience of Benedict's fiction in the *Los Angeles Times* (27 March), Chris Goodrich wrote:

"Benedictland is neither a particularly comic nor a particularly tragic place but it brims with odd characters and creatures driven by primal, irrefutable urges."

Debra Spark's *Coconuts For the Saint* (Faber) caught the eyes of critics and book editors, partly because of its setting and ethnicity. It is the story of Sandolfo, a Puerto Rican baker (his shop is named La Madeleine), and his triplet daughters – Tata, Melone, and Beatriz – told from multiple points of view. Perhaps also profiting from the honest ethnic curiosity of readers were Nina Vida's *Goodbye, Saigon* (Crown), in large part about Vietnamese in southern California, and Carol Edgarian's *Rise the Euphrates* (Random House), telling the history of three generations of Armenian American women.

Heather Lewis's *House Rules* (Doubleday) had a more primal appeal. She tells the tale of fifteen-year-old Lee, a champion horseback rider who encounters sex, violence, abuse, and drug addiction. "The erotic, the nurturing, and the horrific elements of the story stand uneasily but resolutely side by side," wrote *The New Yorker* (13 June), "each stubbornly refusing to explain away the existence of the others."

From the crowd of first novels published in 1994, here are a few selected by this reviewer and recommended to readers. None is flawless, but each is marked by commitment, integrity, and quality writing. Karl Ackerman, *The Patron Saint of Unmarried Women* (St. Martin's Press). Described by Roz Spafford in the *Washington Post* (1 May) as "both rueful and funny, one of a kind," it is set firmly in Washington, D.C., and details the ins and outs of a love affair between two interesting people – Jack Townsend and Nina Lawrence.

William Carpenter, a Maine poet and evidently a bit of an unreconstructed hippie, writes a first-person story told by a radical young woman named Penguin in *A Keeper of Sheep* (Milkweed). *Sweetbitter* (Broken Moon), by Reginald Gibbons, editor of *TriQuarterly,* is set in the years 1896–1916 and placed in east Texas. It is a large novel whose protagonist, Reuben S. Sweetbitter, is half Choctaw, half white man. It is a love story and a story of the violent clash of cultures.

A female bluegrass fiddler, Carrie Marie Mullins by name, the only woman in the Hawktown Road band, is at once the protagonist and the voice of *Come and Go, Molly Snow* (Norton), by Mary Ann Taylor-Hall, a gifted story writer from Kentucky. The story, and the lively, singing, and sensuous prose that clothes it, are admirable and authentic.

Bobbie Ann Mason is only about half kidding in her blurb when she says "Elvis would have loved it!"

Even including books mentioned elsewhere in this piece, it is safe to say that it was not a boom year for the historical novel (not counting the innumerable romance novels set lightly in past time). Nevertheless, the genre lives, and there were some good and fair-to-middling examples. *The Mutiny Run* (St. Martin's Press), Frank Eccles's fourth novel, joins Captain Brewster and his ship H.M.S. *Adamant* in 1797 doing battle against the French and the Dutch and English mutineers. Perhaps it more properly belongs among the year's translations, but a first novel by Uruguayan literary critic Napoleon Baccino Ponce de Leon, *Five Black Ships* (Harcourt Brace), was widely and favorably reviewed. Narrated by Juanillo, the jester for the fleet, it follows the voyage of Ferdinand Magellan in 1519. Rita Mae Brown enjoyed some success with *Dolley* (Bantam), a story of (and partly by) Dolley Madison, set in Washington during the War of 1812. Robert Skimin brought out *Ulysses: A Biographical Novel of U. S. Grant* (St. Martin's Press), and John Lovejoy's *Halo* (Harcourt Brace) was set on the Oregon Trail in the mid–nineteenth century. In her first novel, *Sherman's March* (Villard), Cynthia Bass, recounted in several voices – one of them that of William Tecumseh Sherman – tells the story of Sherman's march from Atlanta to the sea. Sherman's last words: "Oh, well. It's hard to become immortal without being misunderstood. Look at Christ."

Several historical novels were by black authors about black experience or, anyway, aimed at an African American audience. In *Black Gold* (Dutton) Anita Bunkley follows two African American families in Texas from 1906 to the early 1920s. Barbara Chase-Riboud, whose *Sally Hemings* was published in 1979, wrote of Sally Hemings's daughter Harriet, who seems to have been a witness to most of the significant events of mid-nineteenth-century America, in *The President's Daughter* (Crown). In Louise Meriwether's *Fragments of the Ark* (Pocket) a slave named Robert Smalls steals a Confederate gunboat and delivers it safely to the U.S. Navy. *Cape Fear Rising* (Blair), by Philip Gerard, is based on the "Wilmington riot" of 1898. Elizabeth Wilde Mayerson's *Miami: A Saga* (Dutton) offers a history of Miami, featuring black families, from the 1880s through Hurricane Andrew. Good fiction, but on a fragile historical background is *The Falling Hills* (1967), brought out in a new edition by the University of South Carolina Press, by Professor Perry Lentz of Kenyon College. This novel depicts a real event, the so-called Fort Pillow massacre

of 12 April 1864. An interesting new preface by Lentz, together with some excellent writing, make this a worthwhile piece of historical fiction in spite of the fact that the overwhelming evidence and several serious studies by disinterested parties, during the Civil War and later, seem to indicate that this atrocious event did not take place, at least not at all as here described. Finally, in *Masters of Illusion* (Warner) by Mary-Ann Tirone Smith, we have a novel about the great Connecticut circus fire of 1944 where, in July of that year, 169 people were killed and many more seriously injured.

Probably the most important translation in a fairly quiet year was not a new book. Fyodor Dostoyevsky's *Demons* (Knopf) is the latest translation of a work by that author by the much-praised team of Richard Pevear and Larissa Volokhonsky. There are four versions of this 1871 novel, under various titles, in print; but this one has earned kudos as the best. Writing in the *Los Angeles Times* (16 October), Michael Henry Helm said, "The introduction, the helpful but unobtrusive notes, and most of all the fine translation make the new 'Demons' a capital job of restoration." "Without irony it's simply impossible to get through these heroic times," says Nina Gradov, one of the Russian family which is the subject of Vassily Aksyonov's large (529 pages) and widely and prominently reviewed *Generations of Winter* (Random House). We follow the family Gradov, closely engaged as witnesses and participants in public affairs from the Kronstadt revolt of 1921 through the end of World War II in 1945. Also from the Russian is *Incidences* (Serpent's Tale), a collection of brief, intense stories by Daniil Kharms, who died in his thirties during 1942. Ludmilla Petrushevskaya writes *Chernukha* ("black stuff") in her novella *The Time: Night* (Pantheon).

From long-suffering Poland came *Rat* (Arcade), told as an autobiography by a "real" rat, by Andrzej Zaniewski. The rat says things like: "Terror will increase your strength. Later you will learn to hate and kill." In his own commentary the author has a few things to say, also. "Don't forget, then, dear reader," he writes, "that in describing a rat's life in this detailed naturalistic way, I had you in mind." Serbian writer Milos Tsernianski is represented by the first volume of *Migrations* (Arcade). Set in the eighteenth century, the novel centers on a Serbian officer, Vuk Isakovic, serving the Austro-Hungarian Empire. Czech writer Ivan Klima had his seventh book to be translated into English – *My Golden Trades* (Scribners). It is based on his own experiences as an out-of-favor writer under the Com-

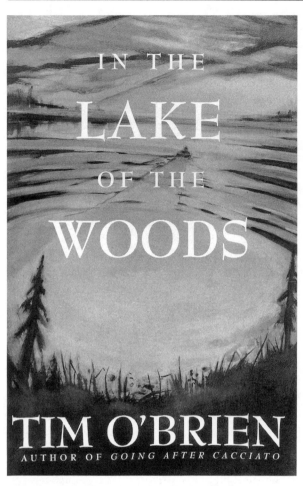

Dust jacket for Tim O'Brien's novel about politics, the My Lai massacre, and the long-term effects of the Vietnam War

munists, one who was forced to earn a living in unlikely occupations. In an afterword he says: "The hero of my book, most involuntarily, tries his hand at a number of jobs, none of which he is really suited for. There is no gold in any of them, unless you count the unexpected gains experience brings. The book is autobiographical to the extent that I actually did most of the jobs mentioned in the stories." *My Golden Trades* was widely and favorably reviewed.

Danish writer Peter Høeg, who won abundant critical praise in 1993 for *Smilla's Sense of Snow*, tells the complex story of the rebellion of three children – Peter, Katarina, and August – in a Danish school for a variety of special children in *Borderlines* (Farrar Straus Giroux). From the Dutch came *Nightfather* (Persea), by Carl Friedman. Narrated by an unmarried girl in the 1960s, *Nightfather* is concerned with her father Ephraim and his continuing recollections of the Holocaust. Also from the Dutch is Cees Nooteboom's brief, mysterious, and highly sym-

bolic *The Following Story* (Harcourt Brace), a surreal tale of Herman Mussert, who looks like Socrates and is/was a teacher of Latin and Greek and who has somehow or other ended up in a Lisbon hotel. Any number of works came out of Germany. Among them *The Silent Angel* (St. Martin's Press) by Nobel laureate Heinrich Boll, stands out. Boll died nine years ago, and this was an early unpublished novel, part of the postwar works by Boll called *Trümmer-Literatur* (rubble literature). Set in an unnamed German city much like Boll's own Cologne, it is the story of Hans Schwitzler, a deserter from the army who owes his life to Willy Gompertz and must deliver Willy's coat to his family. Alfred Andersch is represented by *The Father of a Murderer* (New Directions). Set in 1928 it deals mainly with a school and a classroom presided over by Headmaster Himmler, father of the infamous Heinrich. A reflection or an example of newer developments on the European scene is *Mother Tongue* (Coach House), by Emine Seugi Ozdamar, four short stories about immigrant life by this Turkish-born German writer. From Turkey itself we have *The Black Book* (Farrar Straus Giroux), by Orhan Pamuk. The book is set in Istanbul and alternates between two narrators – Jelal, a newspaper columnist, and Galip, a lawyer – evoking layers of Istanbul's history as the surface narrative of their rivalry for Ruya (who happens to be Galip's wife) plays out. Taking the form of a writer's notebook and a work in progress and described by its publisher as a "metafictional anatomy of the modern soul," is *Night* (Louisiana State University Press), by Bilge Karasu. The last line of the story is a single question on an otherwise blank page – "Can writing all this keep one from going mad?" Egyptian writer Nawal El Saadawi sets *The Innocence of the Devil* (University of California Press) in a mental institution where both God and Satan are patients. The story is at once realistic and surreal. Israeli writer Yehoshva Kenaz enters the life of a seventy-six-year-old woman in Tel Aviv in *The Way to the Cats* (Steerforth). *The Three-Inch Golden Lotus* (Hawaii), by Chinese novelist Feng Jicai, is advertised as "a novel on foot binding."

From France there is *A Singular Man* (Marlboro), by Ammanuel Bove, a writer admired by Samuel Beckett, Rainer Maria Rilke, and André Gide. Isi Beller's *Sacred Fire* (Arcade) is a thriller, a what-if whose protagonist is a French psychoanalyst. The premise is that a retrovirus has managed to infect human sperm with HIV.

Spanish author Arturo Perez-Reverte's *The Flanders Panel* (Harcourt Brace) is an intellectual thriller set in the art world of Madrid. Argentine metafictionist Juan José Saer's *Nobody Nothing Never* was published by Serpent's Tail. A more important Argentine writer, once a collaborator with Jorge Luis Borges, Adolfo Bioy Casares saw his second collection of stories, *Selected Stories* (New Directions), Englished. His translator, Suzanne Jill Levine, describes him as "an urban comedian, a parodist who turns fantasy and science fiction inside out to expose the banality of our scientific, intellectual, and especially erotic pretensions." The fifteen adventurous stories in this volume live up to that billing. The most widely noticed among the Latin American works of fiction published here in 1994 was *The Orange Tree* (Farrar Straus Giroux) by Carlos Fuentes. The book is composed of five novellas distinctly different in time and space and (sometimes) style – "The Two Shores," a first-person story by Jeronimo de Aguilar, one of Cortes's men who acted as translator with the Indians; "Sons of the Conquistador," narratives told separately and together by Martin 2 and Martin 1, two of Cortes's children; "The Two Numantias," an account of the eight months' siege of Numantia, in Spain, by the Romans; "Apollo and the Whores," set in modern times in Acapulco and told by Oscar-winning movie actor Vincente Valera (what he tells is a wild, acted-out, erotic version of Snow White and the Seven Dwarfs; Valera ends up dead); finally, "the Two Americas: Fragments from the Diary of a Genoese Sailor," which treats the arrival of Columbus in the Caribbean among other things. These pieces are linked by the general theme of culture shock and clash and by the image of the orange tree which appears in and haunts them all.

And then there are the generally and genuinely unusual books, one way or another one of a kind. For example, two books brought out simultaneously by the University of Chicago Press: a novel, *Bengal Nights,* by Romanian author Mircea Eliade, together with the memoir *It Does Not Die,* by Indian poet Maitreyi Devi. Written forty years apart, they both deal with a "real" love affair between Eliade and Devi. Robert Littel's *The Visiting Professor* (Random House) is an unusual and satiric mix of academic novel and spy novel, featuring an allusive protagonist, Lemuel Falk. Bob Baylus, writing in the *Baltimore Sun* (19 April) had this to report: "Robert Littel has earned a reputation for off-beat spy novels; in *The Visiting Professor* he has written a post–cold war work that has more in common with Jonathan Swift than Ian Fleming." In *The Devil's Own Work* (Knopf), English writer Alan Judd, who published a biography of Ford Maddox Ford in 1991, offers a rewrite and revision, in new terms

and voices, of *The Good Soldier* (1915), Ford's most famous novel, described in the *Boston Globe* (3 July) as "a careful but spooky reconstruction of the Ford novel." A vaguely similar homage is Christopher Bigsby's *Hester: A Novel About the Early Hester Prynne* (Viking). The book is exactly what it says, telling Hester's story, in England and colonial America up to the time depicted in *The Scarlet Letter* (1850). *Di and I* (Random House), by screen and television writer Peter Lefcourt, who scored a few years ago with *The Deal* (Random House), lifts Charles Berns, the protagonist of that novel, into a new situation and a new relationship, in this case with Britain's Princess Diana. Carolyn See judged (in the *Washington Post,* 24 June) – "It seems less funny than crazy." In *Biografi: A Traveller's Tale* (Harvest), by Lloyd Jones, the protagonist goes to Albania in 1991 to search for dictator Enver Hoxha's double, a former dentist named Petar Shapallo. Shapallo tells his own story in interview form. The relation of this fiction to the factual world is complicated by the truth that there was (is?) a real Petar Shapallo who acted as a stand-in for Hoxha. Petar, fictional or "real" or a little of both, recognizes the complexity of his vocation: "I had known I would have to act, like an actor, but until that moment it had never occurred to me that Enver had been doing the same." Donald McCaig's latest book about Border collies, *Nop's Hope* (Crown), received widespread critical praise, including a highly favorable notice from Christopher Lehmann-Haupt in *The New York Times* (7 July). In *Nop's Hope* parts of the novel are told from dogs' points of view and in their own words. Emma Donoghue's *Stir-Fry* (HarperCollins) is an upside-down working out (a "fractured fairy tale") of the Cinderella story as a lesbian coming-of-age novel. The author is a playwright in Dublin. For mystery and originality few writers can match the story of B. Traven, author of *The Treasure of the Sierra Madre* (1935). This year saw the completion of the publication of the six novels he called "Jungle Novels" with *Trozas* (Ivan R. Dee). Set in a *monteria,* a jungle logging camp for mahogany, *Trozas* is a bleak and savage story of men living at extremes. As Traven himself describes it: "The jungle, and work in the jungle allow no privileges – the master is like the slave, the officer like the soldier; come evening they are both as tired and the last spark of ambition and love of cleanliness are lost to both." Eliot Asinof and former big-league pitcher Jim Bouton produced a collaborative novel, *Strike Zone* (Viking), in which Bouton wrote the part and words for Sam Ward, the pitcher, and Asinof created a voice for the umpire – Ernie Kolacka. The novel concerns an (imaginary) fixed game between the Phillies and the Cubs. In a contemporary sense all of the work of Susan Straight, a white novelist who writes exclusively about black characters, including her third and latest book, *Blacker Than a Thousand Midnights* (Hyperion), is unusual. With this book she continues her fictional exploration of a black community in southern California – Rio Seco. This one is written from the point of view of Darnell Tucker, a laid-off firefighter.

Two of the more interesting odd books of 1994 involve a conjunction of visual and verbal art – *The Wild Party* (Pantheon), a rhyming poem written in 1928 by Joseph Moncure March (who was the first managing editor of *The New Yorker*), in its new version illustrated with drawings by Art Spiegelman; and *Stations: An Imagined Journey, Story & Paintings* (Pantheon), by artist Michael Flanagan. *Stations*, described by its publisher as "a fictional archeology of time and place, where the past asserts itself as an unfathomable mystery at the heart of everyday life," comes to us as an album of photographs concerning two imaginary railroad lines in the Shenandoah Valley – The Buffalo and Shenandoah and the Powhatan Railroad. In addition to beautiful pictures of the places along the line, there is the text, which (among other things) has characters and situation and story. This is an extraordinary book and the first giant step forward I have seen in the wedding of text to visual image in book form. This book began with the encouragement of the late Jacqueline Kennedy Onassis.

Something needs to be said about the doings during this year of the university presses in the care and maintenance of American letters. With the exception of Louisiana State University Press, which was long a leader in the field, many of the presses – Georgia, Iowa, Southern Methodist, Pittsburgh, Illinois, Missouri, and some others – continue to publish original fiction, both collections of stories and novels. Louisiana State was forced to discontinue its ambitious program of bringing out new fiction because of budgetary constraints; but still in the pipeline (and due out early in 1995) are a new novel, *A Time to Dance*, by Walter Sullivan, and *Omniphobia*, a collection of stories by R. H. W. Dillard. And Louisiana State continues to publish poetry and to promote their new series of reprints – Voices of the South. Illinois, after years of publishing stories, brought out its first novel in 1994. Milton Wolff, who rose from recruit to commanding officer of the Abraham Lincoln Brigade during the Spanish civil war of the 1930s, has produced *Another Hill: An Autobiographical Novel*, centering on two main charac-

ters – Mitch Castle and Leo Rogin. The war is presented as a raw experience, at once different from and, in many ways, more complex than the more familiar versions of a variety of professional writers. Near the end, as the war is ending badly for the Loyalists, Castle defines his vision: "Castle, seeing things his own way – often so different from the way they were seen by others, and too often quite different than the truth – experienced this as certain. It was his own reality, and he had to live by it even if in the end it killed him."

Among the outstanding collections of short stories coming from university presses are *Mississippi History* (University of Missouri Press), by Steve Yarbrough, his second collection; and a first collection, also from Missouri – *Kneeling on Rice*, by Elizabeth Denton, eleven stories about women aptly described by the publisher: "Outrageous situations made entirely believable, and eccentric characters caught up in life and chaotic entanglements, are the hallmarks of Elizabeth Denton's funny, often moving, fiction." Prizewinning author John Casey may be carried away, going a wee bit too far in his book jacket claim that this collection puts "Elizabeth Denton in a league with Alice Munro," but it is, indeed, an excellent collection. Also from Missouri comes Gordon Weaver's latest collection, his seventh (he is also the author of four novels) – *The Way We Know In Dreams*. Eleven various stories in various voices were judged in *The New York Times Book Review* (31 July) to be "the sort of inspired, clever and unexpected fiction that stays with a reader a long time." The Iowa Short Fiction Award, judged by Francine Prose, went to *Macauley's Thumb*, by Lex Williford, ten solidly constructed, straightforward stories touched with good humor and a strong sense of character and set variously and firmly in Texas, Mexico, New Mexico, Oklahoma, Arkansas, and Alabama. Southern Methodist, which also does novels and new editions, brought out two first-rate first collections – *River Street*, by Phil Condon, and *Can You Get There From Here?*, by Donley Watt. Another first collection coming from a southwestern university press is *Letters from the Horse Latitudes* (Texas Christian University Press), by C. W. Smith. Smith, a professor of English at Southern Methodist, is the author of four novels. One of the finest short-story writers of our time, William Hoffman, author of ten novels and, with the brand-new *Follow Me Home* (Louisiana State University Press), three collections of stories, earned highest praise for this latest collection of eleven stories. Writing in *The Sewanee Review* (Fall 1994), Robert Buffington said simply and directly enough: "He is the best pure storyteller I have read in these two years." The late Frederick Schiller Faust, who wrote under the name Max Brand, is represented by *The Collected Stories of Max Brand* (University of Nebraska Press), edited by Robert and Jane Easton. Surprisingly, for a writer associated in the public mind with the Western, the stories are various and few are set in the West. From the University of Washington Press came *The Soup of Salanda,* by H. Arlo Nimmo, a series of tales drawn from his experience as an anthropoligist living among the boat-dwelling Bajau people in the Sulu Islands of the Philippines.

Louisiana State University Press continues to publish the annual Pegasus Prize for Literature, this year's winner being the Turkish novel *Night,* by Bilge Karasu. Highly experimental, Karasu's "text" is praised by Mary Lee Settle as "evocative and sensuous" and, in another blurb by poet Richard Howard, as "a kind of scathing aleatory mosaic."

Perhaps equally important in our present age of publishing without sustained or significant backlists, some of the university presses are bringing worthwhile books back into print in new editions and, as well, translations which would otherwise be unavailable. The University Press of Mississippi offered a new novel, *Anabasis: A Journey to the Interior,* by Ellen Gilchrist, all about a slave girl named Auria in ancient Greece, as well as the Banner Books series, with its new editions of Richard Wright's *Savage Holiday* (1954) and *The Color Curtain* (1956) and Ellen Douglas's *Apostles of Light* (1973), with an introduction by Elizabeth Spencer. Both Douglas and Spencer have titles in the new Voices of the South series from Louisiana State University Press. The first year's list was as follows: Fred Chappell, *The Gaudy Place* (1973); Ellen Douglas, *The Rock Cried Out* (1979); George Garrett, *Do, Lord, Remember Me* (1965); Lee Smith, *The Last Day the Dogbushes Bloomed* (1968); Elizabeth Spencer, *The Voice at the Back Door* (1965); Peter Taylor, *The Widows of Thornton* (1954); *Poor Fool* (1930), by Erskine Caldwell; *The Last of the Southern Girls* (1973), by Willie Morris; *Band of Angels* (1956), by Robert Penn Warren; and *The Morning and the Evening* (1961), by Joan Williams. MIT Press brought out a critical edition of George Santayana's *The Last Puritan* (1935). The University Press of New England republished Lawrence Millman's *Hero Jesse* (1982). The University of Nebraska Press in its Bison Books series published *The Job* (1917), Sinclair Lewis's first novel. From the University of Oklahoma Press there was a new edition of *Harvesting Ballads* (1984), by Philip Kimball, described in the *DLB Yearbook: 1984* as "a writer who here takes his

Playwright David Mamet, whose first novel, The Village, *was published in 1994*

place, with one wonderful novel, among our very best." Oklahoma University Press also has a Native American series, regularly publishing fiction by Native American authors, including, in 1994, *Bone Game,* by Louis Owens, and *The Light People,* a first novel by Gordon Henry, Jr., telling the story of Oskinaway, a Chippewa boy. Southern Methodist University Press has become a major player in a short time, publishing new editions of earlier books as well as original fiction. Among the reprints of the year for Southern Methodist University Press were *The Grandmothers' Club* (1986), by Alan Cheuse, with an afterword by John Aldridge; *Thief of Dreams* (1991), by John Yount; *The Old Army Game,* consisting of the novel *Which Ones Are the Enemy?* (1961) and nine short stories (1955–1993), by George Garrett. A smaller Texas institutional press, Texas Review Press, had added the novel to its Breakthrough Award series, already publishing books of poetry and collections of stories. The first-place award winner for 1994 was JoAllen Bradham for her first novel, *Some Personal Papers,* described by Madison Smartt Bell as "a novel about serial murder with charitable intent." Duke University Press republished two novels by Susan Petigru King, a nineteenth-century South Carolina novelist – *Gerald Gray's Wife* (1864) and *Lily* (1855). Rice University Press now has a Fiction Reprint series, which published two novels by Daniel Stern – *Who Shall Live, Who Shall Die* (1963) and *After the War* (1965).

I have no statistics, but it seems clear from book lists and book reviews that the number of titles of translated fiction published by commercial houses is slowly and inexorably shrinking. To an extent the university presses are beginning to enter the translation scene. Duke University Press, for example, published *Stella Manhattan,* a 1985 novel about gay life in New York, by Brazilian author

Stella Santiago. The University of Texas Press brought out Mexican writer Sergio Galindo's 1986 novel *Otilia's Body*. The University of Arkansas Press published *In the Land of Silence,* a 1987 Bolivian novel involving one central character with three interior selves, by Jesus Urzagasti; it will shortly publish *Horses into the Night,* a postmodernist novel in the Catalan language by Baltasar Porcel.

Not only the university presses are engaged in the republication of significant literary novels now out of print. This year, for example, Coyne and Chenowith brought out a new edition of *Cooper* (1987), by Hilary Masters, the second novel of his Hudson Valley trio. Editor Tim Page put together *Dawn Powell at Her Best,* consisting of two novels and eight stories by Powell.

The New Yorker may be the last major market for the short story where they pay real money for fiction; and Jonathan Yardley (among others) may be on their case. See "The New Yorker & Fiction: A Sad Story," *Washington Post,* 27 June, wherein he describes all but two of the stories in the special fiction issue, "The New Yorker Celebrates Fiction," as "limp, airless, and unengaging." But, come what may, the short story seems to be thriving, judging by the many and various collections published in 1994 and by the major anthologies which are a starting place for many readers searching for a new voice. Judging by *Prize Stories 1994: The O. Henry Awards* (Anchor) and *The Best American Short Stories 1994* (Houghton Mifflin) (guest editor this year – Tobias Wolff), there are many new voices and not much overlapping – less than usual, in fact. This is the twenty-eighth volume of the O. Henry Awards to be edited by William Abrahams, and he notes with pride and surprise that of the twenty-one stories on board this time, eighteen are by newcomers to the awards. After many years of moderate reluctance, Abrahams has gradually accepted the idea that first-rate stories can and do appear in little magazines. To my count, fifteen of the twenty-one first appeared there. Wolff is not quite so bold. Eight of his stories came from the little-magazine league and, in general, he has better-known writers. But there is a lot of talent, old and new, and there is ample variety. Shannon Ravenel of Algonquin Books seems to have come to terms with pop culture in this, the ninth volume of the series New Stories From the South. Ravenel writes, "Popular culture has blurred lines once so clearly drawn between races and classes. Tabloid TV has stirred our melting pot into froth. No topic is taboo today. But it is the writers, not the talk show hosts, who will take us deep into the regions inside those lines." She has put together

a nice eclectic group, leaning a little more toward the tried and true, but a solid and exemplary anthology.

There was a multitude of anthologies of every kind, usual and unusual, during the year. Here are three that are unusual enough to merit notice. *Listening to Ourselves: More Stories from "The Sound of Writing"* (Anchor), edited by Alan Cheuse and Caroline Marshall. All of the thirty-seven stories included here were written for radio broadcasting on *The Sound of Writing* program. They are, then, short and intended to be heard. But, for any number of reasons, the editors have put together a more diverse group of writers and a wider variety of form and content than the other mentioned anthologies. *The Quotable Moose: A Contemporary Maine Reader* (University Press of New England), edited by Wesley McNair, includes work by forty writers and includes poetry as well as fiction; but there are nineteen stories, some published for the first time, some by nationally known writers – Carolyn Chute and Cathie Pelletier – and others by good writers not yet known beyond the limits of Maine. *Wild Women: Contemporary Stories by Women Celebrating Women* (Overlook Press) is, obviously, a trendy, gimmicky stratagem, an "idea" anthology. But ignoring the obvious, shrugging off the *excuse* for this gathering, one finds forty-seven stories by forty-six writers, some of them good indeed and all of them worth knowing. This anthology is good enough to stand alongside its chief competition – *The Oxford Book of Modern Women's Stories* (Oxford), which brings together forty stories from 1905 (Willa Cather's "Paul's Case") to the 1990s.

Anthologies may serve to indicate the general good health of the short story, but it is the individual collections which keep the form alive and well. The new collections came in all kinds. There were stories by old masters – *A Frank O'Connor Reader* (Syracuse) and *John O'Hara, Gibbsville, Pa: The Classic Stories* (Carroll and Graff). The late John Cheever is represented in *Thirteen Uncollected Stories* (Academy). A story goes with this one – four years and more than one million dollars in legal expenses in a fuss between the Cheever family and academy. It was finally settled out of court, allowing this volume of thirteen out-of-copyright stories to be published. Another master, Grace Paley, brought out *The Collected Stories* (Farrar Straus Giroux), which, in fact, contains no new work but puts her three previous collections – *The Little Disturbances of Man* (1959), *Enormous Changes at the Last Moment* (1974), and *Later the Same Day* (1985) – into one volume. Paley is greatly admired, though not by everyone.

Writing in *The New Criterion* (September), Brooke Allen made a valid point: "The fact is that Paley has so identified her writing with the various causes she espouses – peace, environmentalism, prison reform, feminism – that in criticizing her work one runs the risks of being perceived as a kind of ogre who is out to get the world's oppressed."

There were any number of worthy collections of short fiction by established artists. Topping the list is John Updike's eleventh collection of stories, *The Afterlife* (Knopf), twenty-two stories, mostly dealing with men and women of middle age: "Again and again in *The Afterlife*, men and women in their 50s and 60s are forced to confront death with that special intensity brought on by its hoary imminence." (Jay Parini, *The New York Times Book Review*, 6 November). These stories are also shadowed and haunted by the memory of other, earlier Updike stories and by some aspects of his own life. The special quality of them is described by critic Jonathan Yardley (*The Washington Post*, 26 October) as "a mixture of sadness, and stoicism, anger and humor, realism and nostalgia." Another outstanding and exemplary collection of stories is William Hoffman's third (he is also author of ten novels) – *Follow Me Home* (Louisiana State University Press). The stories in this collection are all set in and concerned with his native Virginia. Robert Buffington, writing in the *Sewanee Review* (Fall), argues for Hoffman's singularity: "His world is the South – specifically Virginia – but he labors in no one's long shadow within that dense fictional tradition. Hoffman's Virginia is not yet a classless society, though the best class is fraying at the edges; and his characters range from farmhands to the hunt-club set." Louis Auchincloss's *Tales of Yesteryear* (Houghton Mifflin) is his fiftieth book, bringing together stories written over forty years and covering the upper-class world of New York City for seven decades. In *Women and Ghosts* (Doubleday) Alison Lurie has nine stories, each of which has some kind of ghost in it. (In "The Pool People" there are blue ghosts at the deep end of a swimming pool.) The settings for these stories include Key West, the Lake District of England, New Delhi, and Cape Cod. R. K. Narayan, the writer whom Graham Greene once described as "the novelist I most admire in the English language," has a mixture of old and new stories, all set in and around the town of Malgudi, in *Grandmother's Tale* (Viking). A sequence of loosely linked, often surreal stories set in New Orleans, *Arise and Walk* (Hyperion) is the latest collection of the author of *Wild at Heart* (1990) – Barry Gifford. Montana's Rick Bass has three long stories – "Mahatma Joe,"

"Field Events," and "Platte River" – in *Platte River* (Houghton Mifflin). Of the essence of his stories, fellow story writer Christopher Tilghman cautioned in the *Baltimore Sun* (1 May), "His argument with the world can feel a little incoherent." The prolific Stephen Dixon brought out two collections, *The Stories of Stephen Dixon* (Holt) and *Long Made Short* (Johns Hopkins University Press), the former containing sixty stories in 642 pages. In "The Victor" the wife of the equally prolific writer Robert Burmeister says this of him: "Don't worry about this guy. Living is writing, writing is living, even the stomach flu along with a death in the family hardly stop him for a day. . . ." The singular quality of Dixon's art is aptly noted by Merrill Leffler in the *Baltimore Sun* (17 April): "He is an improvisational writer and plot is generally not his interest, nor is character development, nor is epiphany nor illumination nor resolution, at least not in any traditional way." Scotland's Alasdair Gray produced *Ten Tall Tales & True* (Harcourt Brace) concerning his home country. And the amazing Patrick O'Brian has twenty-seven stories, written from 1950 to the present, in *The Rendezvous and Other Stories* (Norton). Of this collection, his American editor, Starling Lawrence, has written (in a letter dated 7 March): "The stories in this collection are not about the sea, but they are graced with all the qualities that distinguish O'Brian's novels: humor, lyricism, scrupulous attention to detail, and insight into human passions." Under protection and with time on his hands, Salman Rushdie has produced his first collection of stories, *East, West* (Pantheon), nine stories in a wide variety of forms and presented in three sections, "East," "West," and "East, West." Perhaps the most surprising element in these stories is the unquenchable good humor that shines through many of them. Six of the stories were previously published in other places, two in *The New Yorker*. The veteran Fielding Dawson has a novella and two stories in *The Orange in the Orange* (Black Sparrow), the title novella dealing with a writing teacher's prison classroom. Of the collection Dawson says, "It's this book that reveals me as an activist, radical author rather than literary." The prolific and gifted Frederick Busch, author of nineteen books since 1973, produced *The Children in the Woods: New and Selected Stories* (Ticknor and Fields). Eight of the twenty-three stories here are previously uncollected. Busch was the 1991 winner of the P.E.N./Malamud Award for excellence in the short story.

Two writers prominent in the practice of other forms have composed interesting blendings of fact and fiction. Poet Maxine Kumin's *Women, Animals, and Vegetables* (Norton) is a mixture of personal essays and short stories. Critic Frank Lentricchia's autobiographical *The Edge of Night* (Random House) is described by its publisher as a "soulful confession" and argues that it pushes "expository writing to its limits and sometimes beyond"; but this book may be best approached as narrative, if not "pure" fiction, a sequence of related stories linked by a common literary protagonist who was once described in *The New York Times* as "the Dirty Harry of contemporary literary theory." Other collections which appeared in 1994 were many and various. From among them this reviewer highlights and recommends the following: Jim Harrison's *Julip* (Houghton Mifflin), three novellas; *Field Notes* (Knopf), by Barry Lopez, twelve stories; Ralph Lombreglia's second collection, *Make Me Work* (Farrar Straus Giroux); Janice Daugharty's first collection (set in the Okefenokee Swamp country of south Georgia), *Going Through the Change* (Ontario Review); Abigail Thomas's *Getting Over Tom* (Algonquin); *Stealing Time* (Random House), by Mary Grimm; *Barrel Fever* (Little, Brown), by David Sedaris, sixteen pieces in first person on the subject of vengeance; Tom Perrotta, *Bad Haircut: Stories of the Seventies* (Bridge Works); winner of the annual Flannery O'Connor award, Alyce Miller's *The Nature of Longing* (Georgia); *Jack Kerouac Is Pregnant* (Dalkey Archive), by Aurelie Sheehan; *Epiphany* (Longstreet), by Ferrol Sams, three long stories; Alan Sternberg's *Camaro City* (Harcourt Brace), ten stories mostly set in a decaying Connecticut factory city; Rikki

Ducornet, *The Complete Butcher's Tales* (Dalkey Archive); from the University of Iowa Press come two collections, *Igloo Among Palms,* by Rod Val, and *The Good Doctor,* by Susan Onthank Mates; and from New Zealand, *Dangerous Desires* (Viking), by Peter Wells. Scotland's Duncan McLean created *Bucket of Tongues* (Secker and Warburg). In *The New York Times Book Review* (14 August) Walker Gaffney placed the collection's sociological importance: "Duncan McLean's gritty collection of short stories charts the cruel indifference that chronic unemployment instills in Scotland's working-class youth."

There were reprints such as Douglas Woolf's *Hypocrite Days & Other Tales* (Black Sparrow), consisting of his first novel (1955) and a group of stories. Dalkey Archive brought out his *Wall to Wall* (1962). From Chronicle Books arrived a new series of individual novellas, including Les Galloway's *The Forty Fathom Bank,* about commercial fishermen, and David Knowles's artful *The Secrets of the Camera Obscura.* The whole series is worthwhile if only because of William Kotzwinkle's *Swimmer in the Secret Sea,* a deeply moving account, set in Maine, of the birth and death of a child.

Finally, the adventurous Southern Methodist University Press (see *DLB Yearbook: 1993*) produced an interesting and perhaps influential combination – the anthology *Texas Bound: 19 Texas Stories,* together with *Texas Bound 8 by 8,* an audiocassette with eight of the stories from the anthology.

Dictionary of Literary Biography Yearbook Awards for Distinguished Novels Published in 1994

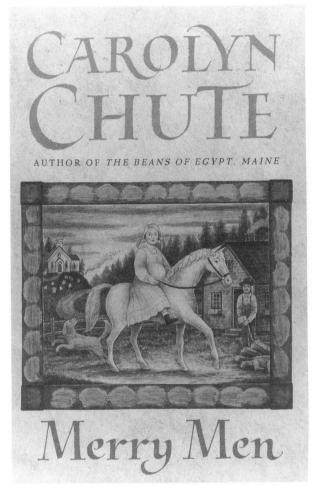

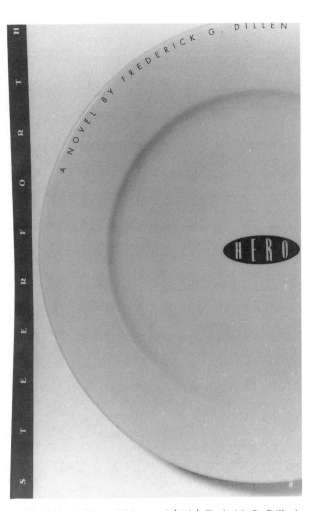

Dust jackets for (left) Carolyn Chute's third novel about the inhabitants of the fictional Egypt, Maine, and (right) Frederick G. Dillen's novel about an aging waiter in a Manhattan steak house

NOVEL

With her two earlier novels — *The Beans of Egypt, Maine* (1985) and *Letourneau's Used Auto Parts* (1988) — Carolyn Chute laid claim to a literary territory that, until her arrival, had been terra incognita. Now with *Merry Men* she goes deeper and wider in a large story inclusive of all classes and kinds. Evoking echoes of Robin Hood, she creates an elaborate and complex plot, brimming with almost too many memorable characters to remember. This is a powerful book, nothing tentative or hesitant about it. It is an exercise and pure example of mythmaking. The myth, large and small, is all about ourselves.

FIRST NOVEL

In a busy field of excellent first novels, any number of them first-rate by all the usual standards, Frederick G. Dillen's *Hero* (Steerforth) stands out for its intensity, for the resolute purity of its concentration and focus, and for its powerful, unflinching (and often wildly funny) vision of the raggedy rainbow coalition that is contemporary urban America. Hard-nosed, harsh, and utterly unsentimental, this small and powerful story is also strangely beautiful and deeply touching. *Hero* is an experience, real enough to become a memory. Dillen is a writer of great gifts, accomplishment, and promise.

Dictionary of Literary Biography Yearbook Award for a Distinguished Volume of Short Stories Published in 1994

Dust jacket for Richard Bausch's collection of a novella and eight stories

With his third collection of stories, *Rare & Endangered Species: A Novella & Stories* (Houghton Mifflin), Richard Bausch arrives at a firm mastery of the forms of short fiction. Two earlier collections — *Spirits* (1987) and *The Fireman's Wife* (1990) — earned him attention and honor, but these eight stories and the title novella demonstrate a higher artistry and a deeper commitment to the strong, subtle domestic themes that have concerned him from the outset of his career. His characters are, as he hopes, "exactly, wholly, and lovingly intended," and his writing is as clear as a clean window.

— George Garrett

The Year in Literary Biography

William Foltz
University of Hawaii

If nothing else, 1994 offered variety. There was Abbé Jean-Paul Migne, a sloppy follower of Zenodotus of Ephesus; another editor and biographer, Samuel Johnson; and, finally, eras and cultures later, my coeval, Erica Jong. Americans were subject and subjected to the biographer; as subjects, Henry David Thoreau, Sarah Orne Jewett, and a superb edition of Elizabeth Bishop's letters; as subjected, Nathaniel Hawthorne and his country's suffering families. Two treatments of Anna Akhmatova and her suffering Soviet Union were balanced by William Shirer's final book, on Leo Tolstoy and his suffering wife. An interpretation of the Russian novelist's exact contemporary, George Eliot, joined those of four other novelists: Akhmatova; north Britain's Robert Louis Stevenson; Alan Paton in South Africa; and Ireland's Sean O'Faolain. Anomalous, though not shared, sensibilities met with sympathy in the lives of Charles Baudelaire and Oscar Wilde. Bertolt Brecht met with the fury of an impatient man.

Nineteenth-century Europe, like Alexandria twenty-three centuries earlier, was an era of compilation: English readers are most familiar with the thirteen volumes of the *Oxford English Dictionary,* edited by Sir James Murray. The 1977 life of Murray, *Caught in the Web of Words,* by Katherine Murray, was as scholarly as his dictionary. Before Murray gathered his slips, Theodor Mommsen had encouraged the Royal Prussian Academy in 1863 to fund publication of some sixteen volumes of Latin inscriptions. More monumental (and more imperfect) was August Boechk's *Corpus of Greek Inscriptions* (1825–1877), another subsidized work. But nothing can match the one-million-plus pages, in 469 volumes, of Greek and Latin that church fathers published, but not exactly edited, by Abbé Migne (1800–1875). Migne himself compared his accomplishment to surviving all twelve labors of Hercules, constructing ten different cathedrals, and digging the tunnel through Mont Cenis.

There is now a witty biography of Migne, *God's Plagiarist: Being an Account of the Fabulous Indus-*

Dust jacket for the study of the nineteenth-century French Catholic priest who published 469 volumes of the Greek and Latin church fathers

try and Irregular Commerce of the Abbé Migne, by R. Howard Bloch (University of Chicago Press). Bloch is probably best known for his earlier book, *Medieval Misogyny and the Invention of Western Romantic Love* (1991), that linked medieval antifeminism to romantic love. This biography links two other seemingly disparate topics: commerce and patristics, or, as he puts it, "Wholesale Drygoods and the Fathers of the Church."

What unites the topics is the industry rather than the scholarship of Abbé Migne, whose name has become a substantive for the most available collection of church fathers. Information about the private or even family life of the abbé is scarce in this biography. Bloch's discoveries of correspondence in Paris reveal a man with a public face whose workday was one of sixteen hours and whose diet was that of a monk. Born in the Auvergne in a regional culture of stubbornness into a family of prosperous merchants, Migne took holy orders. In 1831 he was chastised by the bishop of Orléans for protesting the desecration of a church by secularists on the feast of Corpus Christi. Not only did his bishop chastise him, but he also confiscated Migne's two-hundred-page protest. This event, Bloch argues, crystallized his opposition to the secular world, complaisant bishops, and everything after the Reformation. Migne's revenge was to publish whole libraries. He left for Paris to set up his Ateliers catholique whose workmen, both lay and defrocked, were invariably underpaid. Before he started the patrologies, Migne ran, with his brother, a series of newspapers that stole their news from others. Bloch argues convincingly that Migne's journalistic experience – hiding behind legal fictions, editing with scissors, and exploiting the mechanical stream press – led him to the patrologies: he refused to pay for news of this world or the next. The biographer wisely does not go into the traditions of patristic scholarship in the nineteenth century, but he does document Migne as part of the Catholic revival, a revival not simply in doctrine but also in numbers: as the Catholic Church recovered from 1789, as the number of religious increased, so did the tomes of the patrologies. Bloch's sure focus on France does, however, obscure Migne's colleagues across the channel: the same year Migne decided to start the patrologies (1833) marks the beginning of the Oxford movement, whose members edited, and not simply published, the anti-Nicene fathers. If John Henry Newman's study of the Donatists led him to Rome, Migne hoped his project would even undo the Great Schism of 1054 and reunite "foreigners, Protestants and Greeks."

Bloch is good on the progress of printing technology behind this "industrio-spiritual project"; his equating of Migne with the Balzacian hero of *Illusions perdues* (1837) is cogent; best is his exposure of Migne as a self-publicist as effective as Henry Ford, Buffalo Bill, or Norman Mailer. Publicity replaces truth, and the testimony of Christian witnesses furnishes a prospectus. Further, Migne

and his successors into the twentieth century are geniuses of retail distribution. Today's equivalent is the commemorative Christmas plate.

Bloch gracefully acknowledges the assistance of the University of California for affording him "delicious time" in the Bibliothèque nationale and Archives nationales. Occasionally he seems not to have left, as Latin, French, and English run together in a happy jumble. The bishop of Hippo is both Augustin and Augustine on the same page; Ulfilas, the apostle to the Goths, is translated as Evangiles; and then there is S. Grégoire the Great.

To lift a volume of Migne is a heavy experience: at four pounds, eleven ounces per volume, the complete set weighs in at over twenty-three hundred pounds and stretches over ninety-one feet. To turn to the title page is equally impressive: one almost feels virtuous. It is too bad the publisher did not include a photograph of the many typefaces Migne employed: I count fifteen in volume 120 of the Greek fathers. Ironically, or perhaps appropriately since Migne's aim was availability, the 218 volumes of the Latin fathers can now be lifted in one hand. This assumes that your other hand has fifty thousand dollars: the CD-ROM has arrived. In 1870, five years before the then-blind Migne died, the patrologies would have cost in today's money about forty-five hundred dollars. Chadwyck-Healy, the purveyors of the CD, have succeeded, as Migne did, in plundering the past.

Samuel Johnson also made money preparing compilations, but Richard Holmes in *Dr. Johnson & Mr. Savage* (Hodder and Stoughton), gives us not magisterial middle-aged lexicographer and editor but the young Johnson. The ostensible period of this biography is the three years from 1737 to 1739, the central years of intimacy between Johnson and Richard Savage. It moves beyond that focus to argue that during their night walks and later, when he wrote an apology for his friend, Johnson saw the possibilities of a new form of intimate life writing. Holmes's study frees Johnson from James Boswell even more than James Clifford's *Young Samuel Johnson* (1955). Clarence Tracy's *The Artificial Bastard: A Biography of Richard Savage* (1953) was a monograph. This dual life adds forty years of scholarship and one hundred pages. Savage's name was appropriate: he hounded his reputed mother Lady Macclesfield, killed a man in a barroom brawl, and died in ungrateful poverty.

This is the poet that Johnson defended in his *Life of Savage* (1743). Savage was popular. Some of his male friends, Holmes hints, were attracted to his possible sexual ambiguity, an ambiguity – if I am reading this right — that explains, in part, why Savage took the title role in his *The Tragedy of Sir Thomas Overbury* (1723), written about a courtier whose death in 1613 was caused by a poisoned clyster. Better is Holmes's analysis of Savage's appeal to Johnson, the young man not yet a Tory. Biographically, Johnson's political anger, naive romanticism, stubborn loyalty, and credulity were matched by Savage. Philosophically, the impoverished Johnson saw in Savage's misfortunes a test case for a benevolent God. Consequently, Holmes concludes that Johnson defended his older friend often at the expense of moral truth. The modern biographer shows us a too-credulous Johnson, but at the same time he argues that Johnson was not taken in but was merely too sympathetic.

We see Johnson's rhetoric at work in his account of Savage's trial. Holmes concludes — unlike the judge — that it was not premeditated murder. We have a masterful analysis of what Johnson left out; a demonstration of how Johnson's parliamentary reports helped him re-create a dialogue he never heard and made Savage a double ventriloquist. What did Johnson leave out? The answer to this question is Savage's Jacobite politics, his obscene detestation of Horace Walpole, his erotic verse, and the irascible manipulation of his friends.

Readers will be grateful that Holmes makes available the text of some of Savage's early verse; whether the music to which they were set reflects "a gasping orgasm of sound" is probably a matter of taste. The biographer argues strongly for the merits of Savage's poetry: the unique confessional mode of *The Wanderer* (1726) could startle a postmodernist. This is a large and (to some) a not impressive claim. There is a larger claim: jumping over almost eighty years and to a new sensibility, Holmes promotes both poets to Shelleyan rank as unacknowledged legislators. Was Savage Lady Macclesfield's bastard? This is an irrelevant question: it is enough that he thought he was.

Holmes has thoroughly untangled four conflicting accounts of the famous night ramble; a map would help. But the fifteen cuts from Hogarth are a graceful addition to the text. In this biography of a biography Holmes, without the usual sources of letters, eyewitnesses, or diaries, sees himself as a biographical Charon, traveling between past and present. This is too modest: Holmes has brought both writers back to the light.

Johnson's debate on marriage in *Rasselas, A History of the Prince of Abyssinia* (1762) concludes that if marriage has many pains, celibacy has no pleasures. Two Americans might agree with the apodosis. In *Dearest Beloved: The Hawthornes and the Making*

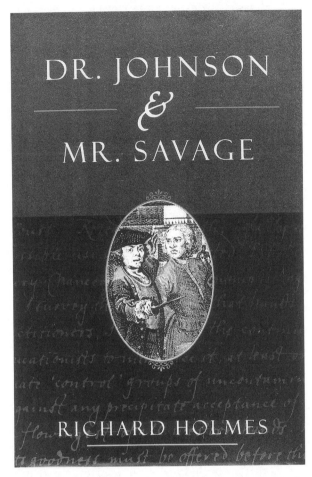

Dust jacket for the book about the relationship between the author of Lives of the Poets *(1779–1781) and the controversial eighteenth-century poet and dramatist*

of the Middle-Class Family (University of California Press) T. Walker Herbert pursues the sins of the father that Frederick Crewes discovered almost thirty years ago. Crewes has since repented but not the generation that succeeded him. Two years ago Edwin Haviland Miller's *Salem is My Dwelling Place* (1992) gave us Nathaniel Hawthorne's deprived childhood. Herbert's dense study, informed by recent feminist scholarship and theory, gives us the depraved American family of the mid–nineteenth century. In fact, Hawthorne's entry under the index exceeds that of his wife, Sophia, and daughter Una by only a dozen lines. This biography is an illuminating and infuriating work of extraordinary interest. Herbert moves laterally between two poles: the Hawthornes' psyches and their society's beliefs. By the biography's end some readers will be unable to disentangle the lives from the works, the paradigm from the exception, and, what is most important, the biographical source from the literary text.

Herbert begins with a modern biographer's in medias res: Hawthorne's midlife crisis which starts as he leaves for Europe in 1858, the successful author of two novels and about to write the third, *The Blithedale Romance* (1852), that shapes the opening chapters. This is followed by a retrospective view of fifty pages focusing on the New England that read Ralph Waldo Emerson and Samuel Taylor Coleridge; the sexual milieu that formed Hawthorne and his wife (seen in *The House of Seven Gables,* 1851); and the preservation of gentility in an entrepreneurial society.

Part 3, the longest part of the biography at some one hundred pages, examines the marital politics of the Hawthornes and *The Scarlet Letter* (1850). The biography ends in Rome as does Hawthorne as a writer (*The Marble Faun,* 1860). In all of these sections Herbert travels nearly effortlessly from letters to novels, from contemporary documents to critical theory. His biography encompasses the American psychosocial concerns as much as it redefines a native writer.

Hawthorne – in order to be self-made, an American ideal – had to deny that his family assisted him after his father's death in Surinam. Sophia helped him in refashioning this myth of self-dependency. To this extent Hawthorne is an American type and their marriage the new marriage of the early nineteenth century. Rather than the censor with a dirty mind (Crewes's view), Herbert wishes to present a Sophia who is playfully warm, intellectually feverous, and fiercely independent. She comes across as sort of a Dorothy Wordsworth whose creative powers were employed for the male. Her type is that of the domestic angel under the control of the husband god, an American pattern. The androgynous beatitude of their marriage is interrupted by the birth of children. After the birth of their last child, Rose, they had no more sex. Later Sophia was to say that her husband's "passions were under his feet." This leads Herbert to witty excursus, one of many interesting ones, on birth control: " 'under his feet' implies a degree of self-denial inconsistent with penetration." No doubt. But the major liturgical text of Hawthorne's time asks assistance to "beat down Satan under our feet."

And speaking of beating, Herbert's close and often convincing explication of *The Scarlet Letter* presents us with the two husbands, the two male natures that fitfully appeared in Hawthorne's marriage. Chillingworth is the Emersonian self-made man carried too far: man as masturbator. Dimmesdale is the guilt-ridden postmasturbator undergoing the torture of a self-abused selfhood. Both,

Herbert argues, reflect the nineteenth-century male sexual dilemma. Hester saves Dimmesdale; Sophia almost saved Nathaniel. This analogy will surprise many readers of Hawthorne, as will the next.

The birth of their daughter Una upset the Hawthornes' marriage. Of all their children, and an epilogue pursues them to their deaths, it is Una who suffered most. Sophia merges her psychic identity with her, but Nathaniel cannot. Hawthorne saw in Una's temper that of an ill-behaved angel, the failure of his marriage. She becomes the Pearl of *The Scarlet Letter,* and Pearl becomes, accordingly, a prophecy of Una's psychic and physical breakdown.

We return to the beginning event of the biography: the successful novelist, his marriage unraveling, arrives in Italy where all will undergo "Roman Fever," the title of the last section of the book. Here, in her fifteenth year, Una's illness disrupts the sacred marital collusion of Nathaniel and Sophia. The famous portrait of Beatrice Cenci and the statue which gives the title to *The Marble Faun* explain the tensions of the extended Hawthorne entourage.

Herbert reads the story of Cenci into the family dynamics of the Hawthorne ménage but fails to wonder if Hawthorne read Percy Bysshe Shelley. Cenci was beheaded in the late sixteenth century for killing the father who raped her; Hawthorne, Herbert would have us believe, "squirmed with loathing" when his young daughter cavorted naked. The "earthly monster" that Hawthorne said possessed his daughter when she opened her shirt is actually her father's own sexual disgust, an incestuous imposition of patriarchal sexuality which is tantamount to rape. Una fought back through her illness, a form of patricide, and in so doing disrupted the marriage further. *The Marble Faun* records Hawthorne's subsequent failure to write. We are meant to conclude that this tale of horrors should be predicated of the nineteenth-century American middle class. Traditional family values have taken on new meaning.

Though Herbert includes fourteen illustrations of scribblings, people, and art to bolster his points (one is of Hawthorne with a "soft phalloid hat"), had he dated the letters he cites, his arguments would be more convincing. How old was Una when she cavorted, and how soon did Hawthorne comment about it? It is easy to dismiss some of Herbert's wilder assertions: an uppity Irish maid is actually a woman "skilled in the stratagems of the oppressed," the Concord River becomes an image of contaminated masculine sexuality. But it is not easy to come from this book without reviewing Hawthorne and his culture.

After the Hawthornes' experience Thoreau and his biographer might disagree with Johnson's opinion of celibacy's few pleasures. Henry Salt, an Englishman and acolyte of Thoreau, wrote much on his subject. Of these the most important work is *The Life of Henry David Thoreau;* the first edition came out in 1890, a second in 1896. The full publication of his subject's *Journals* (fourteen volumes) sixteen years later and the Centenary Edition of Emerson (1904) led Salt to prepare a new edition in 1908.

Unfortunately, this proposed edition found no publisher. Today we should be grateful that the University of Illinois Press has brought it to light with the help of three scholars, George Hendrick, Willene Hendrick, and Fritz Oehlschlaeger. These editors analyze Salt's changes: he included new anecdotes, he praised Thoreau's ability as a lecturer, and he separated him from the usual transcendentalists (Thoreau's transcendentalism was "an innate habit of mind," not a creed acquired from Emerson, Salt insisted). However, this version of *The Life of Henry David Thoreau* is not just a reprint of a book that almost existed. Two of the editors, the Hendricks, have published on Salt; Oehlschlaeger on Thoreau. All three have annotated and corrected Salt's account. Furthermore, the manuscript published here has been augmented by the notes of Raymond Adams at the University of North Carolina at Chapel Hill, to whom Salt sent his original manuscript in 1929. Adams never finished his own projected life of Thoreau, but his notes fill out certain details. It was Salt, via Thoreau, who provided Mahatma Gandhi with the moral reasons for being a vegetarian. The biography, then, does contain some new material.

Salt and his immense list of publications are still of interest; in fact, one-fifth of this volume covers his life. On his death the *Daily Telegraph* (London) saw him as "the most thorough-going faddist in Britain." He was more, as the editors' introduction makes clear. An Eton headmaster, he heard John Ruskin attack Alfred Tennyson's *Maud* (1855); reread Shelley; and met Bernard Shaw, who became the "Sunday husband" of Salt's wife, a practicing lesbian. Salt joined an organization that seems to have been a depoliticized Fabian Society. This, the Fellowship of the New Life (the future prime minister Ramsay MacDonald was a member), introduced him to Thoreau. He became a vegetarian, saw his fellow masters as cannibals, and resigned from Eton. It is tempting to dismiss Salt as the author of *The Secrets of the Reptile House: Snake Feeding at the Zoological Gardens* (1909), but his works on Shelley, Lucretius, and Virgil probably have merits; his biography of the poet James Thomson ("B. V.,"

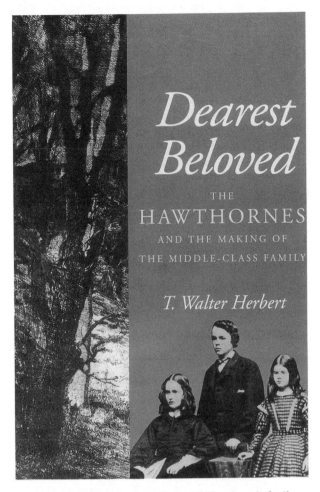

Dust jacket for the study of Nathaniel Hawthorne's family and marriage

1843–1882) remains valuable, an achievement not noted in this volume. If Thoreau is still read in Britain it is because of Salt. The editors of this book refrain from drawing some of the obvious analogies between Salt and Thoreau: classics, sexual alignment, political independence, eccentricity, and choice of dwelling. This is too bad.

But perhaps the major reason for reading this life is the grace with which it is written. Consciously literary with an Olympian disregard of scholarly details (we take his sources on trust), Salt's style is clearly indebted to the limp tricolons of Newman and occasionally to the mechanical balance and antitheses of Thomas Basington Macaulay. Chapters on "Doctrines" and "Writings" are kept to the end, and Thoreau's psyche has been kept firmly in its place. But there is no doubt that Salt is his subject's follower. The events of Salt's biography are what we might expect: Concord and then Walden, a Walden already a "mere holiday resort" in 1909.

This is a late-Victorian life: Thoreau dies smelling a bunch of hyacinths. We hear his last audible words, "moose" and "Indian," and read Salt's comments on their meaning: childhood, nature, and his bequest of antiquities to a learned society in Boston. A tradition that began with philosophical speculation about Johann Wolfgang von Goethe's "Light! More Light!" now ends with smarmy debates over "rosebud" in *Citizen Kane*. Salt's 1908 bibliography and three portraits of Thoreau end this concise and well-printed biography.

William Shirer, a best-selling journalist and historian, almost finished his *Love and Hatred: The Troubled Marriage of Leo and Sonya Tolstoy* (Simon and Schuster) before his death at age eighty-nine. In this biography he aimed to explain the strange, irrational tragedy of Tolstoy's dying in a village stationmaster's cottage, while his wife of forty-eight years, by whom he had thirteen children, waited outside in the cold. Some of her children had forbidden her access until just before his death on 28 October 1910 (old style). The most poignant of the twenty-six photographs included shows her, on tiptoe, peering in the window. The recent publication of her later diaries led Shirer to his task in which his Russian-speaking wife assisted him.

Shirer begins with a fluid one-hundred-page narrative of the first twelve years of the marriage. We have a quick look at two potential brides, one pregnant peasant and Tolstoy's final choice of Sonya. She accepts, and in two weeks they marry. But first Tolstoy shows her his diaries: the buxom wench is in there, and this begins the jealousy that intermittently destroys their marriage. Sonya's anger at having her husband's bastard underfoot is understandable. But Sonya's own mother was illegitimate, and her father had an affair with Ivan Sergeyevich Turgenev's mother. What effect this had on Sonya — and it must have had some — is one of many questions this biography never poses. Shirer, like other equally convincing biographers, turns to *Anna Karenina* (1875) and, later, *The Kreuzer Sonata* (1890) to portray the Tolstoys' marital tension: tears alternate with forgiveness for nearly a half century.

Then the fifty-year-old novelist suffers the "Great Midlife Crisis," perhaps one of the silliest names for a chapter that should explain Tolstoy's change. In reality Tolstoy's crisis was not the usual: he acquired neither a convertible and/or mistress (Vance Packard's paradigm) nor found religion. Instead he founded his own religion. This ten-page chapter should explain the failure of Tolstoy as father and husband. It does not. We get a summary of

his subject's turgid *Confession* (1879). The dying Turgenev implored Tolstoy to return to literature. He did not. Instead he listened to Vladimir Chertkov for the rest of his life. Chertkov, twenty-five years younger than the master, became Tolstoy's apostle and the enemy of his wife. Exiled for assisting Tolstoy's attempt to settle other religious fanatics in Canada, he was recalled to Russia and fought with Sonya over copyright and the possession of Tolstoy's and Sonya's diaries during the last two years of the master's life.

Sonya's midlife crisis in her fifties resulted from the death of her youngest child in February 1895 and led to a transfer of affection, but not sexual activity, to the still-obscure composer Sergei Taneyev half a year later. Even though Sonya kept no diary for twenty-eight months after her child's death, Shirer presents a convincing picture of a woman who became increasingly maddened by an impossibly inconsistent husband. The two hundred pages of this section end with two failures: her appeal to the czar over censorship and her attempt to run away.

Her husband runs away in October's snows. The final section of this biography examines the last month, week, and day of the marriage, and it reads like a Fyodor Dostoyevsky novel: cosmic unhappiness told with masterful suspense. Tolstoy wanted to give away his interest in his copyrights, but Sonya objected to the potential impoverishment of her family and accused Chertkov of being her husband's lover. The master planned his escape. He ran off with some of his children, and the world found out. Sonya rented a train, traveling with the rest of the children, and found him. The press arrived, the provincial governor arrived, and the militia arrived; the metropolitan of Saint Petersburg urged repentance, and the police chief issued live ammunition. Shirer discovered what must be the world's first mega–media event. It makes O. J. Simpson look like *TV Guide* gossip. What we do not see is the "rubbishy old man" of which Anna Akhmatova writes.

Shirer, as always, writes quickly and gracefully integrates his sources into the narrative. But an editor should have caught the occasional clichés (daughters "flew the coop"), explained what might be obscure (Dostoyevsky's speech at the Pushkin unveiling "was to electrify Russia"). The portentous needs excising: Anna Karenina asks "Who are we? Where did we come from? Where are we going? What is the meaning, if any, of life — and death?"

Tolstoy's contemporary George Eliot led an easier life. Rosemarie Bodenheimer, the author of an earlier study in narration, *The Politics of Story in Victorian Social Fiction* (1988), takes an allied approach to Eliot in *The Real Life of Mary Ann Evans: George Eliot, Her Letters and Fiction* (Cornell University Press): here narration extends to what most readers would see as letters. But following the lead of recent scholars, the letter has become a coded genre, particularly for women. In fact, nearly fifty pages of this three-hundred-page book consist of a review of epistolary criticism from the mid–eighteenth century to the present. Eliot's letters, novels, and stories can be read as fiction, that is, another presentation of the evolving self, meditations on her experience.

This argument moves along turgidly in sentences over thirty-five words long and with critical panache: dialogical, characterological, and a suppressed Gallic difference. What this means, I think, is that Henry James's sister was right: Eliot's letters – and Bodenheimer fearlessly cites the passage – were a "monument of ponderous dreariness." This is okay: Eliot's letters "do not make the cut" if readers wish to revel in personality. If they are dull, they were meant to be: it was bad manners for a lady to write in a confessional mode. Bodenheimer's evidence for this comes from the experience of the Brontë family and contemporary etiquette books: the books convince more than do her remarks about the Brontës. Jane Carlyle's letters are fun to read. Perhaps Eliot's are, to paraphrase Macaulay, dull in a new way.

Once we get through theory, this work improves immeasurably and will illumine many aspects of Eliot's life and work. Bodenheimer zeroes in on major events or "intractable issues in Eliot's mental and emotional life." She comments on these issues as she moves from the letters to published works. Further, since some of these issues extend over "biographical time," they can be understood by works written later than the events that took place in a defined "biographical time." This sounds like The Opinions of George Eliot. An internalized Victorian sage has returned.

Bodenheimer persuasively locates the origins of Eliot's distinctive narrative tone in those letters that differ, even in handwriting, from her early ones. This distinctive tone is heard clearly in *Adam Bede* (1859), whose readers, oppositional or actual, Eliot is forced to construct: Eliot's earlier correspondents will become the novel's readers.

Of major interest to readers will be the material that focuses on three major events: The holy war (1841–1843), when Eliot frees herself from family ties and traditional Christian belief; her elope-

ment with the married George Henry Lewes some eleven years later; and, finally, her marriage to John Cross in 1880, a man twenty years her junior. All these events share a repeated action: Eliot, after intense debate, chooses an action incomprehensible to the world. She then writes her friends. Ditto her fiction: the letter writer has become the narrator explaining and justifying a character's conduct. The biographer thoroughly explicates the tone of the letters in which Eliot explains her elopement with Lewes. This event, a final break from her family, is paralleled by events, moral problems, and, at times, even the narrator's tone in *The Mill on the Floss* (1860). Bodenheimer suggests three readings of the novel. The most convincing is the autobiographical: both Maggie and Eliot were torn between loyalty to family and self-development. Less convincing is her explanation of Eliot's marriage with Cross as a return to the traditional respectability that Maggie lost. Maggie drowned, but Eliot married.

The dangers of gossip, which is defined rather humorlessly as "the externalization of a repressed truth," figure heavily in Eliot's later novel, *Middlemarch* (1871). The biographical crux here is not an illicit relationship with a still-married man but "The Outing of George Eliot" (to quote the chapter's title). London gossiped about the identity of George Eliot and Middlemarch about Bulstrode. Both the novelist and the banker share a "cross-dressing situation." The events in this chapter could have comic possibilities – one man claimed he was George Eliot – but Eliot's quandary is too serious.

Bodenheimer presents an important aspect of Eliot's life, her relationships with Lewes's officially legitimate children. Three of the surviving were his; four more had Leigh Hunt's son Thornton as their father. Rosemary Ashton's thorough *G. H. Lewes: A Life* (1992) presents more strictly biographical information on what must have been trying times. Eliot came to know these stepsons through their letters. Given what happened to many of Eliot's letters (they were lost, destroyed, or censored), Bodenheimer's reading of *Silas Marner* (1861) as a fairy tale of substitute parenthood is less authoritative than the sure links she had drawn between the letters and other novels. Since the two restless young men, Vincy and Ladislaw, in *Middlemarch* (1872) both fall under patriarchal domination, Bodenheimer's argument that their original was Thornton, Lewes's feckless and subsidized son, rings true.

This is an often somber but valuable work about a woman who, among other things, looks after her husband's children by a first marriage. Bodenheimer's use of the letters helps our under-

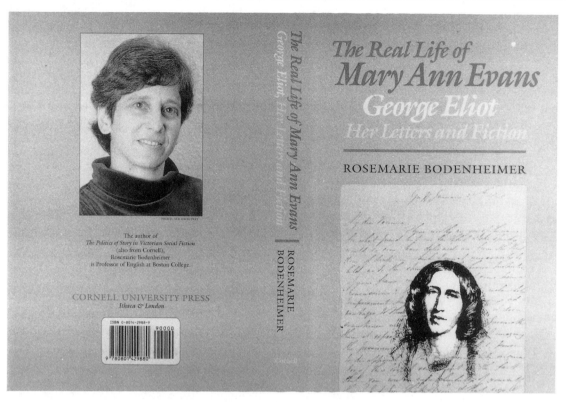

Dust jacket for the study of George Eliot's life and letters

standing of a novelist who is coming to be regarded as the equal of William Makepeace Thackeray. It would be more valuable with a bibliography and a list, with page numbers, of the letters she cited.

The next biography moves more convincingly from writings, private or published, to her subject's life. Joanna Richardson examines the author of the often-anthologized saying "The dead, the poor dead, have great sorrows" and investigates his sorrows in her superb, comprehensive, and gracefully written *Baudelaire* (St. Martin's Press). Richardson makes available many of the recent productions of the immense French Charles Baudelaire industry. Genealogies, court transcripts, and publishers' contracts supplement but do not bury her subject. As biographers have come to realize, Baudelaire, like all dandies, lived a fiction. He acted the life he wrote. What Richardson does, and does splendidly, is reveal the man behind his mask. Her new Baudelaire is less bizarre but more convincing. Drugs are more often recreational than addictive; concupiscence is more contemplated than enjoyed. Throughout her book, poems and correspondence almost imperceptibly merge with her narrative. Letters are translated, but since the correspondence of sound and word would be destroyed, she wisely refuses to translate poems.

Richardson avoids the temptation of joining her subject's primary subject: his interior. Rather than constant psychoanalysis — surely a temptation — she gracefully allows other critics to have their brief say. The problems of the poet who created a new emotion (Victor Hugo's succinct phrase) go back to his mother, and this is Richardson's major contribution to the understanding of the poet. To avoid the devil, the granddaughter of Mme Aupick (the poet's mother's name from her second marriage) burnt masses of her grandmother's correspondence to Baudelaire, yet Richardson's argument remains convincing.

Since Baudelaire was formed by his early years, the biographer examines them closely in two of the book's six parts. His father, the possessor of an eighteenth-century sensibility in art, manners, and sensuality (traits his son Charles was to inherit), died at the age of sixty-eight, when Charles was six years old. Free from the chores of domesticity and neglecting even to erect a funeral monument, in thirteen months Baudelaire's mother was impregnated by Jacques Aupick, and after half a year she married him (the child was stillborn). The rapidity of this change created an alliance with his mother that was profound, complex, and domineering on both sides. Baudelaire, neither a virgin nor a voluptuary, recorded in his verse what his actions anticipated: sexual betrayal. If, as André Gide says, European poetry would never be the same after Baudelaire, the poet was not the same after his mother's remarriage.

His letters to her, even when he was age forty ("You were both an idol and a friend"), reveal a pattern of emotional blackmail. So do his mother's actions. The retrospective vision of Baudelaire's poetry, Richardson concludes, is an eternal attempt, always doomed, to recapture a vanished past, the curse of unfulfilled desire. Her comments about her son, gathered from the letters she wrote others, reveal a "pathetic inability" to understand him. Financial indifference and maternal neglect led to bouts of emotional suffocation joined with bank drafts. He threatened suicide, she ignored him; he fell ill, she invaded with a priest.

Richardson's book is a study in mother/son relationships. If her first husband, Joseph-Françoise Baudelaire, was a vanishing aristocrat, her second, Jacques Aupick, was the century's paradigm of a bureaucratic winner: whether his ruler was Napoleon, Louis XVIII, Louis-Philippe, or Napoleon III, he hung on. And General Aupick, later ambassador to Turkey and Spain, was perhaps the worst stepfather a future poet could have. If the mood of Baudelaire's poetry is conditional, General Aupick's verbs were imperative.

In 1841, outraged that his stepson flunked out of school, he and his mother sent their extravagant and possibly syphilitic son to Calcutta. He made it as far as Réunion; the captain sent him back uncured of his "exclusive taste for literature." A maritime Baudelaire returned with a knowledge of Africa's smells, an appreciation for that continent's women, and an early draft of "L'Albatros."

Back in Paris, again in debt, a family council appointed a conservator. Baudelaire, embittered by this lack of trust, began a career as an art critic and formed friendships with Théophile Gautier and Gérard de Nerval; later he met Gustave Flaubert and praised Richard Wagner. Richardson, in addition to a portrait of a tormented soul, gives us the social and aesthetic milieu, but it is Baudelaire in time and not Baudelaire and his times. The balance is just. Baudelaire also formed the first of three serious liaisons. The first, which lasted on and off for nineteen years, was with his Creole *Vénus noire,* Jeanne Duval, earlier the mistress of his friend, the famous photographer Nadar (Felix Tournachon). Of the twenty-two photographs in this volume, seven are by Nadar. Duval, a drug-addicted, unfaithful, and grasping Creole became, Richardson

argues, the catalyst for poetic creation in *Les Fleurs du Mal* (1857). She was also sinful pleasure and its punishment at the same time. Of the 125 chapters in Richardson's biography, the twelve pages on *Les Fleurs du Mal,* in fact all of part 3, serve as a finely perceptive essay of literary analysis, reception criticism, and confident judgment.

His next mistress, who also inspired many poems in *Les Fleurs du Mal,* was La Président (Apollonie Sabatier). Despite missing, incomplete, and undatable letters, Richardson's part 4 presents a most sympathetic *Vénus blanche,* the poet's unattainable ideal woman. Baudelaire had idealized her for the five preceding years. Then "she did what to her was most natural, and offered herself to him." Richardson then rehearses the arguments of earlier biographical critics to explain why this affair did not work out (she was too old, his affections could now revert to his mother, sex was repugnant). This biographer's explanation is linked to her thesis. However devoted La Président was, however much her love could have redeemed him, Baudelaire, betrayed by his mother, was beyond salvation. Richardson, with dignity and pity, follows this madonna and muse to her death in 1890.

If the poet's love for Duval was carnal, for La Président spiritual, his love for the third was equivocal. This was Marie Daubrun, a golden-haired actress and the inspiration for "L'Invitation au voyage." Concluding that she had betrayed him twice, he gave up on her and gave up any future attempt to find, or even possess, an ideal.

Richardson, whose subject demands psychological explanation, does not neglect Baudelaire's literary relationships. Often these took the form of fraud, outright lies to his publishers, or grandiose schemes to duplicate in Brussels the success of Charles Dickens in the United States. However poorly the poet comes out, it is the famous critic Charles-Augustin Sainte-Beuve who is worse. Duval betrayed Baudelaire's bed, Sainte-Beuve his reputation. It was his feline jealousy that prevented him from public praise of *Les Fleurs du Mal* and from its public defense. In 1949 six of the poems were finally restored to the collection. Sainte-Beuve encouraged Baudelaire to apply to the Académie Français and then ridiculed him for doing so. That Baudelaire thought he had a chance is remarkable. After a stroke felled Baudelaire, Sainte-Beuve promised Mme Aupick he would visit. He sent his secretary.

As Baudelaire dies we see his death through the recollection of thirteen people: these recollections show him aphasic, addicted, and hounded by the woman who understood him least, his mother. She buried him next to General Aupick.

Only rarely does Richardson get too close to her subject. Many will have more sympathy with General Aupick's uncomprehending ire at what his training would call a wastrel. The same is true of the conservator, Narcisse-Désiré Ancelle, appointed in 1844 to run the wastrel's finances: fiduciaries are supposed to say no, especially to those who demand money almost every fourth page in this biography. Richardson's biography is the culmination of over twenty earlier biographical studies from Colette to Tennyson: the French edition of her 1985 *Judith Gautier* won a Prix Goncourt in 1989; the dedicatee of *Les Fleurs du Mal,* Théophile Gautier, was treated in 1958. We look forward to her *Flaubert.*

Catherine Peters, whose *Thackeray's Universe* (1987) gave us 300 solid pages, has written a longer (440 pages) and more than competent life of a novelist whose reputation is enjoying a comeback in her *The King of Inventors: A Life of Wilkie Collins* (Princeton University Press). She brings to her work not only the experience of the earlier biography but also her work as the editor of three novels by Collins. She has the texts down cold. The temptation to bleed Thackeray's life into Collins's is firmly avoided, as is an excessive amount of purely literary criticism.

Wilkie Collins's private life reads like one of his novels; Peters explains the complications of his two "morganatic marriages" (Collins's words) with a good deal of sympathy. More details, particularly about the unfortunate financial arrangements for his survivors, can be found in William Clark's often too breathless *The Secret Life of Wilkie Collins* (1988). Peters reaches her conclusions independently of Clark, and, since her work's scope is larger, she keeps them in perspective.

The author makes extensive use of many unpublished letters and begins her life with a newly identified manuscript of Collins's mother that almost establishes a family tradition of statistically anomalous marriages. In much of Collins's family the unconventional was often the convention: the exception was his father, William. Collins comes out a throwback as much as a radical; in his circle were the clandestinely, bigamously, irregularly, and disastrously married. Collins, opposed to marriage as an institution, seems to be between Eliot's openness and Dickens's reticence. There is much in this splendid biography on the Collins family: it spreads over three columns of blinding five-point type in the extensive index and covers nearly 275 separate topics.

Peters moves easily between the life, with Collins's travels in Europe and the United States, and the works, from the early journalism and his first novel, *Antonia: or the Fall of Rome* (1850), written when he was twenty-three to the uncompleted *Blind Love* (1890); the former is perhaps the only Gothic novel to contain actual Goths, and the latter contains those doubled characters that are featured in all his novels. Peters has read everything – even his plays. Her thorough bibliography is not a start but a conclusion.

The major event in Collins' life was his meeting with Dickens (sixty topics in the index). Despite the twenty years' difference in age that separated them, from 1852 to 1870 Dickens found in Collins not simply a bohemian companion with whom he could share his nocturnal rambles and marital discord, nor only an admiring disciple. Collins became a collaborator in the elder's journalism and literary productions. Often it seems this biography was organized around the life of Dickens. Their joint play, *The Frozen Deep* (1856), to which Peters devotes an entire chapter, cemented their friendship, heightened Dickens's infatuation with and love for the eighteen-year-old actress Ellen Ternan, and encouraged Dickens to begin his course of public readings in England and abroad. Another of their joint productions was emotional: Peters suggests that it was Dickens's courage to separate from his wife in 1858 that allowed Collins to live openly with his first morganatic wife, Caroline Graves.

Before presenting this liaison, Peters adds to our knowledge of another odd marriage: that of Collins's brother Charles with Dickens's favorite child, Kate. Charles, according to a newly analyzed letter from John Everett Millais, began his irregularity as early as 1856 (two years before Collins began living with his first wife). Like George Gissing's mistress, Charles's was disreputable; unlike Gissing, Charles broke with her, married Catherine, and was so overcome with religious scruples that he was impotent. Information such as this, and Peters devotes a brief appendix to it, fleshes out our understanding not only of Collins but also helps to explain Catherine's lovers and Dickens's grief over the marriage, a grief that puzzled Peter Ackroyd in *Dickens* (1990).

To re-create Collins's liaison with Graves, a widow with one daughter, is difficult since no letters survive from him to Graves. Nevertheless, Peters' conclusions are based on thorough research: birth, marriage, and death certificates; post office and trade directories; letters in various libraries and private hands; and judicious and clearly labeled speculation from his novels and articles. If anything, his relationship with Graves is handled almost too sympathetically. After the death of Collins's mother in 1868, Graves apparently expected Collins to do the right thing. He was at a marriage: he witnessed a twenty-seven-year-old liquor salesman marry his thirty-eight-year-old Caroline. Amazingly, Graves's daughter chose to stay with Collins as his devoted housekeeper and amanuensis; more amazingly, by 1868 the forty-one-year-old Collins moved into the third year of his liaison with the pregnant nineteen-year-old Martha Rudd; most amazingly, Graves returned to Collins's fold in two years. The other fold, that with Martha, was a tube stop away.

"Wilkie's affairs," as Dickens said, "defy all prediction." Peters does not try to justify morally what seems to be a plot from her subject's novels. She explains it: Wilkie was a conventional Victorian with two households. This would be more convincing could she locate other gentlemen with two morganatic marriages going on simultaneously. Though Collins followed the Prayer Book's advice (his wills left money to both families), the Rudd family rarely figures in his surviving correspondence, though Graves is mentioned often by name.

Marital and even sexual confusion figure in Collins's novels also. The biographer's analyses, especially in the chapters on *No Name* (1862) and *Armadale* (1866), are good, particularly those on the later novel. Peters assumes the reader's recollection of the plot – as I recall five people have the same name; the untangling of the plot becomes an epistemological enquiry into the unconsciousness. These forays into the psychological are often interesting, as is the biographer's ability to tie the events in the novels to the scandals, legal problems, and social issues of their respective decades.

Peters's fine work will encourage us to read the novels of Collins's last decades. Her interpretations and useful summaries of unfamiliar novels – *Man and Wife* (1870), iniquitous English and Scottish marriage laws; *The New Magdalen* (1873), reformed prostitute; *The Law and the Lady* (1875), the Scottish "not proven" verdict; and *The Legacy of Cain,* genetics – suggest that late Collins may become a subindustry: alas, the last three novels are no longer in print nor are they separate articles in John Sutherland's guide to Victorian fiction. The decline in Collins's ability to devise the impossibly clever plot, Peters argues, was not solely due to opium: by the time of *The Moonstone* (1868) he was already addicted. Further, the manuscripts she examined at the University of Texas included elabo-

Dust jacket for the biography of the nineteenth-century British novelist who was a friend and colleague of Charles Dickens

rate plans for his later novels. Her explanation for Collins's falling sales is Algernon Charles Swinburne's explanation elaborated: many are novels with a mission or, as she says, novels that lack the "mythic, fairy-tale quality" that moved beyond mere mystery and melodrama.

The last twenty years of Collins's life show us a man overworked and overdrugged, whose eyesight and digestion were both failing. This decline can be seen clearly in some of the twenty-six clear illustrations. His readings in the United States brought in hardly a tenth of Dickens's haul. Others succeeded in the genre he established and polished, the murder mystery and sensation novel. Peters's judicious biography has already become the standard life.

Paula Blanchard's *Sarah Orne Jewett: Her World and Her Work* (Addison Wesley) moves her subject back and forth from Berwick, Maine, to Boston and thrice to Europe in a series of clearly written chapters. Can a life of Jewett be of compelling interest?

Perhaps, if we peered at the possible erotics of her existence, but this Blanchard eschews. There is much on setting and genealogy. With all her relatives and cognates, the young Jewett hardly needed anyone out of her immediate genetic group for friendship. The result is, Blanchard argues, the often childlike point of view in her fiction. The Maine and Berwick the biographer renders differ from the rest of New England: socially, for there were many unmarried women and widows; and morally, in that down easterners accept suffering as do Jewett's characters.

For Blanchard, Jewett is still the regional writer whose lean and understated problems of suffering and endurance are linked to a specific place. The biographer's chapter 18 rehearses the rediscovery of Jewett but steps back from the complexities of modern feminist criticism. Jewett's relationships with other women are based on friendship rather than on mystical bonds of compassion and womanly wisdom which, in her fiction, are passed through an oral culture. Compassion for others rather than passion for another marks her life and works.

Chief among her friends was Annie Fields, the subject of much speculation. One of the sixteen illustrations is her undated portrait by John Singer Sargent. Fifteen years older than Jewett, they became friends after the death of Fields's husband in 1881. Fields was already a famous literary hostess to American and English writers, a published poet — but never very good in Blanchard's judgment — and a social reformer. She moved Jewett's mind and body from Berwick to Boston for half the year. Fields was not her first close friend, but she did open Jewett to a world more cosmopolitan than Maine. Yet, as Blanchard shows, Jewett already had literary and intellectual connections (some by marriage) with Cambridge and Boston: Ralph Waldo Emerson, Charles Eliot Norton, Henry Wadsworth Longfellow, Julia Ward Howe, Harriet Beecher Stowe, John Greenleaf Whittier, and a dense list of literati and academics now forgotten except by specialists. Blanchard, unlike some scholars, rejects a possible lesbian relationship. She sees Fields and Jewett as partners without power plays, her definition of a Boston marriage. Blanchard, however, should have emphasized that Fields, the survivor of this partnership, controlled their surviving letters.

Before her meeting with Fields, Jewett's mentor was Theophilus Parsons, a fuzzy Swedenborgian, who encouraged her to write. Her letters to him ceased after she and Fields began to live together. William Dean Howells succeeded Parsons

as her mentor as he succeeded Fields's husband as the editor of the *Atlantic Monthly*.

Perhaps a good fifth of this biography is literary commentary on plot summary and character analysis of Jewett's major decade, 1879–1888. Of the novels, *Deephaven* (1877) and *The Country of the Pointed Firs* (1896) receive the most attention; but Blanchard also examines briefly and cogently some seventy-six short stories, especially, as we might expect, "A White Heron." Blanchard's assessments are honest. The children's stories are impossible nowadays; *Deephaven* has structural faults and can be compared to Elizabeth Gaskell's *Cranford* (1851) (but is this any literary recommendation?). *The Story of the Normans* is a mishmash of racism. Blanchard's earlier *Margaret Fuller: from Transcendentalism to Revolution* (1978) is the source of the solid treatment of Fuller's influence on the polemics of *A* [female] *Country Doctor* (1884). The biographer has located the originals and, more important, the places of Jewett's fiction. In almost all her fiction "moral commentary intrudes" too often. It should not surprise us then that Jewett's models included Eliot as well as Tobias Smollett and Ouida.

The Country of the Pointed Firs gets its own chapter. Mrs. Todd is the sibylline healer — perhaps even Bona Dea. Readers will not find Enna's grieving Demeter searching for Persephone. Notes direct us to feminist critics, the text to place names.

Jewett traveled to Europe three times with Fields. Whether these detailed trips had any intellectual effect on Jewett is "difficult to say," but they did bind her to Fields. We get masses of facts: Berwick's way of life, preservation societies, and trees and gardens; crowds of writers, readings, and arts and crafts in Boston. But a social calendar is not a life. Even the teas of middle-aged women (Henry James, Jewett, and Fields), once at Rye, later on Charles Street, are mainly skillful vignettes. Much better is Blanchard's treatment of the last year of Jewett's life: the western Willa Cather sought and received eastern advice: to write, to find her own voice as a woman, and to live with her friend.

Blanchard follows F. O. Matthiessen's often-criticized 1929 study in emphasizing the importance of Jewett's physician father. Ironically, what Matthiessen praised Jewett for, a regional voice, has come back into favor. All in all, this is an admirably sane biography written clearly for general readers and not just for English majors and their teachers.

If Jewett's geography and perhaps even vision were limited, the same is not true of the next novelist. Frank McLynn, who has four biographical studies centered on Africa and five on Scotland, has moved further and wound up in Samoa with *Robert Louis Stevenson: A Life* (Random House). McLynn considers Stevenson Scotland's best writer and the writer who married the worst woman, the American divorcée Fanny Vandegift Osbourne. The general movements of Stevenson are clear: university study at Edinburgh, a trip to France where he met the married Fanny, and back to Britain before he pursued her in San Francisco. He returned with a bride ten years his senior, wound up in Bournemouth, traveled again to the United States, sailed from San Francisco through the South and North Pacific, and settled and died on a Samoan hillside barely middle-aged. This much is clear, and McLynn follows his subject around clearly: throughout this biography the reader knows where Stevenson was, what he was writing, and how he was published. What all biographers have been trying to do since the first authorized biography of Graham Balfour in 1901 is to make the geographical psychological. McLynn also presents a map of the mind but one that may confuse readers. In all, it is a useful, solid life that cuts through the fog of hagiography and vituperation and makes skillful use of letters, novels, poetry, and, at times, dreams.

A Scottish nativity must be fraught with dangers: like Sir Walter Scott he was an invalid, like George Gordon, Lord Byron he had a terrifyingly religious nurse, and like James Boswell he had a dogmatic father. But Stevenson's father was also dour, moody, and designed lighthouses. In 1873 his cousin Bob joined him in the great row: the father's Jerusalem quarreled with his son's Athens. His mother, "sweet natured, devout," is the most shadowy family member in this biography but should not be: to move from Scotland to Samoa in her late sixties and then nurse a dying son demands fuller comment. McLynn locates the source of her son's illnesses in her DNA pool: Samoan high chiefs agreed it was not tuberculosis; perhaps, the biographer argues, it was fibronous bronchitis (his first hemorrhage of the lungs was in 1880) or some unspecified "thyroid abnormality." A youthful bout with syphilis appears briefly. In any event a stroke killed him.

McLynn leaves the impression that Fanny should have died. Instead Fanny survived and flourished after Stevenson's death: her earlier attacks of hypochondria, which she threw either to compete with her husband or to cause him to move, vanished. The biographer will not let loose of Fanny and her family; he follows them to their graves. Fanny died at age seventy-four in 1914.

That same year Belle, her daughter by her first marriage, then age fifty-six, married her mother's lover, a man in his midthirties.

Immediately apparent are the age discrepancies in these marriages. McLynn resurrects and elaborates upon the Victorian whore-madonna complex to explain Stevenson's marriage. Some explanations seem odd: if Stevenson's interest in women was a way of warding off depression, replacing Eros with Thanatos, why not younger women?

McLynn does dispel the buzz of inference and innuendo about Stevenson's college years. Stevenson was unpopular, disruptive, and seen as an English poseur. His inattendance "allowed him to become an autodidact." McLynn takes issue with J. C. Furnas's biography of the 1950s and would with Ian Bell's more recent *Dreams of Exile* (1993). The evidence may be "tantalizingly exiguous," but Stevenson whored: "Claire" was not the title of a lost literary work, an elaborate joke, or another name for the first Fanny, Mrs. Fanny Sitwell (later the wife of Sidney Colvin, the Slade Professor of Arts and the editor of bowdlerized letters). Sitwell, twelve years his senior, became the first older woman. McLynn sees 1873–1874 as marking the "great love of his life" but can only argue from Stevenson's letters since he destroyed Sitwell's at her request. This unconsummated love led to another, this time in France with a Georgian princess. He pitched woo and hinted as much to Sitwell – perhaps to pique her. The princess responded, but with "iron [and guilt] in his soul" Stevenson turned her not only down but into a maternal figure.

This seems reasonable. Then Stevenson, again the typical Victorian with an either/or view of women, turned Sitwell into the madonna, a sacred mother figure. Sitwell replaced the mother who sided with his father during the great row of 1873. Oedipal confusion reigned. McLynn wisely admits that this psychoanalytic approach will infuriate some, especially Jenni Calder (one assumes he means her 1980 *R.L.S.: A Life Study*). But McLynn persists. To buttress the Oedipal approach, the biographer notes that Stevenson first got the attention of the princess, Sitwell, and Osbourne by playing with their children! Further: few men marry women ten years their senior.

If we were to extend McLynn's argument, would not the second Fanny (Osbourne) be both whore (divorcée) and madonna (a mother of two living children)? Is not "Fanny" more than a proper name in Stevenson's time? Nineteenth-century Theban misbehavior cannot account for all the following confusion: Sitwell was first attracted to cousin

Dust jacket for the biography of the nineteenth-century British novelist long characterized as merely a writer for children

Bob; cousin Bob turned her infatuation toward cousin Louis for Bob was smitten by her daughter Belle; but daughter Belle may have asked cousin Louis to marry her instead of her mother. McLynn says the later, probable event could account for the ensuing tension between Belle and Stevenson. But three hundred pages later Belle replaces Fanny as Stevenson's literary confidante. In any event, Stevenson's compassionate father was glad his son married someone, even if she was middle-aged.

McLynn does not like Fanny Osbourne. We have a "pioneering gun-toter" and a "bourgeois spendthrift"; but McLynn says Stevenson also was a spendthrift (and the bills in Samoa prove it). She also burnt an earlier draft of *The Strange Case of Dr. Jekyll and Mr. Hyde* (1886), prevented Stevenson from writing a social history of the Pacific, and, worse, her interest in him was primarily financial. (Then why the affair – the source is Henry James – with a man forty years younger after Stevenson's

death?) McLynn does not like her children, and he is right about them: Lloyd, he concludes, was Judas to his Christlike stepfather. He is also correct that Osbourne's plagiarism destroyed Stevenson's long-standing friendship with W. E. Henley, leading that poet to do a hatchet job on Stevenson in a 1910 book review.

In Samoa some might have some sympathy for Osbourne fighting the tropical jungle, misinterpreting local customs, and trying to keep her caps starched in eighty-seven degrees and 90 percent humidity. She administered three hundred acres of tropical land; she corresponded with Kew Gardens; she protected and spoiled her leechlike children. Then in 1891 "psychic overload" led to a breakdown in her. Surely her age, fifty-two, and the islands' civil unrest contributed something. And did she not drink? If the portrait of Fanny varies from biographer to biographer, from desexed nurse to an eroticized harridan, what are we to make of her husband?

In the last 150 pages, on Stevenson's final five years in Samoa, both his actions and his writing are clear. They should be: McLynn relies heavily on Barry Menikoff's *Robert Louis Stevenson and the Beach of Falesá* (1984). We understand Stevenson's place in colonial politics. Stevenson always liked the underdog, and perhaps he did try to retain or even re-create a society close to the Highlands: kilts become lava-lavas and High Chief Mataafa another Young Pretender. Sometimes the Samoans liked Osbourne: a high chieftess should be older. The evisceration of Stevenson's last works by Sidney Colvin becomes obvious.

McLynn's literary analysis is often acute and succinct. *An Island Voyage* (1878) contains "Panglossian reassurances to the dimmer kind of Victorian reader." His reading of *The Strange Case of Dr. Jekyll and Mr. Hyde* densely mixes doppelgängers from ten other authors with a mélange of thematic, familial, philosophical, and marital observations as Jung joins Freud. McLynn argues if his poetry (as sex-saturated as that of D. H. Lawrence) argues with Eros; his fiction argues with father. His readings of *Treasure Island* (1883), *Kidnapped* (1886), and *The Master of Ballantrae* (1889) illuminate family and national conflicts. It is in the unfinished *Weir of Hermiston* (1896) that Stevenson finally comes to terms with his father and mother.

Thirty-five photographs supplement the text; the index is most useful. For some reason a few letters appear in a mixture of typefaces. Now, the Pacific Oceans are large; we could use a map of Stevenson's voyage. The names of their islands are so vowelly that you do not initially believe them. It is remarkable and commendable that only one mistake slips in (Ha-pu in the Marquesas becomes Ka-pu). Since there have been more biographies of Stevenson than any other nineteenth-century writer, it cannot be said that McLynn's work fills a gap. But it comprehends a whole life with sympathy and a passionate concern for the subject's works.

After Richard Ellmann's massive biography *Oscar Wilde* of five years ago, Melissa Knox decided to fill in the internal picture of Wilde, to integrate material Ellmann did not touch: she aims in *Oscar Wilde: A Long and Lovely Suicide* (Yale University Press) to connect her subject's literary, psychological, and sexual development. Having done this, it is her hope that we, like her, will love him. Her aim is ambitious, her purpose difficult of achievement. Knox has brought underused material to light: the letters of Wilde's wife, Constance; the uncatalogued letters of Robert Sherard, Wilde's first biographer; extensive material at the William Andrews Clark Memorial Library at UCLA. Her investigation into Wilde's mother's psyche and fervent Irish nationalism, relying as it does on sure documentation, establishes her subject's tension: was he Saxon or Celt?

As an orthodox Freudian, Knox begins with Wilde's childhood and his sister Isola, who died at age nine and with whom, Knox argues, Wilde had some sort of sexual relations. Knox acknowledges that she is not the first to speculate about this relationship, but she has taken it further than other critics and biographers of the last twenty years. Though these relations are not spelled out, this episode was "central to the course of his life and art" (somewhat similar claims have been made for Henry James). Such an important claim deserves attention.

Knox's argument from the poetry develops over some seven pages. Beginning with a "sexual current flowing between them" we meet a "frightened but erotically eager girl." Then both develop a classic "pregenital type of intimacy," and perhaps their "sexual play" continues to her death (Wilde is now twelve); after she dies, Wilde will re-create his love for her with his catamite Bosie Douglas so that going to prison is the emotional equivalent of being buried with her. The only evidence for this incestuous love can be found in Wilde's style in his poems and in *Salome* (1893). Knox's arguments from the poems may convince some: Thomas Hood's "Bridge of Sighs" ("Take her up tenderly . . .") is about a dead prostitute, and its meter is vaguely like the twenty-year-old Wilde's "Requiescat," so Knox links them. Unfortunately the line that follows the

two cited stanzas of Wilde's poem (much of which is a pastiche of Thomas Nashe) begins "Lily-like, white as snow" – not the traditional epithets of a worker in the sex industry. Isola, the "seductive little sister," also comes hiddenly alive in "The Harlot's House." Here the iambic tetrameters should remind us of *In Memoriam* (1842) so the suppressed eroticism of Tennyson's poem can be sensed in the final line of Wilde's poem:

And down the long and silent street,
The dawn with silver-sandelled feet
Crept like a frightened girl.

Knox may have a point about Tennyson (in which case a comparison to Tennyson's sections 7 and 123 would have been in order), but the "silver-sandelled feet" are those of Thetis (over fifteen times in the *Iliad*); further, the effectiveness of the concluding line, which is not pastiche, is created by a trimeter.

Later, in his early forties, Wilde wrote *The Ballad of Reading Gaol* (1898): here associative connection rather than direct reference reveals that Coleridge's resurrected sailors stand for Wilde's dead sister. The borrowing is clear. What is also clear, I think, is that Wilde liked the sound of saraband from his earlier poem "The Harlot's House" (in a line Knox does not quote) and plopped it back in *The Ballad of Reading Gaol*. Wilde came to quote himself. There is one poem which is a morass of sexual anomalies: *The Sphinx* (1894). Here an analyst can find a shivering dawn that leads a tongueless ghost of sin into a student's cell, a ghost which, among other things, presented mouths of flame to a horned god who had a secret name. Not once does Knox cite it.

Better, because Wilde's highest achievement is his drama (despite Max Beerbohm's opinion), are Knox's analyses of the plays. *Salome* reveals his earliest interest in martyrdom (*The Importance of Being Earnest* [1895] is the script of his tragedy). The cast is crowded: Herodias is Lady Wilde in her dress; Herod the anal Wilde and his promiscuous father; Jokanaan as martyr is both Wilde and Wilde as Christ the martyr; and beneath Salome's mask Knox sees the oral Wilde, his dead sister, and his present lover, Bosie Douglas. Even *De Profundis* (1905), in Knox's view, becomes a drama of dialectic dialogue. Fortunately, Knox abandons this approach and sees the late poem as an example of Victorian autobiography in the mode of John Henry Newman and John Stuart Mill. In Wilde's case, however, he sought what Knox and Wilde see as Christian martyrdom. Whether the reader can come to love Wilde whose "resurrection" from prison "was really reerection" and a return to pedophilia is another matter.

Knox's most successful chapter examines *The Importance of Being Earnest,* a drama in which Wilde outs himself as a homosexual challenging the world. That this homosexual was also Irish and his world English is linked to his mother's fervent Irish nationalism. The biographer proceeds act by act and argues that the play is a carbon copy of Wilde's sexual dilemmas. The misplaced cigarette case that Cecily presented to her Uncle Jack which Algernon seizes upon as a reason to prevent Jack's marriage to Gwendolen parallels Wilde's similar gifts to rent boys. The play's text and actions reflect Wilde's unconscious fear of future blackmail. By inverting Victorian truisms on class and marriage, Wilde revealed the paradoxes of his society: the gobbling of cucumber sandwiches is the grab for African colonies; divorces rather than marriages are made in heaven. These insights are convincing. What could have helped her case is that the word *earnest* was camp for *homosexual.*

The subsequent trial against Douglas's father, the marquess of Queensberry, becomes another drama in which Wilde achieves an Oedipal victory: Wilde kills and submits to two fathers, his own and Douglas's at the same time.

Wilde's syphilis was not the immediate cause of his death, but Wilde thought it was killing him. The mannered prose of *The Picture of Dorian Gray* (1890) and his 1887 short story "The Canterville Ghost" was Wilde's attempt to defeat medical horrors. Knox's dense reading of the story is a new and convincing one: learning a year earlier that he had the disease, Wilde's story is an autobiography that tries to hide his guilt over infecting his wife by mocking a ghost which not only bumbles about but has the symptoms of tertiary syphilis. Overall, this biographer's discussion of the disease in Wilde's time is extensive and more thorough than Ellmann's, but at times it is inconsistent. One chapter asserts it was not until seven years after Wilde's death in 1900 that arsenic became a standard therapy; a later one claims it was a standard remedy in the nineteenth century. Knox finds references to syphilis in many poems. Jonathan confesses to Saul (1 Sam. 14:43) that "I did but taste a little honey with the end of the rod"; Wilde adapts these words in his 1881 "Hélas" where it is his "little rod" that gets syphilis. But William Pater cited the same biblical text in his *Life of Winckelmann* (1867) to contrast Christian asceticism with Hellenism (hence, I think, Wilde's title). The biographer may be pushing it

here. She does need to check the text of the King James Version she cites and the poem itself.

Ellmann's biography, almost four times the length of Knox's, will remain the standard treatment; it will also put much of Knox's study back in context. There are times in this biography when we miss the context: Wilde may have flunked one Greek exam for insolence, but he did take a First Class degree in Greats while at Magdalen College in 1878. The reference to "bloody sweats" in *De Profundis* is from the Litany in the Book of Common Prayer; it is not simply a "vivid image of disease." Isa. 35:5 is the basis for Jokanaan's description of Christ, not Wilde's otological fantasies. When Wilde calls himself improbable rather than impossible for remaining in town during the trial, it is an adaption of Aristotle's *On Tragedy,* not merely wit. In some of the above cases, the context would have assisted Knox's arguments: that Wilde saw himself as a martyred Christ who played in the Greek tragedy of his life. If it was Wilde who first "defined psychoanalytic literary criticism," its practitioners have a way to go.

There were two books in 1994 on Anna Akhmatova. In *Anna Akhmatova and Her Circle* (translated by Patricia Beriozkina with compilation and notes by Konstantin Polivanov; University of Arkansas Press) we have the recollections of fourteen people, including two by Akhmatova, of the poet and her friends. Twenty years ago this would have been the special issue of some journal, but this is a translation of the Moscow edition. And much of it is Anna Akhmatova-ana; valuable, of course, but not material that immediately illumines her life and writings. Many of the recollections were written long after the events they describe. Part 1 of this book contains ten contemporaries on Akhmatova arranged roughly to follow the subject's life; part 2 is on her friends.

The reminiscences which will be of less value to the general reader are those of Valeria Sreznevskaya, memories of her childhood and Akhmatova's first husband, the poet Nikolai Gumilev; Georgy Adamovich remembers her before World War I and after the Khrushchev thaw of 1953. Boris Anrep covers the last two periods more poignantly and expands his remarks in part 2. Kornei Chukovsky's diaries present the 1920s; Akhmatova's second husband, Vladimir Shileiko; and then jump to the 1950s. Lydia Ginzburg's words perceptibly focus on Akhmatova's poetry from 1926 through the 1940s. We return to the life of Akhmatova in the recollections of Emma Gershtein (the 1930s) and the comments of Nina

Olshevskaya-Ardova. Akhmatova, even after her expulsion from the writers' union in 1946, often stayed with the Ardovs (but she thought the apartment was bugged). In these seven brief memoirs the literary feuds of prerevolutionary Russia appear with bewildering frequency, the symbolists led by Aleksandr Blok, the futurists of Vladimir Mayakovsky, and the acmeists, including Akhmatova, Osip Mandelshtam, and Gulimev. Vladislav Khodasevich, who left Russia in 1922, sheds light on these feuds and Gumilev's arrest in part 2.

Then there are two better sections, one by Nadia Mandelshtam, the wife of Osip, and the other by Natalia Roskina. Roskina, a literary historian, wrote her "Good-bye Again" in 1966. This "contemporary" forty years younger than Akhmatova whom Roskina met in 1945 when she was seventeen gives us in twenty-five pages a fuller picture of Akhmatova's life: the effects of the expulsion, the improvements after Stalin's death, her continued love for the dead Gumilev. Since she is a literary historian, Roskina's subject has strong opinions about writers: Ernest Hemingway, and two future Nobel laureates, Boris Pasternak and Joseph Brodsky ("a kindred spirit"). Her characterization of Andrei Voznesensky and Yevgeny Yevtushenko as "pop poets" was prescient.

Nadia Mandelshtam, who Akhmatova called the first twentieth-century poet, has written the most poignant chapter of this compilation. Moving back and forth in time, from arrests by the Chekists to Akhmatova's chaotically Russian funeral, Mandelshtam's essay on courage, the courage to write, the courage to hang a picture of Akhmatova on the wall, the courage to oppose the "theoreticians of force" with one's own truth, remains the center of this book. Mandelshtam insists that more than artists or musicians, it is the poet who most directly connects sexuality with art. The link between the personal, whether in Akhmatova's poetry or in relationships with others, including Mendelshtam's husband, forms the other half of this passionate memorial tribute. Speaking of her own life, Akhmatova's life, and Sylvia Plath's suicide (a reference the editors did not catch), Mandelshtam concludes that we pay "a heavy price for every drop of joy."

Oddly enough the two sections from Akhmatova's writings (sketches, notes, lectures, diaries) are less interesting. "Even a wonderful memory can and should forget some things," the poet admits. What is remembered and re-created in part 1 is her childhood. Her other reminiscences in part 2, still apparently in manuscript form, were meant to correct her relationship with Osip Mandelshtam.

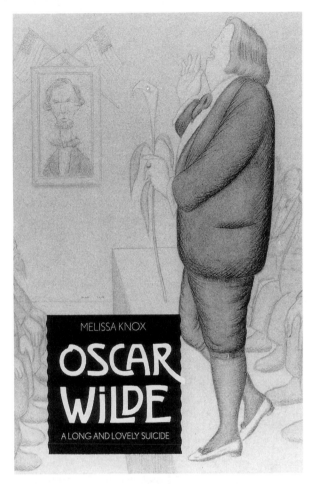

Dust jacket for the biography of the fin de siècle British poet and dramatist that attempts to link Wilde's literary achievement with his psychological and sexual history

Akhmatova wrote them between 1957 and two years before her death in 1966; they recall her first meeting with his wife, the arrest of Osip in 1934, and the assistance of Pasternak to save him from the Reign of Terror. Akhmatova also paid off many old scores both personal and poetic.

The twenty-five illustrations, including Amedeo Modigliani's spare sketch, give us the poet from high-school girl to suffering icon and finally to the dignified recipient of a D.Litt. at Oxford in 1965.

This compilation will be of some value to students of Akhmatova. But the general Russianless reader may be puzzled. My Russian was never more than shaky, but that language lurks behind the syntax and idioms of the preface and foreword. This is tolerable, except the foreword is by Akhmatova's secretary from the 1960s, Anatoly Naiman. Naiman's essay on the poet in Judith Hemschemeyer's recent translation (1989, 1992) is much better. Equally irritating is the inconsistent transliteration. The index gives us Vsevolod Meierkhold, the film director, who Artur Lurye mentions in his memoir of Olga Glebova-Sudeikina; the index does not give us "Meyerhold," who figures in Akhmatova's recollection of the 1910s. Perhaps the original text lacked a bibliography and failed to document the sources of these reminiscences. I think a university press owes us more than "published in various editions." Readers of this compilation should consult the next text. Are we expected to remember that Marya Fyodorovna was the dowager empress?

This year's second book on Akhmatova by a commercial company (Farrar Straus Giroux) is more than admirably produced and organized. In 1980 volume two (1952–1962) of Lydia Chukovskaya's *The Akhmatova Journals* was published. This year sees the printing of volume one (1938–1941), a revised and expanded version of the original 1989 Moscow edition. Missing from the original (perhaps the notebook was lost) are entries from November 1940 to October 1941; the rest of 1941 covers only eight pages. In fact, the journals themselves take up about two-thirds of the three hundred pages. A ten-page publisher's glossary provides information for the general reader on topics, people, places, and institutions that are not in Chukovskaya's exhaustive twenty-five pages of notes. Like Akhmatova – and Herodotus – she pays off many scores: who helped her, and who injured her, and who stole her journals.

Lydia Chukovskaya, a novelist, was the daughter of Kornei Chukovsky, a famous writer of children's stories. Eight pages of his diaries are included in *Anna Akhmatova and Her Circle*. Chukovskaya's husband, Matvey Petrovich Bronshteyn, was both tried and shot on the same day in 1937. Chukovskaya avoided a similar fate. She has fulfilled in this volume what Nadia Mandelshtam's memoirs promised: "We will remember the unwritten poems, we will collect them, and we will not forget them."

Most of the journals are set in Leningrad, and most of the entries are of what Chukovskaya calls a "historical-literary nature." We have Akhmatova's views on fifty Russian writers. By jumping around, a reader can begin to re-create the literary sensibilities of Russia just before and during the revolution. Then there are Chukovskaya's comments on 175 of her own works. The latter are often brief: problems with publisher's proofs, misprints. This is deliberate on Chukovskaya's part. The sufferings of both women, Akhmatova for her imprisoned son, Chukovskaya for her imprisoned husband, and the

terrors of the Big House (NKVD headquarters), can be garnered from this book but generally only from the footnotes. Much of what Chukovskaya wrote in 1967 comes from the brief notes she took and from her memory; to record too much was to endanger Akhmatova, an Akhmatova almost invariably "sad and pale."

Occasionally the personal lives of these two women interrupt literary talk. Akhmatova recalls her childhood, brief moments with Modigliani in Paris, her illnesses, her first marriage with Nikolai Gumilyov (the transliterations from this journal are consistent). However, Pasternak features more in her thoughts than Nikolay Punin, her third husband. Punin had married what he thought was a girl of wax; he got a woman of "reinforced concrete." One realizes from this journal that it is Akhmatova's poetry that counts, not the suffering that produced it.

Chukovskaya treasures the poems. Akhmatova would read a new poem to her; she would memorize it. Then followed an act which defined the terror of the times: Akhmatova would burn the manuscript in the stove. Chukovskaya insists her recollections are the primary text. An appendix provides fifty-four of Akhmatova's poems keyed to the text of the journals; Peter Norman's translation of them reads well. Their content is often unbearable.

After twenty years John Fuegi, the founder of the International Brecht Society, has done himself out of a job. He had the assistance of a few others, especially John Willett. But it was Fuegi who tracked down and interviewed survivors in both East and West Germany and explored Soviet archives. We are forced to conclude that though Bertolt Brecht the lyricist still exists, the dramatist does not. There is potentially no longer a Brecht, the author of *The Threepenny Opera, Mother Courage, The Good Woman of Setzuan,* or *Caucasian Chalk Circle.* What replaces him is a writer who betrayed his collaborators onstage and in bed and who used their bodies and their lines. Fuegi does not deny Brecht's genius as a poet nor his skills as a director, but the 730 pages of his *Brecht and Company: Sex, Politics and the Making of the Modern Drama* (Grove Press) chronicles a writing workshop, not a garret. Massively factual (there are two wars and three political movements to cover) and meticulously researched, this is an indignant biography; at times the author's fury gets the better of his rhetoric and, more important, of his argument. Readers can forgive the youthfully periphrastic "emptying his gonads" because Fuegi provides sharp and telling details of time and place, but Brecht as this century's Antichrist?

Baptized Berthold in 1898, he changed his name to Bertolt. This flattered his lover, Arnolt Bronnen, a lover who introduced the then-married Brecht to the actress Helene Weigel; Brecht finally married her in 1929 despite a bastard child, an aborted child, and a promise to another. Bronnen, having been officially Aryanized (his mother denied her Jewish husband was the father), also married: his wife left their nuptial bed and spent the next twenty-four hours with a rising gauleiter, Joseph Goebbels. This biography, then, becomes a tale of genital confusion, political timeserving, and shameless plagiarism.

Fuegi has discovered a series of patterns that marks Brecht's life in shifty politics, shifty affairs, and shifty plays. All began early: the affairs with women – and men – when he was nineteen in 1917. His lovers would discover, after having been assured of their exclusivity, that Brecht was not. Reassured, they would continue as would Brecht with them and with others. The playwright's courtship ritual over twenty years was reduced to the spare "Say yes." The promises remained the same: marriage or fame.

But despite the sexual allure and rhetoric of Brecht, Fuegi also argues that the loyalty of at least three women – Elizabeth Hauptmann, Ruth Berlau, and Margarete Steffin (the last oft aborted) – was also rooted in their commitment to Communism and world peace, two programs Brecht promoted (the latter sincerely) after he moved to East Berlin in 1948. Fuegi's Brecht is a self-believing monster of egoism and sexual charm; his women are self-deluded, politicized, effaced, and "marginalized" (the caption assigned to a woman in one of the 103 photographs). This work restores the urtext and shows us Brecht balancing "desire and repulsion, magnetism and distance, passion and coldness, commitment and aversion" whenever sex and politics intersected. Coming of age as World War I began and ended is offered, not too convincingly, as one explanation for Brecht's sexual fear and abuse of powerful women.

Of all the women in Brecht's life, it is Hauptmann, the actual (he wrote about 80 percent) author of *The Threepenny Opera,* who suffered the greatest number of betrayals. Hauptmann, who had the languages the Ausberger Brecht lacked, met him in 1924, by which time Brecht had children by two mistresses and another by his abandoned wife. Hauptmann and Brecht intertwine textually and sexually from *A Man's a Man* (1926) to after World War II. Their collaboration came notably together when they met Kurt Weill and his wife, the singer

Lotte Lenya. Brecht's major, and almost only, contribution to *The Threepenny Opera* was the song "Mack the Knife." Fuegi argues that the success of Brecht's plays beginning with *The Threepenny Opera* and including both *Mother Courage* and *The Good Woman of Setzuan* resulted from the balance of Brecht's misogyny (found in his earlier plays) with the strong women of his fellow writers, first Hauptmann and then Steffin. Brecht, then, by himself was little.

Fuegi establishes the contributions of both contributors by close examination of the manuscripts; even the typescripts left their traces. Hauptmann's diaries, previously, selectively, and incompetently published by the German Democratic Republic, are supplemented by material contained in Harvard's Brecht Collection, which is fast disintegrating.

Brecht's plays have heroines. His life had heroines: Hauptmann who dealt with and was briefly arrested by the gestapo when Brecht fled Berlin in 1933 after the Reichstag fire (two months after he apparently toasted the Nazis' rise to power); the tubercular Steffin who tried to recover her lover's papers in purge-ridden Moscow a year earlier; the Danish Communist Berlau who left her country just as the Nazis arrived. But Brecht was no hero in the Weimar Republic nor in the Soviet Union where he lay exhausted from entertainment. In New York he horrified Sidney Hook; in Finland, where he fled after the invasion of Denmark and where Berlau joined him along with Weigel and Steffin, he remained comfortable. Here, outside Helsinki, he and his two mistresses and his wife were befriended by Hella Wuolijoki, from whom Brecht stole money, plots, and lines. He was and remained rich. By 1923 Brecht had learned to sequester funds, to bank in Switzerland, and, above all, to avoid shared copyright. The heirs of Steffin, who Fuegi visited in 1989, lived in converted garden sheds. Brecht had hunkered down in a fourteen-room suburban villa.

The biography takes him from the cabarets of Munich to those of Berlin; then, after the Reichstag fire, to Copenhagen and to Sweden (avoiding the penalties for having run down a child). As Russia was invaded, Brecht and Company escaped. Steffin died in Moscow, and Brecht dickered for tickets for the Trans-Siberian Express. The rest of the company eventually arrived in Hollywood, where Brecht wrote scripts and was tracked by the incompetent Federal Bureau of Investigation (FBI). (The bureau's files are, as always, masterfully illiterate.) Copying and copulating, he visited the now more famous Weills in New York, a city that saw Brecht

Dust jacket for the biography of the German playwright documenting that Brecht wrote only a small amount of the work attributed to him

as a short, grubby has-been. He returned to California and the red scare.

In 1948, as Hollywood replaced sixteenth-century Rome and House Un-American Activities Committee her Inquisitors, Brecht became a Galileo whose tacit complicity, Fuegi insists, led to McCarthy as much as his earlier waffling apparently supported Hitler and Stalin. The irony is that Brecht's own *Galileo* is, Fuegi argues, Brecht's most perfectly crafted work.

What of the making of modern drama? Fuegi notes a jettisoning of earlier theater practices after World War II. Brecht's still-influential idea of "epic theater" (cool acting, cool audience, montage mixed with narrative and song) disappeared as a critical theory in *A Short Organum* and as technique – if, in fact, the audience ever was cool; and if, in fact, the term ever had any consistent meaning. Brecht's critical theories as early as 1921 were never consistent. The producer, Fuegi argues, went forward by going backward: Christopher Marlowe and Japanese No led to *The Threepenny Opera*. Worse, or more interesting, since this is a biography and not a history of theater, Brecht would dump the avant-garde production when a major star became available (in both senses).

Finally leaving the United States, Brecht settled in East Berlin and became a socialist icon. Fuegi's icon tenuously vibrates between Walter Ulbricht and Moscow while directing the Berliner Ensemble. Brecht viewed the 1953 uprisings as an economic glitch and offered his services to support repression. Privately his criticism of the Ulbricht regime remained unpublished ("dissolve the people and elect another"); publicly he moved closer to the regime. In Moscow he received the Stalin Prize; in Berlin he betrayed his many lovers still exhibiting to the end what Fuegi claims he shared with both Stalin and Hitler: charismatic and irrational power. Fuegi wishes us to see Brecht as somehow responsible for these two tyrants; this is a serious confusion of the ethical and political.

In 1931 Sean O'Faolain (born John Whelan) at the age of thirty-one published *Midsummer Night Madness; The New York Times* called it the best book of Irish stories since James Joyce's *Dubliners* (1914), and the *Bookman,* focusing on the introduction, found it a "tactless diatribe against the Irish people." Maurice Harmon's *Sean O'Faolain: A Life* (Constable) tries to cover the tensions between O'Faolain's split loyalties to his country, to his country's church, to his craft, and to himself. The attempt is not as successful as one might wish. This is surprising for Harmon has written much on modern Irish literature and not merely academic studies. Harmon's earlier *Sean O'Faolain: A Critical Introduction* (1966) may assist. This present biography does correct the subject's autobiography *Vive Moi!* (1993). Harmon writes from personal knowledge of his subject. He knows everyone who knew O'Faolain, interviewed at least fifty people, and makes good use of many letters. The twenty photographs are clear. Precise documentation is shaky; some people simply seem to disappear.

A jerky beginning with a parade of simple sentences moves O'Faolain from his birth in Cork in 1900 to his early education at University College Cork. Then we have twenty pages covering the years crucial to his fiction. He took Irish classes, he met his future wife Eileen; the Irish-Anglo war is followed by the truce (1921). O'Faolain volunteered, demonstrated, and received his B.A.; he had, as Harmon points out, a good revolution. It was only during the civil war (1922–1923), that his political conscience was formed. He made bombs, wrote press releases, and became disillusioned. In three short years he will be presented to the Prince of Wales at the Court of Saint James. What happened?

Harmon's comments on O'Faolain's *Newman's Way* (1952) are acute: like the cardinal, he transforms experience and creates a new reality. But readers will want more of his experiences during these important early years. By the 1930s O'Faolain was, along with Frank O'Connor, the leading literary figure of his generation. How he got there remains a question not entirely answered in this biography. His work as editor of *The Bell* from 1940 to 1945 can account for some reasons.

We do have the events of his life, but they often seem curiously divorced from his literary achievements: two master's degrees from Cork, in 1926 a Commonwealth Fellowship to Harvard where O'Faolain took a third master's degree. He sent for Eileen, married her, and seemed to have spent almost two years unaware of the United States (a later fellowship to Princeton in 1953 showed him more of the country). Then to London and initial success with his short stories in 1931. Harmon argues that a cabal of Gaelic League supporters and a sloppy résumé led to O'Faolain's defeat when he sought the English chair at Cork. His defeat was a blessing for Irish letters (though Harmon does not suggest this). Forced to live by his writings, Ireland read a banned novel, more stories, and more biographies. Financial stability finally

came in the late 1940s when he took up travel writing. The thorough bibliography shows that in the thirty years before his death, O'Faolain placed his material in well-paying magazines: *Holiday, Ladies' Home Journal, Mademoiselle, Saturday Evening Post, Redbook, Playboy,* and *Atlantic Monthly.*

We need to see more links between his art and his life. In 1939 he returned to Cork to visit his sick, stubborn, and pathetic mother:

> The experience upset him.... Once, in exasperation, Sean threw her down the stairs and broke her leg. At the end of August Eileen and Sean went to the first night of Daniel Corkey's *Fohnam the Sculptor* at the Abbey.

That is it, and that is not enough. Nor did we learn much about his affair with Elizabeth Bowen two years earlier: she accompanied him to the Salzburg Festival along with Isaiah Berlin. After the death of Eileen in 1988, O'Faolain asked Harmon to tell the story of those women who had been important in his life. His biographer has not quite met that challenge. In 1945 O'Faolain began an affair with Honor Tracey, an editorial assistant at *The Bell.* Harmon, drawing on an unpublished manuscript for *Vive Moi!,* describes her on a balcony during a storm in Taranto: she, a "red-haired, splendid pagan goddess upstretching her breasts to the black downpour"; he is described as a Zeus. Then confession and contrition and back to Eileen: "Honor was very upset." That is it, and that is not enough.

Peter Alexander's *Alan Paton: A Biography* (Oxford) is an authorized life and a huge one; 501 pages is more than enough. Official biographies have their advantages and disadvantages; so does this one. Advantages are full access to letters and manuscripts and interviews with family members. In fact, the indebtedness began earlier for his biographer. In 1974 Paton not only turned over his notes for a proposed biography of the poet Roy Campbell to Alexander, but he also supported Alexander in his legal troubles to get his work published. The relationship between the author and his subject here is one of generally sympathetic honesty. The events or proclivities Paton himself ignored in his autobiographies, *Towards the Mountain* (1980) and *Journey Continued* (1988), are investigated. They include his tyranny as a father and as a schoolteacher, his failed first marriage, and his serious affairs. The presence of crabs confirms in Alexander's judgment what many suspected in 1968: Paton did solicit a twenty-nine-year-old black woman and was mugged. That Alexander is South African helps greatly: countrysides are made plain, manners explained, and if, in the last third of his work, the narrative sinks Paton into the morass of his country's politics, it probably cannot be helped.

We have masses of unpublished material from York to South Africa to New York; Alexander has read everything by Paton including the drafts of his novels; his poetry, published and still in manuscript; his journalism (a copious and squeezed list in the bibliography); even the obscure plays in which Paton acted. In the two chapters on *Cry, the Beloved Country* (1948), Alexander includes fifty-five letters, Paton's diary, interviews, manuscripts, and government reports. The narrative itself can get heavy with detail: the events at Kent State and the poem it provoked, rehashes of synod meetings, schoolboys' anecdotes, a second trip to Bryce Canyon, prison reforms. The sixteen illustrations are clear; only three predate his first novel. What are missing are the love letters and poems of his marriage to his first wife, Dorrie, and those around the time of *Too Late the Phalarope* (1953). Whether Paton and his first wife destroyed them together – for Paton had confessed to having had or having resumed an affair in both cases – or whether Paton and his second wife did so is unclear. Fortunately, those around the time of *Cry, the Beloved Country* survive.

The disadvantages of this sort of official biography are twofold: excessive sympathy at times for his subject and excessive reliance on family material. To take the latter first: what did others think of this former prison warden when he arrived in New York after the success of *Cry, the Beloved Country*? We know what he thought, but are there no letters of others or first impressions? True, we get interviews and excerpts from press accounts but not as much primary material from others as we should. His publisher, Charles Scribner, Jr., could supply some material in his 1991 reminiscences *In the Company of Writers*. But this would inflate an able and balanced biography into a second volume.

Alexander, following Paton's lead, argues that his subject's rebellion against authority began with his passionate dislike for his father, an embittered, brutal, and repressed Scot. The pattern repeats. Paton himself became a less than admirable father to his sons, one of whom was Alexander's teacher at Witwatersrand. The murder of his father remains a mystery Paton, but not his biographer, tried to ignore. Alexander speculates that an illicit affair or misunderstood copulation with a Zulu girl led to his father's death and led Paton to the plot of *Too Late the Phalarope*.

Within one year of his father's murder in 1930, the birth of a son, and his confirmation as an Anglican we begin to hear the spareness of Paton's style in an unpublished story. His confirmation, an event which later made him the political ally of his archbishop, Geoffrey Clayton, also isolated him from his family's Christadelphianism. Paton's *Apartheid and the Archbishop* (1973) records Clayton's struggles with the middle way in politics while forecasting his own.

Today Paton is seen as too slow (just as his novels are seen as too white), but Alexander supplies the political and theological context that explains and justifies what was not a condescending gradualism. Paton's opposition to racism may have developed gradually, but his sympathy for blacks dates back to 1934, as a manuscript of an unfinished novel shows. Readers may wish to consult the concise treatment of this theme by Paton's friend Edward Callan in *Cry, the Beloved Country: A Novel of South Africa* (1991).

Even after the success of his first two novels, we see a man bitterly disappointed in his private life. If his political rebellion stems from parental tyranny, his novels issue from the domestic misery of his first wife: "*Cry, the Beloved Country* kept me off sex." The first Mrs. Paton – the first woman Paton ever kissed – had married a man about to die. He did. She kept his marriage band on for the next five years as Mrs. Paton. Their beds were separate, but hers was shared with her son until he was ten. To Alexander this suggests that Paton "had for years been emotionally deprived in an important sense." This is, I think, too kind. Paton also seems to have been too kind.

The misery of his marriage led to an affair with a nineteen-year-old student teacher when he was thirty-two. Forty years later Paton adopted the elegiac mode in speaking of her "sad salute" at a parting that was a "relief and pain" to both. Did she feel betrayed? We never get her name, we never get her feelings, we never get the biographer's judgment. In any event Paton confessed, and on that very night, after five years of marriage, Mrs. Paton took off her first husband's wedding ring. On that very night their second son was conceived. This might have happened in a novel – and does in *Wuthering Heights* (1847) – but is it probable?

Alexander's introduction of Mary Benson, a fellow South African, is gradual and initially confusing. She starts as a fan in May 1948 who ranks Paton's novel with *War and Peace;* since she is working for David Lean, Paton asks her to provide him with a play in a correspondence already "regular and warm" six months later. We do not learn much about her until September 1949. My math shows

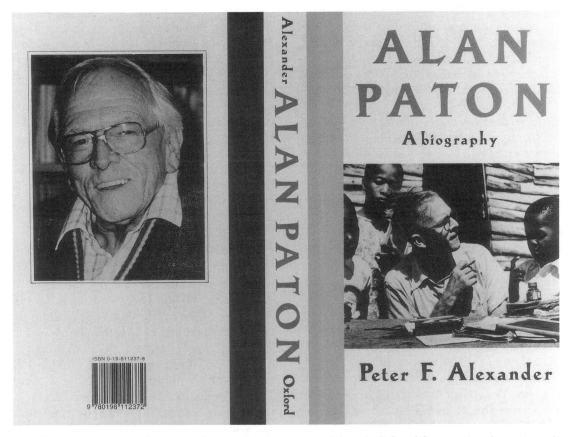

Dust jacket for the biography of the South African novelist whose 1948 novel, Cry, the Beloved Country, *brought attention to the racial problems of his country*

her an unsuccessful starlet in Hollywood at the age of sixteen or seventeen who returned to London and met the forty-six-year-old successful Paton when she was twenty-six. The discrepancy in ages is important psychologically and emotionally: readers should not have to work it out. We might be skeptical over her version of the romance, a version she recorded almost forty years later in her autobiography *A Far Cry* (1989). More convincing, because he does analyze it, is Alexander's application of Paton's sermon delivered at Saint Paul's to his affair with Benson. In this sermon, ostensibly about race relations, we hear the novelist's anguish.

The biographer, then, presents much, but we miss his comments. This is particularly true when Paton wrote successfully. Paton's ability, creativity, and happiness as a writer only flourished when separated from his wife. In Norway and the United States he started and finished *Cry, the Beloved Country* in three months; in 1951 in London he wrote *Too Late the Phalarope* while resuming his friendship with Benson (all the letters to his wife at this time were destroyed); there was also an aborted novel written in two months at a motel near Eureka, California.

What was it about his wife that prevented Paton from writing when at home? Was she a negative muse? If much of Paton's emotional life was self-repressed, so was his aesthetic – until he could free himself physically from her. Surely the biographer owes us some comments here.

The extraordinary success of *Cry, the Beloved Country* in the United States puzzled even Paton's publisher. It will puzzle readers of this biography also. Was the timing good? That Truman integrated the army and Strom Thurmond bolted the Democratic Party in the same year, 1948, may be significant. Alexander ventures no explanation. Nevertheless, we do have a full and sympathetic biography that modifies our understanding of a once-mythic figure.

Elizabeth Bishop is not mythic, yet; but she was a poet's poet, both cerebral and concrete. Both these characteristics are now even more apparent in a selection of her letters ably edited by Robert Giroux in *One Art* (Farrar Straus Giroux). This edition expands and includes a fuller text of many letters David Kalstone used in his study of Bishop, *Becoming a Poet* (1989); Giroux has located 3,000 letters and from them selected 541 to fifty correspondents over fifty years – this takes up an almost unwieldy 649 pages of text. Giroux's editorial practice is rational: cut salutations, closings, and sequential addresses; correct obvious misspellings; keep editorial material in brackets (this keeps Bishop's parentheses).

We have then a rather austere text probably best read along with Brett Millier's *Elizabeth Bishop: Life and the Memory of It* (1993). Failing Millier as a guide, readers will do well to consult the ten-page biography in this volume's introduction and the subsequent three-page chronology. Both will help follow Bishop from Vassar to Key West, from Brazil to Seattle. Regrettably her letters, except one, to Lota (Maria Macedo Soares), her aristocratic Brazilian companion of fifteen years, were destroyed. Some of the tensions and joys of this friendship can be recovered secondhand from the 250 pages of letters from 1951 to 1967.

The letters reveal some of Elizabeth's emotions: often grief, as her close friends Randall Jarrell and Dylan Thomas die. At times anguish: Lota, whose doctors should have forbidden her trip to see Bishop in New York, died of an overdose the next day. The sorrow she felt at her lover's suicide by drugs in 1965 is poignantly and almost embarrassingly apparent in her letters: she tried but was unable to blame herself. It is also apparent in the 1976 poem "One Art," which lends its title to this collection of letters:

> I lost two cities, lovely ones.
> And vaster, some realms I owned, two rivers, a continent.
> I miss them, but it wasn't a disaster.
> – Even losing you (the joking voice, a gesture
> I love) . . .[.]

What we cannot get from the letters is what causes the emotional separation between Bishop and Lota. Brazilian politics and the lure of a well-paying teaching job at the University of Washington do not explain it. What or who may explain it is the mysterious XY (Giroux's pseudonym), a schizophrenic divorcée with a young child, whom Bishop met in Brazil. She surfaces in a letter to Dr. Amy Baumann a few months before Lota's suicide. Bishop wishes to leave her fifteen thousand dollars, and Lota is not to know. No letters to or from XY survive, but Bishop's sympathy is clear from forty other references.

In this case Giroux exerts a control of which Bishop would have approved. Her letters possess what Otavio Paz said of her poetry: "the enormous power of reticence." Her letters cannot be used to document the vaster realms she lost in "One Art." Perhaps, she wonders, she should have included the additional loss of an island in Maine. We see her sympathy and good sense in her second to last letter of the almost forty to Robert Lowell. After praising his poem *Dolphin,* she implores him not to indulge in the confessional mode: good manners forbid the use of others' lives in our work (she said the same thing about Mary McCarthy's novel *The Group*). Perhaps Lowell should have listened. He did earlier: we have his letter proposing marriage and her two responses which politely ignore it by praising his poetry.

This concern for others rather than herself marks her letters. She gets closest to confessing the misery of being a poet in a "thoroughly disgusting world" in a 1953 letter. Yet even here her sympathies are for Dylan Thomas, Robert Lowell, and Marianne Moore. The letters will illuminate, in often trenchant comments, the poetry of Thomas, T. S. Eliot, W. H. Auden, Theodore Roethke, William Carlos Williams, Richard Eberhart, Robert Frost, Wallace Stevens, and Elizabeth Hardwick. They also present publishers, and the luckiest of them is this book's editor: he got to read much of her work first. Also fortunate was the aspiring poet who had the courtesy to send a stamped, self-addressed envelope; Bishop's advice: read past poets and read them all the time. Most unfortunate was Jean-Paul Sartre: "can you imagine a worse fate for your declining years than being read aloud to by Simone de Beauvoir?"

Of the poets to which she wrote, Giroux has given us almost fifty letters to Moore, forty to Lowell, twenty to James Merrill, six to Randall Jarrell. These numbers do not suggest how often her correspondents figured sympathetically as topics in her letters: Moore is mentioned 120 times, Lowell 133, Merrill 26, Jarrell 52. Not unexpectedly, there is only one letter to McCarthy but 50 references.

Bishop's acquaintance was vast: her friends were not all poets. In her 144 letters to Amy Baumann, her physician, we can hear at times her unhappiness. Baumann and Lowell became Bishop's friends and correspondents within months of each other in summer 1947 when Bishop was thirty-six. Baumann remained her mentor; Bishop became Lowell's. Perhaps it is in one of her 30-odd letters to painter Lorin MacIver that we read her personal despair most clearly articulated. The almost 50 letters to Frani Blough, a high-school friend, keep us informed of her surface life. Few of these 500 letters are dull: almost all display the particularity of her eye for the apparently trivial but always concrete and witty: toucans, *Quo Vadis,* berserk squirrels, Jacqueline Kennedy's byzantine hat, the plural of phallus, the best fish market. Then, in a letter written on the day Bishop died, the Harvard student who found no creativity in her course because Bishop "wants you to look up words in the dictionary!"

The index is usually full, copious, and rarely mystifying. Her poems and books appear twice: once under Bishop and then by title – this is most helpful. Some people are missing. Though Bishop's comments on U.S. politics are sparse (our embassy comes off poorly in the 1950s), she read John F. Kennedy's speeches in Portuguese and condemned Barry Goldwater. Since her lover Lota was often warring with the government, Bishop's comments on Brazilian politics are extensive. Kennedy is listed, but the senator from Arizona is not indexed. Obviously not every name Bishop wrote can be included; yet there seems to be no system for what is included: within half a page we get six artists; two are indexed (Walter Gropius and Patrick Heron, the gouache maker), the others, including Oscar Kokoschka, are not.

All readers of Bishop's poetry will remain indebted to her publisher and editor for this splendid assortment. In the last four to five years, there have been almost a dozen studies and almost fifty articles on Bishop. *One Art* will put them in a clearer perspective.

Bishop's letters are models of self-restraint; she ages quietly. Erica Jong has reached fifty, a not unusual event; she does not like it, another not unusual event. In her autobiography *Fear of Fifty: A Midlife Memoir* (HarperCollins) she attempts to persuade readers that her life is the universal and particular at the same time. Jong offers us a mediation on what it is like to be fifty and how she got there. Readers will admire the honesty and gusto of her self-analysis, but often many of her confessions move toward otiose whining interrupted, perhaps every fourth page, by sardonic wit. Mediation in divorce means the fair person gives in, the crazy person wins by yelling; in East Side condominiums Jews are encouraged to grow foreskins and pass as WASPs. This is a practical *Cosmopolitan* with wit: the logistics of affairs, a dozen fallacies women believe about men. Jong's book is a text in need of an anthologist. Like her second novel, *Fanny,* the 325

pages here need pruning, an editor who can excise the clichés, and some sort of index.

The organization of *Fear of Fifty* is generally event, then what it means. Readers have her beginning her sexual life at age fourteen, then worried about pregnancy, and then in her forties brooding over AIDS. We get her first boyfriends from the 1950s and the obligatory litany of the lately dead from the 1980s. Like Laurence Sterne, she comments on her writing as it proceeds. Unlike Sterne, she is disorganized: friends of twenty years' standing are introduced twenty years later and then die.

Intellectually Jong puts herself in the whiplash generation (along with some whips): from Betty Crocker to Betty Friedan and then back to motherhood. Her penultimate chapter suggests, as does Camille Paglia (to whom Jong is silently indebted), that men are not the problem. She reaches this conclusion in a process she knows she shared with George Sand, Anna Akhmatova, Elizabeth Browning, the Brontë sisters, Mary Shelley, and Sylvia Plath. All these writers as young women were liberated by falling in love with an archetypal bad boy. Jong's twenty-six-year-old boy was a gun-toting, barbell lifting motorcyclist of good family who had a literary bent ("it curves upward like a burnished scimitar"). Now at fifty she no longer needs him for she has become her own good boy and bad boy at the same time.

More than twenty years ago *Fear of Flying* (1974) took off: some twelve million copies have been printed. Jong rightly objects to its epitomization as praise of the zipless fuck, the phrase she fears as an epitaph. There is little of that novel here. What we get instead, and halfway through since this book does have an inchoate structure, are some remarks on movie rights. Jong spends more time on giving birth to her daughter and to *Fanny: Being the True History of the Adventures of Fanny Hackabout-Jones* (1980). The birth and education of her daughter on the East Coast, among Tuscan hills, and in Venice are among the most attractive parts of this book. Her chapter devoted to both Venice and her erotic life there forms the climax of *Fear of Fifty.* Jong presents a paean to the city as a setting for love: ripples on the ceiling of the Gritti Palace (it is not John Ruskin's city, but Byron's). With a bright daughter, happily married to a divorce lawyer, financially secure, reconciled to her parents and her Jewishness, what is to fear at fifty?

Dictionary of Literary Biography Yearbook Award for a Distinguished Literary Biography Published in 1994

Dust jacket for Joanna Richardson's biography of the nineteenth-century French poet who was a precursor of modernism

The almost notorious events that we thought we knew about Charles Baudelaire's life could become a novel. Joanna Richardson's *Baudelaire* (St. Martin's Press) is better: his life, his works, and his setting join to become a lucid narrative that reads as richly as any novel. The author, the winner of a Prix Goncourt for an earlier biography on Judith Gautier, has done it again. Biography should please and illuminate a subject for the general, literate reader. Richardson has succeeded. Her scholarship is thorough but not fact-ridden; she re-creates the poet in and apart from his domestic, cultural, and literary background. We never lose sight of nineteenth-century France; we join the conclaves of his family in the provinces and meet the poet's mistresses in Paris. Most remarkable is Richardson's calm sympathy for his suffering, a sympathy which helps clarify his poetry. This biography presents Baudelaire both as a maddened son emotionally blackmailed by his mother and as the paradigmatic herald of a new sensibility to language.

– William Foltz

The Year in Drama

Howard Kissel
New York Daily News

Early in 1993 Esther Sherman, one of the last of a generation of agents who had an exalted notion of the theater and toiled relentlessly on behalf of playwrights who shared her belief, brought a new play by the most celebrated of her clients, Edward Albee, to a producer whose virtues include taste, intellectual acumen, and, perhaps most important, access to investors with large sums of money. He read the play and shared Sherman's enthusiasm for it. He was delighted that she had attached no strings to it, which was unusual given the eminence of the playwright. But when he thought about it, it was perhaps not so unusual. Albee, after all, had not had a play produced on Broadway since the 1983 *Man With Three Arms,* an unsatisfying work that was interpreted as a petulant attack on his critics. For years a work called *The Marriage Play,* which had been produced at an English-speaking theater in Vienna and in Princeton, had been announced for Broadway but was eventually produced Off-Off-Broadway at the Signature Theater, which devoted its 1993–1994 season to a retrospective of Albee's works, largely one-acts.

The producer contacted his potential investors and told them how excited he was by the play. He was dismayed to find that their lack of interest in Albee was so total that none even wanted to read it. He returned it to Sherman with profound regret. She then shopped it around to the various subscription theaters that have for the last twenty years been the most vital forum for new plays in New York.

These theaters, whose operating expenses and artistic salaries tend to be low, offer their subscribers an average of four or five plays a season, which is to say four or five pigs in a poke. In theory these Off-Off-Broadway theaters scorn commerce and present the plays they do because of their commitment to serious theater. But in fact each of the four or five pigs has been selected with an eye to bringing the animal to market. If any of these plays can be transferred to Off-Broadway or Broadway, the producing theater will receive a royalty that will en-

Edward Albee, circa 1980

able it to continue its commitment to serious theater.

The company Sherman found to produce the new Albee play, the Vineyard Theater, was a relative newcomer, but its success with this play – *Three Tall Women* – enhanced its reputation enormously. The Vineyard opened its production of *Three Tall Women* in February 1994 and received enthusiastic reviews. By April the play had transferred to a theater Off-Broadway where it eventually turned a $40,000-a-week profit. Around the time of the transfer Sherman died. Coincidentally, on the day of her

Neil Simon, whose London Suite *opened in New York under the terms of the Broadway Alliance, a plan to lower costs for producing plays*

memorial service the Board of Trustees of Columbia University announced that *Three Tall Women* had won the 1994 Pulitzer Prize for drama. Her belief in the play had been vindicated. *Three Tall Women,* the first Albee play to win a Pulitzer in almost twenty years (the last time was in 1975 for *Seascape*), was more than merely a literary event. It marked Albee's return to a position of central rather than marginal significance.

This story with a happy ending seems a useful way to begin a survey of drama at a time when the prospects for serious theater have never seemed bleaker. One of the reasons for this pessimism became apparent late in 1994, when it was announced that a new play by Neil Simon, *London Suite,* which was being tried out in Seattle, Washington, would be produced at a theater Off-Broadway.

As Emanuel Azenberg, who has produced Simon's plays for the last twenty-odd years, explained, it would cost $175,000 a week to run *London Suite* on Broadway but only $60,000 a week to run it Off-Broadway. There were numerous reasons for the disparity, but one of the most significant was

that on Broadway union stagehands are costly; Off-Broadway, nonunion stagehands are not. (Nor is there featherbedding Off-Broadway. One of the more amusing items about New York theater in 1994 was that Patrick Stewart, who does a brilliant one-man version of Charles Dickens's *A Christmas Carol,* wears a single costume all evening long and nothing at all on his bald head. But he had to hire a chief wig maker – which helps explain why this show, with one actor and a few pieces of furniture on a bare stage, cost $500,000 to mount.)

At one point attempts were being made to bring the Simon play to Broadway under a complex plan called the Broadway Alliance. The alliance, devised a few years ago by a consortium of concerned theater people headed by the distinguished producer Robert Whitehead, is a scheme in which all the Broadway unions and theater owners grant concessions on their normal fees in order for serious plays to be produced on Broadway. It is cheaper to produce plays Off-Broadway or in the subscription theaters Off-Off-Broadway, but Broadway remains the only place where a playwright's work can be rewarded sufficiently to encourage him to continue writing for the theater rather than abandoning it for the more lucrative fields of movie or television screenwriting. The idea that Neil Simon, one of the most successful playwrights in Broadway history, can now only be brought to Broadway under the terms of the alliance is a situation of quite breathtaking irony.

The play with which Albee returned to traditional rather than coterie audiences is not without its innovations. The characters in *Three Tall Women* do not have names. They are A, B, and C. This is to be expected in a writer who has often aimed to make his plays abstractions, but this is the only touch of the abstract in an otherwise deeply absorbing play.

A is an extremely old and wealthy woman. B is her middle-aged companion, accustomed to her crotchetiness and a useful softening agent for the outside world. C is a young woman, a lawyer, trying to get the nonagenarian A's affairs in order. At the end of the first act A has a seizure.

In a marvelous coup de théâtre, when the lights come up on the second act, a mannequin of A, who appears to be in a coma, lies on the bed, an oxygen mask over her face. Meanwhile, the three actresses playing A, B, and C have now become the three stages of A's life – eager, hopeful youth; regretful middle age; and aloof, accepting old age.

While the three ages of A wrangle with one another in the foreground, a silent drama takes place in the background. A young man enters and takes up his vigil at the mannequin's bedside. There is a sense of his making peace with the difficult old woman. This upstage drama has generally been interpreted as autobiographical, Albee's depiction of a reconciliation with his own contentious mother, from whom he was bitterly estranged. Very little in the old woman's spoken remarks about her homosexual son in the foreground suggests a softening, but there is a quiet dignity to their silent confrontation, a genuine compassion on his part that implies that even if she has not made her peace, he has.

The depiction of the three ages of life never feels genteel. Throughout the play the women's (the woman's) self-consciousness and self-realization invariably have a sexual component. One of A's clearest memories in the first act, in which her memory is often unreliable and her suspiciousness about the world around her often makes it impossible to see clearly, is of an evening many years earlier when she and her husband were undressing after a party. He entered her bathroom naked, his penis (which, in her dotage, she calls his "pee-pee") erect, with a new bracelet for her displayed on it. When it softened the bracelet fell into her lap.

In the second act B, A's middle-aged incarnation, recalls the moment when, after years of not understanding anything about sexuality because of the obfuscation of all the women around her, she suddenly understands in a moment of infidelity: "No wonder one day we come back from riding, the horse all slathered, snorting, and he takes the reins, the groom does, his hand touching the back of our thigh, and we notice, and he notices we notice, and we remember that we've noticed him before, most especially bare chested that day heaving the straw, those arms, that butt. And no wonder we smile in that way he understands so quickly, and no wonder he leads us into a further stall – into the fucking hay, for God's sake – and down we go, and it's revenge and self pity we're doing it for until we notice it turning into pleasure for its own sake, for our own sake, and we're dripping wet, and he rides us like we've seen in the pornos, and we actually scream, and then we lie there in the straw – which probably has shit on it – cooling down, and he tells us he's wanted us a lot, that he likes big women, but he didn't dare, and will he get fired now?"

It is hard to avoid noting the homoerotic cast of both these moments of reminiscence. But both have an undeniable pungency that transcends their specific details. This is also a case where the homosexual orientation (which, despite Albee's openness about his own sexuality, has never really played

Program cover for the Vineyard Theater production of Edward Albee's Pulitzer Prize–winning play

much of a role in his work, except, perhaps, as a reason for its often opaque, impersonal quality) is an instance of the play's intense personalness. The richness of the language and the uncharacteristically unrestrained fervor of the emotions this ripe language depicts both mark a return to the youthful vigor of Albee's early writing, before he became involved in verbal games to keep the audience at an intellectual and emotional distance.

Many of Albee's plays have a cerebral quality that undercuts their theatricality. *Three Tall Women*, without abandoning Albee's intellectual approach to playwriting, has an emotional core that irradiates its somewhat schematic structure. *Three Tall Women* marks a vibrant return of one of the American theater's most prodigious talents to the top of his form.

Terrence McNally, though he has been represented on the New York stage for thirty years (his first play, *And Things That Go Bump in the Night*, was

Program cover for the Manhattan Theatre Club production of Terrence McNally's play about the romantic interludes of gay men in a New York country house

produced in 1965), has never achieved the eminence of his onetime mentor, Albee, but in recent years his muse has been enormously fertile, and in *Love! Valour! Compassion!* he has achieved a new maturity and depth. *Love! Valour! Compassion!* is set in a country house about two hours north of New York on three holiday weekends over a summer. The house belongs to a highly regarded middle-aged choreographer, Gregory, who fears his artistic powers are waning. He has a young lover, who is Indian and blind.

All of the guests are gay, and their lives over the last few decades have been intertwined. Buzz, a musical-comedy fanatic, has AIDS, does volunteer work in a clinic, and designs costumes for Gregory's dance company. John, an Englishman who was once Buzz's lover, composes musicals. He had one done on Broadway many years earlier. It flopped. He remained in America and now is a re-

hearsal pianist for Gregory's company. John's current lover is an earthy Hispanic dancer, Ramon, who arouses many of the other characters. As the play progresses we learn that John has lost any sexual interest in Ramon but continues bringing him to the country to tease the other guests. Later in the play we meet John's twin brother, James, who is also dying of AIDS. James is as lovable as John is obnoxious. The final guests are a male couple, Arthur and Perry, who have been together fourteen years and feel "the stress of being role models." Perry does legal work pro bono for Gregory's company.

Like any comedy set in a country house, *Love! Valour! Compassion!* is about the various couplings and uncouplings that take place on summer nights. If it were not for the sexual orientation of the characters, these flings and infatuations might seem all too conventional. What enlivens them is McNally's lively wit.

Perhaps the most remarkable scene in the three-act play is one toward the end, when Buzz, who for most of the evening has seemed merely someone whose chief purpose is to be amusing, starts one of his comic tirades. The character was played by Nathan Lane, who had appeared in one of McNally's most outrageous, funniest plays, *The Lisbon Traviata,* in which he played a maniacal "opera queen." Buzz seems a near relation, a man for whom musical theater is at the center of everything. (Early in the play he has a nightmare – he dreams there will be a revival of *The King and I* starring Tyne Daly and Tommy Tune.)

In his third-act monologue he begins on a light level, expressing yet again his love for musical comedy. But in an uncharacteristically sober moment, his verbal flight does not veer toward the giddy. Instead he suddenly turns realistic and bitter. One of the other characters tells him that not all musicals end happily. "Yes, they do," Buzz says. "That's why I like them, even the sad ones. The orchestra plays, the characters die, the audience cries, the curtain falls, the actors get up off the floor, the audience puts on their coats and everybody goes home feeling better. That's a happy ending, Perry. Once, just once, I want to see a WEST SIDE STORY where Tony really gets it, where they all die, the Sharks and the Jets, and Maria while we're at it, and Officer Krupke, what's he doing sneaking out of the theater, get back here and die with everybody else, you son of a bitch! Or a KING AND I where Yul Brynner doesn't get up from that little Siamese bed for a curtain call. I want to see a SOUND OF MUSIC where the entire Von Trapp Family dies in an authentic Alpine avalanche. A KISS ME KATE where she's got a big cold sore on her mouth. A FUNNY THING HAPPENED ON THE WAY TO THE FORUM where the only thing that happens is nothing and it's not funny and they all go down waiting, waiting for what? Waiting for nothing, waiting for death, like everyone I know and care about is, including me. . . ."

Buzz's monologue is one of the darker moments in a play whose moods are pastel – this is a world where gaiety is never unalloyed, a world where the remembrance of misfortune and early death is never far. Even one of its most lighthearted moments – a rehearsal scene where all the guests wear tutus and do the Dance of the Little Swans from *Swan Lake* – has a muted quality. An idea that might once have seemed merely silly or campy takes on a bittersweet quality in the age of AIDS.

Despite its moments of anger and sadness, despite characters and scenes that sometimes seemed forced, what made *Love! Valour! Compassion!* a more interesting and moving work than many "AIDS plays" was its spirit of affirmation. Its central character, after all, is a choreographer who begins in self-doubt but ends with a new confidence in spite of all the unhappy things going on around him. Even the characters who have AIDS frequently assert their attachment to life. If nothing else, the play demonstrates their devotion to one another, their commitment to friendship, which transcends their disappointments in love. Moreover, the play, with its unabashed theatricality, is an expression of belief in the power of the theater itself to transcend the forces that darken our lives.

Affirmation is increasingly rare in the American theater. Much of its negative energy is simply that of the political landscape in which it is created. Over the last few decades the theater has been heavily politicized, to the point where plays sometimes seem barely disguised newspaper editorials. The sense of theater as an exercise in journalism was strong in one of the year's most talked-about productions, Anna Deavere Smith's *Twilight: Los Angeles, 1992*.

Smith, who teaches at Stanford University, first came to the attention of New York audiences a few years ago with *Fires in the Mirror,* a piece based on the Crown Heights riots that took place in Brooklyn in 1991. The riots, which continue to have political repercussions, took place in a poor Brooklyn neighborhood where blacks – some native, some Caribbean – and Hasidic Jews live uneasily side by side. In the aftermath of the riots, Smith interviewed some of the focal figures, but mainly average people who live in the neighborhood. She impersonated her subjects, weaving their voices into a sometimes illuminating, often touching collage.

Twilight: Los Angeles, 1992 is based on another riot – that which struck Los Angeles in the wake of the not-guilty verdict in the Rodney King case. Where the earlier piece was a form of reportage, Smith's polemical intentions are more noticeable in *Twilight.*

Like a good documentarian, she presents a wealth of people who reveals themselves in telling monologues. She has Rodney King's aunt, for example, share memories of her nephew "hand-fishing" when he was a boy. For her, catching fish without a hook or worm conjures up images of Africa: "I'm talkin' about them wild Africans / Not them well-raised ones." Some of the figures she interviewed are well known (King himself, Reginald Denny, Los Angeles Police Chief Darryl Gates). Some are thoughtful observers (Lani Guinier and Sen. Bill Bradley). Some are simply bystanders to these events: a pregnant woman whose fetus stopped a bullet, saving both their lives; and a bookkeeper indignant that rioters were assaulting Magnin's – "How dare you loot a store rich people go to!"

Almost none of the figures Smith depicts here elicit any emotional response. Her most successful characterizations are satiric – like a Beverly Hills real estate agent who, like many of her friends and clients, seeks refuge in the Polo Lounge of the Beverly Hills Hotel.

An interesting aspect of Smith's approach to her characters is an attempt to render their speech with photorealistic accuracy. She left in, for example, all the "uhs" and "ahs" that litter everyday speech. This is theatrical superrealism, a welter of carefully rendered details creating an impassive surface that does not necessarily illuminate anything below.

Moreover, Smith's range as an actress is not diverse enough to bring more than a few of these characters to credible life. Also, she has an unmusical voice. Admittedly, none of her characters (with the obvious exception of Jessye Norman) is vocally mellifluous, but two and a half hours of a flat voice, often rhythmically monotonous, is wearing.

What Smith has captured is less the twilight of Los Angeles, which can be quite haunting, than its distinctive glare, a harsh and enervating light that heightens what is comic about its subjects but leaves most of them diminished.

A new Arthur Miller play, *Broken Glass,* focuses on civil disorders of more than half a century

*Program cover for the Manhattan Theatre Club production of
Diane Samuels's play about German Jewish children who are
sent to England to escape the Holocaust*

ago. The title reflects *Kristallnacht,* in November 1938, when Nazis broke the windows of Jewish homes and shops all over Germany, the prelude of grislier events to come. The event has reverberations a world away, in Brooklyn, New York. At the heart of the play are an American Jew who has devoted his life to pretending he is not Jewish and his wife, who is literally paralyzed with fear at the increasing incidence of anti-Semitism in Europe.

The conjunction of the self-loathing Jew and a woman crippled by the loathing of Jews that she perceives in others is potentially explosive, but Miller clutters his play with naturalistic touches that have little vitality of their own and do not amplify his main concerns. Much of the plot concerns the sexless marriage of the Gellburgs (it is implied that the name has been changed from Goldberg). The imagery of sexual aversion and marital discord does not jell with the more-powerful images of the Nazi

era. Ultimately, *Broken Glass* seems more the outline for a play than the finished product.

Although the Holocaust has cast a shadow over the theater for many years, the enormity of the subject confounds most playwrights. This year there were two engrossing plays on this theme. One is English, Diane Samuels's *Kindertransport,* which focuses on German Jewish children whose parents have the foresight, just before the war, to send them to England, where there are families willing to take them in. Their lives are saved, but the psychic cost is incalculable. Samuels's play jumps back and forth between the present, when a young woman learns for the first time about the trials her seemingly stoic mother underwent, and the past, when the mother was a child, when she was torn from her family, harboring a resentment that, whatever their fate, she could not share it with them. What lifts the play above a series of naturalistic confrontations between mothers and daughters is Samuels's artful use of a children's book, one of the few objects remaining from the dark past, a German story called "Ratcatcher," which ties the various strands of nightmare together.

The other Holocaust play of interest is French, Charlotte Delbo's *Who Will Carry the Word?* Delbo, a Frenchwoman who spent three years in Auschwitz, wrote a play one of whose strengths is that it is nonsectarian. We learn virtually nothing about the religion or the politics of the women she describes. Since their pasts are vague, we must concentrate on their present, on the chilling reality of minute by minute in a camp.

Delbo shaped her play around the routines of everyday camp life – the lineups, the forced marches, the "selections." This deadening round of repeated actions gives the play the aura of ritual, albeit a ritual of nihilism. In its small, measured movements, it gives the audience an inkling of the numbing experience of the camps, something more disturbing than stories of torture or survival, which can have a reassuring finality.

What is interesting about Delbo's play is that it was written in 1974, well before what we might call "Holocaust consciousness" existed. It is equally interesting that it should have taken twenty years to reach New York.

This year even the imports from London were few. Apart from *Kindertransport* and a stimulating "deconstructionist" version of J. B. Priestley's 1945 *An Inspector Calls,* there were only three memorable English plays.

The most impressive was *Vita and Virginia,* in which Eileen Atkins drew on the love letters between Vita Sackville-West and Virginia Woolf to create a literate, scintillating, witty play. These women were as elegant in person as they were in their prose. Both were married but traveled in sophisticated circles, where their love affair raised few eyebrows.

A great part of their relationship is conveyed in the letters. Although they were addressing one another in print, Atkins has selected passages that make their interchanges onstage seem quite spontaneous and natural. These were not, after all, women who made idle chitchat. They valued words. If their sentences suggest calculation, it was not a case of artifice – the respect and love they had for one another were too great to admit sloppy sentiment. Atkins played Woolf, and Sackville-West was played by Vanessa Redgrave. The year offered no more civilized evening of theater.

Timberlake Wertenbaker, an American who lives and works in London, wrote a satire of the art world, *Three Birds Alighting on a Field*. Needless to say, the art world is so self-satiric that specific lampoons are almost too close to reality to be funny. (The play begins with a seemingly blank canvas being sold at auction. The totally white work, titled "No Illusions," is sold in less than a minute for a million pounds.)

The original part of the play had to do with a wealthy woman whose social-climbing husband urges her to take an interest in art to help his climbing. She expresses a vague interest in morality ("I actually want to be good," she remarks. "The women's magazines only tell me how to be thin."). Almost against her will she develops an interest in art for art's sake.

Like many of Tom Stoppard's works, his 1988 *Hapgood,* presented in New York for the first time this year, five years after it was produced in Los Angeles, is in large part an intellectual guessing game. It is set in a British spy agency run by a woman who must determine which of her employees is a double agent. One of the men in her charge, Kerner, is a Russian physicist with whom she had an affair – and a son – some years back.

Early in the play the physicist explains that certain elements in nature have a dual reality. They appear sometimes as particles, sometimes as waves. "Every time we don't look we get wave pattern," Kerner says in his slightly broken English. "Every time we look to see how we get wave pattern, we get particle pattern. The act of observing determines the reality."

A double agent has a similar identity. The same action can be perceived in quite different ways

Program cover for the Lincoln Center Theater production of Tom Stoppard's play about the search for a double agent in a British spy agency

by the two sides for which he works. Among other things, Kerner is describing the action of the play, which deals in several sets of twins. Under surveillance their behavior varies markedly.

Stoppard is also engaging in a bit of witty self-criticism. At one point Kerner (who, like Stoppard, is a refugee from the Soviet world) expresses his annoyance with Western spy novels. "I don't understand this mania for surprises," he says. "If the author knows [the identity of the spy], it's rude not to tell. In science this is understood: what is interesting is to know what is happening. When I write an experiment I do not wish you to be *surprised,* it is not a *joke*. This is why a science paper is a beautiful thing: first, here is what we will find; now here is how we find it; here is the first puzzle, here is the answer, now we can move on. This is polite. We don't save all the puzzles to make a triumph for the author — that is the dictatorship of the intelligentsia."

There are, it turns out, several double agents, one of whom is Kerner himself. The play, written a year before the fall of the Berlin Wall, contains an interesting "scientific" comment on the difference between East and West: "The West is morally superior," Kerner says. "It is in different degrees unjust and corrupt like the East. Its moral superiority lies in the fact that the system contains the possibility of its own reversal — I am enthralled by the voting, to me it has the power of an equation in nature, the masses converted to energy. Highly theoretical, of course, but it means the responsibility is everybody, you cannot pass the blame to a few gangsters."

Stoppard's verbal and intellectual prestidigitation is without peer, but a comparable magic is evident in a collection of six sketches by David Ives titled *All in the Timing*. In one, "Words, Words, Words," three monkeys — John Milton, Jonathan Swift, and Franz Kafka — are typing away in a room observed by a scientist.

"Ping drobba fft fft fft inglewarp carcinoma," Swift reads from his manuscript. "That's as far as I got."

Kafka likes the "fft fft fft" part. Swift agrees it is "onomatopoeic."

"But do you think it's *Hamlet?*" Swift asks.

"Don't ask me," Milton says. "I'm just a chimp."

This intellectual vaudeville proceeds through a discussion of just what *Hamlet* might be and why, given infinity, the three monkeys might eventually, accidentally type it, and, when they do, whether they will then have to tackle *Ulysses*.

In another sketch a teacher and a pupil fall in love in an artificial language like Esperanto. In "Variations on the Death of Trotsky" Ives presents a series of possibilities for how Trotsky met his bloody end. Throughout the play Trotsky appears onstage with a mountaineer's ax through his head.

Ives's sketches purport to be no more than sketches. But they have a wit, a magic, a theatricality far greater than many full-length plays with weightier intentions.

There was a hope of playfulness in Donald Margulies's *What's Wrong With This Picture?*, a play presented on Broadway about four years after an Off-Off-Broadway incarnation. The premise of Margulies's play is simple. A mother who died swallowing Chinese food in a restaurant returns to get her household in order, to the befuddlement of her grieving husband and son. In the earlier production the play seemed slight but beguiling. On Broadway

it was done so heavy-handedly that all its modest virtues disappeared.

Another intellectual vaudeville was Tony Kushner's *Slavs*, several scenes of which are "outtakes" from *Perestroika*, the second half of his epic *Angels in America*. While there is a modicum of plot about a pair of lesbians in Siberia, the most interesting part of the play is Kushner's sketches about bewildered Soviet apparatchiks contemplating life in a postideological, post-Marxist world.

Eric Bogosian, who is known mainly for his monologues, has written several plays for more than one actor. The latest, *SubUrbia*, is about a group of disaffected youths, a few years out of high school, who lounge about the parking lot of a convenience store talking about their largely useless lives. (Their slovenly manner and garb are in marked contrast to that of the owners of the convenience store, Indian immigrants preparing for American citizenship, well dressed and well spoken.)

Several of the denizens of the parking lot are, in a manner of speaking, artists. Much of the action of the play, for example, consists of waiting for the arrival of their old friend Pony, who has become a second- or third-tier rock star.

Not all of them are awed by his success. When he mentions he has just been interviewed, the most cynical of the group asks him what they interview him about. "My work," he says. "I explain the message of my songs: 'Tear down the walls, find honesty, reach out to another naked human being, help the revolution.' How I write it, get my ideas, you know."

Pony has achieved a certain measure of artistic visibility if not profound success. One of the others wants to go to New York "to make art." Another, who has a job packing boxes, wants to "make something that shatters the world." Buff, a pizza-joint operator, possibly the crudest of the lot, declares, "I'm a video artist, man. I been making these tapes. I ripped off a camcorder up at the mall, and I've been making these tapes. I thought, it could be, you know, something I *do*. I sent one to 'America's Funniest Home Videos.'" The cynic calls him a "post-modern idiot savant!"

As its title implies, *SubUrbia* is a comment on the mind-set of the suburbs. Pony, on his return to his roots, asks his limo driver "to roll the windows down, just so I could smell the air. The smell of freshly cut grass . . . great! I could see into the picture windows of the houses. Families watching TV, eating dinner, guys drinking beer. It's . . . the suburbs! They don't call it the American dream for nothing."

Earlier Jeff, who wants to make something "that shatters the world," screams at Buff, the "video artist," "SARAJEVO! HAITI! ARMENIA! You ever watch the news, Buffman? There's a world outside this tar pit of stupidity. This cauldron of spiritual oatmeal. It's the end of the world, man — no ideas, no hope, no future. The fucking apocalypse. You don't even know what 'apocalypse' means, do you, Buff-cake?" Buff replies, "Of course I do, man. It was a movie."

SubUrbia is at its most successful in its satiric look at feckless, pretentious youth. As the play grows darker, more nihilistic, more violent, it is less persuasive.

Over the last dozen years Chicago has been a notable source of interesting theater. This year the most worthwhile ventures from the Windy City were two works by Mary Zimmerman. One is based on tales of the Arabian Nights. A troupe of actors tells several of the lesser-known fables from that fascinating collection, the most arresting of which is a breathtaking parable of wisdom called *Sympathy the Learned,* in which learning itself comes to seem elegant and bewitching. *Arabian Nights* is notable for its reminder of how difficult and spellbinding good storytelling is.

An odder piece was Zimmerman's *The Notebooks of Leonardo Da Vinci,* in which she uses eight actors to "illustrate," in movements sometimes balletic, sometimes vaudevillean, Leonardo's theories of weight and force. At one point she has a hapless actress demonstrate his theories of flight in a complex bird costume in which rickety pieces of wood attempt to imitate feathers. In between Zimmerman depicts bits and pieces of Leonardo's life, the most interesting of which is his relationship with a ten-year-old "wild child." The overall effect is exhilarating.

A play that has made the rounds of regional theaters but has yet to be mounted in New York is *Keely and Du* by the pseudonymous Jane Martin. The play, which deals with the issue of abortion in ways that avoid the soapbox, seems notable in that it was on the short list to win the Pulitzer. A woman who is about to have an abortion is kidnapped and held captive by a "right-to-life" group until she must give birth. The "right-to-lifers" were tipped off about her visit to the abortion clinic by her abusive former husband. During her pregnancy she develops a bond with the older woman who looks after her, despite the divergence in their views.

Program cover for the Lincoln Center Theater production of Eric Bogosian's play about the lives of disaffected youths in the suburbs

All the men in the play are patriarchal brutes. The women's bond is so strong that, sometime after the captivity is over, the younger woman tends to the older one, who has had a stroke in the prison where she is paying for her crime against the younger one. Though the play achieves some balance in its presentation of the "issues," it does not transcend its status as a topical play, a theatrical editorial.

Within the last few years New York has seen more and more academic theater, plays that appeal to the arbiters of taste who give academic awards and, more important, literary grants and commissions. One such example was Suzan Lori-Parks's *The America Play.* The play focuses on an elderly African-American gravedigger who bears a resemblance to Abraham Lincoln. He sets up an amusement park where patrons can put coins into a bust of Lincoln, then step into a reproduction of the box in Ford's Theater, where the Foundling Father (as he calls himself) sits in a rocking chair enjoying *Our American Cousin.*

The patron takes a gun from a nearby table and, when Lincoln roars with laughter at the play, shoots him in the head. As Lincoln slumps forward, the customer can imitate Booth's flight from the presidential box into history, declaiming "Thus to the tyrants."

The portentous title, the reduction of American history to an amusement-park diversion or a minstrel show, ought to be provocative. But it is all curiously juiceless. Parks tries to echo the wordplay of Samuel Beckett and James Joyce, but where their verbal games derive from the unconscious poetry of everyday Dublin speech, her playfulness seems merely collegiate.

Parks is the recipient of numerous academic awards. So is Phyllis Nagy, whose play *The Scarlet Letter* is not a dramatization of Nathaniel Hawthorne's novel but rather a "sequel" to it. Its action begins after the novel ends. Where the novel derives its strength from indirection, from what remains unsaid, the characters in Nagy's adaptation never shut up.

Hawthorne's characters all operate under the cloud of Puritanism. Nagy's characters dress seven-teenth century but talk New Age. When, for example, Hester's aggrieved husband, Chillingworth, meets her lover Arthur Dimmesdale, whom he suspects (rightly, of course) of being the father of Hester's child, their encounter ends all touchy-feely. Dimmesdale himself, instead of embodying Puritan repressiveness and dishonesty, is here the very model of hip modern masculinity when he declares: "I have a femininity about me that sometimes appeals to children."

Nagy's most obnoxious touch is the character of Pearl, who in the novel is a silent reminder of Hester's sin. In this version Pearl is a nagging scold. Played by a middle-aged woman clad in scarlet, the supposedly seven-year-old Pearl constantly mouths off to her elders.

Nagy offers no real insight into the novel. She has created an evening of smart-ass dialogue, which was acted in a tiresome, declamatory style. Nagy is the recipient of two NEA playwriting fellowships as well as numerous other honors. It is to be hoped that, in the debate over whether Congress will continue to fund the NEA, no one notices that the agency must take responsibility for this joyless, witless gloss on a haunting American classic.

The Year in Children's Books

Caroline C. Hunt
College of Charleston

It was an election year in the United States, and campaigns at all levels focused on issues that affected children and their reading, directly or indirectly. This influence was not apparent at first. The early months of 1994 promised a reprise of 1993 as far as the juvenile publishing scene was concerned: a year of caution, nostalgia, and (often) mediocrity, driven by increased censorship and other social pressures, by limited funding, and by competition from other media. Though these factors continued to play a part, as the year progressed observers noted a new focus on the content of children's books. Campaign rhetoric raised awareness of some hot issues affecting juvenile publishing, especially "family values" and the ill-understood subject of multiculturalism. Politics and marketing intersected in the election year of 1994, and children's books were examined, more than usual, for what they said and what "values" they seemed to support. The results of this intersection were mixed, as publishers found their separate constituencies demanding quite different things. My annual review begins with a look at trends in publishing and censorship, with an emphasis on multiculturalism, then surveys several categories of children's books by individual title: picture books, nonfiction, books for the middle grades, and young-adult books. (This year there is no separate section for poetry; books in verse are integrated into the other sections.) Alphabets, counting books, and holiday books are excluded, as are nursery rhyme collections and most other collections of nonoriginal verse. An obituary section lists children's writers and illustrators who died in 1994, and the last portion of the review treats a related issue, the "death" of children's books. All titles are 1994 United States publications unless otherwise indicated.

Money was on publishers' minds all year – in terms not merely of profits but of possibly disastrous declines in revenue. The book fair at Bologna, Italy (Fiera del libro per ragazzi), normally an occasion for festivity, was uncharacteristically subdued; a lead article in the 9 May issue of *Publishers Weekly*

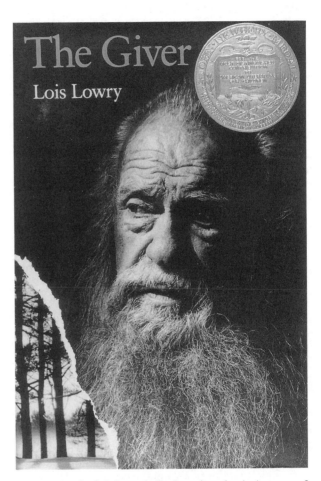

Dust jacket for Lois Lowry's Newbery Award–winning story of a young man's search for individual responsibility

was titled, appropriately, "Caution Sets The Tone." There was widespread concern that children's book buying was declining and would continue to do so. In domestic business news the acquisition of Macmillan by Paramount caused the merger of Macmillan's many imprints for children with the corresponding imprints of Simon and Schuster, Paramount's company. A total of eighteen imprints, originally scheduled to merge into seven, dwindled to only six survivors (nonfiction lines eventually went to Silver Burdett). Layoffs and resignations claimed some well-known figures in juvenile publishing. The new, leaner organization will produce a smaller number of books than before — a financial decision of concern to readers and reviewers alike. Less spectacular but equally troublesome, the children's divisions were downsized at Random House and at Western, the industry's largest juvenile publisher. Not everyone reported bad news, however. Candlewick's sales were up 30 percent in 1993, its second year in operation; Candlewick expects to break even for 1994 when its annual sales figures are analyzed. The Children's Book of the Month Club, begun in 1991, also reported healthy gains (40 percent) for 1993 and anticipated further growth in 1994. A new store, featuring Golden Books, opened in New York City in October.

Nowhere was the focus on content more evident than in the selection of the Newbery and Caldecott medal winners, traditionally announced early in the year. (The Newbery honors the best children's book of the year and the Caldecott the best illustrations; both are selected by committees of the American Library Association.) Lois Lowry garnered her second Newbery for *The Giver* (Houghton Mifflin), a dystopian fantasy about a society which a young man eventually leaves in exchange for the possibility of individual responsibility — or, perhaps, for an early death; the ending is ambiguous, unlike most Newbery winners. Lowry's book provoked widespread discussion among both professionals and young readers; *The Giver* went immediately into classroom use, and unofficial teacher's guides were distributed over the Internet as well as through more conventional sources. Though most agreed that Lowry's Newbery book was less well written than many and derivative in theme, the provocative content overrode those concerns. *The Giver* attracted censorship attempts from both sides. Some conservative adults objected to the portrayal of society as oppressive and of adults as being no wiser than children; more specific objections concerned the reversal of gender roles and the inclusion of euthanasia. Ironically, liberal readers also disliked what they perceived as gender bias; both sides expressed reservations about the suitability of the work for children in elementary school. The Caldecott Medal for best picture book went to Allen Say's *Grandfather's Journey* (Houghton Mifflin), also about a young man who leaves one society, Japanese, for a new one, American; in this case the protagonist returns to his native land but remains divided between two cultures. Coincidentally, both Say and Lowry lived in the same neighborhood in Japan as adolescents and both have the same editor, Walter Lorraine. Both books treated serious themes in age-appropriate fashion, a change from the more lightweight winners of several previous years.

In keeping with the message-oriented mood of 1994, other awards also stressed serious themes of current interest. The Coretta Scott King award for story went to Angela Johnson's moving family tale, *Toning the Sweep* (Orchard, 1993), and the award for illustration to Tom Feelings's *Soul Looks Back in Wonder*. Russell Freedman's biography of Eleanor Roosevelt (Clarion) received a well-deserved Boston Globe–Horn Book Award for nonfiction; the picture-book award went to *Grandfather's Journey* and the fiction award to Vera Williams's family story, *Scooter* (Greenwillow). Britain's Carnegie Medal attracted attention when some judges were apparently unhappy with the eventual winner, Robert Swindell's *Stone Cold* (Hamish Hamilton, 1993), a shocker about homeless adolescents preyed on by a serial killer. The Greenaway Medal took a more conventional turn with Rosemary Sutcliff's posthumous *Black Ships Before Troy*, illustrated by Alan Lee (Frances Lincoln, 1993; U.S. publication, Delacorte, 1993). Some awards bucked the trends, particularly those depending overtly on popularity or sales. The Texas Bluebonnet award, longest of the various state awards chosen by young readers, went to Phyllis Reynolds Naylor's *Shiloh* (1991), the 1992 Newbery winner. Other state awards followed similar lines. One national award delighted many: Janell Cannon's luminous *Stellaluna* (1993) won the ABBY for a title most frequently recommended by booksellers. Many readers had hoped for at least Caldecott Honor designation for this story of a young fruit bat raised as a bird, but since first-time authors and illustrators are rarely serious contenders for the big awards, the ABBY was a satisfying recompense. *Stellaluna* outsold most 1994 Caldecott Honor designees in reporting bookstores throughout 1994. A toy bat, displayed with the book but available separately, also sold nicely.

The Giver and *Grandfather's Journey* touched upon the most important issue in children's-book publishing during the year: in examining individuals and their cultures, they raised the question of just what children's books should say about society. Focused religious objections to certain kinds of books have been increasing for several years, notably in attempts by Fundamentalist parents to ban books about witchcraft and the like. Schools and public libraries across the country reported a continuation of this trend, heightened by the election of Christian Right candidates to school boards. (For example, in Charleston, South Carolina, there was a complaint against the C. S. Lewis classic allegory, *The Lion, the Witch, and the Wardrobe* [1950], despite its distinctly Christian teachings; the witch, apparently, caused the problem. The district kept the book and awaited an appeal while several of us gathered pro-Lewis materials. The appeal never came.) However, the 1994 debate also took a broader form as parents, educators, and critics — joined, in an election year, by an array of political figures — tried to define what ideals they wanted children's books to present. In this attempt the educators' ideals of multiculturalism and toleration came up against an opposing conservative ideal of (and, sometimes, specifically "American") moral standards. Two books from adult best-seller lists exemplify the trend: James Garner's *Politically Correct Bedtime Stories* (Macmillan) and William Bennett's *The Book of Virtues* (Simon and Schuster). Portions of the wickedly funny Garner book had been circulating widely before official publication; "Little Red Riding Hood," for instance, appeared early on various Internet lists. A series of cartoons about bedtime stories in *The New Yorker,* though unrelated, made the same point about the excesses of the ultraliberal approach. Bennett's book, ostensibly intended for actual reading aloud, took the straightforward approach that children can be made virtuous by reading about virtue – in this case, virtue of a very traditional kind. Significantly, the only other child-related books on the adult best-seller list of *The New York Times* for any length of time during 1994 were a holdover from the previous year, *Oh, the Places You'll Go!* (Random House) by Dr. Seuss, and *Zlata's Diary* (Viking), a journal kept by young Zlata Filipović in Sarajevo, treated in greater detail in the nonfiction category below.

Anniversaries and exhibits, less nostalgic as a group than last year's, ranged from the sentimental to the controversial. On the sentimental side Heineman Galleries in New York mounted a show of Ludwig Bemelmans's work (Bemelmans created the Madeline books), and an exhibit called *Three Picture Book Writers Who Established the Golden Period of American Picture Books, 1920–1940,* from the Kerlan Collection at the University of Minnesota, toured Japan for ten months. The three illustrators were Virginia Lee Burton, Marie Hall Ets, and Wanda Gág. The Little House on the Prairie industry revved up its expansion into toys, activities, and crafts, marking the centenary of Laura Ingalls Wilder's family migration to Missouri. In a similar venture the American Girls series — though not marking any anniversary — continued to expand into toys and related ac-

Dust jacket for Allen Say's Caldecott Medal–winning story about a young man's experiences in two cultures, Japanese and American

tivities; some librarians removed the advertisements and order forms from American Girls books before shelving them. The Peter Rabbit mania of last year's centenary gradually abated. Mercer Mayer's "Little Critter" turned twenty-five. Enthusiasts marked the eightieth birthday of Tove Jansson, creator of the Moomintrolls, with a conference in Finland, and a new Moomintroll title was announced (but not available when this article went to press). On the more controversial side San Francisco International Airport exhibited *Multicultural Children's Literature* from the Kerlan Collection, and the seventy-fifth anniversary of Children's Book Week brought various celebrations, most of them resolutely multicultural. The twenty-fifth anniversary of John Steptoe's *Stevie* (1969) showed how much has changed in children's books in a quarter of a century: Steptoe's strikingly illustrated story, which appeared in *Life* when the author-illustrator was only eighteen, shocked many with its depiction of ghetto children's life and language. Now it is regarded as a classic. Less change has come about in another area: John Donovan's *I'll Get There, It Better Be Worth the*

Trip (1969) also reached the quarter-century mark, but books depicting homosexuality are still almost as controversial as then. Marion Dane Bauer, interviewed in the summer 1994 *Bookbird* about her new anthology, summed this up by quoting a librarian's statement to her: "It's all right to write about homosexuality as long as your characters die in the end." Harcourt Brace observed the fiftieth anniversary of master ironist James Thurber's story, *The Great Quillow* (1944), with a colorful new edition. And, as if to remind critics and readers how wrong committees can be, Peter F. Neumeyer brought out a splendid version of the finest children's book ever to be denied the Newbery Award: *The Annotated Charlotte's Web* (HarperCollins).

Censorship attempts in 1994, whether narrowly focused or not, took place in an increasingly conservative atmosphere linking individual reading not merely to good individual morals but to good (or bad) citizenship. A new organization called Of the People, founded in January and based in Arlington, Virginia, announced its intention to push for a parental rights amendment in state legislatures throughout 1994–1995: "The rights of parents to direct the upbringing and educating of their children shall not be infringed." Some professional groups felt that this amendment could adversely affect libraries, both school and public; the amendment was slated for discussion in several states. On the other side of the ideological fence People for the American Way reported 462 censorship cases in 1993–1994; the count and also the tenor and the numerical accuracy of the report were challenged by Focus on the Family, a conservative group based in Colorado. In August an amendment to the Elementary and Secondary Education Act proposed to cut off funds to school systems in which any part of the program "has either the purpose or effect of encouraging or supporting homosexuality as a positive lifestyle alternative" – language which disappeared in later committee revisions. Many public figures, even those with moderate views, hesitated to oppose would-be censors in 1994 – apparently because they might appear to be opposing "morality" or "American" values. In May the Oconee County (Georgia) Board of Education engaged in a prolonged debate about profanity in schoolbooks; one member, James Hunter, wanted to pull John Steinbeck's *The Red Pony* (1937) – along with many other classics – from school shelves because of its language. "I don't care who the author is or how good or great they might be," he was quoted as saying. "If they cuss, they lower their standards." The board's attorney advised that a lawsuit would prob-

ably ensue on First Amendment grounds; Hunter urged going to court if necessary, but fellow board members declined to bring the matter to a vote. One of them, Chuck Horton, made an impassioned statement in favor of students' need to read, concluding that if Hunter's motion were to pass, "you won't have to worry about progress in Oconee County. You won't have to worry about our school system growing." Commenting on the entire Oconee County nonevent, Bruce Murray of the University of Georgia wryly observed, "Finally, a workable motivational proposal to actually get high school kids reading Steinbeck!"

The first major censorship case of the year was also one of the most striking: a library aide in Kalispell, Montana, lost her job after lending two books from her own collection to two students researching a paper on witchcraft. After complaints from parents the principal (backed by all but one of the school's teachers) fired the aide, Debbie Denzer. Support for Denzer came from many quarters, including the American Library Association's Office for Intellectual Freedom, an op-ed piece in *The New York Times,* the Montana Library Association (which awarded Denzer its intellectual freedom award), the Montana ACLU, and the Freedom to Read Foundation. After several reversals the school board eliminated Denzer's position; meanwhile, the two students did their research on bison.

A high percentage of censorship cases involved the explicitly stated idea that reading the questioned materials would directly affect children's behavior and/or family relationships. In El Paso, Texas, Andrea Berkenkemper requested the removal of Maurice Sendak's *In the Night Kitchen* (1970); she was quoted by *American Libraries* as saying that she and her young son "were offended by the fact the little boy pictured did not have any clothes on and it pictured his private area. Please remove this book from your shelves. *It discourages family reading time* [my italics]." Though the book has been a frequent censorship target – sometimes leading librarians to paint little diapers on the main character, according to widespread reports – the expressed connection with family reading time is new. (Sendak's illustrations for Iona and Peter Opie's collection *I Saw Esau* were challenged in San Antonio, Texas, in April.) Another parent, this time in Putnam County, Florida, filed a request to remove Anthony Browne's *Zoo* (1992), winner of Britain's prestigious Greenaway Medal, from the public library's juvenile collection – based largely on the portrayal of a verbally abusive father. This parent, too, cited family reading time ("I read to my children every night but had to change the harshness of [the] father's comments"). Carol D. Fiore of the State Library of Florida reports that a review committee retained the book; no appeal has yet been filed. In a similar case *American Libraries* reported a parental objection to David Greenberg's rhymed picture book, *Slugs* (1983), on the grounds that it "is frightening, has no educational value, and *promotes bad behavior* [my italics]." The school reclassified the book as poetry.

More-general attacks on books by Stephen King (Bismarck, North Dakota) and on Joanna Cole's *Asking About Sex and Growing Up* (1988) (Anchorage, Alaska) were not successful. However, another behavior-oriented protest worked: the Mediapolis, Iowa, school board reversed a committee decision to retain Judy Blume's often-censored *Forever* (1975), which its opponents said "does not *promote abstinence and monogamous relationships* [and] lacks any aesthetic, literary, or social value" (my italics). Again, the protest and its target are old, but the explicitly behavior-oriented argument is the current language of successful censors. Ironically, the same book came under another kind of attack from professionals corresponding via an Internet group; some felt that the unprotected sex in Blume's pre-AIDS romance might promote risk-taking among young readers. The possibility of adding a disclaimer at the beginning of the book was also discussed (and rejected by most).

Many of the behavior-oriented arguments focused on multiculturalism, which was perceived very differently by its proponents and by its enemies. To many, multiculturalism means, simply, considering other cultures than the dominant middle-class American ethos – for instance, third-world cultures. To others it means looking at "minority" cultures such as the African American and Native American, or at the subcultures of "disenfranchised" groups such as lesbians and gays. A helpful article on this confusion appeared in *Publishers Weekly* on 18 July: "The Cult of Multiculturalism," by Michael Thomas Ford (who makes distinctions more detailed than the simple ones I have outlined). In terms of my own roundup, since most participants in the various multicultural arguments do not distinguish between one brand of multiculturalism and another, I will consider examples from all of these categories. Frank Borzellieri of the District 24 school board in Queens, New York, announced on 17 February a plan to find and pull "anti-American" books from school libraries in all boroughs. *Newsweek* (10 March) quotes Borzellieri as calling multiculturalism "an anti–Western Euro-

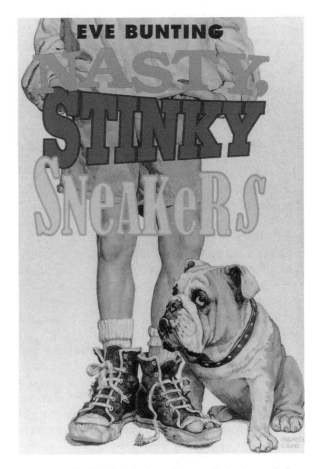

Dust jacket for Eve Bunting's comic story of a boy's search for his odoriferous shoes

pean focus in a lot of curriculums in this country." (*The New York Times* did not cover his statement; an anonymous editor is quoted in *Publishers Weekly* as calling the speech "not newsworthy.") Opponents rallied, and Borzellieri's attempt failed. Conservative talk shows also targeted the idea of multiculturalism as an unhealthy interest in things foreign, linking it to a lack of patriotism. Meanwhile, however, publishers found the production of "foreign" (especially Latino) books to be very profitable – certainly a fine example of "American" free enterprise, as I shall describe shortly. Supporting the minority concept of multiculturalism, the Young Adult Library Services Division of the ALA gave its Margaret A. Edwards Award, for lifetime achievement, to the noted African American author Walter Dean Myers – not only a well-deserved honor for this prolific and popular writer but a clear political statement. Outside of the library world, publishers sought multicultural titles (in all senses) to balance their offerings, and textbook writers were admonished to include multicultural considerations in discussing children's books. (In one case known to me, an author was advised by nearly all the expert reviewers of his first edition to increase the multicultural content for a second edition.)

In another area of multiculturalism, gay and lesbian materials, censorship attempts continued unabated while most librarians and critics, and some publishers, went in the opposite direction. The American Library Association's Social Responsibilities Round Table sponsored a program called "Beyond *Daddy's Roommate*" at the ALA's midwinter conference; participants at the program came from the *Bulletin from the Center of Children's Books* and the Missouri State Library, as well as from ordinary public libraries and from publishers. Marion Dane Bauer's collection, *Am I Blue? Coming Out from the Silence* (HarperCollins), was featured at the same conference, enthusiastically reviewed, and promoted boldly by its publisher; the lead item in the *Harper-Collins Chronicle,* a newsletter about the firm's juvenile books, discussed Bauer's book for a full page under the header "Reflections on Children's Book Publishing on the 25th Anniversary of the Stonewall Riots." Proceeds from the book, according to the newsletter, will go to PFLAG (Parents and Friends of Lesbians and Gays). Another noteworthy collection came from Alyson Press, which specializes in gay/lesbian materials: *Two Teenagers in Twenty: Writings by Gay and Lesbian Youth,* edited by Ann Heron. The subtitle is significant: unlike the other collection, Heron's consists of writing *by* gay and lesbian teenagers, while the (fictional) stories in Bauer's anthology come from established adult authors, many of whom are not themselves gay or lesbian.

Publishers advertised their multicultural wares (in all senses) widely in the professional journals. August House Publishers took out a full-page ad in *School Library Journal* touting "New Multicultural Tales," showcasing, somewhat improbably, a book by Ed Stivender called *Raised Catholic — Can You Tell?* Other titles included *Race With Buffalo and Other Native American Stories for Young Readers,* adapted by Richard and Judy Dockrey Young, and Jackie Torrence's *The Importance of Pot Liquor,* a collection of African American tales, carefully chosen and crisply told. Lee and Low, specializing in "Multicultural Literature for Young Readers," continued to promote *Joshua's Masai Mask* (1993), by Dakari Hru, with pictures by Anna Rich. Meanwhile, Rich teamed up with Angela Shelf Medearis to produce two books in the new Rainbow Biographies series from Lodestar ("an important series of biographies of well-known and lesser-known people

of color," according to the catalogue). The first titles were *Dare to Dream: Coretta Scott King and the Civil Rights Movement* and *Little Louis and the Jazz Band: The Story of Louis "Satchmo" Armstrong.* Both books used an interesting mix of drawings and photographs. (Medearis also had six other minority-oriented titles out for 1994, of which the most notable was *Our People,* for Atheneum, a gentle tale of parent and child examining their heritage.) The Rosen Publishing Group promoted a series for library collections, The Heritage Library of African Peoples, of which each volume is devoted to a separate ethnic group. Lodestar, not noted hitherto as a champion of multiculturalism, announced another new series, A World of My Own, by Kathleen Krull, with photographs by David Hautzig (son of the writer Esther Hautzig). The Dutton/Cobblehill/Lodestar summer catalogue pronounced that the enterprise "spotlights some 'hidden' communities in the United States through the voices and faces of children who actually live there." *City Within a City: How Kids Live in Chinatown* attempted to portray the everyday lives of Chinese Americans in New York, but reviewers felt it was simplistic and, in places, condescending, despite Hautzig's fine photographs. *The Other Side: How Kids Live in a California Latino Neighborhood,* which received less attention, was similar. Multiculturalism received a sort of official imprimatur with Susan Auerbach's six-volume *Encyclopedia of Multiculturalism* (Marshall Cavendish).

Individual books, whether fiction or nonfiction, were expressly marketed as multicultural whenever possible. One example was Naomi Shihab Nye's story, *Sitti's Secret* (Four Winds), about a young Arab American girl's visit to her Palestinian grandmother; advertising by Four Winds stressed the scarcity of material about Arabs and Arab Americans. Virtually every mention of *How Rabbit Tricked Otter and Other Cherokee Trickster Stories* (HarperCollins), by Gayle Ross with pictures by Murv Jacobs, talked about the heritage of the authors. (A recommendation in the NCTE *Council Chronicle* began, "a Cherokee storyteller and a Cherokee artist collaborate to record stories that have been passed orally through generations of the Cherokee Nation." Other reviews, and HarperCollins promotions, followed suit.) Even Puffin, scarcely a multicultural publisher in any ordinary sense, put a Native American boy on the cover of its summer catalogue — marking the arrival of Clyde Robert Bulla's *Eagle Feather* in paperback ("Originally published in 1953 — now available for the first time in paperback!"). A blurb inside the catalogue reassures readers that this aged title is genuinely multicultural: Bulla, according to Puffin, gathered "authentic background" by visiting Navajo lands, and "Tom Two Arrows [the illustrator] is a pure-blood Iriquois [*sic*], born and educated on the Onondaga reservation in New York. An authority on Indian folklore, Mr. Two Arrows has designed exhibits for the American Museum of Natural History." Hugh Lewin's *Jafta: the Homecoming* (Knopf / Random House), illustrated by Lisa Kopper, capitalized on recent events in South Africa in its moving depiction of a father's long-awaited return to his family. As has been increasingly the case, most reviewers failed to indicate, or perhaps were not aware, that this was not technically a new title; its original British publication date was 1992 (Hamish Hamilton). Another import was Nancy Farmer's science-fiction thriller *The Ear, the Eye, and the Arm* (Orchard), set in Zimbabwe; the original version appeared in 1989 as *The Eye, the Ear, and the Arm* (College Press, Harare, Zimbabwe). Morrow brought out an attractive picture book showing people of different skin tones, Sheila Hamanake's *All the Colors of the Earth,* and Little, Brown offered Mary Ann Hobermann's *My Song Is Beautiful: Poems and Pictures in Many Voices.* Nearly every publisher featured retellings and collections of Native American, African, and African American folktales.

The most significant developments in multicultural publishing, however, involved the increasingly aggressive marketing of Latino materials. From an almost total absence of books in this area a decade or so ago, publishing houses have increased their output dramatically in the last few years. The first step, for most established publishers, was the inclusion of Latino authors and characters. More recently three further developments have occurred: the proliferation of books in Spanish and bilingual books; an increasing emphasis on treating, in books, the experience of growing up Latino in the United States; and the emergence of new specialty publishers in this field. An example of the first trend is a HarperCollins bilingual book, *Radio Man/Don Radio,* by Sandra Dorros, following the example of last year's *Hermanas/Sisters,* by Gary Paulsen, from Harcourt Brace. For the read-aloud set another mainline publisher, Little, Brown, offered bilingual songs: *Los pollitos dicen / The Baby Chicks Sing,* by Nancy Abraham Hall and Jill Syverson-Stork, with pictures by Kay Chorao. A bilingual book that analyzes the Latino experience more consciously is a collection edited by Lori M. Carlson for Edge Books, *Cool Salsa: Bilingual Poems on Growing Up Latino in the United States.* New publishing ventures were ambitious in scope. Piñata Books, an imprint

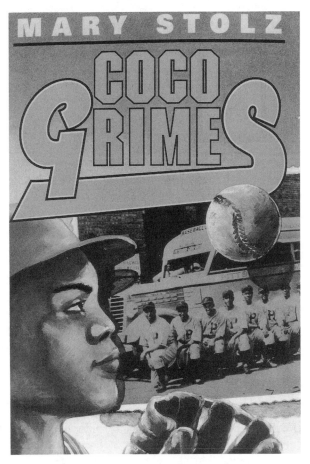

Dust jacket for Mary Stolz's story about a boy's visit with his grandfather to see a veteran of baseball's Negro League

of Arte Público Press (University of Houston), is "devoted to providing materials for children that authentically and realistically portray themes, characters and customs unique to U.S. Hispanic culture." Early offerings included a bilingual picture book, Pat Mora's *The Desert Is My Mother / El desierto es mi madre,* illustrated by Daniel Lechón; three attractive anthologies; and a short novel for middle-grade readers, *Juanita Fights the School Board,* by Gloria Velásquez. Atheneum introduced a new line of books in Spanish, Libros Colibrí, selected in consultation with the noted educator, translator, and children's author Dr. Alma Flor Ada. All titles were simultaneously released in English-language "co-editions." Some early double releases were Karen Ackerman's *By the Dawn's Early Light,* illustrated by Catherine Stock, and the Spanish edition, *Al amanecer,* translated by Flor Ada, who also wrote the imprint's first major critical and popular success, *Dear Peter Rabbit* (Spanish edition *Querido Pedrín*), illustrated by Leslie Tryon.

The impact of increasingly available children's books in Spanish and/or parallel or bilingual editions has won rapid acceptance. *School Library Journal* now regularly reviews Spanish titles in its February, August, and November issues. In spite of efforts in some communities to restrict the purchase of foreign-language materials with public funds, the titles are selling well and being widely distributed, both in libraries and through retail outlets; I noted several handsome Dorling-Kindersley board books, entirely in Spanish, in a local Kmart. In addition to Spanish materials from large U.S. publishers and the new ventures listed above, Spanish-language books are being imported from Madrid and from several outlets in Mexico. Distributors and retailers advertising specialized inventories include Astran and Fiesta Book Company (both in Miami), Lectorum Publications and Bilingual Publications (New York), Hispanic Books Distributors (Tucson, Arizona), Libros Sin Fronteras (Olympia, Washington), and Mariucca Iaconi Book Imports (San Francisco). Twenty years ago these advertisements would not have appeared in mainstream professional reviewing journals.

Picture books, always a large and miscellaneous category, became even harder to classify in 1994. The traditional rule (picture books for the very young, then a transitional type of narrative for those beginning to read, and "chapter books" for the middle grades and above) has given way to a greater separation between form (or, at least, format) and content. Many picture-intensive publications are marketed and reviewed for "all ages" – for instance, the stunningly successful "Magic Eye" books issued by N. E. Thing and the various cross-section books, particularly those by Stephen Biesty. At the upper end of the age scale, "graphic" fiction – a sophisticated form of what used to be called comic books – appeals to many young adults.

The idea that picture books are not only for the very young makes possible the most talked-about children's book of 1994, Patricia Polacco's *Pink and Say* (Philomel), frequently mentioned as an award contender. In format *Pink and Say* is a typical "large picture book" with glossy paper, a color picture on every page, and a modest amount of text. However, the story is not what one might expect in this format: Polacco retells a tale passed down in her family, about a wounded young Union soldier, Sheldon ("Say"), who is rescued by an equally young Union soldier ("Pink") from the "48th Colored" regiment. The narrative is brief and bleak; sheltered by Pink's mother, Moe Moe, the boys witness her death at the hands of marauding soldiers, then are captured and taken to Andersonville, where they are forcibly separated and Pink is

hanged (though his death is not part of the actual text). The sensation caused by *Pink and Say* eclipsed other 1994 offerings by the ever-popular author. *My Rotten Red-Headed Older Brother* (Simon and Schuster Books for Younger Readers) outlines a progression of sibling rivalry, crisis, and reconciliation. *Firetalking* (R. C. Owen), a short illustrated autobiography in the new Meet the Author series, describes Polacco's storytelling heritage. Forthcoming in 1995 is a collection showing her masterful use of that heritage, *Babushka's Mother Goose* (Philomel).

Another picture book that many considered unsuitable for the very young was *Night of the Gargoyles* (Clarion), with text by the prolific writer-for-all-ages Eve Bunting and illustrations by David Wiesner, who won the 1993 Caldecott for his surrealistic *Tuesday* (1992). Wiesner's sinister black-and-white pictures and Bunting's imaginative text did not combine as well as might have been expected; the result is interesting but not wholly successful. Chris Raschka, author-illustrator of the popular 1994 Caldecott Honor Book *Yo! Yes?* (1993) and the unjustly neglected 1992 picture book *Charlie Parker Played Be Bop* (Orchard), produced an ambitious look at fantasy and reality in *Elizabeth Imagined an Iceberg* (Orchard). Many major 1994 picture books fit more neatly into the traditional preschool category. Pam Conrad's *The Tub Grandfather* (HarperCollins), illustrated by Richard Egielski, reunites the little wooden family introduced in her earlier book, *The Tub People* (1989). Karla Kuskin's *City Dog* (Clarion), with illustrations by the author, takes an urban character out into the countryside where, predictably, he is at a loss. The verse story and Kuskin's pastel pictures complement each other beautifully. Leo Lionni once again performed the magic of his colorful collage work in *An Extraordinary Egg* (Knopf), an appealing tale of an alligator hatched by some frogs who believe him to be a chicken.

Several perennially popular illustrators continued their output of high-quality traditional picture books for the very young. Molly Bang's *One Fall Day* (Greenwillow) was a pleasant, if predictable, tale of everyday life, as was Nancy Tafuri's *This Is the Farmer,* also from Greenwillow. Emily Arnold McCully's *My Real Family* (Browndeer / Harcourt Brace), third in her series about the Bear Family, explored issues of jealousy and alienation in a reassuring manner. Gloria Jean Pinkney teamed up again with husband Jerry Pinkney to produce *The Sunday Outing* (Dial), a parallel to their touching 1992 story, *Back Home. The Sunday Outing* details a young girl's weekend trips to the Philadelphia train station, her wish to visit family in North Carolina, and the way her wish comes true. Mem Fox's *Sophie* (Harcourt Brace), illustrated by Aminah Brenda Lynn Robinson, follows a young girl's relationship with her grandfather from love to loss. Natalie Babbitt highlighted the normalcy even of royal families in *Bub, or the Very Best Thing* (HarperCollins), about a king and queen who differ about how to raise their young son – a book which seemed rather ironic in a year of highly publicized royal-family problems. An important picture book of the year came from an author who usually writes for older children; this was *All the Places to Love* (HarperCollins), by Patricia MacLachlan, who won the Newbery for *Sarah, Plain and Tall* (1985). Although *All the Places to Love,* with relentlessly sentimental pictures by Mike Wimmer, took criticism from adult readers who disliked its idealization of farm and family life, the book sold steadily.

For slightly older picture-book readers, a brace of veteran authors extended successful series. Betsy Byars's *The Golly Sisters Ride Again* (Harper-Collins), with pictures by Sue Truesdell, continued the comic saga of the sisters for the I Can Read Series, and Helen Cresswell recycled another popular comic character in *Posy Bates, Again* (Macmillan), illustrated by Kate Aldous. Another comic series addition was *Sheep Take a Hike* (Houghton Mifflin), by Nancy Shaw, with pictures by Margot Apple, showing the popular sheep trekking through the countryside in a series of amusing incidents. Cynthia Rylant, whose 1994 Henry and Mudge book was widely discussed at the end of 1994 in prepublication, produced three other early reader books: *Mr. Putter and Tabby Pour the Tea, Mr. Putter and Tabby Bake the Cake,* and *Mr. Putter and Tabby Walk the Dog,* all from Harcourt Brace. Another series story for beginning readers was Barbara Baker's *One Saturday Morning* (Dutton), with pictures by Kate Duke, an Easy Readers book about a bear family.

Several highly popular animal characters reappeared in 1994. After an absence of several years, a beloved crocodile returned to delight his many fans in Bernard Waber's *Lyle at the Office* (Houghton Mifflin), an updated, still hilarious adventure. (Lyle first appeared in 1961.) A well-received sequel was Susan Meddaugh's wonderful *Martha Calling* (Houghton Mifflin), in which the intrepid mongrel wins a radio call-in contest and takes her family off for a free holiday – only to find "no dogs allowed." The pictures of Martha disguised as an old granny are as satisfying as the eventual happy ending; Martha, who first appeared in *Martha Speaks* (1992), is surely the most appealing picture-book dog since Harry of

Dust jacket for Knopf's new edition of Langston Hughes's 1932 book of poems for young readers

Gene Zion's *Harry, the Dirty Dog* and its sequels. Another popular dog hero stars in Alexandra Day's *Carl Makes a Scrapbook* (Farrar Straus Giroux), in which the kindly Rottweiler engages in some interactive fun with young readers. Imaginary animals populate Ursula LeGuin's 1994 series book, *Wonderful Alexander and the Catwings* (Orchard), illustrated by S. D. Schindler, another attractive little volume in the Catwings series.

Nonseries books included contributions from new writers and new ventures by more established ones. Newcomer Susan Grohmann's book, *The Dust Under Mrs. Merriweather's Bed* (Whispering Coyote Press, Gloucester, Massachusetts), offered a whimsical account of an earthling boy's observation of skydweller Mrs. Merriweather's housecleaning, which results in clouds. Two other stand-alone titles deal with music. Carol Purdy solved the music-lesson doldrums in *Mrs. Merriwether's Musical Cat* (Putnam), and Bill Martin, Jr., portrayed a bizarre one-man band in *The Maestro Plays* (Holt), brilliantly illustrated with cut-paper illustrations by Vladimir

Radunsky. In the realm of outright fantasy, Mitra Modaressi's *The Dream Pillow* (Orchard) concerns a pillow which brings bad dreams and how its effect is changed. A favorite with young readers and professionals was *Harvey Potter's Balloon Farm* (Lothrop, Lee, and Shepard), by Jerdine Nolen, with pictures by Mark Buehner, a piece of inspired whimsy. Caroline Binch's *Gregory Cool* (Dial) tells of a young boy's visit to relatives in Tobago. (Binch is the illustrator of Mary Hoffman's 1991 hit, *Amazing Grace*, which coincidentally was reissued in Britain in a parallel English/Urdu version. A sequel called *Boundless Grace*, from the same author/illustrator team, is forthcoming in 1995.) Lois Ehlert's unusual artwork, incorporating beads and other collage materials, put *Mole's Hill: A Woodland Tale* (Harcourt, Brace) on many "best" lists for 1994; the story itself concerns a mole literally creating a mountain. Another collage artist, Elisa Kleven, came up with a winner in *The Paper Princess* (Dutton), a fantasy. Roy Gerrard's *Croco'nile* (Farrar Straus Giroux) combines an ancient history lesson, an introduction to hieroglyphics, an engaging brother/sister team, and a snappy adventure plot. An extended pun forms the basis of *Truman's Aunt Farm* (Houghton Mifflin), by Jama Kim Rattigan, with pictures by G. Brian Karas, in which an expected "ant" farm turns out to be a surplus of "aunts." Rattigan does wonders with this idea. Mark Teague's *Pigsty* (Scholastic) also uses comic literalism, introducing real pigs into a small boy's messy room.

Among well-established picture-book authors and illustrators, some excellent (and some mediocre) stand-alone titles emerged. A popular British import was Helen Oxenbury's rollicking *It's My Birthday* (Candlewick), in which comic animals make a cake. (Oxenbury's numerous other 1994 titles were reissues.) A more subversive British import was Anthony Browne's *The Big Baby* (Knopf), about a not-very-grown-up father. From New Zealand's Margaret Mahy came *The Rattlebang Picnic* (Dial), in which a family visits a volcano that turns out to be active. Amy Tan, better known for her adult books, made another attempt to capture the juvenile audience with *The Chinese Siamese Cat* (Macmillan), illustrated by Gretchen Shields; this was not generally well received. *The Three Golden Keys* (Doubleday), by Peter Sís, tells of a balloonist's trip to Prague (where Sís grew up). The main body of the book adapts local legend. The irrepressible Jon Scieszka produced another self-reflexive work, *The Book that Jack Wrote* (Viking), illustrated by Daniel Adel. Paul Zelinsky, who has illustrated many Beverly Cleary books and written his own (including a

delightful Rumplestiltskin), teamed up with newcomer Anne Isaacs in the sleeper of the year, *Swamp Angel* (Dutton), a Tennessee tall tale which was being mentioned as an award contender by year's end and was named a Best Illustrated Book of the Year by *The New York Times*. Finally, the old master, William Steig, forged a charming story of a young pig with a harmonica in *Zeke Pippin* (HarperCollins) – a welcome addition in a year when several other masters of illustration, notably Maurice Sendak and Chris Van Allsburg, published no picture books at all.

Several picture books extended the realm of historical fiction to very young readers. Jennifer Armstrong, whose *Chin Yu Min and the Ginger Cat* (1993) was a favorite with critics, scored again with *Little Salt Lick and the Sun King* (Crown), illustrated by Jon Goodell, an upbeat tale of a turnspit boy at Versailles. Another Armstrong historical book, *The Whittler's Tale* (Tambourine), was less well received, with the perception that Valery Vasiliev's elaborate illustrations overwhelmed the text. From the British author Leon Garfield, known for his novels of eighteenth-century London for older children, came *The Saracen Maid* (Simon and Schuster), with pictures by John O'Brien. This beginning chapter book, set in the twelfth century, follows a young boy's adventures far from his English home. Native American historical books, again, caused concern about the line between fiction and nonfiction; Jewel Grutman's *The Ledgerbook of Thomas Blue Eagle* (Thomasson-Grant), with artwork by Gay Matthaei and Adam Cuijanovic, is a fictional narrative set up in the form of a journal written by a student at a nineteenth-century Indian school. Though reviewers were positive, some professionals felt that the book did not clearly identify itself as fictional and might be mistaken for fact – a legitimate concern in the wake of Susan Jeffers's *Brother Eagle, Sister Sky: A Message from Chief Seattle* (1991), which was so heavily "adapted" from the ideas of Chief Seattle as to have virtually no connection with him yet has been accepted unquestioningly by readers as an account of a famous speech (which never existed). Robert Sabuda, who last year illustrated Roy Owen's *The Ibis and the Egret*, adapted the early life of a pharaoh in a fine pictorial biography, *Tutankhamen's Gift* (Atheneum).

As usual, many picture books were retellings of folk and fairy tales, legends, and familiar stories, sometimes with a revisionist twist. Two leaders in this category were from well-established artists. Tomie de Paola's *Christopher: The Holy Giant* (Holiday House) lovingly re-creates the traditional story, complete with an afterword explaining why the beloved Christopher is no longer considered, officially, a saint. Very different, but equally popular, was Julius Lester's *John Henry* (Dial), with strong and compelling pictures by Jerry Pinkney. Many offerings were new versions of well-known Native American tales; best among these was Gerald McDermott's *Coyote: A Trickster Tale from the American Southwest* (Harcourt Brace), which actually came out in 1993 but was not widely promoted (or reviewed) until 1994; McDermott, who has been producing imaginative versions of trickster and other folk stories for over twenty years, received a 1994 Caldecott Honor Book designation for another retelling, *Raven: A Trickster Tale from the Pacific Northwest* (1993). Another contender was David Wisniewski's *Wave of the Sea Wolf* (Clarion), a Tlingit legend with stunning illustrations. Less widely distributed but well received was *Heetunka's Harvest: A Tale of the Plains Indians* (Roberts Rinehart), retold by Jennifer Berry Jones and illustrated by Shannon Keegan, a book which has been officially approved by the Council for Indian Education. An outstanding entry in the crowded field of African folktales was Verna Aardema's *Misoso: Once Upon a Time-Tales from Africa* (Knopf / Apple Soup), illustrated by Reynold Ruffins. Two retellings of well-known Russian stories were new author-illustrator Christopher Denise's *The Fool of the World and the Flying Ship* (Philomel) and J. Patrick Lewis's *The Frog Princess* (Dial), with lavishly beautiful illustrations by Gennady Spirin. The illustrator, who now lives in Princeton, New Jersey, was recently honored with a display of his work at the Leonard L. Milberg Gallery for the Graphic Arts, Princeton University. Among other European-sourced retellings was a meticulous rendition of the Grimms' story *The Seven Ravens* (HarperCollins), adapted by Laura Gerlinger and illustrated by Edward S. Gazsi. From Great Britain came Mollie Hunter's *Gilly Martin the Fox* (Hyperion), with pictures by Dennis McDermott, a spirited retelling of a Scottish folktale.

A frequent complaint by professionals in recent years has been that many retellings do not specify the source of the story or do not do so accurately. A model to follow in this regard is the distinguished group of retellings put out by Holiday House this year, all of them, like the retellings listed above, carefully listing their exact provenance. Two of the Holiday House books are told by Eric A. Kimmel: *Anansi and the Talking Melon,* illustrated by Janet Stephens; and *The Three Princes: A Tale from the Middle East,* illustrated by Kimmel himself. Ellin Greene retold *Billy Beg and His Bull: an Irish Tale,*

Angela Johnson, the author of Toning the Sweep, *which won the Coretta Scott King Award*

with pictures by Kimberly Root, and Joanne Compton offered *Ashpet: An Appalachian Tale,* illustrated by Ken Compton.

Some writers varied the familiar folk/fairy tale format considerably. A favorite with reviewers was Jan Brett's *Town Mouse, Country Mouse* (Putnam), a jaunty version which made the "Best" list at the end of the year in *Publishers Weekly.* Jane Yolen's *The Girl in the Golden Bower* (Little, Brown), illustrated by Jane Dyer, has a very twentieth-century ending. Two independent presses brought out distinctly nontraditional tales. Treasure Chest Publications (Tucson, Arizona) published Judith Cole's *Another Tortoise and Another Hare,* illustrated by Anke Van Dun, and Nadja Publishing (Lake Forest, California) brought out *Princess Jessica Rescues a Prince* by Jennifer Brooks. Most widely read of the revisionist stories was probably *Cinder Edna* (Lothrop), by Ellen Jackson, with illustrations by Kevin O'Malley, the story of Cinderella's assertive neighbor; a rap version set in New York City (and sometimes confused with Jackson's book) was *Cinder-Elly* (Viking), by Frances Minters, with modernistic illustrations by G. Brian Karas. Imported nontraditional stories included two individual reprints from the collection *Fairy Tales* (1981), with text by Terry Jones (formerly of Monty Python's Flying Circus) and pictures by Michael Foreman; the tales are *The Beast with a Thousand Teeth* and *A Fish of the World,* both from Peter Bedrick. Another British writer, William Mayne, usually known for his works for older children and winner of both the Carnegie Medal and the Guardian award, used a traditional figure from English folklore to fashion an original story, *Hob and the Goblins* (Dorling Kindersley), illustrated by Norman Messenger. As always, Mayne's plot is compelling and his language rich and varied.

In addition to Polacco's *Pink and Say* and Bunting and Wiesner's *Night of the Gargoyles,* both discussed earlier as award contenders, many other picture books transcended their usual age grouping. Notable among these was Michael Foreman's *War Game* (Arcade; British publication by Pavilion, 1993), a companion volume to his earlier *War Boy.* Like that volume, *War Game* is a picture book in format but, in its portrayal of the experience of war, clearly not intended for small children. Unlike *War Boy,* Foreman's new book deals not with his own life as a boy during World War II but with trench warfare in World War I. Adults also formed the most appreciative audience for Eric Rohmann's wordless *Time Flies* (Crown), in which a bird flying through a museum is time-warped back into prehistory. Another book by Eve Bunting confronted mature subject matter in a picture-book format: *Smoky Night* (Harcourt Brace), illustrated by David Diaz, takes place during the Los Angeles riots. Though some critics objected to the simplification of complex racial issues, the striking modernistic pictures were widely admired. Several books-for-all-ages were developed posthumously from the work of favorite authors who have died. A reference to unpublished work by Langston Hughes led to the recovery of his manuscript for *The Sweet and Sour Animal Book,* from archives at Yale; in an inspired decision the Oxford University Press agreed to have the illustrations supplied by students at the Harlem School of the Arts. The result is unusual enough to transcend this report's normal exclusion of alphabet and counting books. Knopf reissued *The Dream Keeper and Other Poems,* a selection of poems edited by Hughes for young readers with pictures by Brian Pinkney. In a more comic vein, Roald Dahl's widow has compiled bizarre recipes for all ages in *Roald Dahl's Revolting Recipes* (Viking), by Roald Dahl and Felicity Dahl, with illustrations by Quentin Blake. Various other Dahl titles appeared in paperback, some for the first time.

In the wake of last year's oddest juvenile bestseller, *Everyone Poops,* Kane/Miller published two successors: Genichiro Yagyu's *The Holes in Your Nose* and Shinta Cho's *The Gas We Pass: the Story of Farts,* both translated from the Japanese by Amanda Mayer Stinchecum. These two books, like *Everyone Poops,* were (in the opinion of many booksellers) often purchased by adults as presents for other adults.

Two other illustrated books for a wide range of ages defy categorization. One is Russell Freedman's powerful *Kids At Work: Lewis Hine and the Crusade Against Child Labor* (Clarion), with Hine's photographs, a carefully documented account of child labor in the earlier years of the century. Freedman has surpassed even his own usual high standard with this book; it made a slow start in the professional community (like many nonfiction books unless they are on popular topics) but was being discussed as a contender for several awards by year's end. A second hard-to-define book seemed to defy the odds: it is a retelling of a religious allegory, it comes from a small publisher, and it is written by a college professor. This is Gary D. Schmidt's version of *The Pilgrim's Progress* (Eerdmans), by John Bunyan, illustrated by Barry Moser. It works. Young readers who would never dream of tackling the original will enjoy this rendition.

Nonfiction offerings proliferated in 1994, continuing a recent trend. Though often overlooked by reviewers (and award committees), nonfiction titles form a distinguished group, often of higher quality than other types. Dorling Kindersley offered elegant books like Anita Ganeri's *The Oceans Atlas,* illustrated by Luciano Corbella; series additions included David Burnie's *Seashore* and Steve Parker's *Human Body* in the Eyewitness Explorer series, and another Burnie title, *Life,* in the Eyewitness Science series. The nonfiction market's almost insatiable demands show up in the activity of competent authors: Ganeri, for instance, had more than thirty book-length publications in 1994, many of them entirely new.

Like Kindersley, most publishers of nonfiction promoted series books. Franklin Watts brought out revised editions of several Passport books (*Passport to France* and so forth) and launched several new series: the Places and People series featured Julia Waterlow's *China,* Anita Ganeri's *India,* and Vince Bunce's *Japan.* Two Watts series of the popular how-it-works type were Visual Guides (all by Norman Barrett: *Flying Machines, Space Machines*) and X-ray picture books (such as Gerald Legg's *Amazing Animals,* which received mixed reviews). Peter Bedrick Books added to its Inside Story series with Scott Steedman's *A Frontier Front on the Oregon Trail* and Fiona Macdonald's *A Medieval Cathedral,* among others, and also extended its World Mythology series (Anne Ross, *Devils, Gods and Heroes from Celtic Mythology*; Brian Branton, *Gods and Heroes from Viking Mythology*) and the What Do We Know About series, a multicultural offering (Anna Levingston's, *What Do We Know About the Amazonian Indians?* and

Dr. Colin Taylor's, *What Do We Know About the Plains Indians?*).

Many nonfiction series were "interactive" books with removable parts, add-on materials, and so on. Most widely praised of these was a new line from Scholastic, the Voyage of Discovery series (*Exploring Space, Musical Instruments*). In the same category Kindersley marketed "Action Packs" which contained no real "book" at all (*Pyramid, Night Sky, Dinosaur*) but resembled what used to be called activity kits. Even among ordinary "books," there was increased interest in related forms; Beth Wagner Brust revealed a little-known side of a famous storyteller in *The Amazing Paper Cuttings of Hans Christian Andersen* (Ticknor and Fields).

Several successful authors and author/illustrator teams from 1992 and 1993 repeated their success in 1994 with nonseries books. A best-seller of this type was Richard Platt's *Castle,* with the now-familiar cutaway drawings by Stephen Biesty. Another encore was Kathleen Krull's *Lives of the Writers: Comedies, Tragedies (and What the Neighbors Thought),* illustrated by Kathryn Hewitt (Harcourt Brace), following up on their 1993 title, *Lives of the Musicians.* (A third book, *Lives of the Artists,* is forthcoming in 1995.) Milton Meltzer, a champion of good nonfiction long before it became fashionable, followed his wonderful book on potatoes with *Gold: The True Story of Why People Search for It, Mine It, Trade It, Mint It, Hoard It, Shape It, Wear It, Fight and Kill for It* (HarperCollins). Dorothy Hinshaw Patent teamed up again with photographer William Munoz for *Looking at Bears* (Holiday House) — also *The American Alligator* and *Deer and Elk* (both from Clarion) and *What Good Is a Tail?* (Cobblehill); the duo's outstanding book of the season, also from Dutton's Cobblehill imprint, was *Hugger to the Rescue,* about the use of Newfoundland dogs in search-and-rescue missions.

Somber topics appeared in juvenile nonfiction too. Holocaust books maintained a high standard; one that many liked was David A. Adler's *Hilde and Eli: Children of the Holocaust* (Holiday House); Adler was also responsible for last year's *A Picture Book of Anne Frank* (Holiday House), which had its first British publication in 1994 (Pan Macmillan). *Images of War* (UNICEF/HarperCollins) collects impressions from children in what used to be Yugoslavia. The juvenile nonfiction hit of the year was *Zlata's Diary* (Viking), a journal kept by young Zlata Filipović. The book was heavily promoted, and Zlata toured extensively in the United States. Some found the journal moving, while others doubted its authorship (though, as one Internet contributor put it, the very

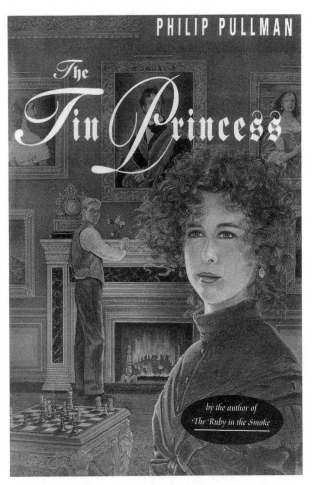

Dust jacket for Philip Pullman's period story of Victorian Great Britain

banality of the book suggests authenticity). Within months *Zlata's Diary* was in translation in various languages and also available on videocassette with paperback publication scheduled for early 1995. On another cheerless subject, AIDS books considered many different aspects of the disease. Lori S. Wiener, Aprille Best, and Philip A. Pizzo, M.D., compiled *To Be a Friend: Children Who Live with HIV Speak* (Albert Whitman); some of the contributors are themselves HIV positive, while others have family members who are.

Among distinguished biographies were Mary E. Lyon's *Master of Mahogany: Tom Day, Free Black Cabinet Maker,* from Scribners, and a multiple biography, Patricia and Fredrick McKissack's *African American Inventors,* from Millbrook's Proud Heritage series. Diane Stanley and Peter Vennemer produced another attractive pictorial biography, *Cleopatra* (Morrow). Andrea Davis Pinkney and Brian Pinkney selected telling details from the life of an eighteenth-century free black in *Dear Benjamin Banneker* (Harcourt Brace). Reviewers praised a scholarly but accessible account of Ulysses S. Grant's life, Albert Marrin's *Unconditional Surrender: U. S. Grant and the Civil War* (Atheneum). From the same period Jean Fritz brought to life the background of a famous author in *Harriet Beecher Stowe and the Beecher Preachers* (Putnam). Notably, a large number of juvenile biographies concerned minorities and women. An autobiographical winner was *Fear No Evil: The Passion and Politics of a Life in Gymnastics* (Hyperion), by the legendary coach Bela Karolyi.

Fiction books were not a particularly distinguished group in 1994. The sales of horror books, particularly in series, remained steady; so did criticism of the genre, already apparent in the previous eighteen months. Patty Campbell's column on horror books in the March/April issue of *Horn Book* aroused considerable comment, with the lines predictably drawn as some experts entirely rejected the genre while others felt that voluntary reading of any sort was laudable. It was noticeable that most of the books frequently mentioned for the Newbery were either quasi-picture books or else close to the young adult category — with *Pink and Say* and *All the Places to Love* at one end of the spectrum and Karen Cushman's *Catherine, Called Birdy* (Clarion) at the other. Many fiction offerings for the middle grades concerned family responsibilities and, indeed, the very definition of family. Most frequently discussed among these was Avi's *The Barn* (Orchard), a rather slender historical novel set in 1850s Oregon in which a boy and his siblings struggle to build a barn to fulfill their dying father's dream. *The Barn* was expected to be a contender for the Newbery in a year the competition was perceived to be less intense than usual. The same time period underlies Jean Van Leeuwen's *Bound for Oregon* (Dial), about the Oregon Trail. The Civil War gets an unusual treatment in Gloria Houston's *Mountain Valor* (Philomel), illustrated by Thomas B. Allen, centering on a girl left on the home front who finds herself driven to take a part in the action. Veteran author Mary Stolz, producing children's books for more than forty years, offered *Cezanne Pinto: A Memoir* (Knopf), about a young African American before, during, and immediately after the Civil War; the title was listed among the best fiction entries of the year by *Publishers Weekly*. The most ambitious of the family/ history offerings (and perhaps the finest) also begins in Civil War times but then follows a family over five generations: Walter Dean Myers's *The Glory Field* (Scholastic).

A grimmer version of long-ago family life than the American ones is Gillian Avery's *A Likely Lad* (Simon and Schuster), a tale of class and family in Edwardian England; though reviewed as a new book, this story was originally published more than twenty years ago in Britain. Another British import from Simon and Schuster, also a historical story about child and family, was Joan Aiken's *The Shoemaker's Boy,* illustrated by Victor Ambrus (original British publication, 1991). A new offering from Britain is Berlie Doherty's *Street Child* (Orchard; British publication, 1993), which defines family by the lack of it: based on a true story, this describes the rescue of a homeless boy by Dr. Bernardo, who subsequently founded the famous children's home.

Some distinguished (and some not-so-distinguished) middle-grade fiction was set in the twentieth century. These books, too, tended to focus on the family to a greater degree than in some previous years. An outside contender for the Newbery was Janet Hickman's *Jericho* (Greenwillow), a well-written account of a young girl's relationship with her great-grandmother. Marion Dane Bauer's *A Question of Trust* (Scholastic) shows two brothers trying to cope with their mother's desertion by sheltering some stray kittens. Ouida Sebestyen presented another young boy deserted by his mother in *Out of Nowhere* (Orchard); more harrowing than Bauer's tale, this one combines an odd assortment of losers (the boy, an abandoned pit bull, an old woman, an eccentric tenant, and other misfits) into a surrogate family. Zilpha Keatley Snyder's *Cat Running* (Delacorte) shows family life in California during the Depression. Eve Bunting's *The In-Between Days* (HarperCollins), with pictures by Arthur Pertzoff, depicts a family facing difficult changes as a child tries to avoid gaining a stepmother. In *When the Water Closes Over My Head* (Dutton), Donna Jo Napoli treats the intertwined issues of fear and family relationships. Maude Casey, a newcomer, offered *Over the Water* (Holt/Edge), about day-to-day life in rural Ireland (original British publication, 1987, by Women's Press).

Some family stories were comic. Bunting's *Nasty Stinky Sneakers* (HarperCollins) follows a boy's attempt to locate his revolting sneakers in time for a contest at school. The ever-popular Joanna Hurwitz's *A Llama in the Family,* illustrated by Mark Graham (Morrow), concerns a family in the llama-trekking business. A nicely rendered London setting distinguishes Paula Danziger's family comedy, *Thames Does Not Rhyme With James* (Putnam); an imaginary cartoon world, created by a disaffected young boy, is skillfully portrayed in *Frankenlouse,* by Mary James (who writes for young adults under the more familiar name of M. E. Kerr), from Scholastic.

For the middle grades, as for younger readers, much of the year's fare consisted of series additions. The ever-prolific Margaret Mahy produced the final installments of the "Cousins Quartet" with *A Fortune Branches Out* (Delacorte), with pictures by Marian Young (British publication, 1993), and *Tangled Fortunes,* also from Delacorte. Robert Newton Peck added a thirteenth installment to his Soup series with *Soup Ahoy,* illustrated by Charles Robinson (Knopf). Mary Stolz offered *Coco Grimes,* illustrated by Pat Cummings (HarperCollins), about a boy's trip with his grandfather to visit a player from the old Negro League; three previous books have featured the same family. Paula Danziger's latest series character faces school and family dilemmas in *Amber Brown Is Not a Crayon* (Putnam). Barbara Robinson capitalized on the success of *The Best Christmas Pageant Ever* (HarperCollins, 1972) with a follow-up, *The Best School Year Ever* (HarperCollins), chronicling the further adventures of the six fearsome Herdman children.

Some titles outside the topic of family achieved distinction. Michael Dorris, author and anthropologist, explored a clash of cultures in *Guests* (Hyperion). Sonia Levitin, better known for her young adult books, contributed *Adam's War* (Dial), an examination of group thinking and the role of violence in young lives. Two distinguished titles dealt with AIDS. In *My Brother Has AIDS,* by Deborah Davis (Atheneum), the effects of the disease on family members are unsentimentally presented. An outstanding title, which would probably be classified by most as a young-adult book if the protagonists were slightly older, is Theresa Nelson's *Earthshine* (Orchard), a quest story in which two preteens undertake to find a cure for their AIDS-ridden parents. This book, which borders on fantasy, was a favorite with librarians and reviewers.

Several imports escaped the neat categories of most of this year's fiction for middle grades. Ian McEwan's *The Daydreamer* (HarperCollins; British publication, also 1994), illustrated by Anthony Browne, explores the intersections of fantasy and reality in a young boy's mind and daily life. Two mouse fantasies came from Britain. *Time and the Clockmice, Etcetera* (Delacorte; British publication, 1993), by Peter Dickinson, illustrated by Emma Chichester Clark, falls into the tradition of *The Borrowers, Mistress Masham's Repose,* and, in this country, *Stuart Little* and *Mrs. Frisby and the Rats of NIMH.* In spite of these antecedents, there is little in Dickinson's book that is derivative. A lighter but still enjoyable mouse book is Dick King-Smith's *Three Terrible Trins* (Crown; British publication data not

Dust jacket for Michael Williams's story of an adolescent growing up in postapartheid South Africa

available), with pictures by Mark Teague. Sylvia Waugh's doll fantasy, *The Mennyms* (Greenwillow), bears a 1993 U.S. publication date but did not get much attention until 1994; it has become a cult favorite with adults. A sequel, *Mennyms in the Wilderness,* is scheduled for 1995 release.

The young-adult (YA) field underwent considerable analysis and self-analysis in 1994. Several respected YA authors produced speeches and articles about the state of YA literature, generally arguing against the perception that books for this age group were declining in quality as well as quantity. Among reviewers the best assessment came from Michael Cart, whose article ("Of Risk and Revelation: The Current State of Young Adult Literature") in the winter issue of *Journal of Youth Services in Libraries* defines the situation clearly and persuasively. Cart's article is a must-read for students of young-adult literature, even though "*JOYS,*" as the journal is affectionately known to its readers, does

Advertisement for Gerald McDermott's Caldecott Honor Book retelling a Native American folktale

received wisdom that young adults will not read history. Set at the end of the thirteenth century, Cushman's book takes the form of a young girl's diary. Though there is a central plot (Birdy's attempts to ward off a series of arranged marriages), the main interest of the book lies in its portrayal of everyday life – fears, smells, and all. Birdy herself is an engaging character.

Three other major offerings for young adults came from well-established writers and focused on once-taboo topics in the young-adult tradition of the "problem novel." Most widely read and discussed of the three was M. E. Kerr's *Deliver Us From Evie,* an evenhanded account of a midwestern family with a lesbian teenager. After several years spent writing (under another name) for younger children, Kerr returned to the young-adult category in 1993 with *Linger,* which was well received critically but did not succeed as well with its readership as some of her earlier books. *Deliver Us from Evie* is vintage Kerr and should restore her popularity. Both of the other major young-adult books of 1994 concern incest. Cynthia Voigt, winner of the 1983 Newbery for *Dicey's Song,* took off in a new direction with *When She Hollers* (Scholastic). This account of a girl's attempts to ward off an abusive stepfather is entirely different from the author's beloved Tillerman books and from her Kingdom trilogy, a Renaissance-style fantasy series. *When She Hollers,* focusing on the events of a single day, was described as "searing" both by reviewers and by Internet contributors; for once, the adjective fits. Francesca Lia Block's new book, *The Hanged Man* (Harper-Colllins), makes a less disturbing impression, partly because incest is not its only theme and partly because of Block's uniquely surrealistic prose style. This writer, too, broke away from a popular series, the Weetzie Bat books, to go off in a new direction; the result justifies her decision.

Two other established writers chose to write sequels. Jean Craighead George's long-awaited *Julie* (HarperCollins), considered by many to be fully the equal of its predecessor, *Julie of the Wolves,* picks up Julie's life as she settles in with her father and his new, non-Eskimo wife. Madeleine L'Engle added to her popular Austin series with *Star* (Farrar Straus Giroux), which has an unusual Antarctic setting. Though *Troubling a Star* received positive ratings from most, *Julie* was one of the season's hits with both reviewers and young readers. So was Anne Fine's *Flour Babies* (Little, Brown), a British import (but not a series book). Though the topic of an assignment in parenting is hardly new, having been ably covered by Eve Bunting and Louise Moeri in

not circulate much outside the library community. Cart's title parodies the colon-infested chapter titles of the authoritative textbook in the field, Donelson and Nielson's *Literature for Today's Young Adults* (HarperCollins), in its first three editions ("Of Sudden Shadows," "Of Heroes and Hopes"); mercifully, all the "of" designations, and the colons, have been removed in the 1994 edition.

While authors, publishers, and critics bemoaned the state of the field, young-adult books continued to be published. As usual they did not follow the same trends as other juvenile publishing. (Anita Silvey's fine editorial in the September/October *Horn Book* skewers overeager generalizers in discussing "The Problem with Trends." Though she writes of children's books in general, the warning is particularly apt in the young-adult field.) The surprise hit of the year was *Catherine, Called Birdy* by first-time author Karen Cushman. So much for the recent years, Fine's book deserves the Carnegie Medal it won in 1993 for its portrayal of a disturbed fourteen-year-old and his peers.

Many young-adult books, some distinguished and some not, dealt with abusive or neglectful families or with family problems. In Sharon Creech's *Walk Two Moons* (HarperCollins), a girl deserted by her mother sets out on a quest of self-discovery. The actual situation becomes clear only gradually in this carefully constructed intergenerational story marking Creech's American debut. (Two earlier books were published in Britain.) The title character of James Deem's *The 3 NBs of Julian Drew* (Houghton Mifflin) is also in flight, but from abuse rather than neglect. Another horrifying story of casual brutality is Chris Lynch's *Gypsy Davey* (Harper-Collins). Julie Johnston explored the aftermath of neglect and abuse in *Adam and Eve and Pinch-Me* (Little, Brown), about a vulnerable girl in foster care. Parental kidnapping is the subject of Susan Beth Pfeffer's *Twice Taken* (Delacorte), and Alzheimer's disease provides the plot machinery in Ron Koertge's *Tiger, Tiger, Burning Bright* (Orchard), an endearing (though somewhat implausible) tale of a boy and his grandfather. Incest again surfaces in *I Hadn't Meant to Tell You This,* by Jacqueline Woodson (Delacorte). Michael Williams portrayed the quest of a muddled white teenager from a dysfunctional family in *The Genuine Half-Moon Kid* (Lodestar), with a postapartheid South African setting. (Williams had previously written about the black experience in South Africa in *Crocodile Burning,* 1992, also from Lodestar and recently released in paperback by Puffin.) An Australian setting adds to the effect of John Marsden's *Letters from the Inside* (Houghton Mifflin), about two pen pals, one of whom is in prison.

As usual, dozens of young-adult books ignored family life to focus on peer interactions. Caroline Cooney showed the tragic results of a high school prank in *Driver's Ed* (Delacorte). Lesléa Newman's *Fat Chance* (Putnam) was a plausible narrative about a girl who develops a life-threatening eating disorder. (Newman is best known for 1993's oft-censored *Heather Has Two Mommies.*) Sid Hite's intricate but satisfying new book, *It's Nothing to a Mountain,* portrays efforts to conceal and help a runaway teen; the scenes following the landslide are particularly memorable. Two excellent young-adult books are story collections. Robin McKinley returned to the field with *A Knot in the Grain and Other Stories* (Greenwillow), in the tradition of her full-length fantasies, and Lori M. Carlson edited *American Eyes: New Asian-American Short Stories for Young Adults* (Holt/Edge).

Several established writers for young adults returned to the historical genre. Isabelle Holland's *Behind the Scenes* (Scholastic) follows the experiences of an Irish servant girl during the Civil War, providing an excellent account of the system that enabled the rich to buy the military service of poorer men (often Irish). Another Civil War story, its theme reminiscent of *Pink and Say,* was the Colliers' *With Every Drop of Blood* (Delacorte). Philip Pullman, British author of Victorian-period books, produced *The Tin Princess* (Knopf), returning to his favorite period after several successful contemporary books. Two of the outstanding young-adult books of the year were historical — one widely publicized, the other less so. Malcolm Bosse's *The Examination* (Farrar Straus Giroux) takes place in the seemingly unpromising setting of sixteenth-century China. A tale of two radically different brothers, this one has everything: period detail, characterization, and a plot with something for everyone. Graham Salisbury's *Under the Blood-red Sun* (Delacorte) depicts a Japanese American family in 1941 — probably the best treatment of this painful subject since the 1945 classic by Florence Crannell Means, *The Moved-Outers.*

The world of children's books lost some of its best-known citizens in 1994. Elizabeth George Speare, who was the second author to earn two Newbery medals (Lowry is the third), died in November in Arizona. She was eighty-four. The better-known of her two medal winners, *The Witch of Blackbird Pond* (1958), focuses on a witch-hunt mentality in late-seventeenth-century Connecticut; *The Bronze Bow,* her other winner (1961), is set in the time of Christ. *The Witch of Blackbird Pond* is still a staple of recommended reading lists for middle-grade students. More controversial than Speare was Alice Childress, a South Carolina native who was active in the New York writing scene for decades until her death at seventy-seven. In addition to work in the theater, Childress was known in the juvenile field for *A Hero Ain't Nothin' but a Sandwich* (1973), an unsentimental tale of a young drug user, Benjy, and his surroundings. *A Hero Ain't Nothin' but a Sandwich* has been the target of numerous objections. Childress was also the author of *Rainbow Jordan* (1981). Nancy K. Robinson died of cancer on 15 March at the age of fifty-one; she was best known for the Veronica books.

Several important illustrators also died in 1994. Richard Scarry, whose books appeared in nearly thirty languages, died in Gstaad, Switzerland, on 30 April. Trained at the Museum of Fine Arts in Boston, Scarry became a children's book illustrator in 1946, by chance, and went on to cre-

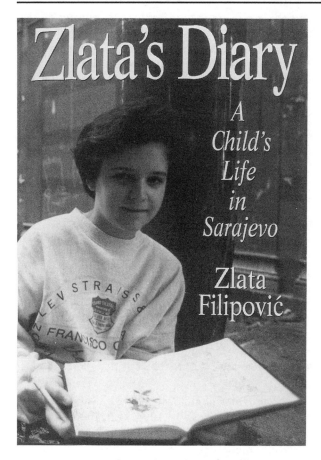

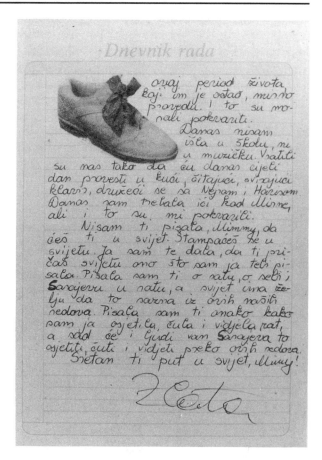

Dust jacket and page from Zlata Filopović's diary of life in the capital of Bosnia-Herzegovina

ate perennial best-sellers like *What Do People Do All Day?* and *Richard Scarry's Best Word Book Ever.* More than a hundred million copies of Scarry's books have been sold, and most have remained continuously in print. Scarry had a 1994 publication, *Richard Scarry's Busy, Busy Town* (Golden), crammed with his now-familiar characters from Lowly Worm on up. Warwick Hutton, best known for his work in mythology, died on 28 September. His 1994 book is *Persephone* (McElderry). In addition to retellings of myth, Hutton was known for his illustration of fantasy novels by Susan Cooper. Taro Yashima died on 30 June at the age of eighty-five. A naturalized American citizen born in Japan, he served the U.S. government during World War II, subsequently becoming a well-known author-illustrator of children's books. In a long career he produced three Caldecott Honor Books: *Crow Boy* (1955), *Umbrella* (1958), and *Seashore Story* (1967) — all from Viking. A tragic end to an exciting career came with Janet Ahlberg's death at fifty-one from cancer; she and her husband, Allen, collaborated on some of the most talked-about and loved British picture books of the postwar period, from *Each Peach*

Pear Plum (1978), which won the Greenaway award, to the imaginative Jolly Postman books, the second of which, *The Jolly Christmas Postman* (1991), also took the Greenaway. The Ahlbergs were responsible for numerous titles in the Wacky Families series, the Foldaway series, the Funnybones series, and several more early-reader series; Janet Ahlberg also illustrated several books by other authors.

The death of children's books was more discussed in 1994 than the deaths of individuals. Conservative parents and the politicians whose constituency they formed lamented the death of old-fashioned books with traditional "American" values and pronounced most of the current crop to be trash. Young-adult literature, as usual, was said to be on its deathbed. The linkage between books and other media came in for particular attention: for instance, the summer movie hit from Disney, *The Lion King,* spawned dozens of booklike products; on 22 August the children's best-seller list in *Publishers Weekly* showed Lion King books in three of the five top spots for picture books, while the top fiction title was also a Lion King book. The same phenomenon had happened with *Aladdin* and with *Beauty and the Beast,* though the 1994 sales were more spectacular. The success of the Disney offerings worried many critics, who feared that a taste for Disney (and for Disney versions of classic stories, in particular) would not lead to "good" reading. The same concerns applied to the film (and novelized-from-the-film, or simply abridged) versions of *The Secret Garden* (1993) and *Little Women* (1994), with accompanying questions of whether the adaptations were "authentic." However, the fact that much of children's "literature" did not consist of books in 1994 is demonstrable from any professional publication. *School Library Journal,* for example, has steadily expanded its reviewing of audiovisual materials; the audiovisual section is now, normally, at least as long as any of the "book" sections.

Even the most traditional bookstores now stock card sets, activity kits, and various other quasi-booklike items as well as related toys and the like. More change is on the way. The whole computer field is about to explode with hundreds of new titles for children; the success of educational software suggests that a whole range of computer materials for home use will be available shortly in ordinary retail outlets (some of which are beginning to carry a selection). Among ordinary "books" themselves, the components are very unlike what existed a decade or two ago: much of children's book illustration, for instance, no longer consists simply of drawings and paintings. The Ahlbergs pioneered books in which pieces – for instance, tiny letters – can be taken in and out; they now have a host of imitators. Pop-ups, fold-outs, and "books" consisting of separate pieces without binding are commonplace. Even what looks like ordinary illustration often turns out to be computer generated, as in Otto Walsh and Vivian Seabold's Mr. Lunch books from Viking (*Mr. Lunch Takes a Plane Ride,* 1993; *Mr. Lunch Borrows a Canoe,* 1994).

One very popular series illustrates neatly the complex interrelationship among the various forms of children's "literature." The Magic School Bus series originated as a publishing concept; Scholastic brought together Joanna Cole and Bruce Degen to flesh out the concept in a series of picture books about science, grouped around the eccentric Ms. Frizzle, her science class, and a yellow bus. The series was a great success. (The duo's 1994 title is *The Magic School Bus in the Time of the Dinosaurs.*) Enter television: Public Broadcasting System's animated Magic School Bus series debuted in 1994, with the voice of Lily Tomlin as Ms. Frizzle – another success. However, for various reasons the television adventures were not, generally, quite the same as the book ones. Hence, there is now a parallel series of Magic School Bus books from Scholastic – not by Cole and Degen but by lesser authors and artists; these books are illustrated, abridged versions of the television scripts. There are also Magic School Bus activity books and interactive CD-ROM presentations of some Magic School Bus adventures.

Because of the political impact of the 1994 U.S. elections, this year's roundup has stressed domestic trends. The domestic children's book industry as it existed in the 1950s is indeed dying. Most of the literary houses are gone or so changed as to defy recognition; some familiar names are now foreign owned. Of the great children's book editors, only two or three remain. In place of what has disappeared is an internationalized marketplace; chilen in the United States are now exposed to books and other media from all over the world and to an ever-growing variety of media. Next year's roundup will branch out internationally and will discuss some of those other media as part of the contemporary children's book scene.

Book Reviewing in America VIII

George Garrett
University of Virginia

A good critic is someone who reads a text with a clear mind; most people are merely reading to find out what they already know.
 – V. S. Naipaul, as quoted in the *Times Literary Supplement,* 2 September 1994.

From the standpoint of getting good books published and read, the belles lettres, as we used to call them, are in woeful shape and getting worse.
 – Louis D. Rubin, Jr., "Our Absolutely Deplorable Literary Situation – And Some Thoughts On How To Fix It Good," *Sewanee Review,* Fall 1994.

After a fairly general look at the literary scene (*plus ça change, plus c'est la meme chose*) and some commentary on book reviewing during the year, there is an interview with D. T. Max, conducted by Kristin van Ogtrop, who has recently been promoted to the rank of a senior editor at *Vogue.* At the time Ogtrop interviewed him, Max was the literary editor of the *New York Observer* and one of the most highly regarded reviewers and literary journalists in the country. A little later, in keeping with the Year of the Revolving Door in American publishing, Max left the *New York Observer* to become a senior editor, charged with features, at *Harper's Bazaar.* Following the van Ogtrop–Max conversation there is a brief contribution and accounting of "Book Reviewing in Texas," by Paul Ruffin, editor of the *Texas Review.* This is the first in a series we are planning, dealing with regional book reviewing (and the accompanying literary scene). As sales representatives and booksellers never fail to point out, Texas is, for better or worse, almost like another country. A book can succeed there, and only there, and still be a genuine commercial success, even a best-seller.

Notes on the scene – 1994

Within the business only a few things seriously matter, chiefly personnel and money, not necessarily in that order. For those who must follow the news of comings and goings, who is in and who is out, it was a busy, revolving-door year, week after week in *Publishers Weekly* or quarterly in the

new and improved, expanded *Authors Guild Bulletin,* where veteran book reviewer Campbell Geeslin edits the lively section "Along Publishers Row." Along that row editors came and went, some to new and better jobs, others out of action. There were enough of the latter, unemployed but veteran editors, to arouse the interest of Bill Strachan, editor in chief at Holt who announced a new imprint, Editors Press, to draw on "a selected group of distinguished – and currently unemployed – veteran editors." ("Veteran Editors To Be Tapped for New Holt Imprint," *Publishers Weekly,* 2 January 1995.) A good deal of ink was splashed and space devoted to the resignation of "Captain Fiction," Gordon Lish, after eighteen years at Knopf. One of the better pieces dealing with this event was by Peter Stevenson in the *New York Observer* (19 December) – "Editor Overboard! Knopf Jettisons Lish/Jumpsuited Superguru of New Fiction": "It was a muted exit for the former talk radio host who had parlayed genius and weirdness into a career as New York's most infamous book editor – without having edited a book that made any real money." Some of Lish's writers included Raymond Carver, Barry Hannah, Cynthia Ozick, Amy Hempel, Nancy LeMann, and Mary Robison. More widely discussed than the decline and fall of Lish was a series of changes at *The New York Times Book Review, The New Yorker,* and *Granta.* In November it was announced that *Book Review* editor Rebecca Pepper Sinkler was retiring and would be replaced, beginning in February 1995, by Charles "Chip" McGrath from *The New Yorker.* In "Times Steals McGrath From New Yorker; Book Review Gets Hockey-Playing Gent" (*New York Observer,* 21 November), Celia McGee asked, "Did he want to do battle with clamoring constituencies of readers, the publishing community, the intellectual and academic worlds, the in-fighting bureaucracy of *The Times?*" In a few weeks *The New Yorker* signed on Bill Buford of the Cambridge-based literary magazine *Granta.* He begins 1 April 1995. Writing in the *Washington Post* ("Taken From Grant: Magazine Editor Hired by the New Yorker," 14 December),

David Streitfeld wondered out loud how Buford will fit in: "At the New Yorker, Buford will oversee a fiction department that is still regarded, mostly by default, as the premier showcase for short stories." He continues, "Under the reign of Tina Brown, fiction in the New Yorker has been relegated to second-class status. There's only one story per issue and it runs as far back in the magazine as possible – way behind the latest developments in the O. J. Simpson case." (See also Jim Windolf, "Granta Claus Coming to New Yorker Town," *New York Observer,* 19 December.) Meantime, in October Michiko Kakutani was named senior critic for *The New York Times.* The other critic in daily rotation is Christopher Lehman-Haupt, the third critic, Margo Jefferson, having been named the Sunday drama critic at *The New York Times.* Earlier than that (3 August), Random House raided *The New Yorker* and hired senior fiction editor Daniel Menaker onto their team. Harcourt, Brace severely reduced its trade-books department in New York, sending several highly regarded editors (and thus writers), including veteran Cork Smith, out into the street. (Max, "For Some at Harcourt Brace, a House Is Not a Home," *New York Observer,* 18 July.) And the Book-of-the-Month Club, after a sixty-eight-year run, decided to drop its editorial board. Although it was a bad time for some editors, others seemed to be doing well. Writing for the *New York Observer* (15 August), "Book Biz Isn't Thriving, but Some Young Editors Are," Max briefly profiled Jon Karp (Random House), Eamon Dolan (HarperCollins), Elisabeth Dyssegaard (Farrar Straus Giroux), and Will Schalbe (Morrow) to prove his point. Farrar Straus Giroux, after forty-nine years on its own, was sold to Verlagsgruppe Georg von Holtzbrinck, which also owns Holt. (See "FSG, Holtzbrinck: So Far *Sehr Gut,*" *New York Observer,* 7 November; also Streitfeld, "Book Report," *Washington Post Book World,* 13 November.)

But nothing mentioned so far, nor any other inside story, captured the attention of the press as much as the fall from power at Simon and Schuster of Richard Snyder. Snyder's problems began, though he apparently did not know or imagine it at the time, when Viacom bought Paramount Communications (including Simon and Schuster) for $10.1 billion. This was front-page news in the *Washington Post* (16 February). Under the leadership of Sumner M. Redstone, Viacom combined Paramount-Blockbuster-Viacom. Redstone was quoted by the *Washington Post:* "We are going to build a global super powerhouse." A few months later (20 June) *Publishers Weekly* headlined "Richard Snyder Is Dismissed as S & S Head by Viacom: Industry Stunned." This had

Richard Snyder, who was fired in June from his position as head of Simon and Schuster (photograph by Maureen O'Brien)

already been a front-page story in the *Washington Post* (14 June) and *The New York Times* (15 June). Wrote Paula Span of the *Washington Post:* "Snyder is not a widely beloved figure. In 1984, *Fortune* named him one of the country's toughest bosses, jokingly comparing him to the Ayatollah Khomeini." It was likewise the lead front-page story in the *Wall Street Journal* – "How The Despotic Boss of Simon & Schuster Found Himself Jobless," by Meg Cox and Johnnie L. Roberts. Even the *Authors Guild Bulletin,* where one might reasonably expect dancing in the street and fireworks in honor of the giant's tumble, found cause to praise Snyder . . . a little: "Even Mr. Snyder's fiercest enemies, and he managed to acquire many outspoken detractors in his 33-year career at Simon & Schuster, would not have charged him with neglect of the bottom line." Snyder was replaced by Jonathan Newcomb, already chief operating officer at the publishing house. (Jane Allison Hausy, "Richard Snyder Out At Simon & Schuster," *Authors Guild Bulletin,* Summer).

Not surprising in such a litigious age as our own is that literary lawsuits made news in 1994. *Authors Guild Bulletin* now boasts a regular column,

"Legal Watch," to keep the membership abreast of the latest pertinent decisions. There were plenty of nice little cases involving nice little legal niceties such as *Alternative Thinking Systems Inc* v. *Simon & Schuster; Ayeni* v. *CBS, Inc; Davis-Kidd Booksellers, Inc.* v. *McWherter; Kretschmer* v. *Warner Brothers,* and *Norse* v. *Henry Holt and Co.* (this last has gone on and on and continues). But three cases caught the roving eyes of journalists and received considerable attention. The most complex was a four-year battle between author Dan E. Moldea and *The New York Times.* Writing in the *Authors Guild Bulletin,* Kay Murray noted the beginning, "The dispute arose in September 1989 when the *Times Sunday Book Review* [*sic*] published *Times* football beat reporter Gerald S. Eskenazi's savagely critical review of Moldea's book, *Interference: How Organized Crime Influences Professional Football.*" On 24 August 1990 Moldea sued the *The New York Times* for defamation and "false light invasion of privacy." Since then the suit has gone up and down in the court system, ending (apparently) in 1994 with victory by *The New York Times.* This suit, since it involved book reviewing, generated a lot of interest. Jack Miles of the *Los Angeles Times* produced a thorough and major piece on the Moldea case – "Can a review be libelous?"– in *The National Book Critics Circle Journal* (August), published together with "Select bibliography on the Moldea case," by Steve Weinberg. Miles argues persuasively for a moderate and reasonable position: "Treating the book section as a zone of utter impunity is bad for the intellectual health of the country, quite apart from the occasional libel such a policy would entail." In October a second libel trial, in a suit that had been cooking for ten years, was brought by Jeffrey Masson against *The New Yorker* writer Janet Malcolm. Defendant Malcolm finally won this one, but the irrepressible, indefatigable Masson (a psychologist) resurfaced as a professor of journalism at the University of California, Berkeley ("Revenge of Masson: Teaching Journalism," *New York Observer* 5 December). The problems for David Leavitt and his novel *While England Sleeps* (1993) continued. Sir Stephen Spender, charging that much in the book was based on his own life and work, brought suit in Britain. At which point Viking capitulated and settled out of court (Streitfeld, "Publisher Kills Novel Over Pilfered Plot," *Washington Post,* 17 February). Leavitt's admirers in the literary establishment leaped to his defense. Biographer James Atlas managed to get his piece into *The New York Times* Sunday editorial section "The Week in Review" (20 February). In "Who Owns a Life? Asks a Poet, When His Is Turned Into Fiction,"

Atlas somewhat disingenuously made the best possible case for Leavitt: "There is nothing scandalous about this sort of borrowing. Mr. Leavitt intended his book as an act of homage; he said he planned to acknowledge his debt to Mr. Spender in his dedication until a lawyer for his American publisher advised him against it."

More-ordinary, commonplace plagiarism made news in 1994. The Rockford Institute published *The Martin Luther King, Jr. Plagiarism Story,* edited by Theodore Pappas, which makes a strong case, with strong evidence, that King borrowed freely from the texts of others when it suited his purposes. The usual answer to these charges was not to deny the facts but to redefine the nature of plagiarism and to argue that thoughts and words are more communal than private property. This particular story remains to be played out. Another concerns poet and professor Neal Bowers, who discovered that some of his published poems were being published again under another name. A profile of Bowers and his quest for justice appeared in the *Chronicle of Higher Education* (26 October), "Portrait: A Professor's Campaign Against Plagiarism." Bowers covered his own story in some detail in "A Loss for Words: Plagiarism and Silence," *American Scholar* (Autumn): "Finding such mixed attitudes among friends and associates, I decided that legal assistance might be the answer to my problems. I quickly learned that the absence of money in poetry publication makes lawyers wonder why it matters if a poet's work is stolen."

And, as if the urge to plagiarize were contagious, there were other examples. For instance, Sarah Lyall's "Novels in plagiarism case are identical in long passages," *The New York Times* (20 April): "There is no doubt about it: In her recent novel, the Indian writer Indrani Aikath-Gyaltsen copied long passages from 'The Rosemary Tree,' a novel published in 1956 by the English novelist Elizabeth Goudge." William Logan does not allege plagiarism; he simply demonstrates it in his review of Paul Mariani's *Lost Puritan: A Life of Robert Lowell* (Norton), writing in the *New Criterion* (December), "Lowell in the Shadows," of the many parallels between Mariani's work and an earlier biography by Ian Hamilton: "There are dozens of such parallel passages, and many others where the writing seems to have been done with one eye on Hamilton and one eye on the computer screen. Hamilton's prose and Hamilton's quotations are the paraphrased and filleted matter of this book."

As usual for the last few years (five in fact), the familiar image of the bearded face of Salman

Rushdie appeared in public places, and his plight, as he is protected against the unrelenting *fatwa,* was widely discussed and written about. *Profession 94* (a publication of the Modern Language Association) was devoted to articles about Rushdie by prominent literary figures. Canadian novelist Margaret Atwood offered "Silencing the Scream." Wayne C. Booth tried to make it a learning experience in "The Subtler Constraints, Or, What Can We Learn from Rushdie's Persecution?" Novelist William H. Gass reached a high adrenalin level in "Tribalism, Identity, and Ideology": "The *fatwa* was pronounced against us all. It commanded the murder of a mouth yet issued from the mouth of a murderer." On the fifth anniversary of the *fatwa* (14 February), the United States officially condemned Iran for continuing to threaten Rushdie, and British prime minister John Major made a "strong appeal." (See "U.S. Stands Behind Rushdie," *Washington Post,* 16 February, an unsigned Reuter story.) Shortly thereafter, Rushdie's friend, British novelist Julian Barnes, published "Staying Alive" in *The New Yorker* (21 February). Here Barnes noticed some improvement: "And at the political level there are now, perhaps for the first time, mild grounds for optimism: the inactivity and glacial indifference of the Bush and Thatcher Administration have been replaced by the comparatively more sympathetic presences of Clinton and Major." Barnes took time to chastise Roald Dahl, Germaine Greer, Hugh Trevor-Roper, and Marianne Wiggins for being, in his view, insufficiently sympathetic. A generally more interesting piece about Rushdie appeared in *Vanity Fair* (August) by Toby Young, "Guarding Salman: backstage at the Fatwa follies with Rushdie's Special Branch detail." Here Young focused on the six-man squad from the Special Branch of New Scotland Yard which, at the expense of roughly five million pounds (so far) guards the life of Salman Rushdie night and day. Young points out that they accompany him to literary parties and events, but that they fit in quite well. He quotes an anonymous publisher as saying: "They're much better read than Rushdie."

Rushdie's problems seemed paler in comparison to the fates of two other Muslim writers. On 14 October, while sitting in his car, Nobel Prize–winner Najīb Mahfūz was stabbed and nearly killed by Muslim radicals, mainly, it seems, on account of his novel *The Children of Gebeiawi,* written in 1959, but not published in Egypt until 1994. Egyptian justice moved relatively quickly, as on 11 January 1995 thirteen Muslim radicals were convicted for the crime, eleven sentenced to jail and two sentenced to

Najīb Mahfūz, winner of the 1988 Nobel Prize, who was attacked and stabbed by Islamic radicals in Cairo, Egypt, in October

death. Most press coverage was devoted to the case of Taslima Nasrin, a Bangladeshi feminist writer who, like Rushdie, was charged with blasphemy. In the absence of a squad from Special Branch, she kept on the move – Sweden, France, and back to Bangladesh; and the newspapers followed her every move and the moves against her: "Thousands March In Bangladesh To Demand Execution Of Writer"; "Blasts Hurt 15 In Call For Death Of Writer." She had an interview with *Time* magazine (22 August): "They May Kill Me Anytime." *The New Yorker* (12 September) published a piece by Mary Anne Weaver, "A Fugitive From Injustice," who presented a mixed view of Nasrin: "She is an Eastern fatalist by birth, a Marxist by conviction, a self-proclaimed atheist who often reflects on God. She is an introverted loner who craves the attention of the press." The attention of the press turned elsewhere, and at this writing her story and her danger continue.

Other miscellaneous news from the literary scene

Scribners dropped the apostrophe; Aleksandr Solzhenitsyn left Vermont and returned to Russia;

Amy Hempel (one of the judges) protested against the National Book Award going to William Gaddis; a survey conducted by sociologist Steven Brint asserted the *New York Review of Books* to be the most influential periodical among American intellectuals; the Book-of-the-Month Club reissued a pornographic novel – Chester Himes's *Pinktoes; Publishers Weekly* published an interview with a poet – "Galway Kinnell: Poets Are Not a Special Breed" (5 December), by Molly McQuade; poet Allen Ginsberg sold his papers to Stanford University for $1 million; the Association of Literary Scholars and Critics, headed by Ricardo Quinones and aimed to compete seriously with the MLA, was founded and merited a *New York Times* article (7 December) – "An Upstart Alliance of Traditional Literati," by William Grimes.

Meanwhile the desire for cultural diversity created modest changes in certain genres. Marj Charlier ("Gang of Offbeat Western Novels Takes Genre by Storm," *Wall Street Journal,* 18 July) took note of the changing world of the Western: "These books, which dare to step outside the game's traditional time frame, are now often written by or about women, blacks, Native Americans, Hispanics and gays." Even the popular romance genre was not immune to the cult of diversity. See Eleena De Lisser, "Romance Books Get Novel Twist And Go Ethnic," *Wall Street Journal,* 6 September: "Beyond physical descriptions ('cascading blond hair' becomes 'curly brown locks'), the multicultural books may feature black colloquialisms and references to the music, foods and traditions of African-American culture." Perhaps in keeping with the diversity theme, the venerable *Hollins Critic* for the first time turned to film for its subject – "All Things to All People: Opposing Agendas and Ambiguous Purpose in the Films of Spike Lee," (October), by Brooke Horvath and Melissa Prunty Kemp.

Meanwhile everybody from the tabloids to Joe McGinniss (who signed on to do a book for Random House) was getting into the O. J. Simpson act. Dominick Dunne is on the case for *Vanity Fair;* and Faye Resnick, friend of the family, has already brought out *Nicole Brown Simpson: The Private Diary of a Life Interrupted* (Dove), which managed to get the attention of trial judge Lance Ito, who banned it from jurors.

Finally, on 11 November *TLS* reported that a group calling itself Daughters of Eve, centered in (where else?) California, is waging an occult campaign against selected British male writers, namely Ted Hughes, Harold Pinter, and John Osborne. They held a mock trial of Osborne in absentia on 22

October. He was found guilty on all counts and described as "a censor, misogynist, homophobe, destroyer of the fragile, vulnerable, talented." Osborne died in December, though no connection to the verdict was found. More trials are scheduled to follow.

Money is, finally (also first and foremost), what it is all about – money spent and money earned. Under the former category are the much-publicized advances against royalties paid by eager publishers for potentially lucrative properties. To be sure, the advance that seized the most attention was the advance that was never meant to be – Newt Gingrich's $4-million-plus advance on a two-book contract from HarperCollins that he was forced, by the press and political pressure, to refuse in favor of a symbolic $1 advance. Other writers, old and new, had better luck. Among them are James Patterson, whose forthcoming *Kiss the Girls* (HarperCollins) received a publisher's advance of $650,000, a Book-of-the-Month Club advance of $315,000, and a movie sale of $1 million; and Pat Conroy, whose *Beach Music* (Doubleday) was taken by the Literary Guild for $1 million. Dell paid $3.15 million for *The Horse Whisperer,* an unfinished first novel by Nicholas Evans; Robert Redford meanwhile paid $3 million for the film rights. Random House paid out seven figures for a discovered manuscript by Louisa May Alcott titled *A Long Fatal Love Chase.* Clive Cussler signed a two-book contract for adventure novels for a princely $14 million. David Ramus signed on with HarperCollins with *Thief of Light,* an autobiographical first novel about the world of a fine-arts dealer, for $1 million. George Dawes Green's *The Juror* (Warner) picked up an advance of $500,000, together with $1.5 million for the film rights. These are only a few of the people who cut a large piece of the publishing pie in 1994. At least one advance made headline news in *Publishers Weekly* ("Pope to Publish With Knopf for $6 Million," 18 July) as Pope John Paul II contracted for *Crossing the Threshold of Hope.* A sense of how literary writing fares, top of the line, was the story in *Publishers Weekly* (12 December) of how Philip Roth, after stints at Random House, Farrar Straus Giroux, and Simon and Schuster, returned to his first publisher, Houghton Mifflin, for a $300,000 advance on his new novel *Sabbath's Theater.* The same story announced that someone named Andrew Klavan was earning a seven-figure advance for a book-to-be called *True Crime.*

Not all of these large advances pay off by any means. Writing in the *Wall Street Journal* (9 December), Patrick M. Reilly followed the fates of three

1994 books which had received huge advances ("Books That Bombed Go on Early Sale"): Marlon Brando's *Songs My Mother Taught Me* (Random House); Robert Lacey's *Grace*, a biography of Grace Kelly (Putnam); and *Dolly* (HarperCollins), by Dolly Parton: "This season's big mistakes point up a weakness in publishing: a near-absence of market research that, for example, might have predicted the waning appeal of stars past their prime." Sarah Lyall's piece in *The New York Times* (1 August), "Publishers' Aces in the Hole: Books That Sell Well Quietly," dealt with "the hidden best sellers, books that sell tens or even hundreds of thousands of copies year after year but for various reasons do not make any lists." Among those titles cited, together with estimated annual sales: *The Audubon Field Guide To North American Birds* (Knopf; 300,000), *Stretching*, an exercise book (Random House; 80,000), *Mathematics for the Million* (Norton; 10,000 a year since the 1930s), and Kahlil Gibran's *The Prophet* (Knopf; 100,000 a year since 1923). Then there are the very expensive books which can add up to big bucks. Craig R. Whitney wrote in *The New York Times* (9 November) about a facsimile of an eleventh-century German manuscript, published by S. Fischer and available to the reading public at a noteworthy price, "A Rare Book Copy For a Mere $16,425." Sometimes the author wins in spite of himself. In "Little, Brown Dumps Kunstler" (*New York Observer*, 9 May), D. T. Max reported that after paying an advance of more than $90,000, Little, Brown dropped the book *My Life as a Radical Lawyer*, by William Kunstler, which was immediately accepted by Carol. Perhaps the most surprising and pleasing money story of the year concerns the poet whose poem, whimsically and almost accidentally, was picked up by a rock star, set to music, and made into a major hit in the music scene. See David Streitfeld, "Book Report," *Washington Post Book World*, 13 November: "In a rare fusion of poetry and pop music, Marlboro College professor Wyn Cooper sold his poem 'Fun' to Sheryl Crow, who made it the basis for her hit song 'I Wanna Do' on the album 'Tuesday Night Music Club.'"

As for money coming in to fuel the publishing industry, we are still months away (in some areas a year or more) from being able to examine hard and accurate numbers for the year. Nevertheless, there are enough recent figures to mark and measure some trends, significant signs, and portents. In spite of dirges, uniforms of sackcloth, and ashes by major publishers (and their terrified stables and flocks of authors), *Publishers Weekly* (5 December) reported that the publishing industry overall had grown from $11.6 billion in business during 1987 to $15.4 billion in 1992, a growth of 38.7 percent. Earlier, on 29 August, *Publishers Weekly* reported that figures on the four largest bookselling chains for the first half of 1994 were up 15 percent. Books-A-Million, the large discount chain in the Southeast, announced a stock split for its shareholders. Bantam Doubleday Dell reported record profits so far in 1994. The downside of things was expressed by former Knopf and *The New Yorker* editor Robert Gottlieb, who was quoted in a *Newsweek* article ("The New Publisher's Row," 21 February): "At least 30 publishing acquaintances of mine have said to me in the last eight years, you got out just in time, it's so horrible." He pointed out that the big players have established control of the market: "Last year the seven big corporate groups accounted for more than 80 percent of all best sellers."

Speaking of best-sellers, the *Wall Street Journal* took a certain relieved pride in their discovery that the buying and reading habits of college students are not significantly different from those of the general public. In an editorial, "Campus Bestsellers" (22 July), they saluted the incorruptible students: "The loudest voices on campus decry the oppressive dictatorship of the racist, sexist, ethnocentric patriarchy, but the book that's flying out of the stores is 'In the Kitchen With Rosie' – recipes from Oprah Winfrey's cook."

But, despite the power and glory of the big publishers and the big economy, other contradictory forces are at work. More and more attention is being paid to the small presses and the university presses, which, with small staffs and a low overhead, can reach a break-even point, at a much lower figure, much sooner than the big houses. Until recently their biggest problems have been distribution and the difficulty of getting their books reviewed; and even though everything is not (yet) coming up roses, modern communication has made it much easier for customers to order small-press and university-press books even from the big chains, which do not, as a matter of course, carry many of these books on their shelves. And nowadays small-press and university-press books are a seriously competitive presence in the book pages, earning regular reviews check by jowl with the blockbusters. A *New York Times* piece by Sarah Lyall, "Defending New York's Publishing Dominance" (4 July), acknowledges that hard numbers prove that New York, center of the present publishing system, is in trouble: "In fact the industry is growing at a much larger rate nationally than it is in the city, meaning that New York's share of the nation's publishing work-

Paul Mariani, whose Lost Puritan: A Life of Robert Lowell *was the subject of a plagiarism controversy (photograph by Stephen Long)*

force has fallen significantly in the last 15 years." Lyall pointed out that nevertheless the city has a large, experienced, and qualified publishing work force and "was also seen as satisfying the publishers' desires to be near other publishers and near the national newspapers, magazines, and television shows that they depend on to promote books." About the only other strong attraction of the New York setting was said to be more a matter of appetite than corporate strategy: "The wide variety of restaurants in Manhattan was frequently cited by publishers as a factor weighing in favor of staying in New York." The *Wall Street Journal* took note of the fact that more and more university presses are successfully publishing fiction, both originals and reprints. In "Seeking Profits, College Presses Publish Novels" (20 September), Marj Charlier writes: "University presses, with their low budgets and overhead, can breakeven on novels and short story collections that sell as few as 3000 copies, compared with the 15,000-copy breakeven point for commer-

cial presses." One of the leaders in the successful publication is (as was noted in last year's *DLB Yearbook*) Southern Methodist University Press. (See Olin Chism, "SMU Press fills void left by the big boys," *Dallas Morning News,* 21 August.) Finally, shrewdly targeted advertising has allowed these presses to make the most of very modest promotional budgets. They now advertise in places like *Poets & Writers,* the *AWP Chronicle,* the little magazines, and quarterlies. Some sense of the size and variety of the small-press world can be gained from the reviews and the advertisements in *The Review of Contemporary Fiction* or *American Review,* which focused an entire issue (volume 15, February–March 1994) on small-press and university-press fiction. Among the small presses represented by new books which were reviewed in the issue were Asylum Arts, Sun and Moon, Fiction Collective Two, Dalkey Archive, Carpenter Press, Coffee House Press, Spillway, Zoland, Godine, Signal Books, Autonomedia, Phrygian Press, Maize Press, Four Walls Eight Windows, Lincoln Springs Press, Arcade, Q.E.D. Press, Arte Publico Press, Cinco Puntos Press, Curbstone, and West End Press.

In the world of newspaper book reviewing there were few significant changes, though the announcement that editor Rebecca Sinkler is to be replaced in early 1995 at *The New York Times Book Review* by Charles McGrath promises at least some changes in the flagship in the foreseeable future. Newspapers we followed closely were: (dailies) *The New York Times,* the *Washington Post,* and the *Wall Street Journal;* and the following Sunday papers: *The New York Times Book Review, Washington Post Book World, Chicago Tribune Books, Boston Globe, Philadelphia Inquirer, Baltimore Sun, Washington Times,* and *Los Angeles Times Book World.* Several other Sunday papers were examined on an irregular basis, including the *Denver Post, Miami Herald, Houston Chronicle,* the *Birmingham News, Atlanta Journal* and *Atlanta Constitution.* By and large the quality of the individual book pages remained roughly the same as last year, roughly the same size and space, give or take; and the quality of the individual book reviews was generally impressive. The *Washington Post Book World* remains in black and white format. *The New York Times Book Review, Los Angeles Times Book Review, Chicago Tribune,* and the *Washington Times* made more and more use of color in their layouts. On the basis of size, commercial and literary influence, and the number of books reviewed week after week, *The New York Times Book Review* is unquestionably the national leader. But judging only by the quality of reviewers and their reviews as well as careful editorial selection of books to be covered, the other major players offered close competition in 1994. I can offer no hard and fast numbers, but my considered impression is that the *Washington Post Book World* (not surprisingly) devoted itself more to nonfiction than fiction, especially historical, political, and social books. Among the others the *Boston Globe* and the *Washington Times* deserve particular praise for their regular, in-depth fiction reviews. For literary journalism Michael Dirda's "Readings" and Streitfeld's "Book Report," both written for the *Washington Post Book World,* continued to set a high standard.

Most interesting to this somewhat jaded reviewer of book reviews were a couple of belated discoveries made in this year. The book pages of the *Raleigh News and Observer* are first rate. Editor David Perkins deserves high praise for his choice of books and reviewers and for his delicate balance of regional and national literary concerns. To be sure, North Carolina these days is home and headquarters for a remarkable number of leading literary writers, but Perkins has found a way to draw on this resource without overemphasizing the local at the expense of the general. Next year we hope to present a survey of "Book Reviewing in the South." As of this writing it is hard to imagine any serious competition to Perkins's book pages except perhaps Michael Skube's in the *Atlanta Journal* and the *Atlanta Constitution.* Another paper and book editor deserving of mention and praise, however, is William Starr of the Columbia, South Carolina, *State* newspaper. Starr does not have the space enjoyed by Perkins or Skube, but within the space he is given, he has created a high-quality literary review. Starr can and does draw on writers and faculty at the University of South Carolina, but the driving force is himself. He writes first-rate reviews and is an excellent literary-cultural journalist, covering events and conferences, and so forth, throughout the South. The second discovery is the *New York Observer,* a hip, energetic, trendy, and (yes) regional weekly from the Big Apple. Under the literary editorship of Max, the *New York Observer* offered more coverage of the publishing scene, from inside that scene, than its grander New York competitors, as well as book reviews of the highest quality. By year's end Max had moved on to *Harper's Bazaar* but continues to review books, from time to time, for the *New York Observer,* and their staff writers continue to report on the cutting edge of the New York literary scene.

Our annual review of the place of magazines in book reviewing begins appropriately with *The New Yorker* for two reasons. First, even though in her second year as editor Tina Brown has significantly reduced the allotted space for book reviewing (and, as well, cut back on the place of fiction in the magazine), *The New Yorker* nevertheless published important literary pieces, not the least of which was an entire issue (27 June and 4 July, "The New Yorker Celebrates Fiction") that from its cartoon cover of sixteen familiar popular and "serious" American writers under the blessing of Miss Liberty draped in an American flag to the final page, Frank Gannon's satiric "Authors With the Most: Mr. Blackwell, the fashion arbiter, rates the great American writers," is, as claimed, fully devoted to fiction. One of the more interesting and talked-about pieces was a profile of novelist James Wilcox – "Moby Dick in Manhattan" – by James B. Stewart: "Can an acclaimed writer devote himself purely to his work and still make money? James Wilcox tried, and he's paying a high price for the literary life." And there were other superior literary essays and articles in other issues. Noteworthy was Nobel Prize–winner Joseph Brodsky's "On Grief and Reason" (26 September) which offered a classic close reading of two poems by Robert Frost (both reprinted in full in the essay), "Home Burial" and "Come In," and concluded, somewhat modestly, "To make a long story short, Frost is a very Virgilian poet." Biographer James Atlas produced "Holmes On the Case" (2 September), profiling the English biographer Richard Holmes. James Park Sloan did some detective work to ascertain the "truth" behind Jerzy Kosinski's wartime experiences in "Kosinski's War" (10 October): "To say that Kosinski never claimed every incident in 'The Painted Word' to be the literal truth is a bit like saying that Jesus never claimed to be the Son of God: it may be accurate in some narrow, legalistic sense, but such an edifice came to be constructed upon the assumption that the legalistic niceties were a moot point." If book reviewing, in and of itself, diminished in *The New Yorker,* literary journalism captured more than usual space and attention. If this journalism is more than a little like that of *Vanity Fair* in the days when Brown edited that magazine, why should that surprise us?

A second reason for beginning our overview of the magazine scene with *The New Yorker* is that this year a *New Yorker* staffer, Lauren MacIntyre, followed the ups and downs of the literary year in the fashion magazines for *DLB Yearbook.* MacIntyre placed two magazines, *Mirabella* and *Esquire,* at the top, praising the "thoughtful book reviews" in *Mirabella* and literary journalism and singling out for special mention *Esquire* literary editor Will Blythe as a critic whose judgments are fair and

Salman Rushdie at a book signing in London; the fifth anniversary of his death sentence was marked in February (photograph by Julian Calder – Impact).

whose style is "keen and funny." She cites his review (June) of E. L. Doctorow's *The Waterworks* (Random House): "It's hard to say which is the more prominent American tradition, beating up on the rich or sucking up to them." MacIntyre rates *Gentlemans Quarterly* and *Vogue* as close seconds to *Mirabella* and *Esquire*. Of *GQ* she notes that literary editor Thomas Mallon is "forthcoming in his reviews and essays," adding: "Overall the magazine's tone is less cynical than the other slicks." In the case of *Vogue* she points out the variety of good writers who review books, contrasting the reviews with the shorter listings: "The book notes tend to be overly kind, a jarring contrast to many of the reviews." *Vanity Fair* and *Elle* she rates a distinct cut below the above mentioned magazines: "Though *Vanity Fair's* coverage is suave and lengthy, it has become perhaps too focused on the cult of personality. Books are not discussed nearly as much as authors and the substance of the former is far less important than the flair of the latter. Author profiles take up all the book department's space (Bret Easton Ellis and Michael Crichton were 1994's biggest features), and while these profiles are engaging, there is little room left over to devote to new books and unfamiliar au-

thors." She notes that *Elle* had a "singular focus" on women all year long which somewhat limited its literary coverage; still *Elle* was not wholly beyond praise: "*Elle's* format is much blurbier than the other slicks and it is the only magazine to publish regular interviews – a nice change of pace. *Elle's* articles were lively and well-written, it's just a shame the focus had to be so narrow." MacIntyre's report praises *Harper's Bazaar* for its breadth of coverage including "audio taped books and books on *CD-ROM,* adding that some of the book reviews were of the highest quality." Concluding: "Unfortunately, although *Bazaar's* content was top rate, there wasn't enough of it to put the magazine in the competition." Finally, at the bottom of the barrel, she examined *Details:* "Its literary coverage was the slightest of all the magazines surveyed." She noted, however, that while it was refreshing to be introduced to some books from lesser-known publishers (Serpent's Tale, New Directions, City Lights), the editorial focus of the magazine remained oddly narrow. "Sex was the hot topic this year . . . "

One slick magazine not dealt with by MacIntyre (and in a certain sense a kind of competitor to *The New Yorker*) is *New York* magazine, which, while not devoting much space to books or literary news, nevertheless is the showcase for one of the best and brightest reviewers, the hard-nosed, sharp-tongued Walter Kirn.

Moving from slick to serious, we find that with the *Kenyon Review* and the *Yale Review* still suffering from editorial shellshock, the major quarterlies – *Sewanee Review, Virginia Quarterly Review,* and *Hudson Review,* followed at a distance by *Southern Review* and *Georgia Review* – held the line, maintained the standards of literary criticism and book reviewing. Of the three leaders the *Virginia Quarterly* continues to review more titles, closely followed by the the *Sewanee Review,* which offers more classic literary articles and essays than either of the other two. All three have a stable of regular critics and reviewers, though there is, inevitably, some overlapping. Not new on the quarterly scene but recently renewed (and improved), the *Southern Quarterly* has had an increased impact and looks likely to become a major player on the scene within a few years. The *New Criterion* (monthly) continues to publish first-rate reviews and critical articles, as does the *New York Review of Books.* Of the latter we learn in an article in *The Chronicle of Higher Education* titled "Hot Type" (20 July) that, according to a survey conducted by sociologist Steven Brint, the *New York Review of Books* is "the most influential periodical among American intellectuals." That may be the case, but if so then American intellectuals care less and less about fiction; for the fiction coverage by the *New York Review of Books* is minimal. Incidentally, the "Hot Type" section of *The Chronicle of Higher Education,* written by staffer Liz McMillen, has become a useful, if brief, newscaster for publishing and literary news. Otherwise that magazine has only occasional literary pieces as, for example, Thomas J. DeLoughry's "Textbook on Demand" (October), dealing with the growing importance of "customized textbooks" being created by Prentice Hall; Harcourt, Brace; Addison Wesley; Primis (McGraw-Hill); and American Heritage Publishing Group; and McMillen's "Literature's Jeremiah Leaps Into the Fray" (September), a profile of critic Harold Bloom; and Scott Heller's "Novelist's Champion Vows to Keep the Flame Burning" (November), an account of editorial changes in the Cambridge University Press critical edition of the works of F. Scott Fitzgerald.

The three issues of *The Review of Contemporary Fiction* remained our best source of information on and reviews of avant-garde fiction in America. The regular back pages of *The World & I* and of *Chronicles* continued to present excellent reviews of a wide va-

riety of books. Finally, a kind of discovery. Until 1994 I had not seen *First Things: A Monthly Journal of Religion and Public Life.* Allowing for the limits of the magazine's specific concerns, the "Books" section, including a "Briefly Noted department," is composed of significant book reviews by highly regarded scholars and critics.

Another magazine made some news and may have some impact on the upcoming literary year. Begun quietly in 1992, *The Oxford American* (out of Oxford, Mississippi) came under the patronage of John Grisham in 1994. Grisham is now the publisher, and the editor is the magazine's original founder, Marc Smirnoff, who has also worked as a personal editor for the Grisham novels. In the January 1995 issue of *GQ,* Ed Hinton ("The Great John Grisham") interviewed Smirnoff and discussed the direction *The Oxford American* will be taking, noting that under Grisham there will be "no graphic sex or violence" and no "foul language," a position which has brought cries of censorship from some literary figures. Still, there are plans to do bold things with this new magazine "of and about the South."

Another word about magazine book reviewing. Spring 1994 saw the appearance of *Re-Publish: A Magazine of the Literary Arts,* whose purpose is to "select entertaining, informative and instructive works from literary publications world wide for reprinting in *Re-Publish* magazine." The contents of the first issue were divided among fiction (Gordon Weaver, Jesse Lee Kercheval, Gladys Swan, and others), poetry (William Stafford, X. J. Kennedy, David Ray, Richard Moore, and others) and, roughly one-third, critical essays by the likes of Fred Chappell, F. D. Reeve, Jonathan Baumbach, and Lance Olsen. Materials in *Re-Publish* came from a variety of publications: *Poetry, Virginia Quarterly Review, Quarterly West, New Letters,* and *The Journal of Danish English Teachers,* among others.

Tomahawk Chops

For those who have not been keeping up, a Tomahawk Chop is awarded to an outstanding negative review. Tomahawk Chops for 1994 go to the following:

Michiko Kakutani, "Wandering Within the Idioms of Glasgow," *The New York Times* (16 December). Review of *How Late It Was, How Late* (Norton), by James Kelman: "Think of one of Nathanael West's black comedies without the humor, combined with one of David Mamet's obscenity-laced plays without the poetry, combined with one of Samuel Beckett's novels without the philosophical subtext, and that should give you a pretty good idea

Charles McGrath (left) editor of The New York Times Book Review, *with his predecessor, Rebecca Pepper Sinkler (photograph by Maureen O'Brien)*

of what this year's winner of the Booker Prize in Britain is like."

"The Examined Life Isn't Worth Living," *The New York Times* (20 September). Review of *Prozac Nation* (Houghton Mifflin), by Elizabeth Wurtzel: "Such self-pitying passages make the reader want to shake the author and remind her that there are far worse fates than growing up during the 70s in New York and going to Harvard."

"Some Familiar Terrain After 'American Psycho,'" *The New York Times* (2 August). Review of *The Informers* (Knopf), by Bret Easton Ellis: "Many of these passages verge on parody, so cartoonlike are the people, so willfully sensational are the events related. If it's satire that Mr. Ellis is after, however, it is a mission in which he utterly fails; his book completely lacks the social detail upon which satire depends. In fact, the animating emotion of 'The Informers' seems to be contempt: the author's contempt for his characters and for his readers."

Walter Kirn, "Freak Chic," *New York* (29 August). Review of *Son of the Circus* (Random House), by John Irving: "With vastly more preparation than payoff, explanation than action, background than foreground, and almost as many pause-and-review commas as stop-and-proceed periods, *A Son of the Circus* is constructed much like this sentence, but at epic length."

Richard Stratton, "Mutant Ninja Turtles Go to Prison," *Prison Life* (January 1995). Review of *Green River Rising* (Morrow), by Tim Willocks:

"This novel is a gross caricature of prison life. The characters are comic book superheroes and villains. It's dumb, it's cartoonish, it's insulting to prisoners, and the writing is overwrought and riddled with cliches."

Gerald Weissmann, "Haunted by Science," *New Criterion* (November). Review of *The Waterworks* (Random House), by E. L. Doctorow: "Doctorow's ideas are public and the wisdom conventional. Industry and science are wasted, commerce and government corrupt; the poor and savage noble. That hair shirt has been worn to the bank before."

J. O. Tate, "Tally Halt!," *Chronicles* (October). Review of *The Columbia History of the British Novel* (Columbia University Press): "A quick impression goes something like this: the British novel from its beginnings has been obsessed by feminist stridency, Stalinist politics, and a homosexual agenda."

Robin Darling Young, "Gay Marriage: Reimagining Church History," *First Things* (November). Review of *Same-Sex Unions in Premodern Europe* (Villard), by John Boswell: "All in all, then, this book does not begin to accomplish what it set out to do.... Indeed, the author's painfully strained effort to recruit Christian history in support of the homosexual cause that he favors is not only a failure, but an embarrassing one."

Thomas McGonigle, "The Ginger Man's genesis," *Chicago Tribune* (5 June). Review of *The History of 'The Ginger Man'* (Houghton Mifflin), by J. P. Donleavy: "Donleavy has seemingly taken a perverse delight in seeing how much he can abuse the reputation created by 'The Ginger Man': Each subsequent book of his, each worse than the previous, either through overwriting or pretentious posturing, has been greeted with less and less enthusiasm."

Camille Paglia, "Plighting Their Troth," *Washington Post Book World* (17 July). Review of *Same-Sex Unions in Premodern Europe* (Villard), by John Boswell: "The cause of gay rights, which I support, is not helped by this kind of slippery, self-interested scholarship, where propaganda and casuistry impede the objective search for truth."

Allen Barra, "Are We Having Fun Yet?," *Los Angeles Times* (17 April). Review of *My Idea of Fun* (Grove/Atlantic), by Will Self: "Self is attempting something very ambitious in 'My Idea of Fun,' but he doesn't have the depth to pull it off and when he tries to cover that fact he does it in typically modern British novelist style with a nasty quip or a smarmy joke."

Gary L. McDowell, " 'Tyrrany' of Lani Guinier," *Washington Times* (13 March). Review of *The Tyrrany of the Majority* (Free Press), by Lani Guinier: "Will the public be saddened at having been deprived of her services? Probably not. Will they breathe a collective sigh of relief that the Constitution and the country have been shielded from her? Perhaps. But for the most part they will simply be bored out of their skulls. What her friends gently call 'nuanced' language, the average reader will see as unrelenting tedium."

Neal Karlen, "Attack of the Anti-Heroes," *Los Angeles Times* (21 August). Review of *The Informers* (Knopf), by Bret Easton Ellis: "Joe McGinniss' gravest crime against literature was not 'The Lost Brother,' the author's recent and ridiculous faux biography of Ted Kennedy. Rather McGinniss' worst felony was rushing Bret Easton Ellis, his fiction-writing student at Bennington College, to publish 'Less Than Zero' at age 21."

Gold Star reviews

Gold Star reviews are positive or mixed reviews deemed to be exemplary, among the year's best and here presented in a kind of honor roll of book reviewers. With the exception of *The New Yorker,* where book reviewing is only one, often occasional aspect of staff work, none of the full-time professionals – staff members of magazines or papers – are here included. Among all these, however, two regulars who write first-rate reviews week after week throughout the year deserve special mention – Colin Walters of the *Washington Times* and Richard Eder of the *Los Angeles Times.* Both of these editors are worthy critics who

produce outstanding work and serve as an example for all other book reviewers.

• Jennifer Howard, "Taking Ties to the Desert," *Newsday* (30 January). Review of *In Touch: The Letters of Paul Bowles* (Farrar Straus Giroux): "For those who already know something about Bowles and his work, this collection offers much: a taste of his loathings and loyalties, his sure sense of place and the necessity of exile, his working habits and writing philosophy (including why he sometimes chose to write under the influence). It's a tantalizing glimpse of a charming, elegant, slightly eccentric traveler known for taking a suitcase full of ties with him into the desert."

• Irving Malin, untitled review in *Southern Quarterly* (Fall) of *In the Tennessee Country* (Knopf), by Peter Taylor: "He (Taylor), like James, knows that our lives are determined by an odd mixture of choice and circumstance. We are all in the 'Tennessee Country' of our origins, despite our attempts to find salvation, freedom and health."

• David W. Madden, untitled review in *Review of Contemporary Fiction* (Fall) of *Robert Crews* (Morrow), by Thomas Berger: "Berger has never been misanthropic, but this novel is an affirmation of life, renewal, and human resourcefulness."

• Richard Dyer, "Following his father through 'Raintree County,' " *Boston Globe* (2 August). Review of *Shade of the Raintree* (Viking), by Larry Lockridge: "It is a biography of a compelling figure written with a compelling urgency and depth of feeling by a son seeking the father he never got the chance to know."

• Thomas McGonigle, "Men in suits," *Chicago Tribune* (9 January). Review of *A Frolic of His Own* (Poseidon), by William Gaddis: "One hopes that 'A Frolic of His Own' will find the readers it deserves, readers who can testify to its power, its humor and even its sexiness. This is a book of genuine – and difficult – merit."

• John Updike, "Posthumous Output," *New Yorker* (30 May). Review of *The Road to San Giovanni* (Pantheon), by Italo Calvino, and *Thirteen Uncollected Stories* (Academy Chicago), by John Cheever: "Ever the playful metaphysician, Calvino wonderfully evokes the sensations of the innocent movie addict – the disturbing discrepancies between weather and time within the movie and conditions outside the theatre, and the narrative puzzles posed by arriving in the middle of the plot, in that era of continuous showings."

• Fred Chappell, "Respect for the real world," *Raleigh News & Observer* (10 April). Review of *Souls Raised from the Dead* (Knopf), by Doris Betts: "It

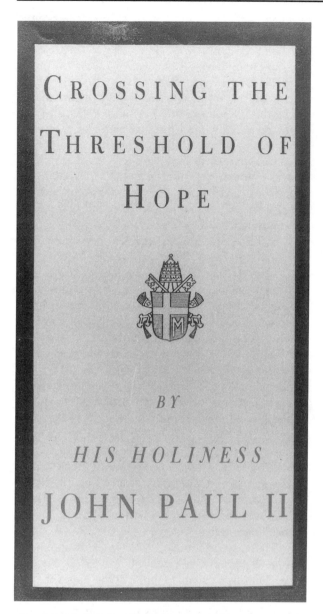

Dust jacket for John Paul II's meditations in the form of an interview. Knopf paid an advance of $6 million for the book.

requires a strong narrative and full-fleshed characters to absorb the kind of attention and mature wisdom that Betts can bring to fiction, and her new book supplies both in plenty."

• William Mills, "Negative Capability," *Chronicles* (December). Review of *The Crossing* (Knopf), by Cormac McCarthy: "McCarthy has an immense capacity for what Keats described as negative capability. Like Hamlet turning a skull in his hand, McCarthy turns the world of *The Crossing* this way, now that, asking us to consider the matter with him."

• Chaim Potok, "Doctorow's tale is saved by the telling," *Philadelphia Inquirer* (12 June). Review of *The Waterworks* (Random House), by E. L. Doctorow: "Yet the book is a dazzling romp, an extraordinary read, given strength and grace by the telling, by the poetic voice and controlled cynical lyricism of its streetwise and world-weary narrator."

• R. S. Gwynn, "Labors of Love," *Hudson Review* (Autumn). Review of *Life Work* (Beacon), by Donald Hall: "In effect, Hall's free-lance writing has become the equivalent of the subsistence farming of his forebears; like theirs, his is essentially a two-person operation; in separate rooms the work of husband and wife goes on in separate yet parallel courses, just as his grandfather Wesley's dominion of the farm ended whenever he set foot inside his wife Kate's kitchen."

• Stephen Margulies, "In Avedon's photos, the famous and the unknown are fashionable," *Baltimore Sun* (3 July). Review of *Evidence, 1944–1994* (Random House), photographs by Richard Avedon: "Mr. Avedon turned foolish clothing styles in *Harper's Bazaar* and *Vogue* into immortal leaping life. Later, he would turn the giant sadness of impoverished human flesh into astonishing style, world-famous glamour."

• Madison Smartt Bell, "'Gal' is a story of extraordinary power and pain," *Boston Globe* (26 June). Review of *Gal: A True Life* (Harcourt, Brace), by Ruthie Bolton: "Putting aside the familiar reasoning that such suffering is possible only at the bottom of the social system, 'Gal' isn't particularly a book about being black. It's a book about being human, and as enthralling as any ever written; every word of it has the clarion ring of truth."

• David Nicholson, "'Wounds': A Masterpiece For the Content of Its Characters," *Washington Post* (12 July). Review of *And All Our Wounds Forgiven* (Arcade), by Julius Lester: "Part poem, part polemic, part prayer, it is a wistful elegy to the civil rights movement, a celebration of its achievements and an acknowledgement of its failings threaded with the muted hope that the spirit of the movement remains alive somewhere in our hearts."

• R. H. W. Dillard, "Who Is the Man in the Boat?," *New York Times Book Review* (3 July). Review of *Once Upon a Time: A Floating Opera* (Little, Brown), by John Barth: "It also runs the changes on its titles with the skill of a jazz musician: time splits and runs at different speeds throughout the novel, and its 'once' or 'now' is, at one and the same time, the present of the novel's plot, the remembered and reported past of its narrator's (and author's) life, the carefully footnoted present of its writing and, of course, the now of the reader's reading."

• Ernest J. Gaines, "Easy Rawlins, Just a Little Older," *Los Angeles Times* (5 June). Review of *Black Betty* (Norton), by Walter Mosley: "His descriptions of the homes of the haves and have-nots of Los Angeles, and his description of that hot Santa Ana wind, and of the desert (of a *single flower* in the desert) is as good as you would find in Chandler at his best. And his dialogue is just as good, whether he is dealing with the hoods in the street, or the police, or children, or matrons in their grand Beverly Hills mansions."

• Richard Bausch, "Success and the American Novelist," *Los Angeles Times* (15 May). Review of *Shade of the Raintree: The Life and Death of Ross Lockridge, Jr.* (Viking), by Larry Lockridge: "And the thing that becomes most clear about Ross Jr. is that he was possessed of an astonishing amount of energy. . . . And he excelled at almost everything he tried (while at the University of Indiana, for instance, he achieved the highest grade-point average in the school's history)."

• Bland Simpson, "Down that dusty trail," *Raleigh News & Observer* (26 June). Review of *The Crossing* (Knopf), by Cormac McCarthy: "McCarthy is effective in 'The Border Trilogy,' describing the lengthy navigations of basin and range, the physical motions of both horse and human in all their Vaqueru-county interrelations. Yet the similarities between the stories of John Grady Coles of 'All the Pretty Horses' and 'The Crossing's' Billy Parham will almost certainly leave many of the master writer's most devoted readers with the uneasy sense that they are now hearing a twice-told tale."

Gold Star book reviewer

Last year we selected Fred Chappell, poet and novelist, as best all-around reviewer for 1993. This year my choice is Jennifer Howard, reviewer and literary journalist, who during the year published book reviews, articles, and interviews in *The New York Times Book Review, Newsday, Washington Post Book World, Los Angeles Times Book Review, Chicago Tribune, St. Petersburg Times, Publishers Weekly, Princeton Alumni Weekly,* and others.

Literary Journalism

Not completely separate from book reviewing, the publication of a new book often being the occasion for a profile or interview of an author, literary journalism in both newspapers and magazines seems to be more active than ever. Certainly a large number of pieces clearly characterized as literary journalism were published in 1994. Here are a few outstanding examples worth noting.

• John Calvin Batchelor, "Left Alone in Miami," *New York Observer* (5 December). An account of a *New York Review of Books* conference on the topic "Writing in Our Hemisphere: South and North," and including such luminaries as Susan Sontag, Robert Stone, Frank Conroy, and William Gass, among others: "The proof of masterful dirty tricks was upstairs in the concluding session. No audience. I was the only one present who was actually a member of the public. Everyone else of the three dozen in this Cape Canaveral–sized chamber was a major novelist, a relative of a major novelist or an indentured graduate student of a major novelist."

• Katherine Dalton, "The Work of Romulus Linney," *Chronicles* (December): "'I look at (my plays) as one huge, long, subtextual autobiography, which nobody can read but me.' He tapped his coffee cup and added (graciously), 'we'll keep it that way.'"

• Jim Windolf, "Tina At Two," *New York Observer* (3 October). An article on the second anniversary of Tina Brown's elevation as editor of *The New Yorker:* "A myth the press-friendly Ms. Brown has helped generate in selling her magazine is that *The New Yorker* was stuffy and stilted under Shawn, a mildewy grandmother's attic. In fact, it was a mysterious publication under his direction, strange and utterly independent."

• Helen Dunbar, "An Author Finds Inspiration in a Pair of Painted Frogs," *Wall Street Journal* (1 November). Profile of Lorrie Moore, author of *Who Will Run the Frog Hospital?* (Knopf): "To Ms. Moore, emotional pain is never widely separated from funny; her narratives are threaded with memorably askew witticisms."

• Adam Begley, "Colossus Among Critics: Harold Bloom," *New York Times Magazine* (25 September): "The legend of his genius ratified by a 1985 MacArthur fellowship, spans four decades. His notorious ego has grown vast as all literature – which is just about the scope of his new book, 'The Western Canon: The Books and School of the Ages,' a sweeping study of 26 canonical authors, from Chaucer and Cervantes to Kafka and Beckett."

• Craig R. Whitney, "A Literary Critic and His Critics: The Hazy Past," *The New York Times* (22 July). Concerned with the exposure of Marcel Reich-Ranicki as a secret agent for Poland in the Cold War: "With the cat out of the bag, he then admitted in an interview with the weekly news magazine *Der Spiegel,* 'Yes, I was also a permanent employee of the Polish secret service.'"

• Alice Steinbach, "Rediscovering Love," *Baltimore Sun* (17 July). Deals with the collaboration of

D. T. Max, formerly of the New York Observer, *now senior editor at* Vogue *(photograph courtesy of D. T. Max)*

novelist Josephine Humphreys and Ruthie Bolton to create *Gal: A True Life* (Harcourt, Brace): "'Gal: A True Life' is a literary success story, absolutely. But it is also a story about how friendship can flourish in the unlikeliest places."

• Rebecca Mead, "The Next Big Lit-Crit Snit," *New York* (15 August). Concerns Harold Bloom and *The Western Canon:* "It does, at least, provide the makings of a great parlor game – why no Thomas Wolfe, no Tom Wolfe, no Tobias Wolff? – for people who still read serious books in America."

• D. T. Max, "The Last Resort," *New York Observer* (20 June). Satirically treats a literary event at the posh resort, La Samanna on the French-owned island Saint Martin: "This May, for the second year in a row, the resort, managed by the trust of Dallas billionaire Carolyn Rose Hunt, hit on a quixotic idea: ship a quartet of pasty-skinned writers down from New York for a 'literary weekend,' hoping rich people who love books would follow."

• Louis D. Rubin, Jr., "Our Absolutely Deplorable Literary Situation – And Some Thoughts On How To Fix It Good," *Sewanee Review* (Fall): "The melancholy fact is that other than getting a prominent review in the *New York Times,* which is possible but unlikely, the only way that a good novel by an unknown writer can receive any attention other than of a local or at most regional nature, is to get noticed on National Public Radio."

• John Blades, "Bellow's Latest Chapter: One year after leaving Chicago, the novelist reflects on his new life," *Chicago Tribune Magazine* (19 June): "As he checks off Boston's virtues, Bellow still sounds a little uncertain about the wisdom of the move. The best thing about Boston, he indicates, may be that it's only two hours from his isolated weekend/vacation home in Vermont."

• Joanne Kaufman, "Doctor, Author, Hunk All Rolled Into One," *Wall Street Journal* (22 March). Profile of author Ethan Canin: "Deciding to become a doctor, he says, was a failure of the imagination. 'I was a Jewish kid. It seemed like a reasonable thing: You're working with people and you're not trying to screw them like you would in the law, the only other job I could think of. It seemed like the safest thing I could do.'"

• Alice Steinbach, "American Original," *Baltimore Sun* (15 May). Interview with E. Annie Proulx: "A single mother, Ms. Proulx supported her three sons by doing freelance journalism. From 1975 to 1988 she 'wrote articles on weather, apples, canoeing, mountain lions, mice, cuisine, libraries, African beadwork, cider and lettuces for dozens of magazines.'"

• John de St. Jorre, "The Unmasking of *O,*" *The New Yorker* (1 August). Identifies the writer who used the pseudonym "Pauline Reage" for *Story of O* (Grove): "The name of the French Scheherazade who wove her compelling story night after night to save her relationship with the man she loved is Dominique Aury. . . . She wrote 'Story of O' for an audience of one; she had never written anything like it before."

• David Streitfeld, "The Bookends of a Life," *Washington Post* (15 February). Profile of author Henry Roth: "Okay, so maybe Wagner isn't an appropriate model for a Jewish writer. Better, in any case, to be the role model yourself, to offer an upbeat example, for every artist who feels defeated and silenced by his art."

• Streitfeld, "It's Not Easy Being Weird," *Washington Post* (23 August). Profile of Hunter S. Thompson: "Some friends show up. Thompson tells some jokes and they laugh. He empties out his pack of Dunhills and, after saying it's almost impossible to make the box fly straight, proceeds to prove it. It never gets anywhere near the wastebasket, which is about six feet away."

• Liz McMillen, "Tulsa's Literary Treasures," *Chronicles of Higher Education* (20 April): "The state of oil rigs and windswept plains is also the home of the University of Tulsa, which has built an unusual collection of manuscripts, papers, and special editions of 20th century writers."

• John Schwartz, "Books of a Lifetime," *Washington Post* (3 February). Profile of William Gaddis: "The onetime fact checker for The New Yorker would probably be uncomfortable telling you the time unless he had acquired a profound understanding of how a watch is made."

• Madison Smartt Bell, "William T. Vollman: The writer as empiricist, obsessive and (nearly) corpse," *New York Times Magazine* (6 February). Profile of William T. Vollman: "Vollman almost always places himself within his work, sometimes as a simple observer, sometimes as an active participant. Yet he is not the sort of writer who can write only about himself. . . . His self-presentations do not convey the variety of Hemingway or Hunter Thompson or Charles Bukowski."

• Jennifer Howard, "Doris Betts," *Publishers Weekly* (25 April). Interview with novelist Doris Betts: "Although it is understated in *Souls Raised from the Dead* (Knopf), a strong feminist current also runs through Betts' work. That, too, explains some of her ambivalence towards the old South, which has tended to exclude women."

• Susanna Moore, "Travels With My Novel," *Travel & Leisure* (March). An account, in the form of a travel article with photographs, of a sixteen-city book tour: "During my stay in Denver the taxi drivers, the men at the reception desk, the bellhop,

and the elevator operator all speak about the Rockies with a kind of mysticism."

PART II

AN INTERVIEW WITH D. T. MAX

Kristin van Ogtrop, senior editor at *Vogue* magazine, interviewed D. T. Max, then book editor of the *New York Observer,* for *DLB*. This luncheon interview took place on 23 August 1994 at the Jewel of India restaurant in midtown Manhattan.

I think that each year the standard four-square Honest Abe book review sort of goes down a notch in terms of how much anyone cares about it.
                                   – D. T. Max

DLB: What do you think of Walter Kirn? [new book reviewer for *New York* magazine]

MAX: I think he's a first-class book reviewer.

DLB: But he slams a lot of things.

MAX: He slams a lot of books. But a lot of books aren't very good. So he tells the truth.

DLB: Do you think it's the duty of a book reviewer to from time to time pick a book that he likes?

MAX: Well, Walter's under a lot of specific pressure, which is that at *New York* magazine you can't really pick minor books. He's *got* to review the John Irving, and he's *got* to review the Bret Easton Ellis, and he's *got* to review Cormac McCarthy. So he's stuck. He can't reach into the pile of books — at least this is my guess — and pull out a little gem. That would be in a kind of "readings" or short section that they don't have. Maybe they can put it in the front of their books, in that "Hot Type" section. So he has to review the big books, and he can't dance around it. John Irving's book I haven't read; Random House said it was wonderful, but Walter makes a very convincing argument that it's this little book hiding in this enormous shell.

DLB: Although I thought it was interesting, I had a really hard time making heads or tails of his review of Bret Ellis's book. I finished reading it and thought, "Is he slamming this book?" He keeps going back to saying, "But it's just a satire" and I thought "Is this Walter Kirn saying this, or is this Walter Kirn pretending to be a Bret Ellis defender?"

MAX: You should read a review of Bret Ellis that Rich Moody wrote [in the *New York Observer*] which I think got to the core of the thing, which is that the book was recycled, and we were all racking our brains to figure out what Bret Easton Ellis was up to and he really wasn't up to anything. I think Rich had it right — he was up to getting out of his contract at Knopf. And this was the quickest way to do it.

DLB: Let's talk about what you do at the *New York Observer*. Your job there is broader than I thought it was.

MAX: It includes writing a publishing column, assigning the book reviews, as well as a certain number of feature pieces on writers and so forth. Mostly writers. The publishing column was weekly last year, this year it will be every other week.

DLB: What do you like better, writing the publishing column or assigning reviews?

MAX: They're so different. The industry is so far from the books it produces that it's a little hard to explain. Whether a given editor is hot or not has absolutely nothing to do with the quality of the books that he or she produces. So that, for instance, this year Ann Godoff at Random House had three best-sellers simultaneously.

DLB: She's the Caleb Carr editor?

MAX: Right. But that has nothing to do with whether Caleb Carr [*The Alienist*] or John Berendt [*Midnight in the Garden of Good and Evil*] or Nathan McCall [*Makes Me Wanna Holler*] wrote good books or lived up to their expectations or anything else. So the jobs almost exist on different planets.

DLB: Did you like the John Berendt book?

MAX: I never read it. I have a lot of friends who aren't in the business who are from Savannah who said that he got it exactly right. But I don't know what the "it" is. It's not that clear what the book is about from the jacket copy.

You know, the Caleb Carr book — I wrote the first piece on Caleb Carr.

DLB: I remember, last summer.

MAX: Right, and at the time the manuscript was in very rough form. I never wound up reading the finished manuscript. I assigned a review to Nicholas Meyer, who as a very young man wrote a book called *The Seven Percent Solution,* which was a Sherlock Holmes imitation. So I thought since he had done a book set in the past, we should have him review it. But he was very busy doing a polish on some screenplay for which I'm sure he was paid — you know, $150,000, and the *Observer* was paying $350 a book review, so you can see the problem right off. He did a good job, but he had to squeeze it in between high-level meetings at Paramount.

DLB: When you assign book reviews, do you pick the books, or do writers pitch the books to you?

MAX: We do two book reviews an issue, and generally speaking, I, in consultation with the editors at the paper, especially the editor, Peter Kaplan, select the books. We try and make them New York–focused books, but sometimes we break that rule if a book is going to be widely enough read in New York. So we'll review the Carville-Matalin book. Last year there were a lot of novels set in New York and that was fun. This year — you know, I look often for oddities, I look for books on university press lists that are about New York. We did a wonderful review of a book called *The Kingdom of Mathias* last year, which was about a mid nineteenth-century snake-oil salesman who was also a prophet and had a huge following in New York. The stuff that went on was so weird. The effect of the book reviews of that sort is to make people realize that New York has always been a really weird, violent town. And I like those reviews.

DLB: What do you think is the most powerful book reviewing vehicle in the country? Do you think it's *The New York Times Book Review?*

MAX: Some people say that *USA Today* has a lot of power, but I think that a certain kind of *New York Times* cover review can make it happen for a book, all alone. There are many cover reviews in *The New York Times Book Review* that only sell five thousand copies of the book. When you think that a million-plus pairs of eyes have read this book review, or looked at it or scanned it or noted it briefly on their way to the automobile section, it's amazing.

There's a difference between a selling book review and a "think-y" book review. You can tell it instantaneously and so can the publicist.

DLB: Explain the difference between a selling book review and a thinking book review.

MAX: Most reviewers are working in a different world. They're working on the question of whether the book is good or not. The two are not always the same question.

So, for instance, I think there was a book on psychology and the Third Reich – there was a great deal of abuse of psychology under the Nazis. It was originally a science they considered tainted and then they made their own awful uses of it. I think the university press that published that told me they had a front-page review and they sold five thousand copies. But the review itself didn't say "You must buy this book." It said the book was important. Saying the book is important very rarely sells it. A lot of things have to come together for a book to sell and one of them can be a *New York Times Book Review* cover that really makes the book sound fun. When they make it sound like really good medicine people still don't buy the book. More people buy it than if it hadn't been on the cover, but not by a lot.

DLB: Are there books that came out in 1994 that were surprise hits for you?

MAX: The book that I think has surprised us all is this biography of Moe Berg, the baseball catcher who was an OSS spy. That was a book that was destined for the best-seller lists even before *The New York Times Book Review* cover review. It was written by a guy who is about our age, Nick Davidoff, and it was just a wonderful book about a subject of curiosity to enough people that could be sort of explained quickly and it became a best-seller. I remember going to a bookstore – we ran a very early review on it – and seeing that many copies of it were already sold, and this was before the *Times* book review ran.

You know there are these reviewers in other cities who are also very important. Jonathan Yardley at the *Washington Post* or Richard Eder [*Los Angeles Times*] does a book review that means something to everyone. If they choose to review a book. And unlike Walter Kirn, I think they often will choose a book because they like it. Maybe Walter can choose anything he wants, I'm just speculating.

Jennifer Howard, 1994 Gold Star Book Reviewer (photograph courtesy of Jennifer Howard)

DLB: What other reviewers besides Walter Kirn do you like?

MAX: We have a very good reviewer named Peter Kirth who I think writes very good reviews. I think there are very very few book reviewers that people read for the pleasure of reading their book reviews. Kirn is enormously entertaining, and when you think of other enormously entertaining reviewers one problem is that the way the industry is structured, very few names appear often enough for you to remember. I think that Adam Begley writes a very good column for *Mirabella,* but part of what we're doing here is we realize that these people appear regularly enough to remember how they write. There are probably several hundred people who write for all the papers around the country but whom you and I never quite know the names of. At the *Observer* we have a specific goal, which is to make the review as interesting as the rest of the paper. And I think that probably *New York* magazine is under similar pressure. Those papers that have separate book sections don't have that pressure. They try and make the book review more of a kind of sales tool: should you buy the book? Is it important? In a lot of ways at the *Observer* you may never know if you should buy the book or not. What we'd like you to do is buy the *Observer*. And I think *New York* magazine is probably the same way – they don't want that page to be quieter. Book reviews are dying all across the country. I have no numbers, but you can see pages being eliminated from midsized cities.

DLB: Are there any trends happening right now in book reviewing or in the book world that you feel are really coming to a head in 1994?

MAX: I think that with each year the standard four-square Honest Abe book review sort of goes down a notch in terms of how much anyone cares about it. Years ago you would find these book reviews everywhere, then by the time you and I came on the scene only the more affluent or independently owned newspapers and the magazines would run them. Now I think everyone really is trying to dance around the idea of a book review; I think most editors regard book reviews as a potential liability.

DLB: Why?

MAX: Because the space tends to be handled in a very quiet way and what all editors fear is quiet pieces. So they're very happy with books, and they want books in their magazines and their newspapers, but they just want them in any way but the four-square book review. And we're all working on solutions to the question. Before Rhoda Koenig [the current book columnist] *Vogue* used to do the combination profile-review type things, and that was one way to liven up the question. You see, book publishers don't advertise. You don't get that traditional one-to-one – you do an article on health, you get two pages of advertising. It's part of the culture, the same way theater doesn't advertise. Movies do advertise, although they don't use monthlies very much for their advertising actually, when you think about it. They do like weeklies, though. Because they don't know far enough ahead when their movies are going to open. But books don't advertise because there's not enough money, and they have the same problem with shifting release dates that the movies have. So it becomes part of the overall tone and tenor and attempt to attract the right demographics for newspapers and magazines. And that's

why I think they have endured as long as they have and in as many forms as they have. I suspect that for newspapers a book review is a sign that you're the better newspaper in the town. Now in towns where there's only one newspaper, that no longer becomes so important because you get every reader anyway.

DLB: What else has been happening in writing and publishing?

MAX: There have recently been two big changes. One is that writers have learned to write more like screenwriters: the fast cut, to open a story without an intro, without a prefatory narrative, the way the nineteenth-century book opened. The second is the rise of the woman reader, who now dominates the market for quality and semiquality fiction to an enormous extent, so that a white, male writer, good as he may be – say Thomas McGuane, or even a Robert Stone – is facing a tremendous uphill battle. And they know it. Whereas for Amy Tan or Terry McMillan it's like a slide down a very smooth and comfortable slope. The world is made for them right now; it's their moment. Take the case of Tina Ansa. Her first story collection and novel sold for about $150,000. When Harcourt broke up a few years later, partially because she had sold well and partially because this trend had continued her agent moved her for $903,000 for two novels to Doubleday.

DLB: I know that multiculturalism has really affected the way books are being published. But – something like John Berendt's book, though, really gives me hope. Every time I open up *The New York Times Book Review* and I see that it's still on the best-seller list, knowing the publishing history of his book, that his agent didn't want to sell it, that he couldn't get a publisher, and now – that just makes me think that there are books that a discerning public can champion and that can break through. But I guess those things are very few and far between. I guess the reason I'm so astounded is because he's outside of the loop. He's not Danielle Steele, he's not – even Caleb Carr has written a very predictable, thrillerish kind of book. It's no surprise to me that Caleb Carr's book is on the best-seller list, even though it's a historical book. It's totally a page-turner.

MAX: It's been a while, though, since a book like that was a best-seller. I don't know, but I think so. It's been really since *Ragtime*.

Michael Skube, book-section editor at the Atlanta Journal *and the* Atlanta Constitution *(photograph courtesy of Michael Skube and the* Atlanta Journal *and the* Atlanta Constitution*)*

There are a lot of conferences on the death of the serious book, but it's mostly writers whose careers just aren't moving forward – the serious book is dying because they're the ones who are writing it. What happened is publishers cut back their lists. They certainly didn't cut Danielle Steele. They cut people who were going nowhere in terms of their sales track record. They weren't black, or Hispanic, or women writing on multigenerational themes – those people tend to do okay. And for those people the serious novel is disappearing. Or, for other people, this may be the heyday of the serious novel. Amy Tan believes she writes serious books – I've never heard her describe them, but I've spent time with her.

DLB: I've never read any of her books.

MAX: They're very light. Very fast. And they're all about family. Jane Smiley also. Jane Smiley had about twelve books, none of which went anywhere, until she wrote a book about a multigenerational family saga involving incest and ecological violations and then she had a bestseller.

Think of what's happened to minimalism. Boy, did that disappear. Those writers were in their late twenties, early thirties; I don't know what they'll write now. There are a lot of them, too. Everyone wanted them. There's a theory that short attention spans meant that thin books would always sell better. None of that seems to be true. People seem to like these big fat books. Publishers will bulk up a book – I remember that Random House paid $500,000 for Carol Edgarian's *Rise the Euphrates,* and she was referred to as "the Armenian Amy Tan." And no one bought that book.

DLB: Would you ever consider working in book publishing again?

MAX: I definitely would consider working in book publishing again. For a while book publishing looked like a kind of dismal profession, with all these cutbacks and so forth. But I think that most of the cutbacks have happened – except perhaps at the Random House group – and that they'll probably start hiring again as the economy picks up. The market on literary and semiliterary books is really very sound. It loses ground gradually, but it hasn't suffered any catastrophic hit. In fact, I really think that if you consider the competition, from everything from video to television to newspapers to magazines, CD-ROM to on-line to just sitting there staring out the window, it's phenomenal that people will devote twenty-five hours to an Amy Tan novel. And I think the reason is that people enjoy reading. And these are people who are young and should therefore be uninterested. I don't see any catastrophic falling off in literacy, and even the computer world requires a kind of literacy that would permit the book to flourish. The real fear was image: image at this point is not very imagistic. It's much more wordy. It's a good effort to send an E-mail letter, despite what everyone says. If you can write any letter, then you can read Amy Tan.

DLB: Amy Tan is your –

MAX: Well, she's a benchmark because she sells fabulously well, she's taken fairly seriously, and she's very much socked into the politically correct world, which is really the world of the book today. If publishers weren't slow to respond, they could cut many many of the male authors on their lists with absolutely no effect on their sales. I think because a lot of them are men, they won't do it. But as women go after the few positions in the industry they don't have, I think we may see the opposite of the Chinese birth situation: dozens of women writers and a handful of male writers. In the *fiction* world. In the nonfiction world people are sort of gender blind.

DLB: I know we've been spending most of our time talking about fiction, but nonfiction is obviously extremely important. Isn't that where a lot of publishers really make their money?

MAX: Yes, and it's where you'll find male readers often. Nonfiction is in its own crisis that corresponds to the book-review crisis which is: do you really want to read eight hundred pages on Brecht? Or is that really a reference book disguised as a biography? The treat in a book like the John Berendt – which I have not read – is that it reads like a novel, as they used to say. It's a narrative. I'm not sure people have much patience with books that don't have strong narratives. I can't think of a book that was a best-seller this year that didn't have a strong narrative.

DLB: What about *The Celestine Prophecy?*

MAX: Well, the New Age is its own weird enormous cult that you and I will only glimpse in small pieces. I haven't read it. If it turns out we all have an afterlife, people who have read those books will have an advantage.

DLB: Do you like going to book parties as part of your job, or is that tedious?

MAX: Book parties are basically selling events in which the publisher is making people notice the existence of an author who might otherwise have escaped their attention. The conversation tends to be almost exclusively about the fate of other authors as well as editors, publishers, and so forth, so in that sense it's probably no more interesting than a reception given by a chemical company. But because there's a certain inherent interest in people who tend to create beautiful works, there's a kind of inherent interest in those book parties. Creative people have always attracted other interesting people or other simply rich people. So they're better parties than they might be. They're also different from the huge movie parties in that they tend to be small. You'll go to the opening for a major movie and that resembles more an open restaurant than it does a party. These book parties are still often held in people's homes. You meet the sort of doyenne who hosted the party, that kind of thing.

DLB: Are they really selling parties, or is it mostly the author's friends and book editors at magazines? Because oftentimes the parties are upon publication of the book, so it's too late.

MAX: You're right – too late for anything we can do.

DLB: So why? Just to be nice to the author?

MAX: I think there is a genuine sense of hope at somebody's party, that it marks the debut of a successful new book. Also the author comes around again for another book in a couple of years, and if you can get the company to pay for drinks and a cab, why not? People in publishing don't make a lot of money. They like that sense of comradeship that comes out of meeting after hours. They're not extravagant events – they're often paid for secretly not by the publisher but by a wealthy friend of the author.

DLB: Do you get information for your column at these parties? Do you find them useful?

MAX: It saves a lot of phone calls. But information is really fairly public in publishing. There's not a lot of looking in garbage cans. Word spreads through the industry instantaneously.

DLB: It's amazing how so many people know how much an author's advance is. People know how much movie actors make, but unless you're a top executive at General Motors or something, your salary is very often private.

MAX: It's definitely unfair to the authors. Why should we have their tax returns when they don't have ours? Unless the publisher goes to a great effort to keep the advance secret, and the author and agent cooperate, most things are known.

DLB: Why would they want to keep it secret? If they paid too much and they're embarrassed?

MAX: No. Generally it's the author who is embarrassed because the advance went down, and they ask the publisher to keep it secret.

DLB: I can't really think of anything else to ask you. Is there something we haven't covered?

MAX: The big question of the future of literary books is still in the air, but I think if you look at it from year to year the trends that you and I have been talking about are three or four years old, and I think everyone's waiting for the next truly literary group of writers to come along. There's been nothing since the mid 1980s.

DLB: Do you think they're being allowed to come along?

MAX: Writing schools are still cashing their checks, so I assume they're being allowed to come along.

DLB: Do you mean a young generation of literary writers?

MAX: Right. That whole mid-1980s generation seems to be missing in action.

DLB: Well, they're still writing, they're just not living up to their promise.

MAX: But they're missing in action. It's now 1994. Who's the new sacrificial lamb? Who's the

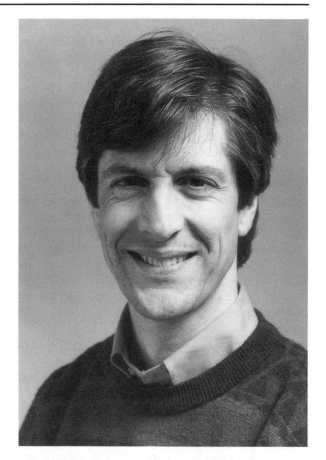

David Perkins, book-section editor at the Raleigh, North Carolina,
News and Observer

new highly touted writer, male or female? Young, old. It's a mystery. They always say a first novel is easier to publish than a second novel, but where are the first novelists? The whole machine waits: you wait and I wait, but nothing is being offered. The discovery level has been very low for the last couple of seasons. Nonfiction has been more of a revelation than fiction.

DLB: I wonder why. You know there are good books out there. Are they being poorly published, or are they being rejected because they're too literary, or are they authors who aren't good-looking enough and so they're not being publicized? What is it?

MAX: It could be economic. It could be that the country's mostly interested in hot young writers when people have jobs. We've been in this kind of slow but long recession and it seems inappropriate for the machine that's ready to push twenty-three-year-old kids.

PART III

BOOK REVIEWING IN TEXAS
Paul Ruffin

Boastful though Texas may be in most arenas of human endeavor – and perhaps, in some things, rightly so – its newspapers, magazines, and journals do not do an impressive a job of book reviewing, especially given the population of the state and its number of large metropolitan areas.

Texas Monthly is the only major commercial magazine in the state published on a monthly basis, but, mostly glitter and glare, it does little major book reviewing and, as might be expected, concerns itself largely with Texas affairs, or what is trendy, or, as one observer has put it, what is in their best interest. One might conclude upon an examination of the magazine that its primary function is to *advertise*. *American Way,* the magazine of American Airlines, published in Fort Worth twice a month, has an enormous potential reading public of nearly a hundred million passengers a year, but the last time I examined a copy it featured only three reviews.

Texas Books in Review, published through the Center for Texas Studies at the University of North Texas, is a quarterly review that features nearly thirty full reviews each number and occasional omnibus reviews, but it focuses exclusively on Texas writers and books on Texas. With a staff of regular and occasional reviewers, this exceptionally well-done publication features thorough, insightful reviews of everything from novels to public-school textbooks and makes a major regional contribution (though I suspect that, given its limited circulation, its impact on sales is negligible). A similar publication in format and frequency of publication, though restricted to reviews of fewer than a hundred words, is *Review of Texas Books,* published in Beaumont. Another review that deserves mention is *Roundup Quarterly* (an adjunct of the Western Writers Association out of El Paso), which reviews Westerns published in the Southwest.

It is somewhat surprising to discover how few literary journals in Texas offer reviews. *Concho River Review* never really got into reviewing, and *Southwest Review* stopped reviewing a few years ago, leaving only *Sulphur River Review* (Austin), *Southwest American Literature* (Southwest Texas State), and *Texas Review* to do what little reviewing is done. *Sulphur River* suffers from limited exposure, and *Southwest American Literature* concerns itself, logically enough, with southwestern books. Published biannually and with insignificant circulation (though it does go to several major national and international libraries), *Texas Review* typically features fifteen to twenty full reviews of five hundred to one thousand words along with ten to twenty shorter reviews each year. The pillar of this journal's review section is the nationally known New York reviewer Irving Malin, whose insightful assessments account for more than half those published each issue. (In truth, I suspect that the sales generated by reviews in national literary journals would not pay for the few cans of ink used in printing most books; as George Garrett put it in *DLB Yearbook 1993,* most of the literary magazines are, "at least as far as book reviews are concerned, too late, too uneven, and too erratic to matter.")

Since newspapers print most of the book reviewing done in Texas, one might get a pretty good idea of what is going on in the field by examining the Sunday papers and supplements, but this approach does not yield much of an overview. The best way to get a broader perspective would be by querying the book-review editors of three of the state's most influential newspapers in the three largest population areas – Austin, Dallas/Fort Worth, and Houston. Having done this, I have come to the conclusion this adjunct enterprise of reviewing books is merely a burden to bear for these papers, like having to go to church on Sunday; you may not have sinned significantly, you see no genuine moral reasons for going, and certainly there is little profit in going (unless you are a politician), but you go because of a perceived expectation or out of tradition or because it's good for the children. Among these book-review editors there seems to be little joyousness or satisfaction at fulfilling some high purpose in what one editor described as "a greatly underpaid profession."

Perhaps one reason these editors appear dispassionate about their calling is that they all seem to believe that the reviews they run have very little ultimate impact on a book's fate. Fritz Lanham, of the *Houston Chronicle,* said that reviews in the state's major newspapers "influence the visibility and sales of a book locally, and to the extent that Texas is one of the bigger book markets because of its population, that affects the national fate of the book," but like Ann Morris, of the *Austin American-Statesman,* he suggested that the influence on national book sales is "very little." Bob Compton of the *Dallas Morning News,* one of the state's most honored newspapers (Pulitzer Prizes in 1986 and 1989) and with a circulation surpassed only by the *Houston Chronicle* (both of which have a Sunday circulation in excess of half a million copies), concurred that reviews in the state's newspapers can certainly enhance the sales potential of regional books. One editor made the remark that perhaps the only newspapers that really have much impact on national sales are the big guns like *The New York Times* or the *Washington Post.*

There is little doubt in the minds of these editors, though, that state newspapers have a decided influence on local sales of books they review, especially regional books. Compton reported that he has been told by Dallas booksellers "that they usually have increased requests for books the week following a favorable review of our Sunday Books page," and, while admitting that readers of reviews are only a "slice of the newspaper readership," Lanham did say that these people are "swayed to a certain extent by reviews."

One of the big problems these editors face, since book reviewing is hardly a major function of their newspapers, is the limitation on numbers of books they can review and reviewers to assess them. The reviews are almost always restricted to the Sunday papers (as is the case across the country), and rarely do they run more than seven full reviews. Compton devotes about two pages per week to book reviews in the "Sunday Reader" section, typically featuring up to seven major reviews, and in the *Houston Chronicle* Sunday supplement *Zest* Lanham runs six or seven major reviews, plus brief mentions, collectively representing four or five pages. (The competitor of the *Chronicle*, the *Post*, whose book reviews are handled by Liz Bennett in their Arts and Entertainment supplement, probably devotes a little less space to books.) Morris said that she prefers and runs "mini-reviews of 350 words most often."

Finding reliable, insightful reviewers seemed to be a source of concern for these editors, who, of course, rely on a staff of regulars but keep an eye out for new talent. Lanham tries to find people "who can write lively, intelligent reviews, produce them in a timely fashion, and want to do them on a fairly regular basis," but he admitted that such reviewers "are more rare than you might imagine." In his search for people with "expertise . . . judgment . . . clear writing," Compton, who early on limited his reviewers to Texas writers, now has reviewers all over the country. Morris said simply that she looks for "intelligent, well-read, diligent, good writers who will work for twenty dollars a review." Limited budgets clearly play a significant role in this business: almost no one pays more than fifty dollars a review, and even the high-end stipends work out to a fraction of minimum wage, given the time a reviewer has to put into reading a book critically, then

Bill Starr, book-section editor at the Columbia, South Carolina, State *newspaper*

writing the review. (Smaller papers pay five to ten dollars for reviews.)

When asked whether they attempt to achieve any sort of balance in their review sections, the editors responded uniformly that they did, though Morris admitted quite bluntly that "it's not a science." Compton said that he tries to balance fiction and nonfiction, steering clear of the "huge popular bestselling authors" such as James Michener, Danielle Steele, and Jackie Collins, and reviewing as many regional publishers as he can, paying particular attention to Texas and southwestern writers. Lanham confessed a bias toward "the high culture end of the spectrum of books" with "a fair amount of crime fiction because it's so popular"; he strives, he said, to produce "a lively mix."

There was quite a lot of agreement among the editors on the merits of running negative reviews. Morris said that she usually hesitates to run them; Lanham responded that when he gets a negative review he wonders "whether I'm making best use of my limited space in devoting it to a book that (in the reviewer's opinion) is lousy"; and Compton said that though he will run them on occasion, if he feels that a review is "unwarrantedly harsh," he will "call and talk it over with the reviewer, and if he or she agrees, we will soften it."

With the rise to prominence of several small and university presses, among them Southern Methodist University Press, which in the fall of 1993 had three major (half-page) reviews of books of fiction in *The New York Times Book Review,* I asked these editors whether they paid much attention to books published by these presses. Morris responded that the *Austin American-Statesman* reviewed the university press books "fairly often," while Compton said unless he feels it is an "extraordinary book," which will get a full review, "I have one or two reviewers who do roundups of books from small publishers and university presses. That column runs on a 'space available' basis, which means infrequently." Lanham advised that because he is "very much aware that the small and university presses are producing fine books of wide interest to readers," he makes a "conscious effort to select for review books from those sources. . . . "

I asked these editors a series of more general questions about the state of writing in the country and region. First of all, I wanted to know what their assessment was of the New York publishing scene. Lanham, citing his brief tenure as a book editor and lack of contact with New York publishers, declined to respond, but Morris gave her typical pointed answer: "Ever-changing and in some peril." Compton's response was that he is "in agreement with many other critics of New York." The New York publishers, he feels, "are pursuing the sure best-sellers and are letting midlist writers slip away, either by not publishing them, or not promoting them. I think literary taste is disappearing, with publishers pursuing the John Grishams, the Robert Wallers, the Danielle Steeles, the Jackie Collinses."

Can the university presses, as David Slavitt suggested in his "The Year in the Short Story" section of the *DLB Yearbook 1993,* take up the slack in fiction publication? (I think that Slavitt was not restricting himself to short fiction.) These editors, with reservation, seem to think so. Morris said, again in her pithy fashion, "Sure. Don't you [think so]?" Lanham responded, "Yes indeed. I hope that small presses and university presses can play a role in publishing books that have real value but may not have blockbuster potential," mentioning specifically the fiction publications of Rice, Texas Christian University, and Southern Methodist University Presses and the nonfiction productions of Texas and Texas A & M. Compton, a bit less sanguine,

said, "I hope that university and small presses can fill that gap. But the rise of the huge chain bookstores may further stifle literary publishing, with the big retail chains demanding surefire sellers from publishers."

I asked whether these editors saw any current trends in American publishing that particularly disturbed or delighted them. Morris replied simply, "The decline of midlist fiction . . . Oprah's power to sell books." (Morris was not the only one to mention Oprah Winfrey's influence on national book sales.) Compton answered, "I am encouraged by university presses, such as TCU Press and SMU Press in Texas. They are printing new fiction and reprinting Texas classics. If there is anything on the national scene that delights me, it is the several series of quality paperback fiction (and nonfiction) that is being kept in attractive editions." (Though Compton did not specifically mention this, I would like to point out that SMU is also reissuing books by non-Texas writers with major name recognition, such as W. P. Kinsella, Alan Cheuse, and George Garrett.)

Finally, I wanted to know how these editors felt about the writing and publishing scene in Texas. Morris said that to her, Texas writing and publishing appear to be "alive and well," though "more people are writing books than are reading them or so it seems." She noted further that there is "an increase in use of Texas as a background for fiction, also more ethnically varied fiction and nonfiction being published." Compton lamented, "A generation of our most admired writers is aging (Elmer Kelton, John Graves, A. C. Greene). Some of the next generation are not often heard from (C. W. Smith, Joe Coomer, and so forth)." On an upbeat note, though, he pointed out that we have "some very attractive Hispanic writers coming to maturity (witness Dagoberto Gilb)." As for Texas publishing, Compton stressed once again that the "burden right now seems to be on university presses to carry the torch."

I would like to mention a few other newspapers who do their part to keep book reviewing alive in the state: the *Dallas Times Herald,* the *Fort Worth Star-Telegram,* and two San Antonio papers, the *Express-News* and the *San Antonio Lights.* All have excellent Sunday supplements and offer a fairly broad spectrum of reviews each week. Hats off to these editors and their review staffs — and to the hundreds of little papers scattered across the state — for carrying on this noble if hopelessly futile enterprise, this "labor of love," as Ann Morris put it. Long may they thole!

There is no genuine book-review leader among the state's major papers, their distribution and influence limited largely to the metropolitan areas they serve. One must remember that a paper printed in Boston or Washington or New York City, if distributed the distance between Dallas and Austin or Houston, could reach several heavily populated states. Whereas some Houston readers with Dallas or Austin backgrounds or connections (or vice versa) might subscribe to papers from those cities, more-sophisticated readers — those most likely to be interested in book reviews — would just as soon pay for a subscription to *The New York Times Book Review,* which, though perhaps not delivered quite as promptly, is well worth the wait.

The most active book reviewer I know in Texas is novelist and freelance writer Clay Reynolds, whose book reviews have been published in everything from *The New York Times Book Review* to the *Texas Review* and appear regularly in the *Dallas Morning News, Fort Worth Star-Telegram, San Antonio Express-News,* and *Houston Chronicle.* I asked Reynolds which Texas newspaper seemed to be doing the best job of reviewing these days. He said that though the *Dallas Morning News* had headed the pack for a long time, the *Houston Chronicle,* under the leadership of Lanham, was fast gaining ground; the *Austin American-Statesman,* according to Reynolds, is a bit too liberal and trendy to suit his tastes. He mentioned another newspaper that seems to him to be doing a fine job of book reviewing: the *Express-News,* out of San Antonio.

Reynolds said that one of the big problems facing newspapers all over the country is the lack of budgets for book reviewing. Many of their reviewers are not paid at all, or are paid very little, citing one case in which a book editor admitted that for years a cleaning lady in the newspaper office building wrote reviews for him, a woman who had "never completed high school and wrote out her reviews by hand. She needed the money [such as it was], and the arts editor, who had neither the time nor interest to invest in book reviews, was glad to have her do the work."

With so little reward for their efforts, Reynolds noted, oftentimes reviewers "write about books they haven't finished . . . or have merely skimmed through. For both substance and opinion, they often rely on the plot summaries and scenarios that publishers enclose in review copies or even on other reviews." Still, reviews are reviews. "As with the cast of a Broadway show," he said, "the future of the artist's work is sometimes directly dependent upon the reaction of a small number of people, whose job it is to fill space in newspapers and magazines."

Given its size and population and the great many well-known writers at work in the state, one can conclude that simple geography and demographics keep Texas from being more involved and more influential in book reviewing. After all, beyond the glow of population centers such as Houston, Austin, San Antonio, and the Fort Worth/Dallas complex, these little oases of culture, Texas is largely desert and prairie and piney woods dotted with towns like Junction and Groesbeck and Cut-and-Shoot, where the nearest Wal-Mart is the bookstore of choice and where a book review would stand as much a chance of being read as Hillary Clinton would of being elected Woman of the Year.

Writers and their Copyright Holders: the WATCH Project

Cathy Henderson
University of Texas at Austin

and

David Sutton
University of Reading

"Whom do I need to contact to get permission to publish a previously unpublished Ezra Pound letter?"

"Who can give me permission to put on a production of a play by Maurice Baring?"

"How do I find out about John Ruskin's copyright now that Messrs. Allen & Unwin no longer exist?"

"Which authors' copyrights are now in the public domain?" Until now, getting answers to questions such as these and finding out about copyright holders has been a haphazard and serendipitous process, and this has been a long-standing concern for those who work with primary, largely unpublished, source materials. The problem has been much the same in the United States, the United Kingdom, and all other countries of which we have made enquiries, despite their differing copyright laws. (Unpublished papers always seem to have special and extended copyright protection.) There exist specialized files, such as those maintained by the Copyright Office in Washington, D.C., and the Society of Authors and the Authors Licensing and Collecting Society in London, but these are concerned primarily with the published writings of living authors and are not designed to assist those working on archives and manuscripts. Librarians and archivists are asked frequently by researchers to help identify and locate copyright holders for papers in their collections, and many maintain informal files for this purpose, but the absence of any central reference work or database has continued to be at the heart of a problem recognized by the whole profession. Now there is a new solution to the problem.

In 1987 the ad hoc Literary Rights Committee of the Rare Books and Manuscripts Section (RBMS) of the American Library Association sought, unsuccessfully, to identify an organization that would create and maintain a file of literary copyright holders. Those approached responded favorably to the idea, but the committee could find no one to undertake the initiative. The committee succeeded in identifying a good number of locally maintained files in a range of United States, Canadian, and British libraries whose managers were willing to contribute information to a central database, but there was no willing compiler. The committee shifted its focus and produced in 1991 a text sheet titled "Locating Copyright Holders," which, in a question-and-answer format, explains basic copyright considerations governing publication of manuscripts and lists steps scholars can take to locate copyright holders.

"Locating Copyright Holders" has established itself as an invaluable aid and will undoubtedly continue to be widely used. From now on, however, we believe that the first point of reference for scholars seeking particular copyright holders will be an electronic file newly available on the Internet through the General Libraries server at the University of Texas at Austin. The name of the file is Writers and their Copyright Holders, which gives us the pleasing acronym of WATCH (although a graduate intern at Austin, after a long day's inputting, queried whether we had considered ACHE – Authors, Copyright Holders, Estates). The WATCH file is also available through the World Wide Web.

The establishment of WATCH, as an innovative collaboration between the Universities of Texas and Reading, followed two breakthroughs in 1993, one in the United States and one in the United Kingdom. First, the Harry Ransom Humanities Research Center, University of Texas at Austin decided to create on its own a file of copyright holders for authors represented in its collections. Shortly afterward the Strachey Trust, a charity established in 1972 to further the pursuit of scholarship especially in areas connected with literary manuscripts, agreed to provide funding for a small-scale project on literary copyright based at the University of Reading Library. The director of the Harry Ransom Humanities Research Center initiative was Cathy Henderson, and David Sutton was appointed to direct the Reading scheme. In a short space of time, agreement was reached between the two institutions that they would work together on a single project rather than two separate ones, and the first publicity for the joint venture was released in March 1994.

The objective is to make information on copyright holders available free of charge for use by anyone with access to the Internet. It is hoped that wide availability of the information will make it easier for scholars to identify whom to contact to seek permission to publish from unpublished manuscripts housed in libraries and archives. It is also possible that this initiative may grow into a much larger program of copyright research, in line with an all-embracing feasibility study prepared for the Strachey Trust by the Authors Licensing and Collecting Society.

At the moment WATCH is an indexed text file that contains primarily the names and addresses of copyright holders or contact persons for English-language authors whose papers are housed, in whole or in part, at the Harry Ransom Humanities Research Center. Records from the Reading team have now been added to the file, and it is anticipated that the principal area of growth in the coming months will be further Reading-generated records. The Reading team draws extensively on its predecessor project, the Location Register of English Literary Manuscripts and Letters, which provides valuable data about manuscripts of literary authors which are to be found in British repositories. Workers at Reading are also seeking to confirm and then include information from various locally maintained files, including those of the British Library; the Bodleian Library; King's College, Cambridge; and Trinity College, Cambridge. The help and cooperation of such institutions is testimony to British recognition of the importance of the project. Staff at the Harry Ransom Humanities Research Center are similarly engaged.

In order to compile the initial file, staff at the Harry Ransom Humanities Research Center mailed letters to all the copyright holders of whom they had record and asked each to confirm that it was the copyright holder for a given individual and to give permission to include its name and address in the proposed WATCH file. The responses were affirmative. Fewer than fifteen of approximately one thousand respondents asked for their name not to be included in the file.

The individuals listed in WATCH have indicated that they are the copyright holders for the authors listed, or the copyright holder's appointed representatives, and have given written permission to have their names and addresses included. As compilers, we have made no attempt to verify an individual's claim to copyright ownership or representation and in the WATCH "read me" are indemnified against any claims brought for violations of copyright law. We suggest that scholars using the list verify copyright claims themselves before publishing anything on the basis of permissions received from people named in the list.

Occasionally information that an author's copyrights are in the public domain is received, and this assertion is recorded; other authors or executors reply that they do not wish to exercise their rights. We also come across situations where copyright in unpublished materials is still protected under United States and United Kingdom law but we cannot identify anyone who will claim the copyright. Consequently, some entries are worded cautiously and inconclusively, as in this example: "Copyright in unpublished papers of William Heinemann was believed to be held by the publishers William Heinemann Ltd. and was assumed to have passed to their present parent company Reed International, whose legal department, however, states that they do not hold any such rights [letter to the United Kingdom WATCH office, 20 May 1994]."

We would like to encourage anyone who has copyright information to contact us. WATCH is a not-for-profit public service and will be that much more effective if it has the active support of the archivists, librarians, and writers whose workload it aims to lighten. The continuing work of the project is dependent upon funding from charitable and cultural bodies. Subject to fund-raising progress, the two teams in Austin and Reading will continue their research, using everything from telephone directories and probate registers to anecdotal accounts and newspaper reports, but we will especially appreciate voluntarily contributed information.

The file now consists of up to a thousand records and is organized alphabetically by author surname. The entry underneath each surname will normally consist of a contact name and address for copyright inquiries, the date when the information was collected, and which of the compilers created the record. Telephone and fax numbers, e-mail addresses, and explanatory notes are included in some cases, and dates of the authors' births and deaths will be added as part of a future editorial review, since this information is useful in calculating the term of copyright protection.

A plan has been devised for the future evolution of the file, if this first stage is successful and if funders are prepared to continue their backing. We envisage progress from the present list of primarily literary authors to a second stage, which would include any English-language authors working in the humanities whose papers are in repositories in Europe or North America. A third stage would extend the project to non-English-language authors in the humanities, and a fourth would cover English-language authors outside the humanities. Clearly there is a tremendous amount of work ahead of us, but we believe that the start we have made is already providing a major new service to scholarship.

For more information, contact Cathy Henderson at the Harry Ransom Humanities Research Center, Austin; e-mail: Cathy.Henderson@utxvm.cc.utexas.edu or David Sutton at the University of Reading Library, England; e-mail: D.C.Sutton@reading.ac.uk

Letter from Japan

Kiyohiko Tsuboi
Okayama University

and

Nobuko Tsuboi
Toyo University

In modern Japanese literature the concept of the pure and serious novel (atheistic literature or belles lettres) was born in the 1920s and has been discussed repeatedly. The year 1993 began with the debate of belles lettres and pop literature again, when Kiyoshi Kasai, a writer of popular novels, published an article in *Kaien* magazine stating that belles lettres is dead, and that the novels in the literary magazines are written only by the established writers older than Kenji Nakagami; by a few young writers such as Kazumi Saeki and Yoko Ogawa, who are still cherishing the desire to write belles lettres; and by such minimalist writers as Haruki Murakami, Ryu Murakami, and Banana Yoshimoto. Recently, the borderline between belles lettres and pop literature has become less distinct than ever. However, Japanese popular literature is now almost all occupied by science fiction, fantasies, and mysteries. Haruki Murakami and Jay McInerney discussed the issue of belles lettres versus pop literature in the March 1994 issue of *Subaru*. Murakami states that in the present era literature itself is not in decline, but only the criteria in society have changed. McInerney contends that the young writers copossess internationally the common media named "pop culture." In short their conclusion is that those who claim the decline of serious literature are writers on the traditional side, and their criteria are quite different from those of the young. In the round-table discussion in the December issue of *Gunzo,* Minato Kawamura draws too hasty a conclusion that such writers as Yasutaka Tsutsui, Genichiro Takahasi, and Hisashi Inoue are simply writing for the intellectual minority of readers and the rest of the writers are writing popular literature. For contemporary writers all over the world, the phrase *pop culture* is the international lingua franca of which the older

Haruki Murakami (photograph by Nancy Coplon)

and more established and traditional writers are very critical.

In the meantime many foreign books, most of which are American literature, have been translated into Japanese. Some of Toni Morrison's works were translated into Japanese after she received the Nobel Prize in literature. Raymond Carver sells well. Ernest Hemingway, William Faulkner, and F. Scott Fitzgerald are still popular. The translation of the complete works of John Steinbeck is now being prepared. Many American popular novels are also translated. Over two million copies of *The Bridges of*

Madison County, by Robert James Waller, were sold in Japan.

Friction between freedom of speech and political correctness caused a controversy in 1994. When a support group for epileptics found a biased expression in a galley proof of a high-school textbook, they immediately took action to stop the publication of the textbook. It was in an excerpt from a novel by Yasutaka Tsutsui. When Tsutsui was accused of his alleged "biased" description, he reacted in an unforeseen way. He declared that instead of fighting a legal battle, he would not write any longer, claiming that his freedom of expression was being abridged and under such circumstances he was not able to write. And his *Thinking over my breaking the pen* became an instant best-seller. There had been pros and cons among writers over the issue; some sided with Tsutsui, others did not. Among those against Tsutsui, Kenzaburo Oe criticized Tsutsui's negative attitude, saying that rather he should make it a social controversy.

Oe highlighted 1994 with his Nobel Prize in literature. He is the second Japanese Nobel laureate. He is recognized for his universal theme of absurdity in society and his strong antinuclear and antiwar stance, not simply for the exquisite beauty particular to the Japanese language as in the case of Yasunari Kawabata, the first Japanese laureate. Since the 1960s he has been writing serious and satiric stories and novels criticizing the modern Japanese society after World War II. There no longer exists such a national literature as the literature of Japan or of any other particular country, due to the international media. Kobo Abe, known for his metafiction, *The Woman in the Dune* (1962), died 22 January 1993, leaving a floppy disk containing the unfinished story, "A Flying Man," which was posthumously published in the April 1994 issue of *Shinchou*. He had been using a computer, while Oe uses a fountain pen. In this metaphoric story the protagonist calls up his brother by cellular phone and proposes to fight together against the patriarchy of the supposedly dead father. While flying he is shot by a woman. Though how the story would end is not known, this is indeed a postmodernist, allegorical story, as are Oe's later works.

The recent literary trend in Japan leans toward nonrealistic, metaphoric, allegorical, metaphysical fiction.

Building the New British Library at St Pancras

Charles Egleston
University of Colorado

The new British Library building at St Pancras, on Euston Road, north London, finally will be completed in 1996; and the hope is that it will be fully functional and open to the public by late 1996 or early 1997 (specifics of the handover program await a final date of construction). Construction problems have plagued the project, but the only two remaining problems — low-voltage wiring and fire sprinklers — are minor. The St Pancras station, next to which the new library sits across Midland Road, is one of the transportation hubs of London, and the library consequently will be more accessible to readers and tourists than it has been at its longtime location on Great Russell Street. The British Library press office expects that over one million people will visit the building each year. Over twelve million volumes will be on site in climate-controlled areas, many of them for the first time so protected.

The major themes guiding the construction of the new library are the unity of knowledge and providing expanded access to it. Readers in the Science, Technology and Industry complex will be able to order material usually sent to the Humanities Reading Room, and vice versa. The age for entrance to the reading rooms is to be lowered to eighteen, and access to reader tickets will be much less restrictive than it has been in the past. The collections will be accessible through an on-line catalogue, and the books, most of which are to be held on movable ranges in four huge basements below the piazza next to Euston Road, will be delivered via a mechanical system that will shorten the time that readers will have to wait (rare and fragile materials will continue to be delivered by hand).

The emphasis on the unity of knowledge is to be represented by a twelve-foot-high statue of a seated Sir Isaac Newton by Sir Eduardo Paolozzi based on a rendering by William Blake. The statue will be situated on the west side of the Euston Road piazza, directly in line with the main entrance to the building. The head of the statue will face east toward the science wing. Inside the entrance this theme of unity will be represented by the massive presence of the King's Library, the collection of over sixty thousand volumes brought together by King George III and given to the nation in 1823 by his son, King George IV, who stipulated that the collection was to be kept "entire and separate." The King's Library, the books of which will continue to be retrievable for readers, are to be placed in a six-story glass tower along the back of the great entrance hall that will provide access to the different parts of the library.

There will be 1,433 reader places (including study carrels and catalogue, microfilm, and CD-ROM desks) in the new building. The Humanities Reading Room, on the top west side of the building, will be interlinked with the "specialist" reading areas for Western Manuscripts, Rare Books and Music, and the Maps collections. Readers will occupy its central space, and there will be general reference literature on open shelving around the perimeter. The Science, Technology, and Industry Complex, on the east side of the building alongside Midland Road, will be on three levels. The first level focuses on patents, the second level focuses on science and technology, and the third level focuses on business and public affairs. Many periodicals and reference sources will be available on open shelving in the complex.

The Philatelic collections will be located off the entrance hall. Also located off the entrance hall will be the exhibit areas, which will be much more elaborate than the exhibit areas at Great Russell Street. There will be three galleries (one named the Digital Gallery). Along with the treasures of the library which visitors expect to see, such as the Lindisfarne Gospels and the Magna Carta, there will be a gallery displaying interactive videos and live demonstrations of such processes as papermaking, typesetting, printing, book illustration, and bookbinding. There will also be changing exhibits. A 260-seat auditorium on the east side of the building will be part of a conference center.

The British Library at St Pancras will hold the core of Great Britain's library heritage except for the National Sound Archive in South Kensington and the Newspaper Library at Colindale, which will remain in their locations. The following libraries, now separate units, will move to the new location: the three parts of the Science Reference and Information Service (Southampton Buildings, Chancery House, Kean Street); all parts of the British Library now sharing space with the British Museum (to include library administration and the conservation studios); and the Oriental and India Office Collections (now on Blackfriars Road).

The genesis of this new complex, the largest cultural public building in London built in the twentieth century, was in 1962. In that year architect Colin St John Wilson was commissioned to design a building for the humanities collections of the British Museum so that these collections, long scattered about London, could be brought together and protected from the deterioration items were suffering in non-climate-controlled storage. For example, the stack space behind the famous Round Reading Room (built in 1857) is overheated in winter because the heating system was added after construction; the skylights there, necessary for light in 1857, have had to be painted over to cut down on the deleterious effects of sunlight.

The original plan for the humanities library was to tear down buildings across Great Russell Street from the front of the museum and create a large square that would feature the British Museum, the new humanities library, and Nicholas Hawksmoor's Church of St George, Bloomsbury, but this plan had to be abandoned when it was opposed by local tradesmen and conservationists, who did not want to disrupt the neighborhood of bookshops, pubs, and shops (most of them built in the 1920s). There was also opposition from those readers who did not want to leave the Round Reading Room. (It has been decided finally that the book collections of the British Museum officially separated from the British Library in the 1970s will be moved into the Round Reading Room when the library at St Pancras is opened.)

In 1972 the humanities library plan was expanded to bring all of the library's collections, now held in nineteen sites across London, into a large, climate-controlled building somewhere in London that would have large storage capacity and a modern book-retrieval system. (This plan has been scaled back.) St John Wilson redesigned his humanities library plans, and a disused rail storage yard of twelve acres abutting St Pancras Station was acquired in 1975. Aside from its access to mass transit, the site had other attractions. It is only three-

The entrance hall of the new British Library at St Pancras (photograph courtesy of the British Library Board)

fourths of a mile from the British Museum, so a planned staged construction, with each building stage fully occupiable, meant that readers would be able to use both library sites as building progressed. The government hoped that the presence of the library would revive the station neighborhood, which was then frequented by prostitutes and hard-drug users.

The St Pancras project has had many delays, the most serious of which was caused by the inflation and recession of the 1980s, for the original funding plan presupposed a booming economy. Financial problems were exacerbated by minor delays; these financial problems in turn delayed construction as the recession deepened. The first delay was caused by a dispute between the library and the Camden Council (governing agency in the area around the station), who demanded that the eastern side (Midland Road) of the building, where it abutted the station, should be lowered in height so as not to obscure the station's Victorian facade. To force compliance of the architect and the British Library, the government, said the London Sunday *Times* on 6 November 1988, resorted to "the slow drip of public funds to finance [the library]."

By the groundbreaking in 1982 there was a three-staged plan that was to be completed at some point before the end of the first half of the twenty-first century. (Apparently no official estimate was ever made for completion of the whole because funding was going to have to be sought for each

Artist's impression of the Rare Books and Music Reading Room at St Pancras (courtesy of the British Library Board)

stage.) Each of the stages of construction was to have been self-contained so as to enable the building to go into use by the first-stage target date of 1991. The Prince of Wales, who has of late been highly critical of the design (see his *A Vision of Britain* [1989]), dedicated the cornerstone on 8 December 1982. The government of Margaret Thatcher committed itself to £90 million to pay for start-up (estimating £116 million to complete the whole of stage I by the target date of 1991).

A substantial part of the cost of stage I was caused by the book storage basements at St Pancras, which are the depth of an eight-story building. So as not to disturb both the Metropolitan line, which runs under Euston Road beside the site, or the Victoria and Northern lines, which run through the site itself and through the basement levels, it was decided to build the top basement first, and the three subsequent basements then one under the other (in reverse of the normal order). The resulting basements were to have movable shelving — 186 miles of it — made by Brynzeel, a Dutch company, the longest movable shelves in the world; so, of course, the

shelves had to be custom-made in Holland (then assembled on site).

Meanwhile, the background chorus of those who did not want to leave the Round Reading Room grew, led by an adviser to Prime Minister Thatcher, Hugh Thomas, now Lord Thomas of Swynnerton, who in October 1983 proposed (apparently seriously, although the idea was never acted upon) that the Euston Road site be used as a giant storehouse only for all the books that the current building could not accommodate. His idea was that this storehouse would be linked to Bloomsbury by an underground railway that he estimated would cost "not much more than" the £88 million (in 1981 prices) earmarked for stage I, and certainly less than the £600 million cost of all three stages (a 1983 estimate that some were making). The Round Reading Room advocates were encouraged by fiscal conservatives in the Thatcher government, who saw that cutting the library would improve the worsening national economic picture. In the London *Times* writing in support of Thomas's plan, Lord Bruce-Gardyne, who had been created life baron in that

A 1928 photograph of the main reading room at the British Library, Great Russell Street

year, proposed raiding the library plan, even selling the Euston Road site, to help make up for a £1.25 billion shortfall in the budget of Chief Secretary to the Treasury Peter Rees. Bruce-Gardyne questioned the value of placing books in climate control when they had been without it, some of them for hundreds of years, and he cast doubts on the growth in the British Library staff in the previous fifteen years and the need for an even larger staff projected for the finally completed St Pancras building.

In spite of the odd theories and unfair criticism, in December 1985 Richard Luce (minister for the arts 1985–1990, knighted 1991) announced funding of £61 million for the second part of stage I of the library plan; this first stage was reprojected to be completed in 1993.

January 1987 was the public beginning of the government's distancing itself from the St Pancras project, apparently so as to force the library management to agree to a refinancing plan for the library. They allied themselves with those in the Labour Party who were opposed to local arts and library cuts that had been made (as had been said) "to fund the project." The London *Times* reported that the government was "investigating the manage-

ment of a big British Library building project" after learning of increased and spiraling costs. In February the investigation was referred to Sir Gordon Downey, the comptroller and auditor general. An article in the London *Times* that month reported that "informed guesses put the likely final cost at more than £1 billion." Buried away in the article was the fact that rather than investigating British Library management, the "review was limited to improving the liaison between the library and the property services agency," and that in fact the chief reason for the rise in costs was inflation coupled with the growing recession, something of which the government was already very much aware.

In the London *Sunday Times* of 20 March 1988 the government launched its refinancing plan, even though the headline seemed to announce the end of the St Pancras library: "New building in St. Pancras to remain unfinished because of prohibitive cost; architects to decide of priority areas to complete." The article continued, "Richard Luce, minister for the arts, says he is calling a halt because the project has been taking too long and is swallowing up too much money. The final cost, if building continued, might be as high as £1 billion." Luce was said to be awaiting outcome of a feasibility study to see how the building might be finished. St John Wilson was quoted as saying, "I was certainly rather shocked when the thought of a complete halt was introduced. It is going to be a very substantial building, and it's a hairy business deciding where the line is going to be drawn."

News of the retrenchment found its way into the U.S. library press that year. There was a brief note in *Library Journal* (15 April 1988) incorrectly repeating the first impression of the 20 March *Sunday Times* article that said the library would never be completed. In May 1988 *American Libraries* interviewed British Library Chief Executive Kenneth Cooper, who said that the reports of the library's demise were not true. They quoted him as saying that St John Wilson's original plans were in fact "speculative drawings." Wilson's response to this, if any, was not noted.

In the London *Sunday Times* of 20 October 1988 a new issue was raised that did not affect the St Pancras library but did tend to cloud the support for the library. The last will and testament of George Bernard Shaw, in appreciation for the use of the Round Reading Room, had been interpreted by the courts in 1959 to mean that royalties from his works – in 1988 two hundred thousand pounds – went to the British Museum. Michael Holroyd, Shaw's biographer, said that bequest should now go to the British Library because it was left in gratitude for use of the library, not the room. This argument provoked much debate, but the position of the British Museum was that the decision was made for them to keep the money; after all, they retained care of the Round Reading Room in 1972. Wisely, the British Library chose not to enter the discussion.

In early November 1988 Luce announced a final £90 million for completion of a scaled-down library. What Luce did not announce, and which is apparent only from reading the architect and library's response, was that Luce approved redesign of the budget to set a cash limit for the project of £450 million, which effectively cut 10 percent from the redesign he had previously commissioned from the architects and the British Library – which required yet further study and replanning. Wilson commented, "there is now a tremendous amount of more work to be done. In the time this takes, further costs will be incurred from having to abort or change work already done on site."

In 1990 a successful scheme was launched for the government to grant £1 million for artworks to

be commissioned for the new building, perhaps in part a response to *A Vision of Britain,* which had lamented the fact that no art had been planned for the library; but quickly the fund was, without warning, cut by the treasury. The government had promised the money to commission over a hundred works of art for the new building, and three works had been selected by a committee (to include the Paolozzi sculpture and a seven-meter square tapestry based on a painting by R. B. Kitaj that includes literary references for the west wall of the entrance hall). The committee resigned in protest on 12 October, claiming its role had been made redundant by the government's refusal to donate the grant. The arts ministry said that public money might be forthcoming at a later stage and private sponsorship should be sought for the three commissioned works. Funding has been found for the Paolozzi sculpture, and fund-raising is under way for the tapestry and "The Gormley Stones," a piazza sculpture by Anthony Gormley.

The London *Times* of 14 January 1992 announced a problem with the book-storage shelving which was soon to have been used so that the library could begin storage on site (book storage now will not take place until the British Library takes possession). Testing by government inspectors revealed that the shelves, which cost £8.5 million, might have been insufficiently rustproofed. (Not all shelves, but only some on the first level, eighty-two feet below the surface, had been installed.) In May 1991 it was further reported by the London *Times* that the mechanism of shelves that had been installed jolted and shuddered, shaking books to the floor, and that the shelves stuck together. The problems with the bookshelves were reported to Parliament as fixed (at the contractor's expense) by National Heritage Secretary Peter Brooke in February 1994.

The London *Times* editorialized on 29 April 1993 that changes in plans had been frequent and that delays and allegations of wasted taxpayers' money had embarrassed the government and the library. Their view was shortsighted, for it failed to take into account that most, if not all, of the financial problems were beyond the control of library management, or even the government. Once the building is finally opened to readers and tourists, the many problems of the project will cease to be an issue.

The University of South Carolina Press

Joyce Harrison
University of South Carolina Press

Established in 1944 and housed on the university's Columbia campus, the University of South Carolina Press is one of the oldest and most prestigious publishing houses in the South and the only university press in the state. It has been an important element in enhancing the scholarly reputation and worldwide visibility of the University of South Carolina. (The press is a member of the Association of American University Presses, the Society for Scholarly Publishing, the American Booksellers Association, the Southeast Booksellers Association, the International Association of Scholarly Presses, and the Publishers Association of the South.) As a not-for-profit publisher, the press operates both as an academic unit of the university and as a business and currently receives a stipend from the university that contributes to its operating expenses.

The press director reports to the provost of the university, and the press is overseen by a press committee of eight faculty members appointed by the provost. The committee is responsible for supervising the press's operations, including its finances and publishing program. The committee meets regularly with members of the press staff to discuss sales and promotional activities and to vote on projects brought to the committee by the acquisitions editors.

The press's first book was *South Carolina: Economic and Social Conditions,* edited by W. H. Callcott and published in the year of the press's founding, 1944. The press's commitment to publishing the best research and writing on South Carolina history, culture, and wildlife was strong and remains strong today, with regional books serving as an important and profitable part of the press's publishing program. The first press director was Frank Wardlaw, appointed in 1946. He was succeeded in 1950 by Louise Jones Dubose, who retired in 1966. The existence of a woman press director in such an early period of the press's history is noteworthy. Robert T. King served as director from 1966 to 1984, when the press published its five hundredth title, *Art and Artists of the South: The Robert P. Coggins Collection,* by

Bruce W. Chambers. In 1985 Kenneth J. Scott, an editor at Macmillan in New York, was hired.

Few subjects that were prominent in the press's catalogue two decades ago are part of the list today. A perusal of the 1974 subject catalogue reveals titles in anthropology, European history, philosophy, and psychology, as well as books in the physical sciences and medicine. The 1974 catalogue also contains books in areas in which the press continues to publish: American history, business, international studies, and religious studies, along with books of regional interest. In the recent past the press has added more subjects, including southern history, the Civil War, other military history, social work, speech/communication, and legal history.

The vicissitudes of scholarship have a direct effect on university presses, and to keep afloat in those stormy seas one must have a firm command of the craft of publishing, a keen eye for trends in academic work, and an appreciation for and understanding of the importance of positive cash flow. By the early 1980s the press was hovering on the brink of extinction, publishing an average of eight books a year and working out of a trailer. The small number of annual new titles, coupled with the press's wide-ranging, diffuse list, resulted in poor sales. Recognition, even from the university community, was all but nonexistent. The university administration and the press committee decided that it was time for a change. When Scott was hired in 1985, he was presented with the challenge of transforming the press from a small publisher, heavily weighted toward regional books, to one that would be a major presence in the world of scholarly publishing.

Under Scott's leadership, and with the support of the university administration and press committee, the press moved forward. By 1990 its annual sales topped $1 million, and by 1992 the number of titles published per year reached forty-seven. The press increased its promotion and sales activities, exhibiting at national and international conferences and conventions, and established sales representation throughout the world. Review attention in-

The University of South Carolina Press staff at the former press location. The press moved to new headquarters in 1995.

creased by 43 percent in 1991, and press books received major awards from organizations and publications.

A large portion of the press's books are in publication series. At present there are fourteen ongoing series representing many of the fields in which the press publishes. Eight of the series editors are members of the University of South Carolina faculty, and four of these are members of the press committee. The series were established as a way simultaneously to build the press's list, increase its revenue, and raise its visibility in certain scholarly disciplines.

Until the mid 1980s the press was known primarily for works in the physical and social sciences – not for titles in the humanities – and its publishing program in literature had never really gotten off the ground. In 1984 Matthew J. Bruccoli, Emily Brown Jefferies Professor of English, launched a series titled Understanding Contemporary American Literature (UCAL). Each volume provides instruction in

how to read a particular author's work, identifying and explicating his or her material, themes, use of language, point of view, structure, symbolism, and responses to experience. The first three books in the UCAL series, all published in 1985, were *Understanding James Dickey,* by Ronald Baughman, *Understanding Bernard Malamud,* by Jeffrey Helterman, and *Understanding John Hawkes,* by Donald J. Greiner; the latter was named an Outstanding Academic Book of 1986 by *Choice* magazine. There are now over thirty UCAL titles in the series, and four or five new books appear each year. Individual volumes are devoted to such authors as Robert Bly, Joseph Heller, John Irving, Ursula K. LeGuin, Denise Levertov, Carson McCullers, Vladimir Nabokov, Joyce Carol Oates, Tim O'Brien, Katherine Anne Porter, Isaac Bashevis Singer, Anne Tyler, Kurt Vonnegut, and Tennessee Williams; other titles in the series focus on genres or on groups of writers, such as the Beats or Chicano literature. All but the first three series volumes, on Dickey, Malamud, and Hawkes, are still in print — a testimony to their usefulness and longevity. The two most successful volumes in the series are *Understanding Edward Albee,* by Matthew C. Roudané, and *Understanding Contemporary American Drama,* by William Herman. Both titles appeared in 1987, and each has sold over two thousand copies.

The success of the UCAL series led Bruccoli in 1987 to establish another — Understanding Contemporary British Literature (UCBL). Like the UCAL books, the titles in the UCBL series provide a concise introduction to their subjects' work. At present there are seven books in the series. The first two, both published in 1990, were *Understanding Doris Lessing,* by Jean Pickering, and *Understanding Graham Greene,* by R. H. Miller. These were followed by books on Arnold Wesker, Paul West, Kingsley Amis, Iris Murdoch, and John Fowles.

James N. Hardin, professor of German at the University of South Carolina, launched his own "Understanding" series in 1986: Understanding Modern European and Latin American Literature (UMELL). UMELL books emphasize the sociological and historical background of the writers treated, as well as serving as guides to the authors' works. The emphasis is on canonical figures of the twentieth century; series books include works on Ingeborg Bachmann, Italo Calvino, Albert Camus, Günter Grass, Eugène Ionesco, Mario Vargas Llosa, Federico García Lorca, Jean-Paul Sartre, and Peter Weiss, among others. The *Journal of European Studies* said of Stephen D. Dowden's *Understanding Thomas Bernhard,* published in 1991: "In this clear and confident reading of Bernhard's works a great deal of ground is effectively covered in a crisp, often epigrammatic style. . . . This is not only an excellent introduction to Bernhard for the uninitiated, but also a sound interpretative overview which squarely addresses the central problems posed by the works." Of Hans Wagener's *Understanding Erich Maria Remarque* (1991), *Monatshefte* remarked that "the reader is provided with a judicious literary assessment of Remarque's work in a most compact, readable form." Wulf Koepke's *Understanding Max Frisch* was designated an Outstanding Academic book for 1992 by *Choice.* The most popular UMELL volume by far is *Understanding Gabriel García Márquez* by Kathleen McNerny, of which more than twenty-five hundred copies have been sold since it was published in 1989.

One of the university's most prominent and celebrated faculty members is the poet and fiction writer James Dickey, First Carolina Professor of English and poet in residence. A collection of poems by Dickey's students at South Carolina, *From the Green Horseshoe,* appeared in 1987. (The Horseshoe is part of the university campus; the oldest and most historic buildings are set around a U-shaped cobblestone path surrounded by grass and trees.) Baughman, author of the UCAL volume *Understanding James Dickey,* edited a collection of interviews and conversations with Dickey that was published in 1989 under the title *The Voiced Connections of James Dickey.*

One of the members of the acquisitions staff is Warren Slesinger, who holds an M.F.A. in creative writing from the University of Iowa, where he studied with poet Donald Justice. Slesinger is well acquainted with and enthusiastic about creative writing. He was the impetus behind three collections of stories by southern authors that, he says, "demonstrate that Southern writing is much more diversified than most people realize; it's not just gothic novels and the Civil War. Our books deal with themes of displacement and change, as the idea of permanence, stability, and community continues to erode." The first of these collections, *New Stories by Southern Women,* was edited by Mary Ellis Gibson and published in 1989. It contains twenty-one selections by such authors as Alice Adams, Alice Walker, Lee Smith, Toni Cade Bambara, Elizabeth Spencer, Gail Godwin, Sallie Bingham, and Marianne Gingher. A similar collection, *Homeplaces: Stories of the South by Women Writers,* also edited by Gibson, was published in 1991. Some of the authors from *New Stories by Southern Women* reappear in *Homeplaces,* joined by Ntozake Shange, Opal Moore, and Molly Best Tinsley. The publication *On the Issues* called *Homeplaces* "an ambitious book, one that reflects changing politics and changing social mores . . . a must-read for anyone interested in the burgeoning genre of Southern women's fiction." The third of the southern writing anthologies was the 1993 book *That's What I Like (About the South) and Other New Southern Stories for the Nineties,* edited by George Garrett and Paul Ruffin. The collection contains selections from thirty-two authors, including Heather Ross Miller, R. H. W. Dillard, Fred Chappell, Madison Jones, Madison Smartt Bell, Beverly Lowry, Bobbie Ann Mason, and Dabney Stuart.

Slesinger's interest in creative writing led him to write to the editors of twenty-four literary magazines across the country — such as *Georgia Review, New England Quarterly, The Gettysburg Review,* and *The Sewanee Review* — and ask them to recommend writers who wrote nonfiction essays and personal memoirs about contemporary American life and whose work was especially promising. The editors responded enthusiastically, eager to suggest authors for the new publishing venture. The first book to be published was *A Geometry of Lilies: Life and Death in an American Family,* by Steven Harvey, a professor of English at Young Harris College in Georgia who has published poetry, fiction, and nonfiction in *Harper's, The Iowa Review, Georgia Review,* and *Southern Poetry Review,* among other publications. When the book appeared in 1993, *Kirkus Reviews* called it a collection of "unpretentious essays that explore – sometimes amusingly, sometimes movingly – the patterns and meanings to be found in the mundane details of family life." Essayist James Kligo said that the book was "alive with poetic energy. . . . These essays, like good poems, shape experience exactly as the experience requires."

Judith Kitchen, who wrote *Understanding William Stafford* for the UCAL series in 1989, was another author recommended to Slesinger by one of the literary-magazine editors. The result was *Only the Dance: Essays on Time and Memory,* a collection of autobiographical writing published in 1994. Peter Stitt, editor of *The Gettysburg Review,* called the book "extraordinarily poetic," and the poet and National Book Award winner Lisel Mueller said it was "like a simultaneous translation of thought (mind at play) into language, and the operative word is *simultaneous.* I know of no precedent for this."

One of the press's most eagerly anticipated projects is a collection of the complete poems and translations of Katherine Anne Porter; it is being compiled by Darlene H. Unrue, who wrote the book on Porter for the UCAL series. Also forthcoming is a collection of Wallace Stevens's letters to his wife, which will be published in conjunction with the Huntington Library, which houses the Stevens papers. Bruccoli is compiling a companion volume to F. Scott Fitzgerald's 1934 novel *Tender is the Night* that will identify events, people, places, and other things that are referred to in the text but that are no longer current, thus providing clarification that will make the book more enjoyable and understandable to students, scholars, and general readers.

In the past decade academia has seen a blurring of divisions between disciplines, with scholars increasingly combining the methods and ideas of one field with those of others. In the field of religious studies the tools of other disciplines are used to look at religion as a broad enterprise that goes beyond traditional boundaries. The press took advantage of these new developments when it launched its series Studies in Comparative Religion in 1988, with Frederick M. Denny, professor of religious studies at the University of Colorado, Boulder, as

Cover for the Spring/Summer 1995 catalogue of the University of South Carolina Press

series editor. Since that time the press has become a leader in the field, publishing over twenty books that have been on the forefront of scholarship. *Religion and Personal Autonomy: The Third Disestablishment in America* (1992), by sociologist Phillip E. Hammond, demonstrates that, although religion is important to Americans, it most often finds expression in private, individual ways. *The Christian Century* advises its readers to "find out here why today's parishes are based less on friendship; why they once were; why even little local churches look bureaucratized; why a new kind of search for identity continues." *Minoan Religion: Ritual, Image, and Symbol* (1992), by the archaeologist and classicist Nanno Marinatos, represents a significant breakthrough in

Former director Ken Scott, left, and George Garrett

the analysis and interpretation of Minoan religious sites, artifacts, and symbols. In 1993 the American Academy of Religion presented its award for Excellence in the Study of Religion – historical category – to religious historian Juan Eduardo Campo's *The Other Side of Paradise: Explorations into the Religious Meanings of Domestic Space in Islam,* a book that brings together evidence from a wide variety of sources and explains for the first time the complex array of religious meanings associated with Islamic houses. *Charismatic Christianity as a Global Culture* (1994), a collection of essays edited by anthropologist Karla Poewe, is a rarity in the literature on comparative religion. By treating what many would consider marginal, idiosyncratic, and even odd varieties of Christian experience and witnessing as a mainstream dimension extending back to Pentecost, the book informs, surprises, and delights. The year 1994 also saw the publication of a new, revised edition of Ronald G. Grimes's *Beginnings in Ritual Studies,* a pathbreaking study of ritual that combines the research and methodologies of religious studies, anthropology, sociology, art, and performance.

Three nonseries books in the press's religious studies list shed light on particularly timely issues: *Islam in the Balkans: Religion and Society between Europe and the Arab World* (1993), by H. T. Norris, traces the development of Muslim communities in Bosnia,

Albania, Kosovo, and Macedonia. Oliver P. Rafferty's *Catholicism in Ulster, 1603–1983: An Interpretative History* (1994) was praised by historian Lawrence J. McCaffrey as "an interesting, informative, and readable discussion of the essence of the Northern Ireland situation. . . . Rafferty's research is commendable, his knowledge of the details of Catholicism in Ulster and the rest of Ireland is considerable, and his conclusions are fair and thoughtful." Walter H. Capps's *The New Religious Right: Piety, Patriotism, and Politics* (1994) provides the reader with an understanding of the New Religious Right as seen through the eyes of the leaders of the movement, including Pat Robertson, Jerry Falwell, and Bob Jones.

The press's publishing program in religious studies is rounded out by two other series, both of which are edited by faculty members of the Duke University Divinity School. James M. Crenshaw is the editor of Studies on Personalities of the Old Testament, and D. Moody Smith edits Studies on Personalities of the New Testament. The volumes in each series provide examinations of the life and work of, and scholarly discourse on, figures in the Bible. The Old Testament series has produced works on Esther, Daniel, Ezekiel, Jonah, Joseph and his family, and Noah; the latter was named an Outstanding Academic Book for 1989 by *Choice*. The New Testament series has produced works on Mark, Peter, and John.

Two South Carolina faculty members are coeditors of the successful Studies in International Relations series. Charles W. Kegley, Jr., is Pearce Professor of International Relations and past president of the International Studies Association; Donald J. Puchala, Charles L. Jacobson Professor of Public Affairs, is director of the university's Institute of International Studies. Studies in International Relations, established in 1985 and comprising over twenty volumes to date, provides a showcase for work on the frontiers of scholarship. Volumes in the series have brought worldwide recognition to the press's publishing program in the field; series authors number among the most prominent figures in the fields of political theory, foreign policy, peace and war studies, international organization, and national security. Many of the volumes in the series have become instant classics, presenting research and methodologies that have become important contributions to the discourse on international relations. These include Marvin Soroos's *Beyond Sovereignty: The Challenge of Global Policy* (1986), Yale H. Ferguson and Richard W. Mansbach's *The Elusive Quest: Theory and International Politics* (1988), and

Robert L. Rothstein's *The Evolution of Theory in International Relations* (1991). Three series books have been named Outstanding Academic Books by *Choice:* William T. Thompson's *On Global War: Historical-Structural Approaches to World Politics* (1989); Michael P. Sullivan's *Power in Contemporary International Politics* (1991); and Ethan Kapstein's *The Political Economy of National Security* (1992).

The field of rhetoric is experiencing a renaissance. Scholars have become interested in going beyond the Greco-Roman tradition to examine contemporary issues and to look at the interface between rhetoric and other disciplines. Studies in Rhetoric and Speech Communication, a series established in 1984 and edited by Thomas W. Benson, professor of speech communication at Pennsylvania State University, presents some of the most exciting work in this new area. In *Symbolic Inducement and Knowing: A Study in the Foundations of Rhetoric* (1984), Richard B. Gregg draws on anthropological, neurophysiological, psycholinguistic, psychological, literary, and rhetorical theories and findings to explore the support for and implications of saying that humans belong to a peculiarly symbol-using, symbol-making, symbol-misusing species. The book won the Speech Communication Association's 1984 Winans-Wichelns Award for Distinguished Scholarship in Rhetoric and Public Address. Lawrence J. Prelli's *A Rhetoric of Science: Inventing Scientific Discourse* (1989) casts a fresh light on the process by which scientific claims are validated. *The Presidency and the Rhetoric of Foreign Crisis* (1993), by Denise M. Bostdorff, examines presidential crisis management – or the way U.S. presidents portray foreign crises to the American public – as a potent tool for the accumulation, and at times the forfeiture, of political power.

Leon Ginsberg, Carolina Research Professor in the College of Social Work at the University of South Carolina and a member of the press's editorial board, is the editor of a new series on interdisciplinary social work, Social Problems and Social Issues. Its aim is to present new developments that go beyond traditional areas and to examine how different elements in the community play an important part in the field of social work; forthcoming titles include books on family preservation, elder practice, and religious diversity.

The University of South Carolina Press is the only press that has a series in maritime history: Studies in Maritime History, edited by William N. Still, Jr., of East Carolina University. The series, with over twenty-five titles published so far, presents studies in all aspects of maritime history, in-

Catherine Fry, who replaced Ken Scott as director of the University of South Carolina Press in March 1995

cluding military campaigns and strategies, trade routes and ports, and river systems. Books in the series have accumulated a great deal of recognition. As an example, the North American Society for Oceanic Historians has presented awards to four series titles: *Stoddert's War: Naval Operations During the Quasi War with France, 1798–1801* (1987), by Michael A. Palmer; *"We Will Stand by You": Serving in the Pawnee, 1942–1945* (1990), by Theodore Mason; *Predators and Prizes: American Privateering and Imperial Warfare, 1739–1748* (1991), by Carl E. Swanson; and *Lejeune: A Marine's Life, 1867–1942* (1991), by Merrill L. Bartlett.

The press has a strong and highly visible list of books on military history, southern history, and the Civil War. *U.S. Army Heraldic Crests: A Complete Illustrated History of Authorized Distinctive Unit Insignia,* by Barry Jason Stein, was published in 1993 and is the best-selling book in the press's history. *A Confederate Nurse: The Diary of Ada W. Bacot, 1860–1863* (1993), edited by Jean V. Berlin, was reprinted in a paperback edition shortly after its clothbound release. *"When I Can Read My Title Clear": Literacy, Slavery and Religion in the Antebellum South* (1992), by Janet Duitsman Cornelius, was called "a remarkable piece of history, comprehensively and eloquently documented" by the *Chicago Tribune*. Other noteworthy titles are *Charleston! Charleston! The History of a Southern City* (1990), by Walter J. Fraser, Jr.; *Soldiers Blue and Gray* (1988), by James I. Robertson, Jr., an in-depth treatment of military life during the Civil War; *A Woman Doctor's Civil War: Esther Hill Hawks' Diary* (1985), edited by Gerald Schwartz; and *Gate of Hell: Campaign for Charleston Harbor, 1863* (1994), by Stephen R. Wise, which retraces the day-to-day action of the two-month assault, including the Battle for Battery Wagner made famous by the movie *Glory* (1989).

A significant portion of the press's list is devoted to books on the state and the region. Many are large, lavishly illustrated coffee-table books. *South Carolina: A Timeless Journey,* with color photographs by Robert C. Clark and text by Thomas M. Poland, was published in the spring of 1994 and is a companion volume to another book by the same team, with additional text by Stephen H. Bennet, *South Carolina: The Natural Heritage* (1989) — one of the press's all-time best-sellers. Photographer Joseph F. Thompson's work is featured in the 1993 publication *Atlanta: A City of Neighborhoods,* accompanied by a text by Robert Isbell. The press has also published books on nature and wildlife, including the immensely successful *Tideland Treasure* (1991), by Todd Ballantine — an illustrated guide to the beaches and marshes of the eastern United States coast — and *Wildflowers in the Carolinas* (1987), by Wade T. Batson.

The press publishes two multivolume scholarly editions on South Carolinians who figured prominently in U.S. history and politics; both are edited by university faculty members in the Department of History. The Papers of Henry Laurens, now in its fourteenth volume, is edited by David R. Chesnutt, and The Papers of John C. Calhoun, edited by Clyde N. Wilson, comprises, at present, twenty-two volumes.

As part of its effort to keep up with its competitors and maintain an edge in the academic publishing community, the press has moved quickly and efficiently into the electronic age. Copyediting for the majority of projects is done on-screen rather than using the manuscript-and-blue-pencil method, and the production staff prepares some of the camera-ready copy for its books in-house rather than sending text to typesetters. Jacket designs, advertisements, and direct-mail pieces are created using sophisticated graphics software, and the press's finances and inventory are well maintained by computer systems. In 1993 the press set up a local area network, or LAN, that in effect links all press staff together by computer. The press has also taken advantage of on-line systems, and staff members use Internet not only to communicate with authors, series editors, and each other, but also to transmit entire manuscripts via FTP — file transfer protocol — which allows an author to send a text electronically rather than mailing a hard copy. In 1990 the press established a "gopher server," which can burrow through the large amounts of material found on the Internet and direct the user to information quickly and easily. At present, ordering and staff information, pointers to other university-press gophers, and a basic version of the press catalogue exist on the press gopher server.

In March 1995 Catherine Fry became the press's fifth director, replacing Scott, who left the press to take up the directorship of the University Press of Florida. Fry had been associate director and marketing manager at Louisiana State University Press, where she had worked for fifteen years. In January 1995 the South Carolina newspaper *The State* quoted Fry as saying that she looked forward to the challenge of leading the press. "Watching the development of the USC Press over the last decade," she said, "I am convinced that it is now poised to become more prominent."

As one looks back at where the press was several years ago compared to where it is today one can see a remarkable — and admirable — difference. The amount of recognition, the increase in revenue, the establishment of a clear editorial policy, and the support of authors, series editors, press committee members, and the university administration have put the University of South Carolina Press firmly on the publishing map.

Conversations with Rare Book Dealers II: An Interview with Ralph Sipper

Ralph B. Sipper grew up in New York City. He earned a bachelor of arts degree in American literature from the City College of New York and took classes toward a master's degree at The New School. Joseph the Provider/Books was established in San Francisco in 1970. Sipper has been a book critic for over thirty years and is the editor of several books, the most recent being *Inward Journey* (Cordelia Editions, 1984). This telephone interview between Matthew J. Bruccoli and Ralph Sipper, "Joseph the Provider," Books, took place on 15 November 1994.

DLB: How long have you been a rare-book dealer?

SIPPER: Twenty-five years, officially. We established Joseph the Provider in San Francisco. But I had been involved with books all of my life, really.

DLB: Most book dealers start off as collectors. Had you been a serious collector before you commenced bookselling?

SIPPER: Well, I never thought of myself as one. A more accurate description would be that I was a book accumulator. Somehow books have always passed through my hands. I first began to accumulate them while indolently pursuing a master's degree in American literature. The indolence did not extend to the piling up of books. I passed them on for many years by way of gift or trade. Occasionally I sold some. Then I bought some more. One day my wife said to me: "You constantly run in and out of bookstores, dragging me along. Why don't we just open our own bookstore?" And that, as we say, was the beginning of the end. You must understand that I started late as a bookseller. I was in my late thirties. But after only two or three weeks I knew that bookselling was what I was meant to do, perhaps all I was fit to do.

Ralph Sipper

DLB: I can't improve on that, Ralph. As you know I have the strong conviction that a good bookseller is a scholar, a researcher, to use a fancy term, a patron of literature. Would you accept that statement with a few blushes?

SIPPER: I would accept it in a collective vein. I think it true of many booksellers. Probably as a group we are what D. H. Lawrence referred to as "Soldiers of Literature." Bibliographical grunts, if you will. But there is another group who are better patrons. Just as booksellers sometimes educate librarians, good collectors educate and influence booksellers. Even more than booksellers, they can influence literary scholarship. Some of the best collectors I know are among the most knowledgeable bibliophiles imaginable. Would you agree with that?

DLB: I would say that they are supposed to be. That is what a good book collector is suppose to be – someone who knows what he is doing, who in fact knows more about the bibliography of the author than anybody in the world.

SIPPER: Exactly.

DLB: So we don't have any argument there.

SIPPER: No.

DLB: Could you express your rationale for operating a rare-book business? What should a proper antiquarian bookshop attempt to do?

SIPPER: Should is a strong word when you speak of a group as independent-minded as booksellers are. What we have done through the years, I think, is a little different than what others have done. Many booksellers try to find the buyer first. This is an economically sound way to operate. My associates and I, on the other hand, have always had the perverse idea that if we get the books the world will beat a path to our doorstep. "They will come," as W. P. Kinsella said. This may not be the safest way to proceed, but it is, for better or worse, our way. We have always tried to find the best copies of the best books, the rarest books, and then just put them out there for anyone to buy. We do this principally through our catalogues, which we research thoroughly, spearheaded by our chief cataloguer, Lee Campbell, trying to make them as accurate and interesting as possible. A secondary mode of selling is to exhibit at ABAA book fairs. The last major way is to respond to particular requests from collectors by locating particular books for them. What we have not done really is work the selling end as aggressively as the buying. We have bought well over the years, in part because we are a bicoastal operation. With our main office being on the West Coast and our associate Larry Moskowitz living in the East, we manage to see as much modern literature as anyone. That's where the fun lies – in the seeing. We choose our books carefully, one

by one really, and only after we have them do we concern ourselves with their marketing.

DLB: You form collections?

SIPPER: Yes, chiefly author or subject collections. I think we were the first booksellers to systematically catalogue Vietnam War fiction. We have also offered and sold collections of California novels, Hollywood novels, and baseball fiction. We even put together a group of agrarian works of fiction, novels in which the principal setting is the American farm. One of the ways in which we like to function is to identify all the books available on the subject and then go out to find the best possible copies of those titles.

DLB: When you build a collection do you then intend to sell it as a collection? En bloc?

SIPPER: That is always the aim, to unify a group of books and then keep the family together. In these days of beleaguered library budgets it is much more difficult to accomplish.

DLB: I should have backed up and asked you why you chose your specialty, which is modern literature and in particular modern American literature. My impression is that you handle major works of modern British literature but your primary interest is American literature.

SIPPER: We handle British literature as well. Modern literature is the easiest way to enter the antiquarian book business.

DLB: Easiest in the sense of easy to build a stock and affordable.

SIPPER: It's easier to learn. For almost thirty years I have moonlighted as a book critic. During that time I have reviewed several hundred volumes of modern fiction, literary history, and biography. These are areas I know intimately, so perhaps that is why we began as we did. But once we established ourselves, we began to expand from within. Instead of just covering, say, American literature and then going back in time or forward, what we did was to identify smaller areas within that broad field and then do variations on those themes, to develop some of the less trodden paths. For example, through the years we have specialized in proletarian literature. Of course, there are some obvious proletarian books that many other dealers also offer reg-

Larry Moskowitz

ularly. During the thirties, a period of social discontent in America, many writers went about expressing their dissatisfaction through fiction. Much of this proletarian literature is not very good because the author's point was less to create art than to improve social conditions. And, of course, art and politics have never been compatible. Nevertheless, because the field itself is historically important, we decided to resurrect it bibliographically on a grander scale before the books disappear for good. We are comprehensively doing this in the field of black literature, not only Richard Wright, Ralph Ellison, James Baldwin, and the Harlem Renaissance, but hundreds of other black writers, and right now we are beginning to pick up books in the fields of Chicano literature and American Indian literature.

DLB: It has been said that smart rare-book librarians, rare-book curators, cultivate the book dealers who can make them look good. But, of course, there are librarians who are notorious for their hostility toward book dealers. The whole area of antiquarian book dealer/librarian relationships is a very thorny one. Would you care to comment?

SIPPER: What you say is true. I can only comment, though, on the basis of personal experience. We have never actively pursued or wooed librarians.

DLB: Do they woo you?

SIPPER: I'm tempted to paraphrase John Cheever by ruefully noting that Joseph the Provider has always been the lover and never the beloved. The fact of the matter is that historically we have been reluctant to hike up our corporate skirts in quest of book orders. I am not denigrating the time-honored practice of making the acquaintanceship of librarians at social functions or visiting them with book-bulging valises. We enjoy long-standing professional relationships with a fair number of libraries. But I like to think that these relationships have evolved naturally rather than by cold calculation. Anyway, there are not all that many great librarians around. There are people at top institutions like Bill Cagle and Tom Staley and others like Austin Mclean, Pat Willis, Tim Murray, and Frank Walker (who just retired) to whom we have paid a fair amount of attention. We stay in touch with them, sending along advance copies of offerings if we think that they will fit into their existing collections. But these are more or less isolated cases. Too many librarians sleepwalk through their jobs. The better ones, more than you might think, become booksellers.

DLB: Yes, I've spent much of my professional life working with university librarians, and some of them are, of course, wonders. I agree with you on Bill Cagle, for example, but most of them seem to really hate books. Baffling.

SIPPER: When you did your Ross Macdonald research at UC – Irvine, what would you have done without Roger Berry? I mean, there was nobody else there who knew the collection, and now that Roger has retired, the collection is not being developed further.

DLB: I could not have written either book without his help.

SIPPER: But what does a Macdonald researcher do now when there is nobody to guide him through the collection?

DLB: I don't know. Certainly booksellers have performed great services for literature, for authorship as well as for themselves. They've made money doing it by in effect serving as archivists for an author and keeping the author's material together through one sale, placing everything in one library. You have had the honor and pleasure of achieving such a deal in the case of Ross Macdonald.

SIPPER: Yes. It was through our offices that his papers wound up at UC – Irvine. He wanted them placed there. A major component of our business is appraising and placing archives. As a natural extension of being a bookseller I have come to know many contemporary authors. Some of them have approached us from time to time and asked us to find a home for their papers. The John Fowles ar-

chive, for example, went to the University of Texas through our offices. I traveled to England three times to accomplish this. The first time, I met with John in Lyme Regis to propose the sale. Next, I went back with the director of the library to iron out the details. Finally, I returned (with my wife as designated packer) to post five hundred pounds of paper to Austin, Texas, from bucolic Devon. Federal Express flew the papers across the Atlantic, and they arrived in Austin thirty-six hours later while I was still in the early throes of jet lag.

DLB: Do you see any positive developing trends in the field of modern first editions?

SIPPER: Well, as I was thinking last night what I could contribute to this interview, I came up negative. I see discouraging signs down the road.

DLB: Such as what?

SIPPER: Such as the homogenization of book values. *The Great Gatsby* without a dust jacket is a five-hundred-dollar book, while *The Great Gatsby* with a jacket and inscribed by Fitzgerald to someone of note is worth perhaps fifty thousand dollars – big difference. Pick up a price guide, though, which attempts to inform through generalization, and you will see *Gatsby* pegged somewhere in between, information which means less than nothing. What price guides and auction records encourage is a misleading shortcut toward understanding book values. They undermine the very rationale of book collecting, which is the status of the individual copy – for example: Is it a poor copy? Is it a decent one? A spectacular one? Did the author sign it? And if he did, is he a literary lion, turning up regularly in public with his pen in hand? Or is he reclusive like, say, J. D. Salinger or Thomas Pynchon, whose autographs are rare? Is the book merely signed, or is it inscribed to someone? To someone of note? And where does this title fit in with the author's body of work? With the work of his peers? Where does it float in the literary mainstream? Are there enough copies available of this particular book to satisfy the market? Or is it scarce? Rare? Now, no single reference work or price guide can even hope to begin to answer such fundamental questions, and yet we get three phone calls a week from some innocent asking, "What is *Catch 22* going for these days?" I mean, surely you must have heard some of this?

DLB: Yes.

SIPPER: How does one answer such a question?

DLB: The answer is, which copy do you have in mind?

SIPPER: Exactly. The concept of the individual copy is a cornerstone of book collecting.

DLB: That's the only answer.

SIPPER: When it comes to collecting, literary merit is only part of the equation. If content only is what you crave, there is always the public library or a paperback edition to fall back on. Antiquarian bookselling is about the book as artifact. The best collectors I have known are the independent-minded ones. Toby Holtzman, who sold his collection of American literature some years ago, collected hundreds of modern authors and on a comprehensive scale, including book contributions, periodicals, you name it. But most of his books he bought new. He kept up with his authors. Only what he could not find new did he pursue in the rare-book market. Toby collected in an individual way. The worst way to collect is to chase books by the new guy on the block. This month it is Cormac McCarthy. Now, the truth of the matter is that Cormac McCarthy is a fine writer, but he was also a fine writer twenty years ago when only a handful of collectors cared.

DLB: Ralph, there was a whole class of book collectors who were trained at 3 West 46th Street, Seven Gables Book Shop. It's been said that Michael Papantonio and John Kohn created more good collectors than any other dealers in America. Would you like to talk about the synergism between book dealer and book collector? Do you educate each other? What do you do for each other?

SIPPER: I did not get to know Mike Papantonio and John Kohn very well because they were phasing out as we were coming in. People like Margie Cohn, Warren Howell, and David Magee are among the dealers who were my mentors. But bookselling has changed since their day. Forty or fifty years ago, if you were a San Francisco gentleman who collected books, you went to your bookseller, either Warren Howell or David Magee – but not both – just as one man cut your hair or made your suits. Dealers in those days guarded their customers jealously. Today it has gotten a lot more egalitarian.

At a book fair in New York or Los Angeles, collectors peruse our books as well as those of Serendipity, Pepper and Stern, Heritage, Ken Lopez, and twenty others. It's more competitive because you don't have the field to yourself. And that makes it more fun and challenging – to a point.

DLB: What, in your view, makes for a good bookseller?

SIPPER: Most of the good booksellers I know have good reference libraries. They spend many hours studying that will not necessarily translate into extra dollars or sales. They research the material they are offering because they understand that knowledge is the difference between creative bookselling and selling by rote.

DLB: What kinds of book scholarship would you like to see being done?

SIPPER: I think if you deal in an author's work you ought to know, at the very least, which of his books are the important ones. Most dealers learn quickly which of an author's books are scarce, but scarcity is only one factor in evaluating a book. Too many dealers don't really do their homework. To me that presages trouble down the line for everyone.

DLB: I'd like to go back to my question about what the customer means to the dealer. Is it fair to say that some of your customers have educated you?

SIPPER: Certainly.

DLB: Got a for instance?

SIPPER: Well, I mentioned Toby Holtzman. Carl Peterson was a most knowledgeable collector. And you, my friend, are no slouch as a scholar or a collector.

DLB: I've never been a good customer. I wish I had been.

SIPPER: It's not too late to start, Matt.

DLB: Thank you, but I was thinking in terms of someone walking in and asking for a book, an author you didn't even recognize, and the guy proceeding to explain to you why this was a great book and why the author was terribly underrated, and as you began looking for books for this customer you got educated. Has that happened?

SIPPER: Yes, but you have to remember that critical opinion is only as good as the critic dispensing it. I've learned to trust certain people's judgment. But they have had to earn that trust from me.

DLB: Impossible question, but this is the kind of question that readers like to see: What is the greatest book or manuscript you have ever handled? And define, please, the basis of greatness.

SIPPER: I don't know that I can or care to isolate one. We've become famous for the fine condition of our books, though some would say *notorious* or *fetishistic* are better descriptive words. But even more thrilling to me than exceptional condition is a book's emotional connection or literary association. One could collect association copies and theoretically write a cultural history by cross-pollinating literary relationships with established canons. Someone right now is collecting important books inscribed by authors to their mothers. You can't get any more bibliographically intimate than that.

DLB: Would you like to say something about condition? Because I think you and I do not agree on the value of condition, and the point is not to argue, but I think I am closer to how civilians feel. Civilians are baffled for the most part by the existence of two copies of a book – neither one inscribed. One is a copy that looks better than the other. It looks newer, looks nicer, and it doesn't cost twice as much; it costs ten times as much. Could you do a brief disquisition on how condition affects value and why?

SIPPER: Because collectors like beautiful objects. Of course, fine copies are harder to find than ordinary ones. When we started out in business the value of a dust jacket was considered minimal. Yet the jacket is an integral part of the book, having been issued with it, after all. The jacket contains biographical information, bibliographical information, and artwork that imparts a visual feel for the book's time. Dust jackets are beautiful things, and people with the taste and wherewithal to own beauty will go to extraordinary lengths to obtain such things, the more so if they are hard to find. Call it preservation of the dubiously valuable; call it anal if you like. I call it human propensity.

DLB: So the dust jacket is in fact not a dust jacket.

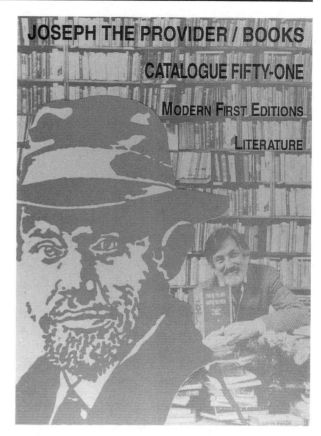

Cover for a Joseph the Provider catalogue featuring a large image of the company logo

SIPPER: Come again?

DLB: It hasn't been a dust jacket for damn near seventy-five years.

SIPPER: Right.

DLB: It is the way in which the publisher attempts to introduce the book to the reader. And in some cases, of course, it has an authorial statement.

SIPPER: Well, yes. Twenty years ago we began to pursue some of these scarce jackets with a vengeance. Now, if at that point nobody had cared, then undoubtedly we would have abandoned our search for them. But it quickly became apparent to us that what collectors really wanted was what their fellow collectors lacked. Having a jacketed *This Side of Paradise* was a way for a collector, who after all enjoys the pride of acquisition, to acknowledge that while he and his friend both had nice copies of the same title, his was the more desirable one. There are only five or so copies known of Vladimir

Nabokov's *Despair,* published in England some sixty years ago, and only two in jacket. The publisher's building was destroyed by a bomb during World War II. For such an important rarity we will pay what we have to, add something onto that figure, and hope that someone agrees with our notion of value. And we had better not be wrong too many times. When you really think about it, bookselling is just about the purest form of capitalism extant.

DLB: I have no response. You've made the case perfectly. You know, we've all heard the story about the guy who got married and his wife removed all the dust jackets and threw them all away because they spoiled the color scheme.

SIPPER: My parents did that. When I was growing up in the Bronx, my parents and my friends' parents normally removed the jackets just as you say. The green bindings were arranged together, etc. I will grant you that someday the whole dust jacket thing could blow up in our faces.

DLB: Good point. You were saying?

SIPPER: Buyers will resist at some level, if they think a book price is inflated. Value when it comes to art objects is really only a perception. Today, a little thing like a clipped price from dust jacket can alter a book's price significantly. You must remember that the absence of a price on a jacket can in some cases leave one in the dark as to whether or not he actually has a first edition. So there are sound bibliographical reasons for insisting on a dust jacket, too. But things may change. Styles of book collecting usually do.

DLB: Of course. We all understand that, but when people come to the house, the one out of one hundred who notices there are these things on the bookshelves ask the question about why do you have all these pieces of paper on the books, and, of course, book collectors come in two sizes, the devout and the infidels. The great Louis Armstrong said, when asked after one of his gigs by a gushing fan what jazz is, "Lady, if you don't know by now, you never will." I don't know why you should want to tell them. However, this is turning into my interview and not yours. You're going to have to do the mandatory explanation of why your business is called Joseph the Provider.

SIPPER: Really?

DLB: I know the story, but do it, please, for the record.

SIPPER: Well, I thought that the Book Nook would not do. I wanted a name for our enterprise that people would remember. I was first introduced to books by my grandfather, Joseph Sipper, who when I was three or four sat me on his knee and read from his books, which he obviously loved. The books under discussion happened to be Hebrew prayer books, which were not then my cup of tea — and still aren't. But grandfather's passion for them shone through. His death was my first intimate experience with that grim reality. Suddenly it all came together: the desire to resurrect a loved one, the literary allusion, the implicit idea that we would be finding books for those who also loved them. Our logo derives from an old photograph of my grandfather. Having inflicted this old story on you, I must also tell you that more often than I like we get phone calls that ask: "Are you a religious bookstore?"

DLB: It's been lucky for you. Some names are lucky, and its been a lucky name.

SIPPER: I've been lucky to be a bookman.

Conversations with Publishers II:
An Interview with Charles Scribner III

Charles Scribner III received his Ph.D. in art history in 1977 from Princeton University, where he taught baroque art in the department of art and archaeology. In 1975 he joined his family's publishing firm, Charles Scribner's Sons, founded in 1846. When Scribners merged into Macmillan Publishing Company in 1984, he went to work for the president of the new parent company, where he became a vice-president of Macmillan and editor of their Scribner imprint. In 1993 Macmillan was acquired by Paramount, and Scribners became an imprint of Simon & Schuster. There Dr. Scribner oversees the publishing of the classic Scribner authors F. Scott Fitzgerald and Ernest Hemingway. At the same time, he has continued to write and lecture on art, especially on the art of the baroque masters Peter Paul Rubens, Gran Bernini, and Michelangelo da Caravaggio. He has made a PBS television documentary on Rubens's "Eucharist" tapestries, and his book on the subject was published in 1982. His two recent books for Abrams's Masters of Art series are *Rubens* (1989) and *Bernini* (1991). A frequent lecturer at the Metropolitan Museum of Art in New York, he also has served as a trustee of the Homeland Foundation, Princeton University Press, and Saint Paul's School (New Hampshire). This telephone interview took place on 16 November 1994.

Charles Scribner III

DLB: Does the publisher have a duty to a dead author? Whether or not the dead author appointed the publisher an executor in a will, what is the publisher's responsibility to an author that the publisher has been associated with or identified with? In other words, Scribners's and F. Scott Fitzgerald, and Ernest Hemingway, and Thomas Wolfe.

SCRIBNER: I've often described (and not in complaint) my job at Scribners as "curator of dead authors." As someone who loves our dead authors as much as my grandfather loved them when they were alive, I would say that the publisher's responsibility to an author should not be subject to any-

thing as ephemeral as death. That is to say, the responsibility to publish the author in his best light is just as strong and binding after an author has died as it was when the author was alive. It may be more difficult to achieve insofar as one doesn't have the benefit of the author at hand to converse with — at least not in *my* experience, although some other publisher may have a more "spiritualistic" relationship with his departed authors! Nonetheless, the responsibility does not decline. I might add — and I know I'm flying in the face of our whole American legal establishment and First Amendment missionaries —

200

but I have to confess that my own view of libel is much the same. I don't believe in printing things about people that would be considered libelous if they were alive. Their bad fortune to have died should not (as it does now) provide a carte blanche to print anything about them, however malicious and false. That doesn't speak to your precise question, but it does illustrate my underlying conviction that one's moral responsibilities to someone do not evaporate when that person has passed the threshold of the grave.

DLB: If an author, one of your authors, were to come to you and ask you to suggest, recommend the best way to dispose of or to arrange for the treatment of his or her literary property, how would you advise the author?

SCRIBNER: My first advice would be either make sure you don't die — and p.s. don't lose your marbles either — or if you can't be certain of success in that effort, then like the emperor Caesar Augustus prepare to die virtually every day. And in so doing please keep your affairs in the kind of order that you would want them to remain in for eternity, i.e., an up-to-date, thorough housecleaning of manuscripts, letters, and the other artifacts that will become your archives someday.

DLB: Anything that you don't want to have published posthumously, you'd better destroy while you're alive.

SCRIBNER: Yes. And if you don't destroy it, please be aware of the fact that your request that your works in progress or any writings be destroyed by someone else cannot be taken as an absolute pronouncement, an infallible pronouncement. Why? Well, think of the case of Ernest Hemingway, who left verbal instructions that his letters were not to be published, but at the same time had joked with my grandfather that someday his letters would, of course, be published. He then later remarked to my father that he had a lot of manuscripts in a safe deposit vault that would earn a lot for his heirs someday. So Hemingway seemed to indulge in some deliberate ambivalence about these matters. And perhaps he was genuinely of two minds about the publication of his letters. I think of a more classical example involving the emperor Augustus. Virgil, we know . . .

DLB: Did Scribners publish him too?

SCRIBNER: Well, not while he was alive. But still my father was, I think, guided by the example of Virgil leaving instructions that his manuscript for the *Aeneid* be burned after his death. Fortunately, the emperor Augustus did not permit that to happen. As my father noted in his memoir, *In the Company of Writers* (1991), fortunately not all literary executors obey such requests. You know, one can't help but speculate whether Virgil was absolutely serious about his request. It may have been his way of going on record for posterity that he wasn't entirely happy with what he had written. But the only definitive way for an author to proclaim his dissatisfaction with a work is to destroy it himself.

DLB: Would you, if you were instructed by an author to destroy material after the author's death, be able to do it?

SCRIBNER: After his death? It would depend on my appraisal of the works in question.

DLB: You would interpose your own judgment.

SCRIBNER: Absolutely.

DLB: And I absolutely agree with you.

SCRIBNER: Absolutely. Why? Because if the letters in question or works in question were clearly libelous and harmful to somebody whom the author cared about, or harmful to his own reputation, and it was clear that the author, had he had the opportunity to destroy them would have done so in good conscience, then yes, of course, I would carry out his wishes, because the *basis* for those instructions would be crystal clear. On the other hand, if the works in question were not harmful either to other people or to the author's own reputation, it would seem to me strange, perhaps even an act of folly, and perhaps not entirely a serious request, that the author had asked for them to be destroyed. I think an appraisal of the material in question would have to be taken into consideration. Mozart, for example, but for financial needs might well otherwise have asked his wife and soon-to-be widow Constanze to destroy the unfinished *Requiem* he was struggling so hard to complete. Instead, she turned it over to a pupil of his, Süssmayr, who did an absolutely faithful job of completing it according to the master's design. And we're all the beneficiaries of that decision today. So let's put it this way: if the author does not physically attempt – he needn't succeed, but he must *try* — to destroy this material himself while alive, it seems to me that requesting somebody else to do it *later* (when he has had plenty of time to do it himself) has to be a request taken under consideration.

DLB: Let me revert briefly to the situation with Hemingway's letters. Would you agree that it's a fair statement that Hemingway himself made it impossible for his letters to remain unpublished — by writing letters of such great literary interest and moreover by making himself such a giant among American writers that it was inevitable that his letters would be published sooner or later — but that his letters would be published, would have to be published? It's his fault that Mary Hemingway, the widow, could not have successfully blocked, impeded, perhaps impeded publication of his letters.

SCRIBNER: I think that's true — with this one important qualification. I think that his request that they not be published was his way of saying that not *all* his letters could be published and do him a service at the same time, that he had some valid reservations, as indeed we all do. I mean, who of us, except perhaps a lifelong career diplomat who never wrote a personal note in his life, would wish to have all his letters published without some form of sifting and value judgments? Again, I'm recalling what my father said on the subject of Hemingway's instructions that his letters not be published. With Mary's (the executor's) approval he eventually published them, and he was convinced he did the right thing. His explanation was as follows: To begin with, he, Hemingway, had kidded his friend and publisher (my grandfather) about someday publishing his letters — so he had envisioned such a thing. It wasn't an unthinkable act in Hemingway's mind. Second — and this is my father speaking — "I believed his letters show a side of him that nothing else in his work does. And it is a very nice side. I considered that I was justified." And then my father went on to explain the analogy with Virgil that I mentioned earlier. Both Virgil and the public benefited from the emperor's disobeying his instructions that the *Aeneid* be burned. Of course, it is true that there was always a danger that a malicious scholar or editor or a stupid executor might have allowed a selection of Hemingway's letters to be published that reflected poorly on him. They might have unfairly emphasized letters that Hemingway wrote in moments of anger and never sent (which showed a great deal of judgment on Hemingway's part). We all do that. We write a letter and perhaps may

throw it out or stick it in a bottom drawer. One could publish a very unkind and unfair selection of any author's letters, and I think that Hemingway wanted to protect himself against that, and I think rightfully so. The ultimate justification in the letters that were published lies in the fact that they were well selected and that they reveal him in a very favorable and humane light. My father says that he'll have to account to Ernest for this in the hereafter, but he's not all that fearful of that encounter.

DLB: Related to this matter of literary remains and the proper disposition of them is the question of fair use, that is, the right of biographers, scholars, critics to quote a reasonably small amount of copyrighted material in their work about an author. I'm sure that we all, you and I, agree that the concept of fair use — although you'll find no place in the copyright act, the American Copyright Act, is there a stipulation of what constitutes fair use — there is a vague description of a certain amount of words, but nowhere does it say how many words or what percentage of the work. I think you and I are agreed that the concept of fair use is necessary to allow scholarly work or biographical work to be done in the field of literary history. But there's that question of what about unpublished material — unpublished letters, unpublished documents, unpublished manuscripts. And, of course, the J. D. Salinger case comes to mind immediately — where a biographer quoted from unpublished Salinger letters and claimed fair use — although before that case the doctrine of fair use was understood to apply only to previously published material, not previously unpublished material. How do you as a publisher feel about loose or stringent interpretation of fair use?

SCRIBNER: I would have to answer that when I came into publishing out of academia in the mid 1970s this issue was a live one, insofar as there were scholars constantly seeking to quote under the "fair use" rubric from unpublished Hemingway letters and manuscripts. And like a schoolteacher my father drilled into me what was in the law and I don't think that has fundamentally changed, though it may have been modified somewhat. The maxim he drilled into me was that fair use only applies to *published* materials. So fair use cannot be invoked for something unpublished. That was the way I was brought up.

DLB: The courts are reinterpreting that.

SCRIBNER: Then they do so at the expense of someone's privacy, and perhaps someone's literary property. And I am not sympathetic. I must say that I am not sympathetic.

DLB: But Congress has amended the copyright code, and I happen to have the wording in front of me. In August 1992 the 102nd Congress revised the copyright act as follows: "Be it enacted by the Senate and the House of Representatives of the United States of America in Congress assembled, that section 107 of Title 17 United States Code is amended by adding at the end the following quote, 'The fact that a work is unpublished shall not itself bar a finding of fair use if such finding is made upon consideration of all the above factors.' Pass the House of Representatives August 11, 1992." So that fair use as was taught to you by your father and was taught to me has now been modified. So the fact that a work is unpublished shall not itself bar a finding of fair use. Is that going to cause problems not just for literary executors but for publishers?

SCRIBNER: Well, it may. I don't see how it cannot cause problems for them. I must say my own sympathies are very much on the side of privacy and not to open unpublished materials to scholars and/or vultures. It's as simple as that.

DLB: Who sometimes look very much the same.

SCRIBNER: Yes. But I don't want to sound hypocritical. As someone who has worked in the field of biography myself I can think of some cases (to take my own subject, Rubens) where heretofore unknown and certainly unpublished letters have popped up. Now, Rubens has been dead since 1640, so it's been awhile. And, yes, they are quoted without a search being made of who, three and a half centuries later, his present-day heirs and family might be. So perhaps there should be some time limit. To pick an example closer to home, if we were to find an unpublished letter of Abraham Lincoln or an unpublished manuscript or speech of Thomas Jefferson, would anyone in his right mind not apply the concept of fair use to those materials after so long a period of time? Yet apropos of a recently deceased author with living children, grandchildren, relatives, I think that to modify the previous prohibition against quoting from unpublished sources without the formal permission of the family is wrong. You have to draw a line. It may be a temporal line; it may be for the first fifty years after an

author's death, or a hundred years, or whatever. Now, "drawing a line" is usually denigrated by opponents as an arbitrary matter. But somebody once said – I thought quite brilliantly – that art as well as civility both begin with the drawing of a line. Perhaps we shouldn't give up our attempt to do so.

DLB: Wearing two of your hats as publisher and as historian, do you feel that the present term of copyright protection is adequate or inadequate? That is, life plus fifty years, because, as you know, in Europe it's life plus seventy. In England the life plus fifty will almost certainly be extended to life plus seventy. Does that seem about right? Or do you feel that copyright should be as close to perpetual as can be arranged?

SCRIBNER: I think that copyright was always intended to strike a balance between the needs of society to advance through publications and research and the needs of artists and authors to be given encouragement to earn a living for themselves and for their families. So I don't think realistically that the idea of perpetual copyright makes any sense. Are we going to pay royalties on the Epistles to the descendants of Saint Paul? Or was it only Saint Peter who was married? I forget. In any event, Moses was married, was he not? Are his descendants to be paid royalties on the Book of Exodus?

DLB: And the Ten Commandments?

SCRIBNER: Now that's an even better example.

DLB: Now there's a valuable property.

SCRIBNER: And what royalty do they get? Ten percent royalty on the Ten Commandments? It has to be within reason.

DLB: What is reasonable, though?

SCRIBNER: If life plus fifty used to be reasonable or deemed reasonable, I think the fact that Europe has extended life plus fifty to life plus seventy sounds as if they are simply being biologically consistent. As the average human life span has been extended, why not copyright as well? People live longer than they did a couple of generations ago; maybe their copyrights should survive commensurately longer.

DLB: Life plus seventy, assuming normal life span of the author, means through the lifetime of the children and well into the life of the grandchildren.

SCRIBNER: That seems sensible. That seems sensible insofar as most people – unless their grandparents died at an early age – most people have the opportunity to know their grandparents. Very few have an opportunity to know their great-grandparents. Perhaps the benefits of copyright should extend to only those who in the normal course of life would have the experience of knowing the creator of the works. What I'm suggesting – only half in jest – is that there was once a time when a fifty-year-old was considered an old man; today seventy is considered still young (well, at least "too young too die"). So why not view copyright the same way?

DLB: What bothers me is there's the element of the tontine about it. If an author lives to a ripe old age his heirs profit. If an author is knocked over by a taxicab at age twenty-eight his heirs are penalized. There's that element of lottery about it that I don't like. I prefer publication plus. The old twenty-eight plus twenty-eight, fifty-six years, wasn't enough.

SCRIBNER: No.

DLB: But I would think publication plus one hundred years might be defendable.

SCRIBNER: Well, how about an "either/or" provision?

DLB: Whichever is longer.

SCRIBNER: Publication plus a hundred or life plus seventy, whichever is longer.

DLB: Whichever is longer.

SCRIBNER: That makes sense. I know in our own case as publishers that "life plus fifty" would have created an enormous disparity between the families of Scott Fitzgerald and Ernest Hemingway, for example. And that does seem unfortunate. But, again, I think a fair formula can be devised.

DLB: It seems to me that the notion that publishers and authors have different stakes in copyright is completely erroneous. I think that the publisher is as interested in protecting the copyright as

is the author. Surely a publisher would rather control a valuable work of literature than have the thing in public domain and have to compete with every publisher who wants to put out a cheap, quick edition of the work. But yet the notion persists that publishers favor short copyright and authors favor long copyright. I would like to hear your response to that, please.

SCRIBNER: I agree with you entirely. I'd be very suspect of a publisher who did not value an author's copyright and wish to extend it for as long as possible. It seems to me that's a publisher whose primary concern is not in nourishing and maintaining the authors he's signed up. Now it's fair to recall that when Scribners first began in 1846, American publishers were not subscribers to any international copyright code, and they were a little bit like – not a little bit like, but very much like – some of our present-day South Pacific "pirate" publishers. There were recently countries (there may yet be a few) in Southeast Asia that specialized in this art of literary piracy. They routinely disregarded foreign authors' copyrights. America was in that position in the nineteenth century. But as our nation came of age, our national interests were deemed to parallel those of our authors. I can't imagine any *real* publisher (as opposed to a bargain-basement reprinter) not feeling that his interests in sustaining copyright are every bit as strong as those of his authors who are protected by those copyrights.

DLB: Your great-grandfather, Charles the Great, viewed the rise of the literary agent with dismay. Does the literary agent perform any service beyond acting as a bargainer? And is that worth ten or fifteen percent?

SCRIBNER: There is one literary agent with whom I felt very close ties of friendship; he was the agent for Louis Auchincloss and C. P. Snow in this country, a man named James Oliver Brown. He had his own company, James Brown Associates, and later towards the end of his life headed Curtis Brown. There's no doubt in my mind that he more than earned his percentage, in his devotion to his authors and the many services he performed for them – among which, and by no means the least of which, his unerring good taste, and judgment, and advice.

DLB: Do you know of editing agents, agents who also function as first editor?

SCRIBNER: He did. And having said that, Jim was of a generation that came about midpoint between my father and grandfather. I'd like to think and hope that there are successors today to agents like James Oliver Brown. Beyond that expression of hope, I will take the Fifth in answering your question.

DLB: You mean you've consumed a fifth already? It's not three o'clock in the afternoon. It's true what they say about publishers.

SCRIBNER: The Fifth Amendment.

DLB: Thank you, Charles. Is there anything that you want to add to this conversation?

SCRIBNER: Only that as I brooded upon the role of the literary executor, an analogy that came to mind . . . well, let me backtrack a bit first. The analogy often used for publishers is that of an obstetrician who has to oversee the author's offspring into the world and make sure it gets off to a healthy start. The publisher cannot guarantee the long life or success of the offspring, but the publisher does have a responsibility to at least see that the offspring (I'm really straining to be sexually neutral here, or rather, gender neutral) makes it into the world safely, after which, it belongs to the parent, not the obstetrician. The obstetrician must take a backseat role in this, must play a backseat role. The analogy that comes to mind for literary executor is somewhat different and is drawn from a later stage of the offspring's life. The phrase that came to mind, one that is very close to heart at the moment as I visit boarding schools with my son, is the old phrase *in loco parentis,* which in the good ole days boarding schools sought to be: "in place of the parent." They were in loco parentis. Now, that loaded Latin phrase prompts an equivalent Latin phrase to sum up my view of the role of the literary executor: *In loco scriptoris,* "in place of the writer." And the really good literary executor must know, of course,

that he or she can never be that writer and must never have the arrogance to think that he or she is the writer. But to the extent possible, the literary executor should place himself or herself in the position of the writer and try to see the issues from the writer's perspective, to see them as the writer would have seen them. And, of course, this presupposes an executor who truly understands the writer well — and, perhaps even more important, thoroughly understands the writer's work.

DLB: I totally agree. We both can think of at least one agent for an American genius who doesn't know the work.

SCRIBNER: When I say "understand the author," I don't mean possessing a detailed knowledge of the author's personal idiosyncrasies so much as having a keen sense of the author's intent and view of the work. In other words, do not mistake an author's comedy for tragedy — and vice versa. Do not mistake satire for a pious tract. Understand the author's intent and perception and the value of the work. "In place of the writer," *in loco scriptoris,* really means to treat the works — that is, the body of literature and material that's been entrusted to the executor — as lovingly as the author would and to care for it with as much good sense and judgment and scrupulosity as the author would care for his or her own work, which is to say as a parent would care for his or her own child. Because I think in the end that's the way authors view their works: as their children. Does that make sense?

DLB: Yes, it makes excellent sense. But I think it's a big mistake for an author to die, because no one can possibly understand the author's feelings about his work except the author.

SCRIBNER: Agreed. Still, a literary executor may, at times, be even more sympathetic and objective and benign in his treatment of a work than the author himself. In any case, that's the ideal.

Who Runs American Literature?

George Garrett
University of Virginia

DLB: Well, who do you feel runs American literature? Editors, agents, publishers, critics?

NAN TALESE: Writers.

Good question, hard to answer. Maybe unanswerable. Still, nothing ventured, nothing gained.

Of course we all know the real answer – that American literature, past and present, is owned and run by its owners, the guys in the suits – thousand-dollar suits these days – with the checkbooks and the power to determine which (among books) lives and which dies. There was a time when the guys in the suits with the checkbooks gained something – status, social respectability, or simple public respect – for being concerned about or, at least, seeming to be concerned about American literature. Alfred Knopf and Bennet Cerf may have been, at heart, hard-nosed businessmen more than anything else. But the old guys still published a lot of good books that mattered. So did the various Scribners, none of whom was ever accused of being a heavyweight intellectual. Things are different now, and everybody senses the change. In a recent piece ("Our Absolutely Deplorable Literary Situation – And Some Thoughts On How To Fix It Good," *Sewanee Review,* Fall 1994) Louis D. Rubin, Jr., begins in the present: "From the standpoint of getting good books published and read, the belles lettres, as we used to call them, are in woeful shape and getting worse." The future does not fare any better in his view. "What we have in sum," he writes, "is about as sour a future outlook for our country's literature as has existed since James Fenimore Cooper began publishing fiction in the early 1820s." Rubin's view seems to be shared by a lot of people in the business.

But maybe there are other ways of looking at things. For example, let's suppose, on the basis of the same evidence everybody else is looking at, that the big boys, those guys in suits, care so little about literature that they cannot be called *hostile* to it, merely indifferent. They are like medieval kings who have their own larger concerns and who rule over a kind of feudal state, delegating authority and responsibility to others. A kingdom of fragments.

Very well. In the kingdom of the blind the one-eyed man is king. And in the fragmented and anarchic American literary scene, out of which literature (if any) must come, even a poet can have power in the tiny precincts of the poetry world.

So in search of answers we went forth, assembled panels of (anonymous, oh yes, and why not?) literati and asked them, if possible, to arrive at some sort of consensus about their part and function in the scheme of things. Who (we asked our anonymous sources) deserves respect and recognition? Who has earned a share of fluttering Bronx cheers? Who are the artists, the real ones and the con artists?

Here are a few of the things we found out.

At the bright, hot, shining center of things (the universe?), New York City (where else?), the word on the street is that the guys with the checkbooks may *run* American literature. But the gatekeepers are the agents who propose, and the editors who dispose. Well, we asked as politely as we could, who, then, are the best and the brightest, the wheeler dealers, the movers and shakers, the ones who matter most?

When the smoke cleared, here is what we learned. First, nobody could agree that there are only ten best agents; "hottest" agents and agencies was how the question was framed. So our sources settled for fifteen, mixing agencies and agents:

(1) Janklow and (Lynn) Nesbit
(2) Ellen Levine
(3) Aaron Priest & Molly Friedrich
(4) Esther Newberg and Amanda ("Binky") Urban of ICM
(5) Robert Gottlieb of William Morris Agency
(6) Candida Donadio
(7) Andrew Wiley of Wiley Aitken and Stone
(8) Jane Gelfman of Gelfman Schneider
(9) Melanie Jackson

(10) Joy Harris of Lantz-Harris Agency
(11) David Black of Black Inc.
(12) Sandra Dijkstra
(13) Wendy Weil
(14) Gail Hochman
(15) Georges Borchardt

You would expect, wouldn't you, that these, the fifteen "hottest" agents in the nation, would mostly be dealing with the fifteen hottest editors (as of 31 December 1994)? And who might these be? Back to our anonymous sources, who promptly reported the following:

(1) Sonny Mehta – Knopf
(2) Dan Frank – Pantheon
(3) Alice Mayhew – Simon and Schuster
(4) Nan Talese – Doubleday
(5) Ann Godoff – Random House
(6) Faith Sale – Putnam
(7) Maureen Egen – Warner
(8) Carole Baron – Delacorte
(9) Barbara Grossman – Viking
(10) David Rosenthal – Villard (Random House)
(11) Bob Miller – Hyperion
(12) Susan Moldow – Scribners
(13) Jonathan Galassi – Farrar Straus Giroux
(14) Morgan Entrekin – Grove Atlantic
(15) Joann Davis – Warner

Our sources were quick to remind us that the list of editors would have been significantly different if made on 31 December 1993, though the list of agents would have been roughly the same. Just so, statistics and experience indicate that at least some of the fifteen hottest editors will be long gone within a calendar year. Agents seem to remain players in the game; though some venerable agencies – Russell and Volkening, Harold Ober, Curtis Brown Ltd. – did not make the cut on any list.

We also note that one and all, agents and editors, are in the New York scene. So far all the wonders of modern communication have not outweighed the importance of being there on the spot where the restaurants are, where the action is. Even allowing that our panel of experts were New Yorkers, is there no place for people like Shannon Ravenel of Algonquin Books, Leslie Phillabaum of Louisiana State University Press, Kathryn Lang of Southern Methodist University Press? More and more the small-press editors and those from the more adventurous university presses are becoming serious players in the literary game. But halfway

into the final decade of the century they remain (at least for the inhabitants of the bright and shining center) out of sight and out of mind.

Let's pretend for a moment that Nan Talese is right, that she was not kidding Kristin van Ogtrop when she answered our question, promptly and emphatically and in one word, *writers*.

The next question is which writers. Clearly, we are not talking about the makers of blockbusters, even though Nan Talese may have been (see for yourself in the full interview). Along with a few unflagging perennials on the backlist, blockbusters are the golden geese of the publishing industry in America. Without blockbusters there can be no poetry, no midlist trade books, indeed no publishing houses, at least on the conglomerate scale. But nobody, except maybe Leslie Fiedler a couple of times, has seriously tried to claim that our American blockbusters are our American literature. Whatever they are, literature they are not. They may *run* American literature . . . somewhat, but they can hardly be said to shape it.

Dealing with writers proved much more troublesome than dealing with New York editors and agents. (Maybe the editors and agents have a valid point in their generalized contempt for writers.) Nobody could or would agree to a consensus about who are the best or even the hottest literary writers on the 1994 scene. Protected by anonymity, our sources allowed that there are not *any* ten novelists, for example, who stand out clearly as superior, the best and brightest of their trade. This, of course, may be an honest and accurate appraisal of the scene, asserting that, agents and editors and book reviewers to the contrary, there are no genuine "stars." At a certain level of achievement, midlist though it may be, all literary writers are equal, a grand democracy of creators like the dream of Walt Whitman. But if there was no consensus about merit and virtue, there was uniform interest and a certain consensus in spotlighting the overrated talents of the times. These, to be sure, are all "stars"; and it follows that if the whole concept is invalid, then all who are professed to be stars are overrated. Even here, however, we could not get our sources to agree enough to form a true consensus. What we are left with is two lists with only the least of overlap:

The Ten Most Overrated Novelists in America

(1) William Gass
(2) William Gaddis
(3) Mary Gordon

(4) Tony Cade Bambera
(5) Tom Robbins
(6) Robert James Waller
(7) Terry McMillan
(8) Stanley Elkin
(9) James Salter
(10) Bob Shacochis

We have no idea, not the slightest, what Robert James Waller is doing on the list in the first place, but there he stands among the others.

The second list (though formed without comparison or contrast) is essentially a minority report, nevertheless a consensus of that minority among our sources:

The Ten Most Overrated Novelists in America

(1) John Irving
(2) Toni Morrison
(3) Grace Paley
(4) Robert Stone
(5) Shelby Hearon
(6) Jim Harrison
(7) William Gaddis
(8) Lurie Moore
(9) Stanley Elkin
(10) Amy Tan

Gaddis and Elkin are the only two to appear on both lists, which may mean (if it means anything) a certain kind of stardom.

The minority report also included a list and ranking that we had not asked for; although it is logical that if you are concerned with writers you believe to be too well known and honored then you may well have in mind a list of writers whose names and works have been undeservedly ignored, if not really forgotten. Here we might expect some or all of the minority sources to sneak in their own names, but they are too clever by half to be caught in that gesture. Instead, since our general topic is American literature, they went back a little in time to bring forward some of the names of outstanding American writers who have been lost in the hierarchical shuffle:

Ten Forgotten American Writers

(1) Gertrude Atherton
(2) Brainerd Cheney
(3) Waldo Frank
(4) Michael Gold
(5) Joseph Hergesheimer

(6) Fannie Hurst
(7) Horace McCoy
(8) Julia Peterkin
(9) Amelie Rives
(10) Carl Van Vechten

We sincerely regret the absence of Floyd Dell from this list. But we have no vote or say in the matter.

This whole business of remembering and forgetting, of who deserves oblivion and who does not, leads us directly to another kind of gatekeeper – the scholar-critic. Even in the age of the sound bite, MTV, CD-ROM, even in the age of canon warfare and galloping diversity, even at a time when the memory of the publishing community is as brief as a mayfly's, still there are those critics who, in reviews and critical articles and essays, seek to honor what is valid and to expose what is fraudulent, to weigh and sift and judge as much for the future as for here and now. After all is said and done, American literature is what they say it is (just as the law and the Constitution is whatever the Supreme Court of the United States says). Do they run it? Well, no. Not exactly. Not hardly. And yet, no denying, unless things change a whole lot more than they have already, it is the literary critics who have the last word and often the last laugh.

Off we went to a new set of (anonymous) sources, at least one of whom is on the list. (Guess who.) And why not?

The Ten Leading Literary Critics in America

(1) Leslie Fiedler
(2) R. W. B. Lewis
(3) John T. Irwin
(4) Harold Bloom
(5) Irving Malin
(6) Denis Donoghue
(7) Jay Martin
(8) Marjorie Perloff
(9) Monroe Spears
(10) John W. Aldridge

A significant number of the above may indeed be members in good standing of the AARP, but there they are, still active and still influential and maybe, in the long run, the true managers of American literature.

In part because it was called to our attention by our scholarly-critical sources, we print without much comment or any marginalia a list we received of another group of American writers, not mentioned by our mainstream novelists,

Ten Best Postmodernist Writers in America

(1) William S. Burroughs (*My Education*)
(2) John Barth (*Once Upon a Time: A Floating Opera*)
(3) Kathy Acker (*My Mother: Demonology*)
(4) Thomas Pynchon (*Vineland*)
(5) Robert Coover (*Pinocchio in Venice*)
(6) R. H. W. Dillard (*Omniphobia*)
(7) Carol Emshwiler (*Verging on the Pertinent*)
(8) William Gibson (*Virtual Light*)
(9) Neil Gaiman (*The Tragical Comedy or Comical Tragedy of Mr. Punch*)
(10) Robert Gluck (*Jack the Modernist*)
(11) Rudy Rucker (*The Hollow Earth*)

to which list was appended the notation: "Okay. So there are eleven of them. When could postmodernists ever count?"

These days poets do not bother to claim that they are the unacknowledged legislators of the world anymore. And we seriously doubt that they, singly or collectively, would assert that they run American literature. But, by the same token, they are not shy about claiming power and honor in their own precincts. They manage their own turf, thank you very much, and with a certain contempt for other forms of literary expression. Among the cognoscenti *storytelling* is a pejorative word. There are also as many quarrels and feuds among the poets as, say, feudal Europe in the darkest of the Dark Ages. What with prizes and grants and awards, fellowships and teaching jobs, a poet can make as much money as a junior corporate executive. So their quarrels and deadly games can make a difference. We approached the poets, then, carefully, on tiptoes. Who knew what they might come up with, especially granted the camouflage of anonymnity? Not surprisingly, our sources offered more lists than any other group we surveyed. And no doubt at all that any other group would produce at least contrasting, if not fundamentally different, lists. So? So we publish what we received in response to (casual enough) inquiry:

Best Living Poets

(1) Richard Wilbur
(2) James Dickey
(3) Philip Booth
(4) Philip Levine
(5) Galway Kinnell
(6) Brendan Galvin
(7) Patricia Goedicke
(8) Dabney Stuart

(9) Rita Dove
(10) R. T. Smith
(11) Dereck Walcott

This list is immediately followed by another:

The Ten Most Overrated Poets in America

(1) John Ashberry
(2) James Merrill
(3) Stanley Kunitz
(4) John Hollander
(5) Robert Bly
(6) Mark Strand
(7) James Tate
(8) Ed Hirsch
(9) Dave Smith
(10) Dana Gioia

Poets being more sensitive than most people, we offer neutrality and condolences to all who made the second list, in the sure and certain knowledge that they would present a different version of both.

The next two lists are interesting, in that our poetry sources thought of them and sent them along on their own. Poets have next to nothing to do with agents or even commercial editors (though, in a poem somewhere, Mark Strand makes mention of going to lunch at Lutece with the prominent, if here unlisted and unmentioned, Harry Ford). Indeed, with exceptions, poets have more to do with university presses and small presses than the big commercial publishing houses in New York. Poets play the game, and play out their lives, in the pages of the literary magazines and quarterlies. The editors of these publications are *their* gatekeepers. Not surprising, then, that our sources sent along two lists of magazines:

Ten Best Magazines for Poetry

(1) *Georgia Review*
(2) *Atlantic Monthly*
(3) *Shenandoah*
(4) *Gettysburg Review*
(5) *Sewanee Review*
(6) *Black Warrior Review*
(7) *Prairie Schooner*
(8) *Ascent*
(9) *Tar River Poetry*
(10) *Southern Humanities Review*

Ten Worst Magazines for Poetry

(1) *American Poetry Review*

(2) *The* ("New Newhouse") *New Yorker*
(3) *Poetry*
(4) *Antaeus* (defunct)
(5) *Field*
(6) *The Nation*
(7) *The New Republic*
(8) *Hudson Review*
(9) *Ohio Review*
(10) *Iowa Review*

Are there really ten commercial American trade publishers who care two hoots about or have diddly-squat to do with American literature these days? That is what this panel wanted to know before they even started fooling around with any kind of a list. Well, not exactly . . . , answered *DLB,* pointing out that with the flurry of mergers and with conglomerate ownership and so forth and so on, there probably are not ten trade houses left. They all belong to each other one way or another, anyway. Who can keep up? Nevertheless there are names, imprints, and the like. And then there is the matter of new directions in economics, how things work – here described by Ed Hinton in "The Great Grisham" *(GQ,* January 1995): "But the fact of the matter is that the big books have begun to consume the good books. Publishers have been swallowed by bigger publishers who have been swallowed by conglomerates who give not a shit for literature and everything for the bottom line."

Still. . . . There's a story (Who knows if it's true? Who cares?) that awhile back Sonny Mehta surprised an editorial meeting by announcing his goal for Knopf author Cormac McCarthy – "I'm going to make this guy a household name." Announced or not, Knopf has succeeded in that goal . . . if you only count households where people buy and read books. We mention the story as an explanation of our panel's list. Some publisher of 1994 must be the model of (relative) excellence. Knopf looks to be it, in terms of literary books published and in terms of their commitment and ability to get the books reviewed and to promote them in the modest marketplace. Knopf and Farrar Straus Giroux are exemplary and close competitors. The reader will notice that Knopf's parent company, Random House, is in the lower half of the list. Why? Because their level and ratio of undisguised schlock put them there. Maybe they figure Knopf can do literature for them.

(1) Knopf
(2) Farrar Straus Giroux
(3) Viking
(4) Norton

(5) HarperCollins
(6) Houghton Mifflin
(7) Simon and Schuster
(8) St. Martin's Press
(9) Random House
(10) Harcourt Brace

More and more, the fate of contemporary American writing (and, thus, in the long run, American literature) is falling into the hands of the university presses. (See "The Year in Fiction.") Some of the old and honorable presses are out of the running, out of *this* running anyway, because these days they deal mostly in the trendy topics of theory and in hot-ticket, amorphous subjects such as gender, race, class, and "culture" and are thus mostly irrelevant to the making of literature or the appreciation thereof. Other presses, often out in the provinces and unable to compete in the big league, *that* big league anyway, have been busily publishing poetry and fiction (short and long and sometimes in translation) and even old-fashioned literary criticism and scholarship. All, without exception, are sorely beset at the present moment by shrinking budgets and (an inevitable corrolary) institutional indifference. But they are carrying on, doing the best they can. The criteria of this list, according to our panel, were that the presses considered were actively in 1994 doing all the above – poetry, fiction, criticism, and scholarship. Although, under those standards, the University of South Carolina Press could not make the list, the panel wished to call particular attention to their extensive and growing Understanding Contemporary American Literature series, which is designed as much for nonacademic readers as it is as a guide and companion for students. The ten best literary university presses are as follows:

(1) Louisiana State University Press
(2) Southern Methodist University Press
(3) University of Missouri Press
(4) University of Arkansas Press
(5) University of Iowa Press
(6) University of Georgia Press
(7) Eastern Washington State University Press
(8) Carnegie-Mellon University Press
(9) University of Chicago Press
(10) Princeton University Press

There is no end to the making of lists. In *The First Man on the Sun* (1983) R. H. W. Dillard celebrates this human habit and impulse, our way of creating a "life reduced for a moment to rows and lists, the game of learning, batting orders, line scores, names and dates. It is a code, a hieroglyph, these lists that mean nothing apart from the context which they describe, and yet to those who have eyes to see, lists that hold the flow and spin of the real, the reel and whirl of things we think we know."

We decided on one more list to wrap up this part of "Who Runs American Literature?" – a list of the ten best creative writing programs in the country. Why? I mean, how far can you get from editors and agents, scholars and critics, best and worst artists, etc.? The fact is that almost all the younger literary writers in America have come out of at least some exposure (and for some it has been significant, degree-earning exposure) to the multitude of creative-writing programs in the country. A large number of the active poets and novelists in the country (and on our lists) have been or are their teachers and mentors, full-time or part-time. For better and for worse (and a little of both) this is the literary system of apprenticeship as the century staggers to an end. A short time ago (at least it seems short enough) people were wondering seriously and in public if writing, "creative" writing, can be taught; and not more than a handful of literary artists were associated with educational institutions – Archibald MacLeish, Robert Frost, Wallace Stegner, Paul Engle, etc. As if overnight, there are now hundreds of creative writing courses, thousands of students at any given instant (what is to become of them God knows); and there is scarcely a community college so remote and deprived that it does not have at least one poet or novelist or both on its faculty. Thus maybe, just maybe, one could argue that the academics, in fact, are running American literature at this time, at least at the entry level. It seemed to us that it would be appropriate to present a list of the best of the institutional writing programs. And for this we did not have to go in search of available and anonymous sources. We are our own sources. For better or worse it is our list, debatable to be sure, but defensible:

The Ten Best Creative-Writing Programs in America

(1) Hollins College
(2) University of Michigan
(3) University of Virginia
(4) University of North Carolina at Greensboro
(5) University of Alabama
(6) George Mason University
(7) University of Iowa
(8) Florida International University
(9) Johns Hopkins University
(10) University of Arkansas

AN INTERVIEW WITH NAN TALESE

Appropriate for this piece is what follows, an interview in depth with one of the most prominent editors (number four on the DLB honor roll) and players on the national scene – Doubleday's Nan Talese. Here she is interviewed on a variety of subjects for *DLB Yearbook* by Kristin van Ogtrop, senior editor at *Vogue*.

DLB: I'd like to know a little bit about your career. Can you give me a brief overview?

TALESE: I started in publishing at Random House, which is where I really "grew up." In 1974 I went to Simon and Schuster, where I started to publish Ian McEwan, Margaret Atwood, Barry Unsworth, A. G. Mojtabi, and others who then came with me when I went to Houghton Mifflin in 1981. At Houghton I was at first head of the New York office and executive editor of the trade division – Houghton was then essentially a Boston publishing house that had a New York office – and then editor in chief and publisher. In 1988 I essentially resigned from the Boston Shuttle and joined Doubleday in New York. In September of 1990, four years ago, I began the imprint.

DLB: Do you feel like the imprint is the most satisfying thing you've done so far?

TALESE: It was something that I really avoided for a long time because I thought imprints only indicated vanity on the part of editors, but I now stand corrected. It is true that when buyers go into a bookstore they care mainly about the author. But Margaret Atwood and Ian McEwan and other authors like the idea of being loyal to one editor and publisher. What the imprint has done is put a stamp on our continuing relationship through all these years.

DLB: Now that you have your own imprint, do you see the advantages of it to the point that you can't ever see yourself going back?

TALESE: Yes, and there are particular advantages for me, because I publish mainly literary fiction and nonfiction, and when booksellers see the imprint, because they know my taste, they know who the readers for the books are. This is particularly good for new writers who have not yet built a reputation. The booksellers know that the books published under this imprint have a certain quality; they read them and they recommend them.

DLB: Do you feel having your own imprint allows you to take risks that you couldn't take before with new writers?

TALESE: No, I don't think it makes that much of a difference. In fact, if anything, because of the financial responsibility of an imprint, I have to be careful not to take on too many new writers. The list as a whole has to be able to support itself within Doubleday and within the whole corporation. Also, there are only so many books that you can publish well.

DLB: How many books do you do a year?

TALESE: I publish about fifteen.

DLB: Do you edit all of them yourself or do you have editors who work for you?

TALESE: I edit many myself, and Jesse Cohen, a superb young editor who works with me, works on some and has his own authors. But we overlap, so each author had both our attention.

DLB: I heard you were down in Charlottesville this summer with Mary Lee Settle, going over her manuscript page by page. I don't know how you have time for that kind of thing – you must be so busy. It's a credit to you as an editor, but everyone says editors don't edit anymore.

TALESE: People have always said that: some editors do, some don't. It's true that much of my time is taken planning the publications of the books. But because an editor is an author's first reader who shares the author's vision, reading and responding is a priority. When a writer is creating, he or she can't also be "on the other side of the net" and be simultaneously critical. Writers can through a certain number of drafts, and most do, but then they need a fresh and careful reading by someone who believes in their talent.

But it is also a great pleasure to talk to a writer about his or her book. If there are certain things that I don't understand, and I talk with the author about either why it slows down the book or what I didn't quite understand, very often something

emerges that he or she thinks is in the book but that actually has never really been developed. This happened with *The Prince of Tides* (1986) and Pat Conroy. He would talk about what he meant specifics to mean, and then I would see how certain scenes and themes connected. I believe these conversations often allow an author to go deeper. A book is only published once, and those I publish I want to be as potentially wonderful as the author can make them.

DLB: And I assume that's why you got into publishing in the first place. Because you love books – not because you want to be totally involved in the business side.

TALESE: I've learned and like the business side – it's essential – but it follows a love of the books.

DLB: Do your authors get editorial advice from their agents too?

TALESE: Some do. There's no single rule. Some books come in and need a lot of work, and some don't. I find most authors are very eager to hear what their editors have to say. John Herman is the former editor of Ticknor and Fields, whose first novel I'm going to publish in June; as I was reading the book I made notes to myself about certain things and then we had conversations about it. The important thing is that John was listening to things that particularly struck me; it's his decision as to what to do about them. And he did rewrite certain things and ask, "Does this solve your problem?" You can't be everything as a writer and reader, which doesn't take away at all from the fact that it is the *author's* book.

DLB: But they couldn't do it without you.

TALESE: Sure they could. And they would. Last week I read Barry Unsworth's new novel entitled *Morality Play.* It is less than two hundred pages long, it is *totally* brilliant, and it seemed to me letter perfect. So I called him – he lives in Italy – and we were talking about the novel when he said that his agent had one question and his editor in England had another – one was at the beginning of the book, one was the end – and he asked me what I thought. Neither page had concerned me, but one of the queries I agreed with, and it was a productive kind of conversation that is valuable to a writer. Writers work in such isolation.

Nan Talese (photograph by Tom Victor, courtesy of Nan Talese)

DLB: And they're so close to it at the end — sometimes it might be easy to overlook the most obvious thing that a reader might ask.

TALESE: I remember when I was at Random House working with Robert Penn Warren (I was just doing line editing) and I would say "I don't understand this," and Warren would sometimes say, "Well, you know, it's back forty pages." But the point is that he saw I didn't pick it up and understood either the scene had to be stronger earlier, or he would add another reference in between. It is the editor's job to be the sounding board, but it is always the writer who effects any changes.

DLB: Let's think about 1994. Were there surprises? A lot of editors, when I asked them about surprises in 1993 — particularly Shannon Ravenel at Algonquin — mentioned *The Bridges of Madison County* as something that was going to change the face of publishing, at least temporarily. Do you feel that there was anything in 1994 similar to that?

TALESE: Perhaps the Price clubs, which buy great quantities of books such as *The Bridges of Madison County* that already have high visibility and an audience. I suspect that over 500,000 of the millions sold

were through the Price clubs. They buy a $25 book and sell it for, say, $13.95, so their profit margin is very narrow. I believe that a single book has to produce a certain amount of revenue a week in order to stay on the shelves; otherwise it's shipped back to the publisher. So, a John Grisham, a Mary Higgins Clark, anything that hits the best-seller list, will be ordered by these outlets by pallets. Next year we will publish a novel by an author whose last book sold 235,000. Because of his reputation, the Price clubs will now order at least 300,000. And that has changed book publishing; you now have, say, 300,000 in addition to what the independent bookstores and the chains would have sold on the previous book. So you have more than doubled a well-known author's initial sales.

DLB: That sounds like it's good for publishing.

TALESE: It's very good for publishing, and it's very good for the well-known authors. But it also creates a problem for less-known writers. Like skyscrapers, the big books cast shadows that are so long they obscure other books from public awareness. This makes the risk that publishers take on new authors and new ideas much greater, and without these our culture becomes static at best and reduced to the lowest imaginative and intellectual level at worst.

DLB: In your career in publishing, do you feel it becomes increasingly harder to get published if you're not commercial? I think about John Calvin Bachelor and how he's written this book that everyone knew in advance was going to be a plot-driven potential best-seller, and so they targeted it that way and it's gotten a lot of publicity. But for someone you're not sure about, who is not identifiable as a blockbuster, is it harder for those kinds of authors to get published now than it was, say, twenty years ago?

TALESE: If we're talking about fiction, yes, because when you publish into a market every other novelist is your competition, whereas if you're writing self-help your core market is people in trouble, and your competitive group is writers of advice, who are fewer in number. Fiction is totally across the board, so your odds of doing well are smaller. The other thing is, there are many more people *writing* books, and you know, inasmuch as the population increases geometrically, so the writers increase. So that in every way you have greater competition. On the one hand, with all of these books you would think publishers have more money to take more chances, but on the other hand, because the expectations are for more money, corporations would prefer publishers only to do the big books. I'm not saying that they only *will* do the big books, but it is the best-sellers that keep a publishing house alive.

DLB: When I talked recently to D. T. Max [then literary editor of *The New York Observer*], for some reason John Berendt's book *Midnight in the Garden of Good and Evil* kept coming up as sort of a surprise book — the agent didn't want to represent it because it couldn't be identified as a specific genre; it reads like a novel, but it's nonfiction. But look at how well that book did.

TALESE: But you see, that's the wonderful thing about publishing: you never can stop taking chances.

DLB: Would you regard Berendt's book as a 1994 surprise?

TALESE: Yes.

DLB: Would you say *The Celestine Prophecy* (Warner) is a surprise?

TALESE: Yes — who in heaven's name was going to know? I wonder whether anyone expected *The Bell Curve* (Free Press) to do what it has done.

DLB: It's so controversial.

TALESE: I know, but do you suppose when it was signed up —

DLB: They knew?

TALESE: It was at the Free Press; I don't think they signed it up because it was controversial. And also it's so non-PC. I think this sort of whole New-Age-book-coming-mainstream is a surprise, that it's really taken hold. The thing that astounds me is that horror, mystery, otherworldish New Age, and very simple books . . .

DLB: Like *The Bridges of Madison County?*

TALESE: Yes. That was sent to me by Warren Cassell from Just Books in March of 1993, before anyone had ever heard of it. He asked me what I thought, and I said I thought it was a charming book. I have this habit of remembering only that which is good, and what I remembered was simply the love story that was the center between those two bookends and realizing the way that it was charmingly told. It's everyone's fantasy, both men and women: a man to be free, a woman to have someone discover the more creative side of herself, but without giving up her marriage.

DLB: And the one great passionate love of your life.

TALESE: Yes — and having your dream fulfilled but being able to live in your ordinary life and not ostensibly betray anyone. So it didn't actually surprise me when that book started taking off. But of course when the critics got a hold of it, they reviewed it as a book of literature — it's never what the book was. The book was a very simple story.

It's very hard to figure out what is going to touch people. I think the fact that *How We Die* has done so well is surprising — Americans do not like to think about death. Our whole mythos is the frontier. Americans talk about "problems," which implies there are "solutions," and because death cannot be "solved," we have tended not to look at it.

DLB: Another book that D. T. Max kept mentioning was the Moe Berg book, about the catcher who was a spy. That book did very well, but I thought, "About a catcher who is a spy?" Go figure. And funny non-PC books, like Christopher Buckley's *Thank You For Smoking.* Maybe it's a backlash.

Maybe we've been so PC for five years or whatever, and now it's coming around a little bit.

TALESE: Well, I think people are beginning to revolt.

DLB: Look how popular Rush Limbaugh is.

TALESE: In 1994 we had both Rush Limbaugh and Howard Stern. That really surprises me and in a way makes me despair for the American mind. There's no thought process. It's the linear sound bite. Books have always been on the cutting edge; it is books that change the way we live, and therefore it is important that good books, not just confirmed prejudices, are read. But again, this is the influence of the Price clubs.

DLB: Thinking about last year and the superstores, and the Price clubs, do you feel that there were any other emerging trends that came up in 1994 that seemed new to you?

TALESE: One trend that I was aware of that may not be evident for a number of years – and this is only in my very small bailiwick – is the number of literary novels that have been bought for films.

DLB: That's a good emerging trend.

TALESE: We'll see if they're made, but I was on panel at the ABA because I am Thomas Keneally's publisher and had commissioned *Schindler's List* (1986). The panel was on Books into Film, and when I looked at my list, I realized that of the forty-five to fifty books I've published in the last four years, seventeen have been bought for films – and they're all literary non-best-sellers. *Mary Reilly,* which will probably come out in the summer, is adapted from a book by Valerie Martin; it's starring Julia Roberts, John Malkovich, and Glenn Close and directed by Stephen Frears; Christopher Hampton wrote the script. Now, if that movie is a success she will be established as a writer with a large audience; her most recent novel, *The Great Divorce,* has already been optioned by Universal. Pat Conroy's *The Prince of Tides* was a best-seller, but not a megaseller. When the movie came out, the Bantam paperback sold another 2.5 million copies over the first 2.5 million. I was walking down Fifth Avenue behind two young women who started to go into a bookstore. One of them said "I want to buy *The Prince of Tides,*" and the other one said, "But we just

saw the movie." And the first replied, "Yes, but now I want to read the book."

And then when people saw *Schindler's List,* the three-hour experience was so absorbing people wanted to extend it, to stay in that world longer. And certainly that was true of *The Age of Innocence* and *The Remains of the Day.*

DLB: The whole Keneally story was so fascinating, how he went into that store and met the man who told him the story and that inspired him to write the book. When that started getting out, when people learned that that was the story behind it, that made the book seem all the more interesting, I think.

TALESE: Yes, but I think it would have happened anyway, because I have seen it with many books that have become films. I don't think it used to be this way at all; I'm aware of it now; maybe other people were aware of it before.

DLB: I keep thinking about *The Remains of the Day.* It's one of my favorite books; I think it's nearly perfect. But I never would have thought of making a movie of it – it's so *not* plot-driven.

TALESE: But you see that's what's happening. Look at Robert Benton's film of Richard Russo's *Nobody's Fool.*

DLB: So do you think filmmakers are just thinking differently?

TALESE: I think what they realize is that they have to have something very solid to build upon at the beginning, and I think they have thus become respectful of the literary novel – which is wonderful, because when you have really good writers whose books are made into films, then the authors have a larger audience for their next books.

DLB: And they make more money.

TALESE: Right. It brings them a larger readership and brings up the level of our culture.

DLB: Schindler's List was published years ago; why do film companies take so long? Did Spielberg buy the rights ages ago?

TALESE: Yes, soon after the book's publication, but he didn't feel that he was yet ready to make it.

DLB: Anything else about 1994? That's a very nice trend.

TALESE: I believe that's true – look at *Like Water for Chocolate* – that was astounding.

DLB: But before the movie, wasn't it selling really well all along?

TALESE: No – we started out printing fifteen thousand copies, and the author did some appearances, speaking mainly Spanish. And then the movie came out, but it was an art-house release, not a wide release. And toward the end of this year, we had sold nine hundred thousand hardcover copies. And the Doubleday Spanish edition has sold seventy thousand copies.

DLB: When we're thinking up all these examples my mind starts spinning because I start thinking, "Okay, there's a reason people like John Grisham and Stephen King sell." But when I start thinking of all these little quirky books, on the one hand it makes me feel good about human nature because you never know what people are going to like, but on the other hand it makes me think it must make it so hard to work in this industry!

TALESE: I think you're absolutely right. The one reason *Makes Me Wanna Holler* and some of those books have become best-sellers is, again, the competition is quite light. It is for blacks, and Hispanics, and Asians. There's a wonderful line in *Shadowlands* when C. S. Lewis asks one of his students why he reads. He answers that he reads to know that he was not alone. Which I think is often why people read. And there has not been much literature for African-Americans, Hispanics, and Asians until recently. The same is true about women's and homosexuals' stories.

DLB: Do you feel like it's increasingly harder for heterosexual white men to get published?

TALESE: Yes. Heterosexual white men seem to read Tom Clancy for escape. They're not great book buyers, and they tend to prefer violence and adventure. I think the white male literary writer has an increasingly diminished market.

DLB: That's difficult

TALESE: It's *very* difficult.

DLB: Say you're a white male writer who's had a very good career, and you're fifty years old, and all of a sudden you're not Amy Tan, you're not Terry McMillan –

TALESE: . . . and you're not John Grisham, and you're not Ludlum, and you're not a genre writer.

DLB: Well, who do you feel runs American literature? Editors, agents, publishers, critics?

TALESE: Writers.

DLB: Because it wouldn't exist without them?

TALESE: Yes. One of the things that we in our industry tend to forget is that without writers none of us have jobs. From the conglomerates' most highly paid CEO to the editorial assistant – each of us is out of a job without writers.
Writers and readers are the significant parties; the rest of us are just the middlemen.

DLB: Do you feel that when a book has a good word of mouth, that's better than any kind of review it could get?

TALESE: Absolutely. Reviewers have become more like book-report writers and rarely create a sense of excitement about a book. But readers recommend books to other readers who buy copies. I'll tell you another phenomenon of 1994 is the little book.

DLB: Little in size?

TALESE: Yes. Margaret Atwood's *Good Bones* is in that small size, and so is *A Mountain Sutra*. The good thing is you can literally put them in your pocket. And I think also when they're discounted the prices go down terrifically, and so it encourages people to buy them for gifts. I love that Danielle Steele has a book that size and it's called *The Gift*. And it's $15, so if you discount it, you're buying a present for $10, or even $7.50.

DLB: Smaller books are cheaper to begin with?

TALESE: Generally – they're less expensive to produce. It's nice for people to be encouraged, if you can do it. It makes sense. But if you have something like a John Grisham book, or a Pat Conroy, you can take a risk at having a higher price because you know most people are going to buy it at a discount, so you're not hurting them. That's the kind of thing that hurts independent bookstores.

DLB: That's something you talked about last year. Do you still feel like the death of the independents is coming?

TALESE: I didn't feel it was the *death,* I felt that they were *threatened.* I think that what the superstores and the independents are doing is just increasing the base of readers. I also think another change this year has been the trade paperback market. Trade paperbacks are, excluding the best-sellers, the highest percentage of bookstore sales.

DLB: Is that new?

TALESE: Yes.

DLB: What was it before? Mass-market paperbacks?

TALESE: Yes.

DLB: Hardcover, never?

TALESE: Well, I can't say because I'm not an expert on this, but mass-market surely – if you sold twenty-five thousand copies of a hardcover book, then you print one hundred thousand in mass-market. But I think that readers are more sophisticated, better educated. Say you come out with a new Margaret Atwood book. In the superstores you'll have her backlist in trade paperback instead of having it in mass-market, books with cheaper paper that don't last. Today's readers want to have in their libraries something that's going to last. Also, they are handsome enough to be given as presents.

DLB: Do you feel that people are reading better books in paperback? Or that more books are being published in trade paperback?
TALESE: More good books are being read and published in quality paperback.

DLB: All the things you've been saying about 1994 have been positive!

TALESE: Well, I think they are, except there is still the long-shadow effect: it's harder to have a new voice heard. And the other thing is new ideas. If you look at the best-seller list, so much of it is for people just wanting to have their already ingrained ideas repeated to them.

DLB: I remember when that two-part series came out in *The New York Times Book Review* last year about Mark Richard and how his book came into being and publicizing it. That piece was so eye-opening to me.

TALESE: That is *really* about how publishing works.

DLB: Isn't that where you talked about the only way to ensure success, publicitywise, was having a beautiful author go around naked on the book tour?

TALESE: Almost – what I said is soon we will have a clause in the contract requiring beautiful authors to tour the country naked.

DLB: It also made me appreciate how much work goes into promoting each author.

TALESE: You also need a lot of luck.

DLB: I'm also so naive. I never think about things like what the author looks like. I have a friend who works at Viking, and she said that comes up all the time. I know working at *Vogue* magazine we have to have beautiful women on the page, but I never thought in the rarefied world of book publishing that it helps to have a good-looking author who can go on the *Today* show.

TALESE: And go into the bookstores and attract a crowd. It's terrible but it's true. The other thing that's happened is that it's not enough now to be an author – you must be a performer. But the reason writers write is because they're *not* performers: they're communicating on a blank piece of paper in an empty room.

DLB: Do you feel sanguine about the future of book publishing? Now that everyone's got a computer, everyone's getting CD-ROM, you can go to the movies, you can do all this other kind of stuff, but do you feel like books will always be here?

TALESE: Yes. In the first place, CD-ROM is extraordinary for nonfiction and for theatrical works – I adore it. The novel is the author's voice. It is the most intimate form of the arts. You can see a picture among many people, you can go to a film, you can go to a concert; but with a novel, it is only the "voice" of the author falling on the "ears" of the reader. It's just the two of you together. It involves the reader's imagination, and I don't think anyone would ever want to lose the imaginative experience, which is one of the reasons that after they see a movie they go back into the bookstores.

DLB: And the experience of holding a book is much different from the experience of working at your computer screen.

TALESE: It's like microfilm – when someone goes into a library they'd much rather get out a book than scroll that microfilm. It's just physically uncomfortable. I think for nonfiction, the computers are going to have a much greater impact. But I think with literary fiction and nonfiction – because literary nonfiction also engages the imagination of the reader – the physical book is going to be very much with us.

I heard something marvelous the other day: "To explain in words takes time and a just and patient hearing" – Robert Louis Stevenson. In this country we have very little time and very little patience. And I think that's particularly true of new ideas. Yes, a lot of books suffer by not being recognized and writers by not being nourished. But that's the law of the world – whether it's bugs or animals or human beings – there's a fast perishability rate for everything. But some will get through. And they will change the way we think.

DLB: That's very encouraging.

TALESE: Well, I'm endlessly optimistic. But I think that's the trait of an editor. If you weren't, you couldn't come into the office because there's too much going against you.

One thing, however, that isn't particularly encouraging is that publishing is now being run by businesspeople who don't read and care overwhelmingly about large profits. So many people who are running publishing houses simply don't read, so they don't really know either the product, to use their word, or the consumer.

DLB: Do you think that that trend would ever reverse?

TALESE: I think eventually that if that's all they think about, such companies will self-destruct.

Because they're not going to be able to know how to make a profit if they are out of touch with their consumers.

DLB: Do you feel that's something you have to fight against a lot, with your own imprint in such a big company?

TALESE: No – because the company supports the imprint. But it is why it's so essential to have editors: publishing executives count on the editors to be in touch. But you see, projections for the future are based on history, and both writers and editors are always seeking new ground – so that, essentially, what excites us is that which is in some way without history.

We thought it would be good to include other voices from the editorial and agent side of the business, to see if they had any insight about the state of the writing and publishing world. Those interviews follow.

AN INTERVIEW WITH CARLO DEVITO

Carlo DeVito is currently editor at Touchtone/Fireside Books, where he edits paperback originals; he also edits hard covers for Simon and Schuster and Scribners. He is a graduate of Fordham University and has been in publishing for seven years. His authors include Arthur Schlesinger, Jr., Dan Rather, Susie Bright, Eleanor Cliff, Vine Daloria, Jr., and Dee Brown. This telephone interview was conducted on 10 February 1995.

DLB: As I told you earlier, for the *Dictionary of Literary Biography Yearbook,* George Garrett has written an article entitled "Who runs American Literature?" and I'm attempting to flush it out with some short interviews by the workers in the vineyard. What I would like for you to tell the *Dictionary of Literary Biography* is what influence does a paperback editor – not necessarily you, but you and your colleagues – what influence do paperback editors have on American literary tastes, high and low. In what ways can you advance an authors career? Establish an author? In what ways can you educate the reading public if that's what you want to do? End of question.

DeVITO: That's a big question. I think I'll take it off in little nuggets. First of all I do extensive work with the Scribners paperback fiction line here at Simon and Schuster, and we combine a series of classic authors like Hemingway and Fitzgerald,

Langston Hughes, Marjorie Kenning Rawlings, Jack Finney into a line with authors like Doris Betts and Annie Proulx, and what we do is attempt to put together I would say, a fairly middle- to highbrow selection of literary fiction. How do we affect things? As a particular editor I can only tell you this: we look for in the paperback side any and everything we think we can sell as literary fiction.

There are two types of paperbacks as you know, there's the trade paperback fiction, which tends to be for the more literary crowd, and there's the mass-market fiction, which tends to be a little more middle of the road to lowbrow. Those are two totally different types of publishing. Mass-market as you probably already know is the kind of stuff you find in airport racks and stuff you bring to the beach, the page turners. Literary fiction tends to sell fewer copies – not that they don't sell a lot, but they tend to sell fewer copies. They tend to be in trade-size paperbacks, five by eight as opposed to four by six, and they are for people who like to read their books and then put them on a bookshelf as opposed to tossing them out or giving them to Goodwill or whatever.

How do we affect what goes on as editors? At this point it's gotten pretty bloodthirsty. When I go to buy the paperback rights of an author, especially for fiction, I'm not only interested in knowing what that author has now, what we're buying now, but what is the next book. Is it written? Is it not written? Is it under contract? Is it not under contract? Can we bring it over here? Can we get a first look before we buy this book? Our goal here at all times is to build an author's career. Authors that sell anywhere from around seventy-five hundred to ten thousand copies in terms of hardcover are pretty much the bottom realm of what you're talking about. Sometimes we get them from university presses, people who publish fiction with a university press, or it's a first time novel with a smaller publisher. We're looking everywhere, in every nook and cranny that we can, to find those kind of things.

How does paperback publishing affect what goes on? There are numerous ways. There is a wonderful story that my boss was talking about the other day. A well-known writer, Mark Helprin – his last book, I always confuse it with Ford Maddox Ford – *A Soldier of the Great War,* was a wonderful, wonderful hit in hardcover, and every trade paperback house in the land was trying to land that book for their paperback line, and I believe it was Avon who won the rights to the paperback. They won it, but they paid such an exorbitant price for it in the

end that to recover it what they needed to do was to go to the mass-market level, to try to bring him to that next level because they had to make it pay off for the amount of money they had paid for it. It proved to be a disaster. His regular readers, people who go for the trade paperback size, are turned off by rack sizes. And generally he lost a lot of people who would normally have read him. Secondly, he didn't appeal to a lot of the people who like to buy fiction in that rack-size format. So as a result they lost sales on all sides, and booksellers had a very bad experience with someone who is otherwise an extremely well known and well respected, highly respected author. To be quite honest, he would probably been better served in a trade paperback format – and you're talking about somebody whose list includes *Winter Tales,* etc., and is a wonderful, wonderful writer – and I do believe the format hurt him. That's my own personal opinion.

Another person to talk about is Annie Proulx. Annie Proulx is exactly what everybody wants. She is an author that you grow with and an author whose audience who can continue to grow. Her first book, *Heartsongs and Other Stories,* got exceptional reviews; we sold about five thousand copies in hardcover and about four thousand in trade paperback. Harpers, I believe, did it. Her second book, *Postcards,* was astonishing. She grew her audience to ten thousand or fifteen thousand hardcovers; the paperback sold well; and with the next book, the Pulitzer Prize winner, *The Shipping News,* she has reached phenomenal levels, and that's what everybody hopes for. She is a wonderfully literate writer who writes absolutely wonderful stories. We were able to get back the rights to the first book, which had not done well, between her first and second books, because there was just not enough about her out there, and all of her books are doing phenomenally well now – and of course she's a Pulitzer Prize winner – and with keeping her in trade paperback we have had a phenomenal success reaching all of the people we really wanted to reach with it. We were able to keep her in the trade paperback size, which is her real and true audience.

Somebody who is exactly different who came from the same house is Patricia Cornwell, whose first book, *Postmortem* (1990), sold five thousand copies in hardcover, and it got nice reviews, and it continued to get nice reviews everywhere. She was a regular first-time Scribners mystery author, and they got a decent paperback sale out of it. Nothing exciting. It got nice reviews all the way around, but it went into the rack-size category because that's the price range in the format that that genre falls into. With each success after her first book her paperback numbers grew and grew. But she was well served by being in a rack-size edition, a mass-market edition, as opposed to being in a trade paperback size. So that's how we as editors or as an industry affect the way a fiction writer gets sold or gets perceived by the public.

AN INTERVIEW WITH JOHN THORNTON

John Thornton began as a book editor in 1968 with Schocken Books, a small family-owned company, and edited nonfiction. He then moved to the New York Graphic Society, which was relocating to Boston. Now Bulfinch Press, they are an illustrated and art-book publisher. From there he moved back to New York City and worked as a trade paperback editor for New American Library and did their Plume, Meridian/Mentor, Signet Classics, and Metro books. He then worked for Washington Square Press for Simon and Schuster, and then for seven years was associate publisher for Facts On File, an information, nonfiction, reference publisher. He then worked at Prentice Hall Press, now defunct, a division of Simon and Schuster, on their general trade program. At the Book of the Month Club he was for two years editorial director of the specialty-book clubs. Then for two and a half years I was editorial director for the Book of the Month Club itself. In the fall of 1993 he struck out on his own and is now associated with the Spieler Literary Agency in New York City.

This telephone interview took place on 10 February 1995.

DLB: George Garrett has written a very intriguing article for the *Dictionary of Literary Biography Yearbook* entitled, "Who Runs American Literature?" He has a good deal to say about the literary opinion makers. But I thought the basic article could be fleshed out with a couple of mini interviews, ten-minute interviews with figures in the publishing world whose influence is not fully understood by civilians. I wanted an agent, and since you're the agent I know best, I flung myself upon your goodwill. What I would like you to talk about is, what influence do agents in general have on American literary tastes, high or low? How much guidance and actual editing do editors perform on a typescript? How much nurturing, developing, guiding of a career do agents sometimes perform? In summary, what is the role of the agent on the literary scene apart from taking a commission, placing the book, and charging the author for the service? What are the good things about agents?

John Thornton

THORNTON: In terms of the actual influence of an agent on the culture, I think that's probably a less-visible and difficult to trace aspect of agenting, because after all they are people who work behind the scenes in the same way that editors, authors editors, and publishing houses work behind the scene.

A good agent, I believe, certainly has to have good antennae whether he's working at the upper end of the quality scale of the culture, or whether he's working down in the mass-market end of the scale. Being able to understand the value of a project, the value of an author's work, of a new author, as it comes into his hands or her hands, I think that is where the taste-making process would begin, where an agent would intercept with taste making in the publishing culture. Like most everyone else, agents range along a spectrum from people who deal almost exclusively in mass-market authors to others who retain only clients of the very highest sort, or of a very specialized sort, such as reference-book authors, or children's-book authors, or poets. I can't imagine there's an agent making a living representing only poets, but hypothetically such a thing could exist.

What do agents do for the work of their authors before publication? Well, I think it's a great deal. There was an article written a few years ago by a friend of mine who is now an editor at W. W. Norton Publishers named Gerry Howard in the *American Scholar*. I think it was called something like, "Mistah Perkins, He Dead," and it was an account of the shifting of the influence away from editors in publishing houses toward the agents on the one hand, and toward the sales-marketing personnel in publishing houses on the other – I think the reason being that the emphasis on financial profitability as more and more publishing houses have been purchased by larger companies. This in turn made more and more demands on editors to bring in books that succeeded not only in the near term, but almost immediately. The result is a kind of nomadic existence that many editors in commercial trade publishing have, where from one year to the next they are not certain whether they'll have their jobs or not, and often they migrate out of anticipated displacements. In the face of instability like that, the agent's role as a kind of first editor, first reader, first helper for the author begins to take on greater importance.

I think the result is that those agents who have the capacity to do it or see the need for it do spend a fair amount of time working on manuscripts, on proposals with their authors, before they enter the hands of an editor, and even sometimes after they've entered the hands of an editor. It's very much again the range of ways in which agents work with their authors. Some really don't have the background and skills. They might come from a background as a lawyer, or a background as a marketing person and be working with authors, but really they don't know how to pencil it. But others edit – I take my own case as an example. I have been a book editor for most of my career, and I'm relatively new at being an agent. I cannot let something leave my hands unless I've worked on it a bit and improved it to my own satisfaction, because I'm able to place myself in the seat of an editor and a reader and to know what it is that will work and won't work for such a person. Another factor is that it is a buyer's market among publishers. I think there is a tremendous amount of literary production going on but a much thinner stream of acquisition and acceptance by publishers, so that whether it's a novel or a book of short stories, a biography, or any kind of fiction or nonfiction, crafting it into a, you might say, bullet-proof product that cannot be easily rejected, that in fact must be taken seriously, and that has its own merits and seductive powers – all those things that are in a good book

proposal or manuscript when it's submitted have to be put there by the author in collaboration with his agent. So the point of the article that I was referring to is that a lot of the available editorial energy has been, in a sense, pushed out of the publishing houses into the arms of agents. Some are prepared for it, and some aren't, and in all cases it's a very labor-intensive activity, and it's very difficult even for willing agents like myself to find the time to work really hard on these projects.

The truth is that a vacuum has been created in which editors and publishing houses are often forced to spend their time serving the needs of sales-marketing people. In some ways they've become not much more than gofers, getting information, getting biographical information on the author, writing tip sheets, preparing materials for presentation, writing catalogue copy, with very little time left over to do the careful work of editing. And what of the traditional work of nurturing and working with an author over not just one project, but over a career, or as much of it as is possible? This business of nurturing and developing a career is again something that falls to literary agents, more and more to do as the constant in an author's life. At the same time I don't want to overly idealize this because literary agenting is a business, and most literary agents ask for a fifteen percent commission of the moneys they obtain by selling books to publishers, and if an author consistently submits projects and they are consistently turned down over a time, what with the overhead and expense of doing that, it's certainly true that agents have to give up clients and can't afford always to try that twentieth or thirtieth submission of a project. In an earlier day there might have been more perseverance than there is now, but at the same time I do think that agents spend a great deal of "free" time acting as psychiatrist and, if you will, nursemaid and friend, listening post, and wailing wall. All of these functions are served for many an author by many an agent.

To sum it up, I guess I would just say that the world of literary agents is a kind of a mirror image of the culture itself. It ranges from high to medium to low. There are agents there present at each of those levels of cultural activity in the book business, so whether it's Danielle Steele or Cormac McCarthy, or I'm trying to think of someone in the middle . . . Ann Tyler. Each of them has an agent chosen, I suppose, after trial and error, to suit his or her needs, and in a way to act as an ambassador to the book world.

For the last word, we turn to poet Henry Taylor for his reflections and animadversions.

WHO OWNS AMERICAN LITERATURE?

Henry Taylor

> "Deion and George Plimpton
> have very little in common."
> — *Steve Young*

On the *Today* show the morning after the 1995 Super Bowl, the victorious, record-setting quarterback of the San Francisco Forty-Niners apologized to the fans of San Diego for the single most insulting play of the game, when Deion Sanders went out — incompletely, as they say — for a long pass. Sanders, a cornerback with a gift for pass interceptions, is the only athlete in the history of competitive sport to have played in both a World Series and a Super Bowl, so why not put him on both defense and offense? Young was asked how the play might have gone if the receiver had been George Plimpton instead of Deion Sanders. The question is not much weirder than "Who Owns American Literature?" — a notion stripped, like wallpaper, from the covers of various newsmagazines asking who owns our schools, our parks, our leisure time, our whole country. Who can say for certain that Sanders wouldn't do a good job editing *The Paris Review?*

What comes to mind is a magazine cover depicting a hand, a fist, actually, with sinuous strips of something or other emerging from between the fingers. It looks like the hand of a stagecoach driver, and the strips look like the harness lines, transformed by the magic of computer graphics to a handful of multicolored ribbons, curling and careering off in various directions, becoming pipelines, mail streams, highways, or cyberducts headed perhaps for New York Commercial Publishing, the Small Press Scene, the Battleground of the Bookstores, the National Book Critics Circle, the Acme Literary Trophy Shop, the Internet, or the offices of the Associated Writing Programs.

To whom does the hand belong? Gary Fisketjon? Sonny Mehta? Toni Morrison? The ghost of Edmund Wilson? Camille Paglia? Sven Birkerts? None of the above. Nor is it the hand of David Lehman, whose grip tightens, but not on the reins. And what of the loosening grip, word of which comes from Daniel Halpern, formerly editor of *Antaeus,* and from Gordon Lish, formerly a youn-

Henry Taylor (photograph by Boris Bohun-Chudynie)

ger man? Among those trying to identify the hand might be various male WASP writers, looking back and forth between fashionable anthologies and the Congress of the United States, muttering, more audibly than they intend to, that the white guys are making a comeback. Then they sit down and do one more draft of the letter they'll never send to their own representatives urging that the National Endowment for the Arts not be terminated.

Those fashionable anthologies, of course, are rarely fashionable outside the colleges and universities, whose share of interest, if not ownership, in American literature is enormous. It would probably be alarming to know what percentage of Emily Dickinson's living readers are enrolled in classes where her work is required reading. In trade bookstores she is often represented in selections from the earliest publications of her poems, which went into the public domain before Thomas Johnson edited *The Complete Poems* (1955). His edition is the joint property of the President and Fellows of Harvard College and the Trustees of Amherst College. However, anyone who wishes may reprint selections from the versions "corrected" and published by Dickinson's immediate survivors.

In terms of numbers, then, the academic sector accounts for most of the readers of literature by famous dead Americans, from Phillis Wheatley and Edward Taylor to Sylvia Plath and Ralph Ellison. Such entities as the National Book Critics Circle are concerned with the contemporary product, most of which is not literature in the good old elitist sense of the term. The academic sector's hold on that realm is so far a matter of the odd anecdote here and there concerning the contemporary theorist who prefers not to say whether Emily Dickinson is a better writer than Danielle Steele, or the journalism class pondering whether Tom Clancy could in a million years think of words that might cause Christopher Buckley any discomfort whatsoever.

The ownership of the contemporary product is just as vastly tangled and confusing as the ownership of the music or petroleum industries. Famous old publishers are owned by less famous larger companies, which are in turn owned by nearly invisible megaholders. Editors move about New York from one desk to another in something very much like Brownian movement, only smaller. Graduate students in writing programs track these movements and plot more strategies than they do novels.

But here and there around the country, there are people with large shelves of books, some of them by American writers, and once in a while one of those people pulls down a book and starts to read. The television is off, the computer has been disconnected from the information superhighway, and a silent, but richly complicated, miracle happens all over again. Charles Baudelaire, who wasn't even an American citizen, got hold of a mighty big chunk of the action when he translated Poe into something that could influence T. S. Eliot, who himself was only a part-time American citizen. Baudelaire probably got it right when he said (well, almost) that the owner of American literature is you, hypocrite reader, my look-alike, my sibling.

The Practice of Biography VIII: An Interview with Joan Mellen

Joan Mellen received her Ph.D. at City University of New York in 1968 and has since taught English and creative writing at Temple University while pursuing an active career as a writer. Her biography of Kay Boyle was published in 1993 by Farrar Strauss Giroux, and at the time this interview was conducted she was completing work on a biography tentatively titled *Hammett and Miss Hellman* to be published in Fall 1995 by HarperCollins. The interviewer is Richard Layman; Dr. Mellen edited the transcript for publication.

DLB: The topics and genres associated with your writing career are movies, Japanese culture, feminism, literature, basketball, film criticism, fiction, true crime, and biographies. Is there some unifying principle to these interests?

MELLEN: Yes. The unifying principle is the search beyond public perception. I'm also interested in tracing causality: how things become the way they are, and how people do. Basketball is the most anomalous of these subjects, of course. In my profile of Bob Knight I was interested in examining the relationship between the public perception of Bob Knight and the man himself and how he conducts the basketball program at Indiana. It was an anthropological search. That book was also about teaching — the only one I've written about what it takes to be a teacher, about how you move people from point A to point B. Bob Knight has an extraordinary ability to teach people how to discover their best talents and then to realize them. Of course as a coach he has a tremendous advantage over an ordinary teacher at a university. The students want to play basketball so much that they are willing to listen to what he has to say: it means their futures, because, like all college athletes, they are unable to relinquish the fantasy that they will be professionals. A teacher in an English composition class can't rely on such dedication from students. I'm interested in exploring how things work, how lives are constructed, and how our choices form the conse-

Joan Mellen (photograph courtesy of Joan Mellen)

quences of our actions. That was also the motivation behind my true-crime book, *Privilege,* with respect to the justice system, and to how one character, a girl named Sasha Bruce, despite having every advantage in intelligence, social position, beauty, and ability, ran out of options.

DLB: So you are a cultural anthropologist?

MELLEN: When it isn't cultural anthropology, biography is history, an interpretation of history. The biographer's method is that of the historian, except that biography is focused on the life of an individual. You get divergent views of a single historical period or event because historians inevitably offer interpretations. You find vastly different biographies of the same figure given the worldview and the talents of the biographer.

DLB: You are a professor of English at Temple.

MELLEN: Yes.

DLB: Do you consider yourself first a teacher or first a writer? Is there any possibility of assigning priorities, or are you simply a scholar fulfilling your responsibilities?

MELLEN: First a writer. I think that makes me a better teacher because, the cliché notwithstanding, I'm engaged in doing what I'm trying to teach students to do. But it also works backwards. I become fierce about the kinds of sentences they write; these days even graduate students find it difficult to write a correct English sentence. When I look at my own work – and my biographies are long, with many, many sentences, and there are times when you are tired and you haven't got a good sentence – I discover I have developed a critical eye toward my own writing that I might not have had if I did not teach. Of course, I'm teaching creative writing. I'm teaching people who are trying to write books themselves, so there is a very direct relationship. I'm very lucky in that. In other kinds of teaching that I do – teaching film, teaching literature – there isn't so close a connection to my writing. Teachers get paid so much less than everyone else – I think of it as a public service. Giving back some of your energy.

DLB: Are your students graduates, undergraduates, or both?

MELLEN: I have both. I teach in Temple's creative writing program. It's a master's program in creative writing, and the students are trying to write books of short stories or novels. I try to help them get agents and try to help them get published. It's a serious business. When it comes to undergraduates – and I've taught since 1967 – the level of literacy and historical literacy has declined so that you're compensating for the woeful inadequacies of elementary and secondary school. Many students have never heard of the Spanish civil war. It is not only their level of literacy and knowledge of literature; they do not know anything about even recent history.

DLB: Why is that?

MELLEN: I think it is the fault of the education system in this country. It is the anti-intellectualism and a kind of defeatism in this society, which insists that it does not really make any difference whether you know what happened in the past. I think there is also a tremendous elitism: the attitude is that there are certain people we expect to study the past; they are at Harvard and Princeton and Yale and they will be our leaders. The rest of the people are expendable; you just push them through. At Temple there are professors who no longer expect students to write correct English sentences. The teachers sometimes do not work hard enough because they are paid at such a low scale compared with other sectors of the society. Meanwhile, the whole system rejects the appreciation of intellect. There is no sense that knowledge will make a difference to the individual or to the culture at large, let alone that education might help us make the world a better place. Ours remains a conservative society in which those in power, those who write the textbooks for children and those who select them, don't encourage the notion of change. That premise, that things should remain as they are, is extremely damaging to education.

DLB: When you write, who is your audience? Does it change from book to book?

MELLEN: It does, although I wish it weren't so. I would like those who read the Kay Boyle biography to enjoy the Bob Knight profile too. I believe you don't have to know anything about basketball, or to like sports, to appreciate that book. Of course there are many people in Indiana who bought the story of Bob Knight because they like to read about him; he's a brilliant man and wonderfully quotable. I'm ecstatic to have any readers, whatever their motive.

DLB: Who is your audience for the literary biographies?

MELLEN: As you can see, I'm quixotic. I don't exclude anyone as a potential reader. My books are not designed for academics, certainly. My style as a biographer is novelistic, so I hope that anyone who likes to read fiction will enjoy the biographies. Yet every line is documented; I do not make up a single detail. But I want all my books to read as if they were stories. Kay Boyle had a fascinating life, but she is largely forgotten as a literary figure. Readers who don't know about her should enjoy the story of that extraordinary life. Many people have not even heard of Lillian Hellman and Dashiell Hammett. I hope for readers interested in the development of their lives. This type of biography draws on dramatic highs, on characterization and dialogue, and, of course, causality. With the demise of realistic fiction, biography has replaced the old-fashioned, juicy family saga. Many readers love biography for that reason.

DLB: So you would be as happy writing a biography of an interesting sports figure or movie star as of a writer?

MELLEN: I choose my subjects according to whether the life points to larger issues, so I don't know about the movie stars, although years ago I wrote a short biography of Marilyn Monroe; this was before Norman Mailer and Gloria Steinem. Mine was very sympathetic to Monroe as a woman.

I don't think of my Bob Knight book as "slumming." I think it's as serious a work as the Kay Boyle. I think that Bob Knight is an immensely valuable and interesting person. He turned out to be kinder, more generous, and easier to deal with than Kay Boyle. He is a far more honest human being than she was.

DLB: What's the point of the biographies? You say they are valuable works. Where is the value?

MELLEN: Each of my books is different. The Bob Knight book illustrates how important teaching is and how difficult. *Kay Boyle: Author of Herself* is as much a history of the twentieth century as it is her biography. I was writing about what it felt like to live in this century as well as how one woman overcame the enormous odds against all women to carve an important place for herself in literary history. How did she achieve this? With what sacrifices? I'm trying to create an appreciation for history even as I'm exploring the details of an individual life. Kay Boyle was no saint. Her life is not a model for women in the sense that somebody could read it and say, "There go I; there I would like to go." She

made enormous mistakes about her work and in her personal life. Nor should biography ever descend into the mire of hagiography with the biographer composing the life of a saint. This is why most authorized biographies are not honest books. The biographer must be free even of well-meaning censorship. Nor is any biography the last word. There remains the opportunity for another interpretation. I was criticized by Kay Boyle's acolytes in San Francisco who had expected me to suppress the realities of her family life and to focus primarily on her literary work. Since her literary work declined in the forties and fifties, that created another problem for the coterie. They certainly didn't want to see the truth of the whole life.

DLB: At least one Pulitzer Prize–winning biographer of recent times has observed that he did not want to let facts get in the way of his work. Do you ever feel overwhelmed by the research, especially in the case of the Kay Boyle book, which is meticulously researched?

MELLEN: Let me invoke one of Lillian Hellman's favorite words: *deplorable*. The achievement of biography is based on your enlisting documents, letters, interviews, diaries; the more information you obtain, the more facts, the better. Biography becomes a work of art when you begin to enlist all this material. When you are interviewing people, they're remembering, and not always accurately. The same artistic discretion is required when the biographer handles letters: people don't necessarily tell the truth in their letters. Enormous judgment is required of the biographer. The goal still must be to get as close as you can to what happened, and toward that end, the more documentation available, the better. I like to think of my method in terms of the camera. Long shots are fine. But you must include scenes in which you come in tight, and for those, extraordinary research – and luck in obtaining that research – is required. Without the facts you have nothing; you're writing a novel and you should call it that.

I was very fortunate because Kay Boyle wrote ten letters or so every day of her life from the time that she was thirteen. I had an enormous amount of material. I was delighted with each new piece of information. It either confirms where you're going, or it creates an antithesis, which is also desirable. You want as much nuance as you can obtain. Your job is to duplicate a life which is invariably full of contradictions. If you don't welcome contradictions, you shouldn't be writing biographies.

DLB: How do you develop the discernment to judge an interview subject who is being self-serving, bending the truth to his or her own uses, or simply lying? Can you teach biographical research? How do you learn biography?

MELLEN: It takes smarts — and total immersion in the project and in the lives of the subjects. That's why I believe you must interview everyone breathing who was even acquainted with the subject. Sometimes two people will tell the same story — differently. That happened in my new Lillian Hellman–Dashiell Hammett book. Lillian Hellman gave a dinner on Martha's Vineyard. There were only two guests: a woman named Lynda Palevsky and the theater critic, Hellman's friend Robert Brustein. Although she professed to regret not having had children, Lillian preferred not to be in their presence. That night she told Lynda Palevsky she didn't want her two-year-old to come to dinner; she should leave him with a baby-sitter at the hotel. Now Lillian was nearly blind by this time, and Lynda, who didn't want to leave her little boy back at the hotel, thought she could have the child eat his dinner without Lillian knowing. In Palevsky's version of the story, the child ate his dinner, Lillian never knew he was there, and all was well. But in Brustein's version of the same dinner party, Lillian immediately sensed the child's presence; she was not one hundred percent blind anyway. She became furious, saying, "Get that child away from the table!" It was one of Lillian's more mean-spirited moments. She was like the little girl in the nursery rhyme: when she was good, she was very very good, but when she was bad, she was horrid. I had to persuade people who loved her to be interviewed because they wanted to be honest and yet didn't want to talk about those mean-spirited moments. I think friends are right to emphasize the best, and I conclude that's what Lynda was doing. I have also found that most people don't lie in interviews. But some do, usually for self-serving ends, which was not the case in this story.

DLB: How did you resolve the conflict between those two stories?

MELLEN: I have not come to the editing of that scene yet, but I'm afraid that I have to go with Brustein's version. Common sense tells you that a mother could not get a two-year-old to sit perfectly still.

DLB: What attracts you to a biographical subject?

MELLEN: I've only done the two full biographies, the Kay Boyle and *Hammett and Miss Hellman.* Both cases were rather extraordinary in the sense that I knew the subjects. I met Kay Boyle in Ireland in 1986. She was an old, old lady; she was born in 1902. She had decided that she was going to travel around Ireland doing interviews for a feminist book about strong Irish women. She was in contact with a close friend of mine named Blair Clark — he plays a role in connecting the two biographies. His father, Judge Clark, was instrumental in helping Kay Boyle get cleared during the McCarthy period of the charges, particularly the charges against her husband, that he was a Communist. He wasn't. She was what they called — I really don't like to use that McCarthyite word — a fellow traveler. But he wasn't a Communist. Judge Clark's son, Blair, stayed friendly with Kay, and then when he knew she was going to be in Ireland and we were in Ireland, we had dinner. She started telling stories about her life, how Marcel Duchamp saved her from being killed by her husband Laurence Vail — these marvelous, exciting stories. Of course, she was a great self-dramatizer, as I was to find out later. I thought: "My God. Has anybody written this woman's biography?" No one had. I asked her right then and there. I said, "Would you be interested in having a biography written?" She said no, because a graduate student was publishing a dissertation about her work and it would conflict. So I said fine. Six months later Kay Boyle wrote me a letter and asked when I was coming to California. So I went, and that's how I started. It began as an authorized biography and wound up being unauthorized.

The same Blair Clark was the person who Lillian had decided in 1962 was going to take Hammett's place in her life. He was tall; he was Anglo-Saxon; he had that cool distance that, as a very insecure woman, she favored. He was extraordinarily handsome. He remained close to Lillian until her death and in the last years of her life he introduced me to her. I invited her to dinner. We went to a party at her house. We took her to a party at her best friend Hannah Weinstein's. I saw her maybe seven or eight times. So she was in my mind, although at the time I had no intention of writing about her. She was also a thorn in my side in a way, because of how demanding she was, even as a very old lady, of this man who never was her lover. He was a person whom she assigned to that role, which he didn't really want. In any case, she always kept her friends and former lovers close. She remained in my mind as a strong character. Then, years after her death, Blair Clark said to me, "She compartmentalized her life so much that people who knew her well didn't know what the others knew and didn't know who the other people were and who she was closest to." At lunch one day he said, "I've always wondered what really happened between her and Hammett." Immediately I thought that would make an interesting story. I decided to do it. My advantage was that I knew Blair Clark, and he knew Lillian Hellman's closest friends, not least Peter Feibleman – her primary heir and one of her literary executors – as well as Billy Abrahams, whom he had known in the late thirties and early forties at Harvard. Billy was her editor, and Hellman in her will named him as her official biographer.

I had an enormous advantage in that these people were acquaintances. I had access to Lillian Hellman's circle in a way that no other biographer has had. I will also be the first author to publish a book about either Lillian Hellman or Dashiell Hammett making full use of the archive at the Harry Ransom Humanities Research Center at the University of Texas at Austin. When the Hammett biographies were written, the full archive wasn't yet in Texas; it arrived only after Lillian Hellman's death in 1984.

DLB: There was what they called a Lillian Hellman archive, but it consisted mostly of drafts of the plays.

MELLEN: That's correct. That's the material Lillian Hellman sold to them in the sixties. After she died, many boxes of material were shipped to Texas out of her apartment. I'll be the first person to publish having worked with those archives. I think that's an enormous advantage. I have also been very fortunate in having unlimited permission to quote from her work, and from Hammett's work owned by her estate, from Peter Feibleman and the other fiduciaries of the literary property of the Hellman-Hammett estate. Peter Feibleman, a writer himself of note, did not ask to see a single line of the book before granting me permission. I don't know how people who write biographies can create a full impression of the subject's life without this freedom to quote from letters and diaries. I am enormously grateful to Peter Feibleman, and to William Abrahams and Richard Poirier, the other literary executors.

DLB: Did your view of Boyle's, Hammett's, or Hellman's writing change after you became involved in the research about their lives?

MELLEN: Sure. Because I first thought of Kay Boyle as what she had been in the twenties and thirties, as a modernist. I think she contributed to the creation of that original *New Yorker* style of the single-episode story – a single emotional moment – a paradigm of a certain kind of modernism. I had no idea that she became a social realist later in life and had lost that great style that she had developed in the twenties and thirties. You learn such essential facts only as you go on. Somehow, as she became political, her style suffered greatly. It does not have to be that way. I don't believe that, but in her case it was that way.

DLB: Did you see the piece in the *Sunday Times* about John Osborne's death? There was a wonderful statement by Philip Larkin that "most people faced with contradictory judgments about an artist and his work will adjust their views until the two elements fall in line rather than accept the ambiguity."

MELLEN: You better not. Why do you have to? In a way the life in a biography has to be as sprawling as the real life. It's an impression of that life. It has to be pretty close and simultaneously retain all those contradictions intact.

DLB: I think the *why* goes to F. Scott Fitzgerald's observation that the mark of a first-rate mind is the ability to hold two contradictory ideas at the same time. Most people can't do it. The resolution of contradictions is part of human nature.

MELLEN: It's also fear.

DLB: Fear of what?

MELLEN: Fear of having nothing to hang onto. I think Hammett had that fear himself, which led him to allow himself to be used by the Communist Party the way he was. And he was used. He felt the kind of emptiness that comes from not having an anchor. If you have two contradictory ideas, where are you? For some people that's frightening.

DLB: To what extent was Hammett a willing puppet? Did he allow himself to be used, or did he simply distance himself to the point that he didn't much care what they put his name on?

MELLEN: Well, no. He was more than a puppet. If you dig, dig, dig, you can actually find reports of meetings he chaired. I have an account of a meeting about gathering petitions to get Earl Browder on the New York State ballot and to discuss defending a Communist who was being "discriminated against." Somebody gets up at the meeting and says, "This is all very well, but are you willing to defend the Democratic rights of," and I think a Socialist is named who was not a member of the happy few. And, boy! Hammett shut him up.

DLB: You have minutes of these meetings?

MELLEN: I have an anecdotal report. It tells where he was, when it was, the name of the dissenter, a man called Mr. Hamilton, who is otherwise unidentified, what committee it was, and how it was set up. There are times, there were many, many times when I think somebody else authored a petition and Hammett signed it, or allowed his name to be used as the sponsor, or the president, or the chair. But as the president of the League of American Writers, after all, he certainly knew what was going on. I don't think he didn't know, I really don't. He fell prey to a certain cynicism, the attitude of "what difference does it make?" He signed certain petitions and not others, after all. He would not condemn the purge trials, or the hounding of Leon Trotsky and his family. He would not condemn the Hitler-Stalin pact. He had to have read what he was signing. I can't believe that he was entirely used without knowing it.

DLB: A critic of one of your movie books suggested that you must have been sitting so far to the left of the screen that your view was distorted. Are you politically motivated?

MELLEN: I'm not politically motivated. I have been called a feminist and a leftist, labels I reject. I'm not a feminist in any narrow sense, nor am I leftist, whatever that means in these times. However, I do consider myself a dissident. I believe that the function of an artist is to attack the status quo. If we lived in a utopia, in a just society, that would not be necessary. Since I don't believe utopia can ever exist, it's a moot point. Insofar as there are abuses, as there will be always among human beings, some of whom, many of whom, are selfish, and this doesn't apply only to Generation X, insofar as the society is not hospitable to all its citizens, it's a writer's function to point the way to how things might be improved, exposing contradictions along the way. Luis Buñuel, one of my favorite film directors, once said, "the responsibility of an artist, everyday, is to kill his father, sleep with his mother,

and betray his country." The artist shakes the order of things, detests complacency, urges change, urges upheaval in the hope that we might move closer to eliminating injustice, inequity, hypocrisy, discrimination against the weak, and violations of people's rights which occur often without the opportunity of redress. If the artist's function is not to suggest a better world, what is it? Luckily, we still believe in the value of dissident voices gaining a hearing, and that's the right we must protect above all others.

DLB: When you say "writer," are you talking about yourself or your subjects?

MELLEN: Actually I'm talking about all of us. Kay Boyle, Lillian Hellman, and Dashiell Hammett were all dissidents who believed in making their protests against various forms of injustice. Lillian Hellman and Dashiell Hammett, for reasons we can go into, subjected themselves to the views of the American Communist Party. Insofar as they did that, they were not free to explore what was in the best interests of this country. They were expressing what the Communist Party expressed, which is what Moscow wanted them to do. It wasn't in the interests of the American dissident movement in the 1930s to support the New Deal. Well, maybe it was; maybe it wasn't. Maybe a labor party might have been a better idea than the New Deal. When the Communist Party said support Roosevelt and the New Deal (and not socialism, by the way, although they were a Communist party), Hammett and Hellman supported Roosevelt and the Democratic Party. And, of course, when the Communist Party said stop opposing Hitler, they did. Now they joined an antiwar group, and Lillian Hellman sat at the League of American Writers with Clifford Odets and wrote antiwar resolutions until such time as Hitler invaded the Soviet Union. So what kind of dissidents are these? I think they betrayed their own cause, if their cause was socialism. I'd like to think that Hammett understood that. Hammett understood that because, at a certain point, Hammett decides to live simply, gives away his money. He has a better value system.

DLB: Gives away his money?

MELLEN: It is true. You could say, well, who did he give it to? He supported many worthy causes.

DLB: He gave it to Communist Party organizations until 1950 or so.

MELLEN: Hammett didn't just help the party. He wanted to use his money to help the weak; maybe he was simply too drunk to inquire too deeply into how his money was being spent. You ask him for a check for a "Win the War Writers Group," and he'd take out his wallet and give you a thousand dollars. If you asked him for a contribution for the Veterans of the Abraham Lincoln Brigade, he would take out money instantly. He was constantly shedding himself of whatever money he had. Lillian, on the other hand, amassed a fortune and did not live as a Socialist, but neither did many in the Communist movement. But Hammett saw that contradiction. He felt uneasy about accumulating wealth and yet calling himself a Marxist.

DLB: I had the sense that he was just oblivious to the details of personal finance until Muriel Alexander came in and organized his affairs.

MELLEN: I think he had always left his business affairs in other people's hands. And, of course, I don't think one can underestimate the effect on Hammett's life of his alcoholism. He didn't pay his income taxes during the war, but this was not a political protest. Yet he was not entirely oblivious. From the Aleutian Islands he wrote a letter to Lillian's secretary, Nancy Bragdon, saying, "I think I'll wait. I'm sure that they'll understand if I pay these taxes after the war. What should I do about it?" It was in his mind to pay those taxes.

DLB: The effect on her memoirs is pretty obvious, but what effect on her plays did Hellman's political notions have?

MELLEN: When it came to her work, Hellman retained her integrity; Stalinist politics do not emerge in her plays. You wouldn't even know that a Communist wrote those plays, although Hellman was a member of the party in the thirties. She had a strong moral sense, and she wrote out of her strong sense of justice. The best example of her freedom from party politics is the well-known case of *Watch on the Rhine* [1941]. When she began to write, the accepted party view was that it was essential to be an anti-Fascist. When Stalin signed his pact with Hitler, Lillian did not change a thing. She wrote and had produced an anti-Fascist play when Communists were supposed to be antiwar, not anti-Fascist.

It was Hammett who was under party discipline and who blanched. There was a period when he was very uneasy with *Watch on the Rhine*. This was during the period when you were not supposed to advocate sacrificing everything for the fight against fascism, which is the theme of that play. Hammett reconciled himself to *Watch on the Rhine* only after Hitler invaded the Soviet Union. Then he sat down and wrote the screenplay. But he did not go to Sardi's to wait for the reviews; for the most part he stayed away from rehearsals, which was not his habit otherwise. He distanced himself. In later years Lillian said she never forgave him for distancing himself from that play because it was against the party point of view.

DLB: I have had difficulty understanding what Hammett's contribution was to *Watch on the Rhine*. The screenplay is no different from the stage play that I can see.

MELLEN: Ah, the screenplay. I did an entire chapter in my book comparing between Hammett's screenplay for *Watch on the Rhine* and Lillian's revisions of it. That screenplay I think represented an enormous turning point for Hammett. When he saw what he had done, versus what she did with it, he realized then that he was no longer a writer. If he had any doubts.

DLB: Can you elaborate?

MELLEN: Yes. What will surprise those who admire *Red Harvest* [1929] and *The Glass Key* [1931] is the didacticism of Hammett's version of the screenplay. People get up and pontificate about the workers, and the rich, and the poor, and the Fascists, and Hitler. Lillian took all of that out; or rather, let me put it this way, where he had a whole page, she had a sentence. He self-indulgently used the opportunity to preach. He created an endless sequence on the train where the Mohler family is going to Washington, D.C., which is not in the original play. Which is understandable – he had to do exteriors for a film. But he became lost in the ideology of the melting pot: he'd have an Italian and an Armenian and a Scandinavian, and they'd all give their points of view, and he'd have naive characters being instructed by the anti-Fascist hero. All of this didactic speech making was removed. He had Popular Front rhetoric about all the monuments of Washington, D.C. – the Communist Party at that time was more American than Americans. He had a lot of that; Lillian Hellman took her Hammett-like eye and went over that script and reduced it to a taut, tight, Hammett-like prose that you would expect from *Red Harvest*. He was wallowing. It was embarrassing, and I think he knew it.

DLB: I've seen the completed version of the screenplay but never Hammett's version, the revised one.

MELLEN: It's available at Texas. It is in pencil. You know the secret of identifying Hammett's handwriting? He dotted his *i*'s with a little circle. You can always tell. In the correspondence between Hal Wallis and Herman Shumlin over the slowness with which Hammett was working on the screenplay and their impatience, you can see how everybody tried to prop him up. Shumlin did. Arthur Kober did. Lillian did. And I think this really showed Hammett where he was. Just at the time that he was working on that script, he returned his advance to Bennett Cerf for the novel he never wrote.

DLB: Advertised as "There was a Young Man."

MELLEN: He was not going to write that novel. Then he enlisted in September in the army.

DLB: I never saw the correspondence with Wallis either.

MELLEN: That correspondence is at the University of Southern California in the Warner Bros. archives.

DLB: Very impressive.

MELLEN: Well, either you do the full investigation or you don't. You leave no stone unturned when you're writing a biography. You should welcome the research and become excited with each new discovery, each new piece of the mosaic. If you suddenly discover a person whom you did not get to talk to, you pack up and find them, even if it's the day before you hand in the final manuscript.

DLB: Did Lillian Hellman ruin Hammett as a writer?

MELLEN: I think that if you look closely at the texture of their lives, that idea is absurd. That he stopped writing cannot be laid at her door. Here is Hammett. He really stops being a writer in 1930.

It takes four years for him to write *The Thin Man* [1934]. Then just at the time that he was finishing that book at last, he begins to help Lillian with her first play, *The Children's Hour* [1934]. I think it was terribly difficult for him to get through *The Thin Man;* it's an afterthought to his career. It must have been a relief for him when he began to help Lillian, to transfer to her the discipline of the writer's life.

DLB: It is not a very good book.

MELLEN: It is not. It is far inferior to the other four novels. There's no comparison to the early novels, and I think helping her with her work allowed him the illusion that he was still involved in writing and creative work. Far from it taking something from him, working with Lillian kept him going. He would not have been involved in literary work at all if not for her. I located one of Hammett's secretaries whom no one had talked to. In 1936 she wrote a diary of Hammett trying to write and she, being his secretary, trying to help him for several months in the spring of 1936. We see Hammett struggling. He is living in a hotel; Lillian rarely appears; they've had a fight, and he rarely speaks to her, although she calls up once in a while. So the Hammett cult cannot invoke the excuse that he did not write because he was working with her on one of her plays. He is struggling, and he is struggling. He simply can't write any longer. He has come to the end. Then, of course, some years later, when we talk about *Watch on the Rhine,* the film, we see that she has become the accomplished writer. She really doesn't need him anymore. She is the better writer. There is no question in my mind about it; all you have to do is compare her version of the screenplay with his.

I'd like to add one more element. Lillian Hellman was an enormously insecure woman. A friend of hers said Lillian was the most insecure person she had ever met. Given Hellman's success so early, this seemed an anomaly. But remember that she grew up in an era where women, especially in the South, were judged by their looks, by how attractive they were as women. She, alas, was plain. As for women writers, there were no great models for that, excepting perhaps Gertrude Stein, who was far away in Paris. For Hellman, the gratification that came from the writing was always secondary to the validation she required from a man. Validation for a woman remained being adored by a man. Hellman still needed Hammett for confidence, although as a writer she no longer needed his advice. He gave her that confidence, at least until a major turning point in their relationship in 1945. Then his support continued in a reprise in 1949 and 1950.

DLB: Did Hammett contribute anything aside from the idea to *The Children's Hour?*

MELLEN: Hammett worked with Hellman closely on *The Children's Hour.* She had included a didactic character, Judge Potter. If the judge were going to remain in the story, there would be no story because he immediately saw through Mary's lie and was not going to allow Mrs. Tilford to ruin the teachers' lives. One of Hammett's crucial suggestions was that Hellman remove this character completely. One point I could never decipher – and there always remain questions in biography for which you have no access to the answers – is whether Hammett had anything to do with the changes Lillian Hellman made in the ending from one draft to another. Originally, she had a very strong ending. Then she weakened it and in the final version she allows the teacher to forgive the old lady. The ending that we see is not the original fierce ending. An educated guess would be that producer Herman Shumlin, thinking of the demands of Broadway, suggested the new ending. I don't believe it was Hammett, but I don't know.

Lillian wrote to him often, but Hammett threw away all her letters. He never saved anything. In keeping with this idea of shedding everything, including his old identity, he shed money, he shed letters, and he left few documents. Lillian, insofar as she was able, asked the recipients to return her letters to her. She never wanted a biography written. She didn't trust the process, nor did Hammett, by the way. One can understand that. There are a lot of bad biographies written; she didn't really want to trust her life to someone who did not know her. Many of her letters she herself destroyed; some were stolen.

There's a netherworld connected to biography too. People steal letters. People sell letters. A secretarial service was in Hellman's house typing, and someone stole a bunch of letters that she wrote to John Melby, her lover, whom she met in Moscow in 1944 and 1945. They recently came on the market at the Swann Gallery in New York. So, although Melby told me that when Lillian received her letters to him back, she destroyed them; some in fact survived. Possession became the law, since legally they belonged physically to the Melby estate, while the copyright belonged to the Hellman estate. They were bought by the University of Texas and are now part of the Hellman archive there.

DLB: Do you think that either Hammett's or Hellman's work will endure?

MELLEN: At their best they were solidly of the second rank. I think she knew it. He admitted it and said that the second rank is a very high rank indeed. Hellman then took that as one of Hammett's lines that she especially liked. It is very difficult to be of the second rank; she is right about that. I think she made a powerful contribution to a realistic, moralistic theater. We don't see the plays revived much; yet *The Children's Hour,* which had been banned, appeared in a major production in London for the first time last fall. I think her plays have a powerful driving force: *The Children's Hour, The Little Foxes* [1939], *Watch on the Rhine,* perhaps *The Autumn Garden* [1951]. I think that his first novel, *Red Harvest,* along with *The Glass Key,* are very fine, are classics of their genre.

Hellman and Hammett both suffer from the same problem in their writing; they stay on the surface. They're very much alike in this. These two people are very much alike in other ways as well. I know that the Hammett fans out in San Francisco prefer to think of him as very different from her. But they are very similar. Lillian actually feared introspection less than he did, although it doesn't emerge in her work. She was a veteran of psychiatry, yet even in her memoirs she doesn't penetrate very deeply. Neither did he, and I believe that was the main reason he stopped writing. He looked down on the detective genre and wanted to go further. But you can't go further unless you are willing to enter the interior life. There was some frightening primal scene, perhaps from his childhood, that frightened him and prevented him from exploring the depths. That's a scene, however, to which no biographer has had access.

DLB: The genre he created, the hard-boiled detective genre, has a built-in limitation that restricts introspection.

MELLEN: The evasion of introspection was true in his personal life as well. Every time he said something loving, he qualified it. In one of the letters he wrote Lillian when she was in Hollywood and he was in the army at Fort Monmouth, in New Jersey, but spending weekends in the city, he wrote, "I really love waking up in your apartment on Sunday mornings. . . ." It sounds committed, domestic. Then he added, "It's better than the barracks." He does that often. He also felt he had to write those letters referring to his sexual desire for other women: "I'm going to meet so and so. I hope they have a grown-up daughter." He always taunted her with the threat of other women, lest she take him for granted. This fear of being possessed was enormous in Hammett.

I believe he loved Lillian more than he ever loved anyone in his life, except for his daughter Jo, although he didn't really know Jo very well; their relationship was conducted largely by mail. From the time he met her, Lillian was the closest person in his life. Hellman's great objection to Diane Johnson's biography of Hammett was that she didn't feel that this truth came through in the book. One of the things that amazed me in the research was that he did love her. He could deny it or not, or he could put Lillian in her place by having her walk in on him when he was in bed with another woman, which he did a lot during the early days. Nonetheless, he really did love her, and he certainly needed her, although he would not admit that either.

DLB: How about his first daughter, Mary?

MELLEN: Are you ready for the revelation? I don't believe Mary was his natural daughter, and I corroborated that with sources other than Lillian Hellman. We know that Lillian didn't always tell the truth, and it may seem that believing that Jose was pregnant with another man's child was in Lillian's interest. Certainly Lillian was always resentful of Hammett's remaining in contact with Jose. Yet I am persuaded that Mary was not his. It is just like Hammett to do his damnedest to cover up such a fact. Lillian was afraid of him until the day he died. She was terrified of his displeasure and anger. So she could never, ever, during his lifetime breathe a word of this truth.

DLB: Is Mary still alive?

MELLEN: No. Mary died without ever knowing.

DLB: What convinces you that Hammett is not her father?

MELLEN: Hammett told it to others. Why would he do that when he was so careful about keeping this truth from Mary herself? He would never have said such a thing if it weren't so; he revealed it in a moment of confidence to a person he trusted, someone he knew wished his family well, someone who was not in any way in Lillian's camp. I believe it. Most people believe he married Jose be-

cause she was pregnant, which is true. But I believe he married her because she was pregnant with another man's child. Now Jo Marshall has argued that her mother would never have slept with more than one man. But she was a Catholic girl who slept with Hammett outside of marriage, a man she scarcely knew. Jose was an abused girl, an orphan. The relatives who took her in treated her like a servant. They locked her in the cellar. She was never given any new clothes; like Cinderella, locked in the cellar or treated like a servant. All this must have had an enormous effect on her subsequent feelings about herself and her life. She became dependent, passive. She was very grateful to Hammett. She would have done anything for him all the rest of her life. She never criticized him. He had saved her and her child.

DLB: But she filed for divorce, didn't she?

MELLEN: He asked her to. Jo described the scene for me. Hammett came to Jose's house. He told the children to stay in the kitchen. He didn't want them to overhear the conversation. Then he asked Jose for a divorce. You have to remember how people felt about divorce in those days, not only Catholics, but non-Catholics as well. Hammett asked for the divorce because Lillian was pregnant with his child, and she wanted him to marry her.

DLB: And she had an abortion, and he changed his mind, or they changed their minds?

MELLEN: He engineered a scene, which Lillian couldn't live with. Namely he arranged a scene in which she'd walk in on him with another woman. Even with a baby, nothing would change, he was telling her. In one of Hammett's very early stories, "On the Way," in which he's called Kipper and she's called Gladys, he predicts everything that's going to happen in their relationship. He offers to marry her, but she doesn't want it that way. This business with the baby in real life occurs later, but Hammett made the point at the start: everything would be on his terms. He made the rules. He was never going to be sexually faithful. And Lillian — can we blame any woman for making the request that a man be faithful to her?

DLB: No. But then she was not sexually faithful to him either, and she seems to have been as cruel to him as he to her.

MELLEN: Later. Much later, not then. I don't think she was cruel to him in the early days. I think her real infidelities were retaliations. Now that doesn't mean she was faithful to her husband, Arthur Kober. She wasn't.

DLB: How about when she was at Liveright?

MELLEN: Lillian Hellman came of age in the twenties. She was what they called a "flaming youth." Young people experimented sexually; they had sex outside of marriage. I think from Dashiell Hammett, Lillian wanted the whole package. Yet he was the most unlikely man to ask that from. That tells us a great deal about Lillian and her damaged sense of self. She had no mother to help her; her mother never functioned as real mother. Her father was a womanizer, rejecting them both. Meanwhile the little girl was plain. What was she going to do? How was she going to navigate her way through life? She was tough; she had the gene for toughness. She said, "I still want whatever there is to have of life." She had an appetite for living. She determined early that she would not settle back into being some sort of wallflower victim. Then she made compromises to get what she wanted.

DLB: You seem to admire her.

MELLEN: I do, in spite of the fact that she became mean-spirited at times later in her life. I admire her grit. I admire her ability to make use of whatever talent she had. She was smart enough to perceive that she needed someone to help her at the beginning. That's true of most writers; someone must show you the way.

DLB: Why are lies the pervasive theme of all her work?

MELLEN: I'm not sure that lies are *the* pervasive theme. Lies are certainly a theme, however. As a lonely only child with neither mother nor father to understand her, Lillian was a liar from early on. She developed a cynicism which matched Hammett's, despite his insistence that he hated lying and hated her lying. He said, "Just don't do it to me. Just knock it off." He saw her lying right away, and he forgave it. I think she lies as a survivor, as that only child who has no one on whom to count. As a child she hated being the Newhouse poor relation. The rich Newhouses from her mother's family flaunted their wealth and looked down on Julia, Lillian's mother, who married a man in trade, a low-class

person and a failure. Lillian had to figure out, "How am I going to escape from all this? How am I going to pull myself out of all this?"

DLB: It seems curious to me that not only did she lie, she announced that she was going to lie.

MELLEN: Finally, as she says in *The Autumn Garden,* don't we all lie to ourselves anyway? At the same time she did not wish to be exposed, because her later persona was built on invention. Mary McCarthy, in accusing her of pervasive lying, threatened to blow a life project. But in 1939 Lillian went to Zilboorg, the psychiatrist, to cure her not only of drinking but also of lying. Even as she fantasized and invented her life, a strong, honest side of her character was repelled by lying. She was a fragmented personality, which is why she called herself *An Unfinished Woman.* That title reveals she was capable of extraordinary honesty.

DLB: Is this the last biography of Hammett and Hellman? There have been so many about each of them.

MELLEN: I have a great deal of new material. And I can use material other biographers had access to but declined to use for fear of Hellman's suing them, which she threatened to do. I'm able to make connections which haven't been made, using new sources, using the archive at Texas. No one has written about the connection between Hammett's discovery of Lilian's involvement with John Melby and the devastating years of drinking and nihilism which followed.

The Hellman-Melby story is very important in the context of Hellman-Hammett. Would they have married? Would Lillian ever have gone to Nanking? Can you imagine Lillian in Nanking without a toilet? Yet I believe she felt loved by Melby in a way she had not been loved for years. That renewed her. There's also the story about what happened to Max Hellman at the end of his life which has not been told. Yet I don't for a minute believe this is the "last biography." A biographer with a sensibility different from mine will produce a different book utilizing the same sources. And of course new letters, new documents, will inevitably surface.

DLB: You are doing final revisions on your book now. Are you satisfied with it?

MELLEN: Who can say? I'm doing the best I can. I learned a fundamental truth from my favorite biographical subject, Bob Knight. Before a game he would tell his team, "When you leave the floor, you should have nothing left!" That line expresses one of the aspects of his teaching that I admire: his ability to teach people that success involves giving nothing short of everything you have to the effort. Students always think they're working hard when you know they could work harder. My graduate students are as guilty of this as the undergraduates. I want them to know what it feels like to give everything. It turns out to be the same for a writer as for an athlete. By the time you're finished, you are exhausted; you have nothing left to give. I know I'm coming to the end of the Hellman-Hammett project because I'm approaching that level of exhaustion.

DLB: Do you have any advice for aspiring biographers?

MELLEN: Here's my advice. Number one, keep yourself as the biographer out of the narrative. No matter how painful some of your experiences might have been – perhaps your subject slammed the door in your face – these incidents should not appear in the text. The book is not about you and how difficult it was for you to write it, nor is it about why you chose this subject instead of another. That is interesting only to you and, perhaps, to your friends and loved ones. A dangerous trend has developed in the last ten years or so in which women biographers enter the narratives of their biographies about women and start addressing their subjects. Or they become involved in talking about their own problems, shoving their subjects off the stage.

In a biography of Manet's model, Victorine Meurent, called *Alias Olympia,* the author Eunice Lipton enters the story to ponder whether or not she should quit her teaching job and whether she should stay married. Elinor Langer actually asks her subject, Josephine Herbst, how to keep her own flagging sixties radicalism alive. In her biography of Simone de Beauvoir, Carol Ascher writes a letter to de Beauvoir, in which she whines, as if she were a child facing an insensitive mother, "Why should I be devoting myself to you when you never did anything for me?" De Beauvoir, of course, did not commission the biography. Nor did readers bargain for the story of the biographer rather than that of the

subject when they paid their thirty dollars. Sometimes these biographers act out their feminist agendas. Francine Du Plessix Gray is so outraged that Flaubert burned the letters of her subject, Louise Colet, that she elevated Colet to being a major poet, which she wasn't.

I don't think there's such a thing as an "objective" biography. The biographer selects, emphasizes, and dramatizes certain scenes and not others according to her own sense of values, psyche, etc. Yet you go too far when you sacrifice the life of your subject to fill unoccupied roles in your own life, when you ask that your biographical subject become mother, sister, friend, lover, even priest or priestess. Above all you should leave the process of writing the biography out of the book. Finally, it's arrogant to bring yourself in.

The second area of advice I would offer is never write about a living subject. There are many reasons for this. But most important is that you interfere in the living subject's life, in her relationships with family and friends. After cooperating with me and encouraging the book, Kay Boyle decided that she didn't want a biography. She changed her mind. She's a human being; she changed her mind. Then she went and told her friends not to talk to the biographer. Jessica Mitford, believing in freedom of discourse, violated that request and gave me an interview.

Kay Boyle, enraged, never spoke to her again, and I believe Jessica Mitford was sorry. She acted on the principle of free speech and choice, but there was a terrible price to pay. At the end, Jessica Mitford did not attend Kay Boyle's funeral or her memorial service, and I don't think that Mitford has forgiven me. There are also feelings children have about parents which they have kept secret but which they may out of frustration reveal to a biographer; the subject discovers them for the first time in print. The biographer should not interfere in the subject's relationships, and this becomes inevitable if the subject is alive.

I will plead that when I began I had Kay Boyle's approval, which is so; I was not writing an unauthorized biography. Then things changed. I would not be so naïve again. It is not appropriate to invade the privacy rights of anyone, including your own subject. I would never do it again. Not ever.

Cleanth Brooks

(16 October 1906 – 10 May 1994)

Mark Royden Winchell
Clemson University

BOOKS: *The Relation of the Alabama-Georgia Dialect to the Provincial Dialects of Great Britain* (Baton Rouge: Louisiana State University Press, 1935);

An Approach to Literature: A Collection of Prose and Verse with Analyses and Discussions, with Robert Penn Warren and John Thibaut Purser (Baton Rouge: Louisiana State University Press, 1936); revised edition, New York: F. S. Crofts, 1939);

Understanding Poetry: An Anthology for College Students, with Warren (New York: Holt, 1938; revised edition, New York: Holt, 1950);

Modern Poetry and the Tradition (Chapel Hill: University of North Carolina Press, 1939; London: Editions Poetry London, 1948);

Understanding Fiction, with Warren (New York: F. S. Crofts, 1943);

Understanding Drama, with Robert B. Heilman (New York: Holt, 1945; London: Harrap, 1947); enlarged as *Understanding Drama: Twelve Plays* (New York: Holt, 1948);

The Well Wrought Urn: Studies in the Structure of Poetry (New York: Reynall & Hitchcock, 1947; London: Dobson, 1949);

Modern Rhetoric, with Readings, with Warren (New York: Harcourt, Brace, 1949);

Fundamentals of Good Writing: A Handbook of Modern Rhetoric, with Warren (New York: Harcourt, Brace, 1950; London: Dobson, 1952);

Poems of Mr. John Milton: The 1645 Edition with Essays in Analysis, with John Edward Hardy (New York: Harcourt, Brace, 1951; London: Dobson, 1957);

Literary Criticism: A Short History, with William K. Wimsatt (New York: Knopf, 1957; London: Routledge & Kegan Paul, 1957);

The Hidden God: Studies in Hemingway, Faulkner, Yeats, Eliot, and Warren (New Haven: Yale University Press, 1963);

William Faulkner: The Yopknapatawpha Country (New Haven: Yale University Press, 1963);

A Shaping Joy: Studies in the Writer's Craft (London: Metheun, 1971; New York: Harcourt Brace Jovanovich, 1971);

American Literature: The Makers and the Making, 2 volumes, with R. W. B. Lewis and Warren (New York: St. Martin's Press, 1973);

William Faulkner: Toward Yoknapatawpha and Beyond (New Haven: Yale University Press, 1978);

The Rich Manifold: The Author, the Reader, the Linguistic Medium, edited, with an interview, by Joseph M. Ditta and Ronald S. Librach (Columbia: Missouri Review, 1983);

William Faulkner: First Encounters (New Haven: Yale University Press, 1983);

The Language of the American South (Athens: University of Georgia Press, 1985);

On the Prejudices, Predilections, and Firm Opinions of William Faulkner (Baton Rouge: Louisiana State University Press, 1987);

Historical Evidence and the Reading of Seventeenth-Century Poetry (Columbia: University of Missouri Press, 1991).

OTHER: "The Poem as Organism: Modern Critical Procedure," *English Institute Annual, 1940* (New York: Columbia University Press, 1941): 20–41;

Thomas Percy, *The Percy Letters,* edited by Brooks and David Nichol Smith (volumes 1–5, Baton Rouge: Louisiana State University Press, 1944–1961; volumes 6–10, New Haven: Yale University Press, 1962–1979);

The Correspondence of Thomas Percy and Richard Farmer, edited by Brooks (Baton Rouge: Louisiana State University Press, 1946);

"Metaphor and the Function of Criticism," in *Spiritual Problems in Contemporary Literature,* edited by Stanley Romaine Hopper (New York: Harper, 1952), pp. 127–137;

An Anthology of Stories from the Southern Review, edited by Brooks and Warren (Baton Rouge: Louisiana State University Press, 1953);

Tragic Themes in Western Literature: Seven Essays, edited, with an introduction, by Brooks (New Haven: Yale University Press, 1955);

"Irony as a Principle of Structure," in *Literary Opinion in America: Essays Illustrating the Status, Methods, and Problems of Criticism in the United States in the Twentieth Century,* revised edition, edited by Morton D. Zabel (New York: Harper & Row, 1962), pp. 729–741;

The Correspondence of Thomas Percy and William Shenstone, edited by Brooks (New Haven: Yale University Press, 1977).

SELECTED PERIODICAL PUBLICATIONS –
UNCOLLECTED: "The Christianity of Modernism," *American Review,* 6 (November 1935–March 1936): 435–446; revised as "A Plea to the Protestant Churches," in *Who Owns America?: A New Declaration of Independence,* edited by Herbert Agar and Allen Tate (Boston: Houghton Mifflin, 1936);

"A Note on the Limits of 'History' and the Limits of 'Criticism,'" *Sewanee Review,* 61 (Winter 1953): 129–135;

"The New Criticism," *Sewanee Review,* 87 (Fall 1979): 592–602;

"God, Gallup, and the Episcopalians," *American Scholar,* 50 (Summer 1981): 313–325;

"Literature and Technology" [fourteenth annual Jefferson Lecture], *Wilson Quarterly,* 9 (Autumn 1985): 88–99;

"T. S. Eliot and the American South," *Southern Review,* new series 21 (Autumn 1985): 914–923.

Cleanth Brooks in his early forties (photograph by Cameron King)

Cleanth Brooks was probably the most important literary critic to come to prominence during the second third of the twentieth century. In the generation before him such pioneers as T. S. Eliot, I. A. Richards, and John Crowe Ransom helped fashion a criticism sophisticated enough to explain the radical innovations being wrought in poetry and fiction. (This approach to literary interpretation came to be called the New Criticism simply because Ransom had given that innocuous title to a book he published in 1941.) Brooks applied the methods of this New Criticism not only to the modernist texts for which they were created but also to the entire canon of English poetry from John Donne to William Butler Yeats. In his many critical works, especially *The Well Wrought Urn: Studies in the Structure of Poetry* (1947) and the textbooks he edited with Robert Penn Warren and others, Brooks taught several generations of students how to read literature without prejudice or preconception. In addition to these

achievements, Brooks helped invent the modern literary quarterly and wrote the best book yet on the works of William Faulkner.

Cleanth Brooks, Jr., the son of the Reverend Cleanth Brooks, Sr., and Bessie Lee Witherspoon Brook, was born in Murray, Kentucky, on 16 October 1906. The elder Brooks was a Methodist minister and an early graduate of Vanderbilt University in Nashville, Tennessee. Because Methodist clergy were reassigned to different churches every few years, the family moved eight times during Brooks's childhood and early adolescence. After receiving his early education in the public schools of southern Kentucky and western Tennessee, Brooks enrolled in the privately run McTyeire School in McKenzie, Tennessee, in the fall of 1920. The curriculum at McTyeire consisted of four years each of English, mathematics, and Latin, three of Greek, and one of United States history. The students were also expected to attend chapel and to participate in sports. By the time he left McTyeire for Vanderbilt in 1924, Brooks had had what he regarded as the equivalent of a British "public school" education.

In the years immediately following World War I, a group of young men from Vanderbilt met on alternate Saturday nights to read and discuss their own poetry. These young men later published a magazine called the *Fugitive*. Through their verse and literary criticism, the three most important Fugitives – Ransom, Allen Tate, and Warren – would profoundly influence the course of twentieth-century literature. Although Brooks was not a part of the Fugitive movement, he remembered it as a "campfire still glowing in the distance." He took a course in advanced composition from Ransom and became casual friends with Warren, who was a nineteen-year-old senior during Brooks's freshman year. Brooks also recalled the indirect influence of another Fugitive poet – Donald Davidson. One day in a literature class Brooks heard a now-forgotten graduate student read an essay that Davidson had written on a story by Rudyard Kipling. It was at that moment that Brooks first realized the value of close reading as a critical technique.

Brooks earned his B.A. from Vanderbilt in the spring of 1928 and entered graduate school at Tulane University in New Orleans that fall. (By this time his father had already transferred to the Louisiana Conference of the southern Methodist Church.) At Tulane there was less creative activity than at Vanderbilt and almost no interest in the "interior life of the poem." Nevertheless, Brooks continued to write verse and to ask the sort of critical questions that the old historical scholarship could not answer. During his year at Tulane, he earned an M.A. in English and entered the competition for a Rhodes scholarship. It was also during this year that he met his future wife, Edith Amy Blanchard, who was always called Tinkum (after Tinkum Tidy, a character in a local comic strip). When he won a Rhodes scholarship and set sail for England in the fall of 1929, it was with the understanding that Tinkum would be waiting for him when he got back.

At Oxford, Brooks was reunited with his old Vanderbilt friend Warren, who was in the final year of his own Rhodes scholarship when Brooks arrived. Although he was still committed to writing poetry, Brooks also became more interested in criticism and scholarship during his three years at Oxford. At this time, a young Cambridge don named I. A. Richards was revolutionizing the teaching of literature by asking his students to evaluate poems without the benefit of historical and biographical information. Richards's belief in an inclusive poetry, which balanced and reconciled conflicting impulses in the reader's mind, seemed to be just the sort of approach demanded by the verse of Eliot and Yeats. While Brooks was assimilating the influence of

Richards, he was also doing historical research on the letters of Bishop Thomas Percy. In collaboration with his mentor at Oxford, David Nichol Smith, Brooks became general editor of Percy's correspondence.

When Brooks completed his B.Litt. degree at Oxford in 1932, the United States was in the depth of an economic depression, and academic jobs were particularly scarce. Nevertheless, Huey Long, the political dictator of Louisiana, was pouring vast sums of money into Louisiana State University. Also, Charles W. Pipkin, chairman of the committee that had awarded Brooks his Rhodes scholarship, was dean of the graduate school at LSU. In 1932 Brooks was hired as a lecturer in the Louisiana State University English department. Then, on 12 September 1934, his long-delayed marriage to Tinkum finally took place. By that time, Cleanth, Sr., who had suffered a paralytic stroke and had no disability insurance, was living with his son. With an annual salary of $2,250, Brooks was the sole support for a wife, two aging parents, and a cousin whom Brooks's parents had adopted in infancy. By the mid 1930s Brooks was teaching a full load of courses, writing a book on the English origins of the southern dialect, and helping edit the *Southwest Review,* a joint venture of LSU and Southern Methodist University. He was assisted in this last project by his old friend Warren, who had been hired by the LSU English department in the fall of 1934.

In 1935 Brooks published his first book, *The Relation of the Alabama-Georgia Dialect to the Provincial Dialects of Great Britain.* (Four years later, this book would be used by the dialect coach for the film version of Margaret Mitchell's *Gone With the Wind.*) Even more important, 1935 was the year that LSU relinquished its role in publishing the *Southwest Review* and launched its own literary quarterly, the *Southern Review.* This magazine, as shaped by its managing editors Brooks and Warren, virtually defined the literary review as a highbrow periodical publishing fiction, poetry, and criticism for the intelligent general reader. During its seven years of existence, the original series of the *Southern Review* was the best magazine of its kind and the standard against which all similar publications would be measured.

More than any other single phenomenon, the *Southern Review* brought southern literature to the attention of a national and even international audience. It also brought national and international writers to the attention of southern readers. In addition to writings by Eudora Welty, Peter Taylor, Katherine Anne Porter, and various Fugitive poets, the

Southern Review published work by Ford Madox Ford, Aldous Huxley, Kenneth Burke, Sidney Hook, Delmore Schwartz, I. F. Stone, F. O. Matthiessen, Mary McCarthy, Nelson Algren, James T. Farrell, John Dewey, Philip Rahv, and scores of other luminaries whom one would never think to associate with southern culture. As one observer noted in 1940, the center of literary criticism in the Western world had moved "from the left bank of the Seine to the left bank of the Mississippi."

If Brooks arrived at Vanderbilt too late to be part of the Fugitive movement, he also missed participating in *I'll Take My Stand,* a collection of essays published in 1930 by twelve southerners, who defended the agrarian tradition of the Old South against the threats of industrialism and cultural assimilation. (Since Ransom, Tate, Warren, and Davidson were among the contributors to *I'll Take My Stand,* literary historians have tended to link the Fugitive and Agrarian movements.) By the mid 1930s Brooks had also become an articulate defender of the Agrarian faith. In 1936 he contributed to *Who Owns America?,* a collection of social and economic essays by cultural traditionalists from both the United States and Great Britain. (The British contributors, G. K. Chesterton and Hilaire Belloc, were leaders of a movement of conservative Roman Catholics who called themselve Distributists.) This volume, which was edited by Tate and the Kentucky journalist Hebert Agar, advocated a more equitable distribution of land and widespread decentralization of economic power.

Brooks's contribution to *Who Owns America?* dealt not with politics or economics but with religion. Entitled "A Plea to the Protestant Churches," his essay warned that liberal Protestantism was abandoning a transcendent supernatural faith for a rather tepid brand of secular humanism. In an attempt to be relevant to the modern world, liberal Protestantism has made the fatal mistake of choosing science as its epistemological model. Brooks believed that religion, properly understood, had more in common with art than with science. By art he means "a description of experience which is concrete where that of science is abstract, many-sided where that of science is necessarily one-sided, and which involves the whole personality where science involves only one part, the intellect." His essay then goes on to make a crucial distinction. "Religion is obviously more than art. A religion is anchored to certain supreme values which it affirms are eternal, not merely to be accepted for the moment through a 'willing suspension of disbelief.'" Unfortunately,

liberal Protestantism had not even reached the level of aestheticism, much less passed beyond it.

At the same time that they were editing the *Southern Review* and pursuing their own writing projects, Brooks and Warren were trying to teach the intricacies of literature to ill-prepared students at a land-grant university in the Deep South. They soon realized that the textbooks they were using were of little help in accomplishing this task. At the urging of their department head, William A. Read, they prepared a thirty-page mimeographed booklet on metrics and imagery. This class handout was first used by Brooks, Warren, and a graduate student named John T. Purser in the spring semester of 1935. By the fall of 1936 the three had published a critical anthology of poetry, fiction, drama, and expository prose under the title *An Approach to Literature.* (Detractors began referring to it as "The *Reproach* to Literature.") In 1975 (nearly forty years after its original publication) the book went into its fifth edition.

In 1938 Brooks and Warren published an even more influential textbook called *Understanding Poetry.* Although they would have preferred the more modest title *Reading Poems,* the phrase "understanding poetry" is a perfect statement of the book's purpose. Its end is critical understanding rather than vague appreciation. And the object of that understanding is poetry, not literary history or biography. After a ten-page "Letter to the Teacher" and a twenty-five-page introduction, the text is divided into seven sections of poems, each preceded by an editorial foreword. (There is also an afterword following the second section, as well as three "notes" of several pages each in section 4.) The distinctive feature of this approach is that the divisions are made according to literary, rather than historical or geographical, considerations. The categories are narrative, implied narrative, objective description, metrics, tone and attitude, imagery, and theme. The main body of the book contains critical discussions of thirty-seven poems and the texts of over two hundred others (many of which are accompanied by exercises). This is followed by a twenty-three-page glossary, heavily emphasizing matters of technique.

In their introduction Brooks and Warren try to define poetry. They begin by comparing it with other kinds of discourse that students (and, indeed, all human beings) habitually use. Unlike technical language, poetry does not give an objective description of facts but expresses an attitude about experience. Thus, in its function it resembles ordinary human speech far more than technical discourse does. As Brooks and Warren point out, "it is highly important to see that both the impulse and methods of poetry are rooted very deep in human experience, and the formal poetry itself represents, not a distinction from but a specialization of, thoroughly universal habits of human thinking and feeling."

One might easily come away from this introduction thinking of poetry as language skillfully used to express an attitude about experience. That, of course, is more nearly a definition of rhetoric than of poetry. In a sense Brooks and Warren see poetry as a kind of rhetoric – one based on dramatic tension rather than on didactic assertion or appeals to pathos (although both of these latter elements appear in many good poems). As Brooks would do often in his subsequent writing, he and Warren make the analogy between a poem and a drama. "[E]very poem," they write, "implies a speaker of the poem, either the poet writing in his own person or someone into whose mouth the poem is put, and . . . the poem represents the reaction of such a person to a situation, a scene, or an idea."

Brooks's first major critical book, *Modern Poetry and the Tradition,* was published by the University of North Carolina Press in 1939. Here, Brooks essentially accepts Eliot's notion that English poetry took a wrong turn at the end of the seventeenth century and that the modernists – under the influence of the French Symbolists – have begun to bring it back. Brooks argues that the eighteenth and nineteenth centuries developed certain aesthetic assumptions that the metaphysical poets did not hold and that the modern poets have rejected. Perhaps the most important of these assumptions is that there is an inherently poetic subject matter. Brooks traces this belief back to Thomas Hobbes's view that the poet is a mere copyist, not a maker. If it is the poet's function simply to hold the mirror up to nature, he can please his audience most by holding that mirror up to pleasant objects.

Another shared assumption of the eighteenth and nineteenth centuries was that intellect was somehow antagonistic to the poetic faculty. Despite superficial differences between the neoclassic and Romantic critics, both saw metaphysical wit as a trivialization of the deep emotion and high seriousness of poetry. Better to whisper sweet nothings into the ear of one's beloved than tax her mind with ingenious metaphors and conceits. Better to worship God in utter simplicity than to write religious poems with puns in them. In opposition to this prejudice, the best critical minds of the seventeenth and twentieth centuries are of one accord. Like Richards, Brooks believes in a poetry that can accommodate a wide range of human experience – a poetry of inclusion, not of exclusion.

Although Brooks more fully discusses his conception of poetry in *The Well Wrought Urn,* it should be clear already that he regards metaphor as being the very essence of a poem. (Here he differs with Housman and others who see it as simply a figure of speech used to dress up a prose statement.) Above all others, Brooks contends, "the metaphysical poets reveal the essentially functional character of all metaphor. We cannot remove the comparisons from their poems, as we might remove ornaments or illustrations attached to a statement, without demolishing the poems. The comparison *is* the poem in a structural sense." What makes the metaphysical conceit different from the sentimental metaphor (other than its superior inclusiveness) is its effect on the reader. The sentimental metaphor may seem apt on first reading; however, closer acquaintance will reveal the disparities that the poet has been unwilling to acknowledge. Hence, it does not wear well. Because the metaphysical poet has acknowledged the disparities from the outset, has actually built his poem around them, his metaphor usually seems more apt with successive rereadings. Or as Brooks puts the matter, "If it does not explode with a first reading, it is extremely durable."

The common view of literary history at the time that Brooks wrote *Modern Poetry and the Tradition* was that the Romantics had effected a literary revolution by breaking with the neoclassic concept of decorum prevalent in the eighteenth century and that the modernist poets of the early twentieth century had taken that revolution several steps farther. Following Eliot's lead, Brooks disputes this view. For one thing, he sees the Romantic revolt as being a bogus revolution. "[T]he Romantic poets, in attacking the neoclassic conception of the poetic, tended to offer new poetic objects rather than to discard altogether the conception of a special poetic material." In their failure to be sufficiently revolutionary, the Romantics simply perpetuated the dissociation of sensibility that Eliot believes infected most English poetry from the late seventeenth century on. At its worst this led to the twin sins of didacticism and sentimentality, both of which were carried to ridiculous extremes during the Victorian era. The modern poets approved of by Brooks and Eliot were not extending the Romantic revolution so much as reversing the dissociation of sensibility, to which the Romantics were just as prone as their neoclassic predecessors and Victorian heirs. These "moderns" are actually counterrevolutionaries or neometaphysicals.

Although Brooks would later modify some of the judgments expressed in this book, one that has

2

But there are some misapprehensions to be avoided at the outset. We
~~This last statement, however, may strike one as odd, for we~~
tend to associate Donne with the self-conscious and witty figure--
his comparison of the souls of the lovers to the two legs of the compass is the obvious example. ~~Yet, because the typical reader takes
the compass comparison as Donne's norm, he may well feel like asking
why our experience with Donne may tell us anything about the
difficulties of Shakespeare.~~ Shakespeare's extended figures are ~~not~~
elaborated in another ~~this~~ fashion. They are, we are inclined to feel, spontaneous comparisons struck
out in the heat of composition, and not carefully articulated, self-
conscious conceits at all. Indeed, for the average reader the connection between spontaneity and seriously imaginative poetry is so
strong that he will probably reject as preposterous any account
of Shakespeare's poetry which sees any elaborate pattern in the
imagery. He will reject it because to accept it means for him the
assumption that the writer was not a fervent poet but a preternaturally
cold and self-conscious monster.

~~One sympathizes with such a reaction.~~ Poems are certainly not made by
formula and blue-print. One ~~should~~ rightly holds/suspect a critical
interpretation that implies that they are. Shakespeare, we may be
sure, was no such monster of calculation. But neither, for that
matter, was Donne. Even in Donne's poetry, the elaborated and
logically developed comparisons are outnumbered by the abrupt and
succinct comparisons-- by what T. S. Eliot has called the"telescoped
conceits." Moreover, the extended comparisons themselves are
frequently knit together in the sudden and apparently uncalculated
fashion of the telescoped images; and if one examines the way in
which the famous compass comparison is related to the rest of the
poem in which it occurs, he may feel that even this elaborately
"logical" figure was probably the result of a happy accident.

~~See the Appendix, p.~~

Corrected typescript for an essay from Brooks's The Well Wrought Urn *(YCAL MSS 30, Series II, Box 52, Beinecke Rare Book and Manuscript Library, Yale University)* clearly stood the test of time is his remarkably perceptive reading of *The Waste Land* (1922). So much has been written about that poem since 1939 that it is easy to forget how incompletely it had been understood before Brooks came along. The explication he gives of the poem is as lucid as any beginning student could possibly want. Brooks utilizes 80 percent of the chapter he devotes to *The Waste Land* to accomplish this. The final pages of that chapter, however, are of immeasurably greater importance. Here, Brooks argues for a startlingly revisionist interpretation of the poem. To read *The Waste Land* as a statement of despair or unbelief, he contends, is to stay far too close to the surface of this supremely ironic text. Instead *The Waste Land* is at least an inchoate affirmation of Christian faith. Making this point, Brooks writes:

> Eliot's theme is not the statement of a faith held and agreed upon (Dante's *Divine Comedy*) nor is it the projection of a "new" system of beliefs (Spenser's *Faerie Queene*). Eliot's theme is the rehabilitation of a system of beliefs, known but now discredited. . . . To put the matter in still other terms: the Christian terminology is for the poet a mass of cliches. However "true" he may feel the terms to be, he is still sensitive to the fact that they operate superficially as cliches, and his method of necessity must be a process of bringing them to life again. The method adopted in *The Waste Land* is thus violent and radical, but thoroughly necessary.

Brooks's discussion of Eliot is followed by a chapter on Yeats as myth maker. Here again, Brooks makes the work of a difficult modern poet understandable without compromising its complexity. Because of his aversion to the modern industrial world, Yeats is a kindred spirit of the Agrarians. And like the southern formalists, he believes that the poetic imagination can divine truths that are inaccessible to science. " 'I am,' Yeats tells us, 'very religious, and deprived by Huxley and Tindall. . . . of the simple-minded religion of my childhood, I had made a new religion, almost an infallible church of poetic tradition, of a fardel of stories, and of personages, and of emotions, inseparable from their first expression, passed on from generation to generation by poets and painters with some help from philosophers and theologians.' "

Modern Poetry and the Tradition concludes by returning to the dissociation of sensibility as the key issue in English literary history. Brooks argues, for example, that Hobbes is responsible not only for the wrong turn that poetry took at the end of the seventeenth century but also for the death of tragedy on the English stage. By emphasizing paradigmatic simplicity, the scientific worldview of Hobbes robbed poetry of the dialectical tension that made metaphysical verse so rich. That same tension, Brooks argues, is essential to tragedy. In order to appreciate tragedy we must be able simultaneously to admire and judge the tragic hero. The Elizabethans could do this (just as they could admire and judge dashing rogues). The heroic drama of the Restoration, however, more nearly resembles melodrama. When character is purged of ambiguity, pathos is still possible, but tragedy is not.

If tragedy fared so badly after the Elizabethan era, one might ask why comedy remained so healthy well into the eighteenth century. More to the point, could wit really have been purged from literature when the appeal of the great Restoration comedies lay in little else? Brooks responds to this objection by distinguishing between the ironic wit that is characteristic of tragedy and the satiric wit that sustains comedy. Tragedy "represents something of a tension between unsympathetic laughter and sympathetic pity — between the impulse to condemn the protagonist and the impulse to feel pity for him." Perhaps the last significant character in seventeenth-century literature to exhibit tragic tension was John Milton's Satan. The Puritan in Milton condemned the Prince of Darkness, while the rebel secretly admired him. Although such an attitude raises logical and theological problems, it is the very essence of the tragic imagination. The epistemological simplification introduced by Hobbes could accommodate a criticism of others but not the criticism of self authored by a truly introspective wit. Yeats said that we make rhetoric out of our arguments with others and poetry out of our arguments with ourselves. By this definition the writing of true poetry became much more difficult after the dissociation of sensibility.

Even as Brooks was earning recognition in the larger academic world, he found his position at LSU to be increasingly embattled. After the assassination of Long and the imprisonment of several of his subordinates for graft and corruption, power in both the state government and the university changed hands. The new president of LSU, Gen. Campbell B. Hodges, was a former commandant at West Point who brought an authoritarian approach to his new position. While he was scrupulously honest, Hodges also supressed much of the creative and intellectual activity at LSU. In what was ostensibly a wartime austerity measure, he suspended the *Southern Review* in 1942. (Many observers believed that this action was, at least in part, an attempt to punish Brooks for his role as a faculty dissident.) Shortly after the suspension of the review, Warren left LSU for a postiion at the University of Minnesota. Over the next five years Brooks himself was wooed by some of the most prestigious schools in the nation. In 1947 he accepted an offer from Yale University.

In March 1947, while Brooks was preparing to make the transition from LSU to Yale, Reynal and Hitchcock published his second major collection of critical essays. If Brooks's reputation as a critic can be said to rest on a single book, that book is *The Well Wrought Urn*. Although this volume includes some lively and trenchant observations on critical theory, Brooks is primarily concerned with offering new readings of ten of the most admired poems in English literature – Donne's "The Canonization," William Shakespeare's *Macbeth,* Milton's "L'Allegro" and "Il Penseroso," Robert Herrick's "Corinna's going a-Maying," Alexander Pope's "The Rape of the Lock," Thomas Gray's "Elegy in a Country Churchyard," William Wordsworth's "Intimations of Immortality," John Keats's "Ode on a Grecian Urn," Alfred Tennyson's "Tears, Idle Tears," and Yeats's "Among School Children." As a look at three representative chapters of this book indicates, Brooks hoped to identify those qualities shared by the great poetry of all ages.

One of the qualities that has enabled *The Well Wrought Urn* to endure when other seasonal classics have fallen by the wayside is the ease with which the book moves between general theory and specific practice. Brooks's critical principles inform his readings, and his readings illuminate his principles. This symbiosis is evident as early as the first chapter, where Brooks illustrates his concept of poetic language by referring to important poems by Wordsworth, Pope, and Gray before reaching back in time to Donne. Brooks's basic assumption (boldly announced in the title of his first chapter) is that poetic language is "The Language of Paradox." He tells us that "it is a language in which the connotations play as great a part as the denotations. And I do not mean that the connotations are important as supplying some sort of frill or trimming, something external to the real matter in hand. I mean that the poet does not use a notation at all – as the scientist may properly be said to do so. The poet, within limits, has to make up his language as he goes." Whereas the scientist (really the technologist) is constantly purging his language of ambiguity, the poet thrives on ambiguity because it allows him to approximate more closely the rich texture of actual experience.

The title *The Well Wrought Urn* is itself remarkably suggestive and ambiguous. Brooks's reference is to the penultimate stanza of "The Canonization," where the speaker argues that the love he shares

with his woman, although it be of no great moment in worldly terms, can serve as an example and inspiration to future lovers (just as the humble lives of saints can be a source of religious inspiration): "We'll build in sonnets pretty roomes; / As well a well wrought urn becomes / The greatest ashes, as half-acre tombes. . . ." "The poem," Brooks writes, "is an instance of the doctrine which it asserts; it is both the assertion and the realization of the assertion. The poet has actually built within the song the 'pretty room' with which he says the lovers can be content. The poem itself is the well-wrought urn which can hold the lovers' ashes and which will not suffer in comparison with the prince's 'half-acre tomb.' "

In order to demonstrate that paradox is the universal language of poetry, Brooks must discuss a representative selection of poems that are widely admired but generally thought to be free of paradox. The first of his texts to fall clearly into this category is Herrick's "Corinna's going a-Maying." By examining the complex attitude that the speaker of this poem takes toward the carpe diem theme (whether or not this was the biographically known attitude of Parson Herrick), Brooks questions whether any true poem can ever be reduced to its paraphrasable prose content.

Brooks titles his chapter on "Corinna's going a-Maying" "What Does Poetry Communicate?" and answers that question by asserting, "The poem communicates so much and communicates it so richly and with such delicate qualifications that the thing communicated is mauled and distorted if we attempt to convey it by any vehicle less subtle than that of the poem itself." Taken too literally, that statement could mean that criticism is virtually impossible. If any critical analysis less subtle than the poem itself is inadequate, only the most discriminating minds are capable of criticism. And that criticism necessarily will be expressed in a prose that is different from the language of poetry. Faced with such a challenge, the prospective critic might well throw up his hands, read the poem verbatim, and say, "*That* is what it communicates." Brooks does not go that far; however, he realizes that any critical theory that would reduce a poem to its prose paraphrase is incapable of answering the exasperated sophomore who asks, "Then, why didn't the poet just come out and say what he meant?"

Brooks's best known and most admired essay in *The Well Wrought Urn* is probably his discussion of Keats's "Ode on a Grecian Urn." Keats may not be as witty as Donne or as densely allusive as Eliot, but his originality of metaphor and sensuousness of imagery set him apart from all other Romantics. And the "Ode on a Grecian Urn" is generally regarded as one of his best poems. But this wonderfully concrete artifact ends with an apparently sententious bit of philosophizing that even Keats's greatest admirers have found hard to defend. If the concluding equation of beauty and truth is inconsistent with the rest of Keats's poem, then it is an affront to logic. If it is not inconsistent, one suspects that it is probably superfluous. Brooks manages to resolve this dilemma by taking seriously Keats's metaphor of the urn as a dramatic speaker. He asks if we might not read "Ode on a Grecian Urn" in such a way that the statement "Beauty is truth, truth beauty" rises as naturally from the dramatic context of the poem as Lear's statement "Ripeness is all" does from the conflicts of Shakespeare's play.

Perhaps a more fundamental problem with the last two lines of the poem is determining what they might mean at a prose level. If the idea itself is merely gibberish, then its appropriateness to the poem becomes irrelevant – unless, of course, one wants to argue that Keats was deliberately writing nonsense verse (inviting a comparison not to *King Lear* but to Edward Lear). Brooks indicates the dilemma as follows: "One can emphasize *beauty* is truth and throw Keats into the pure-art camp, the usual procedure. But it is only fair to point out that one could stress *truth* is beauty, and argue with the Marxist critics of the 'thirties for a propaganda art. The very ambiguity of the statement 'Beauty is truth, truth beauty' ought to warn us against insisting very much on the statement in isolation, and to drive us back to a consideration of the context in which the statement is set." Not surprisingly, Brooks discovers that rather than forcing us to accept either "conflicting" reading of the poem, this procedure allows us to synthesize both readings at a higher level of ambiguity.

The "message" that one gleans from examining the urn is riddled with paradox. Keats calls the urn a "sylvan historian"; however, Brooks reminds us in the title of his essay that the history in question is "without footnotes." The specificity of conventional historical accounts is absent from the scenes depicted on the urn. What we have is no facsimile representation of actual events but an unchanging paradigm of the richness of life – what Keats calls a "cold pastoral." "The sylvan historian," Brooks notes, " . . . takes a few details and so orders them that we have not only beauty but insight into essential truth. Its history . . . has the validity of myth – not myth as a pretty but irrelevant make-believe, an idle fancy, but myth as a valid perception into reality."

Truth for Keats is something far more general and far more beautiful than mere facts. Or, to put the matter differently, myth is all the history that we know or need to know. If we are sensitive to what the entire poem has been saying (largely in terms of paradox), "we shall be prepared for the enigmatic, final paradox which the silent form utters." Thus, our response to those closing lines is a way of testing whether we have been reading the poem correctly. Had Keats simply meant that beauty is truth and written his "Ode on a Grecian Urn" as a declaration of pure aestheticism, the poem would have been much less complex and its concluding statement of theme clearly beside the point. (That that theme is so often simplistically misread indicates how a reader's preconceptions can distort his understanding.) However, by stating the theme as a paradox that cannot be adequately understood except in terms of the entire poem, Keats refuses to allow the careful reader a too-facile understanding of that theme.

Despite the great influence that the New Criticism enjoyed among students and scholars alike, it did not meet with universal approbation. Brooks and company encountered considerable resistance from old historicists, who argued that the New Critics paid too little attention to external evidence in their pursuit of exegetical ingenuity. A case in point is Douglas Bush's attack on Brooks's reading of Marvell's "Horatian Ode." The poem in question was written by Marvell as a celebration of Oliver Cromwell's rise to power and his triumphant return from Ireland. In his essay Brooks attempts to determine what Marvell's poem actually says about Cromwell as opposed to what purely historical evidence might indicate the poet personally thought about the British lord protector. Providing a characteristically close reading of Marvell's poem, Brooks tries to indicate the ambiguity and complexity of the poetic speaker's attitude toward Cromwell.

Unconvinced by Brooks's analysis, Bush questions him on his interpretation of several specific lines. Bush believes that Marvell's opinion of Cromwell was one of unambiguous admiration. The purpose of Brooks's elaborate discriminations, he argues, is simply to educe a needlessly complex reading from a relatively straightforward poetic statement, in effect "to turn a seventeenth-century liberal into a modern one." "This is one reason," Bush concludes, "why historical conditioning has a corrective as well as a positive value."

The problem with Bush's position is that Brooks clearly did do his historical homework before approaching the text of the "Horatian Ode." He simply came to different conclusions from the same evidence. With his continuing work on the Percy letters and his immense scholarly curiosity, Brooks was never simplistically antihistorical. He simply wanted to go beyond what history can tell us about the meaning and merit of a work of literature. As his old friend and colleague Robert Bechtold Heilman put it, "For such a person [as Brooks] to say that history is not all is a rather different thing from an ignorant B.A.'s thinking that history is nothing." It is perhaps significant that the last book Brooks published in his life was entitled *Historical Evidence and the Reading of Seventeenth-Century Poetry* (1991). Among the essays contained in that volume was a revised version of his discussion of Marvell's "Horatian Ode."

Another line of attack on the New Criticism came from democratic nativists such as Archibald MacLeish, Van Wyck Brooks, Alfred Kazin, and Howard Mumford Jones. With varying degrees of sophistication, these socially engaged men of letters accused the New Critics of a precious aestheticism. MacLeish regarded such a stance as morally irresponsible when democracy was fighting for its very survival during World War II. Van Wyck Brooks believed that all of literary modernism represents a break with the vital and progressive spirit of the late nineteenth century. Kazin saw southern formalism (no less than militant Stalinism) as an attack on the liberal democratic ethos of American culture, while Jones urged his fellow countrymen to reject the Anglophile Eliot and the gothic Faulkner in favor of the native optimism of Henry Wadsworth Longfellow and Louisa May Alcott.

Perhaps the most strident attack on the politics of the New Criticism occurred when the Fellows of the Library of Congress, a group heavily stacked with aesthetic formalists, bestowed the 1948 Bollingen Prize for poetry on Ezra Pound's *The Pisan Cantos* (1948). In articles published in two successive issues of the *Saturday Review of Literature,* Robert Hillyer questioned whether an agency of the U.S. government should honor a Fascist collaborator such as Pound and a scurrilously antidemocratic poem such as *The Pisan Cantos.* Not content to attack Pound alone, Hillyer strongly implied that all literary modernists and their New Critical allies were traitors to democratic culture.

Just as he had defended his position against the attacks of historical scholars such as Bush, Brooks rose to the challenge posed by the democratic nativists. In a lecture delivered at the Jewish Theological Seminary in the winter of 1949, he argued that his opponents were begging an important question when they divided the literary world between the moralistic and the amoral. Many of the New Critics (Brooks and Eliot among them) still subscribed to an orthodox religious faith. Having weathered the assaults on religion made by Charles Darwin, Karl Marx, and Sigmund Freud, they saw no need to transform literature into a secular faith. (In the 1950s Brooks would argue that archetypal critics such as Leslie Fiedler and Northrop Frye came close to doing precisely that.) Behind the impulse to make literature into something more than religion (or less than politics) was the well-intentioned but misguided figure of Matthew Arnold. To adopt the Arnoldian position, Brooks argued in the Winter 1953 issue of the *Sewanee Review,* was to do a disservice to both God and art. "[T]hough poetry has a very important role in any culture," he writes, "to ask that poetry save us is to impose on poetry a burden it cannot sustain. The danger is that we shall merely get an ersatz religion and an ersatz poetry."

Although Brooks and Warren were separated for a third time in their careers when Warren left LSU for the University of Minnesota in 1942, their friendship and collaboration continued. In 1943 they published *Understanding Fiction,* a companion volume to *Understanding Poetry,* and in 1949 a composition textbook entitled *Modern Rhetoric.* (In 1945 Brooks and Heilman had published *Understanding Drama.*) In addition to earning substantial royalties, these books helped to establish the New Criticism as the dominant pedagogical method in college classrooms for more than a generation. The team of Brooks and Warren was once again complete when Warren joined the Yale faculty in 1950.

Early in their stay at Yale, Cleanth and Tinkum Brooks resolved that when the opportunity presented itself, they would move out into the country, preferably into a house with some history and character. The right house, they concluded, was a structure built in 1720 on the outskirts of Wallingford, Connecticut, northwest of New Haven. Although they fell in love with the house, they were far from enamored of the location. Railroad tracks ran practically through the front yard, and the adjoining lots belonged to other people, who might well build on them. Over a year's time, the Brookses had a contractor move the house from Wallingford to some isolated property in the country village of Northford, about ten miles north of New Haven. Cleanth and Tinkum substantially redesigned the old house and later constructed a separate building on the same property. This addition contained a study, a garage, and a sizable attic. Brooks figured that it took the entire decade of the 1950s to do everything that he and Tinkum wanted done to the house.

When Brooks came to Yale in 1947, the English department had long been a bastion of historical scholarship. (The legendary eighteenth-century specialist Chauncey Brewster Tinker had brought the James Boswell papers to campus and had determined the direction of the English program for half a century.) Nevertheless, younger professors, such as Maynard Mack and Louis Martz, were far more sympathetic to the innovations of Brooks and Warren. Another strong advocate of the New Criticism was the European scholar Rene Wellek, who had come to Yale to start a program in comparative literature. Finally, Brooks's younger colleague William K. Wimsatt became one of the most articulate theoreticians the new movement would ever produce. In 1957 he and Brooks published their monumental study *Literary Criticism: A Short History*. This was the same year that Northrop Frye's *The Anatomy of Criticism* posed the most substantial challenge the New Criticism had faced since its rise to prominence twenty years earlier.

At a time when the close reading of poetry was falling out of favor among literary trendsetters, Brooks's critical interests became increasingly focused on the fiction of Faulkner. His book *William Faulkner: The Yoknapatawpha Country* (1963) was an attempt to emphasize the traditional and communitarian aspects of Faulkner's vision. Although detractors have accused Brooks of a Proscrustean attempt to turn Faulkner into an honorary Agrarian, the thesis of his book is supported by astute readings of individual novels. This is evident in Brooks's much-anthologized discussion of *Light in August* (1932).

Commenting on what he regards as the most significant unifying theme in *Light in August,* Brooks writes:

One way in which to gauge the importance of the community in this novel is by imagining the action to have taken place in Chicago or Manhattan Island, where the community – at least in Faulkner's sense – does not exist.... The plight of the isolated individual cut off from any community of values is of course a dominant theme of contemporary literature. But by developing this theme in a rural setting in which a powerful sense of community still exists, Faulkner has given us a kind of pastoral – that is he has let us see our modern and complex problems mirrored in a simpler and more primitive world. *Light in August* is, in some respects, a bloody and violent pastoral. The plight of the lost sheep and of the black sheep can be given special point and meaning because there is still visible in the background a recognizable flock with its shepherds, its watchdogs, sometimes fierce and cruel, and its bellwethers.

Brooks makes a similar argument in his essay on Faulkner's first great novel, *The Sound and the Fury* (1929). He argues that the "real significance of the Southern setting" in this novel "resides, as so often elsewhere in Faulkner, in the fact that the breakdown of a family can be exhibited more poignantly and significantly in a society which is old-fashioned and in which the family is still at the center.... [W]hat happens to the Compsons might make less noise and cause less comment, and even bring less pain to the individuals concerned, if the Compsons lived in a more progressive and liberal environment."

If Faulkner's conservative social vision is most often comic, he was capable in his greatest novels of creating truly modern tragedies. Such is the case with *Absalom, Absalom!* (1936). Brooks warns, however, that the reader misconstrues Faulkner's meaning if we read this book as specifically a tragedy of the South. Thomas Sutpen is a completely self-made man, whose character has neither been formed nor constrained by any organic community. Admittedly, he is not a rebel against the community in the sense that Joe Christmas is. He simply tries to establish his identity (which includes his role in society) according to his own private obsessions. In so doing, Thomas Sutpen becomes a victim of his own innocence. "It is," Brooks writes, "par excellence the innocence of modern man, though it has not, to be sure, been confined to modern times. One can find more than a trace of it in Sophocles' Oedipus, and it has its analogies with the brittle rationalism of Macbeth, though Macbeth tried to learn his innocence by an act of the will and proved to be a less than satisfactory pupil. But innocence of this sort can properly be claimed as a special characteristic of modern man, and one can claim further that it flourishes particularly in a secularized society." Perhaps because Sutpen lives in a nonsecularized society, his innocence does not flouish but becomes the cause of his downfall.

The year after *William Faulkner: The Yoknapatawpha Country* was published, Brooks was appointed cultural attaché to the American embassy in London. Surely his most memorable assignment there was to represent the United States government at the memorial service for Eliot in Westminster Abbey in February 1965. During his two years in England, Brooks delivered over 140 lectures throughout Great Britain and the European continent. Several of these were later published in his collection of essays *A Shaping Joy,* which appeared in 1971. The experience in England enabled Brooks to renew contacts with friends from his days at Oxford. In fact his old tutor Nevill Coghill invited him to deliver a lecture at a performance of *Doctor Faustus,* which was to star Coghill's former student Richard Burton and Burton's new wife, Elizabeth Taylor. This production was delayed when the Burtons were summoned to Hollywood for the filming of *Who's Afraid of Virginia Woolf?* (1966). By the time they returned to Oxford, Brooks was already back at Yale.

During the time that Brooks served at the embassy in London, profound changes had taken place in American society. Within the university old-fashioned humanists were frequently vilified as reactionaries. If the New Criticism had once been a radical innovation in literary theory, it was now an embattled orthodoxy. Social activists, reminiscent of the spirit if not the ideology of an earlier generation of democratic nativists, denounced the "bourgeois aestheticism" of those who valued textual autonomy. At the same time, intentionalists such as E. D. Hirsch were championing the primacy of the author, while reader-response critics such as Stanley Fish were asserting the supremacy of the reader. (Both of these men had studied with the New Critics at Yale, Fish having served as a grader for Brooks.) Finally, all forms of traditional literary study were challenged by the cognitive relativism of deconstruction. Ironically, the American center of this new movement was Yale University. By the time that Brooks retired in 1974, Paul de Man, J. Hillis Miller, Geoffrey Hartman, and Harold Bloom had given the term "Yale critic" a far different meaning than it had had in the heyday of Brooks, Warren, Wimsatt, and Wellek.

If Brooks's criticism had become unfashionable in the literary salons of the Northeast, his stature remained high in his native South. During his final years at Yale and for a decade after his retirement, Brooks was guest professor at several southern universities. From 1969 to 1984, he taught on two separate occasions at LSU, the University of Tennessee, and the University of North Carolina, and once each at Tulane University and Millsaps College in Jackson, Mississippi. He also held research fellowships at the University of South Carolina and at the Humanities Center in Research Triangle Park, North Carolina. At the same time, he continued to be a regular contributor to southern magazines, such as the *Sewanee Review* and the *Southern Review,* the latter of which had been resurrected

by LSU in 1965. Although the Brookses never moved back to the South, they regularly attended the annual meeting of the South Atlantic Modern Language Association and formed many close friendships with southern writers and scholars.

Although *William Faulkner: The Yoknapatawpha Country* is Brooks's best-known and most distinguished work on Southern literature, it represented only the beginning of a renewed engagement with the writing of his native region. In 1978 he published *William Faulkner: Toward Yoknapatawpha and Beyond,* a study of Faulkner's writings set outside of his mythic postage stamp of soil. This was followed in 1983 by *William Faulkner: First Encounters,* a collection of introductory essays designed for the beginning student. Finally, in 1987, Brooks published a miscellaneous collection of lectures and discussions titled *On the Prejudices, Predilections, and Firm Opinions of William Faulkner.* Brooks's bibliography also includes a sizable number of uncollected essays on other southern writers.

In April 1984 Cleanth Brooks became the twenty-eighth distinguished scholar to deliver the Dorothy Blount Lamar lectures in southern culture at Mercer University in Macon, Georgia. For his subject he returned to the topic of his first book, the English origins of the southern language. Less technical than that earlier dialect study, these discussions were addressed to a general audience. Nevertheless, Brooks's conclusions had the professional imprimatur of the highly respected linguist Raven McDavid. In 1985, the Lamar lectures were published as *The Language of the American South,* exactly fifty years after Brooks's first book on the southern dialect.

Among the highlights of Brooks's career in the 1980s were two other significant speaking engagements – the Paul Anthony Brick lectures at the University of Missouri, in April 1982, and the Jefferson lecture in Washington, D.C., in May 1985. In the Brick lectures Brooks defended his approach to criticism against some of the recent attacks to which it had been subjected. Specifically, he reasserted his belief in the primacy of the text against those approaches that would privilege the author, the reader, or the linguistic medium. (Bloom, Fish, and Susan Sontag were among the contemporary theorists he challenged.) Not since the appendices to *The Well Wrought Urn* had Brooks so ably validated Wellek's description of him as a "critic of critics." In contrast Brooks's Jefferson Lecture was a more general defense of the humanities in an age of technology. This annual lecture program had been initiated by the National Endowment for the Humanities in

Brooks, right, with Robert Penn Warren

the early 1970s. The thirteen lecturers prior to Brooks had included Sidney Hook, Barbara Tuchman, Edward Shils, C. Vann Woodward, Saul Bellow, John Hope Franklin, Erik Erikson, Lionel Trilling, and Warren.

In fall 1985 Brooks and Warren were invited back to LSU for a program commemorating the fiftieth anniversary of the founding of the *Southern Review*. For three days in October, a host of prominent writers and critics discussed the role of southern letters within the larger modernist movement. The young filmmaker Ken Burns helped recreate the ambience of 1935 by screening his documentary film on Huey Long. The university and the surrounding community celebrated twenty years of the new *Southern Review*. But the real purpose of the conference was to honor the two men who, in launching the original series of the magazine, had brought the South into modern literature and modern literature into the South. Two years later Brooks made his last significant contribution to southern culture by helping to found the Fellowship of Southern Writers. Since 1987 this organization has enabled a select group of creative writers (along with a few editors and historians) to assert their identity as southerners, while encouraging new literary talent in the region. Brooks was the group's first chancellor.

Although Brooks maintained his professional activities until he was literally on his deathbed, advancing age brought changes to his personal life. In 1981 he and his wife sold their remote country home at Northford and moved back into New Haven. Then, in May 1986, Tinkum Brooks was diagnosed with terminal lung cancer. Over the course of the summer and early fall, she died as she had lived – with fortitude and dignity. She passed away in New Haven on the first of October and was buried in Roselawn Cemetery in Baton Rouge. Despite intense grief for his wife of fifty-two years, Brooks proved himself to be a stoic and resourceful survivor. Although nearly blind, he continued to write and lecture and to travel to various parts of the world. When a cataract operation in the late 1980s restored much of his vision, he picked up the pace of his professional activities and seemed to be more vigorous and spirited than ever. At the same time, many of his contemporaries were gone. After a four-year bout with cancer, Brooks's lifelong friend and collaborator Warren died in September 1989.

The end came for Brooks himself in the spring of 1994. The previous year, he had made a large bequest to Yale University. He was at work on several projects, including a collection of essays for the University of Missouri Press. Throughout academia a backlash seemed to be forming against the fashionable critical theories and tendentious moralizing that had recently dominated literary studies. If Brooks had not actually been vindicated, he had lived long enough to see the tide moving back in his direction. Then, in January 1993, he learned that he had cancer of the esophagus. (Not long after that, cancer was discovered in his liver as well.) Over the next few months, Brooks fought valiantly to maintain his life and his career even as his health was deteriorating. In a remarkable display of will, he made one final trip to England to deliver a lecture at the University of London in March. Not long after he returned, it became apparent that he had only weeks to live. After suffering a fall some time during the early morning of 6 May 1994, he began to fail even more rapidly. At 7:30 A.M. four days later, he breathed his last breath. The burial, which was scheduled for the following week in Baton Rouge, had to be postponed because of torrential rains. Finally, on Saturday morning, 21 May 1994, he was laid to rest in a family plot near his parents and his wife Tinkum. Sixty years after he had begun to transform the literary culture of our time, Cleanth Brooks was home to stay.

Letters:

"Cleanth Brooks on *I'll Take My Stand:* A Letter to Donald Davidson," *South Carolina Review,* 26 (Fall 1993): 93–100.

Selected Interviews:

Robert Penn Warren, "A Conversation with Cleanth Brooks," in *The Possibilities of Order: Cleanth Brooks and His Work,* edited by Lewis P. Simpson (Baton Rouge: Louisiana State University Press, 1976), pp. 1–124;

B. J. Leggett, "Notes for a Revised History of the New Criticism: An Interview with Cleanth Brooks," *Tennessee Studies in Literature,* 24 (1979): 1–35;

Joseph M. Ditta and Ronald S. Librach, "Sounding the Past: A Discussion with Cleanth Brooks," *Missouri Review,* 6 (Fall 1982): 139–160;

Reid Buckley, "A *Partisan* Conversation: Cleanth Brooks," *Southern Partisan,* 3 (Spring 1983): 22–26;

Linda Blanken, "Cleanth Brooks: The Fourteenth Jefferson Lecturer in the Humanities," *Humanities* (April 1985): 4–6.

Bibliography:

John Michael Walsh, *Cleanth Brooks: An Annotated Bibliography* (New York: Garland, 1990).

Biography:

Mark Royden Winchell, *A Blossoming Labor: Cleanth Brooks and the Rise of Modern Criticism* (Charlottesville: University Press of Virginia, 1995).

References:

Douglas Bush, "Marvell's Horatian Ode," *Sewanee Review,* 60 (Fall 1952): 363–376;

R. S. Crane, "The Critical Monism of Cleanth Brooks," in *Critics and Criticism: Ancient and Modern,* edited by Crane and others (Chicago: University of Chicago Press, 1952), pp. 83–107;

Thomas W. Cutrer, *Parnassus on the Mississippi: The Southern Review and the Baton Rouge Literary Community 1935–1942* (Baton Rouge: Louisiana State University Press, 1984);

John Edward Hardy, "The Achievement of Cleanth Brooks," *Hopkins Review,* 6 (1953): 148–161;

Robert Bechtold Heilman, *The Southern Connection* (Baton Rouge: Louisiana State University Press, 1991);

Murray Krieger, *The New Apologists for Poetry* (Minneapolis: University of Minnesota Press, 1956);

Thomas L. McHaney, "Brooks on Faulkner: The End of the Long View," *Review,* 1 (1979): 29–45;

D. A. Shankar, *Cleanth Brooks: An Assessment* (Bangalore: G. K. Ananthram, IBH Prakashana, 1981);

Lewis P. Simpson, ed., *The Possibilities of Order: Cleanth Brooks and His Work* (Baton Rouge: Louisiana State University Press, 1976);

Simpson and others, eds., *The Southern Review and Modern Literature: 1935–1985* (Baton Rouge: Louisiana State University Press, 1988);

Monroe K. Spears, " 'Kipper of the Vineyards,' " *New York Review of Books,* 7 May 1987, pp. 38–41;

Rene Wellek, "Cleanth Brooks," in his *A History of Modern Criticism, 1750–1950,* volume 6 (New Haven: Yale University Press, 1986), pp. 188–213;

Marc Wortman, "Shattering the Urn," *Yale Alumni Magazine* (December 1990): 32, 34–35, 38–39.

Papers:

Brooks's papers are held in the Beinecke Rare Book Room and Manuscript Library at Yale University.

A TRIBUTE

from Judith Farr

I first met Cleanth Brooks in the fall of 1958, when I entered his class in Wordsworth and the Romantic Poets at Yale University graduate school. Of course I had "met" him before: in the pages of *Understanding Poetry* and through the conversation of two poets – Marianne Moore and Léonie Adams – who knew and liked him, and who had been kind to me, a student poet, in New York City. As an undergraduate I had won a poetry-writing contest Moore judged, and I was studying with Adams at Columbia. Neither poet was altogether happy with my plan to take a Ph.D. while continuing to write; both thought graduate study sometimes killed the creative spark. But if I had to go to graduate school, each recommended I try to be admitted to Yale so I could study with Cleanth Brooks, who, as Moore said wittily, "certainly understood poetry."

I well remember the first day of class with Cleanth. I had never seen a picture of him, and because he was so powerful a critical force then, I somehow expected that he would be ten feet tall with Dionysian locks, breathing fire. Instead, I found myself walking along the corridor in search of the proper classroom with a rather short and slender, clearly very gentle gentleman with kindly eyes, silver hair, a smart bow tie, and a big briefcase. "Good morning," he said with a mellifluous southern accent, "are you lost?" "It's my first day of class at Yale," I said, "I've come here to study with Cleanth Brooks, and I'm looking for his classroom." "Well, now, you just come along with me," he said, and though it is a deadly cliché, I must report that he said this "with twinkling eyes." I did go along with him for more than thirty years after that; profited from his advice, both professional and personal; was blessed by his friendship; married (as it happened) one of his favorite students, Dr. George Farr, Jr.; cherished the clearest memories of him as a writer, lecturer, teacher; and mourned his loss.

Cleanth's approach to literature and the figure of the artist was one with which I was wholly sympathetic (of course, he had probably helped to form it since I had "grown up" on his textbooks; but I think that in some basic way I also came by this approach naturally, my parents being professionally engaged with the arts). Cleanth's vision was that the critic, however magisterial, however brilliant, essentially served the artist: he was never a rival presence but rather an adroit commentator, the most willing of willing, informed, knowledgeable readers, prepared to assist the public in achieving the richest possible understanding of the artist's work. There was a modesty implicit in this point of view, and I always felt Cleanth's reverence for true writers, though he could certainly be savage in his controlled fashion to a false or poor one. As a teacher, his manner was anything but pyrotechnical. "Now in this poem," he would say mildly, always the first edition of whatever text it was before him if he was teaching modern poetry, or the most scholarly variorum edition if the poetry was older, "let us consider the following." It used to be alleged that the "New Critics," of whom Cleanth was among the most famous, had little interest in biography or history, concentrating only on the formal entity that was the work under discussion. But I found that Cleanth always knew, expected us to know, and passed on a great deal of "information" about whatever work he had assigned. Of course he had such a broad range of knowledge – I remember him once quoting word for word the last paragraph of *Our Mutual Friend,* Dickens being not especially one of what he used to call his "fields of competency," and then passing on to quote Wordsworth – perfectly – before moving to a quotation from *Absalom, Absalom!* I had at one point a mad desire to write a paper for the Romantics course on the glosses to Coleridge's "Rime of the Ancient Mariner" in comparison with Marianne Moore's footnotes. Cleanth regarded this idea with patient dubiety but allowed me to do the paper, and in his comments I was introduced to a great many other poetic glossaries from the Middle Ages to the present. This broad scholarly knowledge, coupled with his own really artistic sense of what was valuable and lasting in a work of art, made Cleanth a fine and sensitive public lecturer. I remember the talk he gave as the Jefferson Lecturer for the National Endowment for the Humanities in Washington: it has great scope, and it also preserved a sense of what might be interesting to the common readers sitting before him.

Cleanth was courtly. In 1958 at Yale we were a group of five women, as it happened, who elected his Romantics course, and I think that, being one who clearly appreciated women, he rather relished that. He was no less strict as a teacher of women than of men, but he *was* courtly. He managed to be terribly tough and yet wonderfully polite. After many years of friendship he would sometimes call me "darling" (as if I were, I always felt, a favorite niece) in the course of providing some cold-blooded counsel about getting on in the academic world. I used to tease him that he was clearly a sexist since he hadn't wanted Yale to go coed and since – somehow! – he always awarded a 92 or 93 percent to my husband's graduate papers while mine seemed to be mired at 91 percent. He received these accusations with good humor, and he never altered. He found almost everything interesting, and one of the best letters I ever received from him contained the best critique of *Gone With the Wind* – which he liked, not because he was southern but because it was "such a great yarn" – that I have ever read. To be with him was to feel part of a larger and grander society – not only the writers of the past but the famous writers who were his friends and associates, though he was no name-dropper, not in the least.

He and his wife Tinkum were immensely devoted to each other, and when she died a few years ago, Cleanth told my husband and me that at first he had not particularly cared what happened to him, so much did he miss her. Therefore, I admired tremendously the way Cleanth continued to go round the country, lecturing, and the way he continued to write, right up to his own death. My last meeting with him was at the University of Maryland a year ago when the library dedicated a room to Katherine Anne Porter. His first words to me were compliments for some poems of mine he had seen, and I was overwhelmed as always by his generosity. I will miss him so much! And I regret so much being now after almost forty years called back to meeting him only on the page, or in fond memory.

A TRIBUTE

from Hugh Kenner

And can it have been forty-six years ago? The arithmetic seems implacable: June 1948, when for two years I had been teaching freshmen and juniors, while equipped with no credential beyond a Toronto M.A. For had not my mentors at Toronto been but Oxford or Cambridge M.A.'s. (The chief exception, A. S. P. Woodhouse, the Miltonist, had gone south for a Harvard Ph.D. and would consequently be referred to, with faintly audible irony, as "DOCtor Woodhouse.") But by 1948 Marshall McLuhan had entered my world, not to say my life; and as much back then as in later days of fame, Marshall was a trend-spotter to be listened to. He'd divined something hidden from me, that by then, even in Canada, the days of a doctorless professoriate were numbered if not ended. So if I expected any future I needed a Ph.D., moreover from Yale, where his old associate Cleanth Brooks, but recently arrived, could be trusted to shield me from

pedantry. And in mid June, in New Haven, behold me in the Brooksian presence, while Marshall makes explicit his own sense of the matter.

It wasn't till many years later, when a large university's English Department put me in charge of graduate admissions, that I began to assess the prodigies Cleanth must next have accomplished. For by later that summer I'd been admitted to Yale and by September was in attendance, an outcome neither Marshall nor I thought remarkable. But graduate admissions, I was eventually to learn, are normally closed by mid March, and what prodigies of patient persuasion must Cleanth Brooks have applied to a major university's bureaucracy, drawing on every nuance of his southern wile, to secure the late admission of a protégé of a friend! "Strategy," Marshall said of Cleanth, "is his most eloquent topic." While I'd never be hearing him eloquent about it, I was to profit repeatedly from his strategic cunning.

For my progress at Yale was highly irregular, not least in being shaped by my need to be finished at the end of the two years I had money for. So I was working on a dissertation from the week I arrived, all the while taking courses meant to prepare me to work on it. (I had many conferences with Cleanth but never a course; he steered me instead toward Bill Wimsatt and Maynard Mack.) The dissertation's open-ended title, suggested by Marshall, was *James Joyce: Critique in Progress,* and Cleanth was its supervisor. He had what I've since tried, imperfectly, to emulate, an uncanny knack of intervening only when intervention mattered. The result was duly accepted; a much-pruned version got published in 1956 as *Dublin's Joyce.*

But the degree required more than a dissertation accepted; it required an ordeal then (I think) unique to Yale: a morning-long oral examination conducted by as many of the English faculty as could be induced to convene, whether they'd had anything to do with the student or not. No matter that in my two years I'd had dealings, formal and informal, with no more than, oh, seven or eight; on a spring morning in 1950 behold a room containing some forty ferocious cranioclasts, and me.

One examiner was W. K. DeVane, author of the revered *Browning Handbook;* and, said he, "Mr. Kenner, I am going to ask you a series of questions, and I expect you to answer each of them in one sentence. Now. *What was the principal contribution of Coleridge to English poetry?* Remember, one sentence!" I began, "Well, technically," only to be interrupted: "Mr. Kenner: technique is a part of poetry; but a *very small part.*" I next ventured on a Jamesian sentence, which was not what he wanted either. No.

"*Coleridge – liberated – the imagination.* Now remember that, Mr. Kenner!"

And here Cleanth moved in deftly, perceiving – and sharing – my dismay: a doctoral oral at a major university reduced to that kindergarten order of cliché! He guessed, too, that many examiners would agree; what they'd value was familiarity with the remote, even the second-rate: the "style of the period." So, What, he asked, did I remember about William Congreve? (His dates are 1690–1728. What does *anybody* remember about him?) Well, I responded, chiefly the passage Dr. Johnson admired. Ah, went on Cleanth suavely, What was it he admired about it? I replied, "He said there was nothing to equal it in Shakespeare. It is a description of a temple; and, said Johnson, you can show me no such description of material objects, without an intermixture of moral notions, which produces such an effect. . . ."

And on the examiners that did produce the effect Cleanth had been aiming for; I was not the fumbler I had earlier seemed to be. Only he and I knew that he'd known that his question wouldn't stall me; that the Congreve passage had come up in a conversation between us, not many weeks before. Generals do not think otherwise, enabling their corporals with the aid of knowledge they're privy to. Strategy, yes, that's certainly what he'd employed.

On leaving Yale I moved to the other side of the country, whereafter, to my regret, we saw each other seldom. In California, though, I found myself teaching sophomores out of the Brooks-Warren *Understanding Poetry,* something radically different from the sort of poetry textbook I'd known. At Toronto we'd used the two-volume *Representative Poetry,* a text edited by a Toronto faculty committee, one member of which at least could be trusted for exquisite taste thanks to his impeccably Bloomsbury manner. ("But isn't it *too* mellifluous?" he'd ask in a seminar. Any poem at all was apt to be *too* something.) *Representative Poetry* was arranged by chronology, the main thing to which poetry testified being the fashion of the period in which it got written. Knowing what fashion expected, poets were apt to let themselves go; hence all that toothsome *too*ness.

The chief Brooks-Warren innovation was to cut clean away from such historical fixations. A poem, for them, wasn't an example of something: of Romantic *Angst,* of Augustan sophistry. It was its sole self, a freestanding artifact, held together not

by a time's pressures but by its own inner tensions. Irony and Paradox were among the ways such tensions manifested themselves. That's one formula for "the New Criticism," which was new chiefly in playing down two sorts of narrative: of the poet's times, of the poet's life. Those had earlier been critical staples.

One way *Understanding Poetry* bespoke the classroom was in tending to value poems according to what complexities discourse could weave around them. That led, in the mid twentieth century, to some odd omissions, notably Williams and Pound, who (except for the Pound of *Hugh Selwyn Mauberley*) didn't go in for Irony, let alone Paradox but sought to set something down and deal with the consequences of doing that. "So much depends upon a red wheel barrow. . . ." That says what it says; whereafter the classroom either falls silent or else is asked to notice that Williams at his typewriter caused the original to look like this:

So much depends
upon

a red wheel
barrow . . .

– something the voice shouldn't try to imitate; no, a purely visual pattern that blocks the printed words off from the spoken.

Which is to venture toward McLuhan territory, not that it's a detail of that territory that ever interested Marshall, strangely locked as he remained all his life inside the poetic parameters of F. R. Leavis, who'd have sniffed a sniff audible the length of the room at any hint that typography might matter. (And for the lore of the Leavisian sniff it's to Marshall I'm indebted. How complex is one's web of indebtedness.)

Cleanth, that sweet man – I saw him, I'd like to say time and again, but no, just a few more times, whenever fate and the logic of conferences manoeuvred us into the same space. We always enjoyed each other. And another thing I'd like to think would be that he took such pleasure in his former students as they took in re-meeting or remembering him. For he was never your rival. He was uniquely your friend. *Et in Arcadia ego* was one of the many things his presence prompted you to think.

Paxton Davis

(7 May 1925 – 27 May 1994)

R. H. W. Dillard
Hollins College

BOOKS: *Two Soldiers* (New York: Simon & Schuster, 1956);
The Battle of New Market: A Story of V.M.I. (Boston: Little, Brown, 1963);
One of the Dark Places (New York: Morrow, 1965);
The Seasons of Heroes (New York: Morrow, 1967);
A Flag at the Pole: Three Soliloquies (New York: Atheneum, 1976);
Ned (New York: Atheneum, 1978);
Three Days: With Robert E. Lee at Gettysburg (New York: Atheneum, 1980);
Being a Boy (Winston-Salem, N.C.: John F. Blair, 1988);
A Boy's War (Winston-Salem, N.C.: John F. Blair, 1990);
A Boy No More (Winston-Salem, N.C.: John F. Blair, 1992).

Paxton Davis

Marlow, in Joseph Conrad's *Heart of Darkness* (1902), says, "I don't like work – no man does – but I like what is in the work – the chance to find yourself. Your own reality – for yourself, not for others – what no other man can ever know. They can only see the mere show, and never can tell what it really means." Strongly influenced by Conrad, Paxton Davis spent a lifetime drawn to and telling the stories in his work of men who come face to face with themselves, with their own reality; who, often in a single moment, find either the stuff of which heroes are made or – to quote Conrad again, this time from *Lord Jim* (1900) – a "weakness that may lie hidden, watched or unwatched, prayed against or manfully scorned, repressed or maybe ignored more than half a lifetime." And, of course, with that singular courage or foolhardiness that marks an artist, he also attempted in his ten books to tell "what no other man can ever know" and "what it really means."

One does not have to look too far to discover the autobiographical sources of Davis's overriding interest in those moments when individual lives undergo transformations or reveal themselves for what they are. His entire generation passed through such a transformation, moving from one world through the ordeal of war and emerging into a brave new world as unfamiliar and alien to them as the foreign lands in which they fought. Their experience, traveling halfway around the world to fight a war that even in victory was permanently to change their lives back home, was unlike that of any previous American generation. Only the Civil War, that massive and bloody upheaval away from which Americans seem unable to turn, made anything like

253

the impact on American life (especially on that of the American South) that World War II did. How natural, then, that Davis, as a veteran of the war and as a southerner, should have concerned himself so deeply with ordeals by fire (or ice) and their results. As one of his characters says in the novel *The Seasons of Heroes* (1967), "We find in war the self we dare not face in peace."

James Paxton Davis, Jr., was born in Winston-Salem, North Carolina, in 1925, but his family on both sides was deeply rooted in Virginia and in American history. His great-great-grandfather on his father's side, James Paxton, was a major in the War of 1812 and later served as commandant of the Virginia state arsenal at Lexington; his great-great-great-grandfather on his mother's side, John Beckley, was the first clerk of the House of Representatives and first librarian of Congress. Davis spent his childhood and adolescence in North Carolina but, naturally enough with his antecedents, attended the Virginia Military Institute (VMI) for the academic year 1942–1943 before entering the army at the age of nineteen. After being trained as a laboratory technician in Texas, he was sent to India and then to Burma, where he served in the Typhus Commission. He returned home shortly before his twenty-first birthday and resumed his college education in 1946. Having discovered, as he put it in *A Boy No More* (1992), that "I was not really a soldier, good as I became impersonating one," he did not return to VMI but entered Johns Hopkins University.

At Johns Hopkins he studied with George Boas and Charles Anderson and became a member of a circle of young would-be writers who clustered around Thomas Chastain. It was there that he found his literary heroes (many of whose pictures he was later to frame and hang about his desk in his study, a practice he picked up from Chastain): F. Scott Fitzgerald, Ernest Hemingway, Henry James, Virginia Woolf, E. M. Forster, Raymond Chandler, and Eric Ambler. He was eventually to write an important essay on Ambler, "The World We Live In: The Novels of Eric Ambler," for *The Hollins Critic* in 1971, which led to his meeting and striking up a friendship with him. Although he had written (and thrown away) a novel while he was in India, it was at Johns Hopkins that he became convinced that if he were to be a writer, he must become a novelist (a decision that he was later to question and abandon as he came into his own as a writer). In *A Boy No More* he explains how the educational bias of the time led him to that conclusion:

. . . if I have a criticism of the way English was taught in the late 1940s, not only at Hopkins but almost everywhere, it is that its emphasis on fiction and poetry, and overwhelmingly on long fiction, left in me the conviction that other prose forms – the essay, history, biography, journalism – were insignificant genres alongside The Novel. No one ever said that outright; but like many of my generation I came away believing that unless I wrote novels, and masterpieces at that, I had subtly but surely seated myself below the salt.

Determined to write novels but also needing to make a living, Davis returned home to Winston-Salem in 1949 and began a career as a newspaper journalist that was to carry him to Richmond (where he won the Virginia Press Association's award for interpretive reporting in 1951) and then back to Winston-Salem. He married Wylma Elizabeth Pooser in 1951, a marriage that was to last twenty years and produce three children (Elizabeth Keith, Anne Beckley, and James Paxton III). In 1953 he accepted a position as an assistant professor of journalism at Washington and Lee University in Lexington, Virginia, where he taught until a major heart attack led to his early retirement as a full professor in 1976. He was also the journalism department's head from 1968 until 1974. An interesting glimpse of Davis's life as a young professor living with his wife and three-year-old daughter in a prefab house appears in French film director and novelist Philippe Labro's prizewinning novel *L'Etudiant Etranger* (1986). In the French edition of the novel, which is based on Labro's year (1954–1955) as a student at Washington and Lee, Davis and his wife appear under their own names, but in the English translation by William R. Byron, *The Foreign Student* (1988), they become Rex and Doris Jennings. The portrait of Davis is a sympathetic one, for he was a good and supportive friend to the young French student and remained in close touch with him for the next four decades.

Despite his academic career, Davis did not leave active newspaper work completely. He became book editor of the *Roanoke* (Virginia) *Times and World-News* in 1961 and for twenty years made the book page of that paper one of the most literate and respected in the country. "I wanted absolute control over every detail," he said in an interview with George Garrett in 1989. "That may be foolish, but I could put out precisely the page I wanted. And I think the results justified that."

Davis also became a contributing editorial columnist for the Roanoke paper in 1976 and continued in that position until early 1994. His columns ranged from slashing attacks on political hypocrisy and foolishness (especially those of Presidents Reagan and Bush) to elegant homages to his literary and cinematic heroes to essays on the books, movies, games, and complex social mores of American boys of his generation. The pieces on boyhood were eventually to develop into Davis's last major work, his three-volume memoir, but the columns on the current political, cultural, and educational scenes drew the most heated response. The paper's conservative readers read his political pieces and branded him a dangerous radical and intellectual provocateur, while his defenses of the canon of Western literature and his comments on the decline of literacy in modern America led the paper's liberal readers to accuse him of being a Tory defender of the patriarchy. The paper's editorial-page editor, Alan Sorensen, said that "By far, he received the most mail and generated the most heat from readers." The newspaper editorialized on his death that "Sometimes caricatured as a liberal because of his oft-noted disdain for Ronald Reagan, Davis was really a conservative, whose beliefs were grounded in the experience of his World War Two generation. He despised the erosion of standards of all kinds." His colleague Bob Fishburn added, "Pax, in short, had many facets, but was never two-faced. In words that I have often used to describe him to those who never knew him, he was an Edwardian anarchist, a punctilious private man with a broad streak of rebel." He regularly received death threats but never stopped writing his provocative columns until his advancing heart disease finally forced him into silence.

But for all his success as a teacher and newspaper editor and columnist, his ten books remain his permanent legacy to American letters. In hindsight they appear very much to be of a piece, a steadily developing body of work built upon and unified by his central concern with what might properly be called heroic moments, but they also fall into three clearly defined periods.

The first group of books, published between 1956 and 1967, marks Davis's effort to write "The Novel": *Two Soldiers* (1956), a pair of short novels set in India and Burma during the war; *One of the Dark Places* (1965), a novel drawn directly out of Davis's experience in the Typhus Commission in Burma; and *The Seasons of Heroes,* a historical novel set in Virginia before, during, and after the Civil War. The books of this period also include *The Battle of New Market* (1963), an account written for younger readers of the VMI cadets' participation in the Civil War battle.

Both of the short novels that make up *Two Soldiers* are set in the China-Burma-India theater where Davis served. The first, "Ledo," tells the story of Goff, a young black soldier who has, for reasons he is unable or unwilling to articulate, refused to perform his duties as a soldier properly and is facing severe punishment. He runs away from his unit, kills an officer in his fear, and flees into the jungle. There he is rescued by Naga tribesmen and becomes a respected member of their society. But when the Nagas find a wounded American lieutenant who will die without proper medical aid, Goff takes him down to Ledo, even though he knows that he will face court-martial and execution there. He approaches his execution with the calm acceptance of a Billy Budd, and the wounded young lieutenant, who had tried and failed to save him, understands that Goff's apparent defeat is a personal victory of great magnitude. Goff fled into the heart of darkness and there found his heroic self.

The second of the short novels, "Myitkina," could be called Paxton Davis's *The Red Badge of Courage* (1895), for like Stephen Crane's novel it is the story of a young soldier's initiation, his passage from fear and confusion through failure and betrayal to maturity as a fighting man. The ironies of Crane's novel are compounded in Davis's story by the young soldier's being a medic, untrained for combat and serving with other medics, most of whom have never even fired a rifle. That he survives his own failures, which include causing the death of one of his comrades by his inability to kill a Japanese soldier, is as strong a personal victory as Goff's discovery of himself in the jungle, but one which will leave its scars as surely as the bullet which wounds him in the shoulder.

Two Soldiers reveals the influence of Crane and Conrad (a passage from *Lord Jim* is used as the epigraph of "Ledo") and, in its spare, disciplined prose, Ernest Hemingway, but, beyond their influence, Davis joins the three of them in his ability to render the look and feel of his scene and the events that take place there with great truthfulness, clarity, and force. Reviewers noted the skill of the writing and the author's ear for the sound and rhythm of prose, but after the great success of such "big" war novels as Irwin Shaw's *The Young Lions* (1948), Norman Mailer's *The Naked and the Dead* (1949), Herman Wouk's *The Caine Mutiny* (1951), and James Jones's *From Here to Eternity* (1951), Davis's small book received neither the critical attention nor the popular success that it deserved.

One of the Dark Places, Davis's first full-length novel, returns to the scene of the first book, but

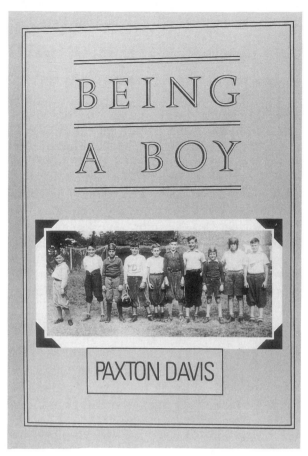

Dust jacket for the first volume of Davis's
autobiographical reminiscences

with characters and a plot much closer to Davis's own experience in the war. It is primarily the story of two men, both seriously wounded by serious losses in their lives, who forge an unlikely alliance and struggle together to gather the data for an understanding of (and possible cure for) scrub typhus while the battle for Burma rages around them. The two ultimately are defeated not by the disease or the Japanese, but by the ambition of their commanding officer, who undercuts their chances in order to enhance his own postwar career. The novel is as vividly and precisely written as *Two Soldiers,* and its two central characters both find themselves and achieve personal victories even in the face of crushing defeat. The novel takes its title from Conrad's *Heart of Darkness,* and it joins Conrad's own work in its effort to speak of dark truths while at the same time asserting the solidarity of human feeling in that darkness.

In his third novel, *The Seasons of Heroes,* Davis turned away from his own war to explore an earlier

war and the nature of heroism in three generations of the same Virginia family. Told in the first person by Robert Gibboney (1864), his father Matthew (1861), and his son William (1912), the novel tells no tale of guns and glory but rather of men who, like Gen. Matthew Gibboney, become rare in their insight, "the soldier who sees in war not the consummation of his dreams but their utmost collapse." As in the earlier books, the heroes here find themselves in defeat, and the most heroic of them all is William, the one who was never a soldier and whose personal heroism is only revealed to him by the testimony of others. Davis also deals directly with questions of racial injustice and the complex relationships between blacks and whites that he had earlier only referred to in "Ledo." The prose is still distinctively Davis's own, although the concluding section of the novel, which tells the story of the Gibboneys and their black employee, the almost mythical Shell (a.k.a. Kid Sonora), is Faulknerian in its honesty, its high humor, and its moral complexity. Again, the novel did not receive the attention it deserved, perhaps because it was overshadowed by the critical furor surrounding the publication the same year of another southern historical novel, William Styron's *The Confessions of Nat Turner* (1967).

The year 1970 marked a major turning point in both the life and literary career of Paxton Davis. His marriage drew to a close (ending in divorce in 1971), and he moved away from Lexington to the colonial Virginia town of Fincastle. His family's roots were deeply planted in Fincastle; local lore has it that one of his great-aunts still haunts her former home, occasionally rocking invisibly in a chair in the parlor. He met (and married in 1973) Peggy Painter Camper, who was to become a major factor of both stability and vitality in his life. A Democratic Party activist and aide to Rep. James Olin during his years in Congress (1983–1993), she shared her husband's artistic and intellectual interests while bringing her own strong interests and concerns to the marriage. She was certainly a major factor in keeping Davis working and active after the heart attack which led to his early retirement from teaching and the series of pin strokes which were severely to hinder his reading and writing in the 1980s. Except for a brief time in Roanoke in order to be nearer to hospital facilities after the heart attack, they continued to live in Fincastle, first in the large house which Ellen Glasgow used as the model for "the Manse" in her novel *Vein of Iron* (1935) and later in a nearby cottage, which Davis enjoyed likening to the cottage of T. E. Lawrence's last years, Clouds Hill.

Davis also began to reconsider the place of the novel in literature and what he wanted to do in his own work in the early 1970s. He began work on a spy novel, to be called "The Ming-Mao Complex," but he was forced to abandon it during his health crisis and as shifts in the geopolitics of the Communist world began to make the complicated triple cross at the heart of the plot unworkable. But more important, realizing that other prose forms were much more suited to the work he wished to do, he abandoned the novel itself, or, as he often wryly put it, he removed himself from "the *War and Peace* Sweepstakes."

The second period in Davis's literary career produced three small volumes, *A Flag at the Pole: Three Soliloquies* (1976), *Ned* (1978), and *Three Days: With Robert E. Lee at Gettysburg* (1980). These three studies of self-revelation in the most trying of circumstances do constitute a turning away from the novel, but they are also a continuation and further focusing of his central concerns, marked by an increasing attention to the sonorities possible with an even more disciplined and spare prose.

The books defy categorization. Neither novels nor works of scholarly history, they are all biographical fictions, accurate in their historical facts but imaginative in their effort to get at the essence of the individuals hidden in (and revealed by) those facts. As Davis points out in an afterword to *Ned,* "I claim for it only fidelity to the facts and its own internal harmony." After *A Flag at the Pole* was rejected by several publishers who, while praising the book's quality, were unable to find a familiar category for it and could not figure out a way to market it, Davis accepted an offer from Atheneum to publish the work as a book for young adults. He went on to write the other two books for the same publisher, all three of them listed as "juvenile fiction," which meant they would not be widely reviewed or read as literary works, but Atheneum did produce the books handsomely (the first two with illustrations by Davis's Fincastle artist neighbor, Harold Little).

All three of the books reexamine the lives of the heroes of Davis's youth: the polar explorers Ernest Shackleton, Roald Amundsen, and Robert Falcon Scott; T. E. Lawrence; and Robert E. Lee. *A Flag at the Pole* finds in each of the three explorers, driven as they were by different needs and desires, a common "courage, dedication and magnanimity, representative of the best of an age still unashamed to value such virtues." Each of the three speaks a soliloquy – Shackleton in 1909, planning new challenges after failing to reach the pole; Amundsen

in 1911 on the day he reaches the pole; and Scott in 1912, on the day he dies in the ice, having failed to be the first to reach the pole but having nevertheless gained the deepest knowledge of himself and humanity.

Ned tells the story of T. E. Lawrence as a chivalric quest, tracing Lawrence's progress from squire to knight to monk. In an effort to engage young readers with this most enigmatic of modern heroes in a direct and individual way, Davis employed the same device Charles Reade used in *The Cloister and the Hearth* (1861); he calls his central character only "Ned" until the closing page, when, at his death, "he seemed to see his Bedouin riders again, rifles raised against the desert sky, turning his way to chant their love and fealty – to them, not Ned, but 'Aurens! Aurens! Aurens!'" Davis's chivalric portrait of Lawrence is an openly romantic and heroic one, written almost defiantly in the face of the darker political and psychoanalytical "interpretations of his character and the significance of his life [which] are as varied as the motives and biases of his many biographers."

The hero of *Three Days,* Robert E. Lee, does not fare so well; he must face up to his own failures perhaps more fully than any of Davis's other defeated characters. Strongly influenced by revisionist historians' reassessments of the role of Generals James Longstreet and Lee at Gettysburg, Davis portrays Lee as a tragic figure, distracted by pain and lost in the illusion that the valor and devotion of his men cannot be overcome or resisted, who makes grave errors which lead to the slaughter of thousands of those devoted men. At the end of the book Lee considers his defeat and honestly assesses the blame:

> What had gone wrong? Everything, everything: Jackson's death, Stuart's absence and silence, Hill's reluctance, Ewell's hesitation, Longstreet's slows; but most of all – central and crucial, ineradicable and unforgivable – himself, his judgment, his rigidity, his pride. They had exacted a price he scarcely dared face, though he must.

The "marble man" of southern hagiography is replaced by a real man whose pain resonates from the pages of the book. This book and the novel *The Seasons of Heroes* should both be considered by future scholars attempting to understand the full range of the southern response to the Civil War in the years that followed it.

After these studies of the seasons of heroes, Davis turned again to his own life and experience for the subject matter of his final three books: *Being*

Davis, 1988

a Boy (1988), *A Boy's War* (1990), and *A Boy No More* (1992). The three books form one extended narrative, the story of a boy's growing up in a small North Carolina city, of his going to war, and of his return to a country and a life quite different from what he had expected and planned. Although they recount the story of one man's coming of age, they both metaphorically and literally also reflect the larger story of a nation's coming of age at the same time. In them Davis's style reached its full maturity as well, a restrained but flexible prose which could move easily from seriousness to humor and irony with only subtle modulations of tone. Readings from the book at his memorial service in Fincastle drew not only tears from those assembled but bursts of laughter; there could have been no greater tribute to the craft and art of his prose than that response. The books were published by a small regional publisher, John F. Blair of Winston-Salem, North Carolina, who spent a great deal of care on the presentation of the work (they are unusually handsome volumes), and the efforts were rewarded by the great success of the books, especially across the South. They were so well received critically and popularly that all three were released on audiocassettes by Books on Tape, read without abridgment by Wolfram Kandinsky.

Although the three volumes are of a piece, marked both by Davis's memory for telling detail and by the precise and disciplined prose style which he honed in the three historical fictions, each performs a different task in the overall design. *Being a Boy,* as the title suggests, is almost an essay on the innocent timelessness of boyhood, and while it does recount the particulars of Davis's life, it always places the events of his life in that larger context. It is organized less by chronology than by topic (the movies, reading, football, radio, neighborhood games) and forms an album of the sights and sounds that formed the life and understanding of every boy in southern America in the 1930s. The book concludes with a visit with three dozen other boys to the World's Fair in New York with its "World of Tomorrow." On 3 September 1939, on their way home, they read of Adolf Hitler's invasion of Poland: "World War Two had begun. We understood that, but not that before it was over we'd all serve, and some die, in it. Nor could we guess that the sweet, safe, innocent America of our birth and boyhood soon would vanish, as boyhood would vanish, forever."

As in the war story "Myitkina," *A Boy's War* is primarily chronological and limited to the individual experiences and perceptions of its central character, as though to indicate that each boy's war is separate and unique, unlike the universal experiences of childhood. Its scene is no longer the neighborhood but the entire world, and Davis's view of the vast war is necessarily focused through his own eyes, for it is too large and complex for anyone to describe or understand – even from the distance of nearly half a century. Davis's war is the real war, however, one fought by boys, not always on the front lines but always in harm's way. It is the story of boys who must come of age early by doing the dangerous work of men, in isolation and discomfort, dealing with deadly typhus, the Japanese enemy, boredom and loneliness, and even the stench and horror of grave disinterment.

The ironic climax of *A Boy's War* occurs when Davis, alone in the jungle, encounters a single soldier, as likely to have been a Chinese deserter as a Japanese soldier, in mortal combat. Both manage to fire at each other in the brief encounter of no more than ten seconds' duration. Davis is hit, but his wound proves to be only a scratch, "no worse than the hundreds of scratches I'd got playing football and baseball as a boy." Then, with the deadly game of war over, he returns home and "two weeks later, less a day, I turned twenty-one and became eligible to vote."

The third volume of the memoir, *A Boy No More,* tells the story of Davis's years at Johns Hopkins and his first newspaper jobs, but, as in the earlier volumes, it leads the reader on a larger journey as well, one to discover what it means to be an adult, to be truly a boy no more. Death, only an event on the radio or the silver screen in a boy's world, became a constant presence in the distant jungles of Burma and then comes inescapably home to that boy's world in *A Boy No More*. One of the liveliest and most memorable of the little boys in *A Boy's World* dies of cancer early in this volume, and it ends, as the first volume began, in the hospital in Winston-Salem where Davis was born and where now his father dies: "The sun had risen by the time we left the hospital for the parking lot, but the downtown streets were empty. I drove my mother

home, where a cluster of their friends were waiting, and was a boy no more." It is only then, possessed existentially of that dark truth, that the boy finally leaves his boyhood behind and becomes the man who, rich in experience, will one day be able to write this powerful account of his passage between worlds.

Paxton Davis was hard at work on a new book based on a nationally notorious Winston-Salem murder when his heart condition worsened. He agreed to heart surgery only because he wished so much to finish this book, but that was not to be. His weakened heart stopped beating on Friday, 27 May 1994. "His artist friends and church friends and music friends and literary friends and town friends and book friends and fellow professor friends and publishing friends and the many former students from Washington & Lee who became close friends," wrote Peggy Davis after his death, "formed a tapestry of individuals who broke all boundaries of clique or club, race, gender or economic standing." I am proud to count myself among the many writers and friends who were influenced by and who will miss Paxton Davis, but I am comforted by his vital presence in the books, which I read again before writing this piece – by the voice which speaks in them of the secret discoveries of the heart in the darkest of places, "what no other man can ever know" but what Paxton Davis managed to tell in his work with discipline and elegance and wit and, above all, with absolute integrity.

A TRIBUTE

from George Garrett

I knew Paxton Davis for a little more than thirty years, starting in the days when I was teaching English at the University of Virginia and he was teaching journalism an hour and a half away at Washington and Lee. We didn't see each other all that often, not enough really, but we and our wives did get together in Virginia and in Maine. In the last few years we would meet for a summer weekend in Warm Springs, where the loudest noise was the sound of the stream bubbling over rocks, maybe fifty yards away from the wide porch where we sat in rockers and drank bourbon and talked about everything under the sun. He was a good and generous friend. Everybody who knew him misses him.

But there was something else, quite aside from the personal, for which he should be remembered and missed – his writing. Pax was a wonderful writer, wonderfully gifted, beautifully and strictly trained (by himself) and, unlike so many of us, getting better, finer all the time. We could learn from him. We could take heart from his example. There was, of course, his book page for the *Roanoke Times and World News,* which he edited for about twenty years, beginning in 1961. (See *DLB Yearbook 89,* pp. 126–129, for an interview with Davis as book editor.) Later there was his lively, often curmudgeonly column which stirred up people all up and down the Shenandoah Valley and in southwest Virginia. And there are the books which are there and will last. The three autobiographical books are remarkable and were remarkably successful. As writing they are so graceful and so *refined,* pared down to a subtle music of evocation and innuendo, that one scarcely notices, at first reading, the magical skill of their making. They are the finest work of a writer who was already very, very good, good enough to create by habit – he had *good* habits – if he had elected to. He didn't. He kept trying and achieving more. Of the earlier books my special favorites, the ones I keep recommending to writers and readers and here recommend to you, reader, are the lean and lovely trilogy – *A Flag at the Pole, Ned,* and *Three Days: With Robert E. Lee at Gettysburg.* He was always a spare writer, no wasted effort or motion just like some

great athletes; but in this three he made a bold move, inventing the methods he perfected in the autobiographical books, able to say more and more with less and less effort.

I do not know if Pax will achieve posthumously some of the honor and reputation he deserved. (Does it matter? Yes, this much. It will be a better world if he does.) But I owe him much and so do a lot of good writers I know. We are beholden to him, and it is an honor for us to be so.

A TRIBUTE

from William Hoffman

To Paxton Davis the manner in which a column, article, essay, story, or novel was crafted became more important than all other considerations. He cared passionately for our language and its honest use. His literary creed built upon the integrity which characterized his life. Readers sensed that integrity in his every utterance. He refused to compromise with the superficial or second-rate. He brought excellence to our language, our literature, and our lives. He stayed the course. Well done, friend Pax.

Ralph Waldo Ellison
(1 March 1914 – 16 April 1994)

Leonard J. Deutsch
Marshall University

BOOKS: *Invisible Man* (New York: Random House, 1952; London: Gollancz, 1953); republished, with an introduction by Ellison (New York: Random House, 1982);
Shadow and Act (New York: Random House, 1964; London: Secker & Warburg, 1967);
Going to the Territory (New York: Random House, 1986).

When Ralph Ellison died of pancreatic cancer at age eighty on 16 April 1994, *The New York Times* called him "one of the major American writers of the 20th century" and *Invisible Man* a "seminal novel... one of the most important works" in our literature. A tribute on 26 May 1994, sponsored by the American Academy of Arts and Letters, included James Earl Jones reading from *Invisible Man,* trumpeter Wynton Marsalis playing selections from the music of Ellison's friend Duke Ellington, and Nobel Prize winner Toni Morrison and colleague Albert Murray sharing recollections.

The essayist, novelist, and short-story writer was born on 1 March 1914 in Oklahoma City. His father, Lewis Ellison, had been a soldier in Cuba, the Philippines, and China; a construction worker; and then a construction foreman before starting a small ice and coal business. His mother, Ida Millsap Ellison, married Lewis in Abbeville, Georgia, before their move to Oklahoma. She was a domestic worker and a political activist. When Ralph was three and his brother Herbert was four months old, their father died in an accident.

As *Shadow and Act* makes clear, Ralph Ellison was eager to learn and experience as much of life as possible. He studied trumpet, soprano sax, and several brass instruments and took private music lessons from the conductor of the Oklahoma Orchestra that he paid for by mowing the maestro's lawn. He read avidly and delighted in constructing his own crystal radio set. He absorbed the tales his elders told in the local drugstore and barbershop. Despite the social segregation imposed upon African

Ralph Ellison, 1985 (photograph by Leon Russell)

Americans, Ellison reveled in the richness of his life and celebrated its beauty and complexity.

He entered the combined primary and secondary Frederick Douglass School at age six and graduated in 1931, after which he worked for two years during the Depression. He was awarded a scholarship by the state of Oklahoma, "supposedly on merit," he said, "but the scholarship program itself was a device through which the state hoped to circumvent applications by Negro students for enrollment in the state universities of Oklahoma." In 1933, at age nineteen, he finally decided to attend Tuskegee Institute. Because he did not have enough money to purchase a train ticket, he traveled to Macon County, Alabama, in hobo fashion. Armed guards ordered him off the box car in Decatur, where the Scottsboro Boys, hobos themselves, were being tried for allegedly raping two white girls. Ellison escaped by running for his life.

At Tuskegee he majored in music theory, participated in the school's drama program, and heard speakers such as Alaine Locke, author of *The New Negro* (1925). He also discovered T. S. Eliot's *The Waste Land*. He was influenced not only by the poem's symbolism, musical rhythms, and organization but also by Eliot's sense of a literary tradition. As Ellison developed as a writer he drew upon both canonical works and African American materials to an extraordinary degree.

In 1936, at age twenty-two, he spent the summer in Harlem to earn money for his senior year in college. Diverted by New York's allure, Ellison did not return to Tuskegee, although he was later to receive an honorary doctorate from this and a host of other institutions. Abandoning his plans for a career in music or sculpture, he became friends with Langston Hughes and Richard Wright. The latter arranged for the publication of Ellison's first piece, a book review, in the 1937 autumn issue of *New Challenge,* a leftist periodical edited by Wright.

After supporting himself through a variety of jobs – food dispenser at the YMCA, freelance photographer, file clerk/receptionist for a psychiatrist, assembler of high-fidelity stereo systems – Ellison found employment with the Federal Writers Project in 1938. Sterling A. Brown served as supervising editor when Ellison did research as a member of the Living Lore Unit. Ellison helped collect New York's urban and industrial folklore, an experience which was later to assist him as a writer.

Between 1939 and 1944 Ellison published eight short stories and served as managing editor of the *Negro Quarterly* in 1942. Toward the end of World War II he was a cook in the merchant marines, and when he was discharged in 1945 he recuperated on a Vermont farm, overcoming the effects of the ship's contaminated water supply. This is where *Invisible Man* began to take form in his mind.

At this creative stage in his life, Ellison entered into his second marriage. He tartly sidestepped "irrelevant" questions about his first, shortlived marriage, but his union with Fanny McConnell lasted until his death almost forty-eight years later. He met James Weldon Johnson's former secretary in 1944 and married the Louisville-born woman on 26 August 1946.

Ellison spent seven years working on *Invisible Man*. Its famous opening lines set the tone and context: "I am an invisible man. No, I am not a spook like those who haunted Edgar Allan Poe; nor am I one of your Hollywood-movie ectoplasms. I am a man of substance, of flesh and bone, fiber and liq-

uids – and I might even be said to possess a mind. I am invisible, understand, simply because people refuse to see me." Thus begins the narrator's story of his journey from the South to New York and finally underground, and his explanation of how he came to understand and contend with his invisibility. The equally famous closing sentence – "Who knows but that, on the lower frequencies, I speak for you" – universalizes his story.

The novel creates some of the most vivid characters in literature. In addition to the unnamed invisible man himself, there is Dr. Bledsoe, the stern and powerful college president who disingenuously defers to whites and deviously betrays the narrator; Reverend Barbee, the blind preacher who casts a Homeric spell over the students with his haunting tale of the sacrificial Founder; Jim Trueblood, a sharecropper who finds deliverance in the blues; Mr. Norton, the college trustee who subconsciously harbors incestuous desires for his daughter and who is simultaneously repulsed and mesmerized by Dr. Trueblood's casual retelling of his commission of actual incest; Mary Rambo, the philosophical landlady who briefly serves as a stabilizing force in the invisible man's life after he arrives in Harlem; Brother Jack, head of the leftist Brotherhood, who recruits the invisible man and initially grooms him as a public figure but later sacrifices him to the interests of the organization; Ras the Exhorter, a black nationalist whose avenging radicalism transforms him into an agent of destruction; Brother Tod Clifton, a defector from the Brotherhood organization who symbolically manipulates Sambo dolls to signal his alienation and sense of betrayal; and Proteus B. Rinehart, the epic shape-shifter, who in assuming multiple roles teaches the invisible man how to master invisibility and, hence, control reality. An amazing collection of minor characters – Peter Wheatstraw, the yam vendor, Brother Tarp, and Dupre, one of the rioters – contributes to the teeming sense of life with which the novel pulsates.

While *Invisible Man* on one level is a bildungsroman that chronicles political turmoil, racial violence, and personal hardship with shocking candor, the book also represents the triumph of style. When it won the National Book Award for 1952, the judges cited Ellison's "positive exuberance of narrative gifts." The vernacular playfully counterpoints the literary. Reverend Barbee, for example, delivers a sermon which intermingles black rhetoric with Whitmanesque imagery. Street talk, with its blues modulations and jazz rhythms, resonates in tension with Shakespearean, Melvillean, and Joycean echoes.

Ellison, in August 1966, testifying before a U.S. Senate subcommittee on the problems of the inner cities (AP/Wide World Photos)

Despite its complexity, *Invisible Man* stayed on the best-seller lists for months, was translated into at least seventeen languages, and sold millions of copies. In a 1965 poll two hundred authors and critics called it the most distinguished novel written since World War II. Critics have considered the book not only artistically timeless but ceaselessly relevant. After Ellison's death the Associated Press characterized *Invisible Man* as "an intricate tale that offered an uncanny blueprint for the next two decades, from the civil rights movement to Malcolm X and the growth of Afrocentricism." Others have seen adumbrations of Farrakhanian polemics and the ascendancy of multiculturalism. As one critic put it, the Brotherhood "stands for all the doctrinaire utopianism and fakery to come."

Immediate critical responses were not uniformly positive, however. The novel's depiction of the Brotherhood (a thinly disguised portrait of the Communist Party) outraged leftist readers. Religious Fundamentalists found the novel's suggestive passages to be worthy of censorship. Ellison's devotion to his craft made him suspect in the eyes of those who saw literature as a social tool. Amiri Ba-

raka (LeRoi Jones), for example, castigated him for "fidgeting away in some college," while Ernest Kaiser denounced him as "an Establishment writer, an Uncle Tom, an attacker of the sociological formulations of the civil rights movement." In 1969 Charles Johnson was told by the librarian of the black-studies program at Southern Illinois University that they did not carry *Invisible Man* "because Ralph Ellison is not a black writer."

By the end of his life, however, Ellison had assumed the stature of a cult hero. The fact that he was not consumed with militant rage was no longer held against him by fellow black writers and racial leaders. He was instead praised for depicting African American life "not in terms of sheer victimhood" but in affirmation of its rich diversity.

In 1964 Ellison published *Shadow and Act,* a collection of essays which dealt with the subtle nuances of African American music; various aspects of American culture, especially the fecund cultural interchange between black and white Americans; and his own critical theory. The ideas in this book have had a profound impact on literary critics and theorists. Henry Louis Gates, for example, in his preface to *The Signifying Monkey* (1988) says, "Ralph Ellison's example of a thoroughly integrated critical discourse, informed by the black vernacular tradition and Western criticism, provided the model for my work." References to Ellison abound in contemporary critiques and analyses of African American literature.

His second collection of essays, *Going to the Territory* (1986), provides further insight into his life and the forces that helped shape it. The book elegantly articulates and extends the ideas found in his earlier work.

As David Remnick observed one month before Ellison died, "Few novels have ever entered the canon so quickly" as did *Invisible Man* (*The New Yorker,* 14 March 1994). Ellison was besieged with offers from academe, and he was frequently invited to testify before congressional committees.

After his fellowship at the American Academy of Arts and Letters in Rome (1955-1957), he taught at Bard College (1958-1961), the University of Chicago (winter of 1961), Rutgers (1962-1969), and New York University as Albert Schweitzer Professor of the Humanities (1970-1979). He also lectured at Columbia University, Harvard, Princeton, Yale, and numerous other universities in the United States and abroad.

In 1969 Ellison received the Medal of Freedom from President Lyndon Johnson. Of even greater satisfaction was his receiving the Chevalier de l'Ordre des Artes et Lettres in 1970 from one of his personal heroes, André Malraux, who was then serving as France's minister of cultural affairs. Having been elected vice-president of P.E.N. and vice-president of the National Institute of Arts and Letters in the 1960s, he was made an honorary fellow of the Modern Language Association in 1974, and he was inducted into the American Academy of Arts and Letters in 1975. He also served as a trustee on many civic, cultural, and academic boards.

Ellison's lean productivity as a writer of fiction includes a dozen or so short stories – among them the widely anthologized "King of the Bingo Game," "Flying Home," and "A Coupla Scalped Indians" – and a much-awaited second novel, which reportedly was almost completed at the time of his death. He labored off and on for forty years on his follow-up novel, parts of which have appeared in literary magazines, and a 360-page chunk of which was destroyed when his summer house in Plainfield, Massachusetts, burned to the ground in the 1970s. Ellison, in his last published interview (March 1994), remarked: "The novel has got my at-

tention now. I work every day, so there will be something very soon."

When Ellison died, the New York *Amsterdam News* proclaimed that he had cut "a brilliant swath . . . through the literary firmament." One of his admirers, Johnson, acknowledged his indebtedness to Ellison when he won the National Book Award in 1990 for *Middle Passage;* he also praised Ellison as a pathfinder who "enables us as a people – as a culture – to move from narrow complaint to broad celebration."

Ellison's richly metaphoric and symbolic art has become part of the world's literature even as it transforms, elevates, and enlarges America's cultural heritage.

Bibliographies:

Jacqueline Covo, *The Blinking Eye: Ralph Waldo Ellison and His American, French, German, and Italian Critics 1952-1971: Bibliographic Essays and a Checklist* (Metuchen, N.J.: Scarecrow Press, 1974);

Joanne Giza, "Ralph Ellison," in *Black American Writers: Bibliographical Essays,* volume 2, edited by M. Thomas Inge, Maurice Duke, and Jackson R. Bryer (New York: St. Martin's Press, 1978), pp. 47-71;

Joe Weixlmann and John O'Banion, "A Checklist of Ellison Criticism, 1972-1978," *Black American Literature Forum,* 12 (Summer 1978), pp. 51-55;

Robert G. O'Meally, "The Writings of Ralph Ellison," in Kimberly W. Benston, ed., *Speaking for You: The Vision of Ralph Ellison* (Washington: Howard University Press, 1987), pp. 411-419;

Leonard Deutsch, "Ralph Ellison," in *Essential Bibliography of American Fiction: Modern African American Writers,* edited by Matthew J. Bruccoli and Judith S. Baughman (New York: Facts On File, 1994), pp. 19-31.

References:

Kimberly W. Benston, ed., *Speaking for You: The Vision of Ralph Ellison* (Washington: Howard University Press, 1987);

Jack Bishop, *Ralph Ellison* (New York: Chelsea House, 1988);

Harold Bloom, ed., *Ralph Ellison: Modern Critical Views* (New York: Chelsea House, 1986);

Henry Louis Gates, Jr., and K. A. Appiah, eds., *Ralph Ellison: Critical Perspectives Past & Present* (New York: Amistad Press, 1994);

Ronald Gottesman, ed., *Merrill Studies in Invisible Man* (Columbus, Ohio: Merrill, 1971);

John Hersey, ed., *Ralph Ellison: A Collection of Critical Essays* (Englewood Cliffs, N.J.: Prentice-Hall, 1974);

Robert N. List, *Dedalus in Harlem: The Joyce-Ellison Connection* (Washington: University Press of America, 1982);

Michael F. Lynch, *Creative Revolt: A Study of Wright, Ellison, and Dostoevsky* (New York: Peter Lang, 1990);

Kerry McSweeney, *Invisible Man: Race and Identity* (Boston: Twayne, 1988);

Alan Nadel, *Invisible Criticism: Ralph Ellison and the American Canon* (Iowa City: University of Iowa Press, 1988);

Robert G. O'Meally, *The Craft of Ralph Ellison* (Cambridge: Cambridge University Press, 1980);

O'Meally, ed., *New Essays on Invisible Man* (Cambridge, Mass.: Harvard University Press, 1988);

Susan Resneck Parr and Pancho Savery, eds., *Approaches to Teaching Ellison's Invisible Man* (New York: Modern Language Association, 1989);

John M. Reilly, ed., *Twentieth-Century Interpretations of Invisible Man: A Collection of Critical Essays* (Englewood Cliffs, N.J.: Prentice-Hall, 1970);

Edith Schor, *Visible Ellison: A Study of Ralph Ellison's Fiction* (Westport, Conn.: Greenwood Press, 1993);

Joseph F. Trimmer, ed., *A Casebook on Ralph Ellison's Invisible Man* (New York: Crowell, 1972);

Jerry G. Watts, *Heroism & the Black Intellectual: Ralph Ellison, Politics & the Dilemmas of Afro-American Intellectual Life* (Chapel Hill: University of North Carolina Press, 1994).

Seymour Lawrence

(11 February 1926 – 4 January 1994)

Darren Harris-Fain

Seymour Lawrence worked as an independent book publisher for nearly thirty years, from the creation of his imprint in 1965 to his death early in 1994. During that period he promoted the careers of many important American writers, including Thomas Berger, Richard Brautigan, J. P. Donleavy, Jim Harrison, Thomas McGuane, Tim O'Brien, William Saroyan, and Kurt Vonnegut. He also helped to publish the work of significant writers outside the United States, among them three recipients of the Nobel Prize for literature: Miguel Angel Asturias, Camilo José Cela, and Pablo Neruda.

Born in New York, Lawrence studied at Harvard University and worked as a book salesman in the late 1940s and early 1950s before joining the staff of *Atlantic Monthly* in 1952. He worked his way up from editorial assistant to director before leaving to become a vice-president at Knopf. The following year he went independent. Known as "Sam" to the writers with whom he worked, Lawrence was an outgoing champion of literature whose lively personality enabled him to pursue a career as an independent publisher who worked with, not for, major publishing houses. He started the Seymour Lawrence imprint in 1965 with Donleavy's *The Ginger Man* (first published in the United States in 1958), beginning an association with Dell that lasted seventeen years and saw his imprint on such novels as Brautigan's *Trout Fishing in America* (1967) and Vonnegut's *Slaughterhouse-Five* (1969), which he accepted after it was rejected by Vonnegut's publisher. This book and others were published by Dell's Delacorte label.

In 1983 Doubleday, the parent company of Dell, eliminated the Lawrence imprint during a period of mergers and cutbacks. Lawrence worked for Dutton for a while, then continued his imprint at Houghton Mifflin, which honored him in 1990 for his contributions to contemporary American litera-ture. He died from complications of a heart attack at age sixty-seven.

A TRIBUTE

from Thomas McGuane

Boca Grande. 4 January 1994, 9:00 P.M.

Sam Lawrence died a couple of hours ago at Englewood Hospital. I had been seeing him every other day or so for the last couple of weeks. I took him to lunch on Thursday. On Sunday he called to tell me that he had liked a story I had just published, a story that was about how life and death are embedded in one another. On Sunday night Bernice Washington, his friend and his nurse, had him taken to the hospital. He didn't want anyone to know he was there. On Tuesday, I was beginning to wonder where he'd gone, and on Tuesday Sam was feeling better. He sent Mrs. Washington back to the Gasparilla Inn for his papers and asked her to call me and tell me where he was. She returned to the hospital in early evening carrying his working supplies, but Sam had already died.

My first response on hearing this was to be overcome by its strangeness. Sam had been so full of life and plans that his death seemed improbable. I could more easily imagine him as he fondly recited his spring list. But I remembered how much I had felt the decline of his health, the psoriasis, the diabetes, the amputation of a leg. And I remember after a meeting next to the Gulf of Mexico, when I was absorbed by Sam's high spirits, that my wife had said, "I just don't see how Sam is going to make it." I remember how sobered I was by her remark; because Sam's courage had sort of fooled me. One day, sitting next to the blue, winter sea, holding up the palms of his hands which were peeling away with psoriasis, his face unshaven because he *couldn't*

Seymour Lawrence (University of Mississippi)

shave, a hardship for a dandy like Sam, he said, "I want a new body." His doctors had denied his cocktails and his cherished cigarettes, though he continued to sneak them. It was clear that he suspected that the experts who had removed his leg and were threatening to soon remove another, were individuals who were prey to useless superstitions in the name of science, whatever that was, certainly nothing that produced his favorite things, which were miracles like those of painting and writing.

Why was I so loyal to Sam? I am speaking now, professionally. Because, among other reasons, he was so loyal to me. I think all of his authors felt that way. Many of us had found ourselves in the hands of some perfidious and conniving individuals when we were published elsewhere. Sam Lawrence's loyalty was blind, the kind of loyalty you wish for in a family, but seldom get. It was unmitigated despite the fact that some of us did not deserve it. Writers flourish on loyalty. Loyalty is what Ponce de León would have been seeking if he had been a writer rather than a man of action. Whether we call Sam a publisher, an editor, or an impresario,

his approach to his own work was something like ours to ours: it was the pursuit of a dream.

Sam and I had in common an incapacity for repose. As a kind of whistling in the dark, I told him, in our last conversation about writing, that Jean Cocteau had said that a writer must never do anything hard. As a sort of riposte, Sam quoted Melville, "To insure the greatest efficiency of the dart, the harpooneers of this world must start to their feet from out of idleness, and not from out of toil." A lovely thought, it was sheer wishful thinking.

I have no idea what happens to us when we die; but I do know that Sam needed this rest and this peace.

A TRIBUTE

from Susan Minot

I met Sam Lawrence over ten years ago at a fund-raising reading for Books & Co. at the Puck Building here in New York. A friend of mine, Morgan Entrekin, who had worked under and learned

Front and back covers of a keepsake published by the University of Mississippi to mark the opening of the Seymour Lawrence Room
(University of Mississippi)

from Sam, introduced us, saying I'd just sold my first story to *The New Yorker*. Sam's eyes lit up. "Watch out," he said, "I might publish you." He asked to see my stories. At the time he was living at the Gramercy Park Hotel, and a few days later I met him there. He held up a bottle of champagne. "Congratulations," he said, and offered me a contract for a novel. I told him I couldn't possibly write a novel. Sam said I could call it whatever I wanted, he was publishing my book. I didn't know any better. I thought all publishers were like this.

Sam had the heart of a celebrator. He liked a fight, and he liked to go to bat for his authors, and he loved to win. To Sam the author knew best, and he encouraged his authors to approve jacket covers, even to suggest format and type. Sam bought books for their literary merit, but he also liked to make money — his eyes shone when he spoke of a deal he had made at Frankfurt.

Last spring many of Sam's authors honored him in Oxford, Mississippi, at the dedication of the room named for him at Ole Miss. One was always hearing about these other authors. Could he be giving each person the same sense of security which he gave me? Apparently so.

It was a privilege to be a part of Sam's group. I don't know quite what I'll do without him.

In the years that I knew Sam we often met at restaurants he liked. At Umberto's on 17th Street we had our last lunches together. In the spring he wore a seersucker suit and pink shirt and his elegant soft shoes. And he told his stories. One might hear, perhaps for the second time, of his bringing Katherine Anne Porter in her white ball gown and emeralds to speak to the all-male Signet Society at Harvard. The next book on his list by Tim O'Brien was a "knock-out." He ordered the veal chop and had another Kier Royale. He told how Jayne Anne Phillips had sought him out to be her publisher, of debauchery with Harrison and Chatham in Key West, all the time urging the waiter to keep grinding the pepper mill. He had been to Montana and finally "got" Tom McGuane; he had awe for the talent of Barry Hannah. There were the new discoveries – Rick Bass and Richard Bausch and Gish Jen and Tom Drury – and of his old ones, Kurt Vonnegut and J. P. Donleavy. The lunches would go on. Sometimes I wondered if he knew a writer needed to write. He never asked how it was going; he never mentioned deadlines except in the mildest way.

He talked about paintings – there was an O'Keefe he was hoping to buy. He had met a woman named Joan Williams again after thirty years. He talked of his early years, as publisher of the *Atlantic,* of being on Beacon Hill raising Nick and Macey. He'd driven cross-country as a traveling salesman and learned it was the bookseller who sold books. He told me the greatest joy in his life had been the birth of his two granddaughters.

When he lost his foot last summer he didn't stop. He was publishing from his hospital bed; there was the museum for his art collection, the house he wanted to build in Washington near his daughter, and Frank Conroy's new book. The last time I saw Sam was in November at Fairmont Hot Springs in Montana, where he'd come with his daughter Macy and her family for a vacation. He looked tired. He did not complain, but one could see he was not pleased with the way things were going. He continued to joke about himself, and with Sam the joke always had a strange solemn meaning. The last note I got from him showed the usual flash of light and that extra maniacal note. Love, he signed it, Uncle Ahab.

A TRIBUTE

from Jayne Anne Phillips

14 February 1994

We've come here today from all over America and Europe to make a valentine for Sam, and the timing is somehow right, since he operated as an empowering saint in the lives of so many of us. I first met Sam in 1978 at the Saint Lawrence Writers Conference in upstate New York, and he has functioned as an angel in my life ever since. "Mr. Lawrence," I asked him at the time, "do you publish short stories?" "Not if I can help it," he replied. But he read "Sweethearts," my collection of one-page fictions published by Truck Press in 1976, and phoned me in West Virginia within the week. "You're a real writer," he said to me, "Bring your stories to Boston." Sam was an artist at what he did, and he understood what artists need. We planned the publication of *Black Tickets* together in

Mendocino, with Sam put up in some spectacular digs and me arriving in my dented Nova on a weekend break from my first teaching job. Somehow we ended up in an old graveyard by the sea at dusk, with fog and gold light swirling around Sam's walking stick, and he looked at me seriously and said, "You're a witch." At that moment something sparkled across a stone, moving fast, and he said, "Look, look, a wizard! I mean a lizard!" He became "the Wizard," and his letters to me began, Dear Witch. He really was in it for the magic. Writing was alchemy, and publishing was the prayer that carried the words. He quoted me as saying, "Sam and I found each other," but I think that statement is representative of how Sam viewed all his relationships with writers. He chose his writers very carefully, and when he committed to our work, he committed for life, and beyond death. He loved us, he took care of us, he yelled at us, he drank with us, he phoned us, daily sometimes, with all the news of the latest foreign sale, swank dinner, advertising budget, he gossiped with us, he ate and drank with us in inimitable Sam style, a style that said, "We're wonderful, and the work we're trying to do is wonderful, and will endure, like this wine." He argued with us, he apologized, sometimes, with an engaging, slightly chastened dignity, he was patient and forbearing. Romance might waver, domestic arrangements collapse, but Sam was steadfast; he helped us in ways our families could not. He did what only he could do: he sustained our spirits, even as he made money for us, and for himself, with utter glee. All that was a lovely game and a passionate life. He loved life, he loved good food and beautiful places and English suits and privilege. He insisted on privilege, yet he said to me more than once, "It doesn't matter where you come from. Katherine Anne came from Indian Creek, Texas, she came from nowhere. It doesn't matter where you come from, it matters what you do; that's why we live in this country." He lived life on his terms, with a kind of crazy bravery. I think of him at ABA in a wheelchair, with a nurse to change the bandages on his bleeding foot. Threatened, he worked. He worked harder. He worked in bed with his papers strewn all around him. We talked about the December sales conference at Houghton. "Should I walk in with the crutches, or should I just be seated at the table when they all walk in? Better if I'm sitting down already, don't you think? Less of a big deal." Faced with his own illness, his own mortality, he was amazingly brave in dealing with us, his writers, like a parent whose first thought is to pro-

Lawrence, center with cane, standing at the University of Mississippi with some of the authors he published during his career
(University of Mississippi)

tect the children. He made himself a myth about Ahab, the swashbuckling publishing pirate, and the voice on the phone was always strong: he was always making progress, he was the star of rehab, he was planning to come along on that upcoming European pub tour, which country should it be? And he convinced us. We'd all been concerned about Sam. But when we got the call from Joan, his much loved companion, or from Camille, his longtime assistant and ally, or from Tom, who was with Sam in Florida, the news — that such an undaunted heart could stop — was unbelievable. The day he died, he dictated a letter to me from his hospital bed, and he ended it — "Love and best wishes for a Great and Glorious '94, the Wizard of Boca Grande."

His was a glorious faith. His belief in us was unconditional, because writing is not founded on conditions. He stood as an elegant bulwark between the writer and the corporation, the writer and the reviews, good or bad, between the writer and self-doubt. He cheered our every endeavor, he railed against our enemies, he told us jokes, he danced with us, he published work that inspired us to work, he repeated our best conversational lines to one another as evidence of our immense stature and the crazy vagaries of the writer's circumstance. He made us a kind of family. And beyond all that, he influenced the course of American literature. Writing was a life, not a career. Publishing was a calling, not a job. He was fiercely uncompromising. He was bull-headed in support of us. He laughed with us, he comforted us.

And having worked with Sam will continue to comfort us, to gird us for battle with the darkest days of his absence. For me, those days will be many. I met him as a nearly unpublished twenty-four-year-old; he was the benefactor and constant of my writing life. He was my friend, through the deaths of my parents and the births of my children. He waited, without complaint, six years for my new book, with never a break in letters, calls, or lunches at the Ritz.

Finally, I phoned him from MacDowell last summer and said, "Sam, I'm packing the car to go home. Today's my birthday and I finished the book."

"Perfect!" he shouted. "I love you!" He promptly dispatched two dozen roses to Boston. He loved the book, but he didn't love the title. Titles came and went over the next few weeks. Finally he said to me, "You've got to let go of this goddamn book. You're driving everyone crazy. I have the title."

"Well – " I said.

"Listen carefully," he said. "It's one word."

There was silence on the line.

"SHELTER," Sam said, with that hesitation that crept into his speech, ". . . And may we all . . . find some."

I felt a little scared, like a shadow had come between us. He'd been in and out of the hospital, but I hadn't known, until that moment, how scared I was of losing Sam. I couldn't quite breathe.

He took my silence for indecision. "It's ominous," he said, "it's mysterious. It's like an offering."

So, Sam, a thousand hearts in this valentine. And today is not our only offering. You don't die while we're alive. We are your writers. In the act of writing, we celebrate you. In reading each other, we celebrate your vision. All of us in this room, in supporting, producing, selling, editing, literary American fiction, protect what you protected, and we honor you.

Peter Taylor

(8 January 1917 – 2 November 1994)

Mark Trainer

BOOKS: *A Long Fourth* (New York: Harcourt, Brace, 1948; London: Routledge & Kegan Paul, 1949);

A Woman of Means (New York: Harcourt, Brace, 1950);

The Widows of Thornton (New York: Harcourt, Brace, 1954);

Tennessee Day in St. Louis (New York: Random House, 1957);

Happy Families Are All Alike (New York: McDowell Obolensky, 1959; London: Macmillan, 1960);

Miss Leonora When Last Seen (New York: Ivan Obolensky, 1964);

The Collected Stories of Peter Taylor (New York: Farrar, Straus & Giroux, 1969);

Presences: Seven Dramatic Pieces (Boston: Houghton Mifflin, 1973);

In the Miro District (New York: Knopf, 1977; London: Chatto & Windus, 1977);

The Early Guest (Winston-Salem, N.C.: Palaemon Press, 1982);

The Old Forest and Other Stories (New York: Doubleday, 1985; London: Chatto & Windus, 1985);

A Stand In the Mountains (New York: Frederic C. Beil, 1986);

A Summons to Memphis (New York: Knopf, 1986; London: Chatto & Windus, 1986);

The Oracle at Stoneleigh Court (New York: Knopf, 1993; London: Chatto & Windus, 1993);

In the Tennessee Country (New York: Knopf, 1994; London: Chatto & Windus, 1994).

Peter Taylor's writing career spanned nearly sixty years, during which he published numerous volumes of short stories as well as a novella, two novels, plays, and narrative poems. From the publication of his first story, "The Party," in 1937 in the journal *River* (another writer enjoying first-time publication in this issue was Eudora Welty) to the appearance of *In the Tennessee Country* shortly before his death in 1994, Taylor created a peculiarly distinctive body of work.

He was most at home in the short-story form, and his best stories truly work as miniature novels in that they circumscribe an entire world of human interaction. He most often used the setting of the Upper South and the generations that peopled that region in the first half of this century. While his eye for the traditions and history of his native Tennessee lent his stories a unique verisimilitude, he managed to imbue their settings – Memphis, Nashville, and his fictional Thornton, Chatham, and Owl Mountain – with a metaphoric strength that raises his work far above that of a regionalist. It is the very obscurity of these Tennessee lifestyles and traditions, only slightly less obscure to readers of the late 1930s when he began publishing than they are to modern readers, that makes them so useful to Taylor.

His collections of stories were published regularly over the years to critical acclaim, and he had a lifelong association with *The New Yorker*. Popular recognition was slow in coming to him, perhaps because of his devotion to the short-story form rather than the novel. Taylor taught writing for most of his career, which kept him from being dependent on publication for a livelihood.

> I feel so strongly against professionalism, against someone's feeling he has to write a book every year to keep his name before the public. I see people pressing themselves, torturing themselves, for that, rather than writing out of a compulsion some story from their own experience. . . . I really don't think you should make money writing. Oh, I'm not going to turn down money, but people worrying about how they are going to make a living writing ought to worry about making a living some other way on the periphery, doing something congenial to them like teaching or editing. We hear a lot of complaints from writers now . . . about the situation of the writer – well it's *always* been awful! I think you should write for yourself, for the joy of it, the pleasure of it, and for the satisfaction that you have in learning about your life.

Peter Taylor

Peter Taylor was born in Trenton, Tennessee, in 1917. His was a family steeped in the politics of the Volunteer State. His grandfather, Robert Love Taylor, served terms both as governor and United States senator. In 1886 this grandfather, his great-grandfather and his granduncle all made bids for the governorship in what came to be known as the War of the Roses. His own father was a lawyer who moved the family around Tennessee – Nashville, Memphis, and Trenton – and to Saint Louis. These locales, their subtle differences, and the cultural exchanges they shared in the post–Civil War era would power much of Taylor's work. It was a world of transition where the traditional conception of the family tried to coexist with the emerging industrial South.

The young Peter Taylor who emerged from this background found himself at odds with his father, who hoped he would pursue a career in law. He briefly attended Southwestern University, where he studied with Allen Tate. "But I found I could not teach him anything," Tate would later write. "The simple truth is that he did not need to

know anything that I could teach him. He had a perfection of style at the age of 18 that I envied." At Tate's urging he enrolled at Vanderbilt the following year, where he studied under John Crowe Ransom. When Ransom moved on to Kenyon College in Gambier, Ohio, Taylor followed. The poet Randall Jarrell, only four years Taylor's senior, was also teaching and coaching tennis at Kenyon. Another student who came to Kenyon to study with Ransom was Robert Lowell. "When I was at Kenyon," Taylor remembered, "there were all these poets around, and I tried to write poetry. Writing a short story depends a lot on compression. That's the main way to differentiate it from a novel. In writing with Ransom, every emphasis was on compression. When you write poetry you have to make a word count for more. In a certain way a short story is somewhere between a novel and a poem. Chekhov's stories are really poems. The best stories can be talked about as poems in the same way. You see the structure, you see it all at once, as you can't in a novel."

Following their graduation from Kenyon, both Taylor and Lowell undertook graduate study at

Louisiana State University under Robert Penn Warren. At this point Taylor had sold work to the *Kenyon Review* and *Southern Review*. Deciding that critical study was not for him, he left the program at Thanksgiving.

The following year, 1941, he was drafted and spent the next two and a half years at Fort Oglethorpe, near Chattanooga, Tennessee. In 1943 he was introduced by his mentor Tate to the poet Eleanor Lilly Ross. After a six-week courtship the two were wed in Sewanee, Tennessee, with Tate, Lowell, and Jean Stafford (then Lowell's wife) in attendance.

Taylor spent two years of the war stationed in England and upon his return took a job with Henry Holt publishers. But the following autumn he joined the English department at the Woman's College of the University of North Carolina, the first of many teaching appointments he would hold over the years.

Taylor published his first collection of stories, *The Long Fourth,* in 1948. "Peter Taylor has a disenchanted mind," wrote Robert Penn Warren in his introduction, "but a mind that nevertheless understands and values enchantment."

Of the stories collected in this premiere volume, "A Spinster's Tale" has been the most anthologized in subsequent years. The title gives context to the narrator's recollection of a few months in her adolescence following by a year the death of her mother during childbirth. Having subconsciously absorbed an idea of the rewards attending mature female sexuality, she spends much of the story at the parlor window poised between terror and anticipation of the appearance of Mr. Speed, a harmless town drunk whom she likens to a "loose horse." The fate promised by the title becomes more and more inevitable as the anxiety she has embodied in Mr. Speed spreads to her father and brother. When Mr. Speed finally shows up on her porch during a rainstorm, she can only treat him as an object of fear, and she has him carried off by the police. At the story's end she tells us not a week has passed in her life since when she has not thought of Mr. Speed and the terror he represented. It is an ambitious and for the most part successful psychological portrait. The preponderance of Freudian symbols invites, and has prompted, extended analysis. Yet for all the grace brought to its telling, the narrative and its narrator insist upon a fairly specific interpretation, something more overt than the rounded understanding of human motivation shown in Taylor's fully matured work.

His stories are often told in the first person by narrators that are, as he said, "seldom completely reliable, but they aren't totally unreliable." They are intelligent and thoughtful men or women who are nevertheless answering a compulsion they might not entirely understand.

Subsequent stories develop the subject matter that would occupy most of his work: the study of community and family membership confronted by a changing social order. Of these, none is more striking than "Venus, Cupid, Folly and Time." A grown man tells of the strange parties held when he was a boy by an aged brother and sister who were leftovers of a grand family that founded and then abandoned the fictional city of Chatham. Although nearly all the parents of the children who attend these parties fear the influence of Mr. and Miss Dorset, it has become a rite of passage for the offspring of the best families that the parents do not dare deny them in this small, closed society. Ned and Emily Meriwether decide to sneak in an outsider, a boy from a lower order named Tom Bascomb, passing off Tom as Ned and Ned as the outsider. This invasion and the implications of Tom's dumb show of romantic advances to his "sister" over the course of the party bring an end to the Dorset parties and leave an indelible impression on the children of Chatham that lasts into the adulthood from which our narrator is writing.

Like his best work, the story can be held up and examined from any number of perspectives. When asked to describe it with a single word, Taylor said, "That's easy. Incest." He went on to explain: "Social incest. Some people cannot function outside a narrow social group. They especially can't marry outside the group. That kind of limitation can incapacitate them for life; it works in all kinds of ways. The whole story, of course, is almost an allegory." But unlike most allegories, Taylor brought to his representative characters an undeniable humanity which saved them from being mere types. Often this representative character suggests the disappearing South of the previous century, whether it be the Civil War veteran grandfather who refuses to allow his history to be appropriated by the gentrified Nashville set in "In the Miro District," or Miss Leonora Logan who goes missing when the values of history and preservation her family embodied become obsolete in a growing industrialized southern town in "Miss Leonora When Last Seen."

Over the years Taylor was building his reputation as a craftsman of distinction, he continued to

"Indeed there is no living American writer whose work I admire so much as Taylor's."
—**Jonathan Yardley**

"No one writing in English can do more with a short story...he is a master."
—**Geoffrey Wolff**, *Newsweek*

"His *Collected Stories* is one of the major works of our literature."
—**Joyce Carol Oates**

"One of the finest short story writers of our time."
—**Albert Griffith**, *Commonweal*

"I am tempted to say that Peter Taylor is the greatest living short story writer, but I shall be prudent and suggest he is the greatest one writing in English today."
—**Linda Kuehl**, *Saturday Review*

ISBN: 0-385-27983-3

PETER TAYLOR

The Old Forest
—*and Other Stories*—

The Old Forest
and Other Stories
PETER TAYLOR

THE DIAL PRESS

Dust jacket for the collection of stories that brought greater public recognition to Taylor's work

teach writing, holding posts at University of North Carolina at Greensboro, Kenyon, and Harvard. He left this last plum appointment to the disbelief of his friends and colleagues:

> I thought I was a great success as a teacher and being at Harvard. But I was known as a fiction writing teacher and I hated being labeled as a teacher ... instead of being a writer. See, my teaching of writing was more than my writing to people and I just hated that. I thought I was a failure. There are a lot of famous writing teachers at Harvard who publish a book or so and they're marvelous with students. They go along and that's their life. But that's not being a writer.

He went from Harvard to the University of Virginia, from that point on teaching only a half year. He retired from teaching in 1983, the same year he was inducted into the American Academy of Arts and Letters.

It was with the publication of *The Old Forest and Other Stories* in 1985 that greater recognition began to come Taylor's way. The volume collected several of his older stories with new ones. Perhaps the most celebrated of Taylor's shorter

works is the title story. In the 1930s Nat Ramsey, a young man of a good Memphis family engaged to be married the following week to a member of the debutante set, has a minor car accident while in the company of a Memphis "demimondain," Lee Ann Deehart. After the wreck Lee Ann runs off into the nearby forest and cannot be found. Her disappearance puts Nat's imminent marriage in danger, and over the next four days the protective and powerful male leadership of the city undertakes the search. As the story unfolds, the delineations and restrictions of this seemingly genteel community become increasingly evident. After mild protest Nat had toed the family line by coming to work in his father's cotton brokerage; his stubborn persistence in a class on Latin odes his only connection to a life other than the one expected of him. Lee Ann and the young women like her are shut out of the Memphis elite, live in boarding houses, and are only considered proper company for a beer garden by young men like the narrator, on whom they look with thinly disguised condescension. But perhaps the most restricted by this social order is Caroline Baxley, Nat's fiancée. She is "one of the innocent,

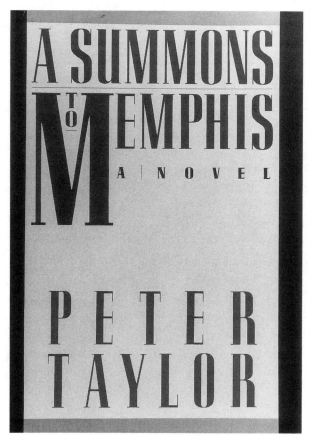

Dust jacket for the novel for which Taylor won a Pulitzer Prize
in 1986

untutored types that we generally took to dances at the Memphis Country Club and whom we eventually looked forward to marrying." It is Caroline who stands to lose the most through this predicament and who cannot wait for the men of the town to solve the mystery of Lee Ann's whereabouts. The story brings together the best elements of Taylor's work and was subsequently made into a film by Steven Ross.

In 1986, just before the publication of his first full-length novel, *A Summons to Memphis,* Taylor suffered a stroke that left him unable to speak or write for a time. While he struggled to regain his health, *A Summons to Memphis* brought him wider praise and recognition than he had ever known. The book won the Pulitzer Prize for fiction and the Ritz/Hemingway Award and was nominated for the National Book Award.

Taylor described the novel as "a comedy about a rich old man whose children try to prevent his remarrying, and it ranges back over their earlier lives. It's about revenge upon and forgiveness of

parents. Maturity, in a way, is forgiving your parents." The laconic narrator, Phillip Carver, is the son of the old widower, and it is his two sisters who are determined to prevent the remarriage and enlist Phillip's aid in doing so. Although Phillip has moved off to New York and considers himself unencumbered by the family squabbles and tensions he left behind in Memphis, the plea for his return inevitably draws him back in.

In the eight years that followed *A Summons to Memphis,* Taylor struggled to continue with his writing in the face of increasingly failing health. Unable physically to write, he was forced to dictate his manuscripts. In 1993 his last collection of stories, *The Oracle at Stoneleigh Court,* was published. These stories emphasized a supernatural strain that had long been present in his work, specters in the Jamesian mold who enter the lives of Taylor's staid characters. "Ghosts and fantasies, I think, are a part of the experience of most people," he said. "I came to realize from reading and from my own experience that people who see ghosts see them because they need to see them, or want to see them. The wish is so strong or the need is so strong."

Taylor's final work, his second full-length novel, *In the Tennessee Country,* brings together many of the themes he had been working with in different guises throughout his career. The story is told to us by Nathan Longfort, a retired professor of art history. "In the Tennessee country of my forebears," Nathan tells us, "it was not uncommon for a man of good character suddenly to disappear." It is one of these men in particular, an illegitimate cousin to his mother named Aubrey Bradshaw Tucker, who is the focus of the novel. The book's extended opening scene takes place when Nathan is a small boy aboard the funeral train carrying the body of his esteemed grandfather, a former Tennessee governor and U.S. senator, from Washington, D.C., to Knoxville. By trip's end, when the senator has been lowered into his Knoxville grave, Aubrey is missing from the funeral party. The nearby woods and stations are scoured, but he is nowhere to be found. This family background of expectation and privilege exerts such an influence on Nathan's life that he becomes fascinated with Aubrey and the Tennesseans like him who chose to withdraw themselves from the world in which they were raised. By the time Nathan is a retired professor (rather than the painter he might have been), his curiosity about Aubrey's fate has nearly become an obsession, and it is then that he locates and eventually comes face to face with Aubrey.

The work of Peter Taylor seems assured a place in the American fiction of this century that will continue to be read well into the next. When some measure of literary celebrity reached him in later life, he was able to receive it with equanimity. "If you're a serious writer, you want to be able to do your work and have warm response to it by intelligent readers and not try to be a movie star, not try to be a culture hero. I don't think it was the road for me. That's just my temperament, I guess."

Interviews:

Stephen Goodwin, "An Interview with Peter Taylor," *Shenandoah,* 24 (Winter 1973): 3–20;

J. William Broadway, "A Conversation with Peter Taylor," *The Chattahoochee Review,* 6 (Fall 1985): 17–44, 61–75.

References:

Hubert H. McAlexander, ed., *Conversations with Peter Taylor* (Jackson: University Press of Mississippi, 1987);

McAlexander, ed., *Critical Essays on Peter Taylor* (New York: G. K. Hall, 1993);

Stuart Wright, *Peter Taylor: A Descriptive Bibliography 1934–87* (Charlottesville: University Press of Virginia, 1988).

A TRIBUTE

from Richard Bausch

I first heard the name of Peter Taylor in 1971, from my then-teacher, who was just a couple of years out of the University of Virginia. We read and discussed "The Spinster's Tale," and of course I knew right away that I wanted to get everything I could of Mr. Taylor's and ingest it, the way I was ingesting things back then. "The Spinster's Tale" remains one of my favorite stories, but there are others, too: "The Dean of Men," "Venus, Cupid, Folly and Time," "The Fancy Woman," "Cookie," "Reservations," "What You Hear From 'em?," "Miss Leonora When Last Seen," "The Old Forest," "Port Corchere," "The Scoutmaster" – the names of the stories come so readily to mind, and are easy to recite, because the stories themselves have stayed with me over the years. And through the years I was always aware of Mr. Taylor, as new stories made their way to the world: "The Captain's Son," "In The Miro District," "The Oracle of Stoneleigh Court" – all these wonderful stories.

I was first introduced to Peter Taylor in 1972, when he read at my university. He signed my book of the collected stories. And though later I became friends with people who were closer to him – with Susan Richards Shreve and Stephen Goodwin, and Robert and Martha Wilson, and others – I saw, through a sort of reflection, what it must have been to him as a teacher and mentor. He was obviously the kind of teacher and mentor who considered that his mentorship extended beyond the confines of the university setting and the classroom, although it could be said, too, that it was a kind of university Mr. Taylor carried with him from place to place. In 1986 I was privileged to be one of those who would speak to introduce Peter at the Folger Shakespeare Library. And after a party the night before the reading, I drove him back to his hotel. On that ride, as we were discussing someone who had made an impression at the gathering, a professorial type who had spoken over and through his wife and had obviously had too much to drink, Peter said that this gentleman reminded him of the professor in my novella *Spirits.* He went on to say why, in terms that clearly demonstrated to me his knowledge of the story. This would have been impressive enough to me, had the book in which that story appeared been out in the world for any period of time – but the book was in galleys and was not scheduled to appear for months. He chattered on, being funny, telling me these things about this fictional someone I had made up, and I had a glimpse of what good fortune my friends had enjoyed, to have actually worked with him.

His work will survive – as long as people read stories, his stories will insist on their place. He may have once despaired of writing as deeply as his one peer, Chekhov, but he need not have. He need not have.

A TRIBUTE

from Madison Smartt Bell

I first began reading Peter Taylor's stories in my early teens, I think, when I was too young to really understand them, but I kept on reading them just the same. I can still remember the shape and color of those volumes, the places they had fetched up on the shoals of other books in our house. It may have been the voice that held me, at once alien and strangely intimate, independently of its matter. That sound reminds me now of the endless conversation between my parents and my grandparents about different Nashville families and their qualities and interrelationships ("no, she married a Caldwell, not a . . ."), which I always seemed to be half-listening to in those days, somewhere in a corner of the room and most likely strumming the pages of some other book. And I kept worrying at the stories, like a puppy with a rawhide toy, till they began to yield the flavor of their intentions.

In later years I met Mr. Taylor a number of times, probably not more than five, and always pleasantly. I was able to participate in minor ways in the renascence of his reputation that followed the publication of *The Old Forest,* and when we met I found that he had read what I had written and been pleased. I had been (am still) especially drawn to the story "A Wife of Nashville," indubitably a major masterpiece of twentieth-century short fiction, and on the several occasions when I wrote about was unable to resist quoting the whole long passage of its conclusion, where twenty-some years of historical recitation come to bear on a space of no more than a few seconds, and with inimitable force. Still for me that is the most spectacular example of Peter Taylor's consummate skills, which so few

writers still living even know how to value, much less master.

My fascination with "A Wife of Nashville" is now itself twenty-some years old, and I came back to the story last fall while working on a creative-writing textbook. I called Mr. Taylor in Charlottesville to get a theoretical and tentative permission to include a heavily annotated edition of the story in the book. Unbeknownst to me he was in bed, recovering from a stroke, but he answered the phone himself, and his speech and mind were both very clear. He was cheerful and vigorous and seemed pleased with the project. I promised to send him the annotated story when I was done.

In the end the commentary was about as long as the story itself and still didn't exhaust all that could be said about it. It was some weeks before I remembered to send it to Mr. Taylor, and then, before I had addressed the package, I thought that I would be in Charlottesville myself in two weeks' time and could deliver it to him in person.

He died two days before I arrived there, I think, and that there won't be writers like him any more is reason enough to grieve his loss. But there was something more to the moment when I got the news, a subtle twist of irony that he himself might have devised. I was reminded of Helen Ruth, holding the phone at the end of "A Wife of Nashville" and poised on the cusp of an unparaphraseable understanding. It made me know that the scriptural warning is addressed to survivors as much as to those we survive: *we are not promised tomorrow.* That moment could have been drawn from one of his stories. I suppose that, in some infinitesimal way, it is part of his story now.

A TRIBUTE

from Fred Chappell

Peter Taylor's commitment to literary excellence was as strong as that of his dear friend Randall Jarrell, but there was a much less personal edge to it. He wouldn't take it as an affront if one of his acquaintances published a less than worthy poem or story. He simply failed to mention such things. Neither was he given to fulsome praise of work he liked. He acknowledged such pieces graciously but almost as it were in passing, and then would go on to discuss his enduring enthusiasms. These included Henry James, Thomas Mann, the short stories of D. H. Lawrence, Anton Chekhov, and – in later years especially – the novels of Anthony Trollope.

His canon of excellence was, then, rather a narrow one, though of course it included a great many more authors than I have mentioned here. But with this list one can extrapolate who the others would be and the qualities that Peter desired and expected in work he could admire. He would talk about the pages of these writers with such pleasure and in such specific detail that he never needed to define in any abstract terms what *excellence* represented for him. It embraced Ernest Hemingway and F. Scott Fitzgerald but excluded Henry Miller and Erskine Caldwell. Even so, he found it difficult to condemn aloud even writing toward which he was quite cool. I recall one time when his friend Tom Molyneux asked his opinion of Djuna Barnes. Peter hesitated for some moments, and then said, "Well, she has . . . *texture*." When pressed for a definition of "texture" he was evasive. But at last as Tom kept on with the question Peter replied: "Texture means that every page is as hard to read as every other page."

I believe that witty replies often rose to Peter's mind and that he suppressed most of them in the interest of good manners. I think he found humor more sociable than wit. Allen Tate's gossip was often sexual; Peter's rarely. His was a gossip of character rather than incident; he was fond of pointing out contrarieties, foibles, and contradictions in the behavior and conversation of friends and acquaintances. "Do you notice how So-and-so always drops her voice when she talks about *Republicans*?" But this gossip was never malicious. I can't remember that he ever spoke against anyone. He would sometimes allude darkly to "his enemies," but in my presence he never derogated or even identified them.

Now and then, however, he would allow his verbal wit to flash out. I remember one instance vividly. Peter and I were sitting with the poet Gibbons Ruark at Greensboro's sad excuse for a literary watering place, a grubby beer joint called The Pickwick. The conversation turned to horseshoe pitching, a recreation Peter rather enjoyed. He claimed, though, to have no interest in any competitive aspect of the game. It was the *sound* a ringer made, he explained, that was so satisfying. He wished he could throw more ringers just to hear that sound.

"What you need," offered Gib, "is someone to stand by the stake and, whenever you pitch a miss, toss on a ringer for you."

"But I'd see them doing it," Peter complained. "It wouldn't be the same."

"You could close your eyes when you pitched," Gib said. "Then the sound would be your own."

"But what if you closed your eyes and pitched and didn't hear anything? Not a sound. Then what?" I asked.

"Well – " said Peter, "it's a dead ringer."

A TRIBUTE

from George Garrett

I doubt that there is anyone who admires Peter Taylor's literary accomplishments more than I do or has a greater respect for his art and craft. He brought something new and wonderful to southern writing even as he sustained our finest and firmest American traditions. There is no question that the work he created, first to last, is here to stay.

The man has left us behind, slipped away into the spirit world, leaving each of us our separate memories of him.

My memory goes back more than thirty years. We first met in (of all places) New York City, doing some work for the Ford Foundation. We pretty much agreed on things and had a good time. Later on I worked with him at some writers' conferences. He was fine to work with. I visited Greensboro a few times while he was teaching there, and I delighted in his company.

Later I had to leave Virginia for the wide world, and Peter Taylor came up from Greensboro and took over my job. To round the story off, when he retired I was chosen, partly by Peter, to replace him at Virginia; and then, entirely by accident, we ended up living next door to each other on Wayside Place. What else did we share? We both had roots in Sewanee where he is now buried. We taught some of the same students and had a good many mutual friends. We belonged to some of the same organizations.

It is the man I mourn. The work is safely alive. I loved and admired Peter Taylor's style – his graceful ways, his special wit and wisdom, his irrepressible sense of humor, and, above all, the courage that never failed him. I will always miss him.

Light perpetual keep him.

A TRIBUTE

from Daniel O'Neill

Washington – past midnight. Tom, Debra and I are walking Peter back to his room at the Capitol Hill Hotel, walking with him down the broad, half-lit sidewalk of Third Street after a long awards ceremony and cocktail reception at the Folger. At the reception Peter allowed himself to be stationed, cane at his side, on a padded bench at a far end of the room. There, nursing the one small scotch he let us bring him, he received – quietly, graciously, with an occasional stir of laughter – wave after wave of younger writers, former students, admirers. Finally, hours into the function, he spotted us in the crowd and glassily signaled that it was time to go. We are all tired; we have walked this far down the street in silence when, inexplicably, Tom starts in: "So, Peter . . . I saw you pounding down that Johnny Walker Red . . . How 'bout it? . . . You slip a fifth under your coat? We gonna knock some back in the room now. . . ?"

In fact it is only Tom who has had too much to drink. The taunting, the blind insistence on a reaction, is meant to be in fun, but surely it is rougher fun than Peter is up to. After all, he is past seventy: his speech is slurred, his gait hobbled by a stroke four years ago. And here, at this dim hour, is a burly New York editor, the friend of a friend and nearly forty years his junior, jabbering away, practically poking him in the ribs as he struggles to make his way down the deserted street.

But when I glance over I see that Peter's mouth is already stretched back into that wonderful deep-cut crescent of a smile, and that the pale blue eyes, still searching for the next placement of the cane on the sidewalk, are open wide as a child's. "Yes, that's right, Thomas," he is saying in a hoarse, delighted voice. "Yes, yes, of course we will – it sounds *marvelous!* You take yours – what? – straight-up?" He seems to me practically floating now as he swings the cane around, elbows splayed, laughing full out – that deep, shuddering kettle drum laugh that seems always on the point of getting away from him: "Uh-huh-huh, huh-huh! *Huh-huh-huh-huh!*"

How many similar scenes had I witnessed over the years I knew Peter? Just when you thought he had been thrown into circumstances he couldn't possibly manage, that his antique formality and seeming innocence were about to run aground on someone's rudeness or egotism or uninvited intimacy . . . it was as if a part of him never before seen, but designed for just such difficult terrain as this, would unfold and, like an ingenious set of wheels, touch down, allowing Peter to roll along every bit as smoothly himself as before.

One could say – and it has been said – that something analogous is going on in the best of Peter's stories, where the energy often seems to be generated by a breaking-through (or near-breaking-through) from the constrained tones of his narrators' measured, decorous speech to the primal longings and passions that underlie them. But this is not the place for such speculations. Because to re-read the stories – gorgeously crafted and enduringly moving as they are – is not really to remember Peter as we knew him. I believe, with many, that Peter's stories are among the best to have been written in this century. And the stories will be there. But also I know that, for me, they can never take the place of this man who, for all his courtly manners and anachronistic charm, was the most natural and unaffected – and very possibly the kindest – person I have ever known.

Helen Wolff

(27 July 1906 – 29 March 1994)

Darren Harris-Fain

Credited with promoting the work of a world-wide body of authors, editor and publisher Helen Wolff was a widely admired figure in the American and international book trade. With her husband she founded Pantheon Books, which they ran for nineteen years, and in 1961 they established a respected imprint with Harcourt, Brace & World. Among the writers with whom she worked are Umberto Eco, Günter Grass, Stanislaw Lem, Anne Morrow Lindbergh, Amos Oz, and Georges Simenon, who called the Wolffs "the most astonishing couple in the world of publishing."

Born Helen Mosel in Macedonia in 1906, she grew up speaking German, Turkish, and Serbian at home. She acquired additional languages easily, beginning with her boarding-school education in Vienna after World War I. She moved to Munich in 1927 to join Kurt Wolff Verlag, where she worked on the publishing company's art books. She married the president of the company, who was twenty years older than she, in 1933. The following year their son, Christian, was born; she also had a stepson and stepdaughter from Wolff's previous marriage. After their marriage the couple settled in Nice, France, due to the increasingly threatening political climate in Germany. Two years later they moved to a village near Florence, Italy, but returned to France after the outbreak of World War II.

They settled in New York in 1941. Though they had little money, the following year they managed to create their own publishing house, Pantheon, by encouraging three investors to contribute seventy-five hundred dollars to the venture. Early successes included a 1944 edition of the Grimms' fairy tales and a translation of Russian novelist Boris Pasternak's masterpiece, *Doctor Zhivago* (1958). They established their own imprint at Pantheon and published several important works by American and international authors – aided by her facility with European languages, which allowed her to read works in the original before other American publishers were able to read them in translation.

They moved to Locarno, Italy, in 1959, two years before they resigned from Pantheon, which was soon acquired by Random House. The same year they were invited by William Jovanovich to create an imprint for Harcourt Brace, Helen and Kurt Wolff Books – probably the first personal imprint in American publishing.

Two years later Wolff's husband was killed in a traffic accident. She returned to New York and continued their imprint, however, aiding in the American publication of such novels as Italo Calvino's *Invisible Cities* (1974) and Eco's *The Name of the Rose* (1983). She remained active in publishing until her retirement in 1986, after which the Wolff imprint remained active at Harcourt Brace Jovanovich. She died at age eighty-eight in her home in Hanover, New Hampshire, of an apparent heart attack.

A TRIBUTE

from Günter Grass

NACHRUF AUF HELEN WOLFF

Ihr Tod hat alles verändert, mehr als zu sagen ist. Und was gesagt werden kann, steht nun auf einem anderen Blatt; denn eigentlich hatte ich Helen Wolff heiter, mit einem alle Feierlichkeit wegräumenden Wort begrüßen wollen: Liebe Helene, wie gut, daß Duzda bist.

Als mich die Deutsche Akademie für Sprache und Dichtung bat, zur Verleihung des Friedrich-Gundolf-Preises eine Laudatio zu halten, fiel mir zur Preisträgerin weit mehr ein, als eine kurze Rede bändigen könnte. Allenfalls bereitete mir der Nimbus des Namens Gundolf einen nicht gelinden, eher einen lähmenden Schrecken. Etwas Hohepriesterliches ging von ihm aus, etwas, das mir unwirklich und entrückt zu sein schien. Diese Distanz war nicht zu überbrücken, ich konnte nur, außer Un-

Helen Wolff

wissenheit, Respekt bezeugen; denn schnell Angelesenes wollte ich weder der Preisträgerin noch dem zur Feierstunde versammelten Publikum zumuten.

Dann holte mich die traurige Nachricht ein. Letzte Gewißheit. Der Verlust. Und doch ist mir immer noch so, als könnte ich zu Dir, liebe Helen, die in meinen geheimsten und monologischen Zwiegesprächen immer als Helene angerufen wird, direkt, vom Freund zu Freundin, als Autor zur Verlegerin sprechen und so tun, als sei nichts geschehen, als dürfe weiterhin Rat eingeholt, der nächste Brief erhofft werden, als erlaube Dein ungeduldiges Warten aufs nächste Manuskript beliebig viele Vertröstungen.

Welch eine Verlegerin! Wo hat es das jemals gegeben: So viel episch andauernde Liebe zu Autoren, so viel Nachsicht mit chronisch egozentrischen Urhebern, so viel Nachsicht mit chronisch egozentrischen Urhebern so viel verläßliche Kritik, die nichts besser, aber manches genauer wissen

wollte, so viel Gastlichkeit und wohnlich einladender Hintergrund, der den oft genug an der Bühnenrampe turnenden, sich selbst erschöpfenden Schriftstellern Zuflucht und mehr als einen Drink geboten hat.

Wenn ich in meinem Nachruf hier lobrede, ist mir bewußt, daß ich stellvertretend für viele Autoren spreche, unter ihnen zwei, denen Vergleichbares eingefallen wäre; denn Max Frisch und Uwe Johnson waren gleich mir Zöglinge der Wolffschen Zucht- und Pflegeanstalt. Sie kannte uns bis in letzte Verliese und Hinterhältlichkeiten hinein. Ihr war nichts vorzumachen. Bei ihr verlegt, das hieß, bei ihr aufgehoben zu sein, auch über Durststrecken hinweg.

Wir Autoren wußten und haben es uns oft genug bestätigt, daß wir – bei aller uns nachgesagten Eigenleistung – vor allem Helen Wolff unsere literarische Präsenz in Amerika zu verdanken hatten. Sie hat uns, dem Wortsinn nach, betreut. Vergleichbare Dankbarkeit mögen die Übersetzer empfunden haben, denen ihr kritischer Rat oder Einspruch bis hin zu den Fahnenkorrekturen gewiß blieb. Ralph Manheim, mein Übersetzer, konnte ein Lied davon singen, ein vielstrophiges, denn seit "Grimms Märchen" – noch zur Kurt Wolffs Lebzeiten – isterder strengsten Disziplinierung unterworfen gewesen.

Kurt Wolff. Welch ein Verleger! Und welch eine Verlegerin, die sich von seinem Schatten nie lösen wollte, die keine Eigenständigkeit betonen mußte, die vielmehr ihr Herkommen – und sei es beiseite gesprochen – durch rückversichernden Kommentar belegte. Ich erinnere Sätze wie: "Kurt hätte in diesem Fall so entschieden . . ." oder: "Kurt wäre hier anderer Meinung gewesen. . . . "

"Helen and Kurt Wolff Books" über Jahrzehnte hinweg. Das war ein Gütesiegel. Diese Buchreihe ist ein Begriff. Wie Frisch und Johnson war ich stolz, mit meinen Büchern in diese Reihe aufgenommen zu sein. Dafür waren wir dankbar; denn bei allem Selbstbewußtsein der genannten Autoren soll festgehalten und daran erinnert werden: ohne die Verlegerin Helen Wolff hätte die erzählende deutschsprachige Literatur in Amerika nur minimale Chancen gehabt. Sie hat die Brücke gebaut. Sie hat keine Mühe gescheut, selbst schwierigste Texte – ich denke an Schädlichs "Versuchte Nähe" – den Lesern von New York bis San Francisco nahezubringen. Uwe Johnsons "Jahrestage" waren ihr jedes Risiko wert. Selbst wenn, was zu hoffen ist, ihre Arbeit fortgesetzt wird, bleibt sie ohne Nachfolge; denn nach Helen Wolffs Tod ist zu befürchten, daß auch in diesem literarischen Bereich die Zukunft entweder dem schnellen Geschäft oder dem amerikanischen Selbstgenügen gehören wird.

So will es mir, aus europäischer Sicht, vorkommen, als sei Amerika ohne Helen verarmt. Plötzlich ist da nichts mehr. Der Brückenpfeiler ist weg. Gewiß spricht aus dieser Sicht panischer Schrecken, doch auch die Erkenntnis, wieviel die Autoren meiner Generation den deutschen Emigranten verdanken. Sie, die aus Deutschland vertrieben wurden, haben mehr für uns getan als zu erwarten, zu erhoffen war. Sie, die in Amerika blieben, bewahrten uns vor provinzieller Verengung, sie machten uns weltoffen.

Diese Gewißheit habe ich seit meinen frühen "Blechtrommel"–Jahren. Im Januar 1960 wurde der junge Autor nach Zürich in ein Hotel gebeten, dessen großbürgerlicher Glanz beklemmend, womöglich bedrückend gewirkt hätte, wenn nicht Kurt und Helen Wolff mit souveräner Geste den geballten Pomp relativiert und alles ganz leicht

gemacht hätten. Kaum war mein Drink bestellt – ich glaube, es war eine Bloody Mary – , überraschte mich das Ehepaar Wolff mit der von Kurt gestellten Frage: "Könnten Sie sich vorstellen, daß Ihr jüngst erschienener Roman "Die Blechtrommel" in Amerika Leser findet?"

Ich antwortete wahrheitsgemäß mit nein, wollte aber mein Nein beweiskräftig untermauern und gab zu, daß mich die inzwischen erwiesene Tatsache, sogar in Bayern Leser gefunden zu haben, einigermaßen überrascht hätte. Um mich deutlicher zu machen, wies ich darauf hin, daß aller was Oskar Matzerath angehe, in entlegener baltischer Region spiele, sich weitgehend und penetrant auf Danzig, genauer gesagt, auf einen unansehnlichen Vorort namens Langfuhr beschränke, daß man dort stubenwarm breit und bedrohlich gemütlich spreche und außerdem immerfort von Kaschuben, einer schwindenden Minderheit die Rede sei; dort rieche es nach Provinz.

Danach sprach Kurt Wolff als Autorität. Sein Beschluß stehe fest. Das Buch werde in Amerika erscheinen. Meine Erklärung habe überzeugend gewirkt, obgleich sie sich aufs Abraten versteift hätte. Er wisse, daß sich alle große Literatur auf die Provinz konzentriere, sich in ihr verkrieche, ohne dabei provinziell zu werden; und deshalb sei sie weltweit verständlich. Helen stimmte dem zu, indem sie zugleich Fragen zu Schwierigkeiten stellte, die sich beim Übertragen von Dialekt und Jargon ergeben könnten: "Sagen Sie mir bitte, was genau ist Glumse?"

So kam es, daß zwei Jahre später "Die Blechtrommel" in der Übersetzung von Ralph Manheim den amerikanischen Lesern zugemutet wurde; offenbar sind die kaschubischen Kartoffelläcker und der miefige Vorort Langfuhr den Texanern ähnlich zugänglich gewesen wie zuvor den Bayern. Der Sprung übers große Wasser war, dank verlegerischer Weitsicht, geglückt.

Bald danach wechselten Helen und Kurt Wolff von Random zu dem Verlagshaus Harcourt Brace Jovanovich. Ich ging mit ihnen. Als Kurt Wolff während eines Besuches in Deutschland tödlich verunglückte, setzte Helen Wolff ihres Mannes Arbeit fort. Ihre verlegerische Sorgfalt war schon zuvor Grundlage meines Vertrauens gewesen. Von Buch zu Buch haben wir uns begleitet. Ihrem prüfenden Blick mußte jede Übersetzung standhalten. Ihrer Beharrlichkeit und Autorität – zum Beispiel dem Verlagseigner Jovanovich gegenüber – konnte Uwe Johnson, wie schon gesagt, die Vermittlung seiner Bücher verdanken. Und sie hat dafür gesorgt, daß er vom Riverside

Drive aus auf sein verlorengegangenes Mecklenburg zurückschauen konnte. In einem Brief an den Literaturwissenschaftler Roland Berbig schreibt sie aus Hanover/New Hampshire am 6. Juni 1991: ". . . Sehr stark empfand ich, bei ihm und bei seiner Frau, Heimweh nach der Landschaft der verlorenen Heimat, die er mit so viel geographischer Akribie beschreibt, Wind und Wellen eingeschlossen. Daß er sich, unwiederbringlich, exilieren mußte, als Unschuldiger den Kriminellen weichen, war ein ewiger Stachel."

So zerbrechlich Helen Wolff wirkte, von ihr ging jene Kraft aus, die über Jahrzehnte hinweg, gepaart mit verlegerischem Mut, dafür gebürgt hat, daß die Reihe "Helen and Kurt Wolff Books" kein Ende fand, selbst nicht in krisenhaften Zeiten, an denen es nicht gefehlt hat: überall verschwanden wohlbekannte Verlage, selbstredend nach den Regeln der Freien Marktwirtschaft.

Helen überstand alles. In Macedonien geboren, in Österreich aufgewachsen und dennoch mit preußischer Haltung, allerdings wie aus einer von Fontane geleiteten Schule, so hat sie, von fragiler Gestalt, leise, aber bestimmt den verlegerischen Kurs ihres Mannes, der ihr Kurs war, auch bei stürmischer Wetter- und Börsenlage bestimmt. Wer wie ich Gelegenheit gehabt hat, als Gast des Verlages bei jeder Veröffentlichung seiner Bücher dabei gewesen zu sein, der wurde einem zwar anstrengenden, doch merkwürdigerweise gleichwohl belebenden Programm unterworfen. Jedenfalls konnte er sicher sein, fachlich qualifizierten Kritikern konfrontiert zu werden; mir wurde wiederholt die Möglichkeit geboten, mich beim Umgang mit amerikanischer Literaturkritik von der deutschen zu erholen. Ich lernte professionelle Qualität und leidenschaftliche Sachlichkeit kennen, Verlagsmitarbeiter, die nicht nur eine schreibtischgebundene Existenz führten, den Wechsel von Tempo und Muße, und während zeitlich terminierter Gespräche saß ich Literaturkritikern gegenüber, die tatsächlich gelesen hatten und sich deshalb nicht in verquaster Rhetorik gefallen mußten.

Über all dem wachte anwesend oder per Distanz Helen Wolff. Sie sorgte dafür, daß der europäische Autor keiner die Moral untergrabenden Langeweile anheimfallen konnte und schützte ihn zugleich vor dem Geschwindigkeitsrausch des ihm ungewohnten amerikanischen Tempos. Bei ihr lernte ich Hannah Arendt kennen. Gespräche an ihrem Tisch verliefen nie beliebig. Nie blieb sie ihren Gästen, als Referenz oder Zugabe, eine gehörige Portion Bestätigung schuldig. Die Verlegerin Helen Wolff ist sich immer bewußt gewesen, daß es die Autoren sind, die die Substanz eines Verlages ausmachen. Sie wußte, daß ein noch so schönes und vielstöckig auf modernsten Stand gebrachtes Verlagshaus ein leeres Gehäuse ist, wenn sich der Verleger und seine Mitarbeiter nicht täglich der Priorität der Autoren versichern. So selbstbewußt nahm sie eine vermittelnd dienende Position ein. Manch deutscher Verleger und manche Verlegerin könnten sich an Helen Wolff ein Beispiel nehmen; zumindest fänden sie Gelegenheit, des Ausmaßes ihrer Selbstherrlichkeit gewahr zu werden.

Die Büchermacherin und Briefstellerin. Über viele Jahre hinweg haben wir einander Nachricht gegeben. Ach, liebe Helene, wie wird mir das fehlen. Meinen langwierigen Arbeitsexzessen bist Du eine geduldige Zuhörerin gewesen. Meine Kinder in ihrer Vielzahl waren Dir oft übersichtlicher als mir. Gelegentlich und nur abschnittsweise erlaubten wir der amerikanischen und der deutschen Politik, unsere Briefe ein wenig einzutrüben; Du warst radikal und konservativ zugleich. Wir sorgten uns in Gespräche wie in Briefen gemeinsam um Uwe Johnson, dem nicht mehr zu helfen war. Unser Briefwechsel überlebte diverse Präsidenten und Kanzler. Ironisch und aus hellwacher Erinnerung hast Du die deutschen Anfälligkeiten kommentiert. Und von Zeit zu Zeit sind uns dahergeplauderte Briefe gelungen; Fontane ließ grüßen.

Mein Nachruf, der eigentlich eine Laudatio sein sollte, schließt mit Dank. Als ich mir noch aus Anlaß einer gewünschten Lobpreisung Gedanken machte, wurde mir bewußt, daß Helen Wolffs Wiedersehen mit der Stadt Leipzig ein langes Stück Geschichte, eine sehr deutsche, also weitläufige Geschichte beschließen würde. Vor zwei Jahren erhielt ich von ihr einen Brief, in dem sie bedauerte, nicht zur Buchmesse kommen zu können – "Ich fühle mich dem Messe-Betrieb nicht gewachsen, besonders in einem mir unvertrauten Leipzig . . ."

Heute hätte Helen Wolff hier sein wollen, in einer Stadt, in der vor wenigen Jahren viele Tausend Menschen den damals Regierenden zugerufen haben: Wir sind das Volk! – Wenig später tauschte man ein Wörtchen aus, wohl in der Hoffnung, daß "ein Volk" zu sein, mehr zähle und gewichtiger sei als nur "das Volk." Wie gerne hätten wir Helen Wolff, über alle Eiertänze deutscher Selbstfindung hinweg, hier, in Leipzig begrüßt. Wie gerne hätte ich ihr gedankt, der Freundin, der Verlegerin. Sie fehlt mir.

copyright © 1994 by Günter Grass

A TRIBUTE_____

from Amos Oz

In her apartment in New York in 1972 Helen Wolff said to me: "You are the only author on my list, whose work I cannot read in the original." Then as we were having coffee (served in a central European manner), she asked me: "Hebrew. Just how un-European is the Hebrew language?" I said: "Very." Helen was astonished, almost bewildered: "So how could Buber, Scholem, Agnon, Max Brod, and the others work in Hebrew? Was their Hebrew vernacular in any way Germanic?" So I told her about the strange revival of the Hebrew language and how various European languages could be traced within the modern Hebrew MELODIES. Helen remarked: "And Kafka tried to teach himself Hebrew, towards the end of his life." Then we talked about Kafka and about Kafka's fantasy about immigrating to Palestine. By the end of the evening I felt I had discovered a distant relative and found that I had a wonderful friend, both in one person.

In this conversation as well as in many others that followed, Helen amazed me by her ability to imagine a language which she did not know. In the course of our working sessions in New York, as well as in our correspondence over problems of editing the English version of my Hebrew works, Helen could more often than not put her finger on a single word or idiom in the draft English translation and guess — or rather, sense — what was there in the Hebrew original, and where the English translation could only be possible through sacrificing some of the nuances.

Helen had this absolute hearing and this magical ability to read subtexts and sub-subtexts. But then she had the same ability in judging human characters.

I cherish her wisdom, her subtlety, and her unique ability to anticipate where her authors were going in their works in progress (or where they were unable to go). She was a warmhearted person, a great editor, a superb conversationalist, and a very dear friend.

Literary Awards and Honors Announced in 1994

ACADEMY OF AMERICAN POETS AWARDS

LAMONT POETRY SELECTION
Brigit Pegeen Kelly, *Song* (BOA Editions).

HAROLD MORTON LANDON TRANSLATION AWARD
Rosemarie Waldrop, for translating Edward Jabes's *The Book of Margins* (University of Chicago Press).

PETER I. B. LAVAN YOUNGER POET AWARDS
Peter Gizzi, Li-Yong Lee, Cynthia Varin.

WALT WHITMAN AWARD
Jan Richman, *Because the Brain Can Be Talked into Anything: Poems* (Louisiana State University Press).

AMERICAN ACADEMY IN ROME FELLOWSHIPS IN LITERATURE
Karl Kirchwey.

AMERICAN ACADEMY OF ARTS AND LETTERS AWARDS

ACADEMY AWARDS IN LITERATURE
Jon Rabin Baitz, Marvin Bell, Stuart Dybek, Adrienne Kennedy, Tony Kushner, Mary Lee Settle, Chase Twichell, Geoffrey Wolff.

ACADEMY MEMBERS
Shelby Foote, Karel Husa, Josephine Jacobsen, David Mamet, Nathan Oliveira, James Ingo Reed, Steve Reich, Paul Resika, Robert Ryman, Kenneth Snelson, Robert Starer, Robert Stone.

E. M. FORSTER AWARD IN LITERATURE
Janice Galloway.

GOLD MEDAL FOR BIOGRAPHY
Walter Jackson Bate.

SUE KAUFFMAN PRIZE FOR FIRST FICTION
Emile Capouya, *In the Sparrow Hills* (Algonquin Books of Chapel Hill).

MEDAL FOR DISTINGUISHED CONTRIBUTIONS TO AMERICAN LITERATURE
Gwendolyn Brooks.

ROME FELLOWSHIP IN LITERATURE
Karl Kirchwey.

RICHARD AND HILDA ROSENTHAL FOUNDATION AWARD IN LITERATURE
Janet Peery, *Alligator Dance: Stories* (Southern Methodist University Press).

JEAN STEIN AWARD FOR FICTION
Chris Offutt.

HAROLD D. VURSELL MEMORIAL AWARD IN LITERATURE
Darryl Pinckney.

WITTNER BYNER PRIZE IN POETRY
Rosanna Warren.

AMERICAN BOOK AWARDS

Miguel Algarin and Bob Holman, eds., *Aloud! Voices from the Nuyorican Poets Café* (Holt).

Eric Drooker, *Flood! A Novel in Pictures* (Four Walls Eight Windows).

Paul Gilroy, *Black Atlantic: Modernity and Double Consciousness* (Harvard University Press).

Rose Glickman, *Daughters of Feminists* (St. Martin's Press).

Janet Campbell Hale, *Bloodlines: Odyssey of a Native Daughter* (Random House).

Lawson Fusao Inada, *Legends from Camp* (Coffee House Press).

Graciela Limón, *In Search of Bernabé* (Arte Público Press).

Gregory J. Reed, *Economic Empowerment Through the Church* (Zondervan).

Giose Rimanelli, *Benedetta in Guysterland* (Guernica Editions).

Ronald Takaki, *A Different Mirror: A Multicultural History of America* (Little, Brown).

Tino Villanueva, *Scene from the Movie GIANT* (Curbstone Press).

CHILDREN'S BOOK AWARD

Virginia Kroll, illustrated by Katherine Roundtree, *WOOD-HOOPOE Willie* (Charlesbridge Publishing).

CRITICISM AWARD

Edward W. Said.

GADFLY AWARD

Jill Nelson, *VOLUNTEER SLAVERY: My Authentic Negro Experience* (Noble Press).

LIFETIME ACHIEVEMENT

Joseph Mitchell.

PUBLISHER/EDITOR AWARD

Joyce Jenkins.

AMERICAN TRANSLATORS ASSOCIATION AWARDS

LEWIS GALANTIERE PRIZE

Tina Nunnelly, for translating Peter Høeg's *Smilla's Sense of Snow* (Doubleday Canada).

HANS CHRISTIAN ANDERSEN AWARDS

AUTHOR AWARD

Michil Madl.

ILLUSTRATOR AWARD

Jorg Muller.

AT&T BOOK AWARD FOR NONFICTION

John Campbell, *Edward Heath: A Biography* (Cape).

BANCROFT PRIZES

Stanley Elkins and Eric McKitrick, *The Age of Federalism: Early American Republic 1788-1800* (Oxford University Press).

Winthrop Jordan, *Tumult and Silence at Second Creek: an Inquiry into a Civil War Conspiracy* (Louisiana State University Press).

David Levering Lewis, *W. E. B. DuBois: the Biography of a Race, 1868–1819* (Holt).

ALBERT J. BEVERIDGE AWARD IN AMERICAN HISTORY

Karen Ordahl Kupperman, *Providence Island, 1630-1641: The Other Puritan Colony* (Cambridge University Press).

IRMA S. AND JAMES H. BLACK AWARD

Eric A. Kimmel, *Three Sacks of Truth* (Holiday House).

JAMES TAIT BLACK MEMORIAL PRIZES

BEST BIOGRAPHY

Richard Holmes, *Dr. Johnson and Mr. Savage* (Flamingo).

BEST WORK OF FICTION

Caryl Phillips, *Crossing the River* (Bloomsbury).

BOOKER PRIZE

James Kelman, *How Late It Was, How Late* (Secker & Warburg).

BOOKER RUSSIAN NOVEL PRIZE

Bulat Okudzhava, *The Closed-down Theatre.*

BOSTON GLOBE–HORN BOOK AWARDS

FICTION

Vera B. Williams, author and illustrator, *Scooter* (Greenwillow).

NONFICTION

Russell Freedman, *Eleanor Roosevelt: A Life of Discovery* (Clarion).

PICTURE BOOK

Allen Say, author and illustrator, *Grandfather's Journey* (Houghton Mifflin).

THE JOHN BURROUGHS LIST OF NATURE BOOKS FOR YOUNG READERS

Joan Anderson, author; Patricia D. Moehlman, photographer; *Jackal Woman* (Charles Scribner's Sons).

Betsy Bowen, author and illustrator, *Tracks in the Wild* (Little, Brown).

Bruce Brooks, *Making Sense, Animal Perception and Communication* (Farrar Straus Giroux).

Barbara Juster Estensen, author; Mary Barrett Brown, illustrator; *Playful Slider: the North American River Otter* (Little, Brown).

J. Edward Evans, *Charles Darwin: Revolutionary Biologist* (Lerner).

Evelyn Gallardo, *Among the Orangutans: The Biruté Galdikas Story* (Chronicle Books).

Bruce Hiscock, author and illustrator, *The Big Storm* (Atheneum).

Andrea Jack and Larry Points, *Assateague, Island of the Wild Ponies* (Macmillan).

Martin and Tanis Jordan, *Jungle Days, Jungle Nights* (Grisewood & Dempsey Kingfisher Books).

Bianca Lavies, author and photographer, *A Gathering of Garter Snakes* (Dutton Children's Books).

Marybeth Lorbiecki, author; Kerry Maguire, illustrator; *Of Things Natural, Wild, and Free: A Story about Aldo Leopold* (Carolrhoda Books).

Bruce McMillan, author and photographer, *A Beach for the Birds* (Houghton Mifflin).

Mary Beth Owens, author and illustrator, *Counting Cranes* (Little, Brown).

Jonathan Pine, author; Julie Zickefoose, illustrator; *Backyard Birds* (HarperCollins).

Howard Tomb, author; Dennis Kunkel, photographer; *MicroAliens: Dazzling Journeys with an Electron Microscope* (Farrar Straus Giroux).

BURROUGHS MEDAL

David G. Campbell, *Crystal Desert* (Secker & Warburg).

RANDOLPH CALDECOTT MEDAL

Allen Say, *Grandfather's Journey* (Houghton Mifflin Company).

CANADA-AUSTRALIA LITERARY PRIZE

Lewis Nowra.

THE CHRISTOPHER AWARDS

BOOKS

Sarah and A. Elizabeth Delany with Amy Hill Hearth, *Having Our Say: The Delany Sisters' First 100 Years* (Kodansha).

Doris Donnelly, *Spiritual Fitness: Everyday Exercises for Body and Soul* (HarperCollins).

Gilbert M. Gaul, *Giant Steps: The Story of One Boy's Struggle to Walk* (St. Martin's Press).

Brian Keenan, *An Evil Cradling: The Five-Year Ordeal of a Hostage* (Viking).

Kay Mills, *This Little Light of Mine: The Life of Fannie Lou Hamer* (Dutton).

Helen Prejean, *Dead Man Walking: An Eyewitness Account of the Death Penalty in the United States* (Random House).

Ronald Takaki, *A Different Mirror: A History of Multicultural America* (Little, Brown).

Luis Alberto Urrea, *Across the Wire: Life and Hard Times on the Mexican Border* (Anchor Books).

BOOKS FOR YOUNG PEOPLE

Phillip Hoose, *It's Our World, Too! Stories of Young People Who Are Making a Difference* (Little, Brown).

Ruud van der Rol and Rian Verhoeven, authors; Tony Langham and Plym Peters, translators; *Anne Frank: Beyond the Diary* (Viking).

Gerda Marie Scheidl, author; Nathalie Duroussy, illustrator; Rosemary Lanning, translator; *The Crystal Ball* (North-South Books).

ARTHUR C. CLARKE AWARD

Jeff Noon, *Vurt* (Crown).

COMMONWEALTH WRITERS PRIZE

Vikram Seth, *A Suitable Boy* (Phoenix House).

JOHN DOS PASSOS PRIZE FOR LITERATURE

Ernest J. Gaines.

ENGLISH CENTRE OF INTERNATIONAL PEN AWARDS

J. R. ACKERLEY PRIZE FOR AUTOBIOGRAPHY

Blake Morrison, *And When Did You Last See Your Father* (Granta Books in association with Penguin).

TIME-LIFE SILVER PEN AWARD FOR NONFICTION

John Rigby Hale, *The Civilization of Europe in the Renaissance* (Time-Life Books).

GEORGE FREEDLEY MEMORIAL AWARD

Rachel M. Brownstein, *Tragic Muse: Rachel of the Comédie Française* (Knopf).

GOLDEN KITE AWARDS

FICTION AWARD

Virginia Euwer Wolff, *Make Lemonade* (Holt).

NONFICTION AWARD

Russell Freedman, *Eleanor Roosevelt: A Lifetime of Discovery* (Clarion).

PICTURE/ILLUSTRATION AWARD

Kevin Hawks, *By the Light of the Halloween Moon* (Lothrop).

GOVERNOR GENERAL'S LITERARY AWARDS

CHILDREN'S LITERATURE – ILLUSTRATION

Murray Kimber, *Josepha: A Prairie Boy's Story* (Red Deer College Press).

Pierre Pratt, text by Rémy Simard, *Mon chien est un éléphant* (Annick Press).

CHILDREN'S LITERATURE – TEXT

Julie Johnston, *Adam and Eve and Pinch-Me* (Lester).

Suzanne Martel, *Une belle journée pour mourir* (Éditions Fides).

DRAMA

Michel Ouellette, *French Town* (Éditions du Nordir).

Morris Panych, *The Ends of the Earth* (Talonbooks).

FICTION

Robert LaLonde, *Le Petit Aigle à tête blanche* (Éditions du Seuil).

Rudy Wiebe, *A Discovery of Strangers* (Knopf).

NONFICTION

John A. Livingston, *Rogue Primate: An Exploration of Human Domestication* (Key Porter Books).

Chantal Saint-Jarre, *Du sida* (Éditions Denoël).

POETRY

Robert Hilles, *Cantos from a Small Room* (Wosak & Wynn).

Fulvio Caccia, *Aknos* (Éditions Guernica).

TRANSLATION

Jude Des Chênes, *Le mythe du sauvage* (Éditions du Septentrion); French version of Olive Patricia Dickason's *The Myth of the Savage* (University of Alberta Press).

Donald Winkler, *The Lyric Generation: The Life and Times of the Baby Boomers* (Stoddart Publishing); English version of François Ricard's *La génération lyrique* (Éditions du Boréal).

THE GUARDIAN AWARDS

AWARD FOR CHILDREN'S FICTION

Sylvia Waugh, *The Mennyms* (Julia MacRae).

FICTION PRIZE

Cinndia McWilliam, *Debatable Land* (Bloomsbury Publishing).

HEINEMANN AWARD FOR LITERATURE

John Rigby Hale, *The Civilization of Europe in the Renaissance* (Time-Life Books).

DRUE HEINZ LITERATURE PRIZE

Jennifer Cornell, *Departures* (unpublished).

DAVID HIGHAM PRIZE FOR FICTION

Fred D'Aguiar, *The Longest Memory* (Chatto & Windus).

HUGO AWARDS

JOHN CAMPBELL AWARD

Amy Thomson.

BEST NONFICTION BOOK

John Coute and Peter Nicholls, eds., *Encyclopedia of Science Fiction* (St. Martin's Press).

BEST NOVEL

Kim Stanley Robinson, *Green Mars* (HarperCollins).

BEST NOVELLA
Harry Turtledove, "Down in the Bottomlands" (*Analog*).

BEST NOVELETTE
Charles Sheffield, "Georgia on My Mind" (*Analog*).

BEST PROFESSIONAL EDITOR
Kristine Kathryn Rusch.

BEST SHORT STORY
Connie Willis, "Death on the Nile" (*Isaac Asimov's Science Fiction Magazine*).

INGERSOLL PRIZES

T. S. ELIOT AWARD FOR CREATIVE WRITING
Wendell Berry.

RICHARD M. WEAVER AWARD FOR SCHOLARLY LETTERS
Dr. Murray N. Rothbard.

JERUSALEM PRIZE

Mario Vargas Llosa.

CORETTA SCOTT KING AWARDS

AUTHOR AWARD
Angela Johnson, *Toning the Sweep* (Orchard Books).

ILLUSTRATOR AWARD
Tom Feelings, *Soul Looks Back in Wonder, Collection of African American Poets* (Dial).

LANNAN LITERARY AWARDS

FICTION
Edward P. Jones, Steven Millhauser, Caryl Phillips, Stephen Wright.

NONFICTION
Jonathan Kozol.

POETRY
Simon Armitage, Eavan Boland, Jack Gilbert, Linda Hogan, Richard Kenney.

THE LIBRARY ASSOCIATION AWARDS

BESTERMAN MEDAL
John McIlwaine, *Africa: A Guide to Reference Material* (Hans Zell).

CARNEGIE MEDAL
Robert Swindells, *Stone Cold* (Hamish Hamilton).

KATE GREENAWAY MEDAL
Alan Lee, *Black Ships Before Troy* (Frances Lincoln).

RUTH LILLY PRIZE FOR POETRY

Donald Hall.

LOS ANGELES TIMES BOOK PRIZES

BIOGRAPHY
Mikal Gilmore, *Shot in the Heart* (Doubleday).

CURRENT INTEREST
Henry Kissinger, *Diplomacy* (Simon & Schuster).

FICTION
David Malouf, *Remembering Babylon* (Pantheon).

HISTORY
George Chauncey, *Gay New York: Gender, Urban Culture and the Making of the Gay Male World 1890–1940* (Basic Books).

POETRY
Carolyn Forché, *The Angel of History* (HarperCollins).

SCIENCE AND TECHNOLOGY
Jonathan Weiner, *The Beak of the Finch: A Story of Evolution in Our Time* (Knopf).

THE ART SEIDENBAUM AWARD FOR FIRST FICTION
Martin M. Šimeúka, translated by Peter Petro with a forward by Vaclav Havel, *The Year of the Frog* (Louisiana State University Press).

MACARTHUR FOUNDATION GRANT

Adrienne Rich.

LENORE MARSHALL *NATION* MAGAZINE PRIZE

W. S. Merwin, *Travels* (Knopf).

MEDAL OF HONOR FOR LITERATURE

Richard Wilbur.

MODERN LANGUAGE ASSOCIATION AWARDS

JAMES RUSSELL LOWELL PRIZE

Eric J. Sundquist, *To Wake the Nations: Race in the Making of American Literature* (Harvard University Press).

PRIZE FOR A FIRST BOOK

Eric W. Lott, *Love and Theft: Blackface Minstrelsy and the American Working Class* (Oxford University Press).

PRIZE FOR INDEPENDENT SCHOLARS

Olga Augustinos, *French Odysseys: Greece in French Travel Literature from the Renaissance to the Romantic Era* (Johns Hopkins University Press).

NATIONAL BOOK AWARDS

FICTION

William Gaddis, *A Frolic of His Own* (Poseidon Press).

NONFICTION

Sherwin B. Nuland, *How We Die: Reflections on Life's Final Chapter* (Knopf).

POETRY

James Tate, *Worshipful Company of Fletchers* (Ecco).

NATIONAL BOOK CRITICS CIRCLE AWARDS

BIOGRAPHY

Edmund White, *Genet* (Knopf).

CRITICISM

John Dizikes, *Opera in America: A Cultural History* (Yale University Press).

FICTION

Ernest J. Gaines, *A Lesson Before Dying* (Knopf).

NONFICTION

Alan Lomax, *The Land Where the Blues Began* (Pantheon).

POETRY

Mark Doty, *My Alexandria* (University of Illinois Press).

NATIONAL JEWISH BOOK AWARDS

AUTOBIOGRAPHY/MEMOIR

Howard A. Schack, *A Spy in Canaan: My Secret Life as a Jewish-American Businessman Spying for Israel in Arab Lands* (Birch Lane Press/Carol).

CHILDREN'S LITERATURE

Adele Geras, *Golden Windows: and Other Stories of Jerusalem* (HarperCollins Children's Books).

CHILDREN'S PICTURE BOOKS

Sheldon Oberman, *The Always Prayer Shawl* (Boyds Mills Press).

CONTEMPORARY JEWISH LIFE

Jack Wertheimer, *A People Divided: Judaism in Contemporary America* (Basic Books).

FICTION

Alan Isler, ·*The Prince of West End Avenue* (Bridge Works).

FOLKLORE AND ANTHROPOLOGY

Samuel G. Armistead and Joseph H. Silverman, *Folk Literature of the Sephardic Jews, Volume III* (University of California Press).

HOLOCAUST

James E. Young, *The Texture of Memory* (Yale University Press).

ISRAEL

Steven Zipperstein, *Elusive Prophet: Ahad Ha'am and the Origins of Zionism* (University of California Press).

JEWISH EDUCATION

H. Deitcher and A. J. Tannenbaum, eds., *Studies in Jewish Education, Educational Issues and Classical Jewish Texts, Vol. 5* (Magnes Press of Hebrew University in Jerusalem).

JEWISH HISTORY

Leonard Dinnerstein, *Antisemitism in America* (Oxford University Press).

JEWISH THOUGHT

Michael Fishbane, *The Kiss of God: Spiritual and Mystical Death in Judaism* (University of Washington Press).

SCHOLARSHIP

Menachem Elon, *Jewish Law: History, Sources, Principles* (Jewish Publication Society).

SEPHARDIC STUDIES

Michael Laskier, *North African Jewry in the 20th Century* (New York University Press).

VISUAL ARTS
Joseph and Yehudit Shadur, *Jewish Papercuts: A History and Guide* (Judah L. Magnes Museum and Gefen).

JOHN T. NEWBERY MEDAL

Lois Lowry, *The Giver* (Houghton Mifflin).

NOBEL PRIZE FOR LITERATURE

Kenzaburo Oe.

NUESTADT INTERNATIONAL PRIZE FOR LITERATURE

Kamau Brathwaite.

SCOTT O'DELL AWARD FOR HISTORICAL FICTION

Paul Fleischman, *Bull Run* (HarperCollins).

PEN/MARTHA ALBRAND AWARD FOR NONFICTION

Michael Kelly, *Martyr's Day: Chronicle of a Small War* (Random House).

PEN/BOOK-OF-THE-MONTH CLUB TRANSLATION PRIZE

André Breton, *Earthlight,* translated by Bill Zavatsky and Zack Rogow (Sun & Moon Press).

PEN/FAULKNER AWARD FOR FICTION

Philip Roth, *Operation Shylock* (Simon & Schuster).

PEN/ERNEST HEMINGWAY FOUNDATION AWARD

Dagoberto Gilb, *The Magic of Blood* (University of New Mexico Press).

PEN/GREGORY KOLOVAKOS AWARD

Helen R. Lane.

PEN/RALPH MANNHEIM MEDAL FOR TRANSLATION

Richard Wilbur.

PEN/RENATO POGGIOLI TRANSLATION AWARD

Moira Madden.

PEN/REVSON FOUNDATION FELLOWSHIP

James Harms.

PEN/SPIELVOGEL-DIAMONSTEIN AWARD

Stanley Fish, *There's No Such Thing as Free Speech . . . and it's a good thing* (Oxford University Press).

PEN/VOELKER AWARD FOR POETRY

Jane Kenyon, *Let Evening Come* (Graywolf) and *Constance* (Graywolf).

PHI BETA KAPPA AWARDS

RALPH WALDO EMERSON AWARD
David Levering Lewis, *W. E. B. DuBois: the Biography of a Race, 1868–1919* (Holt).

CHRISTIAN GAUSS AWARD
John T. Irwin, *Mystery to a Solution* (Johns Hopkins University Press).

EDGAR ALLAN POE AWARDS

GRAND MASTER AWARD
Lawrence Block.

BEST CRITICAL WORK
Burl Barer, *The Saint: A Complete History* (McFarland).

BEST FACT CRIME
Bella Stumbo, *Until the Twelfth of Never* (Pocket Books).

BEST FIRST MYSTERY NOVEL
Laurie King, *A Grave Talent* (St. Martin's Press).

BEST JUVENILE NOVEL
Barbara Brooks Wallace, *The Twin in the Tavern* (Atheneum).

BEST MYSTERY NOVEL
Minette Walters, *The Sculptress* (St. Martin's Press).

BEST ORIGINAL PAPERBACK
Steven Womack, *Dead Folks' Blues* (Ballantine).

BEST SHORT STORY
Lawrence Block, "Keller's Therapy" (*Playboy*).

BEST YOUNG ADULT NOVEL
Joan Lowery Nixon, *The Name of the Game Was Murder* (Delacorte).

PULITZER PRIZES

BIOGRAPHY
David Levering Lewis, *W. E. B. DuBois: the Biography of a Race, 1868–1919* (Holt).

DRAMA
Edward Albee, *Three Tall Women: A Play in Two Acts* (Dutton).

FICTION
E. Annie Proulx, *The Shipping News* (Scribners).

GENERAL NONFICTION
David Remnick, *Lenin's Tomb: The Last Days of the Soviet Empire* (Random House).

POETRY
Yusef Komunyakaa, *Neon Vernacular* (Wesleyan University Press).

QUALITY PAPERBACK BOOK (QPB) CLUB AWARDS

NEW VISIONS AWARD
Kathleen Norris, *Dakota: A Spiritual Geography* (Ticknor & Fields).

JOE SAVAGO NEW VOICES AWARD
Randall Kenan, *Let the Dead Bury Their Dead* (Abacus).

REA AWARD FOR THE SHORT STORY

Tillie Olsen.

W. H. SMITH LITERARY AWARD

Vikram Seth, *A Suitable Boy* (Phoenix House).

SOCIETY OF AMERICAN HISTORIANS AWARDS

BRUCE CATTON PRIZE FOR LIFETIME ACHIEVEMENT
Walter Lord.

ALLAN NEVINS DISSERTATION PRIZE
Dean David Grodzins, *Theodore Parker and the American Transcendentalists* (unpublished).

FRANCIS PARKMAN PRIZE FOR SPECIAL ACHIEVEMENT
David Levering Lewis, *W. E. B. DuBois: the Biography of a Race, 1868–1919* (Holt).

IAN ST. JAMES AWARD

Joshua Davidson.

TEXAS INSTITUTE OF LETTERS LITERARY AWARDS

BOOK PUBLISHERS OF TEXAS AWARD FOR BEST BOOK FOR YOUNG PEOPLE
Dee Stuart, *The Astonishing Armadillo* (Carolrhoda Books).

BRAZOS BOOKSTORE AWARD FOR BEST SHORT STORY
Dagoberto Gilb, "Nancy Flores" (*Sonora Review*).

CARR P. COLLINS AWARD FOR NONFICTION
Howard Swindle, *Deliberate Indifference* (Viking/Penguin).

FRIENDS OF THE DALLAS PUBLIC LIBRARY AWARD FOR CONTRIBUTION FOR KNOWLEDGE
William H. Goetzmann, *Sam Chamberlain's Mexican War: The San Jacinto Museum Paintings* (Texas Historical Museum Association).

JESSE JONES AWARD FOR FICTION
Dagoberto Gilb, *The Magic of Blood* (University of New Mexico Press).

NATALIE ORNISH AWARD FOR POETRY
Jack Myers, *Blindsided* (David Godine).

LON TINKLE AWARD FOR CAREER ACHIEVEMENT
Horton Foote.

STEVEN TURNER AWARD FOR FIRST
BOOK OF FICTION
　　Lee Merrill Byrd, *My Sister Disappears* (Southern Methodist University Press).

ANTOINETTE PERRY AWARDS

BEST PLAY
　　Tony Kushner, *Angels in America: Perestroika* (Theatre Communications Group).

LILA WALLACE–READER'S DIGEST WRITERS' AWARDS

Sherman Alexie, Christopher Durang, Ian Frazier, Jessica Hagedorn, Bell Hooks, June Jordan, W. S. Merwin, David Mura, Lee Smith, Wakaka Yamauchi.

WHITBREAD BOOK OF THE YEAR AWARDS

NOVEL AND BOOK OF THE YEAR
　　Joan Brady, *Theory of War* (Andre Deutsch).

BIOGRAPHY
　　Brenda Maddox, *The Married Man* (Sinclair Stevenson).

CHILDREN'S NOVEL
　　Geraldine McCaughrean, *Gold Dust* (Oxford University Press).

FIRST NOVEL
　　Fred D'Aguiar, *The Longest Memory* (Chatto & Windus).

POETRY
　　James Fenton, *Out of Danger* (Penguin Poetry).

WILLIAM CARLOS WILLIAMS PRIZE

David Ray, *Wool Highways and Other Poems* (Helicon Nine Editions).

YALE SERIES OF YOUNGER POETS

Tony Crunk, *Living in the Resurrection* (unpublished).

Checklist: Contributions to Literary History and Biography

This checklist is a selection of new books on various aspects of literary and cultural history, including biographies, memoirs, and correspondence of literary people and their associates.

Bellow, Saul. *It All Adds Up*. New York: Knopf, 1994.

Berman, Ronald. *The Great Gatsby and Modern Times*. Urbana & Chicago: University of Illinois Press, 1994.

Blanchard, Paula. *Sarah Orne Jewett: her world and her work*. Reading, Mass.: Addison-Wesley, 1994.

Bloch, R. Howard. *God's Plagiarist: Being an Account of the Fabulous Industry and Irregular Commerce of the Abbé Migne*. Chicago: University of Chicago Press, 1994.

Bodenheimer, Rosemarie. *The Real Life of Mary Ann Evans: George Eliot, Her Letters and Fiction*. Ithica: Cornell University Press, 1994.

Booth, Bradford, and Ernest Mehew, eds. *The Letters of Robert Louis Stevenson, volumes I, II, III, and IV*. New Haven: Yale University Press, 1994.

Donleavy, J. P. *The History of The Ginger Man*. New York: Houghton Mifflin/Seymour Lawrence, 1994.

Duran, Leopaldo. *Graham Greene: Friend and Brother*. London: HarperCollins, 1994.

Fitzgerald, F. Scott. *The Love of the Last Tycoon: A Western,* edited by Matthew J. Bruccoli. New York & London: Cambridge University Press, 1994.

Giroux, Robert, ed. *One Art: Elizabeth Bishop Letters*. New York: Farrar, Straus & Giroux, 1994.

Green, Candida Lycett, ed. *John Betjeman: Letters, Volume 1, 1926–1951*. London: Methuen, 1994.

Herbert, T. Walker. *Dearest Beloved: the Hawthornes and the making of the middle-class family*. Berkeley: University of California Press, 1994.

Hobson, Fred. *Mencken: A Life*. New York: Random House, 1994.

Holmes, Richard. *Dr. Johnson & Mr. Savage*. London: Hodder & Stoughton, 1994.

Jackson, Brenda. *Frieda Lawrence*. London: Pandora, 1994.

Keates, Jonathan. *Stendhal*. London: Sinclair-Stevenson, 1994.

Keating, Peter. *Kipling the Poet*. London: Secker & Warburg, 1994.

Leeming, David. *James Baldwin: A Biography*. New York: Knopf, 1994.

Lilly, George. *Anthony Powell: A Bibliography*. London: St. Paul's Bibliographies, 1994.

Lockridge, Larry. *Shade of the Raintree: The Life and Death of Ross Lockridge, Jr.* New York: Viking, 1994.

Maddox, Brenda. *The Married Man: A Life of D. H. Lawrence*. London: Sinclair-Stevenson, 1994.

Malcolm, Janet. *The Silent Woman: Sylvia Plath and Ted Hughes*. New York: Knopf, 1994.

Mellen, Joan. *Kay Boyle: Author of Herself*. New York: Farrar, Straus & Giroux, 1994.

Myers, Jeffrey. *Scott Fitzgerald: A Biography*. New York: HarperCollins, 1994.

Nicholl, Charles. *The Reckoning: The Murder of Christopher Marlowe*. New York: Harcourt Brace, 1994.

Osborne, John. *Damn You, England*. London: Faber, 1994.

Peters, Catherine. *The King of Inventors: a Life of Wilkie Collins*. Princeton: Princeton University Press, 1994.

Redford, Bruce. *The Letters of Samuel Johnson, Volume IV, 1782–1784*. Oxford: Clarendon Press, 1994.

Richardson, Joanna. *Baudelaire*. New York: St. Martin's, 1994.

Sedgewick, Ellery. *A History of the* Atlantic Monthly *1857–1909: Yankee Humanism at High Tide and Ebb*. Amherst: University of Massachusetts Press, 1994.

Shelden, Michael. *Graham Greene: The Man Within*. London: Heinemann, 1994.

Sherry, Norman. *The Life of Graham Greene, Volume 2: 1939–1955*. London: Cape, 1994.

Shirer, William. *Love and Hatred: the troubled marriage of Leo and Sonya Tolstoy*. New York: Simon & Schuster, 1994.

Thompson, E. P. *Witness Against the Beast: William Blake and the Moral Law*. New York: New Press, 1994.

Trevor, William. *Excursions in the Real World*. New York: Viking, 1994.

Welty, Eudora. *A Writer's Eye: Collected Book Reviews*. Jackson: University of Mississippi Press, 1994.

Wrezin, Michael. *A Rebel in Defense of Tradition: The Life and Politics of Dwight Macdonald*. New York: Basic Books/HarperCollins, 1994.

Necrology

Sir Harold Acton – 27 February 1994
Franz Bader – 14 September 1994
Helen B. Baldwin – 28 May 1994
William Barlow – 10 May 1994
Bernard Benstock – 14 July 1994
Paul Berna – 21 January 1994
Jess B. Bessinger, Jr. – 23 June 1994
Robert Bloch – 23 September 1994
Charles G. Bolté – 7 March 1994
Philip Bosakowski – 11 September 1994
Pierre Boulle – 30 January 1994
Joe Brainard – 25 May 1994
Cleanth Brooks – 10 May 1994
Douglas W. Bryant – 12 June 1994
Ann McGarry Buchwald – 3 July 1994
Charles Bukowski – 9 March 1994
Kurt Burnheim – 8 June 1994
Kenneth Neill Cameron – 14 March 1994
Elias Canetti – 13 August 1994
Aleksandr Chakovsky – 17 February 1994
David Leon Chandler – 23 January 1994
Thomas Chastain – 1 September 1994
Alice Childress – 14 August 1994
Georgia B. Christopher – 16 December 1994
Marchette Chute – 6 May 1994
Amy Clampitt – 10 September 1994
Bertram Clarke – 6 February 1994
James Clavell – 6 September 1994
Walter Clemons – 6 July 1994
Christopher Coe – 6 September 1994
Frank Cormier – 9 February 1994
Richard Patrick Critchfield – 10 December 1994
Guy Debord – 30 November 1994
John Devaney – 25 May 1994
Michael Dewell – 4 March 1994
William Dickey – 3 May 1994
Eliseo Diego – 2 March 1994
Frances Donaldson – 27 March 1994
John T. Dugan – 24 December 1994
Frances Duncombe – 27 June 1994
Allan Eady – 9 January 1994
Ralph Ellison – 16 April 1994
Hal Ellson – 31 October 1994
William Everson – 3 June 1994
Richard Falk – 28 January 1994

David Feinberg – 2 November 1994
Philip S. Foner – 13 December 1994
George H. Ford – 6 December 1994
Oscar Fraley – 6 January 1994
Doris C. Frankel – 1 February 1994
Sidney Gilliat – 31 May 1994
Erwin A. Glikes – 13 May 1994
Albert Goldman – 28 March 1994
Irving Goodman – 10 January 1994
John Blair Linn Goodwin – 12 January 1994
Phyllis Goodhart Gordan – 24 January 1994
Lewis Grizzard – 20 March 1994
Philip P. Hallie – 7 August 1994
Charles Henry Hamilton – 7 July 1994
Joan Harrison – 14 August 1994
Alfred Harvey – 4 July 1994
Joan Haslip – 19 June 1994
Robert Hatch – 31 May 1994
Walter Havighurst – 3 February 1994
Elinor Rice Hays – 21 March 1994
Ashley Holden, Sr. – 11 January 1994
Henry Horowitz – 11 April 1994
Barbara Howell – 7 June 1994
Dakari Hru – 31 August 1994
Warwick Hutton – 28 September 1994
Michael Innes – 12 November 1994
Eugène Ionesco – 28 March 1994
Derek Jarman – 19 February 1994
Eric Johnson – 4 August 1994
E. J. Kahn, Jr. – 28 May 1994
Eugene Kamenka – 19 January 1994
Samuel Kaplan – 14 January 1994
Kevin Kelly – 28 November 1994
Robert D. Kempner – 19 February 1994
Sang Man Kim – 26 January 1994
Thomas J. King – 20 May 1994
S. A. Kingsbury – 23 October 1994
Russell Kirk – 29 April 1994
David Kirschenbaum – 19 January 1994
Harry Kondoleon – 16 March 1994
Margaret Lane – 14 February 1994
Christopher Lasch – 14 February 1994
Mary Lasswell – 19 July 1994
Seymour Lawrence – 4 January 1994
Robert E. Lee – 8 July 1994

Leonid M. Leonov – 8 August 1994
Allen Lesser – 13 January 1994
Harry Levin – 29 May 1994
Samuel Lipman – 17 December 1994
Frank Belknap Long – 2 January 1994
John G. Lord – 18 May 1994
Robert Lowry – 5 December 1994
Frederick Manfred – 7 September 1994
Golo Mann – 8 April 1994
Alfred Matthew – 26 November 1994
Neil McCaffrey, Jr. – 8 December 1994
Robert C. McNamara – 12 January 1994
Matthew A. Meyer – 25 November 1994
Margaret Millar – 26 March 1994
Merriam Modell – 1 July 1994
José Luis Montalvo – 15 August 1994
William Morris – 2 January 1994
Ruth Mortimer – 31 January 1994
Franklin D. Murphy – 16 June 1994
N. Danesi Murray – 9 June 1994
Yuri M. Nagibin – 17 June 1994
Yves Navarre – 24 January 1994
Lowry Nelson – 12 November 1994
Daisy Newman – 25 January 1994
Juan Carlos Onetti – 30 May 1994
Janet Oppenhein – 2 December 1994
John Osborne – 24 December 1994
Kenneth Leo Patton – 25 December 1994
Ernst Pawel – 16 August 1994
Robert O. Payne – 9 February 1994
Lois Peyser – 18 February 1994
Aurelia Plath – 11 March 1994
Nathan Polowetsky – 7 August 1994
Karl Popper – 17 September 1994
Dennis Potter – 7 June 1994
Frederick A. Praeger – 28 May 1994
John Preston – 28 April 1994
Lewis Puller, Jr. – 11 May 1994
Sonia Raiziss – 19 March 1994
Derek Raymond – 30 July 1994
Jane Elizabeth Richmond – 6 June 1994

W. Edson Richmond – 11 August 1994
Nancy K. Robinson – 15 March 1994
Berton Roueché – 28 April 1994
John C. Russell – 22 April 1994
Pinchas Sadeh – 29 January 1994
Luis Alberto Sánchez – 6 February 1994
Richard Scarry – 30 April 1994
Andrei Sedych – 8 January 1994
Samuel Selvon – 16 April 1994
Robert Sherrod – 13 February 1994
Randy Shilts – 17 February 1994
Sunny Sloan – 8 January 1994
Carlton Sprague Smith – 19 September 1994
Thomas H. Smith – 26 September 1994
Charles Sopkin – 22 September 1994
Elizabeth G. Speare – 15 November 1994
Ann M. Sperber – 11 February 1994
Marshall Sprague – 9 September 1994
Irwin Stark – 4 June 1994
Francis Steegmuller – 20 October 1994
Jule Styne – 20 September 1994
Julian Symons – 19 November 1994
Peter Taylor – 2 November 1994
Caitlin Thomas – 31 July 1994
Samuel E. Thorne – 7 April 1994
Basil Vlavianos – 27 June 1994
John Wain – 24 May 1994
Terence de Vere White – 17 June 1994
Ella Keats Whiting – 24 November 1994
John R. Wilhelm – 6 June 1994
John Williams – 3 March 1994
Charles Elihu Winer – 4 April 1994
Mildred Wohlforth – 3 January 1994
Helen Wolff – 29 March 1994
Clement Biddle Wood, Jr. – 4 December 1994
Valerie Worth – 31 July 1994
Seishi Yamaguchi – 29 March 1994
Taro Yashima – 30 June 1994
Junnosuke Yoshiyuki – 26 July 1994
Herbert S. Zim – 5 December 1994

Contributors

Leonard J. Deutsch ....*Marshall University*
R. H. W. Dillard ....*Hollins College*
Charles Egleston...*University of Colorado*
William Foltz..*University of Hawaii*
George Garrett...*University of Virginia*
Darren Harris-Fain...*Columbia, South Carolina*
Joyce Harrison ....*University of South Carolina Press*
Cathy Henderson ....*University of Texas at Austin*
Caroline C. Hunt ....*College of Charleston*
Howard Kissel...*New York Daily News*
Robert McPhillips...*Iona College*
David R. Slavitt ....*University of Pennsylvania*
David Sutton ....*University of Reading*
Mark Trainer ....*Charlottesville, Virginia*
Kiyohiko Tsuboi and Nobuko Tsuboi..*Toyo University*
Mark Royden Winchell...*Clemson University*

Cumulative Index

Dictionary of Literary Biography, Volumes 1-151
Dictionary of Literary Biography Yearbook, 1980-1994
Dictionary of Literary Biography Documentary Series, Volumes 1-12

Cumulative Index

DLB before number: *Dictionary of Literary Biography*, Volumes 1-151
Y before number: *Dictionary of Literary Biography Yearbook*, 1980-1994
DS before number: *Dictionary of Literary Biography Documentary Series*, Volumes 1-12

A

Abbey Press DLB-49

The Abbey Theatre and Irish Drama,
1900-1945 ....DLB-10

Abbot, Willis J. 1863-1934 ....DLB-29

Abbott, Jacob 1803-1879 ....DLB-1

Abbott, Lee K. 1947- DLB-130

Abbott, Lyman 1835-1922 ....DLB-79

Abbott, Robert S. 1868-1940 ...DLB-29, 91

Abelard, Peter circa 1079-1142 .....DLB-115

Abelard-Schuman DLB-46

Abell, Arunah S. 1806-1888 ....DLB-43

Abercrombie, Lascelles 1881-1938 ...DLB-19

Aberdeen University Press
Limited DLB-106

Abish, Walter 1931- DLB-130

Ablesimov, Aleksandr Onisimovich
1742-1783 ....DLB-150

Abrahams, Peter 1919- DLB-117

Abrams, M. H. 1912- DLB-67

Abrogans circa 790-800 ....DLB-148

Abse, Dannie 1923- DLB-27

Academy Chicago Publishers DLB-46

Accrocca, Elio Filippo 1923- DLB-128

Ace Books DLB-46

Achebe, Chinua 1930- DLB-117

Achtenberg, Herbert 1938- DLB-124

Ackerman, Diane 1948- DLB-120

Acorn, Milton 1923-1986 ....DLB-53

Acosta, Oscar Zeta 1935?- DLB-82

Actors Theatre of Louisville DLB-7

Adair, James 1709?-1783? DLB-30

Adam, Graeme Mercer 1839-1912 ...DLB-99

Adame, Leonard 1947- DLB-82

Adamic, Louis 1898-1951 ....DLB-9

Adams, Alice 1926- Y-86

Adams, Brooks 1848-1927 ....DLB-47

Adams, Charles Francis, Jr.
1835-1915 ....DLB-47

Adams, Douglas 1952- Y-83

Adams, Franklin P. 1881-1960 .....DLB-29

Adams, Henry 1838-1918 ....DLB-12, 47

Adams, Herbert Baxter 1850-1901 ...DLB-47

Adams, J. S. and C.
[publishing house] DLB-49

Adams, James Truslow 1878-1949 ...DLB-17

Adams, John 1735-1826 ....DLB-31

Adams, John Quincy 1767-1848 .....DLB-37

Adams, Léonie 1899-1988 ....DLB-48

Adams, Levi 1802-1832 ....DLB-99

Adams, Samuel 1722-1803 ......DLB-31, 43

Adams, Thomas
1582 or 1583-1652 ....DLB-151

Adams, William Taylor 1822-1897 .. DLB-42

Adamson, Sir John 1867-1950 ......DLB-98

Adcock, Arthur St. John
1864-1930 ....DLB-135

Adcock, Betty 1938- DLB-105

Adcock, Betty, Certain Gifts DLB-105

Adcock, Fleur 1934- DLB-40

Addison, Joseph 1672-1719 ....DLB-101

Ade, George 1866-1944 ....DLB-11, 25

Adeler, Max (see Clark, Charles Heber)

Adonias Filho 1915-1990 ....DLB-145

Advance Publishing Company DLB-49

AE 1867-1935 ....DLB-19

Ælfric circa 955-circa 1010 ....DLB-146

Aesthetic Poetry (1873), by
Walter Pater DLB-35

After Dinner Opera Company Y-92

Afro-American Literary Critics:
An Introduction DLB-33

Agassiz, Jean Louis Rodolphe
1807-1873 ....DLB-1

Agee, James 1909-1955 ....DLB-2, 26

The Agee Legacy: A Conference at
the University of Tennessee
at Knoxville Y-89

Aguilera Malta, Demetrio
1909-1981 ....DLB-145

Ai 1947- DLB-120

Aichinger, Ilse 1921- DLB-85

Aidoo, Ama Ata 1942- DLB-117

Aiken, Conrad 1889-1973 ....DLB-9, 45, 102

Aikin, Lucy 1781-1864 ....DLB-144

Ainsworth, William Harrison
1805-1882 ....DLB-21

Aitken, George A. 1860-1917 ......DLB-149

Aitken, Robert [publishing house] ...DLB-49

Akenside, Mark 1721-1770 ....DLB-109

Akins, Zoë 1886-1958 ....DLB-26

Alabaster, William 1568-1640 ......DLB-132

Alain-Fournier 1886-1914 ....DLB-65

Alarcón, Francisco X. 1954- DLB-122

Alba, Nanina 1915-1968 ....DLB-41

Albee, Edward 1928- DLB-7

Albert the Great circa 1200-1280 ...DLB-115

Alberti, Rafael 1902- DLB-108

Alcott, Amos Bronson 1799-1888 .....DLB-1

Alcott, Louisa May
1832-1888 ....DLB-1, 42, 79

Alcott, William Andrus 1798-1859 ....DLB-1

Alcuin circa 732-804 ....DLB-148

Alden, Henry Mills 1836-1919 ......DLB-79

Alden, Isabella 1841-1930 ....DLB-42

Alden, John B. [publishing house] DLB-49

Alden, Beardsley and Company DLB-49

Aldington, Richard
1892-1962 ....DLB-20, 36, 100, 149

Aldis, Dorothy 1896-1966 ....DLB-22

Aldiss, Brian W. 1925- DLB-14

Aldrich, Thomas Bailey
1836-1907 . . . . DLB-42, 71, 74, 79

Alegría, Ciro 1909-1967 . . . . DLB-113

Alegría, Claribel 1924- DLB-145

Aleixandre, Vicente 1898-1984 . . . . DLB-108

Aleramo, Sibilla 1876-1960 . . . . DLB-114

Alexander, Charles 1868-1923 . . . . . . DLB-91

Alexander, Charles Wesley
[publishing house] DLB-49

Alexander, James 1691-1756 . . . . DLB-24

Alexander, Lloyd 1924- DLB-52

Alexander, Sir William, Earl of Stirling
1577?-1640 . . . . DLB-121

Alexis, Willibald 1798-1871 . . . . DLB-133

Alfred, King 849-899 . . . . DLB-146

Alger, Horatio, Jr. 1832-1899 . . . . DLB-42

Algonquin Books of Chapel Hill DLB-46

Algren, Nelson
1909-1981 . . . . DLB-9; Y-81, 82

Allan, Andrew 1907-1974 . . . . DLB-88

Allan, Ted 1916- DLB-68

Allbeury, Ted 1917- DLB-87

Alldritt, Keith 1935- DLB-14

Allen, Ethan 1738-1789 . . . . DLB-31

Allen, Frederick Lewis 1890-1954 . . DLB-137

Allen, Gay Wilson 1903- DLB-103

Allen, George 1808-1876 . . . . DLB-59

Allen, George [publishing house] . . . DLB-106

Allen, George, and Unwin
Limited DLB-112

Allen, Grant 1848-1899 . . . . DLB-70, 92

Allen, Henry W. 1912- Y-85

Allen, Hervey 1889-1949 . . . . DLB-9, 45

Allen, James 1739-1808 . . . . DLB-31

Allen, James Lane 1849-1925 . . . . DLB-71

Allen, Jay Presson 1922- DLB-26

Allen, John, and Company DLB-49

Allen, Samuel W. 1917- DLB-41

Allen, Woody 1935- DLB-44

Allende, Isabel 1942- DLB-145

Alline, Henry 1748-1784 . . . . DLB-99

Allingham, Margery 1904-1966 . . . . . DLB-77

Allingham, William 1824-1889 . . . . . DLB-35

Allison, W. L. [publishing house] . . . DLB-49

The *Alliterative Morte Arthure* and
the *Stanzaic Morte Arthur*
circa 1350-1400 . . . . DLB-146

Allott, Kenneth 1912-1973 . . . . DLB-20

Allston, Washington 1779-1843 . . . . . . DLB-1

Alonzo, Dámaso 1898-1990 . . . . DLB-108

Alsop, George 1636-post 1673 . . . . . . DLB-24

Alsop, Richard 1761-1815 . . . . DLB-37

Altemus, Henry, and Company DLB-49

Altenberg, Peter 1885-1919 . . . . DLB-81

Altolaguirre, Manuel 1905-1959 . . . . DLB-108

Aluko, T. M. 1918- DLB-117

Alurista 1947- DLB-82

Alvarez, A. 1929- DLB-14, 40

Amadi, Elechi 1934- DLB-117

Amado, Jorge 1912- DLB-113

Ambler, Eric 1909- DLB-77

*America: or, a Poem on the Settlement of the
British Colonies* (1780?), by Timothy
Dwight DLB-37

American Conservatory Theatre DLB-7

American Fiction and the 1930s DLB-9

American Humor: A Historical Survey
East and Northeast
South and Southwest
Midwest
West DLB-11

The American Library in Paris Y-93

American News Company DLB-49

The American Poets' Corner: The First
Three Years (1983-1986) Y-86

American Proletarian Culture:
The 1930s DS-11

American Publishing Company DLB-49

American Stationers' Company DLB-49

American Sunday-School Union DLB-49

American Temperance Union DLB-49

American Tract Society DLB-49

The American Writers Congress
(9-12 October 1981) Y-81

The American Writers Congress: A Report
on Continuing Business Y-81

Ames, Fisher 1758-1808 . . . . DLB-37

Ames, Mary Clemmer 1831-1884 . . . . DLB-23

Amini, Johari M. 1935- DLB-41

Amis, Kingsley 1922- DLB-15, 27, 100, 139

Amis, Martin 1949- DLB-14

Ammons, A. R. 1926- DLB-5

Amory, Thomas 1691?-1788 . . . . DLB-39

Anaya, Rudolfo A. 1937- DLB-82

Ancrene Riwle circa 1200-1225 . . . . DLB-146

Andersch, Alfred 1914-1980 . . . . .DLB-69

Anderson, Margaret 1886-1973 . . . DLB-4, 91

Anderson, Maxwell 1888-1959 . . . . . . .DLB-7

Anderson, Patrick 1915-1979 . . . . .DLB-68

Anderson, Paul Y. 1893-1938 . . . . . . .DLB-29

Anderson, Poul 1926- DLB-8

Anderson, Robert 1750-1830 . . . . . . .DLB-142

Anderson, Robert 1917- DLB-7

Anderson, Sherwood
1876-1941 . . . . DLB-4, 9, 86; DS-1

Andreas-Salomé, Lou 1861-1937 . . . .DLB-66

Andres, Stefan 1906-1970 . . . . .DLB-69

Andreu, Blanca 1959- DLB-134

Andrewes, Lancelot 1555-1626 . . . . .DLB-151

Andrews, Charles M. 1863-1943 . . . . .DLB-17

Andrews, Miles Peter ?-1814 . . . . . . .DLB-89

Andrian, Leopold von 1875-1951 . . . .DLB-81

Andrić, Ivo 1892-1975 . . . . .DLB-147

Andrieux, Louis (see Aragon, Louis)

Andrus, Silas, and Son DLB-49

Angell, James Burrill 1829-1916 . . . . . .DLB-64

Angelou, Maya 1928- DLB-38

Anger, Jane flourished 1589 . . . . .DLB-136

Angers, Félicité (see Conan, Laure)

Anglo-Norman Literature in the Development
of Middle English Literature DLB-146

The Anglo-Saxon Chronicle
circa 890-1154 . . . . .DLB-146

The "Angry Young Men" DLB-15

Angus and Robertson (UK)
Limited DLB-112

Anhalt, Edward 1914- DLB-26

Anners, Henry F.
[publishing house] DLB-49

Annolied between 1077 and 1081 . . . .DLB-148

Anselm of Canterbury 1033-1109 . . .DLB-115

Anthony, Michael 1932- DLB-125

Anthony, Piers 1934- DLB-8

Anthony Burgess's *99 Novels:*
An Opinion Poll Y-84

Antin, Mary 1881-1949 . . . . Y-84

Antschel, Paul (see Celan, Paul)

Antsey, F. 1856-1934 . . . . .DLB-141

Anzaldúa, Gloria 1942- DLB-122

Anzengruber, Ludwig 1839-1889 . . . .DLB-129

Apodaca, Rudy S. 1939- DLB-82

Apple, Max 1941- DLB-130

Appleton, D., and Company DLB-49

Appleton-Century-Crofts DLB-46

Applewhite, James 1935- DLB-105

Apple-wood Books DLB-46

Aquin, Hubert 1929-1977 . . . . .DLB-53

Aquinas, Thomas 1224 or
  1225-1274 . . . . .DLB-115

Aragon, Louis 1897-1982 . . . . .DLB-72

Arbor House Publishing
  Company DLB-46

Arbuthnot, John 1667-1735 . . . . . . .DLB-101

Arcadia House DLB-46

Arce, Julio G. (see Ulica, Jorge)

Archer, William 1856-1924 . . . . .DLB-10

The Archpoet circa 1130?-? DLB-148

Archpriest Avvakum (Petrovich)
  1620?-1682 . . . . .DLB-150

Arden, John 1930- DLB-13

Arden of Faversham DLB-62

Ardis Publishers Y-89

Arellano, Juan Estevan 1947- DLB-122

The Arena Publishing Company DLB-49

Arena Stage DLB-7

Arenas, Reinaldo 1943-1990 . . . . . . .DLB-145

Arensberg, Ann 1937- Y-82

Arguedas, José María 1911-1969 . . . .DLB-113

Argueta, Manlio 1936- DLB-145

Arias, Ron 1941- DLB-82

Arland, Marcel 1899-1986 . . . . .DLB-72

Arlen, Michael 1895-1956 . . . . . . .DLB-36, 77

Armah, Ayi Kwei 1939- DLB-117

Der arme Hartmann
  ?-after 1150 . . . . .DLB-148

Armed Services Editions DLB-46

Arndt, Ernst Moritz 1769-1860 . . . . . .DLB-90

Arnim, Achim von 1781-1831 . . . . . . .DLB-90

Arnim, Bettina von 1785-1859 . . . . . . .DLB-90

Arno Press DLB-46

Arnold, Edwin 1832-1904 . . . . .DLB-35

Arnold, Matthew 1822-1888 . . . . .DLB-32, 57

Arnold, Thomas 1795-1842 . . . . .DLB-55

Arnold, Edward
  [publishing house] DLB-112

Arnow, Harriette Simpson
  1908-1986 . . . . .DLB-6

Arp, Bill (see Smith, Charles Henry)

Arreola, Juan José 1918- DLB-113

Arrowsmith, J. W.
  [publishing house] DLB-106

Arthur, Timothy Shay
  1809-1885 . . . . .DLB-3, 42, 79

The Arthurian Tradition and Its European
  Context DLB-138

Artmann, H. C. 1921- DLB-85

Arvin, Newton 1900-1963 . . . . DLB-103

As I See It, by Carolyn Cassady DLB-16

Asch, Nathan 1902-1964 . . . . DLB-4, 28

Ash, John 1948- DLB-40

Ashbery, John 1927- DLB-5; Y-81

Ashendene Press DLB-112

Asher, Sandy 1942- Y-83

Ashton, Winifred (see Dane, Clemence)

Asimov, Isaac 1920-1992 . . . . . . DLB-8; Y-92

Askew, Anne circa 1521-1546 . . . . . DLB-136

Asselin, Olivar 1874-1937 . . . . DLB-92

Asturias, Miguel Angel
  1899-1974 . . . . DLB-113

Atheneum Publishers DLB-46

Atherton, Gertrude 1857-1948 . . . . DLB-9, 78

Athlone Press DLB-112

Atkins, Josiah circa 1755-1781 . . . . . DLB-31

Atkins, Russell 1926- DLB-41

The Atlantic Monthly Press DLB-46

Attaway, William 1911-1986 . . . . DLB-76

Atwood, Margaret 1939- DLB-53

Aubert, Alvin 1930- DLB-41

Aubert de Gaspé, Phillipe-Ignace-François
  1814-1841 . . . . DLB-99

Aubert de Gaspé, Phillipe-Joseph
  1786-1871 . . . . DLB-99

Aubin, Napoléon 1812-1890 . . . . DLB-99

Aubin, Penelope 1685-circa 1731 . . . . DLB-39

Aubrey-Fletcher, Henry Lancelot
  (see Wade, Henry)

Auchincloss, Louis 1917- DLB-2; Y-80

Auden, W. H. 1907-1973 . . . . DLB-10, 20

Audio Art in America: A Personal
  Memoir Y-85

Auerbach, Berthold 1812-1882 . . . . . DLB-133

Auernheimer, Raoul 1876-1948 . . . . . DLB-81

Augustine 354-430 . . . . DLB-115

Austen, Jane 1775-1817 . . . . DLB-116

Austin, Alfred 1835-1913 . . . . .DLB-35

Austin, Mary 1868-1934 . . . . .DLB-9, 78

Austin, William 1778-1841 . . . . .DLB-74

The Author's Apology for His Book
  (1684), by John Bunyan DLB-39

An Author's Response, by
  Ronald Sukenick Y-82

Authors and Newspapers
  Association DLB-46

Authors' Publishing Company DLB-49

Avalon Books DLB-46

Avendaño, Fausto 1941- DLB-82

Averroës 1126-1198 . . . . .DLB-115

Avicenna 980-1037 . . . . .DLB-115

Avison, Margaret 1918- DLB-53

Avon Books .DLB-46

Awoonor, Kofi 1935- DLB-117

Ayckbourn, Alan 1939- DLB-13

Aymé, Marcel 1902-1967 . . . . .DLB-72

Aytoun, Sir Robert 1570-1638 . . . . .DLB-121

Aytoun, William Edmondstoune
  1813-1865 . . . . .DLB-32

B

B. V. (see Thomson, James)

Babbitt, Irving 1865-1933 . . . . .DLB-63

Babbitt, Natalie 1932- DLB-52

Babcock, John [publishing house] DLB-49

Baca, Jimmy Santiago 1952- DLB-122

Bache, Benjamin Franklin
  1769-1798 . . . . .DLB-43

Bachmann, Ingeborg 1926-1973 . . . . .DLB-85

Bacon, Delia 1811-1859 . . . . .DLB-1

Bacon, Francis 1561-1626 . . . . .DLB-151

Bacon, Roger circa
  1214/1220-1292 . . . . .DLB-115

Bacon, Sir Nicholas
  circa 1510-1579 . . . . .DLB-132

Bacon, Thomas circa 1700-1768 . . . . .DLB-31

Badger, Richard G.,
  and Company DLB-49

Bage, Robert 1728-1801 . . . . .DLB-39

Bagehot, Walter 1826-1877 . . . . .DLB-55

Bagley, Desmond 1923-1983 . . . . .DLB-87

Bagnold, Enid 1889-1981 . . . . .DLB-13

Bagryana, Elisaveta 1893-1991 . . . .DLB-147

Bahr, Hermann 1863-1934 ..... DLB-81, 118

Bailey, Alfred Goldsworthy
1905- DLB-68

Bailey, Francis [publishing house] ... DLB-49

Bailey, H. C. 1878-1961 .... DLB-77

Bailey, Jacob 1731-1808 .... DLB-99

Bailey, Paul 1937- DLB-14

Bailey, Philip James 1816-1902 ..... DLB-32

Baillargeon, Pierre 1916-1967 .... DLB-88

Baillie, Hugh 1890-1966 .... DLB-29

Baillie, Joanna 1762-1851 .... DLB-93

Bailyn, Bernard 1922- DLB-17

Bainbridge, Beryl 1933- DLB-14

Baird, Irene 1901-1981 .... DLB-68

Baker, Augustine 1575-1641 .... DLB-151

Baker, Carlos 1909-1987 .... DLB-103

Baker, David 1954- DLB-120

Baker, Herschel C. 1914-1990 ..... DLB-111

Baker, Houston A., Jr. 1943- DLB-67

Baker, Walter H., Company
("Baker's Plays") DLB-49

The Baker and Taylor Company DLB-49

Balaban, John 1943- DLB-120

Bald, Wambly 1902- DLB-4

Balderston, John 1889-1954 .... DLB-26

Baldwin, James
1924-1987 .... DLB-2, 7, 33; Y-87

Baldwin, Joseph Glover
1815-1864 .... DLB-3, 11

Baldwin, William
circa 1515-1563 .... DLB-132

Bale, John 1495-1563 .... DLB-132

Balestrini, Nanni 1935- DLB-128

Ballantine Books DLB-46

Ballard, J. G. 1930- DLB-14

Ballerini, Luigi 1940- DLB-128

Ballou, Maturin Murray
1820-1895 .... DLB-79

Ballou, Robert O.
[publishing house] DLB-46

Balzac, Honoré de 1799-1855 ...... DLB-119

Bambara, Toni Cade 1939- DLB-38

Bancroft, A. L., and
Company DLB-49

Bancroft, George
1800-1891 .... DLB-1, 30, 59

Bancroft, Hubert Howe
1832-1918 .... DLB-47, 140

Bangs, John Kendrick
1862-1922 .... DLB-11, 79

Banim, John 1798-1842 .... DLB-116

Banks, John circa 1653-1706 .... DLB-80

Banks, Russell 1940- DLB-130

Bannerman, Helen 1862-1946 ..... DLB-141

Bantam Books DLB-46

Banville, John 1945- DLB-14

Baraka, Amiri
1934- DLB-5, 7, 16, 38; DS-8

Barbauld, Anna Laetitia
1743-1825 .... DLB-107, 109, 142

Barbeau, Marius 1883-1969 .... DLB-92

Barber, John Warner 1798-1885 ..... DLB-30

Bàrberi Squarotti, Giorgio
1929- DLB-128

Barbey d'Aurevilly, Jules-Amédée
1808-1889 .... DLB-119

Barbour, John circa 1316-1395 ..... DLB-146

Barbour, Ralph Henry
1870-1944 .... DLB-22

Barbusse, Henri 1873-1935 .... DLB-65

Barclay, Alexander
circa 1475-1552 .... DLB-132

Barclay, E. E., and Company DLB-49

Bardeen, C. W.
[publishing house] DLB-49

Baring, Maurice 1874-1945 .... DLB-34

Barker, A. L. 1918- DLB-14, 139

Barker, George 1913-1991 .... DLB-20

Barker, Harley Granville
1877-1946 .... DLB-10

Barker, Howard 1946- DLB-13

Barker, James Nelson 1784-1858 ..... DLB-37

Barker, Jane 1652-1727 .... DLB-39, 131

Barker, William
circa 1520-after 1576 .... DLB-132

Barker, Arthur, Limited DLB-112

Barkov, Ivan Semenovich
1732-1768 .... DLB-150

Barks, Coleman 1937- DLB-5

Barlach, Ernst 1870-1938 ...... DLB-56, 118

Barlow, Joel 1754-1812 .... DLB-37

Barnard, John 1681-1770 .... DLB-24

Barnes, Barnabe 1571-1609 .... DLB-132

Barnes, Djuna 1892-1982 ...... DLB-4, 9, 45

Barnes, Julian 1946- Y-93

Barnes, Margaret Ayer 1886-1967 .... DLB-9

Barnes, Peter 1931- DLB-13

Barnes, William 1801-1886 .... DLB-32

Barnes, A. S., and Company DLB-49

Barnes and Noble Books DLB-46

Barnet, Miguel 1940- DLB-145

Barney, Natalie 1876-1972 .... DLB-4

Baron, Richard W.,
Publishing Company DLB-46

Barr, Robert 1850-1912 .... DLB-70, 92

Barral, Carlos 1928-1989 .... DLB-134

Barrax, Gerald William
1933- DLB-41, 120

Barrès, Maurice 1862-1923 .... DLB-123

Barrett, Eaton Stannard
1786-1820 .... DLB-116

Barrie, J. M. 1860-1937 .... DLB-10, 141

Barrie and Jenkins DLB-112

Barrio, Raymond 1921- DLB-82

Barrios, Gregg 1945- DLB-122

Barry, Philip 1896-1949 .... DLB-7

Barry, Robertine (see Françoise)

Barse and Hopkins DLB-46

Barstow, Stan 1928- DLB-14, 139

Barth, John 1930- DLB-2

Barthelme, Donald
1931-1989 .... DLB-2; Y-80, 89

Barthelme, Frederick 1943- Y-85

Bartholomew, Frank 1898-1985 ..... DLB-127

Bartlett, John 1820-1905 .... DLB-1

Bartol, Cyrus Augustus 1813-1900 .... DLB-1

Barton, Bernard 1784-1849 .... DLB-96

Barton, Thomas Pennant
1803-1869 .... DLB-140

Bartram, John 1699-1777 .... DLB-31

Bartram, William 1739-1823 .... DLB-37

Basic Books DLB-46

Basille, Theodore (see Becon, Thomas)

Bass, T. J. 1932- Y-81

Bassani, Giorgio 1916- DLB-128

Basse, William circa 1583-1653 ..... DLB-121

Bassett, John Spencer 1867-1928 ..... DLB-17

Bassler, Thomas Joseph (see Bass, T. J.)

Bate, Walter Jackson 1918- ... DLB-67, 103

Bateman, Stephen
circa 1510-1584 .... DLB-136

Bates, Katharine Lee 1859-1929 ...... DLB-71

Batsford, B. T.
[publishing house] DLB-106

The Battle of Maldon circa 1000 . . . . . .DLB-146

Bauer, Bruno 1809-1882 . . . . .DLB-133

Bauer, Wolfgang 1941- DLB-124

Baum, L. Frank 1856-1919 . . . . .DLB-22

Baum, Vicki 1888-1960 . . . . .DLB-85

Baumbach, Jonathan 1933- Y-80

Bausch, Richard 1945- DLB-130

Bawden, Nina 1925- DLB-14

Bax, Clifford 1886-1962 . . . . . . .DLB-10, 100

Baxter, Charles 1947- DLB-130

Bayer, Eleanor (see Perry, Eleanor)

Bayer, Konrad 1932-1964 . . . . .DLB-85

Bazin, Hervé 1911- DLB-83

Beach, Sylvia 1887-1962 . . . . .DLB-4

Beacon Press .DLB-49

Beadle and Adams DLB-49

Beagle, Peter S. 1939- Y-80

Beal, M. F. 1937- Y-81

Beale, Howard K. 1899-1959 . . . . .DLB-17

Beard, Charles A. 1874-1948 . . . . .DLB-17

A Beat Chronology: The First Twenty-five
Years, 1944-1969 . . . . .DLB-16

Beattie, Ann 1947- Y-82

Beattie, James 1735-1803 . . . . .DLB-109

Beauchemin, Nérée 1850-1931 . . . . . . .DLB-92

Beauchemin, Yves 1941- DLB-60

Beaugrand, Honoré 1848-1906 . . . . . .DLB-99

Beaulieu, Victor-Lévy 1945- DLB-53

Beaumont, Francis circa 1584-1616
and Fletcher, John 1579-1625 . . . .DLB-58

Beaumont, Sir John 1583?-1627 . . . .DLB-121

Beaumont, Joseph 1616–1699 . . . . . .DLB-126

Beauvoir, Simone de
1908-1986 . . . . .DLB-72; Y-86

Becher, Ulrich 1910- DLB-69

Becker, Carl 1873-1945 . . . . .DLB-17

Becker, Jurek 1937- DLB-75

Becker, Jurgen 1932- DLB-75

Beckett, Samuel
1906-1989 . . . . DLB-13, 15; Y-90

Beckford, William 1760-1844 . . . . . . .DLB-39

Beckham, Barry 1944- DLB-33

Becon, Thomas circa 1512-1567 . . . .DLB-136

Beddoes, Thomas Lovell
1803-1849 . . . . DLB-96

Bede circa 673-735 . . . . DLB-146

Beecher, Catharine Esther
1800-1878 . . . . DLB-1

Beecher, Henry Ward
1813-1887 . . . . DLB-3, 43

Beer, George L. 1872-1920 . . . . DLB-47

Beer, Patricia 1919- DLB-40

Beerbohm, Max 1872-1956 . . . . . DLB-34, 100

Beer-Hofmann, Richard
1866-1945 . . . . DLB-81

Beers, Henry A. 1847-1926 . . . . DLB-71

Beeton, S. O. [publishing house] . . . DLB-106

Bégon, Elisabeth 1696-1755 . . . . DLB-99

Behan, Brendan 1923-1964 . . . . DLB-13

Behn, Aphra 1640?-1689 . . . . DLB-39, 80, 131

Behn, Harry 1898-1973 . . . . DLB-61

Behrman, S. N. 1893-1973 . . . . DLB-7, 44

Belaney, Archibald Stansfeld (see Grey Owl)

Belasco, David 1853-1931 . . . . DLB-7

Belford, Clarke and Company DLB-49

Belitt, Ben 1911- DLB-5

Belknap, Jeremy 1744-1798 . . . . . . DLB-30, 37

Bell, Clive 1881-1964 . . . . .DS-10

Bell, James Madison 1826-1902 . . . . . DLB-50

Bell, Marvin 1937- DLB-5

Bell, Millicent 1919- DLB-111

Bell, Vanessa 1879-1961 . . . . .DS-10

Bell, George, and Sons DLB-106

Bell, Robert [publishing house] DLB-49

Bellamy, Edward 1850-1898 . . . . DLB-12

Bellamy, Joseph 1719-1790 . . . . DLB-31

Bellezza, Dario 1944- DLB-128

La Belle Assemblée 1806-1837 . . . . . . DLB-110

Belloc, Hilaire
1870-1953 . . . . .DLB-19, 100, 141

Bellow, Saul
1915- DLB-2, 28; Y-82; DS-3

Belmont Productions DLB-46

Bemelmans, Ludwig 1898-1962 . . . . . DLB-22

Bemis, Samuel Flagg 1891-1973 . . . . . DLB-17

Bemrose, William
[publishing house] DLB-106

Benchley, Robert 1889-1945 . . . . DLB-11

Benedetti, Mario 1920- DLB-113

Benedictus, David 1938- DLB-14

Benedikt, Michael 1935- DLB-5

Benét, Stephen Vincent
1898-1943 . . . . .DLB-4, 48, 102

Benét, William Rose 1886-1950 . . . . .DLB-45

Benford, Gregory 1941- Y-82

Benjamin, Park 1809-1864 . . . .DLB-3, 59, 73

Benlowes, Edward 1602-1676 . . . . . .DLB-126

Benn, Gottfried 1886-1956 . . . . .DLB-56

Benn Brothers Limited DLB-106

Bennett, Arnold
1867-1931 . . . . DLB-10, 34, 98, 135

Bennett, Charles 1899- DLB-44

Bennett, Gwendolyn 1902- DLB-51

Bennett, Hal 1930- DLB-33

Bennett, James Gordon 1795-1872 . . .DLB-43

Bennett, James Gordon, Jr.
1841-1918 . . . . .DLB-23

Bennett, John 1865-1956 . . . . .DLB-42

Bennett, Louise 1919- DLB-117

Benoit, Jacques 1941- DLB-60

Benson, A. C. 1862-1925 . . . . .DLB-98

Benson, E. F. 1867-1940 . . . . .DLB-135

Benson, Jackson J. 1930- DLB-111

Benson, Stella 1892-1933 . . . . .DLB-36

Bentham, Jeremy 1748-1832 . . . . . . .DLB-107

Bentley, E. C. 1875-1956 . . . . .DLB-70

Bentley, Richard
[publishing house] DLB-106

Benton, Robert 1932- and Newman,
David 1937- DLB-44

Benziger Brothers DLB-49

Beowulf circa 900-1000
or 790-825 . . . . .DLB-146

Beresford, Anne 1929- DLB-40

Beresford-Howe, Constance
1922- DLB-88

Berford, R. G., Company DLB-49

Berg, Stephen 1934- DLB-5

Bergengruen, Werner 1892-1964 . . . .DLB-56

Berger, John 1926- DLB-14

Berger, Meyer 1898-1959 . . . . .DLB-29

Berger, Thomas 1924- DLB-2; Y-80

Berkeley, Anthony 1893-1971 . . . . . . .DLB-77

Berkeley, George 1685-1753 . . . .DLB-31, 101

The Berkley Publishing
Corporation DLB-46

Berlin, Lucia 1936- DLB-130

Bernal, Vicente J. 1888-1915 . . . . DLB-82

Bernanos, Georges 1888-1948 . . . . . . DLB-72

Bernard, Harry 1898-1979 . . . . DLB-92

Bernard, John 1756-1828 . . . . DLB-37

Bernard of Chartres
circa 1060-1124? DLB-115

Bernhard, Thomas
1931-1989 . . . . DLB-85, 124

Berriault, Gina 1926- DLB-130

Berrigan, Daniel 1921- DLB-5

Berrigan, Ted 1934-1983 . . . . .DLB-5

Berry, Wendell 1934- DLB-5, 6

Berryman, John 1914-1972 . . . . DLB-48

Bersianik, Louky 1930- DLB-60

Bertolucci, Attilio 1911- DLB-128

Berton, Pierre 1920- DLB-68

Besant, Sir Walter 1836-1901 . . . . . . DLB-135

Bessette, Gerard 1920- DLB-53

Bessie, Alvah 1904-1985 . . . . DLB-26

Bester, Alfred 1913-1987 . . . . .DLB-8

The Bestseller Lists: An Assessment Y-84

Betjeman, John 1906-1984 . . . . DLB-20; Y-84

Betocchi, Carlo 1899-1986 . . . . DLB-128

Bettarini, Mariella 1942- DLB-128

Betts, Doris 1932- Y-82

Beveridge, Albert J. 1862-1927 . . . . . . DLB-17

Beverley, Robert
circa 1673-1722 . . . . DLB-24, 30

Beyle, Marie-Henri (see Stendhal)

Bibaud, Adèle 1854-1941 . . . . DLB-92

Bibaud, Michel 1782-1857 . . . . DLB-99

Bibliographical and Textual Scholarship
Since World War II Y-89

The Bicentennial of James Fenimore
Cooper: An International
Celebration Y-89

Bichsel, Peter 1935- DLB-75

Bickerstaff, Isaac John
1733-circa 1808 . . . . DLB-89

Biddle, Drexel [publishing house] . . . DLB-49

Bidwell, Walter Hilliard
1798-1881 . . . . DLB-79

Bienek, Horst 1930- DLB-75

Bierbaum, Otto Julius 1865-1910 . . . . DLB-66

Bierce, Ambrose
1842-1914? DLB-11, 12, 23, 71, 74

Bigelow, William F. 1879-1966 . . . . . DLB-91

Biggle, Lloyd, Jr. 1923- DLB-8

Biglow, Hosea (see Lowell, James Russell)

Bigongiari, Piero 1914- DLB-128

Billinger, Richard 1890-1965 . . . . . . DLB-124

Billings, John Shaw 1898-1975 . . . . . DLB-137

Billings, Josh (see Shaw, Henry Wheeler)

Binding, Rudolf G. 1867-1938 . . . . . . DLB-66

Bingham, Caleb 1757-1817 . . . . DLB-42

Bingham, George Barry
1906-1988 . . . . DLB-127

Binyon, Laurence 1869-1943 . . . . DLB-19

Biographia Brittanica DLB-142

Biographical Documents I Y-84

Biographical Documents II Y-85

Bioren, John [publishing house] DLB-49

Bioy Casares, Adolfo 1914- DLB-113

Bird, William 1888-1963 . . . . DLB-4

Birney, Earle 1904- DLB-88

Birrell, Augustine 1850-1933 . . . . DLB-98

Bishop, Elizabeth 1911-1979 . . . . DLB-5

Bishop, John Peale 1892-1944 . . .DLB-4, 9, 45

Bismarck, Otto von 1815-1898 . . . . . DLB-129

Bisset, Robert 1759-1805 . . . . DLB-142

Bissett, Bill 1939- DLB-53

Bitzius, Albert (see Gotthelf, Jeremias)

Black, David (D. M.) 1941- DLB-40

Black, Winifred 1863-1936 . . . . DLB-25

Black, Walter J.
[publishing house] DLB-46

The Black Aesthetic: Background DS-8

The Black Arts Movement, by
Larry Neal DLB-38

Black Theaters and Theater Organizations in
America, 1961-1982:
A Research List DLB-38

Black Theatre: A Forum
[excerpts] DLB-38

Blackamore, Arthur 1679-? DLB-24, 39

Blackburn, Alexander L. 1929- Y-85

Blackburn, Paul 1926-1971 . . . .DLB-16; Y-81

Blackburn, Thomas 1916-1977 . . . . . . DLB-27

Blackmore, R. D. 1825-1900 . . . . DLB-18

Blackmore, Sir Richard
1654-1729 . . . . DLB-131

Blackmur, R. P. 1904-1965 . . . . DLB-63

Blackwell, Basil, Publisher DLB-106

Blackwood, Caroline 1931- DLB-14

Blackwood's Edinburgh Magazine
1817-1980 . . . . .DLB-110

Blair, Eric Arthur (see Orwell, George)

Blair, Francis Preston 1791-1876 . . . . .DLB-43

Blair, James circa 1655-1743 . . . . .DLB-24

Blair, John Durburrow 1759-1823 . . . .DLB-37

Blais, Marie-Claire 1939- DLB-53

Blaise, Clark 1940- DLB-53

Blake, Nicholas 1904-1972 . . . . .ΓιB-77
(see Day Lewis, C.)

Blake, William 1757-1827 . . . . .DLB-93

The Blakiston Company DLB-49

Blanchot, Maurice 1907- DLB-72

Blanckenburg, Christian Friedrich von
1744-1796 . . . . .DLB-94

Bledsoe, Albert Taylor
1809-1877 . . . . DLB-3, 79

Blelock and Company DLB-49

Blennerhassett, Margaret Agnew
1773-1842 . . . . .DLB-99

Bles, Geoffrey
[publishing house] DLB-112

The Blickling Homilies
circa 971 . . . . .DLB-146

Blish, James 1921-1975 . . . . .DLB-8

Bliss, E., and E. White
[publishing house] DLB-49

Bliven, Bruce 1889-1977 . . . . .DLB-137

Bloch, Robert 1917- DLB-44

Block, Rudolph (see Lessing, Bruno)

Blondal, Patricia 1926-1959 . . . . .DLB-88

Bloom, Harold 1930- DLB-67

Bloomer, Amelia 1818-1894 . . . . .DLB-79

Bloomfield, Robert 1766-1823 . . . . . .DLB-93

Bloomsbury Group DS-10

Blotner, Joseph 1923- DLB-111

Bloy, Léon 1846-1917 . . . . .DLB-123

Blume, Judy 1938- DLB-52

Blunck, Hans Friedrich 1888-1961 . . .DLB-66

Blunden, Edmund
1896-1974 . . . . DLB-20, 100

Blunt, Wilfrid Scawen 1840-1922 . . . .DLB-19

Bly, Nellie (see Cochrane, Elizabeth)

Bly, Robert 1926- DLB-5

Boaden, James 1762-1839 . . . . .DLB-89

Boas, Frederick S. 1862-1957 . . . . . . .DLB-149

The Bobbs-Merrill Archive at the
Lilly Library, Indiana University . . . Y-90

The Bobbs-Merrill Company DLB-46

Bobrov, Semen Sergeevich
   1763?-1810 . . . . .DLB-150

Bobrowski, Johannes 1917-1965 . . . . .DLB-75

Bodenheim, Maxwell 1892-1954 . . .DLB-9, 45

Bodenstedt, Friedrich von
   1819-1892 . . . . .DLB-129

Bodini, Vittorio 1914-1970 . . . . . . .DLB-128

Bodkin, M. McDonnell
   1850-1933 . . . . .DLB-70

Bodley Head DLB-112

Bodmer, Johann Jakob 1698-1783 . . . .DLB-97

Bodmershof, Imma von 1895-1982 . . .DLB-85

Bodsworth, Fred 1918- DLB-68

Boehm, Sydney 1908- DLB-44

Boer, Charles 1939- DLB-5

Boethius circa 480-circa 524 . . . . . . .DLB-115

Boethius of Dacia circa 1240-? DLB-115

Bogan, Louise 1897-1970 . . . . .DLB-45

Bogarde, Dirk 1921- DLB-14

Bogdanovich, Ippolit Fedorovich
   circa 1743-1803 . . . . .DLB-150

Bogue, David [publishing house] DLB-106

Bohn, H. G. [publishing house] DLB-106

Boie, Heinrich Christian
   1744-1806 . . . . .DLB-94

Bok, Edward W. 1863-1930 . . . . .DLB-91

Boland, Eavan 1944- DLB-40

Bolingbroke, Henry St. John, Viscount
   1678-1751 . . . . .DLB-101

Böll, Heinrich 1917-1985 . . . . . .Y-85, DLB-69

Bolling, Robert 1738-1775 . . . . .DLB-31

Bolotov, Andrei Timofeevich
   1738-1833 . . . . .DLB-150

Bolt, Carol 1941- DLB-60

Bolt, Robert 1924- DLB-13

Bolton, Herbert E. 1870-1953 . . . . . . .DLB-17

Bonaventura .DLB-90

Bonaventure circa 1217-1274 . . . . . .DLB-115

Bond, Edward 1934- DLB-13

Boni, Albert and Charles
   [publishing house] DLB-46

Boni and Liveright DLB-46

Robert Bonner's Sons DLB-49

Bontemps, Arna 1902-1973 . . . . . .DLB-48, 51

The Book League of America DLB-46

Book Reviewing in America: I Y-87

Book Reviewing in America: II Y-88

Book Reviewing in America: III Y-89

Book Reviewing in America: IV Y-90

Book Reviewing in America: V Y-91

Book Reviewing in America: VI Y-92

Book Reviewing in America: VII Y-93

Book Reviewing in America VIII Y-94

Book Supply Company DLB-49

The Book Trade History Group Y-93

The Booker Prize
   Address by Anthony Thwaite,
   Chairman of the Booker Prize Judges
   Comments from Former Booker
   Prize Winners Y-86

Boorde, Andrew circa 1490-1549 . . . DLB-136

Boorstin, Daniel J. 1914- DLB-17

Booth, Mary L. 1831-1889 . . . . DLB-79

Booth, Philip 1925- Y-82

Booth, Wayne C. 1921- DLB-67

Borchardt, Rudolf 1877-1945 . . . . DLB-66

Borchert, Wolfgang
   1921-1947 . . . . DLB-69, 124

Borel, Pétrus 1809-1859 . . . . DLB-119

Borges, Jorge Luis
   1899-1986 . . . . DLB-113; Y-86

Börne, Ludwig 1786-1837 . . . . DLB-90

Borrow, George 1803-1881 . . . . . . DLB-21, 55

Bosch, Juan 1909- DLB-145

Bosco, Henri 1888-1976 . . . . DLB-72

Bosco, Monique 1927- DLB-53

Boswell, James 1740-1795 . . . . . DLB-104, 142

Botev, Khristo 1847-1876 . . . . DLB-147

Botta, Anne C. Lynch 1815-1891 . . . . . DLB-3

Bottomley, Gordon 1874-1948 . . . . . . DLB-10

Bottoms, David 1949- DLB-120; Y-83

Bottrall, Ronald 1906- DLB-20

Boucher, Anthony 1911-1968 . . . . DLB-8

Boucher, Jonathan 1738-1804 . . . . . . DLB-31

Boucher de Boucherville, George
   1814-1894 . . . . DLB-99

Boudreau, Daniel (see Coste, Donat)

Bourassa, Napoléon 1827-1916 . . . . . DLB-99

Bourget, Paul 1852-1935 . . . . DLB-123

Bourinot, John George 1837-1902 . . . DLB-99

Bourjaily, Vance 1922- DLB-2, 143

Bourne, Edward Gaylord
   1860-1908 . . . . DLB-47

Bourne, Randolph 1886-1918 . . . . . . .DLB-63

Bousoño, Carlos 1923- DLB-108

Bousquet, Joë 1897-1950 . . . . .DLB-72

Bova, Ben 1932- Y-81

Bovard, Oliver K. 1872-1945 . . . . . . .DLB-25

Bove, Emmanuel 1898-1945 . . . . .DLB-72

Bowen, Elizabeth 1899-1973 . . . . .DLB-15

Bowen, Francis 1811-1890 . . . . .DLB-1, 59

Bowen, John 1924- DLB-13

Bowen-Merrill Company DLB-49

Bowering, George 1935- DLB-53

Bowers, Claude G. 1878-1958 . . . . . . .DLB-17

Bowers, Edgar 1924- DLB-5

Bowers, Fredson Thayer
   1905-1991 . . . . .DLB-140; Y-91

Bowles, Paul 1910- DLB-5, 6

Bowles, Samuel III 1826-1878 . . . . . . .DLB-43

Bowles, William Lisles 1762-1850 . . . .DLB-93

Bowman, Louise Morey
   1882-1944 . . . . .DLB-68

Boyd, James 1888-1944 . . . . .DLB-9

Boyd, John 1919- DLB-8

Boyd, Thomas 1898-1935 . . . . .DLB-9

Boyesen, Hjalmar Hjorth
   1848-1895 . . . . .DLB-12, 71

Boyle, Kay
   1902-1992 . . . . DLB-4, 9, 48, 86; Y-93

Boyle, Roger, Earl of Orrery
   1621-1679 . . . . .DLB-80

Boyle, T. Coraghessan 1948- Y-86

Brackenbury, Alison 1953- DLB-40

Brackenridge, Hugh Henry
   1748-1816 . . . . .DLB-11, 37

Brackett, Charles 1892-1969 . . . . .DLB-26

Brackett, Leigh 1915-1978 . . . . .DLB-8, 26

Bradburn, John
   [publishing house] DLB-49

Bradbury, Malcolm 1932- DLB-14

Bradbury, Ray 1920- DLB-2, 8

Bradbury and Evans DLB-106

Braddon, Mary Elizabeth
   1835-1915 . . . . .DLB-18, 70

Bradford, Andrew 1686-1742 . . . .DLB-43, 73

Bradford, Gamaliel 1863-1932 . . . . . .DLB-17

Bradford, John 1749-1830 . . . . .DLB-43

Bradford, Roark 1896-1948 . . . . .DLB-86

Bradford, William 1590-1657 . . . .DLB-24, 30

Bradford, William III
  1719-1791 . . . . DLB-43, 73

Bradlaugh, Charles 1833-1891 . . . . . . DLB-57

Bradley, David 1950- DLB-33

Bradley, Marion Zimmer 1930- DLB-8

Bradley, William Aspenwall
  1878-1939 . . . . .DLB-4

Bradley, Ira, and Company DLB-49

Bradley, J. W., and Company DLB-49

Bradstreet, Anne
  1612 or 1613-1672 . . . . DLB-24

Bradwardine, Thomas circa
  1295-1349 . . . . DLB-115

Brady, Frank 1924-1986 . . . . DLB-111

Brady, Frederic A.
  [publishing house] DLB-49

Bragg, Melvyn 1939- DLB-14

Brainard, Charles H.
  [publishing house] DLB-49

Braine, John 1922-1986 . . . . . . DLB-15; Y-86

Braithwait, Richard 1588-1673 . . . . . DLB-151

Braithwaite, William Stanley
  1878-1962 . . . . DLB-50, 54

Braker, Ulrich 1735-1798 . . . . DLB-94

Bramah, Ernest 1868-1942 . . . . DLB-70

Branagan, Thomas 1774-1843 . . . . . . DLB-37

Branch, William Blackwell
  1927- DLB-76

Branden Press DLB-46

Brathwaite, Edward Kamau
  1930- DLB-125

Brault, Jacques 1933- DLB-53

Braun, Volker 1939- DLB-75

Brautigan, Richard
  1935-1984 . . . . DLB-2, 5; Y-80, 84

Braxton, Joanne M. 1950- DLB-41

Bray, Anne Eliza 1790-1883 . . . . DLB-116

Bray, Thomas 1656-1730 . . . . DLB-24

Braziller, George
  [publishing house] DLB-46

The Bread Loaf Writers'
  Conference 1983 . . . . Y-84

The Break-Up of the Novel (1922),
  by John Middleton Murry DLB-36

Breasted, James Henry 1865-1935 . . . DLB-47

Brecht, Bertolt 1898-1956 . . . . . . DLB-56, 124

Bredel, Willi 1901-1964 . . . . DLB-56

Breitinger, Johann Jakob
  1701-1776 . . . . DLB-97

Bremser, Bonnie 1939- DLB-16

Bremser, Ray 1934- DLB-16

Brentano, Bernard von
  1901-1964 . . . . DLB-56

Brentano, Clemens 1778-1842 . . . . . . DLB-90

Brentano's DLB-49

Brenton, Howard 1942- DLB-13

Breton, André 1896-1966 . . . . DLB-65

Breton, Nicholas
  circa 1555-circa 1626 . . . . DLB-136

The Breton Lays
  1300-early fifteenth century DLB-146

Brewer, Warren and Putnam DLB-46

Brewster, Elizabeth 1922- DLB-60

Bridgers, Sue Ellen 1942- DLB-52

Bridges, Robert 1844-1930 . . . . . . .DLB-19, 98

Bridie, James 1888-1951 . . . . DLB-10

Briggs, Charles Frederick
  1804-1877 . . . . DLB-3

Brighouse, Harold 1882-1958 . . . . . . DLB-10

Bright, Mary Chavelita Dunne
  (see Egerton, George)

Brimmer, B. J., Company DLB-46

Brines, Francisco 1932- DLB-134

Brinley, George, Jr. 1817-1875 . . . . . DLB-140

Brinnin, John Malcolm 1916- DLB-48

Brisbane, Albert 1809-1890 . . . . DLB-3

Brisbane, Arthur 1864-1936 . . . . DLB-25

British Academy DLB-112

The British Library and the Regular
  Readers' Group Y-91

The British Critic 1793-1843 . . . . .DLB-110

The British Review and London
  Critical Journal 1811-1825 . . . . . . .DLB-110

Brito, Aristeo 1942- DLB-122

Broadway Publishing Company DLB-46

Broch, Hermann 1886-1951 . . . . .DLB-85, 124

Brochu, André 1942- DLB-53

Brock, Edwin 1927- DLB-40

Brod, Max 1884-1968 . . . . DLB-81

Brodhead, John R. 1814-1873 . . . . . . DLB-30

Brodkey, Harold 1930- DLB-130

Brome, Richard circa 1590-1652 . . . . . DLB-58

Bromfield, Louis 1896-1956 . . . .DLB-4, 9, 86

Broner, E. M. 1930- DLB-28

Bronnen, Arnolt 1895-1959 . . . . DLB-124

Brontë, Anne 1820-1849 . . . . DLB-21

Brontë, Charlotte 1816-1855 . . . . . . .DLB-21

Brontë, Emily 1818-1848 . . . . DLB-21, 32

Brooke, Frances 1724-1789 . . . . . . DLB-39, 99

Brooke, Henry 1703?-1783 . . . . .DLB-39

Brooke, L. Leslie 1862-1940 . . . . . . .DLB-141

Brooke, Rupert 1887-1915 . . . . .DLB-19

Brooker, Bertram 1888-1955 . . . . . . .DLB-88

Brooke-Rose, Christine 1926- DLB-14

Brookner, Anita 1928- Y-87

Brooks, Charles Timothy
  1813-1883 . . . . .DLB-1

Brooks, Cleanth 1906-1994 . . . DLB-63; Y-94

Brooks, Gwendolyn 1917- DLB-5, 76

Brooks, Jeremy 1926- DLB-14

Brooks, Mel 1926- DLB-26

Brooks, Noah 1830-1903 . . . . .DLB-42

Brooks, Richard 1912-1992 . . . . .DLB-44

Brooks, Van Wyck
  1886-1963 . . . . DLB-45, 63, 103

Brophy, Brigid 1929- DLB-14

Brossard, Chandler 1922-1993 . . . . . .DLB-16

Brossard, Nicole 1943- DLB-53

Brother Antoninus (see Everson, William)

Brougham and Vaux, Henry Peter
  Brougham, Baron 1778-1868 . . . .DLB-110

Brougham, John 1810-1880 . . . . .DLB-11

Broughton, James 1913- DLB-5

Broughton, Rhoda 1840-1920 . . . . . . .DLB-18

Broun, Heywood 1888-1939 . . . . .DLB-29

Brown, Alice 1856-1948 . . . . .DLB-78

Brown, Bob 1886-1959 . . . . DLB-4, 45

Brown, Cecil 1943- DLB-33

Brown, Charles Brockden
  1771-1810 . . . . DLB-37, 59, 73

Brown, Christy 1932-1981 . . . . .DLB-14

Brown, Dee 1908- Y-80

Brown, Frank London 1927-1962 . . . .DLB-76

Brown, Fredric 1906-1972 . . . . .DLB-8

Brown, George Mackay
  1921- DLB-14, 27, 139

Brown, Harry 1917-1986 . . . . .DLB-26

Brown, Marcia 1918- DLB-61

Brown, Margaret Wise
  1910-1952 . . . . .DLB-22

Brown, Morna Doris (see Ferrars, Elizabeth)

Brown, Oliver Madox
  1855-1874 . . . . .DLB-21

Brown, Sterling
1901-1989 .... DLB-48, 51, 63

Brown, T. E. 1830-1897 .... DLB-35

Brown, William Hill 1765-1793 ..... DLB-37

Brown, William Wells
1814-1884 .... DLB-3, 50

Browne, Charles Farrar
1834-1867 .... DLB-11

Browne, Francis Fisher
1843-1913 .... DLB-79

Browne, Michael Dennis
1940- DLB-40

Browne, Sir Thomas 1605-1682 .... DLB-151

Browne, William, of Tavistock
1590-1645 .... DLB-121

Browne, Wynyard 1911-1964 .... DLB-13

Browne and Nolan DLB-106

Brownell, W. C. 1851-1928 .... DLB-71

Browning, Elizabeth Barrett
1806-1861 .... DLB-32

Browning, Robert 1812-1889 .... DLB-32

Brownjohn, Allan 1931- DLB-40

Brownson, Orestes Augustus
1803-1876 .... DLB-1, 59, 73

Bruccoli, Matthew J. 1931- DLB-103

Bruce, Charles 1906-1971 .... DLB-68

Bruce, Leo 1903-1979 .... DLB-77

Bruce, Philip Alexander
1856-1933 .... DLB-47

Bruce Humphries
[publishing house] DLB-46

Bruce-Novoa, Juan 1944- DLB-82

Bruckman, Clyde 1894-1955 .... DLB-26

Bruckner, Ferdinand 1891-1958 ....DLB-118

Brundage, John Herbert (see Herbert, John)

Brutus, Dennis 1924- DLB-117

Bryant, Arthur 1899-1985 .... DLB-149

Bryant, William Cullen
1794-1878 .... DLB-3, 43, 59

Bryce Enchenique, Alfredo
1939- DLB-145

Brydges, Sir Samuel Egerton
1762-1837 .... DLB-107

Buchan, John 1875-1940 .... DLB-34, 70

Buchanan, George 1506-1582 ...... DLB-132

Buchanan, Robert 1841-1901 ..... DLB-18, 35

Buchman, Sidney 1902-1975 .... DLB-26

Buck, Pearl S. 1892-1973 .... DLB-9, 102

Büchner, Georg 1813-1837 .... DLB-133

Bucke, Charles 1781-1846 .... DLB-110

Bucke, Richard Maurice
1837-1902 .... DLB-99

Buckingham, Joseph Tinker 1779-1861 and
Buckingham, Edwin
1810-1833 .... DLB-73

Buckler, Ernest 1908-1984 .... DLB-68

Buckley, William F., Jr.
1925- DLB-137; Y-80

Buckminster, Joseph Stevens
1784-1812 .... DLB-37

Buckner, Robert 1906- DLB-26

Budd, Thomas ?-1698 .... DLB-24

Budrys, A. J. 1931- DLB-8

Buechner, Frederick 1926- Y-80

Buell, John 1927- DLB-53

Buffum, Job [publishing house] DLB-49

Bugnet, Georges 1879-1981 .... DLB-92

Buies, Arthur 1840-1901 .... DLB-99

Building the New British Library
at St Pancras Y-94

Bukowski, Charles 1920- DLB-5, 130

Bullins, Ed 1935- DLB-7, 38

Bulwer-Lytton, Edward (also Edward Bulwer)
1803-1873 .... DLB-21

Bumpus, Jerry 1937- Y-81

Bunce and Brother DLB-49

Bunner, H. C. 1855-1896 .... DLB-78, 79

Bunting, Basil 1900-1985 .... DLB-20

Bunyan, John 1628-1688 .... DLB-39

Burch, Robert 1925- DLB-52

Burciaga, José Antonio 1940- DLB-82

Bürger, Gottfried August
1747-1794 .... DLB-94

Burgess, Anthony 1917-1993 .... DLB-14

Burgess, Gelett 1866-1951 .... DLB-11

Burgess, John W. 1844-1931 .... DLB-47

Burgess, Thornton W.
1874-1965 .... DLB-22

Burgess, Stringer and Company DLB-49

Burk, John Daly circa 1772-1808 .... DLB-37

Burke, Edmund 1729?-1797 .... DLB-104

Burke, Kenneth 1897-1993 ...... DLB-45, 63

Burlingame, Edward Livermore
1848-1922 .... DLB-79

Burnet, Gilbert 1643-1715 .... DLB-101

Burnett, Frances Hodgson
1849-1924 .... DLB-42, 141

Burnett, W. R. 1899-1982 .... DLB-9

Burnett, Whit 1899-1973 and
Martha Foley 1897-1977 .... DLB-137

Burney, Fanny 1752-1840 .... DLB-39

Burns, Alan 1929- DLB-14

Burns, John Horne 1916-1953 .... Y-85

Burns, Robert 1759-1796 .... DLB-109

Burns and Oates DLB-106

Burnshaw, Stanley 1906- DLB-48

Burr, C. Chauncey 1815?-1883 ...... DLB-79

Burroughs, Edgar Rice 1875-1950 .... DLB-8

Burroughs, John 1837-1921 .... DLB-64

Burroughs, Margaret T. G.
1917- DLB-41

Burroughs, William S., Jr.
1947-1981 .... DLB-16

Burroughs, William Seward
1914- DLB-2, 8, 16; Y-81

Burroway, Janet 1936- DLB-6

Burt, Maxwell S. 1882-1954 .... DLB-86

Burt, A. L., and Company DLB-49

Burton, Miles (see Rhode, John)

Burton, Richard F. 1821-1890 .... DLB-55

Burton, Robert 1577-1640 .... DLB-151

Burton, Virginia Lee 1909-1968 ..... DLB-22

Burton, William Evans
1804-1860 .... DLB-73

Burwell, Adam Hood 1790-1849 ..... DLB-99

Bury, Lady Charlotte
1775-1861 .... DLB-116

Busch, Frederick 1941- DLB-6

Busch, Niven 1903-1991 .... DLB-44

Bussieres, Arthur de 1877-1913 ...... DLB-92

Butler, Juan 1942-1981 .... DLB-53

Butler, Octavia E. 1947- DLB-33

Butler, Samuel 1613-1680 ..... DLB-101, 126

Butler, Samuel 1835-1902 .... DLB-18, 57

Butler, E. H., and Company DLB-49

Butor, Michel 1926- DLB-83

Butterworth, Hezekiah 1839-1905 .... DLB-42

Buttitta, Ignazio 1899- DLB-114

Byars, Betsy 1928- DLB-52

Byatt, A. S. 1936- DLB-14

Byles, Mather 1707-1788 .... DLB-24

Bynner, Witter 1881-1968 .... DLB-54

Byrd, William II 1674-1744 .... DLB-24, 140

Byrne, John Keyes (see Leonard, Hugh)

Byron, George Gordon, Lord
1788-1824 . . . . DLB-96, 110

C

Caballero Bonald, José Manuel
1926- DLB-108

Cabañero, Eladio 1930- DLB-134

Cabell, James Branch
1879-1958 . . . . DLB-9, 78

Cabeza de Baca, Manuel
1853-1915 . . . . DLB-122

Cabeza de Baca Gilbert, Fabiola
1898- DLB-122

Cable, George Washington
1844-1925 . . . . DLB-12, 74

Cabrera, Lydia 1900-1991 . . . . DLB-145

Cabrera Infante, Guillermo
1929- .DLB-113

Cady, Edwin H. 1917- DLB-103

Caedmon flourished 658-680 . . . . . . DLB-146

Caedmon School circa 660-899 . . . . DLB-146

Cahan, Abraham
1860-1951 . . . . DLB-9, 25, 28

Cain, George 1943- DLB-33

Calder, John
(Publishers), Limited DLB-112

Caldwell, Ben 1937- DLB-38

Caldwell, Erskine 1903-1987 . . . . . DLB-9, 86

Caldwell, H. M., Company DLB-49

Calhoun, John C. 1782-1850 . . . . .DLB-3

Calisher, Hortense 1911- DLB-2

A Call to Letters and an Invitation
to the Electric Chair,
by Siegfried Mandel DLB-75

Callaghan, Morley 1903-1990 . . . . . . DLB-68

Callaloo Y-87

Calmer, Edgar 1907- DLB-4

Calverley, C. S. 1831-1884 . . . . DLB-35

Calvert, George Henry
1803-1889 . . . . DLB-1, 64

Cambridge Press DLB-49

Cambridge Songs (Carmina Cantabrigensia)
circa 1050 . . . . DLB-148

Camden House: An Interview with
James Hardin Y-92

Cameron, Eleanor 1912- DLB-52

Cameron, George Frederick
1854-1885 . . . . DLB-99

Cameron, William Bleasdell
1862-1951 . . . . DLB-99

Camm, John 1718-1778 . . . . DLB-31

Campana, Dino 1885-1932 . . . . DLB-114

Campbell, Gabrielle Margaret Vere
(see Shearing, Joseph)

Campbell, James Dykes
1838-1895 . . . . DLB-144

Campbell, James Edwin
1867-1896 . . . . DLB-50

Campbell, John 1653-1728 . . . . DLB-43

Campbell, John W., Jr.
1910-1971 . . . . DLB-8

Campbell, Roy 1901-1957 . . . . DLB-20

Campbell, Thomas
1777-1844 . . . . .DLB-93, 144

Campbell, William Wilfred
1858-1918 . . . . DLB-92

Campion, Thomas 1567-1620 . . . . . . DLB-58

Camus, Albert 1913-1960 . . . . DLB-72

Canby, Henry Seidel 1878-1961 . . . . DLB-91

Candelaria, Cordelia 1943- DLB-82

Candelaria, Nash 1928- DLB-82

Candour in English Fiction (1890),
by Thomas Hardy DLB-18

Canetti, Elias 1905- DLB-85, 124

Canham, Erwin Dain
1904-1982 . . . . DLB-127

Cankar, Ivan 1876-1918 . . . . DLB-147

Cannan, Gilbert 1884-1955 . . . . DLB-10

Cannell, Kathleen 1891-1974 . . . . DLB-4

Cannell, Skipwith 1887-1957 . . . . DLB-45

Cantwell, Robert 1908-1978 . . . . DLB-9

Cape, Jonathan, and Harrison Smith
[publishing house] DLB-46

Cape, Jonathan, Limited DLB-112

Capen, Joseph 1658-1725 . . . . DLB-24

Capote, Truman
1924-1984 . . . . .DLB-2; Y-80, 84

Caproni, Giorgio 1912-1990 . . . . DLB-128

Cardarelli, Vincenzo 1887-1959 . . . . DLB-114

Cárdenas, Reyes 1948- DLB-122

Cardinal, Marie 1929- DLB-83

Carew, Thomas
1594 or 1595-1640 . . . . DLB-126

Carey, Henry
circa 1687-1689-1743 . . . . DLB-84

Carey, Mathew 1760-1839 . . . . . .DLB-37, 73

Carey and Hart DLB-49

Carey, M., and Company DLB-49

Carell, Lodowick 1602-1675 . . . . . . .DLB-58

Carleton, G. W.
[publishing house] DLB-49

Carlile, Richard 1790-1843 . . . . .DLB-110

Carlyle, Jane Welsh 1801-1866 . . . . . .DLB-55

Carlyle, Thomas 1795-1881 . . . . DLB-55, 144

Carman, Bliss 1861-1929 . . . . .DLB-92

Carmina Burana circa 1230 . . . . .DLB-138

Carnero, Guillermo 1947- DLB-108

Carossa, Hans 1878-1956 . . . . .DLB-66

Carpenter, Stephen Cullen
?-1820? DLB-73

Carpentier, Alejo 1904-1980 . . . . . . .DLB-113

Carrier, Roch 1937- DLB-53

Carrillo, Adolfo 1855-1926 . . . . .DLB-122

Carroll, Gladys Hasty 1904- DLB-9

Carroll, John 1735-1815 . . . . .DLB-37

Carroll, John 1809-1884 . . . . .DLB-99

Carroll, Lewis 1832-1898 . . . . .DLB-18

Carroll, Paul 1927- DLB-16

Carroll, Paul Vincent 1900-1968 . . . . .DLB-10

Carroll and Graf Publishers DLB-46

Carruth, Hayden 1921- DLB-5

Carryl, Charles E. 1841-1920 . . . . . . .DLB-42

Carswell, Catherine 1879-1946 . . . . . .DLB-36

Carter, Angela 1940-1992 . . . . .DLB-14

Carter, Elizabeth 1717-1806 . . . . .DLB-109

Carter, Henry (see Leslie, Frank)

Carter, Hodding, Jr. 1907-1972 . . . . .DLB-127

Carter, Landon 1710-1778 . . . . .DLB-31

Carter, Lin 1930- Y-81

Carter, Martin 1927- DLB-117

Carter and Hendee DLB-49

Carter, Robert, and Brothers DLB-49

Cartwright, William circa
1611-1643 . . . . .DLB-126

Caruthers, William Alexander
1802-1846 . . . . .DLB-3

Carver, Jonathan 1710-1780 . . . . .DLB-31

Carver, Raymond
1938-1988 . . . . DLB-130; Y-84, 88

Cary, Joyce 1888-1957 . . . . DLB-15, 100

Cary, Patrick 1623?-1657 . . . . .DLB-131

Casey, Juanita 1925- DLB-14

Casey, Michael 1947- DLB-5

Cassady, Carolyn 1923- DLB-16

Cassady, Neal 1926-1968 ....DLB-16

Cassell and Company DLB-106

Cassell Publishing Company DLB-49

Cassill, R. V. 1919- DLB-6

Cassity, Turner 1929- DLB-105

The Castle of Perseverance
        circa 1400-1425 ....DLB-146

Castellano, Olivia 1944- DLB-122

Castellanos, Rosario 1925-1974 .....DLB-113

Castillo, Ana 1953- DLB-122

Castlemon, Harry (see Fosdick, Charles Austin)

Caswall, Edward 1814-1878 ....DLB-32

Catacalos, Rosemary 1944- DLB-122

Cather, Willa
        1873-1947 .... DLB-9, 54, 78; DS-1

Catherine II (Ekaterina Alekseevna), "The
        Great," Empress of Russia
        1729-1796 ....DLB-150

Catherwood, Mary Hartwell
        1847-1902 ....DLB-78

Catledge, Turner 1901-1983 ......DLB-127

Cattafi, Bartolo 1922-1979 ....DLB-128

Catton, Bruce 1899-1978 ....DLB-17

Causley, Charles 1917- DLB-27

Caute, David 1936- DLB-14

Cavendish, Duchess of Newcastle,
        Margaret Lucas 1623-1673 .....DLB-131

Cawein, Madison 1865-1914 ....DLB-54

The Caxton Printers, Limited DLB-46

Cayrol, Jean 1911- DLB-83

Celan, Paul 1920-1970 ....DLB-69

Celaya, Gabriel 1911-1991 ....DLB-108

Céline, Louis-Ferdinand
        1894-1961 ....DLB-72

The Celtic Background to Medieval English
        Literature DLB-146

Center for Bibliographical Studies and
        Research at the University of
        California, Riverside Y-91

The Center for the Book in the Library
        of Congress Y-93

Center for the Book Research Y-84

Centlivre, Susanna 1669?-1723 ......DLB-84

The Century Company DLB-49

Cernuda, Luis 1902-1963 ....DLB-134

Cervantes, Lorna Dee 1954- DLB-82

Chacel, Rosa 1898- DLB-134

Chacón, Eusebio 1869-1948 .... DLB-82

Chacón, Felipe Maximiliano
        1873-? DLB-82

Challans, Eileen Mary (see Renault, Mary)

Chalmers, George 1742-1825 .... DLB-30

Chamberlain, Samuel S.
        1851-1916 .... DLB-25

Chamberland, Paul 1939- DLB-60

Chamberlin, William Henry
        1897-1969 .... DLB-29

Chambers, Charles Haddon
        1860-1921 .... DLB-10

Chambers, W. and R.
        [publishing house] DLB-106

Chamisso, Albert von
        1781-1838 .... DLB-90

Champfleury 1821-1889 .... DLB-119

Chandler, Harry 1864-1944 .... DLB-29

Chandler, Norman 1899-1973 ..... DLB-127

Chandler, Otis 1927- DLB-127

Chandler, Raymond 1888-1959 ....DS-6

Channing, Edward 1856-1931 ...... DLB-17

Channing, Edward Tyrrell
        1790-1856 .... DLB-1, 59

Channing, William Ellery
        1780-1842 .... DLB-1, 59

Channing, William Ellery, II
        1817-1901 .... DLB-1

Channing, William Henry
        1810-1884 .... DLB-1, 59

Chaplin, Charlie 1889-1977 .... DLB-44

Chapman, George
        1559 or 1560 - 1634 ...... DLB-62, 121

Chapman, John DLB-106

Chapman, William 1850-1917 ...... DLB-99

Chapman and Hall DLB-106

Chappell, Fred 1936- DLB-6, 105

Chappell, Fred, A Detail
        in a Poem DLB-105

Charbonneau, Jean 1875-1960 ...... DLB-92

Charbonneau, Robert 1911-1967 .... DLB-68

Charles, Gerda 1914- DLB-14

Charles, William
        [publishing house] DLB-49

The Charles Wood Affair:
        A Playwright Revived Y-83

Charlotte Forten: Pages from
        her Diary DLB-50

Charteris, Leslie 1907-1993 .... DLB-77

Charyn, Jerome 1937- Y-83

Chase, Borden 1900-1971 ....DLB-26

Chase, Edna Woolman
        1877-1957 ....DLB-91

Chase-Riboud, Barbara 1936- DLB-33

Chateaubriand, François-René de
        1768-1848 ....DLB-119

Chatterton, Thomas 1752-1770 ....DLB-109

Chatto and Windus DLB-106

Chaucer, Geoffrey 1340?-1400 ....DLB-146

Chauncy, Charles 1705-1787 ....DLB-24

Chauveau, Pierre-Joseph-Olivier
        1820-1890 ....DLB-99

Chávez, Denise 1948- DLB-122

Chávez, Fray Angélico 1910- DLB-82

Chayefsky, Paddy
        1923-1981 ....DLB-7, 44; Y-81

Cheever, Ezekiel 1615-1708 ....DLB-24

Cheever, George Barrell
        1807-1890 ....DLB-59

Cheever, John
        1912-1982 .... DLB-2, 102; Y-80, 82

Cheever, Susan 1943- Y-82

Cheke, Sir John 1514-1557 ....DLB-132

Chelsea House DLB-46

Cheney, Ednah Dow (Littlehale)
        1824-1904 ....DLB-1

Cheney, Harriet Vaughn
        1796-1889 ....DLB-99

Cherry, Kelly 1940 ....Y-83

Cherryh, C. J. 1942- Y-80

Chesnutt, Charles Waddell
        1858-1932 ....DLB-12, 50, 78

Chester, Alfred 1928-1971 ....DLB-130

Chester, George Randolph
        1869-1924 ....DLB-78

The Chester Plays circa 1505-1532;
        revisions until 1575 ....DLB-146

Chesterfield, Philip Dormer Stanhope,
        Fourth Earl of 1694-1773 ......DLB-104

Chesterton, G. K.
        1874-1936 ...DLB-10, 19, 34, 70, 98, 149

Chettle, Henry
        circa 1560-circa 1607 ....DLB-136

Chew, Ada Nield 1870-1945 ....DLB-135

Cheyney, Edward P. 1861-1947 .....DLB-47

Chicano History DLB-82

Chicano Language DLB-82

Child, Francis James
        1825-1896 ....DLB-1, 64

Child, Lydia Maria
1802-1880 . . . . DLB-1, 74

Child, Philip 1898-1978 . . . . DLB-68

Childers, Erskine 1870-1922 . . . . DLB-70

Children's Book Awards
and Prizes DLB-61

Childress, Alice 1920- DLB-7, 38

Childs, George W. 1829-1894 . . . . . . DLB-23

Chilton Book Company DLB-46

Chittenden, Hiram Martin
1858-1917 . . . . DLB-47

Chivers, Thomas Holley
1809-1858 .DLB-3

Chopin, Kate 1850-1904 . . . . DLB-12, 78

Chopin, Rene 1885-1953 . . . . DLB-92

Choquette, Adrienne 1915-1973 . . . . DLB-68

Choquette, Robert 1905- DLB-68

The Christian Publishing
Company DLB-49

Christie, Agatha 1890-1976 . . . . . DLB-13, 77

Christus und die Samariterin
circa 950 . . . . DLB-148

Chulkov, Mikhail Dmitrievich
1743?-1792 . . . . DLB-150

Church, Benjamin 1734-1778 . . . . . . DLB-31

Church, Francis Pharcellus
1839-1906 . . . . DLB-79

Church, William Conant
1836-1917 . . . . DLB-79

Churchill, Caryl 1938- DLB-13

Churchill, Charles 1731-1764 . . . . . . DLB-109

Churchill, Sir Winston
1874-1965 . . . . DLB-100

Churchyard, Thomas
1520?-1604 . . . . DLB-132

Churton, E., and Company DLB-106

Chute, Marchette 1909- DLB-103

Ciardi, John 1916-1986 . . . . DLB-5; Y-86

Cibber, Colley 1671-1757 . . . . DLB-84

Cima, Annalisa 1941- DLB-128

Cirese, Eugenio 1884-1955 . . . . DLB-114

Cisneros, Sandra 1954- DLB-122

City Lights Books DLB-46

Cixous, Hélène 1937- DLB-83

Clampitt, Amy 1920- DLB-105

Clapper, Raymond 1892-1944 . . . . . DLB-29

Clare, John 1793-1864 . . . . DLB-55, 96

Clarendon, Edward Hyde, Earl of
1609-1674 . . . . DLB-101

Clark, Alfred Alexander Gordon
(see Hare, Cyril)

Clark, Ann Nolan 1896- DLB-52

Clark, Catherine Anthony
1892-1977 . . . . DLB-68

Clark, Charles Heber
1841-1915 . . . . DLB-11

Clark, Davis Wasgatt 1812-1871 . . . . DLB-79

Clark, Eleanor 1913- DLB-6

Clark, J. P. 1935- DLB-117

Clark, Lewis Gaylord
1808-1873 . . . . DLB-3, 64, 73

Clark, Walter Van Tilburg
1909-1971 . . . . DLB-9

Clark, C. M., Publishing
Company DLB-46

Clarke, Austin 1896-1974 . . . . DLB-10, 20

Clarke, Austin C. 1934- DLB-53, 125

Clarke, Gillian 1937- DLB-40

Clarke, James Freeman
1810-1888 . . . . DLB-1, 59

Clarke, Rebecca Sophia
1833-1906 . . . . DLB-42

Clarke, Robert, and Company DLB-49

Claudius, Matthias 1740-1815 . . . . . . DLB-97

Clausen, Andy 1943- DLB-16

Claxton, Remsen and
Haffelfinger DLB-49

Clay, Cassius Marcellus
1810-1903 . . . . DLB-43

Cleary, Beverly 1916- DLB-52

Cleaver, Vera 1919- and
Cleaver, Bill 1920-1981 . . . . DLB-52

Cleland, John 1710-1789 . . . . DLB-39

Clemens, Samuel Langhorne
1835-1910 . . . . DLB-11, 12, 23, 64, 74

Clement, Hal 1922- DLB-8

Clemo, Jack 1916- DLB-27

Cleveland, John 1613-1658 . . . . DLB-126

Clifford, Lady Anne 1590-1676 . . . . DLB-151

Clifford, James L. 1901-1978 . . . . . . DLB-103

Clifford, Lucy 1853?-1929 . . . . . DLB-135, 141

Clifton, Lucille 1936- DLB-5, 41

Clode, Edward J.
[publishing house] DLB-46

Clough, Arthur Hugh 1819-1861 . . . . DLB-32

Cloutier, Cécile 1930- DLB-60

Clutton-Brock, Arthur
1868-1924 . . . . DLB-98

Coates, Robert M.
1897-1973 . . . . DLB-4, 9, 102

Coatsworth, Elizabeth 1893- DLB-22

Cobb, Charles E., Jr. 1943- DLB-41

Cobb, Frank I. 1869-1923 . . . . .DLB-25

Cobb, Irvin S.
1876-1944 . . . . DLB-11, 25, 86

Cobbett, William 1763-1835 . . . DLB-43, 107

Cochran, Thomas C. 1902- DLB-17

Cochrane, Elizabeth 1867-1922 . . . . . .DLB-25

Cockerill, John A. 1845-1896 . . . . . . .DLB-23

Cocteau, Jean 1889-1963 . . . . .DLB-65

Coderre, Emile (see Jean Narrache)

Coffee, Lenore J. 1900?-1984 . . . . . . .DLB-44

Coffin, Robert P. Tristram
1892-1955 . . . . .DLB-45

Cogswell, Fred 1917- DLB-60

Cogswell, Mason Fitch
1761-1830 . . . . .DLB-37

Cohen, Arthur A. 1928-1986 . . . . . . .DLB-28

Cohen, Leonard 1934- DLB-53

Cohen, Matt 1942- DLB-53

Colden, Cadwallader
1688-1776 . . . . DLB-24, 30

Cole, Barry 1936- DLB-14

Cole, George Watson
1850-1939 . . . . .DLB-140

Colegate, Isabel 1931- DLB-14

Coleman, Emily Holmes
1899-1974 . . . . .DLB-4

Coleman, Wanda 1946- DLB-130

Coleridge, Hartley 1796-1849 . . . . . . .DLB-96

Coleridge, Mary 1861-1907 . . . . . DLB-19, 98

Coleridge, Samuel Taylor
1772-1834 . . . . DLB-93, 107

Colet, John 1467-1519 . . . . .DLB-132

Colette 1873-1954 . . . . .DLB-65

Colette, Sidonie Gabrielle (see Colette)

Colinas, Antonio 1946- DLB-134

Collier, John 1901-1980 . . . . .DLB-77

Collier, Mary 1690-1762 . . . . .DLB-95

Collier, Robert J. 1876-1918 . . . . .DLB-91

Collier, P. F. [publishing house] DLB-49

Collin and Small DLB-49

Collingwood, W. G. 1854-1932 . . . . .DLB-149

Collins, An floruit circa 1653 . . . . . . .DLB-131

Collins, Mortimer 1827-1876 . . . . DLB-21, 35

Collins, Wilkie 1824-1889 ......DLB-18, 70

Collins, William 1721-1759 ....DLB-109

Collins, Isaac [publishing house] DLB-49

Collyer, Mary 1716?-1763? DLB-39

Colman, Benjamin 1673-1747 ....DLB-24

Colman, George, the Elder
1732-1794 ....DLB-89

Colman, George, the Younger
1762-1836 ....DLB-89

Colman, S. [publishing house] DLB-49

Colombo, John Robert 1936- DLB-53

Colter, Cyrus 1910- DLB-33

Colum, Padraic 1881-1972 ....DLB-19

Colvin, Sir Sidney 1845-1927 ......DLB-149

Colwin, Laurie 1944-1992 ....Y-80

Comden, Betty 1919- and Green,
Adolph 1918- DLB-44

Comi, Girolamo 1890-1968 ....DLB-114

The Comic Tradition Continued
[in the British Novel] DLB-15

Commager, Henry Steele
1902- DLB-17

The Commercialization of the Image of
Revolt, by Kenneth Rexroth DLB-16

Community and Commentators: Black
Theatre and Its Critics DLB-38

Compton-Burnett, Ivy
1884?-1969 ....DLB-36

Conan, Laure 1845-1924 ....DLB-99

Conde, Carmen 1901- DLB-108

Conference on Modern Biography Y-85

Congreve, William
1670-1729 ....DLB-39, 84

Conkey, W. B., Company DLB-49

Connell, Evan S., Jr. 1924- DLB-2; Y-81

Connelly, Marc 1890-1980 ......DLB-7; Y-80

Connolly, Cyril 1903-1974 ....DLB-98

Connolly, James B. 1868-1957 ......DLB-78

Connor, Ralph 1860-1937 ....DLB-92

Connor, Tony 1930- DLB-40

Conquest, Robert 1917- DLB-27

Conrad, Joseph
1857-1924 .... DLB-10, 34, 98

Conrad, John, and Company DLB-49

Conroy, Jack 1899-1990 ....Y-81

Conroy, Pat 1945- DLB-6

The Consolidation of Opinion: Critical
Responses to the Modernists DLB-36

Constable, Henry 1562-1613 ...... DLB-136

Constable and Company
Limited DLB-112

Constant, Benjamin 1767-1830 ..... DLB-119

Constant de Rebecque, Henri-Benjamin de
(see Constant, Benjamin)

Constantine, David 1944- DLB-40

Constantin-Weyer, Maurice
1881-1964 .... DLB-92

Contempo Caravan: Kites in
a Windstorm Y-85

A Contemporary Flourescence of Chicano
Literature Y-84

The Continental Publishing
Company DLB-49

A Conversation with Chaim Potok Y-84

Conversations with Publishers I: An Interview
with Patrick O'Connor Y-84

Conversations with Publishers II: An Interview
with Charles Scribner III Y-94

Conversations with Rare Book Dealers I: An
Interview with Glenn Horowitz Y-90

Conversations with Rare Book Dealers II: An
Interview with Ralph Sipper Y-94

The Conversion of an Unpolitical Man,
by W. H. Bruford DLB-66

Conway, Moncure Daniel
1832-1907 .... DLB-1

Cook, Ebenezer
circa 1667-circa 1732 .... DLB-24

Cook, Edward Tyas 1857-1919 .... DLB-149

Cook, Michael 1933- DLB-53

Cook, David C., Publishing
Company DLB-49

Cooke, George Willis 1848-1923 .... DLB-71

Cooke, Increase, and Company DLB-49

Cooke, John Esten 1830-1886 .... DLB-3

Cooke, Philip Pendleton
1816-1850 .... DLB-3, 59

Cooke, Rose Terry
1827-1892 .... DLB-12, 74

Coolbrith, Ina 1841-1928 .... DLB-54

Cooley, Peter 1940- DLB-105

Cooley, Peter, Into the Mirror DLB-105

Coolidge, Susan (see Woolsey, Sarah Chauncy)

Coolidge, George
[publishing house] DLB-49

Cooper, Giles 1918-1966 .... DLB-13

Cooper, James Fenimore 1789-1851 .. DLB-3

Cooper, Kent 1880-1965 .... DLB-29

Coover, Robert 1932- DLB-2; Y-81

Copeland and Day DLB-49

Copland, Robert 1470?-1548 ....DLB-136

Coppel, Alfred 1921- Y-83

Coppola, Francis Ford 1939- DLB-44

Corazzini, Sergio 1886-1907 ....DLB-114

Corbett, Richard 1582-1635 ....DLB-121

Corcoran, Barbara 1911- DLB-52

Corelli, Marie 1855-1924 ....DLB-34

Corle, Edwin 1906-1956 ....Y-85

Corman, Cid 1924- DLB-5

Cormier, Robert 1925- DLB-52

Corn, Alfred 1943- DLB-120; Y-80

Cornish, Sam 1935- DLB-41

Cornish, William
circa 1465-circa 1524 ....DLB-132

Cornwall, Barry (see Procter, Bryan Waller)

Cornwallis, Sir William, the Younger
circa 1579-1614 ....DLB-151

Cornwell, David John Moore
(see le Carré, John)

Corpi, Lucha 1945- DLB-82

Corrington, John William 1932- DLB-6

Corrothers, James D. 1869-1917 .....DLB-50

Corso, Gregory 1930- DLB-5, 16

Cortázar, Julio 1914-1984 ....DLB-113

Cortez, Jayne 1936- DLB-41

Corvo, Baron (see Rolfe, Frederick William)

Cory, Annie Sophie (see Cross, Victoria)

Cory, William Johnson
1823-1892 ....DLB-35

Coryate, Thomas 1577?-1617 ......DLB-151

Cosin, John 1595-1672 ....DLB-151

Cosmopolitan Book Corporation DLB-46

Costain, Thomas B. 1885-1965 ....DLB-9

Coste, Donat 1912-1957 ....DLB-88

Cota-Cárdenas, Margarita
1941- DLB-122

Cotter, Joseph Seamon, Sr.
1861-1949 ....DLB-50

Cotter, Joseph Seamon, Jr.
1895-1919 ....DLB-50

Cotton, Charles 1630-1687 ....DLB-131

Cotton, John 1584-1652 ....DLB-24

Coulter, John 1888-1980 ....DLB-68

Cournos, John 1881-1966 ....DLB-54

Cousins, Margaret 1905- DLB-137

Cousins, Norman 1915-1990 ....DLB-137

Coventry, Francis 1725-1754 .... DLB-39

Coverly, N. [publishing house] DLB-49

Covici-Friede DLB-46

Coward, Noel 1899-1973 .... DLB-10

Coward, McCann and
  Geoghegan DLB-46

Cowles, Gardner 1861-1946 .... DLB-29

Cowles, Gardner ("Mike"), Jr.
  1903-1985 .... DLB-127, 137

Cowley, Abraham
  1618-1667 .... DLB-131, 151

Cowley, Hannah 1743-1809 .... DLB-89

Cowley, Malcolm
  1898-1989 .... DLB-4, 48; Y-81, 89

Cowper, William 1731-1800 ... DLB-104, 109

Cox, A. B. (see Berkeley, Anthony)

Cox, James McMahon
  1903-1974 .... DLB-127

Cox, James Middleton
  1870-1957 .... DLB-127

Cox, Palmer 1840-1924 .... DLB-42

Coxe, Louis 1918-1993 .... DLB-5

Coxe, Tench 1755-1824 .... DLB-37

Cozzens, James Gould
  1903-1978 .... DLB-9; Y-84; DS-2

Crabbe, George 1754-1832 .... DLB-93

Crackanthorpe, Hubert
  1870-1896 .... DLB-135

Craddock, Charles Egbert
  (see Murfree, Mary N.)

Cradock, Thomas 1718-1770 .... DLB-31

Craig, Daniel H. 1811-1895 .... DLB-43

Craik, Dinah Maria 1826-1887 ..... DLB-35

Cranch, Christopher Pearse
  1813-1892 .... DLB-1, 42

Crane, Hart 1899-1932 .... DLB-4, 48

Crane, R. S. 1886-1967 .... DLB-63

Crane, Stephen 1871-1900 ... DLB-12, 54, 78

Cranmer, Thomas 1489-1556 ...... DLB-132

Crapsey, Adelaide 1878-1914 .... DLB-54

Crashaw, Richard
  1612 or 1613-1649 .... DLB-126

Craven, Avery 1885-1980 .... DLB-17

Crawford, Charles
  1752-circa 1815 .... DLB-31

Crawford, F. Marion 1854-1909 .... DLB-71

Crawford, Isabel Valancy
  1850-1887 .... DLB-92

Crawley, Alan 1887-1975 .... DLB-68

Crayon, Geoffrey (see Irving, Washington)

Creasey, John 1908-1973 .... DLB-77

Creative Age Press DLB-46

Creel, George 1876-1953 .... DLB-25

Creeley, Robert 1926- DLB-5, 16

Creelman, James 1859-1915 .... DLB-23

Cregan, David 1931- DLB-13

Creighton, Donald Grant
  1902-1979 .... DLB-88

Cremazie, Octave 1827-1879 .... DLB-99

Crémer, Victoriano 1909?- DLB-108

Crescas, Hasdai
  circa 1340-1412? DLB-115

Crespo, Angel 1926- DLB-134

Cresset Press DLB-112

Crèvecoeur, Michel Guillaume Jean de
  1735-1813 .... DLB-37

Crews, Harry 1935- DLB-6, 143

Crichton, Michael 1942- Y-81

A Crisis of Culture: The Changing Role
  of Religion in the New Republic
  .... DLB-37

Crispin, Edmund 1921-1978 .... DLB-87

Cristofer, Michael 1946- DLB-7

"The Critic as Artist" (1891), by
  Oscar Wilde DLB-57

"Criticism In Relation To Novels" (1863),
  by G. H. Lewes DLB-21

Crnjanski, Miloš 1893-1977 .... DLB-147

Crockett, David (Davy)
  1786-1836 ....DLB-3, 11

Croft-Cooke, Rupert (see Bruce, Leo)

Crofts, Freeman Wills
  1879-1957 .... DLB-77

Croker, John Wilson 1780-1857 .... DLB-110

Croly, Herbert 1869-1930 .... DLB-91

Croly, Jane Cunningham
  1829-1901 .... DLB-23

Crosby, Caresse 1892-1970 .... DLB-48

Crosby, Caresse 1892-1970 and Crosby,
  Harry 1898-1929 .... DLB-4

Crosby, Harry 1898-1929 .... DLB-48

Cross, Victoria 1868-1952 .... DLB-135

Crossley-Holland, Kevin 1941- DLB-40

Crothers, Rachel 1878-1958 .... DLB-7

Crowell, Thomas Y., Company DLB-49

Crowley, John 1942- Y-82

Crowley, Mart 1935- DLB-7

Crown Publishers DLB-46

Crowne, John 1641-1712 ....DLB-80

Crowninshield, Edward Augustus
  1817-1859 ....DLB-140

Crowninshield, Frank 1872-1947 .....DLB-91

Croy, Homer 1883-1965 ....DLB-4

Crumley, James 1939- Y-84

Cruz, Victor Hernández 1949- DLB-41

Csokor, Franz Theodor
  1885-1969 ....DLB-81

Cuala Press DLB-112

Cullen, Countee 1903-1946 ... DLB-4, 48, 51

Culler, Jonathan D. 1944- DLB-67

The Cult of Biography
  Excerpts from the Second Folio Debate:
    "Biographies are generally a disease of
    English Literature" – Germaine Greer,
    Victoria Glendinning, Auberon Waugh,
    and Richard Holmes Y-86

Cumberland, Richard 1732-1811 .....DLB-89

Cummings, E. E. 1894-1962 ...... DLB-4, 48

Cummings, Ray 1887-1957 ....DLB-8

Cummings and Hilliard DLB-49

Cummins, Maria Susanna
  1827-1866 ....DLB-42

Cundall, Joseph
  [publishing house] DLB-106

Cuney, Waring 1906-1976 ....DLB-51

Cuney-Hare, Maude 1874-1936 .....DLB-52

Cunningham, Allan
  1784-1842 .... DLB-116, 144

Cunningham, J. V. 1911- DLB-5

Cunningham, Peter F.
  [publishing house] DLB-49

Cunquiero, Alvaro 1911-1981 ......DLB-134

Cuomo, George 1929- Y-80

Cupples and Leon DLB-46

Cupples, Upham and Company DLB-49

Cuppy, Will 1884-1949 ....DLB-11

Currie, James 1756-1805 ....DLB-142

Currie, Mary Montgomerie Lamb Singleton,
  Lady Currie (see Fane, Violet)

Cursor Mundi circa 1300 ....DLB-146

Curti, Merle E. 1897- DLB-17

Curtis, Cyrus H. K. 1850-1933 .....DLB-91

Curtis, George William
  1824-1892 .... DLB-1, 43

Curzon, Sarah Anne 1833-1898 ......DLB-99

Cynewulf circa 770-840 ....DLB-146

D

D. M. Thomas: The Plagiarism
   Controversy Y-82

Dabit, Eugène 1898-1936 ....DLB-65

Daborne, Robert circa 1580-1628 ....DLB-58

Dacey, Philip 1939- DLB-105

Dacey, Philip, Eyes Across Centuries:
   Contemporary Poetry and "That
   Vision Thing" DLB-105

Daggett, Rollin M. 1831-1901 ....DLB-79

Dahl, Roald 1916-1990 ....DLB-139

Dahlberg, Edward 1900-1977 ....DLB-48

Dahn, Felix 1834-1912 ....DLB-129

Dale, Peter 1938- DLB-40

Dall, Caroline Wells (Healey)
   1822-1912 ....DLB-1

Dallas, E. S. 1828-1879 ....DLB-55

The Dallas Theater Center DLB-7

D'Alton, Louis 1900-1951 ....DLB-10

Daly, T. A. 1871-1948 ....DLB-11

Damon, S. Foster 1893-1971 ....DLB-45

Damrell, William S.
   [publishing house] DLB-49

Dana, Charles A. 1819-1897 ......DLB-3, 23

Dana, Richard Henry, Jr
   1815-1882 ....DLB-1

Dandridge, Ray Garfield DLB-51

Dane, Clemence 1887-1965 ....DLB-10

Danforth, John 1660-1730 ....DLB-24

Danforth, Samuel, I 1626-1674 .....DLB-24

Danforth, Samuel, II 1666-1727 .....DLB-24

Dangerous Years: London Theater,
   1939-1945 ....DLB-10

Daniel, John M. 1825-1865 ....DLB-43

Daniel, Samuel
   1562 or 1563-1619 ....DLB-62

Daniel Press DLB-106

Daniells, Roy 1902-1979 ....DLB-68

Daniels, Jim 1956- DLB-120

Daniels, Jonathan 1902-1981 ....DLB-127

Daniels, Josephus 1862-1948 ....DLB-29

Dannay, Frederic 1905-1982 and
   Manfred B. Lee 1905-1971 .....DLB-137

Danner, Margaret Esse 1915- DLB-41

Dantin, Louis 1865-1945 ....DLB-92

D'Arcy, Ella circa 1857-1937 ....DLB-135

Darley, George 1795-1846 ....DLB-96

Darwin, Charles 1809-1882 ....DLB-57

Darwin, Erasmus 1731-1802 ....DLB-93

Daryush, Elizabeth 1887-1977 ......DLB-20

Dashkova, Ekaterina Romanovna
   (née Vorontsova) 1743-1810 ...DLB-150

Dashwood, Edmée Elizabeth Monica
   de la Pasture (see Delafield, E. M.)

Daudet, Alphonse 1840-1897 ......DLB-123

d'Aulaire, Edgar Parin 1898- and
   d'Aulaire, Ingri 1904- DLB-22

Davenant, Sir William
   1606-1668 ....DLB-58, 126

Davenport, Guy 1927- DLB-130

Davenport, Robert ?-? DLB-58

Daves, Delmer 1904-1977 ....DLB-26

Davey, Frank 1940- DLB-53

Davidson, Avram 1923-1993 ....DLB-8

Davidson, Donald 1893-1968 ....DLB-45

Davidson, John 1857-1909 ....DLB-19

Davidson, Lionel 1922- DLB-14

Davie, Donald 1922- DLB-27

Davie, Elspeth 1919- DLB-139

Davies, John, of Hereford
   1565?-1618 ....DLB-121

Davies, Rhys 1901-1978 ....DLB-139

Davies, Robertson 1913- DLB-68

Davies, Samuel 1723-1761 ....DLB-31

Davies, Thomas 1712?-1785 ....DLB-142

Davies, W. H. 1871-1940 ....DLB-19

Davies, Peter, Limited DLB-112

Daviot, Gordon 1896?-1952 ....DLB-10
   (see also Tey, Josephine)

Davis, Charles A. 1795-1867 ....DLB-11

Davis, Clyde Brion 1894-1962 ......DLB-9

Davis, Dick 1945- DLB-40

Davis, Frank Marshall 1905-? DLB-51

Davis, H. L. 1894-1960 ....DLB-9

Davis, John 1774-1854 ....DLB-37

Davis, Lydia 1947- DLB-130

Davis, Margaret Thomson 1926- ..DLB-14

Davis, Ossie 1917- DLB-7, 38

Davis, Paxton 1925-1994 ....Y-94

Davis, Rebecca Harding
   1831-1910 ....DLB-74

Davis, Richard Harding
   1864-1916 ....DLB-12, 23, 78, 79

Davis, Samuel Cole 1764-1809 .....DLB-37

Davison, Peter 1928- DLB-5

Davys, Mary 1674-1732 ....DLB-39

DAW Books DLB-46

Dawson, Ernest 1882-1947 ....DLB-140

Dawson, Fielding 1930- DLB-130

Dawson, William 1704-1752 ....DLB-31

Day, Benjamin Henry 1810-1889 ...DLB-43

Day, Clarence 1874-1935 ....DLB-11

Day, Dorothy 1897-1980 ....DLB-29

Day, Frank Parker 1881-1950 ....DLB-92

Day, John circa 1574-circa 1640 .....DLB-62

Day Lewis, C. 1904-1972 ....DLB-15, 20
   (see also Blake, Nicholas)

Day, Thomas 1748-1789 ....DLB-39

Day, The John, Company DLB-46

Day, Mahlon [publishing house] DLB-49

Deacon, William Arthur
   1890-1977 ....DLB-68

Deal, Borden 1922-1985 ....DLB-6

de Angeli, Marguerite 1889-1987 ....DLB-22

De Angelis, Milo 1951- DLB-128

De Bow, James Dunwoody Brownson
   1820-1867 ....DLB-3, 79

de Bruyn, Günter 1926- DLB-75

de Camp, L. Sprague 1907- DLB-8

The Decay of Lying (1889),
   by Oscar Wilde [excerpt] DLB-18

Dedication, *Ferdinand Count Fathom* (1753),
   by Tobias Smollett DLB-39

Dedication, *The History of Pompey the Little*
   (1751), by Francis Coventry DLB-39

Dedication, *Lasselia* (1723), by Eliza
   Haywood [excerpt] DLB-39

Dedication, *The Wanderer* (1814),
   by Fanny Burney DLB-39

Dee, John 1527-1609 ....DLB-136

Defense of *Amelia* (1752), by
   Henry Fielding DLB-39

Defoe, Daniel 1660-1731 ... DLB-39, 95, 101

de Fontaine, Felix Gregory
   1834-1896 ....DLB-43

De Forest, John William
   1826-1906 ....DLB-12

DeFrees, Madeline 1919- DLB-105

DeFrees, Madeline, The Poet's Kaleidoscope:
   The Element of Surprise in the Making
   of the Poem DLB-105

de Graff, Robert 1895-1981 ....Y-81

de Graft, Joe 1924-1978 ....DLB-117

De Heinrico circa 980? DLB-148

Deighton, Len 1929- DLB-87

DeJong, Meindert 1906-1991 . . . . DLB-52

Dekker, Thomas circa 1572-1632 . . . DLB-62

Delacorte, Jr., George T.
1894-1991 . . . . DLB-91

Delafield, E. M. 1890-1943 . . . . DLB-34

Delahaye, Guy 1888-1969 . . . . DLB-92

de la Mare, Walter 1873-1956 . . . . . . DLB-19

Deland, Margaret 1857-1945 . . . . DLB-78

Delaney, Shelagh 1939- DLB-13

Delany, Martin Robinson
1812-1885 . . . . DLB-50

Delany, Samuel R. 1942- DLB-8, 33

de la Roche, Mazo 1879-1961 . . . . DLB-68

Delbanco, Nicholas 1942- DLB-6

De León, Nephtal 1945- DLB-82

Delgado, Abelardo Barrientos
1931- DLB-82

De Libero, Libero 1906-1981 . . . . . . DLB-114

DeLillo, Don 1936- DLB-6

de Lisser H. G. 1878-1944 . . . . DLB-117

Dell, Floyd 1887-1969 . . . . .DLB-9

Dell Publishing Company DLB-46

delle Grazie, Marie Eugene
1864-1931 . . . . DLB-81

del Rey, Lester 1915-1993 . . . . .DLB-8

Del Vecchio, John M. 1947- DS-9

de Man, Paul 1919-1983 . . . . DLB-67

Demby, William 1922- DLB-33

Deming, Philander 1829-1915 . . . . . . DLB-74

Demorest, William Jennings
1822-1895 . . . . DLB-79

Denham, Sir John
1615-1669 . . . . DLB-58, 126

Denison, Merrill 1893-1975 . . . . DLB-92

Denison, T. S., and Company DLB-49

Dennie, Joseph
1768-1812 . . . . DLB-37, 43, 59, 73

Dennis, John 1658-1734 . . . . DLB-101

Dennis, Nigel 1912-1989 . . . . DLB-13, 15

Dent, Tom 1932- DLB-38

Dent, J. M., and Sons DLB-112

Denton, Daniel circa 1626-1703 . . . . . DLB-24

DePaola, Tomie 1934- DLB-61

De Quincey, Thomas
1785-1859 . . . . DLB-110, 144

Derby, George Horatio
1823-1861 . . . . DLB-11

Derby, J. C., and Company DLB-49

Derby and Miller DLB-49

Derleth, August 1909-1971 . . . . .DLB-9

The Derrydale Press DLB-46

Derzhavin, Gavriil Romanovich
1743-1816 . . . . DLB-150

Desaulniers, Gonsalve
1863-1934 . . . . DLB-92

Desbiens, Jean-Paul 1927- DLB-53

des Forêts, Louis-Rene 1918- DLB-83

DesRochers, Alfred 1901-1978 . . . . . DLB-68

Desrosiers, Léo-Paul 1896-1967 . . . . . DLB-68

Destouches, Louis-Ferdinand
(see Céline, Louis-Ferdinand)

De Tabley, Lord 1835-1895 . . . . DLB-35

Deutsch, Babette 1895-1982 . . . . DLB-45

Deutsch, André, Limited DLB-112

Deveaux, Alexis 1948- DLB-38

The Development of Lighting in the Staging
of Drama, 1900-1945 . . . . DLB-10

de Vere, Aubrey 1814-1902 . . . . DLB-35

Devereux, second Earl of Essex, Robert
1565-1601 . . . . DLB-136

The Devin-Adair Company DLB-46

De Voto, Bernard 1897-1955 . . . . DLB-9

De Vries, Peter 1910-1993 . . . . . . DLB-6; Y-82

Dewdney, Christopher 1951- DLB-60

Dewdney, Selwyn 1909-1979 . . . . . . DLB-68

DeWitt, Robert M., Publisher DLB-49

DeWolfe, Fiske and Company DLB-49

Dexter, Colin 1930- DLB-87

de Young, M. H. 1849-1925 . . . . DLB-25

Dhuoda circa 803-after 843 . . . . DLB-148

The Dial Press DLB-46

Diamond, I. A. L. 1920-1988 . . . . . DLB-26

Di Cicco, Pier Giorgio 1949- DLB-60

Dick, Philip K. 1928-1982 . . . . DLB-8

Dick and Fitzgerald DLB-49

Dickens, Charles
1812-1870 . . . . .DLB-21, 55, 70

Dickey, James
1923- DLB-5; Y-82, 93; DS-7

Dickey, William 1928- DLB-5

Dickinson, Emily 1830-1886 . . . . DLB-1

Dickinson, John 1732-1808 . . . . DLB-31

Dickinson, Jonathan 1688-1747 . . . . . .DLB-24

Dickinson, Patric 1914- DLB-27

Dickinson, Peter 1927- DLB-87

Dicks, John [publishing house] DLB-106

Dickson, Gordon R. 1923- DLB-8

*Dictionary of Literary Biography
Yearbook* Awards Y-92, 93

The Dictionary of National Biography
. . . . .DLB-144

Didion, Joan 1934- DLB-2; Y-81, 86

Di Donato, Pietro 1911- DLB-9

Diego, Gerardo 1896-1987 . . . . .DLB-134

Digges, Thomas circa 1546-1595 . . . .DLB-136

Dillard, Annie 1945- Y-80

Dillard, R. H. W. 1937- DLB-5

Dillingham, Charles T.,
Company DLB-49

The Dillingham, G. W.,
Company DLB-49

Dilthey, Wilhelm 1833-1911 . . . . . . .DLB-129

Dingelstedt, Franz von
1814-1881 . . . . .DLB-133

Dintenfass, Mark 1941- Y-84

Diogenes, Jr. (see Brougham, John)

DiPrima, Diane 1934- DLB-5, 16

Disch, Thomas M. 1940- DLB-8

Disney, Walt 1901-1966 . . . . .DLB-22

Disraeli, Benjamin 1804-1881 . . . . DLB-21, 55

D'Israeli, Isaac 1766-1848 . . . . .DLB-107

Ditzen, Rudolf (see Fallada, Hans)

Dix, Dorothea Lynde 1802-1887 . . . . . .DLB-1

Dix, Dorothy (see Gilmer,
Elizabeth Meriwether)

Dix, Edwards and Company DLB-49

Dixon, Paige (see Corcoran, Barbara)

Dixon, Richard Watson
1833-1900 . . . . .DLB-19

Dixon, Stephen 1936- DLB-130

Dmitriev, Ivan Ivanovich
1760-1837 . . . . .DLB-150

Dobell, Sydney 1824-1874 . . . . .DLB-32

Döblin, Alfred 1878-1957 . . . . .DLB-66

Dobson, Austin
1840-1921 . . . . DLB-35, 144

Doctorow, E. L. 1931- DLB-2, 28; Y-80

Dodd, William E. 1869-1940 . . . . .DLB-17

Dodd, Mead and Company DLB-49

Doderer, Heimito von 1896-1968 ....DLB-85

Dodge, Mary Mapes
　　1831?-1905 ....DLB-42, 79

Dodge, B. W., and Company DLB-46

Dodge Publishing Company DLB-49

Dodgson, Charles Lutwidge
　　(see Carroll, Lewis)

Dodsley, Robert 1703-1764 ....DLB-95

Dodson, Owen 1914-1983 ....DLB-76

Doesticks, Q. K. Philander, P. B.
　　(see Thomson, Mortimer)

Doheny, Carrie Estelle
　　1875-1958 ....DLB-140

Domínguez, Sylvia Maida
　　1935- DLB-122

Donahoe, Patrick
　　[publishing house] DLB-49

Donald, David H. 1920- DLB-17

Donaldson, Scott 1928- DLB-111

Donleavy, J. P. 1926- DLB-6

Donnadieu, Marguerite (see Duras,
　　Marguerite)

Donne, John 1572-1631 ....DLB-121, 151

Donnelley, R. R., and Sons
　　Company DLB-49

Donnelly, Ignatius 1831-1901 ......DLB-12

Donohue and Henneberry DLB-49

Donoso, José 1924- DLB-113

Doolady, M. [publishing house] DLB-49

Dooley, Ebon (see Ebon)

Doolittle, Hilda 1886-1961 ....DLB-4, 45

Doplicher, Fabio 1938- DLB-128

Dor, Milo 1923- DLB-85

Doran, George H., Company DLB-46

Dorgelès, Roland 1886-1973 ....DLB-65

Dorn, Edward 1929- DLB-5

Dorr, Rheta Childe 1866-1948 ......DLB-25

Dorset and Middlesex, Charles Sackville,
　　Lord Buckhurst,
　　Earl of 1643-1706 ....DLB-131

Dorst, Tankred 1925- DLB-75, 124

Dos Passos, John
　　1896-1970 .... DLB-4, 9; DS-1

Doubleday and Company DLB-49

Dougall, Lily 1858-1923 ....DLB-92

Doughty, Charles M.
　　1843-1926 ....DLB-19, 57

Douglas, Gavin 1476-1522 ....DLB-132

Douglas, Keith 1920-1944 ....DLB-27

Douglas, Norman 1868-1952 .... DLB-34

Douglass, Frederick
　　1817?-1895 ....DLB-1, 43, 50, 79

Douglass, William circa
　　1691-1752 .... DLB-24

Dourado, Autran 1926- DLB-145

Dove, Rita 1952- DLB-120

Dover Publications DLB-46

Doves Press DLB-112

Dowden, Edward 1843-1913 ... DLB-35, 149

Dowell, Coleman 1925-1985 .... DLB-130

Downes, Gwladys 1915- DLB-88

Downing, J., Major (see Davis, Charles A.)

Downing, Major Jack (see Smith, Seba)

Dowson, Ernest 1867-1900 ..... DLB-19, 135

Doxey, William
　　[publishing house] DLB-49

Doyle, Sir Arthur Conan
　　1859-1930 .... DLB-18, 70

Doyle, Kirby 1932- DLB-16

Drabble, Margaret 1939- DLB-14

Drach, Albert 1902- DLB-85

The Dramatic Publishing
　　Company DLB-49

Dramatists Play Service DLB-46

Draper, John W. 1811-1882 .... DLB-30

Draper, Lyman C. 1815-1891 .... DLB-30

Drayton, Michael 1563-1631 ...... DLB-121

Dreiser, Theodore
　　1871-1945 .... DLB-9, 12, 102, 137; DS-1

Drewitz, Ingeborg 1923-1986 .... DLB-75

Drieu La Rochelle, Pierre
　　1893-1945 .... DLB-72

Drinkwater, John 1882-1937
　　.....................DLB-10, 19, 149

Droste-Hülshoff, Annette von
　　1797-1848 .... DLB-133

The Drue Heinz Literature Prize
　　Excerpt from "Excerpts from a Report
　　of the Commission," in David
　　Bosworth's *The Death of Descartes*
　　An Interview with David
　　Bosworth Y-82

Drummond, William Henry
　　1854-1907 .... DLB-92

Drummond, William, of Hawthornden
　　1585-1649 .... DLB-121

Dryden, John 1631-1700 ...DLB-80, 101, 131

Držić, Marin circa 1508-1567 ...... DLB-147

Duane, William 1760-1835 .... DLB-43

Dubé, Marcel 1930- DLB-53

Dubé, Rodolphe (see Hertel, François)

Dubie, Norman 1945- DLB-120

Du Bois, W. E. B.
　　1868-1963 ....DLB-47, 50, 91

Du Bois, William Pène 1916- DLB-61

Dubus, Andre 1936- DLB-130

Ducharme, Réjean 1941- DLB-60

Dučić, Jovan 1871-1943 ....DLB-147

Duck, Stephen 1705?-1756 ....DLB-95

Duckworth, Gerald, and
　　Company Limited DLB-112

Dudek, Louis 1918- DLB-88

Duell, Sloan and Pearce DLB-46

Duffield and Green DLB-46

Duffy, Maureen 1933- DLB-14

Dugan, Alan 1923- DLB-5

Dugas, Marcel 1883-1947 ....DLB-92

Dugdale, William
　　[publishing house] DLB-106

Duhamel, Georges 1884-1966 ....DLB-65

Dujardin, Edouard 1861-1949 ......DLB-123

Dukes, Ashley 1885-1959 ....DLB-10

Dumas, Alexandre, *père*
　　1802-1870 ....DLB-119

Dumas, Henry 1934-1968 ....DLB-41

Dunbar, Paul Laurence
　　1872-1906 ....DLB-50, 54, 78

Dunbar, William
　　circa 1460-circa 1522 ......DLB-132, 146

Duncan, Norman 1871-1916 ....DLB-92

Duncan, Quince 1940- DLB-145

Duncan, Robert 1919-1988 ....DLB-5, 16

Duncan, Ronald 1914-1982 ....DLB-13

Duncan, Sara Jeannette
　　1861-1922 ....DLB-92

Dunigan, Edward, and Brother DLB-49

Dunlap, John 1747-1812 ....DLB-43

Dunlap, William
　　1766-1839 ....DLB-30, 37, 59

Dunn, Douglas 1942- DLB-40

Dunn, Stephen 1939- DLB-105

Dunn, Stephen, The Good,
　　The Not So Good DLB-105

Dunne, Finley Peter
　　1867-1936 ....DLB-11, 23

Dunne, John Gregory 1932- Y-80

Dunne, Philip 1908-1992 ....DLB-26

Dunning, Ralph Cheever
1878-1930 .... DLB-4

Dunning, William A. 1857-1922 .... DLB-17

Duns Scotus, John
circa 1266-1308 .... DLB-115

Dunsany, Edward John Moreton Drax
Plunkett, Lord 1878-1957 .... DLB-10, 77

Dupin, Amantine-Aurore-Lucile (see Sand,
George)

Durand, Lucile (see Bersianik, Louky)

Duranty, Walter 1884-1957 .... DLB-29

Duras, Marguerite 1914- DLB-83

Durfey, Thomas 1653-1723 .... DLB-80

Durrell, Lawrence
1912-1990 .... DLB-15, 27; Y-90

Durrell, William
[publishing house] DLB-49

Dürrenmatt, Friedrich
1921-1990 .... DLB-69, 124

Dutton, E. P., and Company DLB-49

Duvoisin, Roger 1904-1980 .... DLB-61

Duyckinck, Evert Augustus
1816-1878 .... DLB-3, 64

Duyckinck, George L. 1823-1863 .....DLB-3

Duyckinck and Company DLB-49

Dwight, John Sullivan 1813-1893 .....DLB-1

Dwight, Timothy 1752-1817 .... DLB-37

Dybek, Stuart 1942- DLB-130

Dyer, Charles 1928- DLB-13

Dyer, George 1755-1841 .... DLB-93

Dyer, John 1699-1757 .... DLB-95

Dyer, Sir Edward 1543-1607 ...... DLB-136

Dylan, Bob 1941- DLB-16

E

Eager, Edward 1911-1964 .... DLB-22

Eames, Wilberforce 1855-1937 ..... DLB-140

Earle, James H., and Company DLB-49

Earle, John 1600 or 1601-1665 ..... DLB-151

Early American Book Illustration,
by Sinclair Hamilton DLB-49

Eastlake, William 1917- DLB-6

Eastman, Carol ?- DLB-44

Eastman, Max 1883-1969 .... DLB-91

Eberhart, Richard 1904- DLB-48

Ebner, Jeannie 1918- DLB-85

Ebner-Eschenbach, Marie von
1830-1916 .... DLB-81

Ebon 1942- DLB-41

Ecbasis Captivi circa 1045 .... DLB-148

Ecco Press DLB-46

Eckhart, Meister
circa 1260-circa 1328 .... DLB-115

The Eclectic Review 1805-1868 .... DLB-110

Edel, Leon 1907- DLB-103

Edes, Benjamin 1732-1803 .... DLB-43

Edgar, David 1948- DLB-13

Edgeworth, Maria 1768-1849 ...... DLB-116

The Edinburgh Review 1802-1929 .... DLB-110

Edinburgh University Press DLB-112

The Editor Publishing Company DLB-49

Editorial Statements DLB-137

Edmonds, Randolph 1900- DLB-51

Edmonds, Walter D. 1903- DLB-9

Edschmid, Kasimir 1890-1966 ...... DLB-56

Edwards, Jonathan 1703-1758 ...... DLB-24

Edwards, Jonathan, Jr. 1745-1801 .... DLB-37

Edwards, Junius 1929- DLB-33

Edwards, Richard 1524-1566 .... DLB-62

Effinger, George Alec 1947- DLB-8

Egerton, George 1859-1945 .... DLB-135

Eggleston, Edward 1837-1902 ...... DLB-12

Eggleston, Wilfred 1901-1986 ...... DLB-92

Ehrenstein, Albert 1886-1950 ...... DLB-81

Ehrhart, W. D. 1948- DS-9

Eich, Günter 1907-1972 ....DLB-69, 124

Eichendorff, Joseph Freiherr von
1788-1857 .... DLB-90

1873 Publishers' Catalogues DLB-49

Eighteenth-Century Aesthetic
Theories DLB-31

Eighteenth-Century Philosophical
Background DLB-31

Eigner, Larry 1927- DLB-5

Eikon Basilike 1649 .... DLB-151

Eilhart von Oberge
circa 1140-circa 1195 .... DLB-148

Einhard circa 770-840 .... DLB-148

Eisenreich, Herbert 1925-1986 ..... DLB-85

Eisner, Kurt 1867-1919 .... DLB-66

Eklund, Gordon 1945- Y-83

Ekwensi, Cyprian 1921- DLB-117

Elder, Lonne III 1931- DLB-7, 38, 44

Elder, Paul, and Company DLB-49

Elements of Rhetoric (1828; revised, 1846),
by Richard Whately [excerpt] DLB-57

Elie, Robert 1915-1973 ....DLB-88

Elin Pelin 1877-1949 ....DLB-147

Eliot, George 1819-1880 ..... DLB-21, 35, 55

Eliot, John 1604-1690 ....DLB-24

Eliot, T. S. 1888-1965 ..... DLB-7, 10, 45, 63

Elizabeth I 1533-1603 ....DLB-136

Elizondo, Salvador 1932- DLB-145

Elizondo, Sergio 1930- DLB-82

Elkin, Stanley 1930- DLB-2, 28; Y-80

Elles, Dora Amy (see Wentworth, Patricia)

Ellet, Elizabeth F. 1818?-1877 ....DLB-30

Elliot, Ebenezer 1781-1849 ....DLB-96

Elliott, George 1923- DLB-68

Elliott, Janice 1931- DLB-14

Elliott, William 1788-1863 ....DLB-3

Elliott, Thomes and Talbot DLB-49

Ellis, Edward S. 1840-1916 ....DLB-42

Ellis, Frederick Staridge
[publishing house] DLB-106

The George H. Ellis Company DLB-49

Ellison, Harlan 1934- DLB-8

Ellison, Ralph Waldo
1914-1994 .... DLB-2, 76; Y-94

Ellmann, Richard
1918-1987 .... DLB-103; Y-87

The Elmer Holmes Bobst Awards in Arts
and Letters Y-87

Elyot, Thomas 1490?-1546 ....DLB-136

Emanuel, James Andrew 1921- DLB-41

Emecheta, Buchi 1944- DLB-117

The Emergence of Black Women
Writers DS-8

Emerson, Ralph Waldo
1803-1882 .... DLB-1, 59, 73

Emerson, William 1769-1811 ....DLB-37

Emin, Fedor Aleksandrovich
circa 1735-1770 ....DLB-150

Empson, William 1906-1984 ....DLB-20

The End of English Stage Censorship,
1945-1968 ....DLB-13

Ende, Michael 1929- DLB-75

Engel, Marian 1933-1985 ....DLB-53

Engels, Friedrich 1820-1895 ....DLB-129

Engle, Paul 1908- DLB-48

English Composition and Rhetoric (1866),
by Alexander Bain [excerpt] DLB-57

The English Language:
410 to 1500 ....DLB-146

The English Renaissance of Art (1908),
by Oscar Wilde DLB-35

Enright, D. J. 1920- DLB-27

Enright, Elizabeth 1909-1968 ....DLB-22

L'Envoi (1882), by Oscar Wilde DLB-35

Epps, Bernard 1936- DLB-53

Epstein, Julius 1909- and
Epstein, Philip 1909-1952 ....DLB-26

Equiano, Olaudah
circa 1745-1797 ....DLB-37, 50

Eragny Press DLB-112

Erasmus, Desiderius 1467-1536 .....DLB-136

Erba, Luciano 1922- DLB-128

Erichsen-Brown, Gwethalyn Graham
(see Graham, Gwethalyn)

Eriugena, John Scottus
circa 810-877 ....DLB-115

Ernest Hemingway's Toronto Journalism
Revisited: With Three Previously
Unrecorded Stories Y-92

Ernst, Paul 1866-1933 ....DLB-66, 118

Erskine, Albert 1911-1993 ....Y-93

Erskine, John 1879-1951 ....DLB-9, 102

Ervine, St. John Greer 1883-1971 ....DLB-10

Eschenburg, Johann Joachim
1743-1820 ....DLB-97

Escoto, Julio 1944- DLB-145

Eshleman, Clayton 1935- DLB-5

Espriu, Salvador 1913-1985 ....DLB-134

Ess Ess Publishing Company DLB-49

Essay on Chatterton (1842), by
Robert Browning DLB-32

Essex House Press DLB-112

Estes, Eleanor 1906-1988 ....DLB-22

Estes and Lauriat DLB-49

Etherege, George 1636-circa 1692 ....DLB-80

Ethridge, Mark, Sr. 1896-1981 .....DLB-127

Ets, Marie Hall 1893- DLB-22

Etter, David 1928- DLB-105

Eudora Welty: Eye of the Storyteller Y-87

Eugene O'Neill Memorial Theater
Center DLB-7

Eugene O'Neill's Letters: A Review Y-88

Eupolemius
flourished circa 1095 ....DLB-148

Evans, Donald 1884-1921 ....DLB-54

Evans, George Henry 1805-1856 .....DLB-43

Evans, Hubert 1892-1986 ....DLB-92

Evans, Mari 1923- DLB-41

Evans, Mary Ann (see Eliot, George)

Evans, Nathaniel 1742-1767 ....DLB-31

Evans, Sebastian 1830-1909 ....DLB-35

Evans, M., and Company DLB-46

Everett, Alexander Hill
790-1847 ....DLB-59

Everett, Edward 1794-1865 ....DLB-1, 59

Everson, R. G. 1903- DLB-88

Everson, William 1912- DLB-5, 16

Every Man His Own Poet; or, The
Inspired Singer's Recipe Book (1877),
by W. H. Mallock DLB-35

Ewart, Gavin 1916- DLB-40

Ewing, Juliana Horatia
1841-1885 ....DLB-21

The Examiner 1808-1881 ....DLB-110

Exley, Frederick
1929-1992 ....DLB-143; Y-81

Experiment in the Novel (1929),
by John D. Beresford DLB-36

Eyre and Spottiswoode DLB-106

Ezzo ?-after 1065 ....DLB-148

F

"F. Scott Fitzgerald: St. Paul's Native Son
and Distinguished American Writer":
University of Minnesota Conference,
29-31 October 1982 ....Y-82

Faber, Frederick William
1814-1863 ....DLB-32

Faber and Faber Limited DLB-112

Faccio, Rena (see Aleramo, Sibilla)

Fagundo, Ana María 1938- DLB-134

Fair, Ronald L. 1932- DLB-33

Fairfax, Beatrice (see Manning, Marie)

Fairlie, Gerard 1899-1983 ....DLB-77

Fallada, Hans 1893-1947 ....DLB-56

Fancher, Betsy 1928- Y-83

Fane, Violet 1843-1905 ....DLB-35

Fanfrolico Press DLB-112

Fanning, Katherine 1927 ....DLB-127

Fanshawe, Sir Richard
1608-1666 ....DLB-126

Fantasy Press Publishers DLB-46

Fante, John 1909-1983 ....DLB-130; Y-83

Al-Farabi circa 870-950 ....DLB-115

Farah, Nuriddin 1945- DLB-125

Farber, Norma 1909-1984 ....DLB-61

Farigoule, Louis (see Romains, Jules)

Farley, Walter 1920-1989 ....DLB-22

Farmer, Philip José 1918- DLB-8

Farquhar, George circa 1677-1707 ...DLB-84

Farquharson, Martha (see Finley, Martha)

Farrar and Rinehart DLB-46

Farrar, Straus and Giroux DLB-46

Farrell, James T.
1904-1979 ....DLB-4, 9, 86; DS-2

Farrell, J. G. 1935-1979 ....DLB-14

Fast, Howard 1914- DLB-9

Faulkner, William 1897-1962
........DLB-9, 11, 44, 102; DS-2; Y-86

Fauset, Jessie Redmon 1882-1961 ....DLB-51

Faust, Irvin 1924- DLB-2, 28; Y-80

Fawcett Books DLB-46

Fearing, Kenneth 1902-1961 ....DLB-9

Federal Writers' Project DLB-46

Federman, Raymond 1928- Y-80

Feiffer, Jules 1929- DLB-7, 44

Feinberg, Charles E. 1899-1988 ....Y-88

Feinstein, Elaine 1930- DLB-14, 40

Felipe, Léon 1884-1968 ....DLB-108

Fell, Frederick, Publishers DLB-46

Felltham, Owen 1602?-1668 ...DLB-126, 151

Fels, Ludwig 1946- DLB-75

Felton, Cornelius Conway
1807-1862 ....DLB-1

Fennario, David 1947- DLB-60

Fenno, John 1751-1798 ....DLB-43

Fenno, R. F., and Company DLB-49

Fenton, Geoffrey 1539?-1608 ......DLB-136

Fenton, James 1949- DLB-40

Ferber, Edna 1885-1968 ....DLB-9, 28, 86

Ferdinand, Vallery III (see Salaam, Kalamu ya)

Ferguson, Sir Samuel 1810-1886 .....DLB-32

Ferguson, William Scott
1875-1954 ....DLB-47

Fergusson, Robert 1750-1774 ......DLB-109

Ferland, Albert 1872-1943 ....DLB-92

Ferlinghetti, Lawrence 1919- ...DLB-5, 16

Fern, Fanny (see Parton, Sara Payson Willis)

Ferrars, Elizabeth 1907- DLB-87

Ferré, Rosario 1942- DLB-145

Ferret, E., and Company DLB-49

Ferrier, Susan 1782-1854 .... DLB-116

Ferrini, Vincent 1913- DLB-48

Ferron, Jacques 1921-1985 .... DLB-60

Ferron, Madeleine 1922- DLB-53

Fetridge and Company DLB-49

Feuchtersleben, Ernst Freiherr von
1806-1849 .... DLB-133

Feuchtwanger, Lion 1884-1958 ..... DLB-66

Feuerbach, Ludwig 1804-1872 ..... DLB-133

Fichte, Johann Gottlieb
1762-1814 .... DLB-90

Ficke, Arthur Davison 1883-1945 ... DLB-54

Fiction Best-Sellers, 1910-1945 ....DLB-9

Fiction into Film, 1928-1975: A List of Movies
Based on the Works of Authors in
British Novelists, 1930-1959 ...... DLB-15

Fiedler, Leslie A. 1917- DLB-28, 67

Field, Edward 1924- DLB-105

Field, Edward, The Poetry File DLB-105

Field, Eugene
1850-1895 .... DLB-23, 42, 140

Field, Marshall, III 1893-1956 ..... DLB-127

Field, Marshall, IV 1916-1965 ..... DLB-127

Field, Marshall, V 1941- DLB-127

Field, Nathan 1587-1619 or 1620 .... DLB-58

Field, Rachel 1894-1942 .... DLB-9, 22

A Field Guide to Recent Schools of American
Poetry Y-86

Fielding, Henry
1707-1754 .... DLB-39, 84, 101

Fielding, Sarah 1710-1768 .... DLB-39

Fields, James Thomas 1817-1881 .....DLB-1

Fields, Julia 1938- DLB-41

Fields, W. C. 1880-1946 .... DLB-44

Fields, Osgood and Company DLB-49

Fifty Penguin Years Y-85

Figes, Eva 1932- DLB-14

Figuera, Angela 1902-1984 .... DLB-108

Filmer, Sir Robert 1586-1653 ...... DLB-151

Filson, John circa 1753-1788 .... DLB-37

Finch, Anne, Countess of Winchilsea
1661-1720 .... DLB-95

Finch, Robert 1900- DLB-88

Findley, Timothy 1930- DLB-53

Finlay, Ian Hamilton 1925- DLB-40

Finley, Martha 1828-1909 .... DLB-42

Finney, Jack 1911- DLB-8

Finney, Walter Braden (see Finney, Jack)

Firbank, Ronald 1886-1926 .... DLB-36

Firmin, Giles 1615-1697 .... DLB-24

First Edition Library/Collectors'
Reprints, Inc. Y-91

First International F. Scott Fitzgerald
Conference Y-92

First Strauss "Livings" Awarded to Cynthia
Ozick and Raymond Carver
An Interview with Cynthia Ozick
An Interview with Raymond
Carver Y-83

Fischer, Karoline Auguste Fernandine
1764-1842 .... DLB-94

Fish, Stanley 1938- DLB-67

Fishacre, Richard 1205-1248 .... DLB-115

Fisher, Clay (see Allen, Henry W.)

Fisher, Dorothy Canfield
1879-1958 ....DLB-9, 102

Fisher, Leonard Everett 1924- DLB-61

Fisher, Roy 1930- DLB-40

Fisher, Rudolph 1897-1934 .....DLB-51, 102

Fisher, Sydney George 1856-1927 ... DLB-47

Fisher, Vardis 1895-1968 .... DLB-9

Fiske, John 1608-1677 .... DLB-24

Fiske, John 1842-1901 ....DLB-47, 64

Fitch, Thomas circa 1700-1774 ...... DLB-31

Fitch, William Clyde 1865-1909 ...... DLB-7

FitzGerald, Edward 1809-1883 ...... DLB-32

Fitzgerald, F. Scott
1896-1940 ..... DLB-4, 9, 86; Y-81; DS-1

Fitzgerald, Penelope 1916- DLB-14

Fitzgerald, Robert 1910-1985 ....Y-80

Fitzgerald, Thomas 1819-1891 ...... DLB-23

Fitzgerald, Zelda Sayre 1900-1948 ......Y-84

Fitzhugh, Louise 1928-1974 .... DLB-52

Fitzhugh, William
circa 1651-1701 .... DLB-24

Flanagan, Thomas 1923- Y-80

Flanner, Hildegarde 1899-1987 ...... DLB-48

Flanner, Janet 1892-1978 .... DLB-4

Flaubert, Gustave 1821-1880 .... DLB-119

Flavin, Martin 1883-1967 .... DLB-9

Fleck, Konrad (flourished circa 1220)
.... DLB-138

Flecker, James Elroy 1884-1915 ..DLB-10, 19

Fleeson, Doris 1901-1970 ....DLB-29

Fleißer, Marieluise 1901-1974 .. DLB-56, 124

Fleming, Ian 1908-1964 ....DLB-87

The Fleshly School of Poetry and Other
Phenomena of the Day (1872), by Robert
Buchanan DLB-35

The Fleshly School of Poetry: Mr. D. G.
Rossetti (1871), by Thomas Maitland
(Robert Buchanan) DLB-35

Fletcher, Giles, the Elder
1546-1611 ....DLB-136

Fletcher, Giles, the Younger
1585 or 1586 - 1623 ....DLB-121

Fletcher, J. S. 1863-1935 ....DLB-70

Fletcher, John (see Beaumont, Francis)

Fletcher, John Gould 1886-1950 .. DLB-4, 45

Fletcher, Phineas 1582-1650 ....DLB-121

Flieg, Helmut (see Heym, Stefan)

Flint, F. S. 1885-1960 ....DLB-19

Flint, Timothy 1780-1840 ....DLB-734

Foix, J. V. 1893-1987 ....DLB-134

Foley, Martha (see Burnett, Whit, and
Martha Foley)

Folger, Henry Clay 1857-1930 ......DLB-140

Folio Society DLB-112

Follen, Eliza Lee (Cabot) 1787-1860 ...DLB-1

Follett, Ken 1949- Y-81, DLB-87

Follett Publishing Company DLB-46

Folsom, John West
[publishing house] DLB-49

Fontane, Theodor 1819-1898 ....DLB-129

Fonvisin, Denis Ivanovich
1744 or 1745-1792 ....DLB-150

Foote, Horton 1916- DLB-26

Foote, Samuel 1721-1777 ....DLB-89

Foote, Shelby 1916- DLB-2, 17

Forbes, Calvin 1945- DLB-41

Forbes, Ester 1891-1967 ....DLB-22

Forbes and Company DLB-49

Force, Peter 1790-1868 ....DLB-30

Forché, Carolyn 1950- DLB-5

Ford, Charles Henri 1913- DLB-4, 48

Ford, Corey 1902-1969 ....DLB-11

Ford, Ford Madox 1873-1939 ... DLB-34, 98

Ford, Jesse Hill 1928- DLB-6

Ford, John 1586-? DLB-58

Ford, R. A. D. 1915- DLB-88

Ford, Worthington C. 1858-1941 .... DLB-47

Ford, J. B., and Company DLB-49

Fords, Howard, and Hulbert DLB-49

Foreman, Carl 1914-1984 .... DLB-26

Forester, Frank (see Herbert, Henry William)

Fornés, María Irene 1930- DLB-7

Forrest, Leon 1937- DLB-33

Forster, E. M.
   1879-1970 .... DLB-34, 98; DS-10

Forster, Georg 1754-1794 .... DLB-94

Forster, John 1812-1876 .... DLB-144

Forsyth, Frederick 1938- DLB-87

Forten, Charlotte L. 1837-1914 ...... DLB-50

Fortini, Franco 1917- DLB-128

Fortune, T. Thomas 1856-1928 ...... DLB-23

Fosdick, Charles Austin
   1842-1915 .... DLB-42

Foster, Genevieve 1893-1979 .... DLB-61

Foster, Hannah Webster
   1758-1840 .... DLB-37

Foster, John 1648-1681 .... DLB-24

Foster, Michael 1904-1956 .... DLB-9

Fouqué, Caroline de la Motte
   1774-1831 .... DLB-90

Fouqué, Friedrich de la Motte
   1777-1843 .... DLB-90

Four Essays on the Beat Generation,
   by John Clellon Holmes DLB-16

Four Seas Company DLB-46

Four Winds Press DLB-46

Fournier, Henri Alban (see Alain-Fournier)

Fowler and Wells Company DLB-49

Fowles, John 1926- DLB-14, 139

Fox, John, Jr. 1862 or 1863-1919 ..... DLB-9

Fox, Paula 1923- DLB-52

Fox, Richard Kyle 1846-1922 .... DLB-79

Fox, William Price 1926- DLB-2; Y-81

Fox, Richard K.
   [publishing house] DLB-49

Foxe, John 1517-1587 .... DLB-132

Fraenkel, Michael 1896-1957 .... DLB-4

France, Anatole 1844-1924 .... DLB-123

France, Richard 1938- DLB-7

Francis, Convers 1795-1863 .... DLB-1

Francis, Dick 1920- DLB-87

Francis, Jeffrey, Lord 1773-1850 .... DLB-107

Francis, C. S. [publishing house] DLB-49

François 1863-1910 .... DLB-92

François, Louise von 1817-1893 .... DLB-129

Francke, Kuno 1855-1930 .... DLB-71

Frank, Bruno 1887-1945 .... DLB-118

Frank, Leonhard 1882-1961 .... DLB-56, 118

Frank, Melvin (see Panama, Norman)

Frank, Waldo 1889-1967 .... DLB-9, 63

Franken, Rose 1895?-1988 .... Y-84

Franklin, Benjamin
   1706-1790 .... DLB-24, 43, 73

Franklin, James 1697-1735 .... DLB-43

Franklin Library DLB-46

Frantz, Ralph Jules 1902-1979 .... DLB-4

Franzos, Karl Emil 1848-1904 ..... DLB-129

Fraser, G. S. 1915-1980 .... DLB-27

Frattini, Alberto 1922- DLB-128

Frau Ava ?-1127 .... DLB-148

Frayn, Michael 1933- DLB-13, 14

Frederic, Harold 1856-1898 ..... DLB-12, 23

Freeling, Nicolas 1927- DLB-87

Freeman, Douglas Southall
   1886-1953 .... DLB-17

Freeman, Legh Richmond
   1842-1915 .... DLB-23

Freeman, Mary E. Wilkins
   1852-1930 .... DLB-12, 78

Freeman, R. Austin 1862-1943 ...... DLB-70

Freidank circa 1170-circa 1233 ..... DLB-138

Freiligrath, Ferdinand 1810-1876 ... DLB-133

French, Alice 1850-1934 .... DLB-74

French, David 1939- DLB-53

French, James [publishing house] DLB-49

French, Samuel [publishing house] ... DLB-49

Samuel French, Limited DLB-106

Freneau, Philip 1752-1832 .... DLB-37, 43

Freni, Melo 1934- DLB-128

Freytag, Gustav 1816-1895 .... DLB-129

Fried, Erich 1921-1988 .... DLB-85

Friedman, Bruce Jay 1930- DLB-2, 28

Friedrich von Hausen
   circa 1171-1190 .... DLB-138

Friel, Brian 1929- DLB-13

Friend, Krebs 1895?-1967? DLB-4

Fries, Fritz Rudolf 1935- DLB-75

Fringe and Alternative Theater
   in Great Britain DLB-13

Frisch, Max 1911-1991 .... DLB-69, 124

Frischmuth, Barbara 1941- DLB-85

Fritz, Jean 1915- DLB-52

Fromentin, Eugene 1820-1876 ...... DLB-123

From The Gay Science, by
   E. S. Dallas DLB-21

Frost, Robert 1874-1963 ...... DLB-54; DS-7

Frothingham, Octavius Brooks
   1822-1895 .... DLB-1

Froude, James Anthony
   1818-1894 .... DLB-18, 57, 144

Fry, Christopher 1907- DLB-13

Fry, Roger 1866-1934 .... DS-10

Frye, Northrop 1912-1991 ...... DLB-67, 68

Fuchs, Daniel
   1909-1993 .... DLB-9, 26, 28; Y-93

Fuentes, Carlos 1928- DLB-113

Fuertes, Gloria 1918- DLB-108

The Fugitives and the Agrarians:
   The First Exhibition Y-85

Fuller, Charles H., Jr. 1939- DLB-38

Fuller, Henry Blake 1857-1929 ...... DLB-12

Fuller, John 1937- DLB-40

Fuller, Roy 1912-1991 .... DLB-15, 20

Fuller, Samuel 1912- DLB-26

Fuller, Sarah Margaret, Marchesa
   D'Ossoli 1810-1850 .... DLB-1, 59, 73

Fuller, Thomas 1608-1661 .... DLB-151

Fulton, Len 1934- Y-86

Fulton, Robin 1937- DLB-40

Furman, Laura 1945- Y-86

Furness, Horace Howard
   1833-1912 .... DLB-64

Furness, William Henry 1802-1896 ... DLB-1

Furthman, Jules 1888-1966 .... DLB-26

The Future of the Novel (1899), by
   Henry James DLB-18

G

The G. Ross Roy Scottish Poetry
   Collection at the University of
   South Carolina Y-89

Gaddis, William 1922- DLB-2

Gág, Wanda 1893-1946 .... DLB-22

Gagnon, Madeleine 1938- DLB-60

Gaine, Hugh 1726-1807 .... DLB-43

Gaine, Hugh [publishing house] DLB-49

Gaines, Ernest J. 1933- DLB-2, 33; Y-80

Gaiser, Gerd 1908-1976 .... DLB-69

Galarza, Ernesto 1905-1984 .... DLB-122

Galaxy Science Fiction Novels DLB-46

Gale, Zona 1874-1938 .... DLB-9, 78

Gall, Louise von 1815-1855 .... DLB-133

Gallagher, Tess 1943- DLB-120

Gallagher, Wes 1911- DLB-127

Gallagher, William Davis
1808-1894 .... DLB-73

Gallant, Mavis 1922- DLB-53

Gallico, Paul 1897-1976 ....DLB-9

Galsworthy, John
1867-1933 .... DLB-10, 34, 98

Galt, John 1779-1839 .... DLB-99, 116

Galvin, Brendan 1938- DLB-5

Gambit DLB-46

Gamboa, Reymundo 1948- DLB-122

Gammer Gurton's Needle DLB-62

Gannett, Frank E. 1876-1957 .... DLB-29

Gaos, Vicente 1919-1980 .... DLB-134

García, Lionel G. 1935- DLB-82

García Lorca, Federico
1898-1936 .... DLB-108

García Márquez, Gabriel
1928- DLB-113

Gardam, Jane 1928- DLB-14

Garden, Alexander
circa 1685-1756 .... DLB-31

Gardner, John 1933-1982 ...... DLB-2; Y-82

Garis, Howard R. 1873-1962 .... DLB-22

Garland, Hamlin
1860-1940 .... DLB-12, 71, 78

Garneau, Francis-Xavier
1809-1866 .... DLB-99

Garneau, Hector de Saint-Denys
1912-1943 .... DLB-88

Garneau, Michel 1939- DLB-53

Garner, Hugh 1913-1979 .... DLB-68

Garnett, David 1892-1981 .... DLB-34

Garraty, John A. 1920- DLB-17

Garrett, George
1929- DLB-2, 5, 130; Y-83

Garrick, David 1717-1779 .... DLB-84

Garrison, William Lloyd
1805-1879 .... DLB-1, 43

Garro, Elena 1920- DLB-145

Garth, Samuel 1661-1719 .... DLB-95

Garve, Andrew 1908- DLB-87

Gary, Romain 1914-1980 .... DLB-83

Gascoigne, George 1539?-1577 ..... DLB-136

Gascoyne, David 1916- DLB-20

Gaskell, Elizabeth Cleghorn
1810-1865 ....DLB-21, 144

Gaspey, Thomas 1788-1871 .... DLB-116

Gass, William Howard 1924- DLB-2

Gates, Doris 1901- DLB-22

Gates, Henry Louis, Jr. 1950- DLB-67

Gates, Lewis E. 1860-1924 .... DLB-71

Gatto, Alfonso 1909-1976 .... DLB-114

Gautier, Théophile 1811-1872 ..... DLB-119

Gauvreau, Claude 1925-1971 .... DLB-88

The Gawain-Poet
flourished circa 1350-1400 ..... DLB-146

Gay, Ebenezer 1696-1787 .... DLB-24

Gay, John 1685-1732 ....DLB-84, 95

The Gay Science (1866), by E. S. Dallas
[excerpt] DLB-21

Gayarré, Charles E. A. 1805-1895 ... DLB-30

Gaylord, Edward King
1873-1974 .... DLB-127

Gaylord, Edward Lewis 1919- DLB-127

Gaylord, Charles
[publishing house] DLB-49

Geddes, Gary 1940- DLB-60

Geddes, Virgil 1897- DLB-4

Gedeon (Georgii Andreevich Krinovsky)
circa 1730-1763 .... DLB-150

Geibel, Emanuel 1815-1884 .... DLB-129

Geis, Bernard, Associates DLB-46

Geisel, Theodor Seuss
1904-1991 ....DLB-61; Y-91

Gelb, Arthur 1924- DLB-103

Gelb, Barbara 1926- DLB-103

Gelber, Jack 1932- DLB-7

Gelinas, Gratien 1909- DLB-88

Gellert, Christian Füerchtegott
1715-1769 .... DLB-97

Gellhorn, Martha 1908- Y-82

Gems, Pam 1925- DLB-13

A General Idea of the College of Mirania (1753),
by William Smith [excerpts] DLB-31

Genet, Jean 1910-1986 ....DLB-72; Y-86

Genevoix, Maurice 1890-1980 .... DLB-65

Genovese, Eugene D. 1930- DLB-17

Gent, Peter 1942- Y-82

Geoffrey of Monmouth
circa 1100-1155 ....DLB-146

George, Henry 1839-1897 ....DLB-23

George, Jean Craighead 1919- DLB-52

Georgslied 896? DLB-148

Gerhardie, William 1895-1977 ....DLB-36

Gérin-Lajoie, Antoine 1824-1882 ....DLB-99

German Drama 800-1280 ....DLB-138

German Drama from Naturalism
to Fascism: 1889-1933 ....DLB-118

German Literature and Culture from
Charlemagne to the Early Courtly
Period DLB-148

German Radio Play, The DLB-124

German Transformation from the Baroque
to the Enlightenment, The DLB-97

The Germanic Epic and Old English Heroic
Poetry: Widseth, Waldere, and The
Fight at Finnsburg DLB-146

Germanophilism, by Hans Kohn DLB-66

Gernsback, Hugo 1884-1967 .... DLB-8, 137

Gerould, Katharine Fullerton
1879-1944 ....DLB-78

Gerrish, Samuel [publishing house] ...DLB-49

Gerrold, David 1944- DLB-8

Gersonides 1288-1344 ....DLB-115

Gerstäcker, Friedrich 1816-1872 ....DLB-129

Gerstenberg, Heinrich Wilhelm von
1737-1823 ....DLB-97

Gervinus, Georg Gottfried
1805-1871 ....DLB-133

Geßner, Salomon 1730-1788 ....DLB-97

Geston, Mark S. 1946- DLB-8

Al-Ghazali 1058-1111 ....DLB-115

Gibbon, Edward 1737-1794 ....DLB-104

Gibbon, John Murray 1875-1952 .....DLB-92

Gibbon, Lewis Grassic (see Mitchell,
James Leslie)

Gibbons, Floyd 1887-1939 ....DLB-25

Gibbons, Reginald 1947- DLB-120

Gibbons, William ?-? DLB-73

Gibson, Graeme 1934- DLB-53

Gibson, Margaret 1944- DLB-120

Gibson, Wilfrid 1878-1962 ....DLB-19

Gibson, William 1914- DLB-7

Gide, André 1869-1951 ....DLB-65

Giguère, Diane 1937- DLB-53

Giguère, Roland 1929- DLB-60

Gil de Biedma, Jaime 1929-1990 .... DLB-108

Gil-Albert, Juan 1906- DLB-134

Gilbert, Anthony 1899-1973 .... DLB-77

Gilbert, Michael 1912- DLB-87

Gilbert, Sandra M. 1936- DLB-120

Gilbert, Sir Humphrey
1537-1583 .... DLB-136

Gilchrist, Alexander
1828-1861 .... DLB-144

Gilchrist, Ellen 1935- DLB-130

Gilder, Jeannette L. 1849-1916 ...... DLB-79

Gilder, Richard Watson
1844-1909 .... DLB-64, 79

Gildersleeve, Basil 1831-1924 .... DLB-71

Giles, Henry 1809-1882 .... DLB-64

Giles of Rome circa 1243-1316 ..... DLB-115

Gilfillan, George 1813-1878 .... DLB-144

Gill, Eric 1882-1940 .... DLB-98

Gill, William F., Company DLB-49

Gillespie, A. Lincoln, Jr.
1895-1950 .... DLB-4

Gilliam, Florence ?-? DLB-4

Gilliatt, Penelope 1932-1993 .... DLB-14

Gillott, Jacky 1939-1980 .... DLB-14

Gilman, Caroline H. 1794-1888 ... DLB-3, 73

Gilman, W. and J.
[publishing house] DLB-49

Gilmer, Elizabeth Meriwether
1861-1951 .... DLB-29

Gilmer, Francis Walker
1790-1826 .... DLB-37

Gilroy, Frank D. 1925- DLB-7

Gimferrer, Pere (Pedro) 1945- DLB-134

Gingrich, Arnold 1903-1976 ...... DLB-137

Ginsberg, Allen 1926- DLB-5, 16

Ginzkey, Franz Karl 1871-1963 ..... DLB-81

Gioia, Dana 1950- DLB-120

Giono, Jean 1895-1970 .... DLB-72

Giotti, Virgilio 1885-1957 .... DLB-114

Giovanni, Nikki 1943- DLB-5, 41

Gipson, Lawrence Henry
1880-1971 .... DLB-17

Girard, Rodolphe 1879-1956 .... DLB-92

Giraudoux, Jean 1882-1944 .... DLB-65

Gissing, George 1857-1903 .... DLB-18, 135

Giudici, Giovanni 1924- DLB-128

Giuliani, Alfredo 1924- DLB-128

Gladstone, William Ewart
1809-1898 .... DLB-57

Glaeser, Ernst 1902-1963 .... DLB-69

Glanville, Brian 1931- DLB-15, 139

Glapthorne, Henry 1610-1643? DLB-58

Glasgow, Ellen 1873-1945 .... DLB-9, 12

Glaspell, Susan 1876-1948 ..... DLB-7, 9, 78

Glass, Montague 1877-1934 .... DLB-11

Glassco, John 1909-1981 .... DLB-68

Glauser, Friedrich 1896-1938 .... DLB-56

F. Gleason's Publishing Hall DLB-49

Gleim, Johann Wilhelm Ludwig
1719-1803 .... DLB-97

Glover, Richard 1712-1785 .... DLB-95

Glück, Louise 1943- DLB-5

Gobineau, Joseph-Arthur de
1816-1882 .... DLB-123

Godbout, Jacques 1933- DLB-53

Goddard, Morrill 1865-1937 .... DLB-25

Goddard, William 1740-1817 .... DLB-43

Godey, Louis A. 1804-1878 .... DLB-73

Godey and McMichael DLB-49

Godfrey, Dave 1938- DLB-60

Godfrey, Thomas 1736-1763 .... DLB-31

Godine, David R., Publisher DLB-46

Godkin, E. L. 1831-1902 .... DLB-79

Godolphin, Sidney 1610-1643 ..... DLB-126

Godwin, Gail 1937- DLB-6

Godwin, Parke 1816-1904 .... DLB-3, 64

Godwin, William
1756-1836 .... DLB-39, 104, 142

Goering, Reinhard 1887-1936 ...... DLB-118

Goes, Albrecht 1908- DLB-69

Goethe, Johann Wolfgang von
1749-1832 .... DLB-94

Goetz, Curt 1888-1960 .... DLB-124

Goffe, Thomas circa 1592-1629 ..... DLB-58

Goffstein, M. B. 1940- DLB-61

Gogarty, Oliver St. John
1878-1957 .... DLB-15, 19

Goines, Donald 1937-1974 .... DLB-33

Gold, Herbert 1924- DLB-2; Y-81

Gold, Michael 1893-1967 .... DLB-9, 28

Goldbarth, Albert 1948- DLB-120

Goldberg, Dick 1947- DLB-7

Golden Cockerel Press DLB-112

Golding, Arthur 1536-1606 .... DLB-136

Golding, William 1911-1993 .... DLB-15, 100

Goldman, William 1931- DLB-44

Goldsmith, Oliver
1730?-1774 ... DLB-39, 89, 104, 109, 142

Goldsmith, Oliver 1794-1861 .... DLB-99

Goldsmith Publishing Company DLB-46

Gollancz, Victor, Limited DLB-112

Gómez-Quiñones, Juan 1942- DLB-122

Gomme, Laurence James
[publishing house] DLB-46

Goncourt, Edmond de 1822-1896 ... DLB-123

Goncourt, Jules de 1830-1870 ...... DLB-123

Gonzales, Rodolfo "Corky"
1928- DLB-122

González, Angel 1925- DLB-108

Gonzalez, Genaro 1949- DLB-122

Gonzalez, Ray 1952- DLB-122

González de Mireles, Jovita
1899-1983 .... DLB-122

González-T., César A. 1931- DLB-82

Goodman, Paul 1911-1972 .... DLB-130

The Goodman Theatre DLB-7

Goodrich, Frances 1891-1984 and
Hackett, Albert 1900- DLB-26

Goodrich, Samuel Griswold
1793-1860 .... DLB-1, 42, 73

Goodrich, S. G. [publishing house] ... DLB-49

Goodspeed, C. E., and Company DLB-49

Goodwin, Stephen 1943- Y-82

Googe, Barnabe 1540-1594 .... DLB-132

Gookin, Daniel 1612-1687 .... DLB-24

Gordon, Caroline
1895-1981 .... DLB-4, 9, 102; Y-81

Gordon, Giles 1940- DLB-14, 139

Gordon, Mary 1949- DLB-6; Y-81

Gordone, Charles 1925- DLB-7

Gore, Catherine 1800-1861 .... DLB-116

Gorey, Edward 1925- DLB-61

Görres, Joseph 1776-1848 .... DLB-90

Gosse, Edmund 1849-1928 ..... DLB-57, 144

Gotlieb, Phyllis 1926- DLB-88

Gottfried von Straßburg
died before 1230 .... DLB-138

Gotthelf, Jeremias 1797-1854 .... DLB-133

Gottschalk circa 804/808-869 .... DLB-148

Gottsched, Johann Christoph
1700-1766 .... DLB-97

Götz, Johann Nikolaus
1721-1781 .... DLB-97

Gould, Wallace 1882-1940 .... DLB-54

Govoni, Corrado 1884-1965 .... DLB-114

Gower, John circa 1330-1408 ...... DLB-146

Goyen, William 1915-1983 ..... DLB-2; Y-83

Goytisolo, José Augustín 1928- ... DLB-134

Gozzano, Guido 1883-1916 .... DLB-114

Grabbe, Christian Dietrich
1801-1836 .... DLB-133

Gracq, Julien 1910- DLB-83

Grady, Henry W. 1850-1889 .... DLB-23

Graf, Oskar Maria 1894-1967 ...... DLB-56

Graf Rudolf between circa 1170
and circa 1185 .... DLB-148

Graham, George Rex 1813-1894 .... DLB-73

Graham, Gwethalyn 1913-1965 ..... DLB-88

Graham, Jorie 1951- DLB-120

Graham, Katharine 1917- DLB-127

Graham, Lorenz 1902-1989 .... DLB-76

Graham, Philip 1915-1963 .... DLB-127

Graham, R. B. Cunninghame
1852-1936 .... DLB-98, 135

Graham, Shirley 1896-1977 .... DLB-76

Graham, W. S. 1918- DLB-20

Graham, William H.
[publishing house] DLB-49

Graham, Winston 1910- DLB-77

Grahame, Kenneth
1859-1932 .... DLB-34, 141

Grainger, Martin Allerdale
1874-1941 .... DLB-92

Gramatky, Hardie 1907-1979 .... DLB-22

Grand, Sarah 1854-1943 .... DLB-135

Grandbois, Alain 1900-1975 .... DLB-92

Grange, John circa 1556-? DLB-136

Granich, Irwin (see Gold, Michael)

Grant, Duncan 1885-1978 .... DS-10

Grant, George 1918-1988 .... DLB-88

Grant, George Monro 1835-1902 .... DLB-99

Grant, Harry J. 1881-1963 .... DLB-29

Grant, James Edward 1905-1966 .... DLB-26

Grass, Günter 1927- DLB-75, 124

Grasty, Charles H. 1863-1924 ...... DLB-25

Grau, Shirley Ann 1929- DLB-2

Graves, John 1920- Y-83

Graves, Richard 1715-1804 .... DLB-39

Graves, Robert
1895-1985 ....DLB-20, 100; Y-85

Gray, Asa 1810-1888 .... DLB-1

Gray, David 1838-1861 .... DLB-32

Gray, Simon 1936- DLB-13

Gray, Thomas 1716-1771 .... DLB-109

Grayson, William J. 1788-1863 .... DLB-3, 64

The Great Bibliographers Series Y-93

The Great War and the Theater, 1914-1918
[Great Britain] DLB-10

Greeley, Horace 1811-1872 ....DLB-3, 43

Green, Adolph (see Comden, Betty)

Green, Duff 1791-1875 .... DLB-43

Green, Gerald 1922- DLB-28

Green, Henry 1905-1973 .... DLB-15

Green, Jonas 1712-1767 .... DLB-31

Green, Joseph 1706-1780 .... DLB-31

Green, Julien 1900- DLB-4, 72

Green, Paul 1894-1981 ....DLB-7, 9; Y-81

Green, T. and S.
[publishing house] DLB-49

Green, Timothy
[publishing house] DLB-49

Greenaway, Kate 1846-1901 .... DLB-141

Greenberg: Publisher DLB-46

Green Tiger Press DLB-46

Greene, Asa 1789-1838 .... DLB-11

Greene, Benjamin H.
[publishing house] DLB-49

Greene, Graham 1904-1991
.... DLB-13, 15, 77, 100; Y-85, Y-91

Greene, Robert 1558-1592 .... DLB-62

Greenhow, Robert 1800-1854 .... DLB-30

Greenough, Horatio 1805-1852 ...... DLB-1

Greenwell, Dora 1821-1882 .... DLB-35

Greenwillow Books DLB-46

Greenwood, Grace (see Lippincott, Sara Jane
Clarke)

Greenwood, Walter 1903-1974 ...... DLB-10

Greer, Ben 1948- DLB-6

Greg, W. R. 1809-1881 .... DLB-55

Gregg Press DLB-46

Gregory, Isabella Augusta
Persse, Lady 1852-1932 .... DLB-10

Gregory, Horace 1898-1982 .... DLB-48

Gregory of Rimini
circa 1300-1358 ....DLB-115

Gregynog Press DLB-112

Grenfell, Wilfred Thomason
1865-1940 ....DLB-92

Greve, Felix Paul (see Grove, Frederick Philip)

Greville, Fulke, First Lord Brooke
1554-1628 ....DLB-62

Grey, Lady Jane 1537-1554 ....DLB-132

Grey Owl 1888-1938 ....DLB-92

Grey, Zane 1872-1939 ....DLB-9

Grey Walls Press DLB-112

Grier, Eldon 1917- DLB-88

Grieve, C. M. (see MacDiarmid, Hugh)

Griffith, Elizabeth 1727?-1793 ... DLB-39, 89

Griffiths, Trevor 1935- DLB-13

Griggs, S. C., and Company DLB-49

Griggs, Sutton Elbert 1872-1930 .....DLB-50

Grignon, Claude-Henri 1894-1976 ...DLB-68

Grigson, Geoffrey 1905- DLB-27

Grillparzer, Franz 1791-1872 ....DLB-133

Grimald, Nicholas
circa 1519-circa 1562 ....DLB-136

Grimké, Angelina Weld
1880-1958 .... DLB-50, 54

Grimm, Hans 1875-1959 ....DLB-66

Grimm, Jacob 1785-1863 ....DLB-90

Grimm, Wilhelm 1786-1859 ....DLB-90

Grindal, Edmund
1519 or 1520-1583 ....DLB-132

Griswold, Rufus Wilmot
1815-1857 .... DLB-3, 59

Gross, Milt 1895-1953 ....DLB-11

Grosset and Dunlap DLB-49

Grossman Publishers DLB-46

Grosseteste, Robert
circa 1160-1253 ....DLB-115

Grosvenor, Gilbert H. 1875-1966 ....DLB-91

Groth, Klaus 1819-1899 ....DLB-129

Groulx, Lionel 1878-1967 ....DLB-68

Grove, Frederick Philip 1879-1949 ...DLB-92

Grove Press DLB-46

Grubb, Davis 1919-1980 ....DLB-6

Gruelle, Johnny 1880-1938 ....DLB-22

Grymeston, Elizabeth
before 1563-before 1604 ....DLB-136

Guare, John 1938- DLB-7

Guerra, Tonino 1920- DLB-128

Guest, Barbara 1920- DLB-5

Guèvremont, Germaine
1893-1968 ....DLB-68

Guidacci, Margherita 1921-1992 ....DLB-128

Guide to the Archives of Publishers, Journals,
and Literary Agents in North American
Libraries Y-93

Guillén, Jorge 1893-1984 ....DLB-108

Guilloux, Louis 1899-1980 ....DLB-72

Guilpin, Everard
circa 1572-after 1608? DLB-136

Guiney, Louise Imogen 1861-1920 ...DLB-54

Guiterman, Arthur 1871-1943 ....DLB-11

Günderrode, Caroline von
1780-1806 ....DLB-90

Gundulić, Ivan 1589-1638 ....DLB-147

Gunn, Bill 1934-1989 ....DLB-38

Gunn, James E. 1923- DLB-8

Gunn, Neil M. 1891-1973 ....DLB-15

Gunn, Thom 1929- DLB-27

Gunnars, Kristjana 1948- DLB-60

Gurik, Robert 1932- DLB-60

Gustafson, Ralph 1909- DLB-88

Gütersloh, Albert Paris 1887-1973 ...DLB-81

Guthrie, A. B., Jr. 1901- DLB-6

Guthrie, Ramon 1896-1973 ....DLB-4

The Guthrie Theater DLB-7

Gutzkow, Karl 1811-1878 ....DLB-133

Guy, Ray 1939- DLB-60

Guy, Rosa 1925- DLB-33

Gwynne, Erskine 1898-1948 ....DLB-4

Gyles, John 1680-1755 ....DLB-99

Gysin, Brion 1916- DLB-16

H

H. D. (see Doolittle, Hilda)

Habington, William 1605-1654 .....DLB-126

Hacker, Marilyn 1942- DLB-120

Hackett, Albert (see Goodrich, Frances)

Hacks, Peter 1928- DLB-124

Hadas, Rachel 1948- DLB-120

Hadden, Briton 1898-1929 ....DLB-91

Hagelstange, Rudolf 1912-1984 ......DLB-69

Haggard, H. Rider 1856-1925 ....DLB-70

Haggard, William 1907-1993 ....Y-93

Hahn-Hahn, Ida Gräfin von
1805-1880 ....DLB-133

Haig-Brown, Roderick 1908-1976 ...DLB-88

Haight, Gordon S. 1901-1985 .....DLB-103

Hailey, Arthur 1920- DLB-88; Y-82

Haines, John 1924- DLB-5

Hake, Edward
flourished 1566-1604 ....DLB-136

Hake, Thomas Gordon 1809-1895 ...DLB-32

Hakluyt, Richard 1552?-1616 ......DLB-136

Halbe, Max 1865-1944 ....DLB-118

Haldeman, Joe 1943- DLB-8

Haldeman-Julius Company DLB-46

Hale, E. J., and Son DLB-49

Hale, Edward Everett
1822-1909 ....DLB-1, 42, 74

Hale, Leo Thomas (see Ebon)

Hale, Lucretia Peabody
1820-1900 ....DLB-42

Hale, Nancy 1908-1988 ....DLB-86; Y-80, 88

Hale, Sarah Josepha (Buell)
1788-1879 ....DLB-1, 42, 73

Hales, John 1584-1656 ....DLB-151

Haley, Alex 1921-1992 ....DLB-38

Haliburton, Thomas Chandler
1796-1865 ....DLB-11, 99

Hall, Donald 1928- DLB-5

Hall, Edward 1497-1547 ....DLB-132

Hall, James 1793-1868 ....DLB-73, 74

Hall, Joseph 1574-1656 ....DLB-121, 151

Hall, Samuel [publishing house] DLB-49

Hallam, Arthur Henry 1811-1833 ...DLB-32

Halleck, Fitz-Greene 1790-1867 ......DLB-3

Hallmark Editions DLB-46

Halper, Albert 1904-1984 ....DLB-9

Halperin, John William 1941- DLB-111

Halstead, Murat 1829-1908 ....DLB-23

Hamann, Johann Georg 1730-1788 ..DLB-97

Hamburger, Michael 1924- DLB-27

Hamilton, Alexander 1712-1756 ....DLB-31

Hamilton, Alexander 1755?-1804 ....DLB-37

Hamilton, Cicely 1872-1952 ....DLB-10

Hamilton, Edmond 1904-1977 ....DLB-8

Hamilton, Elizabeth 1758-1816 ....DLB-116

Hamilton, Gail (see Corcoran, Barbara)

Hamilton, Ian 1938- DLB-40

Hamilton, Patrick 1904-1962 ....DLB-10

Hamilton, Virginia 1936- DLB-33, 52

Hamilton, Hamish, Limited DLB-112

Hammett, Dashiell 1894-1961 ....DS-6

Dashiell Hammett:
An Appeal in TAC Y-91

Hammon, Jupiter 1711-died between
1790 and 1806 ....DLB-31, 50

Hammond, John ?-1663 ....DLB-24

Hamner, Earl 1923- DLB-6

Hampton, Christopher 1946- DLB-13

Handel-Mazzetti, Enrica von
1871-1955 ....DLB-81

Handke, Peter 1942- DLB-85, 124

Handlin, Oscar 1915- DLB-17

Hankin, St. John 1869-1909 ....DLB-10

Hanley, Clifford 1922- DLB-14

Hannah, Barry 1942- DLB-6

Hannay, James 1827-1873 ....DLB-21

Hansberry, Lorraine 1930-1965 ...DLB-7, 38

Hapgood, Norman 1868-1937 ....DLB-91

Harcourt Brace Jovanovich DLB-46

Hardenberg, Friedrich von (see Novalis)

Harding, Walter 1917- DLB-111

Hardwick, Elizabeth 1916- DLB-6

Hardy, Thomas 1840-1928 ...DLB-18, 19, 135

Hare, Cyril 1900-1958 ....DLB-77

Hare, David 1947- DLB-13

Hargrove, Marion 1919- DLB-11

Häring, Georg Wilhelm Heinrich (see Alexis,
Willibald)

Harington, Sir John 1560-1612 .....DLB-136

Harjo, Joy 1951- DLB-120

Harlow, Robert 1923- DLB-60

Harman, Thomas
flourished 1566-1573 ....DLB-136

Harness, Charles L. 1915- DLB-8

Harper, Fletcher 1806-1877 ....DLB-79

Harper, Frances Ellen Watkins
1825-1911 ....DLB-50

Harper, Michael S. 1938- DLB-41

Harper and Brothers DLB-49

Harrap, George G., and Company
Limited DLB-112

Harriot, Thomas 1560-1621 ....DLB-136

Harris, Benjamin ?-circa 1720 ....DLB-42, 43

Harris, Christie 1907- DLB-88

Harris, George Washington
1814-1869 .... DLB-3, 11

Harris, Joel Chandler
1848-1908 ....DLB-11, 23, 42, 78, 91

Harris, Mark 1922- DLB-2; Y-80

Harris, Wilson 1921- DLB-117

Harrison, Charles Yale
1898-1954 .... DLB-68

Harrison, Frederic 1831-1923 ...... DLB-57

Harrison, Harry 1925- DLB-8

Harrison, Jim 1937- Y-82

Harrison, Paul Carter 1936- DLB-38

Harrison, Susan Frances
1859-1935 .... DLB-99

Harrison, Tony 1937- DLB-40

Harrison, William 1535-1593 ...... DLB-136

Harrison, James P., Company DLB-49

Harrisse, Henry 1829-1910 .... DLB-47

Harsent, David 1942- DLB-40

Hart, Albert Bushnell 1854-1943 .... DLB-17

Hart, Julia Catherine 1796-1867 .... DLB-99

Hart, Moss 1904-1961 ....DLB-7

Hart, Oliver 1723-1795 .... DLB-31

Hart-Davis, Rupert, Limited DLB-112

Harte, Bret 1836-1902 .... DLB-12, 64, 74, 79

Harte, Edward Holmead 1922- ... DLB-127

Harte, Houston Harriman
1927- DLB-127

Hartlaub, Felix 1913-1945 .... DLB-56

Hartleben, Otto Erich
1864-1905 .... DLB-118

Hartley, L. P. 1895-1972 .... DLB-15, 139

Hartley, Marsden 1877-1943 .... DLB-54

Hartling, Peter 1933- DLB-75

Hartman, Geoffrey H. 1929- DLB-67

Hartmann, Sadakichi 1867-1944 .... DLB-54

Hartmann von Aue
circa 1160-circa 1205 .... DLB-138

Harvey, Jean-Charles 1891-1967 .... DLB-88

Harvill Press Limited DLB-112

Harwood, Lee 1939- DLB-40

Harwood, Ronald 1934- DLB-13

Haskins, Charles Homer
1870-1937 .... DLB-47

Hass, Robert 1941- DLB-105

The Hatch-Billops Collection DLB-76

Hathaway, William 1944- DLB-120

Hauff, Wilhelm 1802-1827 .... DLB-90

A Haughty and Proud Generation (1922),
by Ford Madox Hueffer DLB-36

Hauptmann, Carl
1858-1921 ....DLB-66, 118

Hauptmann, Gerhart
1862-1946 ....DLB-66, 118

Hauser, Marianne 1910- Y-83

Hawes, Stephen
1475?-before 1529 .... DLB-132

Hawker, Robert Stephen
1803-1875 .... DLB-32

Hawkes, John 1925- DLB-2, 7; Y-80

Hawkesworth, John 1720-1773 ..... DLB-142

Hawkins, Sir John
1719-1789 ....DLB-104, 142

Hawkins, Walter Everette 1883-? DLB-50

Hawthorne, Nathaniel
1804-1864 ....DLB-1, 74

Hay, John 1838-1905 ....DLB-12, 47

Hayden, Robert 1913-1980 ....DLB-5, 76

Haydon, Benjamin Robert
1786-1846 .... DLB-110

Hayes, John Michael 1919- DLB-26

Hayley, William 1745-1820 .....DLB-93, 142

Haym, Rudolf 1821-1901 .... DLB-129

Hayman, Robert 1575-1629 .... DLB-99

Hayne, Paul Hamilton
1830-1886 ....DLB-3, 64, 79

Hays, Mary 1760-1843 .... DLB-142

Haywood, Eliza 1693?-1756 .... DLB-39

Hazard, Willis P. [publishing house] .. DLB-49

Hazlitt, William 1778-1830 .... DLB-110

Hazzard, Shirley 1931- Y-82

Head, Bessie 1937-1986 .... DLB-117

Headley, Joel T. 1813-1897 .... DLB-30

Heaney, Seamus 1939- DLB-40

Heard, Nathan C. 1936- DLB-33

Hearn, Lafcadio 1850-1904 ......DLB-12, 78

Hearne, John 1926- DLB-117

Hearne, Samuel 1745-1792 .... DLB-99

Hearst, William Randolph
1863-1951 .... DLB-25

Hearst, William Randolph, Jr
1908-1993 .... DLB-127

Heath, Catherine 1924- DLB-14

Heath, Roy A. K. 1926- DLB-117

Heath-Stubbs, John 1918- DLB-27

Heavysege, Charles 1816-1876 ......DLB-99

Hebbel, Friedrich 1813-1863 ....DLB-129

Hebel, Johann Peter 1760-1826 ......DLB-90

Hébert, Anne 1916- DLB-68

Hébert, Jacques 1923- DLB-53

Hecht, Anthony 1923- DLB-5

Hecht, Ben 1894-1964
...............DLB-7, 9, 25, 26, 28, 86

Hecker, Isaac Thomas 1819-1888 .....DLB-1

Hedge, Frederic Henry
1805-1890 .... DLB-1, 59

Hefner, Hugh M. 1926- DLB-137

Hegel, Georg Wilhelm Friedrich
1770-1831 ....DLB-90

Heidish, Marcy 1947- Y-82

Heißenbüttel 1921- DLB-75

Hein, Christoph 1944- DLB-124

Heine, Heinrich 1797-1856 ....DLB-90

Heinemann, Larry 1944- DS-9

Heinemann, William, Limited DLB-112

Heinlein, Robert A. 1907-1988 ....DLB-8

Heinrich von dem Türlîn
flourished circa 1230 ....DLB-138

Heinrich von Melk
flourished after 1160 ....DLB-148

Heinrich von Veldeke
circa 1145-circa 1190 ....DLB-138

Heinrich, Willi 1920- DLB-75

Heiskell, John 1872-1972 ....DLB-127

Heinse, Wilhelm 1746-1803 ....DLB-94

Heliand circa 850 ....DLB-148

Heller, Joseph 1923- DLB-2, 28; Y-80

Hellman, Lillian 1906-1984 .... DLB-7; Y-84

Helprin, Mark 1947- Y-85

Helwig, David 1938- DLB-60

Hemans, Felicia 1793-1835 ....DLB-96

Hemingway, Ernest 1899-1961
.... DLB-4, 9, 102; Y-81, 87; DS-1

Hemingway: Twenty-Five Years
Later Y-85

Hémon, Louis 1880-1913 ....DLB-92

Hemphill, Paul 1936- Y-87

Hénault, Gilles 1920- DLB-88

Henchman, Daniel 1689-1761 ....DLB-24

Henderson, Alice Corbin
1881-1949 ....DLB-54

Henderson, Archibald
1877-1963 ....DLB-103

Henderson, David 1942- DLB-41

Henderson, George Wylie
1904- DLB-51

Henderson, Zenna 1917-1983 ....DLB-8

Henisch, Peter 1943- DLB-85

Henley, Beth 1952- Y-86

Henley, William Ernest
1849-1903 ....DLB-19

Henniker, Florence 1855-1923 .....DLB-135

Henry, Alexander 1739-1824 ....DLB-99

Henry, Buck 1930- DLB-26

Henry VIII of England
1491-1547 ....DLB-132

Henry, Marguerite 1902- DLB-22

Henry, O. (see Porter, William Sydney)

Henry of Ghent
circa 1217-1229 - 1293 ....DLB-115

Henry, Robert Selph 1889-1970 .....DLB-17

Henry, Will (see Allen, Henry W.)

Henryson, Robert
1420s or 1430s-circa 1505 ......DLB-146

Henschke, Alfred (see Klabund)

Hensley, Sophie Almon 1866-1946 ...DLB-99

Henty, G. A. 1832?-1902 ....DLB-18, 141

Hentz, Caroline Lee 1800-1856 ....DLB-3

Herbert, Alan Patrick 1890-1971 .....DLB-10

Herbert, Edward, Lord, of Cherbury
1582-1648 ....DLB-121, 151

Herbert, Frank 1920-1986 ....DLB-8

Herbert, George 1593-1633 ....DLB-126

Herbert, Henry William
1807-1858 ....DLB-3, 73

Herbert, John 1926- DLB-53

Herbst, Josephine 1892-1969 ....DLB-9

Herburger, Gunter 1932- DLB-75, 124

Hercules, Frank E. M. 1917- DLB-33

Herder, Johann Gottfried
1744-1803 ....DLB-97

Herder, B., Book Company DLB-49

Herford, Charles Harold
1853-1931 ....DLB-149

Hergesheimer, Joseph
1880-1954 ....DLB-9, 102

Heritage Press DLB-46

Hermann the Lame 1013-1054 .....DLB-148

Hermes, Johann Timotheus
1738-1821 ....DLB-97

Hermlin, Stephan 1915- DLB-69

Hernández, Alfonso C. 1938- DLB-122

Hernández, Inés 1947- DLB-122

Hernández, Miguel 1910-1942 ..... DLB-134

Hernton, Calvin C. 1932- DLB-38

"The Hero as Man of Letters: Johnson,
Rousseau, Burns" (1841), by Thomas
Carlyle [excerpt] DLB-57

The Hero as Poet. Dante; Shakspeare (1841),
by Thomas Carlyle DLB-32

Heron, Robert 1764-1807 .... DLB-142

Herrera, Juan Felipe 1948- DLB-122

Herrick, Robert 1591-1674 .... DLB-126

Herrick, Robert 1868-1938 .... DLB-9, 12, 78

Herrick, William 1915- Y-83

Herrick, E. R., and Company DLB-49

Herrmann, John 1900-1959 .... DLB-4

Hersey, John 1914-1993 .... DLB-6

Hertel, François 1905-1985 .... DLB-68

Hervé-Bazin, Jean Pierre Marie (see Bazin,
Hervé)

Hervey, John, Lord 1696-1743 ..... DLB-101

Herwig, Georg 1817-1875 .... DLB-133

Herzog, Emile Salomon Wilhelm (see Maurois,
André)

Hesse, Hermann 1877-1962 .... DLB-66

Hewat, Alexander
circa 1743-circa 1824 .... DLB-30

Hewitt, John 1907- DLB-27

Hewlett, Maurice 1861-1923 .... DLB-34

Heyen, William 1940- DLB-5

Heyer, Georgette 1902-1974 .... DLB-77

Heym, Stefan 1913- DLB-69

Heyse, Paul 1830-1914 .... DLB-129

Heytesbury, William
circa 1310-1372 or 1373 .... DLB-115

Heyward, Dorothy 1890-1961 .... DLB-7

Heyward, DuBose
1885-1940 .... DLB-7, 9, 45

Heywood, John 1497?-1580? DLB-136

Heywood, Thomas
1573 or 1574-1641 .... DLB-62

Hibbs, Ben 1901-1975 .... DLB-137

Hickman, William Albert
1877-1957 .... DLB-92

Hidalgo, José Luis 1919-1947 ...... DLB-108

Hiebert, Paul 1892-1987 .... DLB-68

Hierro, José 1922- DLB-108

Higgins, Aidan 1927- DLB-14

Higgins, Colin 1941-1988 ....DLB-26

Higgins, George V. 1939- DLB-2; Y-81

Higginson, Thomas Wentworth
1823-1911 ....DLB-1, 64

Highwater, Jamake 1942?- ...DLB-52; Y-85

Hijuelos, Oscar 1951- DLB-145

Hildegard von Bingen
1098-1179 ....DLB-148

Das Hildesbrandslied circa 820 ....DLB-148

Hildesheimer, Wolfgang
1916-1991 ....DLB-69, 124

Hildreth, Richard
1807-1865 ....DLB-1, 30, 59

Hill, Aaron 1685-1750 ....DLB-84

Hill, Geoffrey 1932- DLB-40

Hill, "Sir" John 1714?-1775 ....DLB-39

Hill, Leslie 1880-1960 ....DLB-51

Hill, Susan 1942- DLB-14, 139

Hill, Walter 1942- DLB-44

Hill and Wang DLB-46

Hill, George M., Company DLB-49

Hill, Lawrence, and Company,
Publishers DLB-46

Hillberry, Conrad 1928- DLB-120

Hilliard, Gray and Company DLB-49

Hills, Lee 1906- DLB-127

Hillyer, Robert 1895-1961 ....DLB-54

Hilton, James 1900-1954 ....DLB-34, 77

Hilton, Walter died 1396 ....DLB-146

Hilton and Company DLB-49

Himes, Chester
1909-1984 ....DLB-2, 76, 143

Hine, Daryl 1936- DLB-60

Hinojosa-Smith, Rolando
1929- DLB-82

Hippel, Theodor Gottlieb von
1741-1796 ....DLB-97

Hirsch, E. D., Jr. 1928- DLB-67

Hirsch, Edward 1950- DLB-120

The History of the Adventures of Joseph Andrews
(1742), by Henry Fielding
[excerpt] DLB-39

Hoagland, Edward 1932- DLB-6

Hoagland, Everett H., III 1942- DLB-41

Hoban, Russell 1925- DLB-52

Hobbes, Thomas 1588-1679 ....DLB-151

Hobby, Oveta 1905- DLB-127

Hobby, William 1878-1964 ....DLB-127

Hobsbaum, Philip 1932- DLB-40

Hobson, Laura Z. 1900- DLB-28

Hoby, Thomas 1530-1566 .... DLB-132

Hoccleve, Thomas
circa 1368-circa 1437 .... DLB-146

Hochhuth, Rolf 1931- DLB-124

Hochman, Sandra 1936- DLB-5

Hodder and Stoughton, Limited ... DLB-106

Hodgins, Jack 1938- DLB-60

Hodgman, Helen 1945- DLB-14

Hodgson, Ralph 1871-1962 .... DLB-19

Hodgson, William Hope
1877-1918 .... DLB-70

Hoffenstein, Samuel 1890-1947 ..... DLB-11

Hoffman, Charles Fenno
1806-1884 ....DLB-3

Hoffman, Daniel 1923- DLB-5

Hoffmann, E. T. A. 1776-1822 ...... DLB-90

Hofmann, Michael 1957- DLB-40

Hofmannsthal, Hugo von
1874-1929 .... DLB-81, 118

Hofstadter, Richard 1916-1970 ..... DLB-17

Hogan, Desmond 1950- DLB-14

Hogan and Thompson DLB-49

Hogarth Press DLB-112

Hogg, James 1770-1835 .... DLB-93, 116

Hohl, Ludwig 1904-1980 .... DLB-56

Holbrook, David 1923- DLB-14, 40

Holcroft, Thomas 1745-1809 .... DLB-39, 89

Holden, Jonathan 1941- DLB-105

Holden, Jonathan, Contemporary
Verse Story-telling DLB-105

Holden, Molly 1927-1981 .... DLB-40

Hölderlin, Friedrich 1770-1843 ..... DLB-90

Holiday House DLB-46

Holland, Norman N. 1927- DLB-67

Hollander, John 1929- DLB-5

Holley, Marietta 1836-1926 .... DLB-11

Hollingsworth, Margaret 1940- DLB-60

Hollo, Anselm 1934- DLB-40

Holloway, Emory 1885-1977 ...... DLB-103

Holloway, John 1920- DLB-27

Holloway House Publishing
Company DLB-46

Holme, Constance 1880-1955 ...... DLB-34

Holmes, Abraham S. 1821?-1908 ... DLB-99

Holmes, John Clellon 1926-1988 .... DLB-16

Holmes, Oliver Wendell
1809-1894 ....DLB-1

Holst, Hermann E. von
1841-1904 ....DLB-47

Holt, John 1721-1784 .... DLB-43

Holt, Henry, and Company DLB-49

Holt, Rinehart and Winston DLB-46

Holthusen, Hans Egon 1913- DLB-69

Hölty, Ludwig Christoph Heinrich
1748-1776 .... DLB-94

Holz, Arno 1863-1929 .... DLB-118

Home, Henry, Lord Kames (see Kames, Henry
Home, Lord)

Home, John 1722-1808 .... DLB-84

Home, William Douglas 1912- DLB-13

Home Publishing Company DLB-49

Homes, Geoffrey (see Mainwaring, Daniel)

Honan, Park 1928- DLB-111

Hone, William 1780-1842 .... DLB-110

Hongo, Garrett Kaoru 1951- DLB-120

Honig, Edwin 1919- DLB-5

Hood, Hugh 1928- DLB-53

Hood, Thomas 1799-1845 .... DLB-96

Hook, Theodore 1788-1841 .... DLB-116

Hooker, Jeremy 1941- DLB-40

Hooker, Richard 1554-1600 .... DLB-132

Hooker, Thomas 1586-1647 .... DLB-24

Hooper, Johnson Jones
1815-1862 ....DLB-3, 11

Hopkins, Gerard Manley
1844-1889 ....DLB-35, 57

Hopkins, John (see Sternhold, Thomas)

Hopkins, Lemuel 1750-1801 .... DLB-37

Hopkins, Pauline Elizabeth
1859-1930 .... DLB-50

Hopkins, Samuel 1721-1803 .... DLB-31

Hopkins, John H., and Son DLB-46

Hopkinson, Francis 1737-1791 ...... DLB-31

Horgan, Paul 1903- DLB-102; Y-85

Horizon Press DLB-46

Horne, Frank 1899-1974 .... DLB-51

Horne, Richard Henry (Hengist)
1802 or 1803-1884 .... DLB-32

Hornung, E. W. 1866-1921 .... DLB-70

Horovitz, Israel 1939- DLB-7

Horton, George Moses
1797?-1883? DLB-50

Horváth, Ödön von
1901-1938 .... DLB-85, 124

Horwood, Harold 1923- DLB-60

Hosford, E. and E.
[publishing house] DLB-49

Hoskyns, John 1566-1638 ....DLB-121

Hotchkiss and Company DLB-49

Hough, Emerson 1857-1923 ....DLB-9

Houghton Mifflin Company DLB-49

Houghton, Stanley 1881-1913 ....DLB-10

Household, Geoffrey 1900-1988 .....DLB-87

Housman, A. E. 1859-1936 ....DLB-19

Housman, Laurence 1865-1959 ......DLB-10

Houwald, Ernst von 1778-1845 ......DLB-90

Hovey, Richard 1864-1900 ....DLB-54

Howard, Donald R. 1927-1987 .....DLB-111

Howard, Maureen 1930- Y-83

Howard, Richard 1929- DLB-5

Howard, Roy W. 1883-1964 ....DLB-29

Howard, Sidney 1891-1939 ...... DLB-7, 26

Howe, E. W. 1853-1937 .... DLB-12, 25

Howe, Henry 1816-1893 ....DLB-30

Howe, Irving 1920-1993 ....DLB-67

Howe, Joseph 1804-1873 ....DLB-99

Howe, Julia Ward 1819-1910 ....DLB-1

Howe, Percival Presland
1886-1944 ....DLB-149

Howe, Susan 1937- DLB-120

Howell, Clark, Sr. 1863-1936 ....DLB-25

Howell, Evan P. 1839-1905 ....DLB-23

Howell, James 1594?-1666 ....DLB-151

Howell, Warren Richardson
1912-1984 ....DLB-140

Howell, Soskin and Company DLB-46

Howells, William Dean
1837-1920 .... DLB-12, 64, 74, 79

Howitt, William 1792-1879 and
Howitt, Mary 1799-1888 ....DLB-110

Hoyem, Andrew 1935- DLB-5

Hoyos, Angela de 1940- DLB-82

Hoyt, Palmer 1897-1979 ....DLB-127

Hoyt, Henry [publishing house] DLB-49

Hrabanus Maurus 776?-856 ....DLB-148

Hrotsvit of Gandersheim
circa 935-circa 1000 ....DLB-148

Hubbard, Elbert 1856-1915 ....DLB-91

Hubbard, Kin 1868-1930 ....DLB-11

Hubbard, William circa 1621-1704 ...DLB-24

Huber, Therese 1764-1829 ....DLB-90

Huch, Friedrich 1873-1913 ....DLB-66

Huch, Ricarda 1864-1947 ....DLB-66

Huck at 100: How Old Is
    Huckleberry Finn? Y-85

Huddle, David 1942- DLB-130

Hudgins, Andrew 1951- DLB-120

Hudson, Henry Norman
    1814-1886 ....DLB-64

Hudson, W. H. 1841-1922 ....DLB-98

Hudson and Goodwin DLB-49

Huebsch, B. W.
    [publishing house] DLB-46

Hughes, David 1930- DLB-14

Hughes, John 1677-1720 ....DLB-84

Hughes, Langston
    1902-1967 .... DLB-4, 7, 48, 51, 86

Hughes, Richard 1900-1976 ....DLB-15

Hughes, Ted 1930- DLB-40

Hughes, Thomas 1822-1896 ....DLB-18

Hugo, Richard 1923-1982 ....DLB-5

Hugo, Victor 1802-1885 ....DLB-119

Hugo Awards and Nebula Awards DLB-8

Hull, Richard 1896-1973 ....DLB-77

Hulme, T. E. 1883-1917 ....DLB-19

Humboldt, Alexander von
    1769-1859 ....DLB-90

Humboldt, Wilhelm von
    1767-1835 ....DLB-90

Hume, David 1711-1776 ....DLB-104

Hume, Fergus 1859-1932 ....DLB-70

Hummer, T. R. 1950- DLB-120

Humorous Book Illustration DLB-11

Humphrey, William 1924- DLB-6

Humphreys, David 1752-1818 ....DLB-37

Humphreys, Emyr 1919- DLB-15

Huncke, Herbert 1915- DLB-16

Huneker, James Gibbons
    1857-1921 ....DLB-71

Hunt, Irene 1907- DLB-52

Hunt, Leigh 1784-1859 .... DLB-96, 110, 144

Hunt, William Gibbes 1791-1833 ....DLB-73

Hunter, Evan 1926- Y-82

Hunter, Jim 1939- DLB-14

Hunter, Kristin 1931- DLB-33

Hunter, N. C. 1908-1971 ....DLB-10

Hunter-Duvar, John 1821-1899 .....DLB-99

Huntington, Henry E.
    1850-1927 .... DLB-140

Hurd and Houghton DLB-49

Hurst, Fannie 1889-1968 ....DLB-86

Hurst and Blackett DLB-106

Hurst and Company DLB-49

Hurston, Zora Neale
    1901?-1960 .... DLB-51, 86

Husson, Jules-François-Félix (see Champfleury)

Huston, John 1906-1987 ....DLB-26

Hutcheson, Francis 1694-1746 ......DLB-31

Hutchinson, Thomas
    1711-1780 .... DLB-30, 31

Hutchinson and Company
    (Publishers) Limited DLB-112

Hutton, Richard Holt 1826-1897 ....DLB-57

Huxley, Aldous 1894-1963 .....DLB-36, 100

Huxley, Elspeth Josceline 1907- ...DLB-77

Huxley, T. H. 1825-1895 ....DLB-57

Huyghue, Douglas Smith
    1816-1891 ....DLB-99

Huysmans, Joris-Karl 1848-1907 ...DLB-123

Hyman, Trina Schart 1939- DLB-61

I

Iavorsky, Stefan 1658-1722 ....DLB-150

Ibn Bajja circa 1077-1138 ....DLB-115

Ibn Gabirol, Solomon
    circa 1021-circa 1058 ....DLB-115

The Iconography of Science-Fiction
    Art DLB-8

Iffland, August Wilhelm
    1759-1814 ....DLB-94

Ignatow, David 1914- DLB-5

Iles, Francis (see Berkeley, Anthony)

The Illustration of Early German
    Literary Manuscripts,
    circa 1150-circa 1300 ....DLB-148

Imbs, Bravig 1904-1946 ....DLB-4

Immermann, Karl 1796-1840 ......DLB-133

Inchbald, Elizabeth 1753-1821 ... DLB-39, 89

Inge, William 1913-1973 ....DLB-7

Ingelow, Jean 1820-1897 ....DLB-35

Ingersoll, Ralph 1900-1985 ....DLB-127

The Ingersoll Prizes Y-84

Ingraham, Joseph Holt 1809-1860 .....DLB-3

Inman, John 1805-1850 ....DLB-73

Innerhofer, Franz 1944- DLB-85

Innis, Harold Adams 1894-1952 .....DLB-88

Innis, Mary Quayle 1899-1972 ......DLB-88

International Publishers Company ...DLB-46

An Interview with David Rabe Y-91

An Interview with George Greenfield,
    Literary Agent Y-91

An Interview with James Ellroy Y-91

An Interview with Peter S. Prescott Y-86

An Interview with Russell Hoban Y-90

An Interview with Tom Jenks Y-86

Introduction to Paul Laurence Dunbar,
    Lyrics of Lowly Life (1896),
    by William Dean Howells DLB-50

Introductory Essay: Letters of Percy Bysshe
    Shelley (1852), by Robert
    Browning DLB-32

Introductory Letters from the Second Edition
    of Pamela (1741), by Samuel
    Richardson DLB-39

Irving, John 1942- DLB-6; Y-82

Irving, Washington
    1783-1859 ..... DLB-3, 11, 30, 59, 73, 74

Irwin, Grace 1907- DLB-68

Irwin, Will 1873-1948 ....DLB-25

Isherwood, Christopher
    1904-1986 ....DLB-15; Y-86

The Island Trees Case: A Symposium on
    School Library Censorship
    An Interview with Judith Krug
    An Interview with Phyllis Schlafly
    An Interview with Edward B. Jenkinson
    An Interview with Lamarr Mooneyham
    An Interview with Harriet
    Bernstein Y-82

Islas, Arturo 1938-1991 ....DLB-122

Ivers, M. J., and Company DLB-49

J

Jackmon, Marvin E. (see Marvin X)

Jacks, L. P. 1860-1955 ....DLB-135

Jackson, Angela 1951- DLB-41

Jackson, Helen Hunt
    1830-1885 ....DLB-42, 47

Jackson, Holbrook 1874-1948 ....DLB-98

Jackson, Laura Riding 1901-1991 ....DLB-48

Jackson, Shirley 1919-1965 ....DLB-6

Jacob, Piers Anthony Dillingham (see Anthony, Piers)

Jacobi, Friedrich Heinrich 1743-1819 .... DLB-94

Jacobi, Johann Georg 1740-1841 .... DLB-97

Jacobs, Joseph 1854-1916 .... DLB-141

Jacobs, W. W. 1863-1943 .... DLB-135

Jacobs, George W., and Company ... DLB-49

Jacobson, Dan 1929- DLB-14

Jahier, Piero 1884-1966 .... DLB-114

Jahnn, Hans Henny 1894-1959 .... DLB-56, 124

Jakes, John 1932- Y-83

James, C. L. R. 1901-1989 .... DLB-125

James, George P. R. 1801-1860 .... DLB-116

James, Henry 1843-1916 ..... DLB-12, 71, 74

James, John circa 1633-1729 .... DLB-24

The James Jones Society Y-92

James, P. D. 1920- DLB-87

James Joyce Centenary: Dublin, 1982 ... Y-82

James Joyce Conference Y-85

James VI of Scotland, I of England 1566-1625 .... DLB-151

James, U. P. [publishing house] DLB-49

Jameson, Anna 1794-1860 .... DLB-99

Jameson, Fredric 1934- DLB-67

Jameson, J. Franklin 1859-1937 ..... DLB-17

Jameson, Storm 1891-1986 .... DLB-36

Janés, Clara 1940- DLB-134

Jaramillo, Cleofas M. 1878-1956 ... DLB-122

Jarman, Mark 1952- DLB-120

Jarrell, Randall 1914-1965 ...... DLB-48, 52

Jarrold and Sons DLB-106

Jasmin, Claude 1930- DLB-60

Jay, John 1745-1829 .... DLB-31

Jefferies, Richard 1848-1887 .... DLB-98, 141

Jeffers, Lance 1919-1985 .... DLB-41

Jeffers, Robinson 1887-1962 .... DLB-45

Jefferson, Thomas 1743-1826 .... DLB-31

Jelinek, Elfriede 1946- DLB-85

Jellicoe, Ann 1927- DLB-13

Jenkins, Robin 1912- DLB-14

Jenkins, William Fitzgerald (see Leinster, Murray)

Jenkins, Herbert, Limited DLB-112

Jennings, Elizabeth 1926- DLB-27

Jens, Walter 1923- DLB-69

Jensen, Merrill 1905-1980 .... DLB-17

Jephson, Robert 1736-1803 .... DLB-89

Jerome, Jerome K. 1859-1927 .... DLB-10, 34, 135

Jerome, Judson 1927-1991 .... DLB-105

Jerome, Judson, Reflections: After a Tornado DLB-105

Jesse, F. Tennyson 1888-1958 .... DLB-77

Jewett, Sarah Orne 1849-1909 .... DLB-12, 74

Jewett, John P., and Company DLB-49

The Jewish Publication Society DLB-49

Jewitt, John Rodgers 1783-1821 ..... DLB-99

Jewsbury, Geraldine 1812-1880 ..... DLB-21

Jhabvala, Ruth Prawer 1927- DLB-139

Jiménez, Juan Ramón 1881-1958 .... DLB-134

Joans, Ted 1928- DLB-16, 41

John, Eugenie (see Marlitt, E.)

John of Dumbleton circa 1310-circa 1349 .... DLB-115

John Edward Bruce: Three Documents DLB-50

John O'Hara's Pottsville Journalism Y-88

John Steinbeck Research Center Y-85

John Webster: The Melbourne Manuscript Y-86

Johnson, B. S. 1933-1973 .... DLB-14, 40

Johnson, Charles 1679-1748 .... DLB-84

Johnson, Charles R. 1948- DLB-33

Johnson, Charles S. 1893-1956 ... DLB-51, 91

Johnson, Denis 1949- DLB-120

Johnson, Diane 1934- Y-80

Johnson, Edgar 1901- DLB-103

Johnson, Edward 1598-1672 .... DLB-24

Johnson, Fenton 1888-1958 ...... DLB-45, 50

Johnson, Georgia Douglas 1886-1966 .... DLB-51

Johnson, Gerald W. 1890-1980 ...... DLB-29

Johnson, Helene 1907- DLB-51

Johnson, James Weldon 1871-1938 .... DLB-51

Johnson, John H. 1918- DLB-137

Johnson, Lionel 1867-1902 .... DLB-19

Johnson, Nunnally 1897-1977 .... DLB-26

Johnson, Owen 1878-1952 .... Y-87

Johnson, Pamela Hansford 1912- DLB-15

Johnson, Pauline 1861-1913 .... DLB-92

Johnson, Samuel 1696-1772 .... DLB-24

Johnson, Samuel 1709-1784 .... DLB-39, 95, 104, 142

Johnson, Samuel 1822-1882 .... DLB-1

Johnson, Uwe 1934-1984 .... DLB-75

Johnson, Benjamin [publishing house] DLB-49

Johnson, Benjamin, Jacob, and Robert [publishing house] DLB-49

Johnson, Jacob, and Company DLB-49

Johnston, Annie Fellows 1863-1931 .... DLB-42

Johnston, Basil H. 1929- DLB-60

Johnston, Denis 1901-1984 .... DLB-10

Johnston, George 1913- DLB-88

Johnston, Jennifer 1930- DLB-14

Johnston, Mary 1870-1936 .... DLB-9

Johnston, Richard Malcolm 1822-1898 .... DLB-74

Johnstone, Charles 1719?-1800? DLB-39

Johst, Hanns 1890-1978 .... DLB-124

Jolas, Eugene 1894-1952 .... DLB-4, 45

Jones, Alice C. 1853-1933 .... DLB-92

Jones, Charles C., Jr. 1831-1893 ..... DLB-30

Jones, D. G. 1929- DLB-53

Jones, David 1895-1974 .... DLB-20, 100

Jones, Ebenezer 1820-1860 .... DLB-32

Jones, Ernest 1819-1868 .... DLB-32

Jones, Gayl 1949- DLB-33

Jones, Glyn 1905- DLB-15

Jones, Gwyn 1907- DLB-15, 139

Jones, Henry Arthur 1851-1929 ...... DLB-10

Jones, Hugh circa 1692-1760 .... DLB-24

Jones, James 1921-1977 .... DLB-2, 143

Jones, Jenkin Lloyd 1911- DLB-127

Jones, LeRoi (see Baraka, Amiri)

Jones, Lewis 1897-1939 .... DLB-15

Jones, Major Joseph (see Thompson, William Tappan)

Jones, Preston 1936-1979 .... DLB-7

Jones, Rodney 1950- DLB-120

Jones, Sir William 1746-1794 .... DLB-109

Jones, William Alfred 1817-1900 ..... DLB-59

Jones's Publishing House DLB-49

Jong, Erica 1942- DLB-2, 5, 28

Jonke, Gert F. 1946- DLB-85

Jonson, Ben 1572?-1637 ....DLB-62, 121

Jordan, June 1936- DLB-38

Joseph, Jenny 1932- DLB-40

Joseph, Michael, Limited DLB-112

Josephson, Matthew 1899-1978 ....DLB-4

Josiah Allen's Wife (see Holley, Marietta)

Josipovici, Gabriel 1940- DLB-14

Josselyn, John ?-1675 ....DLB-24

Joudry, Patricia 1921- DLB-88

Jovine, Giuseppe 1922- DLB-128

Joyaux, Philippe (see Sollers, Philippe)

Joyce, Adrien (see Eastman, Carol)

Joyce, James 1882-1941 ..... DLB-10, 19, 36

Judd, Sylvester 1813-1853 ....DLB-1

Judd, Orange, Publishing
   Company DLB-49

Judith circa 930 ....DLB-146

Julian of Norwich
   1342-circa 1420 ....DLB-1146

Julian Symons at Eighty Y-92

June, Jennie (see Croly, Jane Cunningham)

Jung, Franz 1888-1963 ....DLB-118

Jünger, Ernst 1895- DLB-56

Der jüngere Titurel circa 1275 ....DLB-138

Jung-Stilling, Johann Heinrich
   1740-1817 ....DLB-94

Justice, Donald 1925- Y-83

K

Kacew, Romain (see Gary, Romain)

Kafka, Franz 1883-1924 ....DLB-81

Kaiser, Georg 1878-1945 ....DLB-124

Kaiserchronik circca 1147 ....DLB-148

Kalechofsky, Roberta 1931- DLB-28

Kaler, James Otis 1848-1912 ....DLB-12

Kames, Henry Home, Lord
   1696-1782 ....DLB-31, 104

Kandel, Lenore 1932- DLB-16

Kanin, Garson 1912- DLB-7

Kant, Hermann 1926- DLB-75

Kant, Immanuel 1724-1804 ....DLB-94

Kantemir, Antiokh Dmitrievich
   1708-1744 ....DLB-150

Kantor, Mackinlay 1904-1977 ....DLB-9, 102

Kaplan, Fred 1937- DLB-111

Kaplan, Johanna 1942- DLB-28

Kaplan, Justin 1925- DLB-111

Kapnist, Vasilii Vasilevich
   1758?-1823 ....DLB-150

Karadžić, Vuk Stefanović
   1787-1864 ....DLB-147

Karamzin, Nikolai Mikhailovich
   1766-1826 ....DLB-150

Karsch, Anna Louisa 1722-1791 .....DLB-97

Kasack, Hermann 1896-1966 ....DLB-69

Kaschnitz, Marie Luise 1901-1974 ...DLB-69

Kaštelan, Jure 1919-1990 ....DLB-147

Kästner, Erich 1899-1974 ....DLB-56

Kattan, Naim 1928- DLB-53

Katz, Steve 1935- Y-83

Kauffman, Janet 1945- Y-86

Kauffmann, Samuel 1898-1971 .....DLB-127

Kaufman, Bob 1925- DLB-16, 41

Kaufman, George S. 1889-1961 ......DLB-7

Kavanagh, P. J. 1931- DLB-40

Kavanagh, Patrick 1904-1967 ....DLB-15, 20

Kaye-Smith, Sheila 1887-1956 ....DLB-36

Kazin, Alfred 1915- DLB-67

Keane, John B. 1928- DLB-13

Keating, H. R. F. 1926- DLB-87

Keats, Ezra Jack 1916-1983 ....DLB-61

Keats, John 1795-1821 ....DLB-96, 110

Keble, John 1792-1866 ....DLB-32, 55

Keeble, John 1944- Y-83

Keeffe, Barrie 1945- DLB-13

Keeley, James 1867-1934 ....DLB-25

W. B. Keen, Cooke
   and Company DLB-49

Keillor, Garrison 1942- Y-87

Keith, Marian 1874?-1961 ....DLB-92

Keller, Gary D. 1943- DLB-82

Keller, Gottfried 1819-1890 ....DLB-129

Kelley, Edith Summers 1884-1956 ....DLB-9

Kelley, William Melvin 1937- DLB-33

Kellogg, Ansel Nash 1832-1886 .....DLB-23

Kellogg, Steven 1941- DLB-61

Kelly, George 1887-1974 ....DLB-7

Kelly, Hugh 1739-1777 ....DLB-89

Kelly, Robert 1935- DLB-5, 130

Kelly, Piet and Company DLB-49

Kelmscott Press DLB-112

Kemble, Fanny 1809-1893 ....DLB-32

Kemelman, Harry 1908- DLB-28

Kempe, Margery
   circa 1373-1438 ....DLB-146

Kempner, Friederike 1836-1904 ....DLB-129

Kempowski, Walter 1929- DLB-75

Kendall, Claude
   [publishing company] DLB-46

Kendell, George 1809-1867 ....DLB-43

Kenedy, P. J., and Sons DLB-49

Kennedy, Adrienne 1931- DLB-38

Kennedy, John Pendleton 1795-1870 ...DLB-3

Kennedy, Leo 1907- DLB-88

Kennedy, Margaret 1896-1967 ......DLB-36

Kennedy, Richard S. 1920- DLB-111

Kennedy, William 1928- DLB-143; Y-85

Kennedy, X. J. 1929- DLB-5

Kennelly, Brendan 1936- DLB-40

Kenner, Hugh 1923- DLB-67

Kennerley, Mitchell
   [publishing house] DLB-46

Kent, Frank R. 1877-1958 ....DLB-29

Kenyon, Jane 1947- DLB-120

Keppler and Schwartzmann DLB-49

Kerner, Justinus 1776-1862 ....DLB-90

Kerouac, Jack 1922-1969 ... DLB-2, 16; DS-3

Kerouac, Jan 1952- DLB-16

Kerr, Orpheus C. (see Newell, Robert Henry)

Kerr, Charles H., and Company DLB-49

Kesey, Ken 1935- DLB-2, 16

Kessel, Joseph 1898-1979 ....DLB-72

Kessel, Martin 1901- DLB-56

Kesten, Hermann 1900- DLB-56

Keun, Irmgard 1905-1982 ....DLB-69

Key and Biddle DLB-49

Keynes, John Maynard 1883-1946 .... DS-10

Keyserling, Eduard von 1855-1918 ...DLB-66

Khan, Ismith 1925- DLB-125

Khemnitser, Ivan Ivanovich
   1745-1784 ....DLB-150

Kheraskov, Mikhail Matveevich
   1733-1807 ....DLB-150

Khvostov, Dmitrii Ivanovich
   1757-1835 ....DLB-150

Kidd, Adam 1802?-1831 ....DLB-99

Kidd, William
   [publishing house] DLB-106

Kiely, Benedict 1919- DLB-15

Kiggins and Kellogg DLB-49

Kiley, Jed 1889-1962 .... DLB-4

Kilgore, Bernard 1908-1967 .... DLB-127

Killens, John Oliver 1916- DLB-33

Killigrew, Anne 1660-1685 .... DLB-131

Killigrew, Thomas 1612-1683 ...... DLB-58

Kilmer, Joyce 1886-1918 .... DLB-45

Kilwardby, Robert
circa 1215-1279 .... DLB-115

King, Clarence 1842-1901 .... DLB-12

King, Florence 1936 .... Y-85

King, Francis 1923- DLB-15, 139

King, Grace 1852-1932 .... DLB-12, 78

King, Henry 1592-1669 .... DLB-126

King, Stephen 1947- DLB-143; Y-80

King, Woodie, Jr. 1937- DLB-38

King, Solomon [publishing house] ... DLB-49

Kinglake, Alexander William
1809-1891 .... DLB-55

Kingsley, Charles 1819-1875 .... DLB-21, 32

Kingsley, Henry 1830-1876 .... DLB-21

Kingsley, Sidney 1906- DLB-7

Kingsmill, Hugh 1889-1949 .... DLB-149

Kingston, Maxine Hong 1940- Y-80

Kinnell, Galway 1927- DLB-5; Y-87

Kinsella, Thomas 1928- DLB-27

Kipling, Rudyard
1865-1936 .... DLB-19, 34, 141

Kipphardt, Heinar 1922-1982 ...... DLB-124

Kirby, William 1817-1906 .... DLB-99

Kirk, John Foster 1824-1904 .... DLB-79

Kirkconnell, Watson 1895-1977 ..... DLB-68

Kirkland, Caroline M.
1801-1864 .... DLB-3, 73, 74

Kirkland, Joseph 1830-1893 .... DLB-12

Kirkpatrick, Clayton 1915- DLB-127

Kirkup, James 1918- DLB-27

Kirouac, Conrad (see Marie-Victorin, Frère)

Kirsch, Sarah 1935- DLB-75

Kirst, Hans Hellmut 1914-1989 ..... DLB-69

Kitcat, Mabel Greenhow
1859-1922 ....DLB-135

Kitchin, C. H. B. 1895-1967 .... DLB-77

Kizer, Carolyn 1925- DLB-5

Klabund 1890-1928 .... DLB-66

Klappert, Peter 1942- DLB-5

Klass, Philip (see Tenn, William)

Klein, A. M. 1909-1972 .... DLB-68

Kleist, Ewald von 1715-1759 .... DLB-97

Kleist, Heinrich von 1777-1811 ..... DLB-90

Klinger, Friedrich Maximilian
1752-1831 .... DLB-94

Klopstock, Friedrich Gottlieb
1724-1803 .... DLB-97

Klopstock, Meta 1728-1758 .... DLB-97

Kluge, Alexander 1932- DLB-75

Knapp, Joseph Palmer 1864-1951 .... DLB-91

Knapp, Samuel Lorenzo
1783-1838 .... DLB-59

Kniazhnin, Iakov Borisovich
1740-1791 .... DLB-150

Knickerbocker, Diedrich (see Irving,
Washington)

Knigge, Adolph Franz Friedrich Ludwig,
Freiherr von 1752-1796 .... DLB-94

Knight, Damon 1922- DLB-8

Knight, Etheridge 1931-1992 .... DLB-41

Knight, John S. 1894-1981 .... DLB-29

Knight, Sarah Kemble 1666-1727 .... DLB-24

Knight, Charles, and Company DLB-106

Knister, Raymond 1899-1932 .... DLB-68

Knoblock, Edward 1874-1945 ...... DLB-10

Knopf, Alfred A. 1892-1984 ....Y-84

Knopf, Alfred A.
[publishing house] DLB-46

Knowles, John 1926- DLB-6

Knox, Frank 1874-1944 .... DLB-29

Knox, John circa 1514-1572 .... DLB-132

Knox, John Armoy 1850-1906 ...... DLB-23

Knox, Ronald Arbuthnott
1888-1957 .... DLB-77

Kober, Arthur 1900-1975 .... DLB-11

Kocbek, Edvard 1904-1981 .... DLB-147

Koch, Howard 1902- DLB-26

Koch, Kenneth 1925- DLB-5

Koenigsberg, Moses 1879-1945 ...... DLB-25

Koeppen, Wolfgang 1906- DLB-69

Koertge, Ronald 1940- DLB-105

Koestler, Arthur 1905-1983 ....Y-83

Kokoschka, Oskar 1886-1980 ...... DLB-124

Kolb, Annette 1870-1967 .... DLB-66

Kolbenheyer, Erwin Guido
1878-1962 .... DLB-66, 124

Kolleritsch, Alfred 1931- DLB-85

Kolodny, Annette 1941- DLB-67

Komarov, Matvei
circa 1730-1812 ....DLB-150

Komroff, Manuel 1890-1974 ....DLB-4

Komunyakaa, Yusef 1947- DLB-120

Konigsburg, E. L. 1930- DLB-52

Konrad von Würzburg
circa 1230-1287 ....DLB-138

Konstantinov, Aleko 1863-1897 .....DLB-147

Kooser, Ted 1939- DLB-105

Kopit, Arthur 1937- DLB-7

Kops, Bernard 1926?- DLB-13

Kornbluth, C. M. 1923-1958 ....DLB-8

Körner, Theodor 1791-1813 ....DLB-90

Kornfeld, Paul 1889-1942 ....DLB-118

Kosinski, Jerzy 1933-1991 ...... DLB-2; Y-82

Kosovel, Srečko 1904-1926 ....DLB-147

Kostrov, Ermil Ivanovich
1755-1796 ....DLB-150

Kotzebue, August von 1761-1819 ....DLB-94

Kovačić, Ante 1854-1889 ....DLB-147

Kraf, Elaine 1946- Y-81

Kranjčević, Silvije Strahimir
1865-1908 ....DLB-147

Krasna, Norman 1909-1984 ....DLB-26

Kraus, Karl 1874-1936 ....DLB-118

Krauss, Ruth 1911-1993 ....DLB-52

Kreisel, Henry 1922- DLB-88

Kreuder, Ernst 1903-1972 ....DLB-69

Kreymborg, Alfred 1883-1966 .... DLB-4, 54

Krieger, Murray 1923- DLB-67

Krim, Seymour 1922-1989 ....DLB-16

Krleža, Miroslav 1893-1981 ....DLB-147

Krock, Arthur 1886-1974 ....DLB-29

Kroetsch, Robert 1927- DLB-53

Krutch, Joseph Wood 1893-1970 .....DLB-63

Krylov, Ivan Andreevich
1769-1844 ....DLB-150

Kubin, Alfred 1877-1959 ....DLB-81

Kubrick, Stanley 1928- DLB-26

Kudrun circa 1230-1240 ....DLB-138

Kumin, Maxine 1925- DLB-5

Kunene, Mazisi 1930- DLB-117

Kunitz, Stanley 1905- DLB-48

Kunjufu, Johari M. (see Amini, Johari M.)

Kunnert, Gunter 1929- DLB-75

Kunze, Reiner 1933- DLB-75

Kupferberg, Tuli 1923- DLB-16

Kürnberger, Ferdinand
  1821-1879 ....DLB-129

Kurz, Isolde 1853-1944 ....DLB-66

Kusenberg, Kurt 1904-1983 ....DLB-69

Kuttner, Henry 1915-1958 ....DLB-8

Kyd, Thomas 1558-1594 ....DLB-62

Kyftin, Maurice
  circa 1560?-1598 ....DLB-136

Kyger, Joanne 1934- DLB-16

Kyne, Peter B. 1880-1957 ....DLB-78

L

L. E. L. (see Landon, Letitia Elizabeth)

Laberge, Albert 1871-1960 ....DLB-68

Laberge, Marie 1950- DLB-60

Lacombe, Patrice (see Trullier-Lacombe,
  Joseph Patrice)

Lacretelle, Jacques de 1888-1985 .....DLB-65

Ladd, Joseph Brown 1764-1786 ......DLB-37

La Farge, Oliver 1901-1963 ....DLB-9

Lafferty, R. A. 1914- DLB-8

La Guma, Alex 1925-1985 ....DLB-117

Lahaise, Guillaume (see Delahaye, Guy)

Lahontan, Louis-Armand de Lom d'Arce,
  Baron de 1666-1715? DLB-99

Laird, Carobeth 1895- Y-82

Laird and Lee DLB-49

Lalonde, Michèle 1937- DLB-60

Lamantia, Philip 1927- DLB-16

Lamb, Charles 1775-1834 .....DLB-93, 107

Lamb, Lady Caroline 1785-1828 ....DLB-116

Lambert, Betty 1933-1983 ....DLB-60

Lamming, George 1927- DLB-125

L'Amour, Louis 1908?- Y-80

Lampman, Archibald 1861-1899 .....DLB-92

Lamson, Wolffe and Company DLB-49

Lancer Books DLB-46

Landesman, Jay 1919- and
  Landesman, Fran 1927- DLB-16

Landon, Letitia Elizabeth 1802-1838 .DLB-96

Landor, Walter Savage
  1775-1864 ....DLB-93, 107

Landry, Napoléon-P. 1884-1956 .....DLB-92

Lane, Charles 1800-1870 ....DLB-1

Lane, Laurence W. 1890-1967 ......DLB-91

Lane, M. Travis 1934- DLB-60

Lane, Patrick 1939- DLB-53

Lane, Pinkie Gordon 1923- DLB-41

Lane, John, Company DLB-49

Laney, Al 1896- DLB-4

Lang, Andrew 1844-1912 ......DLB-98, 141

Langevin, André 1927- DLB-60

Langgässer, Elisabeth 1899-1950 ....DLB-69

Langhorne, John 1735-1779 ....DLB-109

Langland, William
  circa 1330-circa 1400 ....DLB-146

Langton, Anna 1804-1893 ....DLB-99

Lanham, Edwin 1904-1979 ....DLB-4

Lanier, Sidney 1842-1881 ....DLB-64

Lanyer, Aemilia 1569-1645 ....DLB-121

Lapointe, Gatien 1931-1983 ....DLB-88

Lapointe, Paul-Marie 1929- DLB-88

Lardner, Ring 1885-1933 ....DLB-11, 25, 86

Lardner, Ring, Jr. 1915- DLB-26

Lardner 100: Ring Lardner
  Centennial Symposium Y-85

Larkin, Philip 1922-1985 ....DLB-27

La Roche, Sophie von 1730-1807 ....DLB-94

La Rocque, Gilbert 1943-1984 ......DLB-60

Laroque de Roquebrune, Robert (see Roquebrune, Robert de)

Larrick, Nancy 1910- DLB-61

Larsen, Nella 1893-1964 ....DLB-51

Lasker-Schüler, Else
  1869-1945 ....DLB-66, 124

Lasnier, Rina 1915- DLB-88

Lassalle, Ferdinand 1825-1864 .....DLB-129

Lathrop, Dorothy P. 1891-1980 .....DLB-22

Lathrop, George Parsons
  1851-1898 ....DLB-71

Lathrop, John, Jr. 1772-1820 ....DLB-37

Latimer, Hugh 1492?-1555 ....DLB-136

Latimore, Jewel Christine McLawler
  (see Amini, Johari M.)

Latymer, William 1498-1583 ......DLB-132

Laube, Heinrich 1806-1884 ....DLB-133

Laughlin, James 1914- DLB-48

Laumer, Keith 1925- DLB-8

Laurence, Margaret 1926-1987 ......DLB-53

Laurents, Arthur 1918- DLB-26

Laurie, Annie (see Black, Winifred)

Laut, Agnes Christiana 1871-1936 ...DLB-92

Lavater, Johann Kaspar 1741-1801 ...DLB-97

Lavin, Mary 1912- DLB-15

Lawes, Henry 1596-1662 ....DLB-126

Lawless, Anthony (see MacDonald, Philip)

Lawrence, D. H.
  1885-1930 ....DLB-10, 19, 36, 98

Lawrence, David 1888-1973 ....DLB-29

Lawrence, Seymour 1926-1994 ....Y-94

Lawson, John ?-1711 ....DLB-24

Lawson, Robert 1892-1957 ....DLB-22

Lawson, Victor F. 1850-1925 ....DLB-25

Layton, Irving 1912- DLB-88

LaZamon flourished circa 1200 .....DLB-146

Lazarević, Laza K. 1851-1890 ......DLB-147

Lea, Henry Charles 1825-1909 ......DLB-47

Lea, Sydney 1942- DLB-120

Lea, Tom 1907- DLB-6

Leacock, John 1729-1802 ....DLB-31

Leacock, Stephen 1869-1944 ....DLB-92

Lead, Jane Ward 1623-1704 ....DLB-131

Leadenhall Press DLB-106

Leapor, Mary 1722-1746 ....DLB-109

Lear, Edward 1812-1888 ....DLB-32

Leary, Timothy 1920- DLB-16

Leary, W. A., and Company DLB-49

Léautaud, Paul 1872-1956 ....DLB-65

Leavitt, David 1961- DLB-130

Leavitt and Allen DLB-49

le Carré, John 1931- DLB-87

Lécavelé, Roland (see Dorgeles, Roland)

Lechlitner, Ruth 1901- DLB-48

Leclerc, Félix 1914- DLB-60

Le Clézio, J. M. G. 1940- DLB-83

Lectures on Rhetoric and Belles Lettres (1783),
  by Hugh Blair [excerpts] DLB-31

Leder, Rudolf (see Hermlin, Stephan)

Lederer, Charles 1910-1976 ....DLB-26

Ledwidge, Francis 1887-1917 ......DLB-20

Lee, Dennis 1939- DLB-53

Lee, Don L. (see Madhubuti, Haki R.)

Lee, George W. 1894-1976 .... DLB-51

Lee, Harper 1926- DLB-6

Lee, Harriet (1757-1851) and
Lee, Sophia (1750-1824) DLB-39

Lee, Laurie 1914- DLB-27

Lee, Manfred B. (see Dannay, Frederic, and
Manfred B. Lee)

Lee, Nathaniel circa 1645 - 1692 .... DLB-80

Lee, Sir Sidney 1859-1926 .... DLB-149

Lee, Sir Sidney, "Principles of Biography," in *Elizabethan and Other Essays* DLB-149

Lee, Vernon 1856-1935 .... DLB-57

Lee and Shepard DLB-49

Le Fanu, Joseph Sheridan
1814-1873 .... DLB-21, 70

Leffland, Ella 1931- Y-84

le Fort, Gertrud von 1876-1971 ..... DLB-66

Le Gallienne, Richard 1866-1947 .....DLB-4

Legaré, Hugh Swinton
1797-1843 .... DLB-3, 59, 73

Legaré, James M. 1823-1859 ....DLB-3

The Legends of the Saints and a Medieval
Christian Worldview DLB-148

Léger, Antoine-J. 1880-1950 .... DLB-88

Le Guin, Ursula K. 1929- DLB-8, 52

Lehman, Ernest 1920- DLB-44

Lehmann, John 1907- DLB-27, 100

Lehmann, Rosamond 1901-1990 .... DLB-15

Lehmann, Wilhelm 1882-1968 ...... DLB-56

Lehmann, John, Limited DLB-112

Leiber, Fritz 1910-1992 ....DLB-8

Leicester University Press DLB-112

Leinster, Murray 1896-1975 ....DLB-8

Leisewitz, Johann Anton
1752-1806 .... DLB-94

Leitch, Maurice 1933- DLB-14

Leithauser, Brad 1943- DLB-120

Leland, Charles G. 1824-1903 ...... DLB-11

Leland, John 1503?-1552 .... DLB-136

Lemay, Pamphile 1837-1918 .... DLB-99

Lemelin, Roger 1919- DLB-88

Le Moine, James MacPherson
1825-1912 .... DLB-99

Le Moyne, Jean 1913- DLB-88

L'Engle, Madeleine 1918- DLB-52

Lennart, Isobel 1915-1971 .... DLB-44

Lennox, Charlotte
1729 or 1730-1804 .... DLB-39

Lenox, James 1800-1880 .... DLB-140

Lenski, Lois 1893-1974 .... DLB-22

Lenz, Hermann 1913- DLB-69

Lenz, J. M. R. 1751-1792 .... DLB-94

Lenz, Siegfried 1926- DLB-75

Leonard, Hugh 1926- DLB-13

Leonard, William Ellery
1876-1944 .... DLB-54

Leonowens, Anna 1834-1914 .... DLB-99

LePan, Douglas 1914- DLB-88

Leprohon, Rosanna Eleanor
1829-1879 .... DLB-99

Le Queux, William 1864-1927 ...... DLB-70

Lerner, Max 1902-1992 .... DLB-29

Lernet-Holenia, Alexander
1897-1976 .... DLB-85

Le Rossignol, James 1866-1969 ..... DLB-92

Lescarbot, Marc circa 1570-1642 .... DLB-99

LeSeur, William Dawson
1840-1917 .... DLB-92

LeSieg, Theo. (see Geisel, Theodor Seuss)

Leslie, Frank 1821-1880 ....DLB-43, 79

Leslie, Frank, Publishing House DLB-49

Lesperance, John 1835?-1891 .... DLB-99

Lessing, Bruno 1870-1940 .... DLB-28

Lessing, Doris 1919- DLB-15, 139; Y-85

Lessing, Gotthold Ephraim
1729-1781 .... DLB-97

Lettau, Reinhard 1929- DLB-75

Letter from Japan Y-94

Letter to [Samuel] Richardson on *Clarissa*
(1748), by Henry Fielding DLB-39

Lever, Charles 1806-1872 .... DLB-21

Levertov, Denise 1923- DLB-5

Levi, Peter 1931- DLB-40

Levien, Sonya 1888-1960 .... DLB-44

Levin, Meyer 1905-1981 ....DLB-9, 28; Y-81

Levine, Norman 1923- DLB-88

Levine, Philip 1928- DLB-5

Levis, Larry 1946- DLB-120

Levy, Benn Wolfe
1900-1973 ....DLB-13; Y-81

Lewald, Fanny 1811-1889 .... DLB-129

Lewes, George Henry
1817-1878 ....DLB-55, 144

Lewis, Alfred H. 1857-1914 ....DLB-25

Lewis, Alun 1915-1944 ....DLB-20

Lewis, C. Day (see Day Lewis, C.)

Lewis, C. S. 1898-1963 .... DLB-15, 100

Lewis, Charles B. 1842-1924 ....DLB-11

Lewis, Henry Clay 1825-1850 ....DLB-3

Lewis, Janet 1899- Y-87

Lewis, Matthew Gregory
1775-1818 ....DLB-39

Lewis, R. W. B. 1917- DLB-111

Lewis, Richard circa 1700-1734 .....DLB-24

Lewis, Sinclair
1885-1951 .... DLB-9, 102; DS-1

Lewis, Wilmarth Sheldon
1895-1979 ....DLB-140

Lewis, Wyndham 1882-1957 ....DLB-15

Lewisohn, Ludwig
1882-1955 .... DLB-4, 9, 28, 102

Lezama Lima, José 1910-1976 ......DLB-113

The Library of America DLB-46

The Licensing Act of 1737 ....DLB-84

Lichtenberg, Georg Christoph
1742-1799 ....DLB-94

Liebling, A. J. 1904-1963 ....DLB-4

Lieutenant Murray (see Ballou, Maturin
Murray)

Lighthall, William Douw
1857-1954 ....DLB-92

Lilar, Françoise (see Mallet-Joris, Françoise)

Lillo, George 1691-1739 ....DLB-84

Lilly, J. K., Jr. 1893-1966 ....DLB-140

Lilly, Wait and Company DLB-49

Lily, William circa 1468-1522 ......DLB-132

Limited Editions Club DLB-46

Lincoln and Edmands DLB-49

Lindsay, Jack 1900- Y-84

Lindsay, Sir David
circa 1485-1555 ....DLB-132

Lindsay, Vachel 1879-1931 ....DLB-54

Linebarger, Paul Myron Anthony (see Smith,
Cordwainer)

Link, Arthur S. 1920- DLB-17

Linn, John Blair 1777-1804 ....DLB-37

Lins, Osman 1924-1978 ....DLB-145

Linton, Eliza Lynn 1822-1898 ....DLB-18

Linton, William James 1812-1897 ....DLB-32

Lion Books DLB-46

Lionni, Leo 1910- DLB-61

Lippincott, Sara Jane Clarke
    1823-1904 . . . . .DLB-43

Lippincott, J. B., Company DLB-49

Lippmann, Walter 1889-1974 . . . . . . .DLB-29

Lipton, Lawrence 1898-1975 . . . . .DLB-16

Liscow, Christian Ludwig
    1701-1760 . . . . .DLB-97

Lish, Gordon 1934- DLB-130

Lispector, Clarice 1925-1977 . . . . . . .DLB-113

The Literary Chronicle and Weekly Review
    1819-1828 . . . . .DLB-110

Literary Documents: William Faulkner
    and the People-to-People
    Program Y-86

Literary Documents II: *Library Journal*
    Statements and Questionnaires from
    First Novelists Y-87

Literary Effects of World War II
    [British novel] DLB-15

Literary Prizes [British] DLB-15

Literary Research Archives: The Humanities
    Research Center, University of
    Texas Y-82

Literary Research Archives II: Berg
    Collection of English and American
    Literature of the New York Public
    Library Y-83

Literary Research Archives III:
    The Lilly Library Y-84

Literary Research Archives IV:
    The John Carter Brown Library Y-85

Literary Research Archives V:
    Kent State Special Collections Y-86

Literary Research Archives VI: The Modern
    Literary Manuscripts Collection in the
    Special Collections of the Washington
    University Libraries Y-87

Literary Research Archives VII:
    The University of Virginia
    Libraries Y-91

Literary Research Archives VIII:
    The Henry E. Huntington
    Library Y-92

"Literary Style" (1857), by William
    Forsyth [excerpt] DLB-57

Literatura Chicanesca: The View From
    Without DLB-82

Literature at Nurse, or Circulating Morals (1885),
    by George Moore DLB-18

Littell, Eliakim 1797-1870 . . . . .DLB-79

Littell, Robert S. 1831-1896 . . . . .DLB-79

Little, Brown and Company DLB-49

Littlewood, Joan 1914- DLB-13

Lively, Penelope 1933- DLB-14

Liverpool University Press DLB-112

The Lives of the Poets DLB-142

Livesay, Dorothy 1909- DLB-68

Livesay, Florence Randal
    1874-1953 . . . . DLB-92

Livings, Henry 1929- DLB-13

Livingston, Anne Howe
    1763-1841 . . . . DLB-37

Livingston, Myra Cohn 1926- DLB-61

Livingston, William 1723-1790 . . . . . DLB-31

Liyong, Taban lo (see Taban lo Liyong)

Lizárraga, Sylvia S. 1925- DLB-82

Llewellyn, Richard 1906-1983 . . . . . . DLB-15

Lloyd, Edward
    [publishing house] DLB-106

Lobel, Arnold 1933- DLB-61

Lochridge, Betsy Hopkins (see Fancher, Betsy)

Locke, David Ross 1833-1888 . . . DLB-11, 23

Locke, John 1632-1704 . . . . DLB-31, 101

Locke, Richard Adams 1800-1871 . . . DLB-43

Locker-Lampson, Frederick
    1821-1895 . . . . DLB-35

Lockhart, John Gibson
    1794-1854 . . . . DLB-110, 116 144

Lockridge, Ross, Jr.
    1914-1948 . . . . DLB-143; Y-80

Locrine and *Selimus* DLB-62

Lodge, David 1935- DLB-14

Lodge, George Cabot 1873-1909 . . . . DLB-54

Lodge, Henry Cabot 1850-1924 . . . . . DLB-47

Loeb, Harold 1891-1974 . . . . DLB-4

Loeb, William 1905-1981 . . . . DLB-127

Logan, James 1674-1751 . . . . DLB-24, 140

Logan, John 1923- DLB-5

Logan, William 1950- DLB-120

Logue, Christopher 1926- DLB-27

Lomonosov, Mikhail Vasil'evich
    1711-1765 . . . . DLB-150

London, Jack 1876-1916 . . . . . . DLB-8, 12, 78

The London Magazine 1820-1829 . . . . . DLB-110

Long, Haniel 1888-1956 . . . . DLB-45

Long, Ray 1878-1935 . . . . DLB-137

Long, H., and Brother DLB-49

Longfellow, Henry Wadsworth
    1807-1882 . . . . DLB-1, 59

Longfellow, Samuel 1819-1892 . . . . DLB-1

Longley, Michael 1939- DLB-40

Longmans, Green and Company DLB-49

Longmore, George 1793?-1867 . . . . . .DLB-99

Longstreet, Augustus Baldwin
    1790-1870 . . . . .DLB-3, 11, 74

Longworth, D. [publishing house] . . .DLB-49

Lonsdale, Frederick 1881-1954 . . . . . .DLB-10

A Look at the Contemporary Black Theatre
    Movement .DLB-38

Loos, Anita 1893-1981 . . . . .DLB-11, 26; Y-81

Lopate, Phillip 1943- Y-80

López, Diana (see Isabella, Ríos)

Loranger, Jean-Aubert 1896-1942 . . . .DLB-92

Lorca, Federico García 1898-1936 . .DLB-108

Lord, John Keast 1818-1872 . . . . . . .DLB-99

The Lord Chamberlain's Office and Stage
    Censorship in England DLB-10

Lorde, Audre 1934-1992 . . . . .DLB-41

Lorimer, George Horace
    1867-1939 .DLB-91

Loring, A. K. [publishing house] DLB-49

Loring and Mussey DLB-46

Lossing, Benson J. 1813-1891 . . . . . . .DLB-30

Lothar, Ernst 1890-1974 . . . . .DLB-81

Lothrop, Harriet M. 1844-1924 . . . . . .DLB-42

Lothrop, D., and Company DLB-49

Loti, Pierre 1850-1923 . . . . .DLB-123

The Lounger, no. 20 (1785), by Henry
    Mackenzie .DLB-39

Lounsbury, Thomas R. 1838-1915 . . .DLB-71

Louÿs, Pierre 1870-1925 . . . . .DLB-123

Lovelace, Earl 1935- DLB-125

Lovelace, Richard 1618-1657 . . . . . .DLB-131

Lovell, Coryell and Company DLB-49

Lovell, John W., Company DLB-49

Lovesey, Peter 1936- DLB-87

Lovingood, Sut (see Harris,
    George Washington)

Low, Samuel 1765-? DLB-37

Lowell, Amy 1874-1925 . . . . .DLB-54, 140

Lowell, James Russell
    1819-1891 . . . . DLB-1, 11, 64, 79

Lowell, Robert 1917-1977 . . . . .DLB-5

Lowenfels, Walter 1897-1976 . . . . .DLB-4

Lowndes, Marie Belloc 1868-1947 . . .DLB-70

Lowry, Lois 1937- DLB-52

Lowry, Malcolm 1909-1957 . . . . .DLB-15

Lowther, Pat 1935-1975 .... DLB-53

Loy, Mina 1882-1966 .... DLB-4, 54

Lozeau, Albert 1878-1924 .... DLB-92

Lubbock, Percy 1879-1965 .... DLB-149

Lucas, E. V. 1868-1938 .... DLB-98, 149

Lucas, Fielding, Jr.
[publishing house] DLB-49

Luce, Henry R. 1898-1967 .... DLB-91

Luce, John W., and Company DLB-46

Lucie-Smith, Edward 1933- DLB-40

Lucini, Gian Pietro 1867-1914 ..... DLB-114

Ludlum, Robert 1927- Y-82

Ludus de Antichristo circa 1160 ...... DLB-148

Ludvigson, Susan 1942- DLB-120

Ludwig, Jack 1922- DLB-60

Ludwig, Otto 1813-1865 .... DLB-129

Ludwigslied 881 or 882 .... DLB-148

Luera, Yolanda 1953- DLB-122

Luft, Lya 1938- DLB-145

Luke, Peter 1919- DLB-13

Lupton, F. M., Company DLB-49

Lupus of Ferrières
circa 805-circa 862 .... DLB-148

Lurie, Alison 1926- DLB-2

Luzi, Mario 1914- DLB-128

L'vov, Nikolai Aleksandrovich
1751-1803 .... DLB-150

Lyall, Gavin 1932- DLB-87

Lydgate, John circa 1370-1450 ..... DLB-146

Lyly, John circa 1554-1606 .... DLB-62

Lynd, Robert 1879-1949 .... DLB-98

Lyon, Matthew 1749-1822 .... DLB-43

Lytle, Andrew 1902- DLB-6

Lytton, Edward (see Bulwer-Lytton, Edward)

Lytton, Edward Robert Bulwer
1831-1891 .... DLB-32

M

Maass, Joachim 1901-1972 .... DLB-69

Mabie, Hamilton Wright
1845-1916 .... DLB-71

Mac A'Ghobhainn, Iain (see Smith, Iain
Crichton)

MacArthur, Charles
1895-1956 .... DLB-7, 25, 44

Macaulay, Catherine 1731-1791 .... DLB-104

Macaulay, David 1945- DLB-61

Macaulay, Rose 1881-1958 .... DLB-36

Macaulay, Thomas Babington
1800-1859 ....DLB-32, 55

Macaulay Company DLB-46

MacBeth, George 1932- DLB-40

Macbeth, Madge 1880-1965 .... DLB-92

MacCaig, Norman 1910- DLB-27

MacDiarmid, Hugh 1892-1978 ...... DLB-20

MacDonald, Cynthia 1928- DLB-105

MacDonald, George 1824-1905 ..... DLB-18

MacDonald, John D.
1916-1986 ....DLB-8; Y-86

MacDonald, Philip 1899?-1980 ..... DLB-77

Macdonald, Ross (see Millar, Kenneth)

MacDonald, Wilson 1880-1967 ..... DLB-92

Macdonald and Company
(Publishers) DLB-112

MacEwen, Gwendolyn 1941- DLB-53

Macfadden, Bernarr
1868-1955 ....DLB-25, 91

MacGregor, Mary Esther (see Keith, Marian)

Machado, Antonio 1875-1939 ...... DLB-108

Machado, Manuel 1874-1947 ...... DLB-108

Machar, Agnes Maule 1837-1927 .... DLB-92

Machen, Arthur Llewelyn Jones
1863-1947 .... DLB-36

MacInnes, Colin 1914-1976 .... DLB-14

MacInnes, Helen 1907-1985 .... DLB-87

Mack, Maynard 1909- DLB-111

Mackall, Leonard L. 1879-1937 .... DLB-140

MacKaye, Percy 1875-1956 .... DLB-54

Macken, Walter 1915-1967 .... DLB-13

Mackenzie, Alexander 1763-1820 .... DLB-99

Mackenzie, Compton
1883-1972 ....DLB-34, 100

Mackenzie, Henry 1745-1831 .... DLB-39

Mackey, William Wellington
1937- DLB-38

Mackintosh, Elizabeth (see Tey, Josephine)

Macklin, Charles 1699-1797 .... DLB-89

MacLean, Katherine Anne 1925- DLB-8

MacLeish, Archibald
1892-1982 .... DLB-4, 7, 45; Y-82

MacLennan, Hugh 1907-1990 .... DLB-68

MacLeod, Alistair 1936- DLB-60

Macleod, Norman 1906-1985 .... DLB-4

Macmillan and Company DLB-106

The Macmillan Company DLB-49

Macmillan's English Men of Letters,
First Series (1878-1892) DLB-144

MacNamara, Brinsley 1890-1963 .....DLB-10

MacNeice, Louis 1907-1963 ..... DLB-10, 20

MacPhail, Andrew 1864-1938 ....DLB-92

Macpherson, James 1736-1796 .....DLB-109

Macpherson, Jay 1931- DLB-53

Macpherson, Jeanie 1884-1946 ......DLB-44

Macrae Smith Company DLB-46

Macrone, John
[publishing house] DLB-106

MacShane, Frank 1927- DLB-111

Macy-Masius DLB-46

Madden, David 1933- DLB-6

Maddow, Ben 1909-1992 ....DLB-44

Maddux, Rachel 1912-1983 .... Y-93

Madgett, Naomi Long 1923- DLB-76

Madhubuti, Haki R.
1942- DLB-5, 41; DS-8

Madison, James 1751-1836 ....DLB-37

Maginn, William 1794-1842 ....DLB-110

Mahan, Alfred Thayer 1840-1914 ....DLB-47

Maheux-Forcier, Louise 1929- DLB-60

Mahin, John Lee 1902-1984 ....DLB-44

Mahon, Derek 1941- DLB-40

Maikov, Vasilii Ivanovich
1728-1778 ....DLB-150

Mailer, Norman
1923- ... DLB-2, 16, 28; Y-80, 83; DS-3

Maillet, Adrienne 1885-1963 ....DLB-68

Maimonides, Moses 1138-1204 .....DLB-115

Maillet, Antonine 1929- DLB-60

Main Selections of the Book-of-the-Month
Club, 1926-1945 ....DLB-9

Main Trends in Twentieth-Century Book
Clubs DLB-46

Mainwaring, Daniel 1902-1977 ......DLB-44

Mair, Charles 1838-1927 ....DLB-99

Mais, Roger 1905-1955 ....DLB-125

Major, Andre 1942- DLB-60

Major, Clarence 1936- DLB-33

Major, Kevin 1949- DLB-60

Major Books DLB-46

Makemie, Francis circa 1658-1708 ....DLB-24

The Making of a People, by
J. M. Ritchie DLB-66

Maksimović, Desanka 1898-1993 ...DLB-147

Malamud, Bernard
1914-1986 .... DLB-2, 28; Y-80, 86

Malleson, Lucy Beatrice (see Gilbert, Anthony)

Mallet-Joris, Françoise 1930- DLB-83

Mallock, W. H. 1849-1923 ......DLB-18, 57

Malone, Dumas 1892-1986 ....DLB-17

Malone, Edmond 1741-1812 ......DLB-142

Malory, Sir Thomas
circa 1400-1410 - 1471 ....DLB-146

Malraux, André 1901-1976 ....DLB-72

Malthus, Thomas Robert
1766-1834 ....DLB-107

Maltz, Albert 1908-1985 ....DLB-102

Malzberg, Barry N. 1939- DLB-8

Mamet, David 1947- DLB-7

Manchester University Press DLB-112

Mandel, Eli 1922- DLB-53

Mandeville, Bernard 1670-1733 ....DLB-101

Mandeville, Sir John
mid fourteenth century DLB-146

Mandiargues, André Pieyre de
1909- DLB-83

Manfred, Frederick 1912- DLB-6

Mangan, Sherry 1904-1961 ....DLB-4

Mankiewicz, Herman 1897-1953 .....DLB-26

Mankiewicz, Joseph L. 1909-1993 ....DLB-44

Mankowitz, Wolf 1924- DLB-15

Manley, Delarivière
1672?-1724 ....DLB-39, 80

Mann, Abby 1927- DLB-44

Mann, Heinrich 1871-1950 .....DLB-66, 118

Mann, Horace 1796-1859 ....DLB-1

Mann, Klaus 1906-1949 ....DLB-56

Mann, Thomas 1875-1955 ....DLB-66

Mann, William D'Alton
1839-1920 ....DLB-137

Manning, Marie 1873?-1945 ....DLB-29

Manning and Loring DLB-49

Mannyng, Robert
flourished 1303-1338 ....DLB-146

Mano, D. Keith 1942- DLB-6

Manor Books DLB-46

March, William 1893-1954 ......DLB-9, 86

Marchand, Leslie A. 1900- DLB-103

Marchessault, Jovette 1938- DLB-60

Marcus, Frank 1928- DLB-13

Marden, Orison Swett
1850-1924 .... DLB-137

Marek, Richard, Books DLB-46

Mares, E. A. 1938- DLB-122

Mariani, Paul 1940- DLB-111

Marie-Victorin, Frère 1885-1944 .... DLB-92

Marin, Biagio 1891-1985 .... DLB-128

Marincović, Ranko 1913- DLB-147

Marinetti, Filippo Tommaso
1876-1944 .... DLB-114

Marion, Frances 1886-1973 .... DLB-44

Marius, Richard C. 1933- Y-85

The Mark Taper Forum DLB-7

Mark Twain on Perpetual Copyright ... Y-92

Markfield, Wallace 1926- DLB-2, 28

Markham, Edwin 1852-1940 .... DLB-54

Markle, Fletcher 1921-1991 ... DLB-68; Y-91

Marlatt, Daphne 1942- DLB-60

Marlitt, E. 1825-1887 .... DLB-129

Marlowe, Christopher 1564-1593 ... DLB-62

Marlyn, John 1912- DLB-88

Marmion, Shakerley 1603-1639 ..... DLB-58

Der Marner
before 1230-circa 1287 .... DLB-138

The *Marprelate Tracts* 1588-1589 .... DLB-132

Marquand, John P. 1893-1960 ... DLB-9, 102

Marqués, René 1919-1979 .... DLB-113

Marquis, Don 1878-1937 .... DLB-11, 25

Marriott, Anne 1913- DLB-68

Marryat, Frederick 1792-1848 ...... DLB-21

Marsh, George Perkins
1801-1882 .... DLB-1, 64

Marsh, James 1794-1842 .... DLB-1, 59

Marsh, Capen, Lyon and Webb DLB-49

Marsh, Ngaio 1899-1982 .... DLB-77

Marshall, Edison 1894-1967 .... DLB-102

Marshall, Edward 1932- DLB-16

Marshall, James 1942-1992 .... DLB-61

Marshall, Joyce 1913- DLB-88

Marshall, Paule 1929- DLB-33

Marshall, Tom 1938- DLB-60

Marsilius of Padua
circa 1275-circa 1342 .... DLB-115

Marston, John 1576-1634 .... DLB-58

Marston, Philip Bourke 1850-1887 .. DLB-35

Martens, Kurt 1870-1945 .... DLB-66

Martien, William S.
[publishing house] DLB-49

Martin, Abe (see Hubbard, Kin)

Martin, Charles 1942- DLB-120

Martin, Claire 1914- DLB-60

Martin, Jay 1935- DLB-111

Martin, Violet Florence (see Ross, Martin)

Martin du Gard, Roger 1881-1958 ...DLB-65

Martineau, Harriet 1802-1876 ....DLB-21, 55

Martínez, Eliud 1935- DLB-122

Martínez, Max 1943- DLB-82

Martyn, Edward 1859-1923 ....DLB-10

Marvell, Andrew 1621-1678 ....DLB-131

Marvin X 1944- DLB-38

Marx, Karl 1818-1883 ....DLB-129

Marzials, Theo 1850-1920 ....DLB-35

Masefield, John 1878-1967 ......DLB-10, 19

Mason, A. E. W. 1865-1948 ....DLB-70

Mason, Bobbie Ann 1940- Y-87

Mason, William 1725-1797 ....DLB-142

Mason Brothers DLB-49

Massey, Gerald 1828-1907 ....DLB-32

Massinger, Philip 1583-1640 ....DLB-58

Masson, David 1822-1907 ....DLB-144

Masters, Edgar Lee 1868-1950 ......DLB-54

Mather, Cotton
1663-1728 .... DLB-24, 30, 140

Mather, Increase 1639-1723 ....DLB-24

Mather, Richard 1596-1669 ....DLB-24

Matheson, Richard 1926- DLB-8, 44

Matheus, John F. 1887- DLB-51

Mathews, Cornelius
1817?-1889 ....DLB-3, 64

Mathews, Elkin
[publishing house] DLB-112

Mathias, Roland 1915- DLB-27

Mathis, June 1892-1927 ....DLB-44

Mathis, Sharon Bell 1937- DLB-33

Matoš, Antun Gustav 1873-1914 ...DLB-147

The Matter of England
1240-1400 ....DLB-146

The Matter of Rome
early twelfth to late fifteenth
century DLB-146

Matthews, Brander
1852-1929 ....DLB-71, 78

Matthews, Jack 1925- DLB-6

Matthews, William 1942- DLB-5

Matthiessen, F. O. 1902-1950 .... DLB-63

Matthiessen, Peter 1927- DLB-6

Maugham, W. Somerset
    1874-1965 ....DLB-10, 36, 77, 100

Maupassant, Guy de 1850-1893 .... DLB-123

Mauriac, Claude 1914- DLB-83

Mauriac, François 1885-1970 .... DLB-65

Maurice, Frederick Denison
    1805-1872 .... DLB-55

Maurois, André 1885-1967 .... DLB-65

Maury, James 1718-1769 .... DLB-31

Mavor, Elizabeth 1927- DLB-14

Mavor, Osborne Henry (see Bridie, James)

Maxwell, H. [publishing house] DLB-49

Maxwell, John [publishing house] .. DLB-106

Maxwell, William 1908- Y-80

May, Elaine 1932- DLB-44

May, Karl 1842-1912 .... DLB-129

May, Thomas 1595 or 1596-1650 ... DLB-58

Mayer, Mercer 1943- DLB-61

Mayer, O. B. 1818-1891 .... DLB-3

Mayes, Herbert R. 1900-1987 ..... DLB-137

Mayes, Wendell 1919-1992 .... DLB-26

Mayfield, Julian 1928-1984 .... DLB-33; Y-84

Mayhew, Henry 1812-1887 ..... DLB-18, 55

Mayhew, Jonathan 1720-1766 ...... DLB-31

Mayne, Jasper 1604-1672 .... DLB-126

Mayne, Seymour 1944- DLB-60

Mayor, Flora Macdonald
    1872-1932 .... DLB-36

Mayrocker, Friederike 1924- DLB-85

Mazrui, Ali A. 1933- DLB-125

Mažuranić, Ivan 1814-1890 .... DLB-147

Mazursky, Paul 1930- DLB-44

McAlmon, Robert 1896-1956 ..... DLB-4, 45

McArthur, Peter 1866-1924 .... DLB-92

McBride, Robert M., and
    Company DLB-46

McCaffrey, Anne 1926- DLB-8

McCarthy, Cormac 1933- DLB-6, 143

McCarthy, Mary 1912-1989 .... DLB-2; Y-81

McCay, Winsor 1871-1934 .... DLB-22

McClatchy, C. K. 1858-1936 .... DLB-25

McClellan, George Marion
    1860-1934 .... DLB-50

McCloskey, Robert 1914- DLB-22

McClung, Nellie Letitia 1873-1951 ... DLB-92

McClure, Joanna 1930- DLB-16

McClure, Michael 1932- DLB-16

McClure, Phillips and Company DLB-46

McClure, S. S. 1857-1949 .... DLB-91

McClurg, A. C., and Company DLB-49

McCluskey, John A., Jr. 1944- DLB-33

McCollum, Michael A. 1946 ....Y-87

McConnell, William C. 1917- DLB-88

McCord, David 1897- DLB-61

McCorkle, Jill 1958- Y-87

McCorkle, Samuel Eusebius
    1746-1811 .... DLB-37

McCormick, Anne O'Hare
    1880-1954 .... DLB-29

McCormick, Robert R. 1880-1955 ... DLB-29

McCourt, Edward 1907-1972 .... DLB-88

McCoy, Horace 1897-1955 .... DLB-9

McCrae, John 1872-1918 .... DLB-92

McCullagh, Joseph B. 1842-1896 .... DLB-23

McCullers, Carson 1917-1967 ..... DLB-2, 7

McCulloch, Thomas 1776-1843 ..... DLB-99

McDonald, Forrest 1927- DLB-17

McDonald, Walter
    1934- DLB-105, DS-9

McDonald, Walter, Getting Started:
    Accepting the Regions You Own—
    or Which Own You DLB-105

McDougall, Colin 1917-1984 .... DLB-68

McDowell, Obolensky DLB-46

McEwan, Ian 1948- DLB-14

McFadden, David 1940- DLB-60

McFall, Frances Elizabeth Clarke
    (see Grand, Sarah)

McFarlane, Leslie 1902-1977 .... DLB-88

McGahern, John 1934- DLB-14

McGee, Thomas D'Arcy
    1825-1868 .... DLB-99

McGeehan, W. O. 1879-1933 .... DLB-25

McGill, Ralph 1898-1969 .... DLB-29

McGinley, Phyllis 1905-1978 ....DLB-11, 48

McGirt, James E. 1874-1930 .... DLB-50

McGlashan and Gill DLB-106

McGough, Roger 1937- DLB-40

McGraw-Hill DLB-46

McGuane, Thomas 1939- DLB-2; Y-80

McGuckian, Medbh 1950- DLB-40

McGuffey, William Holmes
    1800-1873 .... DLB-42

McIlvanney, William 1936- DLB-14

McIlwraith, Jean Newton
    1859-1938 .... DLB-92

McIntyre, James 1827-1906 ....DLB-99

McIntyre, O. O. 1884-1938 ....DLB-25

McKay, Claude
    1889-1948 ....DLB-4, 45, 51, 117

The David McKay Company DLB-49

McKean, William V. 1820-1903 .....DLB-23

McKinley, Robin 1952- DLB-52

McLachlan, Alexander 1818-1896 ....DLB-99

McLaren, Floris Clark 1904-1978 ....DLB-68

McLaverty, Michael 1907- DLB-15

McLean, John R. 1848-1916 ....DLB-23

McLean, William L. 1852-1931 ......DLB-25

McLennan, William 1856-1904 .....DLB-92

McLoughlin Brothers DLB-49

McLuhan, Marshall 1911-1980 ......DLB-88

McMaster, John Bach 1852-1932 .....DLB-47

McMurtry, Larry
    1936- DLB-2, 143; Y-80, 87

McNally, Terrence 1939- DLB-7

McNeil, Florence 1937- DLB-60

McNeile, Herman Cyril
    1888-1937 .... DLB-77

McPherson, James Alan 1943- DLB-38

McPherson, Sandra 1943- Y-86

McWhirter, George 1939- DLB-60

McWilliams, Carey 1905-1980 .....DLB-137

Mead, L. T. 1844-1914 ....DLB-141

Mead, Matthew 1924- DLB-40

Mead, Taylor ?- DLB-16

Mechthild von Magdeburg
    circa 1207-circa 1282 ....DLB-138

Medill, Joseph 1823-1899 ....DLB-43

Medoff, Mark 1940- DLB-7

Meek, Alexander Beaufort
    1814-1865 ....DLB-3

Meeke, Mary ?-1816? DLB-116

Meinke, Peter 1932- DLB-5

Mejia Vallejo, Manuel 1923- DLB-113

Melançon, Robert 1947- DLB-60

Mell, Max 1882-1971 .... DLB-81, 124

Mellow, James R. 1926- DLB-111

Meltzer, David 1937- DLB-16

Meltzer, Milton 1915- DLB-61

Melville, Herman 1819-1891 ......DLB-3, 74

Memoirs of Life and Literature (1920),
by W. H. Mallock [excerpt] DLB-57

Mencken, H. L.
1880-1956 .... DLB-11, 29, 63, 137

Mencken and Nietzsche: An Unpublished
Excerpt from H. L. Mencken's *My Life
as Author and Editor* Y-93

Mendelssohn, Moses 1729-1786 .....DLB-97

Méndez M., Miguel 1930- DLB-82

Mercer, Cecil William (see Yates, Dornford)

Mercer, David 1928-1980 ....DLB-13

Mercer, John 1704-1768 ....DLB-31

Meredith, George
1828-1909 .... DLB-18, 35, 57

Meredith, Owen (see Lytton, Edward Robert
Bulwer)

Meredith, William 1919- DLB-5

Mérimée, Prosper 1803-1870 ....DLB-119

Merivale, John Herman
1779-1844 ....DLB-96

Meriwether, Louise 1923- DLB-33

Merlin Press DLB-112

Merriam, Eve 1916-1992 ....DLB-61

The Merriam Company DLB-49

Merrill, James 1926- DLB-5; Y-85

Merrill and Baker DLB-49

The Mershon Company DLB-49

Merton, Thomas 1915-1968 ....DLB-48; Y-81

Merwin, W. S. 1927- DLB-5

Messner, Julian [publishing house] ...DLB-46

Metcalf, J. [publishing house] DLB-49

Metcalf, John 1938- DLB-60

The Methodist Book Concern DLB-49

Methuen and Company DLB-112

Mew, Charlotte 1869-1928 ......DLB-19, 135

Mewshaw, Michael 1943- Y-80

Meyer, Conrad Ferdinand
1825-1898 ....DLB-129

Meyer, E. Y. 1946- DLB-75

Meyer, Eugene 1875-1959 ....DLB-29

Meyers, Jeffrey 1939- DLB-111

Meynell, Alice 1847-1922 ....DLB-19, 98

Meyrink, Gustav 1868-1932 ....DLB-81

Michaels, Leonard 1933- DLB-130

Micheaux, Oscar 1884-1951 .... DLB-50

Michel of Northgate, Dan
circa 1265-circa 1340 .... DLB-146

Micheline, Jack 1929- DLB-16

Michener, James A. 1907?- DLB-6

Micklejohn, George
circa 1717-1818 .... DLB-31

Middle English Literature:
An Introduction DLB-146

The Middle English Lyric DLB-146

Middle Hill Press DLB-106

Middleton, Christopher 1926- DLB-40

Middleton, Stanley 1919- DLB-14

Middleton, Thomas 1580-1627 ..... DLB-58

Miegel, Agnes 1879-1964 .... DLB-56

Miles, Josephine 1911-1985 .... DLB-48

Milius, John 1944- DLB-44

Mill, James 1773-1836 .... DLB-107

Mill, John Stuart 1806-1873 .... DLB-55

Millar, Kenneth
1915-1983 ....DLB-2; Y-83; DS-6

Millay, Edna St. Vincent
1892-1950 .... DLB-45

Miller, Arthur 1915- DLB-7

Miller, Caroline 1903-1992 .... DLB-9

Miller, Eugene Ethelbert 1950- DLB-41

Miller, Heather Ross 1939- DLB-120

Miller, Henry 1891-1980 ..... DLB-4, 9; Y-80

Miller, J. Hillis 1928- DLB-67

Miller, James [publishing house] DLB-49

Miller, Jason 1939- DLB-7

Miller, May 1899- DLB-41

Miller, Paul 1906-1991 .... DLB-127

Miller, Perry 1905-1963 .... DLB-17, 63

Miller, Sue 1943- DLB-143

Miller, Walter M., Jr. 1923- DLB-8

Miller, Webb 1892-1940 .... DLB-29

Millhauser, Steven 1943- DLB-2

Millican, Arthenia J. Bates
1920- DLB-38

Mills and Boon DLB-112

Milman, Henry Hart 1796-1868 ..... DLB-96

Milne, A. A. 1882-1956 ..... DLB-10, 77, 100

Milner, Ron 1938- DLB-38

Milner, William
[publishing house] DLB-106

Milnes, Richard Monckton (Lord Houghton)
1809-1885 ....DLB-32

Milton, John 1608-1674 ....DLB-131, 151

Minnesang circa 1150-1280 ....DLB-138

Minns, Susan 1839-1938 ....DLB-140

Minor Illustrators, 1880-1914 ......DLB-141

Minor Poets of the Earlier Seventeenth
Century DLB-121

Minton, Balch and Company DLB-46

Mirbeau, Octave 1848-1917 ....DLB-123

Mirk, John died after 1414? DLB-146

Miron, Gaston 1928- DLB-60

Mitchel, Jonathan 1624-1668 ....DLB-24

Mitchell, Adrian 1932- DLB-40

Mitchell, Donald Grant 1822-1908 ....DLB-1

Mitchell, Gladys 1901-1983 ....DLB-77

Mitchell, James Leslie 1901-1935 ....DLB-15

Mitchell, John (see Slater, Patrick)

Mitchell, John Ames 1845-1918 .....DLB-79

Mitchell, Julian 1935- DLB-14

Mitchell, Ken 1940- DLB-60

Mitchell, Langdon 1862-1935 ....DLB-7

Mitchell, Loften 1919- DLB-38

Mitchell, Margaret 1900-1949 ....DLB-9

Mitchell, W. O. 1914- DLB-88

Mitford, Mary Russell
1787-1855 ....DLB-110, 116

Mittelholzer, Edgar 1909-1965 .....DLB-117

Mitterer, Erika 1906- DLB-85

Mitterer, Felix 1948- DLB-124

Mizener, Arthur 1907-1988 ....DLB-103

Modern Age Books DLB-46

"Modern English Prose" (1876),
by George Saintsbury DLB-57

The Modern Language Association of America
Celebrates Its Centennial Y-84

The Modern Library DLB-46

"Modern Novelists – Great and Small" (1855),
by Margaret Oliphant DLB-21

"Modern Style" (1857), by Cockburn
Thomson [excerpt] DLB-57

The Modernists (1932), by Joseph Warren
Beach DLB-36

Modiano, Patrick 1945- DLB-83

Moffat, Yard and Company DLB-46

Moffet, Thomas 1553-1604 ....DLB-136

Mohr, Nicholasa 1938- DLB-145

Moix, Ana María 1947- DLB-134

Molesworth, Louisa 1839-1921 .... DLB-135

Möllhausen, Balduin 1825-1905 .... DLB-129

Momaday, N. Scott 1934- DLB-143

Monkhouse, Allan 1858-1936 .... DLB-10

Monro, Harold 1879-1932 .... DLB-19

Monroe, Harriet 1860-1936 ..... DLB-54, 91

Monsarrat, Nicholas 1910-1979 ..... DLB-15

Montale, Eugenio 1896-1981 ...... DLB-114

Montagu, Lady Mary Wortley
1689-1762 .... DLB-95, 101

Montague, John 1929- DLB-40

Monterroso, Augusto 1921- DLB-145

Montgomery, James 1771-1854 ..... DLB-93

Montgomery, John 1919- DLB-16

Montgomery, Lucy Maud
1874-1942 .... DLB-92

Montgomery, Marion 1925- DLB-6

Montgomery, Robert Bruce (see Crispin,
Edmund)

Montherlant, Henry de 1896-1972 .. DLB-72

The Monthly Review 1749-1844 ...... DLB-110

Montigny, Louvigny de 1876-1955 .. DLB-92

Montoya, José 1932- DLB-122

Moodie, John Wedderburn Dunbar
1797-1869 .... DLB-99

Moodie, Susanna 1803-1885 .... DLB-99

Moody, Joshua circa 1633-1697 ..... DLB-24

Moody, William Vaughn
1869-1910 .... DLB-7, 54

Moorcock, Michael 1939- DLB-14

Moore, Catherine L. 1911- DLB-8

Moore, Clement Clarke 1779-1863 .. DLB-42

Moore, Dora Mavor 1888-1979 ..... DLB-92

Moore, George
1852-1933 ....DLB-10, 18, 57, 135

Moore, Marianne
1887-1972 .... DLB-45; DS-7

Moore, Mavor 1919- DLB-88

Moore, Richard 1927- DLB-105

Moore, Richard, The No Self, the Little Self,
and the Poets DLB-105

Moore, T. Sturge 1870-1944 .... DLB-19

Moore, Thomas 1779-1852 ..... DLB-96, 144

Moore, Ward 1903-1978 ....DLB-8

Moore, Wilstach, Keys and
Company DLB-49

The Moorland-Spingarn Research
Center DLB-76

Moraga, Cherríe 1952- DLB-82

Morales, Alejandro 1944- DLB-82

Morales, Mario Roberto 1947- ... DLB-145

Morales, Rafael 1919- DLB-108

Morality Plays: *Mankind* circa 1450-1500 and
Everyman circa 1500 .... DLB-146

More, Hannah
1745-1833 ....DLB-107, 109, 116

More, Henry 1614-1687 .... DLB-126

More, Sir Thomas
1477 or 1478-1535 .... DLB-136

Moreno, Dorinda 1939- DLB-122

Morency, Pierre 1942- DLB-60

Moretti, Marino 1885-1979 .... DLB-114

Morgan, Berry 1919- DLB-6

Morgan, Charles 1894-1958 ....DLB-34, 100

Morgan, Edmund S. 1916- DLB-17

Morgan, Edwin 1920- DLB-27

Morgan, John Pierpont
1837-1913 .... DLB-140

Morgan, John Pierpont, Jr.
1867-1943 .... DLB-140

Morgan, Robert 1944- DLB-120

Morgan, Sydney Owenson, Lady
1776?-1859 .... DLB-116

Morgner, Irmtraud 1933- DLB-75

Morier, James Justinian
1782 or 1783?-1849 .... DLB-116

Mörike, Eduard 1804-1875 .... DLB-133

Morin, Paul 1889-1963 .... DLB-92

Morison, Richard 1514?-1556 ...... DLB-136

Morison, Samuel Eliot 1887-1976 .... DLB-17

Moritz, Karl Philipp 1756-1793 ...... DLB-94

Moriz von Craûn
circa 1220-1230 .... DLB-138

Morley, Christopher 1890-1957 ...... DLB-9

Morley, John 1838-1923 ....DLB-57, 144

Morris, George Pope 1802-1864 ..... DLB-73

Morris, Lewis 1833-1907 .... DLB-35

Morris, Richard B. 1904-1989 ...... DLB-17

Morris, William
1834-1896 ....DLB-18, 35, 57

Morris, Willie 1934- Y-80

Morris, Wright 1910- DLB-2; Y-81

Morrison, Arthur 1863-1945 ....DLB-70, 135

Morrison, Charles Clayton
1874-1966 ....DLB-91

Morrison, Toni
1931- DLB-6, 33, 143; Y-81

Morrow, William, and Company DLB-46

Morse, James Herbert 1841-1923 .....DLB-71

Morse, Jedidiah 1761-1826 ....DLB-37

Morse, John T., Jr. 1840-1937 ....DLB-47

Mortimer, John 1923- DLB-13

Morton, Carlos 1942- DLB-122

Morton, John P., and Company DLB-49

Morton, Nathaniel 1613-1685 ....DLB-24

Morton, Sarah Wentworth
1759-1846 ....DLB-37

Morton, Thomas
circa 1579-circa 1647 ....DLB-24

Möser, Justus 1720-1794 ....DLB-97

Mosley, Nicholas 1923- DLB-14

Moss, Arthur 1889-1969 ....DLB-4

Moss, Howard 1922- DLB-5

Moss, Thylias 1954- DLB-120

The Most Powerful Book Review in America
[*New York Times Book Review*] Y-82

Motion, Andrew 1952- DLB-40

Motley, John Lothrop
1814-1877 .... DLB-1, 30, 59

Motley, Willard 1909-1965 ..... DLB-76, 143

Motteux, Peter Anthony
1663-1718 ....DLB-80

Mottram, R. H. 1883-1971 ....DLB-36

Mouré, Erin 1955- DLB-60

Movies from Books, 1920-1974 ....DLB-9

Mowat, Farley 1921- DLB-68

Mowbray, A. R., and Company,
Limited DLB-106

Mowrer, Edgar Ansel 1892-1977 ....DLB-29

Mowrer, Paul Scott 1887-1971 ....DLB-29

Moxon, Edward
[publishing house] DLB-106

Mphahlele, Es'kia (Ezekiel)
1919- DLB-125

Mtshali, Oswald Mbuyiseni
1940- DLB-125

Mucedorus DLB-62

Mueller, Lisel 1924- DLB-105

Muhajir, El (see Marvin X)

Muhajir, Nazzam Al Fitnah (see Marvin X)

Muir, Edwin 1887-1959 .... DLB-20, 100

Muir, Helen 1937- DLB-14

Mukherjee, Bharati 1940- DLB-60

Muldoon, Paul 1951- DLB-40

Mühlbach, Luise 1814-1873 ....DLB-133

Müller, Friedrich (see Müller, Maler)

Müller, Heiner 1929- DLB-124

Müller, Maler 1749-1825 ....DLB-94

Müller, Wilhelm 1794-1827 ....DLB-90

Mumford, Lewis 1895-1990 ....DLB-63

Munby, Arthur Joseph 1828-1910 ....DLB-35

Munday, Anthony 1560-1633 ....DLB-62

Mundt, Clara (see Mühlbach, Luise)

Mundt, Theodore 1808-1861 ....DLB-133

Munford, Robert circa 1737-1783 ....DLB-31

Munonye, John 1929- DLB-117

Munro, Alice 1931- DLB-53

Munro, George
[publishing house] DLB-49

Munro, H. H. 1870-1916 ....DLB-34

Munro, Norman L.
[publishing house] DLB-49

Munroe, James, and Company DLB-49

Munroe, Kirk 1850-1930 ....DLB-42

Munroe and Francis DLB-49

Munsell, Joel [publishing house] DLB-49

Munsey, Frank A. 1854-1925 .....DLB-25, 91

Munsey, Frank A., and
Company DLB-49

Murav'ev, Mikhail Nikitich
1757-1807 ....DLB-150

Murdoch, Iris 1919- DLB-14

Murdoch, Rupert 1931- DLB-127

Murfree, Mary N. 1850-1922 .....DLB-12, 74

Murger, Henry 1822-1861 ....DLB-119

Murger, Louis-Henri (see Murger, Henry)

Muro, Amado 1915-1971 ....DLB-82

Murphy, Arthur 1727-1805 .....DLB-89, 142

Murphy, Beatrice M. 1908- DLB-76

Murphy, Emily 1868-1933 ....DLB-99

Murphy, John H., III 1916- DLB-127

Murphy, John, and Company DLB-49

Murphy, Richard 1927-1993 ....DLB-40

Murray, Albert L. 1916- DLB-38

Murray, Gilbert 1866-1957 ....DLB-10

Murray, Judith Sargent 1751-1820 ...DLB-37

Murray, Pauli 1910-1985 ....DLB-41

Murry, John Middleton
1889-1957 ....DLB-149

Musäus, Johann Karl August
1735-1787 ....DLB-97

Muschg, Adolf 1934- DLB-75

The Music of *Minnesang* DLB-138

Musil, Robert 1880-1942 ....DLB-81, 124

Muspilli circa 790-circa 850 ....DLB-148

Mussey, Benjamin B., and
Company DLB-49

Mwangi, Meja 1948- DLB-125

Myers, Gustavus 1872-1942 ....DLB-47

Myers, L. H. 1881-1944 ....DLB-15

Myers, Walter Dean 1937- DLB-33

N

Nabbes, Thomas circa 1605-1641 ... DLB-58

Nabl, Franz 1883-1974 .... DLB-81

Nabokov, Vladimir
1899-1977 ......DLB-2; Y-80, Y-91; DS-3

Nabokov Festival at Cornell Y-83

The Vladimir Nabokov Archive
in the Berg Collection Y-91

Nafis and Cornish DLB-49

Naipaul, Shiva 1945-1985 .... Y-85

Naipaul, V. S. 1932- DLB-125; Y-85

Nancrede, Joseph
[publishing house] DLB-49

Naranjo, Carmen 1930- DLB-145

Narrache, Jean 1893-1970 .... DLB-92

Nasby, Petroleum Vesuvius (see Locke, David
Ross)

Nash, Ogden 1902-1971 .... DLB-11

Nash, Eveleigh
[publishing house] DLB-112

Nast, Conde 1873-1942 .... DLB-91

Nastasijević, Momčilo 1894-1938 ... DLB-147

Nathan, George Jean 1882-1958 .... DLB-137

Nathan, Robert 1894-1985 .... DLB-9

The National Jewish Book Awards Y-85

The National Theatre and the Royal
Shakespeare Company: The
National Companies DLB-13

Naughton, Bill 1910- DLB-13

Nazor, Vladimir 1876-1949 .... DLB-147

Neagoe, Peter 1881-1960 .... DLB-4

Neal, John 1793-1876 ....DLB-1, 59

Neal, Joseph C. 1807-1847 ....DLB-11

Neal, Larry 1937-1981 ....DLB-38

The Neale Publishing Company DLB-49

Neely, F. Tennyson
[publishing house] DLB-49

Negri, Ada 1870-1945 ....DLB-114

"The Negro as a Writer," by
G. M. McClellan DLB-50

"Negro Poets and Their Poetry," by
Wallace Thurman DLB-50

Neidhart von Reuental
circa 1185-circa 1240 ....DLB-138

Neihardt, John G. 1881-1973 ......DLB-9, 54

Neledinsky-Meletsky, Iurii Aleksandrovich
1752-1828 ....DLB-150

Nelligan, Emile 1879-1941 ....DLB-92

Nelson, Alice Moore Dunbar
1875-1935 ....DLB-50

Nelson, Thomas, and Sons [U.S.] DLB-49

Nelson, Thomas, and Sons [U.K.] ..DLB-106

Nelson, William 1908-1978 ....DLB-103

Nelson, William Rockhill
1841-1915 ....DLB-23

Nemerov, Howard 1920-1991 .. DLB-5, 6; Y-83

Nesbit, E. 1858-1924 ....DLB-141

Ness, Evaline 1911-1986 ....DLB-61

Nestroy, Johann 1801-1862 ....DLB-133

Neugeboren, Jay 1938- DLB-28

Neumann, Alfred 1895-1952 ....DLB-56

Nevins, Allan 1890-1971 ....DLB-17

Nevinson, Henry Woodd
1856-1941 ....DLB-135

The New American Library DLB-46

New Approaches to Biography: Challenges
from Critical Theory, USC Conference
on Literary Studies, 1990 ....Y-90

New Directions Publishing
Corporation DLB-46

A New Edition of *Huck Finn* Y-85

New Forces at Work in the American Theatre:
1915-1925 ....DLB-7

New Literary Periodicals:
A Report for 1987 ....Y-87

New Literary Periodicals:
A Report for 1988 ....Y-88

New Literary Periodicals:
A Report for 1989 ....Y-89

New Literary Periodicals:
A Report for 1990 ....Y-90

New Literary Periodicals:
A Report for 1991 .... Y-91

New Literary Periodicals:
A Report for 1992 .... Y-92

New Literary Periodicals:
A Report for 1993 .... Y-93

The New Monthly Magazine
1814-1884 .... DLB-110

The New *Ulysses* Y-84

The New Variorum Shakespeare Y-85

A New Voice: The Center for the Book's First
Five Years Y-83

The New Wave [Science Fiction] DLB-8

New York City Bookshops in the 1930s and
1940s: The Recollections of Walter
Goldwater Y-93

Newbolt, Henry 1862-1938 .... DLB-19

Newbound, Bernard Slade (see Slade, Bernard)

Newby, P. H. 1918- DLB-15

Newby, Thomas Cautley
[publishing house] DLB-106

Newcomb, Charles King 1820-1894 ...DLB-1

Newell, Peter 1862-1924 .... DLB-42

Newell, Robert Henry 1836-1901 ... DLB-11

Newhouse, Samuel I. 1895-1979 ... DLB-127

Newman, Cecil Earl 1903-1976 .... DLB-127

Newman, David (see Benton, Robert)

Newman, Frances 1883-1928 .... Y-80

Newman, John Henry
1801-1890 .... DLB-18, 32, 55

Newman, Mark [publishing house] .. DLB-49

Newnes, George, Limited DLB-112

Newsome, Effie Lee 1885-1979 ..... DLB-76

Newspaper Syndication of American
Humor DLB-11

Newton, A. Edward 1864-1940 .... DLB-140

Ngugi wa Thiong'o 1938- DLB-125

The *Nibelungenlied* and the *Klage*
circa 1200 .... DLB-138

Nichol, B. P. 1944- DLB-53

Nicholas of Cusa 1401-1464 .... DLB-115

Nichols, Dudley 1895-1960 .... DLB-26

Nichols, John 1940- Y-82

Nichols, Mary Sargeant (Neal) Gove 1810-
1884 ....DLB-1

Nichols, Peter 1927- DLB-13

Nichols, Roy F. 1896-1973 .... DLB-17

Nichols, Ruth 1948- DLB-60

Nicholson, Norman 1914- DLB-27

Nicholson, William 1872-1949 ..... DLB-141

Ní Chuilleanáin, Eiléan 1942- DLB-40

Nicol, Eric 1919- DLB-68

Nicolai, Friedrich 1733-1811 .... DLB-97

Nicolay, John G. 1832-1901 and
Hay, John 1838-1905 .... DLB-47

Nicolson, Harold 1886-1968 ...DLB-100, 149

Niebuhr, Reinhold 1892-1971 .... DLB-17

Niedecker, Lorine 1903-1970 ...... DLB-48

Nieman, Lucius W. 1857-1935 ...... DLB-25

Nietzsche, Friedrich 1844-1900 .... DLB-129

Niggli, Josefina 1910- Y-80

Nikolev, Nikolai Petrovich
1758-1815 .... DLB-150

Njegoš, Petar II Petrović
1813-1851 .... DLB-147

Niles, Hezekiah 1777-1839 .... DLB-43

Nims, John Frederick 1913- DLB-5

Nin, Anaïs 1903-1977 .... DLB-2, 4

1985: The Year of the Mystery:
A Symposium Y-85

Nissenson, Hugh 1933- DLB-28

Niven, Frederick John 1878-1944 .... DLB-92

Niven, Larry 1938- DLB-8

Nizan, Paul 1905-1940 .... DLB-72

Nobel Peace Prize
The 1986 Nobel Peace Prize
Nobel Lecture 1986: Hope, Despair
and Memory
Tributes from Abraham Bernstein,
Norman Lamm, and
John R. Silber Y-86

The Nobel Prize and Literary Politics ...Y-86

Nobel Prize in Literature
The 1982 Nobel Prize in Literature
Announcement by the Swedish Academy
of the Nobel Prize Nobel Lecture 1982:
The Solitude of Latin America Excerpt
from *One Hundred Years of Solitude* The
Magical World of Macondo A Tribute
to Gabriel García Márquez Y-82

The 1983 Nobel Prize in Literature
Announcement by the Swedish Academy
Nobel Lecture 1983 The Stature of
William Golding Y-83

The 1984 Nobel Prize in Literature
Announcement by the Swedish Academy
Jaroslav Seifert Through the Eyes of the
English-Speaking Reader
Three Poems by Jaroslav Seifert Y-84

The 1985 Nobel Prize in Literature
Announcement by the Swedish Academy
Nobel Lecture 1985 .... Y-85

The 1986 Nobel Prize in Literature
Nobel Lecture 1986: This Past Must
Address Its Present Y-86

The 1987 Nobel Prize in Literature
Nobel Lecture 1987 .... Y-87

The 1988 Nobel Prize in Literature
Nobel Lecture 1988 .... Y-88

The 1989 Nobel Prize in Literature
Nobel Lecture 1989 .... Y-89

The 1990 Nobel Prize in Literature
Nobel Lecture 1990 .... Y-90

The 1991 Nobel Prize in Literature
Nobel Lecture 1991 .... Y-91

The 1992 Nobel Prize in Literature
Nobel Lecture 1992 .... Y-92

The 1993 Nobel Prize in Literature
Nobel Lecture 1993 .... Y-93

The 1994 Nobel Prize in Literature
Nobel Lecture 1994 .... Y-94

Nodier, Charles 1780-1844 ....DLB-119

Noel, Roden 1834-1894 ....DLB-35

Nolan, William F. 1928- DLB-8

Noland, C. F. M. 1810?-1858 ....DLB-11

Nonesuch Press DLB-112

Noonday Press DLB-46

Noone, John 1936- DLB-14

Nora, Eugenio de 1923- DLB-134

Nordhoff, Charles 1887-1947 ....DLB-9

Norman, Charles 1904- DLB-111

Norman, Marsha 1947- Y-84

Norris, Charles G. 1881-1945 ....DLB-9

Norris, Frank 1870-1902 ....DLB-12

Norris, Leslie 1921- DLB-27

Norse, Harold 1916- DLB-16

North Point Press DLB-46

Nortje, Arthur 1942-1970 ....DLB-125

Norton, Alice Mary (see Norton, Andre)

Norton, Andre 1912- DLB-8, 52

Norton, Andrews 1786-1853 ....DLB-1

Norton, Caroline 1808-1877 ....DLB-21

Norton, Charles Eliot 1827-1908 .. DLB-1, 64

Norton, John 1606-1663 ....DLB-24

Norton, Thomas (see Sackville, Thomas)

Norton, W. W., and Company DLB-46

Norwood, Robert 1874-1932 ....DLB-92

Nossack, Hans Erich 1901-1977 ......DLB-69

Notker Balbulus circa 840-912 ......DLB-148

Notker III of Saint Gall
circa 950-1022 ....DLB-148

Notker von Zweifalten ?-1095 ......DLB-148

A Note on Technique (1926), by
Elizabeth A. Drew [excerpts] DLB-36

Nourse, Alan E. 1928- DLB-8

Novak, Vjenceslav 1859-1905 ......DLB-147

Novalis 1772-1801 ....DLB-90

Novaro, Mario 1868-1944 ....DLB-114

Novás Calvo, Lino 1903-1983 .....DLB-145

"The Novel in [Robert Browning's] 'The Ring
and the Book' " (1912), by
Henry James DLB-32

The Novel of Impressionism,
by Jethro Bithell DLB-66

Novel-Reading: The Works of Charles Dickens,
The Works of W. Makepeace Thackeray (1879),
by Anthony Trollope DLB-21

The Novels of Dorothy Richardson (1918), by
May Sinclair DLB-36

Novels with a Purpose (1864), by Justin
M'Carthy DLB-21

Noventa, Giacomo 1898-1960 ......DLB-114

Novikov, Nikolai Ivanovich
1744-1818 ....DLB-150

Nowlan, Alden 1933-1983 ....DLB-53

Noyes, Alfred 1880-1958 ....DLB-20

Noyes, Crosby S. 1825-1908 ....DLB-23

Noyes, Nicholas 1647-1717 ....DLB-24

Noyes, Theodore W. 1858-1946 .....DLB-29

N-Town Plays
circa 1468 to early sixteenth
century DLB-146

Nugent, Frank 1908-1965 ....DLB-44

Nusic, Branislav 1864-1938 ....DLB-147

Nutt, David [publishing house] DLB-106

Nwapa, Flora 1931- DLB-125

Nye, Edgar Wilson (Bill)
1850-1896 ....DLB-11, 23

Nye, Naomi Shihab 1952- DLB-120

Nye, Robert 1939- DLB-14

O

Oakes, Urian circa 1631-1681 ......DLB-24

Oates, Joyce Carol
1938- DLB-2, 5, 130; Y-81

Ober, William 1920-1993 ....Y-93

Oberholtzer, Ellis Paxson
1868-1936 ....DLB-47

Obradović, Dositej 1740?-1811 .... DLB-147

O'Brien, Edna 1932- DLB-14

O'Brien, Fitz-James 1828-1862 ..... DLB-74

O'Brien, Kate 1897-1974 .... DLB-15

O'Brien, Tim 1946- Y-80, DS-9

O'Casey, Sean 1880-1964 ..... DLB-10

Ochs, Adolph S. 1858-1935 .... DLB-25

Ochs-Oakes, George Washington
1861-1931 .... DLB-137

O'Connor, Flannery
1925-1964 ....DLB-2; Y-80; DS-12

Octopus Publishing Group DLB-112

Odell, Jonathan 1737-1818 ...... DLB-31, 99

O'Dell, Scott 1903-1989 .... DLB-52

Odets, Clifford 1906-1963 .... DLB-7, 26

Odhams Press Limited DLB-112

O'Donnell, Peter 1920- DLB-87

O'Faolain, Julia 1932- DLB-14

O'Faolain, Sean 1900- DLB-15

Off Broadway and Off-Off Broadway . DLB-7

Off-Loop Theatres DLB-7

Offord, Carl Ruthven 1910- DLB-76

O'Flaherty, Liam 1896-1984 ... DLB-36; Y-84

Ogilvie, J. S., and Company DLB-49

Ogot, Grace 1930- DLB-125

O'Grady, Desmond 1935- DLB-40

O'Hagan, Howard 1902-1982 .... DLB-68

O'Hara, Frank 1926-1966 .... DLB-5, 16

O'Hara, John 1905-1970 ....DLB-9, 86; DS-2

Okara, Christopher 1930-1967 ..... DLB-125

O'Keeffe, John 1747-1833 .... DLB-89

Okigbo, Christopher 1930-1967 .... DLB-125

Okot p'Bitek 1931-1982 .... DLB-125

Olaudah Equiano and Unfinished Journeys:
The Slave-Narrative Tradition and
Twentieth-Century Continuities, by
Paul Edwards and Pauline T.
Wangman DLB-117

Old English Literature:
An Introduction DLB-146

Old English Riddles
eighth to tenth centuries DLB-146

Old Franklin Publishing House DLB-49

Old German Genesis and Old German Exodus
circa 1050-circa 1130 .... DLB-148

Old High German Charms and
Blessings DLB-148

The Old High German Isidor
circa 790-800 ....DLB-148

Older, Fremont 1856-1935 ....DLB-25

Oldham, John 1653-1683 ....DLB-131

Olds, Sharon 1942- DLB-120

Oliphant, Laurence 1829?-1888 .....DLB-18

Oliphant, Margaret 1828-1897 ......DLB-18

Oliver, Chad 1928- DLB-8

Oliver, Mary 1935- DLB-5

Ollier, Claude 1922- DLB-83

Olsen, Tillie 1913?- DLB-28; Y-80

Olson, Charles 1910-1970 ....DLB-5, 16

Olson, Elder 1909- DLB-48, 63

Omotoso, Kole 1943- DLB-125

"On Art in Fiction "(1838),
by Edward Bulwer DLB-21

On Learning to Write Y-88

On Some of the Characteristics of Modern
Poetry and On the Lyrical Poems of
Alfred Tennyson (1831), by Arthur
Henry Hallam DLB-32

"On Style in English Prose" (1898), by
Frederic Harrison DLB-57

"On Style in Literature: Its Technical
Elements" (1885), by Robert Louis
Stevenson DLB-57

"On the Writing of Essays" (1862),
by Alexander Smith DLB-57

Ondaatje, Michael 1943- DLB-60

O'Neill, Eugene 1888-1953 ....DLB-7

Onetti, Juan Carlos 1909- DLB-113

Onofri, Arturo 1885-1928 ....DLB-114

Opie, Amelia 1769-1853 ....DLB-116

Oppen, George 1908-1984 ....DLB-5

Oppenheim, E. Phillips 1866-1946 ...DLB-70

Oppenheim, James 1882-1932 ....DLB-28

Oppenheimer, Joel 1930- DLB-5

Optic, Oliver (see Adams, William Taylor)

Orczy, Emma, Baroness
1865-1947 ....DLB-70

Orlovitz, Gil 1918-1973 ....DLB-2, 5

Orlovsky, Peter 1933- DLB-16

Ormond, John 1923- DLB-27

Ornitz, Samuel 1890-1957 ....DLB-28, 44

Ortiz, Simon 1941- DLB-120

Ortnit and Wolfdietrich
circa 1225-1250 ....DLB-138

Orton, Joe 1933-1967 ....DLB-13

Orwell, George 1903-1950 ...... DLB-15, 98

The Orwell Year Y-84

Ory, Carlos Edmundo de 1923- .. DLB-134

Osbey, Brenda Marie 1957- DLB-120

Osbon, B. S. 1827-1912 .... DLB-43

Osborne, John 1929- DLB-13

Osgood, Herbert L. 1855-1918 ..... DLB-47

Osgood, James R., and
   Company DLB-49

Osgood, McIlvaine and
   Company DLB-112

O'Shaughnessy, Arthur
   1844-1881 .... DLB-35

O'Shea, Patrick
   [publishing house] DLB-49

Osipov, Nikolai Petrovich
   1751-1799 .... DLB-150

Osofisan, Femi 1946- DLB-125

Ostenso, Martha 1900-1963 .... DLB-92

Ostriker, Alicia 1937- DLB-120

Oswald, Eleazer 1755-1795 .... DLB-43

Otero, Blas de 1916-1979 .... DLB-134

Otero, Miguel Antonio
   1859-1944 .... DLB-82

Otero Silva, Miguel 1908-1985 ..... DLB-145

Otfried von Weißenburg
   circa 800-circa 875? DLB-148

Otis, James (see Kaler, James Otis)

Otis, James, Jr. 1725-1783 .... DLB-31

Otis, Broaders and Company DLB-49

Ottaway, James 1911- DLB-127

Ottendorfer, Oswald 1826-1900 ..... DLB-23

Otto-Peters, Louise 1819-1895 ..... DLB-129

Otway, Thomas 1652-1685 .... DLB-80

Ouellette, Fernand 1930- DLB-60

Ouida 1839-1908 .... DLB-18

Outing Publishing Company DLB-46

Outlaw Days, by Joyce Johnson DLB-16

Overbury, Sir Thomas
   circa 1581-1613 .... DLB-151

The Overlook Press DLB-46

Overview of U.S. Book Publishing,
   1910-1945 ....DLB-9

Owen, Guy 1925- DLB-5

Owen, John 1564-1622 .... DLB-121

Owen, John [publishing house] DLB-49

Owen, Robert 1771-1858 .... DLB-107

Owen, Wilfred 1893-1918 .... DLB-20

Owen, Peter, Limited DLB-112

The Owl and the Nightingale
   circa 1189-1199 .... DLB-146

Owsley, Frank L. 1890-1956 .... DLB-17

Ozerov, Vladislav Aleksandrovich
   1769-1816 .... DLB-150

Ozick, Cynthia 1928- DLB-28; Y-82

P

Pacey, Desmond 1917-1975 .... DLB-88

Pack, Robert 1929- DLB-5

Packaging Papa: *The Garden of Eden* Y-86

Padell Publishing Company DLB-46

Padgett, Ron 1942- DLB-5

Padilla, Ernesto Chávez 1944- DLB-122

Page, L. C., and Company DLB-49

Page, P. K. 1916- DLB-68

Page, Thomas Nelson
   1853-1922 ....DLB-12, 78

Page, Walter Hines 1855-1918 ...DLB-71, 91

Paget, Violet (see Lee, Vernon)

Pagliarani, Elio 1927- DLB-128

Pain, Barry 1864-1928 .... DLB-135

Pain, Philip ?-circa 1666 .... DLB-24

Paine, Robert Treat, Jr. 1773-1811 ... DLB-37

Paine, Thomas 1737-1809 ....DLB-31, 43, 73

Painter, William 1540?-1594 .... DLB-136

Palazzeschi, Aldo 1885-1974 ...... DLB-114

Paley, Grace 1922- DLB-28

Palfrey, John Gorham
   1796-1881 ....DLB-1, 30

Palgrave, Francis Turner
   1824-1897 .... DLB-35

Paltock, Robert 1697-1767 .... DLB-39

Pan Books Limited DLB-112

Panamaa, Norman 1914- and
   Frank, Melvin 1913-1988 .... DLB-26

Pancake, Breece D'J 1952-1979 ..... DLB-130

Panero, Leopoldo 1909-1962 .... DLB-108

Pangborn, Edgar 1909-1976 .... DLB-8

"Panic Among the Philistines": A Postscript,
   An Interview with Bryan Griffin Y-81

Panneton, Philippe (see Ringuet)

Panshin, Alexei 1940- DLB-8

Pansy (see Alden, Isabella)

Pantheon Books DLB-46

Paperback Library DLB-46

Paperback Science Fiction DLB-8

Paquet, Alfons 1881-1944 ....DLB-66

Paradis, Suzanne 1936- DLB-53

Pareja Diezcanseco, Alfredo
   1908-1993 ....DLB-145

Parents' Magazine Press DLB-46

Parisian Theater, Fall 1984: Toward
   A New Baroque Y-85

Parizeau, Alice 1930- DLB-60

Parke, John 1754-1789 ....DLB-31

Parker, Dorothy
   1893-1967 .... DLB-11, 45, 86

Parker, Gilbert 1860-1932 ....DLB-99

Parker, James 1714-1770 ....DLB-43

Parker, Theodore 1810-1860 ....DLB-1

Parker, William Riley 1906-1968 ...DLB-103

Parker, J. H. [publishing house] DLB-106

Parker, John [publishing house] DLB-106

Parkman, Francis, Jr.
   1823-1893 .... DLB-1, 30

Parks, Gordon 1912- DLB-33

Parks, William 1698-1750 ....DLB-43

Parks, William [publishing house] DLB-49

Parley, Peter (see Goodrich, Samuel Griswold)

Parnell, Thomas 1679-1718 ....DLB-95

Parr, Catherine 1513?-1548 ....DLB-136

Parrington, Vernon L.
   1871-1929 .... DLB-17, 63

Parronchi, Alessandro 1914- DLB-128

Partridge, S. W., and Company DLB-106

Parton, James 1822-1891 ....DLB-30

Parton, Sara Payson Willis
   1811-1872 .... DLB-43, 74

Pasolini, Pier Paolo 1922- DLB-128

Pastan, Linda 1932- DLB-5

Paston, George 1860-1936 ....DLB-149

The *Paston Letters* 1422-1509 ....DLB-146

Pastorius, Francis Daniel
   1651-circa 1720 ....DLB-24

Patchen, Kenneth 1911-1972 .... DLB-16, 48

Pater, Walter 1839-1894 ....DLB-57

Paterson, Katherine 1932- DLB-52

Patmore, Coventry 1823-1896 ... DLB-35, 98

Paton, Joseph Noel 1821-1901 ....DLB-35

Patrick, Edwin Hill ("Ted")
1901-1964 ....DLB-137

Patrick, John 1906- DLB-7

Pattee, Fred Lewis 1863-1950 ....DLB-71

Pattern and Paradigm: History as
Design, by Judith Ryan DLB-75

Patterson, Alicia 1906-1963 ....DLB-127

Patterson, Eleanor Medill
1881-1948 ....DLB-29

Patterson, Eugene 1923- DLB-127

Patterson, Joseph Medill
1879-1946 ....DLB-29

Pattillo, Henry 1726-1801 ....DLB-37

Paul, Elliot 1891-1958 ....DLB-4

Paul, Jean (see Richter, Johann Paul Friedrich)

Paul, Kegan, Trench, Trubner and Company
Limited DLB-106

Paul, Peter, Book Company DLB-49

Paul, Stanley, and Company
Limited DLB-112

Paulding, James Kirke
1778-1860 .... DLB-3, 59, 74

Paulin, Tom 1949- DLB-40

Pauper, Peter, Press DLB-46

Pavese, Cesare 1908-1950 ....DLB-128

Paxton, John 1911-1985 ....DLB-44

Payn, James 1830-1898 ....DLB-18

Payne, John 1842-1916 ....DLB-35

Payne, John Howard 1791-1852 .....DLB-37

Payson and Clarke DLB-46

Peabody, Elizabeth Palmer
1804-1894 ....DLB-1

Peabody, Elizabeth Palmer
[publishing house] DLB-49

Peabody, Oliver William Bourn
1799-1848 ....DLB-59

Peace, Roger 1899-1968 ....DLB-127

Peacham, Henry 1578-1644? DLB-151

Peachtree Publishers, Limited DLB-46

Peacock, Molly 1947- DLB-120

Peacock, Thomas Love
1785-1866 ....DLB-96, 116

Pead, Deuel ?-1727 ....DLB-24

Peake, Mervyn 1911-1968 ....DLB-15

Pear Tree Press DLB-112

Pearson, H. B. [publishing house] DLB-49

Pearson, Hesketh 1887-1964 ....DLB-149

Peck, George W. 1840-1916 .....DLB-23, 42

Peck, H. C., and Theo. Bliss
[publishing house] DLB-49

Peck, Harry Thurston
1856-1914 .... DLB-71, 91

Peele, George 1556-1596 .... DLB-62

Pellegrini and Cudahy DLB-46

Pelletier, Aimé (see Vac, Bertrand)

Pemberton, Sir Max 1863-1950 ..... DLB-70

Penguin Books [U.S.] DLB-46

Penguin Books [U.K.] DLB-112

Penn Publishing Company DLB-49

Penn, William 1644-1718 .... DLB-24

Penna, Sandro 1906-1977 .... DLB-114

Penner, Jonathan 1940- Y-83

Pennington, Lee 1939- Y-82

Pepys, Samuel 1633-1703 .... DLB-101

Percy, Thomas 1729-1811 .... DLB-104

Percy, Walker 1916-1990 ...DLB-2; Y-80, 90

Perec, Georges 1936-1982 .... DLB-83

Perelman, S. J. 1904-1979 .... DLB-11, 44

Perez, Raymundo "Tigre"
1946- DLB-122

Peri Rossi, Cristina 1941- DLB-145

Periodicals of the Beat Generation ... DLB-16

Perkins, Eugene 1932- DLB-41

Perkoff, Stuart Z. 1930-1974 .... DLB-16

Perley, Moses Henry 1804-1862 ..... DLB-99

Permabooks DLB-46

Perry, Bliss 1860-1954 .... DLB-71

Perry, Eleanor 1915-1981 .... DLB-44

"Personal Style" (1890), by John Addington
Symonds DLB-57

Perutz, Leo 1882-1957 .... DLB-81

Pesetsky, Bette 1932- DLB-130

Pestalozzi, Johann Heinrich
1746-1827 .... DLB-94

Peter, Laurence J. 1919-1990 .... DLB-53

Peter of Spain circa 1205-1277 ..... DLB-115

Peterkin, Julia 1880-1961 .... DLB-9

Peters, Lenrie 1932- DLB-117

Peters, Robert 1924- DLB-105

Peters, Robert, Foreword to
Ludwig of Bavaria DLB-105

Petersham, Maud 1889-1971 and
Petersham, Miska 1888-1960 .... DLB-22

Peterson, Charles Jacobs
1819-1887 .... DLB-79

Peterson, Len 1917- DLB-88

Peterson, Louis 1922- DLB-76

Peterson, T. B., and Brothers DLB-49

Petitclair, Pierre 1813-1860 ....DLB-99

Petrov, Gavriil 1730-1801 ....DLB-150

Petrov, Vasilii Petrovich
1736-1799 ....DLB-150

Petrović, Rastko 1898-1949 ....DLB-147

Petruslied circa 854? DLB-148

Petry, Ann 1908- DLB-76

Pettie, George circa 1548-1589 .....DLB-136

Pfaffe Konrad
flourished circa 1172 ....DLB-148

Pfaffe Lamprecht
flourished circa 1150 ....DLB-148

Pforzheimer, Carl H. 1879-1957 ....DLB-140

Phaidon Press Limited DLB-112

Pharr, Robert Deane 1916-1992 .....DLB-33

Phelps, Elizabeth Stuart
1844-1911 ....DLB-74

Philippe, Charles-Louis
1874-1909 ....DLB-65

Philips, John 1676-1708 ....DLB-95

Philips, Katherine 1632-1664 ....DLB-131

Phillips, David Graham
1867-1911 ....DLB-9, 12

Phillips, Jayne Anne 1952- Y-80

Phillips, Robert 1938- DLB-105

Phillips, Robert, Finding, Losing,
Reclaiming: A Note on My
Poems DLB-105

Phillips, Stephen 1864-1915 ....DLB-10

Phillips, Ulrich B. 1877-1934 ....DLB-17

Phillips, Willard 1784-1873 ....DLB-59

Phillips, William 1907- DLB-137

Phillips, Sampson and Company DLB-49

Phillpotts, Eden
1862-1960 .... DLB-10, 70, 135

Philosophical Library DLB-46

"The Philosophy of Style" (1852), by
Herbert Spencer DLB-57

Phinney, Elihu [publishing house] ...DLB-49

Phoenix, John (see Derby, George Horatio)

PHYLON (Fourth Quarter, 1950),
The Negro in Literature:
The Current Scene DLB-76

Physiologus
circa 1070-circa 1150 ....DLB-148

Piccolo, Lucio 1903-1969 ....DLB-114

Pickard, Tom 1946- DLB-40

Pickering, William
 [publishing house] DLB-106

Pickthall, Marjorie 1883-1922 ...... DLB-92

Pictorial Printing Company DLB-49

Piel, Gerard 1915- DLB-137

Piercy, Marge 1936- DLB-120

Pierro, Albino 1916- DLB-128

Pignotti, Lamberto 1926- DLB-128

Pike, Albert 1809-1891 .... DLB-74

Pilon, Jean-Guy 1930- DLB-60

Pinckney, Josephine 1895-1957 ......DLB-6

Pindar, Peter (see Wolcot, John)

Pinero, Arthur Wing 1855-1934 .... DLB-10

Pinget, Robert 1919- DLB-83

Pinnacle Books DLB-46

Piñon, Nélida 1935- DLB-145

Pinsky, Robert 1940- Y-82

Pinter, Harold 1930- DLB-13

Piontek, Heinz 1925- DLB-75

Piozzi, Hester Lynch [Thrale]
 1741-1821 .... DLB-104, 142

Piper, H. Beam 1904-1964 ....DLB-8

Piper, Watty DLB-22

Pisar, Samuel 1929- Y-83

Pitkin, Timothy 1766-1847 .... DLB-30

The Pitt Poetry Series: Poetry Publishing
 Today Y-85

Pitter, Ruth 1897- DLB-20

Pix, Mary 1666-1709 .... DLB-80

Plaatje, Sol T. 1876-1932 .... DLB-125

The Place of Realism in Fiction (1895), by
 George Gissing DLB-18

Plante, David 1940- Y-83

Platen, August von 1796-1835 ...... DLB-90

Plath, Sylvia 1932-1963 .... DLB-5, 6

Platon 1737-1812 .... DLB-150

Platt and Munk Company DLB-46

Playboy Press DLB-46

Plays, Playwrights, and Playgoers ... DLB-84

Playwrights and Professors, by
 Tom Stoppard DLB-13

Playwrights on the Theater DLB-80

Der Pleier flourished circa 1250 .... DLB-138

Plenzdorf, Ulrich 1934- DLB-75

Plessen, Elizabeth 1944- DLB-75

Plievier, Theodor 1892-1955 .... DLB-69

Plomer, William 1903-1973 .... DLB-20

Plumly, Stanley 1939- DLB-5

Plumpp, Sterling D. 1940- DLB-41

Plunkett, James 1920- DLB-14

Plymell, Charles 1935- DLB-16

Pocket Books DLB-46

Poe, Edgar Allan
 1809-1849 .... DLB-3, 59, 73, 74

Poe, James 1921-1980 .... DLB-44

The Poet Laureate of the United States
 Statements from Former Consultants
 in Poetry Y-86

Pohl, Frederik 1919- DLB-8

Poirier, Louis (see Gracq, Julien)

Polanyi, Michael 1891-1976 .... DLB-100

Pole, Reginald 1500-1558 .... DLB-132

Poliakoff, Stephen 1952- DLB-13

Polidori, John William
 1795-1821 .... DLB-116

Polite, Carlene Hatcher 1932- DLB-33

Pollard, Edward A. 1832-1872 ...... DLB-30

Pollard, Percival 1869-1911 .... DLB-71

Pollard and Moss DLB-49

Pollock, Sharon 1936- DLB-60

Polonsky, Abraham 1910- DLB-26

Polotsky, Simeon 1629-1680 ...... DLB-150

Ponce, Mary Helen 1938- DLB-122

Ponce-Montoya, Juanita 1949- DLB-122

Ponet, John 1516?-1556 .... DLB-132

Poniatowski, Elena 1933- DLB-113

Poole, Ernest 1880-1950 .... DLB-9

Poore, Benjamin Perley
 1820-1887 .... DLB-23

Pope, Abbie Hanscom
 1858-1894 .... DLB-140

Pope, Alexander 1688-1744 .....DLB-95, 101

Popov, Mikhail Ivanovich
 1742-circa 1790 .... DLB-150

Popular Library DLB-46

Porlock, Martin (see MacDonald, Philip)

Porpoise Press DLB-112

Porta, Antonio 1935-1989 .... DLB-128

Porter, Anna Maria 1780-1832 .... DLB-116

Porter, Eleanor H. 1868-1920 .... DLB-9

Porter, Henry ?-? DLB-62

Porter, Jane 1776-1850 .... DLB-116

Porter, Katherine Anne
 1890-1980 ....DLB-4, 9, 102; Y-80; DS-12

Porter, Peter 1929- DLB-40

Porter, William Sydney
 1862-1910 .... DLB-12, 78, 79

Porter, William T. 1809-1858 .... DLB-3, 43

Porter and Coates DLB-49

Portis, Charles 1933- DLB-6

Postl, Carl (see Sealsfield, Carl)

Poston, Ted 1906-1974 ....DLB-51

Postscript to [the Third Edition of] *Clarissa*
 (1751), by Samuel Richardson DLB-39

Potok, Chaim 1929- DLB-28; Y-84

Potter, Beatrix 1866-1943 ....DLB-141

Potter, David M. 1910-1971 ....DLB-17

Potter, John E., and Company DLB-49

Pottle, Frederick A.
 1897-1987 .... DLB-103; Y-87

Poulin, Jacques 1937- DLB-60

Pound, Ezra 1885-1972 .... DLB-4, 45, 63

Powell, Anthony 1905- DLB-15

Powers, J. F. 1917- DLB-130

Pownall, David 1938- DLB-14

Powys, John Cowper 1872-1963 .....DLB-15

Powys, Llewelyn 1884-1939 ....DLB-98

Powys, T. F. 1875-1953 ....DLB-36

Poynter, Nelson 1903-1978 ....DLB-127

The Practice of Biography: An Interview
 with Stanley Weintraub Y-82

The Practice of Biography II: An Interview
 with B. L. Reid Y-83

The Practice of Biography III: An Interview
 with Humphrey Carpenter Y-84

The Practice of Biography IV: An Interview
 with William Manchester Y-85

The Practice of Biography V: An Interview
 with Justin Kaplan Y-86

The Practice of Biography VI: An Interview
 with David Herbert Donald Y-87

The Practice of Biography VII: An Interview
 with John Caldwell Guilds Y-92

The Practice of Biography VIII: An Interview
 with Joan Mellen Y-94

Prados, Emilio 1899-1962 ....DLB-134

Praed, Winthrop Mackworth
 1802-1839 ....DLB-96

Praeger Publishers DLB-46

Pratt, E. J. 1882-1964 ....DLB-92

Pratt, Samuel Jackson 1749-1814 .....DLB-39

Preface to *Alwyn* (1780), by
Thomas Holcroft DLB-39

Preface to *Colonel Jack* (1722), by
Daniel Defoe DLB-39

Preface to *Evelina* (1778), by
Fanny Burney DLB-39

Preface to *Ferdinand Count Fathom* (1753), by
Tobias Smollett DLB-39

Preface to *Incognita* (1692), by
William Congreve DLB-39

Preface to *Joseph Andrews* (1742), by
Henry Fielding DLB-39

Preface to *Moll Flanders* (1722), by
Daniel Defoe DLB-39

Preface to *Poems* (1853), by
Matthew Arnold DLB-32

Preface to *Robinson Crusoe* (1719), by
Daniel Defoe DLB-39

Preface to *Roderick Random* (1748), by
Tobias Smollett DLB-39

Preface to *Roxana* (1724), by
Daniel Defoe DLB-39

Preface to *St. Leon* (1799), by
William Godwin DLB-39

Preface to Sarah Fielding's *Familiar Letters*
(1747), by Henry Fielding
[excerpt] DLB-39

Preface to Sarah Fielding's *The Adventures of
David Simple* (1744), by
Henry Fielding DLB-39

Preface to *The Cry* (1754), by
Sarah Fielding DLB-39

Preface to *The Delicate Distress* (1769), by
Elizabeth Griffin DLB-39

Preface to *The Disguis'd Prince* (1733), by
Eliza Haywood [excerpt] DLB-39

Preface to *The Farther Adventures of Robinson
Crusoe* (1719), by Daniel Defoe ...DLB-39

Preface to the First Edition of *Pamela* (1740), by
Samuel Richardson DLB-39

Preface to the First Edition of *The Castle of
Otranto* (1764), by
Horace Walpole DLB-39

Preface to *The History of Romances* (1715), by
Pierre Daniel Huet [excerpts] DLB-39

Preface to *The Life of Charlotta du Pont* (1723),
by Penelope Aubin DLB-39

Preface to *The Old English Baron* (1778), by
Clara Reeve DLB-39

Preface to the Second Edition of *The Castle of
Otranto* (1765), by Horace
Walpole DLB-39

Preface to *The Secret History, of Queen Zarah,
and the Zarazians* (1705), by Delariviere
Manley DLB-39

Preface to the Third Edition of *Clarissa* (1751),
by Samuel Richardson
[excerpt] DLB-39

Preface to *The Works of Mrs. Davys* (1725), by
Mary Davys DLB-39

Preface to Volume 1 of *Clarissa* (1747), by
Samuel Richardson DLB-39

Preface to Volume 3 of *Clarissa* (1748), by
Samuel Richardson DLB-39

Préfontaine, Yves 1937- DLB-53

Prelutsky, Jack 1940- DLB-61

Premisses, by Michael Hamburger ...DLB-66

Prentice, George D. 1802-1870 ......DLB-43

Prentice-Hall DLB-46

Prescott, William Hickling
1796-1859 ....DLB-1, 30, 59

The Present State of the English Novel (1892),
by George Saintsbury DLB-18

Prešeren, Francè 1800-1849 ....DLB-147

Preston, Thomas 1537-1598 ....DLB-62

Price, Reynolds 1933- DLB-2

Price, Richard 1949- Y-81

Priest, Christopher 1943- DLB-14

Priestley, J. B. 1894-1984
.........DLB-10, 34, 77, 100, 139; Y-84

Prime, Benjamin Young 1733-1791 .. DLB-31

Primrose, Diana
floruit circa 1630 ....DLB-126

Prince, F. T. 1912- DLB-20

Prince, Thomas 1687-1758 .....DLB-24, 140

The Principles of Success in Literature (1865), by
George Henry Lewes [excerpt] .. DLB-57

Prior, Matthew 1664-1721 ....DLB-95

Pritchard, William H. 1932- DLB-111

Pritchett, V. S. 1900- DLB-15, 139

Procter, Adelaide Anne 1825-1864 ... DLB-32

Procter, Bryan Waller
1787-1874 ....DLB-96, 144

The Profession of Authorship:
Scribblers for Bread Y-89

The Progress of Romance (1785), by Clara Reeve
[excerpt] DLB-39

Prokopovich, Feofan 1681?-1736 ... DLB-150

Prokosch, Frederic 1906-1989 ......DLB-48

The Proletarian Novel DLB-9

Propper, Dan 1937- DLB-16

The Prospect of Peace (1778), by
Joel Barlow DLB-37

Proud, Robert 1728-1813 ....DLB-30

Proust, Marcel 1871-1922 ....DLB-65

Prynne, J. H. 1936- DLB-40

Przybyszewski, Stanislaw
1868-1927 ....DLB-66

Pseudo-Dionysius the Areopagite floruit
circa 500 ....DLB-115

The Public Lending Right in America
Statement by Sen. Charles McC.
Mathias, Jr. PLR and the Meaning
of Literary Property Statements on
PLR by American Writers Y-83

The Public Lending Right in the United Kingdom Public Lending Right: The First Year
in the United Kingdom Y-83

The Publication of English
Renaissance Plays DLB-62

Publications and Social Movements
[Transcendentalism] DLB-1

Publishers and Agents: The Columbia
Connection Y-87

A Publisher's Archives: G. P. Putnam ...Y-92

Publishing Fiction at LSU Press Y-87

Pückler-Muskau, Hermann von
1785-1871 ....DLB-133

Pugh, Edwin William 1874-1930 ...DLB-135

Pugin, A. Welby 1812-1852 ....DLB-55

Puig, Manuel 1932-1990 ....DLB-113

Pulitzer, Joseph 1847-1911 ....DLB-23

Pulitzer, Joseph, Jr. 1885-1955 ....DLB-29

Pulitzer Prizes for the Novel,
1917-1945 ....DLB-9

Pulliam, Eugene 1889-1975 ....DLB-127

Purchas, Samuel 1577?-1626 ....DLB-151

Purdy, Al 1918- DLB-88

Purdy, James 1923- DLB-2

Purdy, Ken W. 1913-1972 ....DLB-137

Pusey, Edward Bouverie
1800-1882 ....DLB-55

Putnam, George Palmer
1814-1872 ....DLB-3, 79

Putnam, Samuel 1892-1950 ....DLB-4

G. P. Putnam's Sons [U.S.] DLB-49

G. P. Putnam's Sons [U.K.] DLB-106

Puzo, Mario 1920- DLB-6

Pyle, Ernie 1900-1945 ....DLB-29

Pyle, Howard 1853-1911 ....DLB-42

Pym, Barbara 1913-1980 ......DLB-14; Y-87

Pynchon, Thomas 1937- DLB-2

Pyramid Books DLB-46

Pyrnelle, Louise-Clarke 1850-1907 ...DLB-42

Q

Quad, M. (see Lewis, Charles B.)

Quarles, Francis 1592-1644 .... DLB-126

The Quarterly Review
1809-1967 .... DLB-110

Quasimodo, Salvatore 1901-1968 .. DLB-114

Queen, Ellery (see Dannay, Frederic, and
Manfred B. Lee)

The Queen City Publishing House .. DLB-49

Queneau, Raymond 1903-1976 ..... DLB-72

Quesnel, Joseph 1746-1809 .... DLB-99

The Question of American Copyright
in the Nineteenth Century
Headnote
Preface, by George Haven Putnam
The Evolution of Copyright, by Brander
Matthews
Summary of Copyright Legislation in
the United States, by R. R. Bowker
Analysis of the Provisions of the
Copyright Law of 1891, by
George Haven Putnam
The Contest for International Copyright,
by George Haven Putnam
Cheap Books and Good Books,
by Brander Matthews DLB-49

Quiller-Couch, Sir Arthur
1863-1944 .... DLB-135

Quin, Ann 1936-1973 .... DLB-14

Quincy, Samuel, of Georgia ?-? DLB-31

Quincy, Samuel, of Massachusetts
1734-1789 .... DLB-31

Quinn, Anthony 1915- DLB-122

Quintana, Leroy V. 1944- DLB-82

Quintana, Miguel de 1671-1748
A Forerunner of Chicano
Literature DLB-122

Quist, Harlin, Books DLB-46

Quoirez, Françoise (see Sagan, Françcise)

R

Raabe, Wilhelm 1831-1910 .... DLB-129

Rabe, David 1940- DLB-7

Raboni, Giovanni 1932- DLB-128

Rachilde 1860-1953 .... DLB-123

Racin, Kočo 1908-1943 .... DLB-147

Rackham, Arthur 1867-1939 ..... DLB-141

Radcliffe, Ann 1764-1823 .... DLB-39

Raddall, Thomas 1903- DLB-68

Radiguet, Raymond 1903-1923 ..... DLB-65

Radishchev, Aleksandr Nikolaevich
1749-1802 .... DLB-150

Radványi, Netty Reiling (see Seghers, Anna)

Rahv, Philip 1908-1973 .... DLB-137

Raimund, Ferdinand Jakob
1790-1836 .... DLB-90

Raine, Craig 1944- DLB-40

Raine, Kathleen 1908- DLB-20

Rainolde, Richard
circa 1530-1606 .... DLB-136

Rakić, Milan 1876-1938 .... DLB-147

Ralph, Julian 1853-1903 .... DLB-23

Ralph Waldo Emerson in 1982 .... Y-82

Ramat, Silvio 1939- DLB-128

Rambler, no. 4 (1750), by Samuel Johnson
[excerpt] DLB-39

Ramée, Marie Louise de la (see Ouida)

Ramírez, Sergío 1942- DLB-145

Ramke, Bin 1947- DLB-120

Ramler, Karl Wilhelm 1725-1798 .... DLB-97

Ramon Ribeyro, Julio 1929- DLB-145

Ramous, Mario 1924- DLB-128

Rampersad, Arnold 1941- DLB-111

Ramsay, Allan 1684 or 1685-1758 ... DLB-95

Ramsay, David 1749-1815 .... DLB-30

Ranck, Katherine Quintana
1942- DLB-122

Rand, Avery and Company DLB-49

Rand McNally and Company DLB-49

Randall, David Anton
1905-1975 .... DLB-140

Randall, Dudley 1914- DLB-41

Randall, Henry S. 1811-1876 .... DLB-30

Randall, James G. 1881-1953 .... DLB-17

The Randall Jarrell Symposium: A Small
Collection of Randall Jarrells
Excerpts From Papers Delivered at
the Randall Jarrell
Symposium Y-86

Randolph, A. Philip 1889-1979 ...... DLB-91

Randolph, Anson D. F.
[publishing house] DLB-49

Randolph, Thomas 1605-1635 ..DLB-58, 126

Random House DLB-46

Ranlet, Henry [publishing house] DLB-49

Ransom, John Crowe
1888-1974 ....DLB-45, 63

Raphael, Frederic 1931- DLB-14

Raphaelson, Samson 1896-1983 ..... DLB-44

Raskin, Ellen 1928-1984 ....DLB-52

Rastell, John 1475?-1536 ....DLB-136

Rattigan, Terence 1911-1977 ....DLB-13

Rawlings, Marjorie Kinnan
1896-1953 .... DLB-9, 22, 102

Raworth, Tom 1938- DLB-40

Ray, David 1932- DLB-5

Ray, Gordon Norton
1915-1986 .... DLB-103, 140

Ray, Henrietta Cordelia
1849-1916 ....DLB-50

Raymond, Henry J. 1820-1869 ... DLB-43, 79

Raymond Chandler Centenary Tributes
from Michael Avallone, James Elroy, Joe
Gores,
and William F. Nolan Y-88

Reach, Angus 1821-1856 ....DLB-70

Read, Herbert 1893-1968 ...... DLB-20, 149

Read, Herbert, "The Practice of Biography," in
The English Sense of Humour and Other
Essays DLB-149

Read, Opie 1852-1939 ....DLB-23

Read, Piers Paul 1941- DLB-14

Reade, Charles 1814-1884 ....DLB-21

Reader's Digest Condensed
Books DLB-46

Reading, Peter 1946- DLB-40

Reaney, James 1926- DLB-68

Rèbora, Clemente 1885-1957 ......DLB-114

Rechy, John 1934- DLB-122; Y-82

The Recovery of Literature: Criticism in the
1990s: A Symposium Y-91

Redding, J. Saunders
1906-1988 .... DLB-63, 76

Redfield, J. S. [publishing house] DLB-49

Redgrove, Peter 1932- DLB-40

Redmon, Anne 1943- Y-86

Redmond, Eugene B. 1937- DLB-41

Redpath, James [publishing house] ...DLB-49

Reed, Henry 1808-1854 ....DLB-59

Reed, Henry 1914- DLB-27

Reed, Ishmael 1938- DLB-2, 5, 33; DS-8

Reed, Sampson 1800-1880 ....DLB-1

Reed, Talbot Baines 1852-1893 .....DLB-141

Reedy, William Marion 1862-1920 ...DLB-91

Reese, Lizette Woodworth
1856-1935 ....DLB-54

Reese, Thomas 1742-1796 ....DLB-37

Reeve, Clara 1729-1807 ....DLB-39

Reeves, John 1926- DLB-88

Regnery, Henry, Company DLB-46

Rehberg, Hans 1901-1963 ....DLB-124

Rehfisch, Hans José 1891-1960 .....DLB-124

Reid, Alastair 1926- DLB-27

Reid, B. L. 1918-1990 ....DLB-111

Reid, Christopher 1949- DLB-40

Reid, Helen Rogers 1882-1970 .....DLB-29

Reid, James ?-? DLB-31

Reid, Mayne 1818-1883 ....DLB-21

Reid, Thomas 1710-1796 ....DLB-31

Reid, V. S. (Vic) 1913-1987 ....DLB-125

Reid, Whitelaw 1837-1912 ....DLB-23

Reilly and Lee Publishing
  Company DLB-46

Reimann, Brigitte 1933-1973 ....DLB-75

Reinmar der Alte
  circa 1165-circa 1205 ....DLB-138

Reinmar von Zweter
  circa 1200-circa 1250 ....DLB-138

Reisch, Walter 1903-1983 ....DLB-44

Remarque, Erich Maria 1898-1970 ...DLB-56

"Re-meeting of Old Friends": The Jack
  Kerouac Conference Y-82

Remington, Frederic 1861-1909 .....DLB-12

Renaud, Jacques 1943- DLB-60

Renault, Mary 1905-1983 ....Y-83

Rendell, Ruth 1930- DLB-87

Representative Men and Women: A Historical
  Perspective on the British Novel,
  1930-1960 ....DLB-15

(Re-)Publishing Orwell Y-86

Reuter, Fritz 1810-1874 ....DLB-129

Reuter, Gabriele 1859-1941 ....DLB-66

Revell, Fleming H., Company DLB-49

Reventlow, Franziska Gräfin zu
  1871-1918 ....DLB-66

Review of Reviews Office DLB-112

Review of [Samuel Richardson's] *Clarissa*
  (1748), by Henry Fielding DLB-39

The Revolt (1937), by Mary Colum
  [excerpts] DLB-36

Rexroth, Kenneth
  1905-1982 .... DLB-16, 48; Y-82

Rey, H. A. 1898-1977 ....DLB-22

Reynal and Hitchcock DLB-46

Reynolds, G. W. M. 1814-1879 .....DLB-21

Reynolds, John Hamilton
  1794-1852 ....DLB-96

Reynolds, Mack 1917- DLB-8

Reynolds, Sir Joshua 1723-1792 ....DLB-104

Reznikoff, Charles 1894-1976 ....DLB-28, 45

"Rhetoric" (1828; revised, 1859), by
  Thomas de Quincey [excerpt] ...DLB-57

Rhett, Robert Barnwell 1800-1876 ...DLB-43

Rhode, John 1884-1964 ....DLB-77

Rhodes, James Ford 1848-1927 .....DLB-47

Rhys, Jean 1890-1979 ....DLB-36, 117

Ricardo, David 1772-1823 ....DLB-107

Ricardou, Jean 1932- DLB-83

Rice, Elmer 1892-1967 ....DLB-4, 7

Rice, Grantland 1880-1954 ....DLB-29

Rich, Adrienne 1929- DLB-5, 67

Richards, David Adams 1950- DLB-53

Richards, George circa 1760-1814 ...DLB-37

Richards, I. A. 1893-1979 ....DLB-27

Richards, Laura E. 1850-1943 ......DLB-42

Richards, William Carey
  1818-1892 ....DLB-73

Richards, Grant
  [publishing house] DLB-112

Richardson, Charles F. 1851-1913 ...DLB-71

Richardson, Dorothy M.
  1873-1957 ....DLB-36

Richardson, Jack 1935- DLB-7

Richardson, John 1796-1852 ....DLB-99

Richardson, Samuel 1689-1761 .....DLB-39

Richardson, Willis 1889-1977 ....DLB-51

Riche, Barnabe 1542-1617 ....DLB-136

Richler, Mordecai 1931- DLB-53

Richter, Conrad 1890-1968 ....DLB-9

Richter, Hans Werner 1908- DLB-69

Richter, Johann Paul Friedrich
  1763-1825 ....DLB-94

Rickerby, Joseph
  [publishing house] DLB-106

Rickword, Edgell 1898-1982 ....DLB-20

Riddell, John (see Ford, Corey)

Ridge, Lola 1873-1941 ....DLB-54

Ridge, William Pett 1859-1930 .....DLB-135

Riding, Laura (see Jackson, Laura Riding)

Ridler, Anne 1912- DLB-27

Ridruego, Dionisio 1912-1975 .....DLB-108

Riel, Louis 1844-1885 ....DLB-99

Riffaterre, Michael 1924- DLB-67

Riis, Jacob 1849-1914 ....DLB-23

Riker, John C. [publishing house] DLB-49

Riley, John 1938-1978 ....DLB-40

Rilke, Rainer Maria 1875-1926 ......DLB-81

Rinehart and Company DLB-46

Ringuet 1895-1960 ....DLB-68

Ringwood, Gwen Pharis
  1910-1984 ....DLB-88

Rinser, Luise 1911- DLB-69

Ríos, Alberto 1952- DLB-122

Ríos, Isabella 1948- DLB-82

Ripley, Arthur 1895-1961 ....DLB-44

Ripley, George 1802-1880 .....DLB-1, 64, 73

The Rising Glory of America:
  Three Poems DLB-37

The Rising Glory of America: Written in 1771
  (1786), by Hugh Henry Brackenridge and
  Philip Freneau DLB-37

Riskin, Robert 1897-1955 ....DLB-26

Risse, Heinz 1898- DLB-69

Ritchie, Anna Mowatt 1819-1870 .....DLB-3

Ritchie, Anne Thackeray
  1837-1919 ....DLB-18

Ritchie, Thomas 1778-1854 ....DLB-43

Rites of Passage
  [on William Saroyan] Y-83

The Ritz Paris Hemingway Award Y-85

Rivard, Adjutor 1868-1945 ....DLB-92

Rive, Richard 1931-1989 ....DLB-125

Rivera, Marina 1942- DLB-122

Rivera, Tomás 1935-1984 ....DLB-82

Rivers, Conrad Kent 1933-1968 .....DLB-41

Riverside Press DLB-49

Rivington, James circa 1724-1802 ....DLB-43

Rivkin, Allen 1903-1990 ....DLB-26

Roa Bastos, Augusto 1917- DLB-113

Robbe-Grillet, Alain 1922- DLB-83

Robbins, Tom 1936- Y-80

Roberts, Charles G. D. 1860-1943 ...DLB-92

Roberts, Dorothy 1906-1993 ....DLB-88

Roberts, Elizabeth Madox
  1881-1941 ....DLB-9, 54, 102

Roberts, Kenneth 1885-1957 ....DLB-9

Roberts, William 1767-1849 ....DLB-142

Roberts Brothers DLB-49

Robertson, A. M., and Company DLB-49

Robertson, William 1721-1793 . . . . . DLB-104

Robinson, Casey 1903-1979 . . . . DLB-44

Robinson, Edwin Arlington
1869-1935 . . . . DLB-54

Robinson, Henry Crabb
1775-1867 . . . . DLB-107

Robinson, James Harvey
1863-1936 . . . . DLB-47

Robinson, Lennox 1886-1958 . . . . DLB-10

Robinson, Mabel Louise
1874-1962 . . . . DLB-22

Robinson, Therese
1797-1870 . . . . DLB-59, 133

Robison, Mary 1949- DLB-130

Roblès, Emmanuel 1914- DLB-83

Roccatagliata Ceccardi, Ceccardo
1871-1919 . . . . DLB-114

Rochester, John Wilmot, Earl of
1647-1680 . . . . DLB-131

Rock, Howard 1911-1976 . . . . DLB-127

Rodgers, Carolyn M. 1945- DLB-41

Rodgers, W. R. 1909-1969 . . . . DLB-20

Rodríguez, Claudio 1934- DLB-134

Rodriguez, Richard 1944- DLB-82

Rodríguez Julia, Edgardo
1946- DLB-145

Roethke, Theodore 1908-1963 . . . . . . .DLB-5

Rogers, Pattiann 1940- DLB-105

Rogers, Samuel 1763-1855 . . . . DLB-93

Rogers, Will 1879-1935 . . . . DLB-11

Rohmer, Sax 1883-1959 . . . . DLB-70

Roiphe, Anne 1935- Y-80

Rojas, Arnold R. 1896-1988 . . . . DLB-82

Rolfe, Frederick William
1860-1913 . . . . DLB-34

Rolland, Romain 1866-1944 . . . . DLB-65

Rolle, Richard
circa 1290-1300 - 1340 . . . . DLB-146

Rolvaag, O. E. 1876-1931 . . . . .DLB-9

Romains, Jules 1885-1972 . . . . DLB-65

Roman, A., and Company DLB-49

Romano, Octavio 1923- DLB-122

Romero, Leo 1950- DLB-122

Romero, Lin 1947- DLB-122

Romero, Orlando 1945- DLB-82

Rook, Clarence 1863-1915 . . . . DLB-135

Roosevelt, Theodore 1858-1919 . . . . DLB-47

Root, Waverley 1903-1982 . . . . .DLB-4

Root, William Pitt 1941- DLB-120

Roquebrune, Robert de 1889-1978 . . . DLB-68

Rosa, João Guimarães
1908-1967 . . . . DLB-113

Rosales, Luis 1910-1992 . . . . DLB-134

Rose, Reginald 1920- DLB-26

Rosegger, Peter 1843-1918 . . . . DLB-129

Rosei, Peter 1946- DLB-85

Rosen, Norma 1925- DLB-28

Rosenbach, A. S. W. 1876-1952 . . . . DLB-140

Rosenberg, Isaac 1890-1918 . . . . DLB-20

Rosenfeld, Isaac 1918-1956 . . . . DLB-28

Rosenthal, M. L. 1917- DLB-5

Ross, Alexander 1591-1654 . . . . DLB-151

Ross, Harold 1892-1951 . . . . DLB-137

Ross, Leonard Q. (see Rosten, Leo)

Ross, Martin 1862-1915 . . . . DLB-135

Ross, Sinclair 1908- DLB-88

Ross, W. W. E. 1894-1966 . . . . DLB-88

Rosselli, Amelia 1930- DLB-128

Rossen, Robert 1908-1966 . . . . DLB-26

Rossetti, Christina 1830-1894 . . . . DLB-35

Rossetti, Dante Gabriel 1828-1882 . . . DLB-35

Rossner, Judith 1935- DLB-6

Rosten, Leo 1908- DLB-11

Rostenberg, Leona 1908- DLB-140

Rostovsky, Dimitrii 1651-1709 . . . . . DLB-150

Bertram Rota and His Bookshop Y-91

Roth, Gerhard 1942- DLB-85, 124

Roth, Henry 1906?- DLB-28

Roth, Joseph 1894-1939 . . . . DLB-85

Roth, Philip 1933- DLB-2, 28; Y-82

Rothenberg, Jerome 1931- DLB-5

Rotimi, Ola 1938- DLB-125

Routhier, Adolphe-Basile
1839-1920 . . . . DLB-99

Routier, Simone 1901-1987 . . . . DLB-88

Routledge, George, and Sons DLB-106

Roversi, Roberto 1923- DLB-128

Rowe, Elizabeth Singer
1674-1737 . . . . .DLB-39, 95

Rowe, Nicholas 1674-1718 . . . . DLB-84

Rowlands, Samuel
circa 1570-1630 . . . . DLB-121

Rowlandson, Mary
circa 1635-circa 1678 . . . . DLB-24

Rowley, William circa 1585-1626 . . . .DLB-58

Rowson, Susanna Haswell
circa 1762-1824 . . . . .DLB-37

Roy, Camille 1870-1943 . . . . .DLB-92

Roy, Gabrielle 1909-1983 . . . . .DLB-68

Roy, Jules 1907- DLB-83

The Royal Court Theatre and the English
Stage Company DLB-13

The Royal Court Theatre and the New
Drama DLB-10

The Royal Shakespeare Company
at the Swan Y-88

Royall, Anne 1769-1854 . . . . .DLB-43

The Roycroft Printing Shop DLB-49

Royster, Vermont 1914- DLB-127

Ruark, Gibbons 1941- DLB-120

Ruban, Vasilii Grigorevich
1742-1795 . . . . .DLB-150

Rubens, Bernice 1928- DLB-14

Rudd and Carleton DLB-49

Rudkin, David 1936- DLB-13

Rudolf von Ems
circa 1200-circa 1254 . . . . .DLB-138

Ruffin, Josephine St. Pierre
1842-1924 . . . . .DLB-79

Ruggles, Henry Joseph 1813-1906 . . . .DLB-64

Rukeyser, Muriel 1913-1980 . . . . . . .DLB-48

Rule, Jane 1931- DLB-60

Rulfo, Juan 1918-1986 . . . . .DLB-113

Rumaker, Michael 1932- DLB-16

Rumens, Carol 1944- DLB-40

Runyon, Damon 1880-1946 . . . . . DLB-11, 86

Ruodlieb circa 1050-1075 . . . . .DLB-148

Rush, Benjamin 1746-1813 . . . . .DLB-37

Rusk, Ralph L. 1888-1962 . . . . .DLB-103

Ruskin, John 1819-1900 . . . . .DLB-55

Russ, Joanna 1937- DLB-8

Russell, B. B., and Company DLB-49

Russell, Benjamin 1761-1845 . . . . . . .DLB-43

Russell, Bertrand 1872-1970 . . . . . . .DLB-100

Russell, Charles Edward
1860-1941 . . . . .DLB-25

Russell, George William (see AE)

Russell, R. H., and Son DLB-49

Rutherford, Mark 1831-1913 . . . . . . .DLB-18

Ryan, Michael 1946- Y-82

Ryan, Oscar 1904- DLB-68

Ryga, George 1932- DLB-60

Rymer, Thomas 1643?-1713 ....DLB-101

Ryskind, Morrie 1895-1985 ....DLB-26

Rzhevsky, Aleksei Andreevich
    1737-1804 ....DLB-150

S

The Saalfield Publishing
    Company DLB-46

Saba, Umberto 1883-1957 ....DLB-114

Sábato, Ernesto 1911- DLB-145

Saberhagen, Fred 1930- DLB-8

Sackler, Howard 1929-1982 ....DLB-7

Sackville, Thomas 1536-1608 ......DLB-132

Sackville, Thomas 1536-1608
    and Norton, Thomas
    1532-1584 ....DLB-62

Sackville-West, V. 1892-1962 ....DLB-34

Sadlier, D. and J., and Company DLB-49

Sadlier, Mary Anne 1820-1903 ......DLB-99

Sadoff, Ira 1945- DLB-120

Saenz, Jaime 1921-1986 ....DLB-145

Saffin, John circa 1626-1710 ....DLB-24

Sagan, Françoise 1935- DLB-83

Sage, Robert 1899-1962 ....DLB-4

Sagel, Jim 1947- DLB-82

Sagendorph, Robb Hansell
    1900-1970 ....DLB-137

Sahagún, Carlos 1938- DLB-108

Sahkomaapii, Piitai (see Highwater, Jamake)

Sahl, Hans 1902- DLB-69

Said, Edward W. 1935- DLB-67

Saiko, George 1892-1962 ....DLB-85

St. Dominic's Press DLB-112

Saint-Exupéry, Antoine de
    1900-1944 ....DLB-72

St. Johns, Adela Rogers 1894-1988 ...DLB-29

St. Martin's Press DLB-46

St. Omer, Garth 1931- DLB-117

Saint Pierre, Michel de 1916-1987 ....DLB-83

Saintsbury, George
    1845-1933 ....DLB-57, 149

Saki (see Munro, H. H.)

Salaam, Kalamu ya 1947- DLB-38

Salas, Floyd 1931- DLB-82

Sálaz-Marquez, Rubén 1935- DLB-122

Salemson, Harold J. 1910-1988 ......DLB-4

Salinas, Luis Omar 1937- DLB-82

Salinas, Pedro 1891-1951 ....DLB-134

Salinger, J. D. 1919- DLB-2, 102

Salkey, Andrew 1928- DLB-125

Salt, Waldo 1914- DLB-44

Salter, James 1925- DLB-130

Salter, Mary Jo 1954- DLB-120

Salustri, Carlo Alberto (see Trilussa)

Salverson, Laura Goodman
    1890-1970 ....DLB-92

Sampson, Richard Henry (see Hull, Richard)

Samuels, Ernest 1903- DLB-111

Sanborn, Franklin Benjamin
    1831-1917 ....DLB-1

Sánchez, Luis Rafael 1936- DLB-145

Sánchez, Philomeno "Phil"
    1917- DLB-122

Sánchez, Ricardo 1941- DLB-82

Sanchez, Sonia 1934- DLB-41; DS-8

Sand, George 1804-1876 ....DLB-119

Sandburg, Carl 1878-1967 ......DLB-17, 54

Sanders, Ed 1939- DLB-16

Sandoz, Mari 1896-1966 ....DLB-9

Sandwell, B. K. 1876-1954 ....DLB-92

Sandys, George 1578-1644 .....DLB-24, 121

Sangster, Charles 1822-1893 ....DLB-99

Sanguineti, Edoardo 1930- DLB-128

Sansom, William 1912-1976 ....DLB-139

Santayana, George 1863-1952 ...DLB-54, 71

Santiago, Danny 1911-1988 ....DLB-122

Santmyer, Helen Hooven 1895-1986 ....Y-84

Sapir, Edward 1884-1939 ....DLB-92

Sapper (see McNeile, Herman Cyril)

Sarduy, Severo 1937- DLB-113

Sargent, Pamela 1948- DLB-8

Saroyan, William
    1908-1981 ....DLB-7, 9, 86; Y-81

Sarraute, Nathalie 1900- DLB-83

Sarrazin, Albertine 1937-1967 ......DLB-83

Sarton, May 1912- DLB-48; Y-81

Sartre, Jean-Paul 1905-1980 ....DLB-72

Sassoon, Siegfried 1886-1967 ....DLB-20

Saturday Review Press DLB-46

Saunders, James 1925- DLB-13

Saunders, John Monk 1897-1940 ....DLB-26

Saunders, Margaret Marshall
    1861-1947 ....DLB-92

Saunders and Otley DLB-106

Savage, James 1784-1873 ....DLB-30

Savage, Marmion W. 1803?-1872 ....DLB-21

Savage, Richard 1697?-1743 ....DLB-95

Savard, Félix-Antoine 1896-1982 ....DLB-68

Sawyer, Ruth 1880-1970 ....DLB-22

Sayers, Dorothy L.
    1893-1957 ....DLB-10, 36, 77, 100

Sayles, John Thomas 1950- DLB-44

Sbarbaro, Camillo 1888-1967 ......DLB-114

Scannell, Vernon 1922- DLB-27

Scarry, Richard 1919-1994 ....DLB-61

Schaeffer, Albrecht 1885-1950 ....DLB-66

Schaeffer, Susan Fromberg 1941- ...DLB-28

Schaper, Edzard 1908-1984 ....DLB-69

Scharf, J. Thomas 1843-1898 ....DLB-47

Scheffel, Joseph Viktor von
    1826-1886 ....DLB-129

Schelling, Friedrich Wilhelm Joseph von
    1775-1854 ....DLB-90

Scherer, Wilhelm 1841-1886 ....DLB-129

Schickele, René 1883-1940 ....DLB-66

Schiff, Dorothy 1903-1989 ....DLB-127

Schiller, Friedrich 1759-1805 ....DLB-94

Schlaf, Johannes 1862-1941 ....DLB-118

Schlegel, August Wilhelm
    1767-1845 ....DLB-94

Schlegel, Dorothea 1763-1839 ....DLB-90

Schlegel, Friedrich 1772-1829 ....DLB-90

Schleiermacher, Friedrich
    1768-1834 ....DLB-90

Schlesinger, Arthur M., Jr. 1917- ...DLB-17

Schlumberger, Jean 1877-1968 ......DLB-65

Schmid, Eduard Hermann Wilhelm (see
    Edschmid, Kasimir)

Schmidt, Arno 1914-1979 ....DLB-69

Schmidt, Johann Kaspar (see Stirner, Max)

Schmidt, Michael 1947- DLB-40

Schmidtbonn, Wilhelm August
    1876-1952 ....DLB-118

Schmitz, James H. 1911- DLB-8

Schnackenberg, Gjertrud 1953- ...DLB-120

Schnitzler, Arthur 1862-1931 ....DLB-81, 118

Schnurre, Wolfdietrich 1920- DLB-69

Schocken Books DLB-46

Schönbeck, Virgilio (see Giotti, Virgilio)

Schönherr, Karl 1867-1943 .... DLB-118

Scholartis Press DLB-112

The Schomburg Center for Research
in Black Culture DLB-76

Schopenhauer, Arthur 1788-1860 ... DLB-90

Schopenhauer, Johanna 1766-1838 .. DLB-90

Schorer, Mark 1908-1977 .... DLB-103

Schouler, James 1839-1920 .... DLB-47

Schrader, Paul 1946- DLB-44

Schreiner, Olive 1855-1920 .... DLB-18

Schroeder, Andreas 1946- DLB-53

Schubart, Christian Friedrich Daniel
1739-1791 .... DLB-97

Schubert, Gotthilf Heinrich
1780-1860 .... DLB-90

Schücking, Levin 1814-1883 .... DLB-133

Schulberg, Budd
1914- DLB-6, 26, 28; Y-81

Schulte, F. J., and Company DLB-49

Schurz, Carl 1829-1906 .... DLB-23

Schuyler, George S. 1895-1977 ... DLB-29, 51

Schuyler, James 1923-1991 ....DLB-5

Schwartz, Delmore 1913-1966 ... DLB-28, 48

Schwartz, Jonathan 1938- Y-82

Schwob, Marcel 1867-1905 .... DLB-123

Science Fantasy DLB-8

Science-Fiction Fandom and
Conventions DLB-8

Science-Fiction Fanzines: The Time
Binders DLB-8

Science-Fiction Films DLB-8

Science Fiction Writers of America and the
Nebula Awards DLB-8

Scot, Reginald circa 1538-1599 ..... DLB-136

Scotellaro, Rocco 1923-1953 .... DLB-128

Scott, Dennis 1939-1991 .... DLB-125

Scott, Dixon 1881-1915 .... DLB-98

Scott, Duncan Campbell
1862-1947 .... DLB-92

Scott, Evelyn 1893-1963 .... DLB-9, 48

Scott, F. R. 1899-1985 .... DLB-88

Scott, Frederick George
1861-1944 .... DLB-92

Scott, Geoffrey 1884-1929 .... DLB-149

Scott, Harvey W. 1838-1910 .... DLB-23

Scott, Paul 1920-1978 .... DLB-14

Scott, Sarah 1723-1795 .... DLB-39

Scott, Tom 1918- DLB-27

Scott, Sir Walter
1771-1832 .... DLB-93, 107, 116, 144

Scott, William Bell 1811-1890 ...... DLB-32

Scott, Walter, Publishing
Company Limited DLB-112

Scott, William R.
[publishing house] DLB-46

Scott-Heron, Gil 1949- DLB-41

Charles Scribner's Sons DLB-49

Scripps, E. W. 1854-1926 .... DLB-25

Scudder, Horace Elisha
1838-1902 ....DLB-42, 71

Scudder, Vida Dutton 1861-1954 .... DLB-71

Scupham, Peter 1933- DLB-40

Seabrook, William 1886-1945 .... DLB-4

Seabury, Samuel 1729-1796 .... DLB-31

The Seafarer circa 970 .... DLB-146

Sealsfield, Charles 1793-1864 ...... DLB-133

Sears, Edward I. 1819?-1876 .... DLB-79

Sears Publishing Company DLB-46

Seaton, George 1911-1979 .... DLB-44

Seaton, William Winston
1785-1866 .... DLB-43

Secker, Martin, and Warburg
Limited DLB-112

Secker, Martin [publishing house] .. DLB-112

Second-Generation Minor Poets of the
Seventeenth Century DLB-126

Sedgwick, Arthur George
1844-1915 .... DLB-64

Sedgwick, Catharine Maria
1789-1867 ....DLB-1, 74

Sedgwick, Ellery 1872-1930 .... DLB-91

Sedley, Sir Charles 1639-1701 ...... DLB-131

Seeger, Alan 1888-1916 .... DLB-45

Seers, Eugene (see Dantin, Louis)

Segal, Erich 1937- Y-86

Seghers, Anna 1900-1983 .... DLB-69

Seid, Ruth (see Sinclair, Jo)

Seidel, Frederick Lewis 1936- Y-84

Seidel, Ina 1885-1974 .... DLB-56

Seigenthaler, John 1927- DLB-127

Seizin Press DLB-112

Séjour, Victor 1817-1874 .... DLB-50

Séjour Marcou et Ferrand, Juan Victor (see
Séjour, Victor)

Selby, Hubert, Jr. 1928- DLB-2

Selden, George 1929-1989 ....DLB-52

Selected English-Language Little Magazines
and Newspapers [France,
1920-1939] DLB-4

Selected Humorous Magazines
(1820-1950) DLB-11

Selected Science-Fiction Magazines and
Anthologies DLB-8

Self, Edwin F. 1920- DLB-137

Seligman, Edwin R. A. 1861-1939 ....DLB-47

Seltzer, Chester E. (see Muro, Amado)

Seltzer, Thomas
[publishing house] DLB-46

Selvon, Sam 1923- DLB-125

Senancour, Etienne de 1770-1846 ...DLB-119

Sendak, Maurice 1928- DLB-61

Senécal, Eva 1905- DLB-92

Sengstacke, John 1912- DLB-127

Šenoa, August 1838-1881 ....DLB-147

"Sensation Novels" (1863), by
H. L. Manse DLB-21

Seredy, Kate 1899-1975 ....DLB-22

Sereni, Vittorio 1913-1983 ....DLB-128

Serling, Rod 1924-1975 ....DLB-26

Serote, Mongane Wally 1944- DLB-125

Serrano, Nina 1934- DLB-122

Service, Robert 1874-1958 ....DLB-92

Seth, Vikram 1952- DLB-120

Seton, Ernest Thompson
1860-1942 ....DLB-92

Settle, Mary Lee 1918- DLB-6

Seume, Johann Gottfried
1763-1810 ....DLB-94

Seuss, Dr. (see Geisel, Theodor Seuss)

The Seventy-fifth Anniversary of the Armistice:
The Wilfred Owen Centenary and the
Great War Exhibit at the University of
Virginia Y-93

Sewall, Joseph 1688-1769 ....DLB-24

Sewall, Richard B. 1908- DLB-111

Sewell, Samuel 1652-1730 ....DLB-24

Sex, Class, Politics, and Religion [in the
British Novel, 1930-1959] DLB-15

Sexton, Anne 1928-1974 ....DLB-5

Shaara, Michael 1929-1988 .... Y-83

Shadwell, Thomas 1641?-1692 ....DLB-80

Shaffer, Anthony 1926- DLB-13

Shaffer, Peter 1926- DLB-13

Shaftesbury, Anthony Ashley Cooper,
    Third Earl of 1671-1713 ....DLB-101

Shairp, Mordaunt 1887-1939 ....DLB-10

Shakespeare, William 1564-1616 .....DLB-62

The Shakespeare Globe Trust Y-93

Shakespeare Head Press DLB-112

Shakhovskoi, Aleksandr Aleksandrovich
    1777-1846 ....DLB-150

Shange, Ntozake 1948- DLB-38

Shapiro, Karl 1913- DLB-48

Sharon Publications DLB-46

Sharpe, Tom 1928- DLB-14

Shaw, Albert 1857-1947 ....DLB-91

Shaw, Bernard 1856-1950 ....DLB-10, 57

Shaw, Henry Wheeler 1818-1885 ....DLB-11

Shaw, Joseph T. 1874-1952 ....DLB-137

Shaw, Irwin 1913-1984 .... DLB-6, 102; Y-84

Shaw, Robert 1927-1978 ....DLB-13, 14

Shaw, Robert B. 1947- DLB-120

Shawn, William 1907-1992 ....DLB-137

Shay, Frank [publishing house] DLB-46

Shea, John Gilmary 1824-1892 ......DLB-30

Sheaffer, Louis 1912-1993 ....DLB-103

Shearing, Joseph 1886-1952 ....DLB-70

Shebbeare, John 1709-1788 ....DLB-39

Sheckley, Robert 1928- DLB-8

Shedd, William G. T. 1820-1894 ....DLB-64

Sheed, Wilfred 1930- DLB-6

Sheed and Ward [U.S.] DLB-46

Sheed and Ward Limited [U.K.] DLB-112

Sheldon, Alice B. (see Tiptree, James, Jr.)

Sheldon, Edward 1886-1946 ....DLB-7

Sheldon and Company DLB-49

Shelley, Mary Wollstonecraft
    1797-1851 ....DLB-110, 116

Shelley, Percy Bysshe
    1792-1822 ....DLB-96, 110

Shelnutt, Eve 1941- DLB-130

Shenstone, William 1714-1763 ......DLB-95

Shepard, Sam 1943- DLB-7

Shepard, Thomas I,
    1604 or 1605-1649 ....DLB-24

Shepard, Thomas II, 1635-1677 .....DLB-24

Shepard, Clark and Brown DLB-49

Shepherd, Luke
    flourished 1547-1554 .... DLB-136

Sherburne, Edward 1616-1702 ..... DLB-131

Sheridan, Frances 1724-1766 .... DLB-39, 84

Sheridan, Richard Brinsley
    1751-1816 .... DLB-89

Sherman, Francis 1871-1926 .... DLB-92

Sherriff, R. C. 1896-1975 .... DLB-10

Sherwood, Robert 1896-1955 ..... DLB-7, 26

Shiels, George 1886-1949 .... DLB-10

Shillaber, B.[enjamin] P.[enhallow]
    1814-1890 .... DLB-1, 11

Shine, Ted 1931- DLB-38

Ship, Reuben 1915-1975 .... DLB-88

Shirer, William L. 1904-1993 .... DLB-4

Shirinsky-Shikhmatov, Sergii Aleksandrovich
    1783-1837 .... DLB-150

Shirley, James 1596-1666 .... DLB-58

Shishkov, Aleksandr Semenovich
    1753-1841 .... DLB-150

Shockley, Ann Allen 1927- DLB-33

Shorthouse, Joseph Henry
    1834-1903 .... DLB-18

Showalter, Elaine 1941- DLB-67

Shulevitz, Uri 1935- DLB-61

Shulman, Max 1919-1988 .... DLB-11

Shute, Henry A. 1856-1943 .... DLB-9

Shuttle, Penelope 1947- DLB-14, 40

Sibbes, Richard 1577-1635 .... DLB-151

Sidgwick and Jackson Limited DLB-112

Sidney, Margaret (see Lothrop, Harriet M.)

Sidney's Press DLB-49

Siegfried Loraine Sassoon: A Centenary Essay
    Tributes from Vivien F. Clarke and
    Michael Thorpe Y-86

Sierra, Rubén 1946- DLB-122

Sierra Club Books DLB-49

Siger of Brabant
    circa 1240-circa 1284 .... DLB-115

Sigourney, Lydia Howard (Huntley)
    1791-1865 .... DLB-1, 42, 73

Silkin, Jon 1930- DLB-27

Silko, Leslie Marmon 1948- DLB-143

Silliphant, Stirling 1918- DLB-26

Sillitoe, Alan 1928- DLB-14, 139

Silman, Roberta 1934- DLB-28

Silva, Beverly 1930- DLB-122

Silverberg, Robert 1935- DLB-8

Silverman, Kenneth 1936- DLB-111

Simak, Clifford D. 1904-1988 ....DLB-8

Simcoe, Elizabeth 1762-1850 ....DLB-99

Simcox, George Augustus
    1841-1905 ....DLB-35

Sime, Jessie Georgina 1868-1958 .....DLB-92

Simenon, Georges
    1903-1989 ....DLB-72; Y-89

Simic, Charles 1938- DLB-105

Simic, Charles,
    Images and "Images" DLB-105

Simmel, Johannes Mario 1924- DLB-69

Simmons, Ernest J. 1903-1972 .....DLB-103

Simmons, Herbert Alfred 1930- DLB-33

Simmons, James 1933- DLB-40

Simms, William Gilmore
    1806-1870 .... DLB-3, 30, 59, 73

Simms and M'Intyre DLB-106

Simon, Claude 1913- DLB-83

Simon, Neil 1927- DLB-7

Simon and Schuster DLB-46

Simons, Katherine Drayton Mayrant
    1890-1969 ....Y-83

Simpson, Helen 1897-1940 ....DLB-77

Simpson, Louis 1923- DLB-5

Simpson, N. F. 1919- DLB-13

Sims, George 1923- DLB-87

Sims, George Robert
    1847-1922 .... DLB-35, 70, 135

Sinán, Rogelio 1904- DLB-145

Sinclair, Andrew 1935- DLB-14

Sinclair, Bertrand William
    1881-1972 ....DLB-92

Sinclair, Jo 1913- DLB-28

Sinclair Lewis Centennial
    Conference Y-85

Sinclair, Lister 1921- DLB-88

Sinclair, May 1863-1946 ....DLB-36, 135

Sinclair, Upton 1878-1968 ....DLB-9

Sinclair, Upton [publishing house] ...DLB-46

Singer, Isaac Bashevis
    1904-1991 .... DLB-6, 28, 52; Y-91

Singmaster, Elsie 1879-1958 ....DLB-9

Sinisgalli, Leonardo 1908-1981 .....DLB-114

Siodmak, Curt 1902- DLB-44

Sissman, L. E. 1928-1976 ....DLB-5

Sisson, C. H. 1914- DLB-27

Sitwell, Edith 1887-1964 .... DLB-20

Sitwell, Osbert 1892-1969 .... DLB-100

Skármeta, Antonio 1940- DLB-145

Skeffington, William
[publishing house] DLB-106

Skelton, John 1463-1529 .... DLB-136

Skelton, Robin 1925- DLB-27, 53

Skinner, Constance Lindsay
1877-1939 .... DLB-92

Skinner, John Stuart 1788-1851 ..... DLB-73

Skipsey, Joseph 1832-1903 .... DLB-35

Slade, Bernard 1930- DLB-53

Slater, Patrick 1880-1951 .... DLB-68

Slaveykov, Pencho 1866-1912 ..... DLB-147

Slavitt, David 1935- DLB-5, 6

Sleigh, Burrows Willcocks Arthur
1821-1869 .... DLB-99

A Slender Thread of Hope: The Kennedy
Center Black Theatre Project ... DLB-38

Slesinger, Tess 1905-1945 .... DLB-102

Slick, Sam (see Haliburton, Thomas Chandler)

Sloane, William, Associates DLB-46

Small, Maynard and Company DLB-49

Small Presses in Great Britain and Ireland,
1960-1985 .... DLB-40

Small Presses I: Jargon Society Y-84

Small Presses II: The Spirit That Moves Us
Press Y-85

Small Presses III: Pushcart Press Y-87

Smart, Christopher 1722-1771 ..... DLB-109

Smart, David A. 1892-1957 .... DLB-137

Smart, Elizabeth 1913-1986 .... DLB-88

Smiles, Samuel 1812-1904 .... DLB-55

Smith, A. J. M. 1902-1980 .... DLB-88

Smith, Adam 1723-1790 .... DLB-104

Smith, Alexander 1829-1867 ..... DLB-32, 55

Smith, Betty 1896-1972 .... Y-82

Smith, Carol Sturm 1938- Y-81

Smith, Charles Henry 1826-1903 .... DLB-11

Smith, Charlotte 1749-1806 .... DLB-39, 109

Smith, Cordwainer 1913-1966 ....DLB-8

Smith, Dave 1942- DLB-5

Smith, Dodie 1896- DLB-10

Smith, Doris Buchanan 1934- DLB-52

Smith, E. E. 1890-1965 ....DLB-8

Smith, Elihu Hubbard 1771-1798 ... DLB-37

Smith, Elizabeth Oakes (Prince)
1806-1893 .... DLB-1

Smith, George D. 1870-1920 ...... DLB-140

Smith, George O. 1911-1981 .... DLB-8

Smith, Goldwin 1823-1910 .... DLB-99

Smith, H. Allen 1907-1976 ......DLB-11, 29

Smith, Hazel Brannon 1914- DLB-127

Smith, Horatio (Horace)
1779-1849 .... DLB-116

Smith, Horatio (Horace) 1779-1849 and
James Smith 1775-1839 .... DLB-96

Smith, Iain Crichton
1928- DLB-40, 139

Smith, J. Allen 1860-1924 .... DLB-47

Smith, John 1580-1631 ....DLB-24, 30

Smith, Josiah 1704-1781 .... DLB-24

Smith, Ken 1938- DLB-40

Smith, Lee 1944- DLB-143; Y-83

Smith, Logan Pearsall 1865-1946 .... DLB-98

Smith, Mark 1935- Y-82

Smith, Michael 1698-circa 1771 ..... DLB-31

Smith, Red 1905-1982 .... DLB-29

Smith, Roswell 1829-1892 .... DLB-79

Smith, Samuel Harrison
1772-1845 .... DLB-43

Smith, Samuel Stanhope
1751-1819 .... DLB-37

Smith, Seba 1792-1868 ....DLB-1, 11

Smith, Sir Thomas 1513-1577 ...... DLB-132

Smith, Stevie 1902-1971 .... DLB-20

Smith, Sydney 1771-1845 .... DLB-107

Smith, Sydney Goodsir 1915-1975 ... DLB-27

Smith, William
flourished 1595-1597 .... DLB-136

Smith, William 1727-1803 .... DLB-31

Smith, William 1728-1793 .... DLB-30

Smith, William Gardner
1927-1974 .... DLB-76

Smith, William Jay 1918- DLB-5

Smith, Harrison, and Robert Haas
[publishing house] DLB-46

Smith, J. Stilman, and Company DLB-49

Smith, W. B., and Company DLB-49

Smith, W. H., and Son DLB-106

Smithers, Leonard
[publishing house] DLB-112

Smollett, Tobias 1721-1771 .....DLB-39, 104

Snellings, Rolland (see Touré, Askia
Muhammad)

Snodgrass, W. D. 1926- DLB-5

Snow, C. P. 1905-1980 .... DLB-15, 77

Snyder, Gary 1930- DLB-5, 16

Sobiloff, Hy 1912-1970 ....DLB-48

The Society for Textual Scholarship and
TEXT Y-87

The Society for the History of Authorship,
Reading and Publishing Y-92

Soffici, Ardengo 1879-1964 ....DLB-114

Solano, Solita 1888-1975 ....DLB-4

Sollers, Philippe 1936- DLB-83

Solmi, Sergio 1899-1981 ....DLB-114

Solomon, Carl 1928- DLB-16

Solway, David 1941- DLB-53

Solzhenitsyn and America Y-85

Somerville, Edith Œnone
1858-1949 ....DLB-135

Sontag, Susan 1933- DLB-2, 67

Sorrentino, Gilbert 1929- DLB-5; Y-80

Sorge, Reinhard Johannes
1892-1916 ....DLB-118

Sotheby, William 1757-1833 ....DLB-93

Soto, Gary 1952- DLB-82

Sources for the Study of Tudor and Stuart
Drama DLB-62

Souster, Raymond 1921- DLB-88

The *South English Legendary*
circa thirteenth-fifteenth
centuries DLB-146

Southerland, Ellease 1943- DLB-33

Southern, Terry 1924- DLB-2

Southern Writers Between the
Wars DLB-9

Southerne, Thomas 1659-1746 ......DLB-80

Southey, Caroline Anne Bowles
1786-1854 ....DLB-116

Southey, Robert
1774-1843 .... DLB-93, 107, 142

Soyfer, Jura 1912-1939 ....DLB-124

Soyinka, Wole 1934- DLB-125

Spacks, Barry 1931- DLB-105

Spark, Muriel 1918- DLB-15, 139

Sparks, Jared 1789-1866 .... DLB-1, 30

Sparshott, Francis 1926- DLB-60

Späth, Gerold 1939- DLB-75

Spatola, Adriano 1941-1988 ....DLB-128

Spaziani, Maria Luisa 1924- DLB-128

The Spectator 1828- DLB-110

Spedding, James 1808-1881 ....DLB-144

Speght, Rachel 1597-after 1630 .....DLB-126

Spellman, A. B. 1935- DLB-41

Spencer, Anne 1882-1975 ....DLB-51, 54

Spencer, Elizabeth 1921- DLB-6

Spencer, Herbert 1820-1903 ....DLB-57

Spencer, Scott 1945- Y-86

Spender, J. A. 1862-1942 ....DLB-98

Spender, Stephen 1909- DLB-20

Sperr, Martin 1944- DLB-124

Spicer, Jack 1925-1965 ....DLB-5, 16

Spielberg, Peter 1929- Y-81

Spielhagen, Friedrich 1829-1911 ....DLB-129

"*Spielmannsepen*"
(circa 1152-circa 1500) DLB-148

Spier, Peter 1927- DLB-61

Spinrad, Norman 1940- DLB-8

Spires, Elizabeth 1952- DLB-120

Spitteler, Carl 1845-1924 ....DLB-129

Spivak, Lawrence E. 1900- DLB-137

Spofford, Harriet Prescott
1835-1921 ....DLB-74

Squibob (see Derby, George Horatio)

Staël, Germaine de 1766-1817 ......DLB-119

Staël-Holstein, Anne-Louise Germaine de
(see Staël, Germaine de)

Stafford, Jean 1915-1979 ....DLB-2

Stafford, William 1914- DLB-5

Stage Censorship: "The Rejected Statement"
(1911), by Bernard Shaw
[excerpts] DLB-10

Stallings, Laurence 1894-1968 .....DLB-7, 44

Stallworthy, Jon 1935- DLB-40

Stampp, Kenneth M. 1912- DLB-17

Stanford, Ann 1916- DLB-5

Stanković, Borisav ("Bora")
1876-1927 ....DLB-147

Stanley, Thomas 1625-1678 ....DLB-131

Stanton, Elizabeth Cady
1815-1902 ....DLB-79

Stanton, Frank L. 1857-1927 ....DLB-25

Stanton, Maura 1946- DLB-120

Stapledon, Olaf 1886-1950 ....DLB-15

Star Spangled Banner Office DLB-49

Starkey, Thomas
circa 1499-1538 ....DLB-132

Starkweather, David 1935- DLB-7

Statements on the Art of Poetry DLB-54

Stead, Robert J. C. 1880-1959 ......DLB-92

Steadman, Mark 1930- DLB-6

The Stealthy School of Criticism (1871), by
Dante Gabriel Rossetti DLB-35

Stearns, Harold E. 1891-1943 ....DLB-4

Stedman, Edmund Clarence
1833-1908 ....DLB-64

Steegmuller, Francis 1906- DLB-111

Steele, Max 1922- Y-80

Steele, Richard 1672-1729 ......DLB-84, 101

Steele, Timothy 1948- DLB-120

Steele, Wilbur Daniel 1886-1970 ....DLB-86

Steere, Richard circa 1643-1721 .....DLB-24

Stegner, Wallace 1909-1993 ... DLB-9; Y-93

Stehr, Hermann 1864-1940 ....DLB-66

Steig, William 1907- DLB-61

Stein, Gertrude 1874-1946 ....DLB-4, 54, 86

Stein, Leo 1872-1947 ....DLB-4

Stein and Day Publishers DLB-46

Steinbeck, John 1902-1968 ...DLB-7, 9; DS-2

Steiner, George 1929- DLB-67

Stendhal 1783-1842 ....DLB-119

Stephen Crane: A Revaluation Virginia
Tech Conference, 1989 ....Y-89

Stephen, Leslie 1832-1904 .....DLB-57, 144

Stephens, Alexander H. 1812-1883 .. DLB-47

Stephens, Ann 1810-1886 ....DLB-3, 73

Stephens, Charles Asbury
1844?-1931 ....DLB-42

Stephens, James 1882?-1950 ....DLB-19

Sterling, George 1869-1926 ....DLB-54

Sterling, James 1701-1763 ....DLB-24

Sterling, John 1806-1844 ....DLB-116

Stern, Gerald 1925- DLB-105

Stern, Madeleine B. 1912- ... DLB-111, 140

Stern, Gerald, Living in Ruin DLB-105

Stern, Richard 1928- Y-87

Stern, Stewart 1922- DLB-26

Sterne, Laurence 1713-1768 ....DLB-39

Sternheim, Carl 1878-1942 .....DLB-56, 118

Sternhold, Thomas ?-1549 and
John Hopkins ?-1570 ....DLB-132

Stevens, Henry 1819-1886 ....DLB-140

Stevens, Wallace 1879-1955 ....DLB-54

Stevenson, Anne 1933- DLB-40

Stevenson, Robert Louis
1850-1894 ....DLB-18, 57, 141

Stewart, Donald Ogden
1894-1980 ....DLB-4, 11, 26

Stewart, Dugald 1753-1828 ....DLB-31

Stewart, George, Jr. 1848-1906 ......DLB-99

Stewart, George R. 1895-1980 ....DLB-8

Stewart and Kidd Company DLB-46

Stewart, Randall 1896-1964 ....DLB-103

Stickney, Trumbull 1874-1904 ......DLB-54

Stifter, Adalbert 1805-1868 ....DLB-133

Stiles, Ezra 1727-1795 ....DLB-31

Still, James 1906- DLB-9

Stirner, Max 1806-1856 ....DLB-129

Stith, William 1707-1755 ....DLB-31

Stock, Elliot [publishing house] DLB-106

Stockton, Frank R. 1834-1902 ....DLB-42, 74

Stoddard, Ashbel
[publishing house] DLB-49

Stoddard, Richard Henry
1825-1903 ....DLB-3, 64

Stoddard, Solomon 1643-1729 ....DLB-24

Stoker, Bram 1847-1912 ....DLB-36, 70

Stokes, Frederick A., Company DLB-49

Stokes, Thomas L. 1898-1958 ....DLB-29

Stokesbury, Leon 1945- DLB-120

Stolberg, Christian Graf zu
1748-1821 ....DLB-94

Stolberg, Friedrich Leopold Graf zu
1750-1819 ....DLB-94

Stone, Herbert S., and Company DLB-49

Stone, Lucy 1818-1893 ....DLB-79

Stone, Melville 1848-1929 ....DLB-25

Stone, Ruth 1915- DLB-105

Stone, Samuel 1602-1663 ....DLB-24

Stone and Kimball DLB-49

Stoppard, Tom 1937- DLB-13; Y-85

Storey, Anthony 1928- DLB-14

Storey, David 1933- DLB-13, 14

Storm, Theodor 1817-1888 ....DLB-129

Story, Thomas circa 1670-1742 ......DLB-31

Story, William Wetmore 1819-1895 ...DLB-1

Storytelling: A Contemporary
Renaissance Y-84

Stoughton, William 1631-1701 ...... DLB-24

Stow, John 1525-1605 .... DLB-132

Stowe, Harriet Beecher
1811-1896 .... DLB-1, 12, 42, 74

Stowe, Leland 1899- DLB-29

Stoyanov, Dimitŭr Ivanov (see Elin Pelin)

Strachey, Lytton
1880-1932 .... DLB-149; DS-10

Strachey, Lytton, Preface to *Eminent
Victorians* DLB-149

Strahan and Company DLB-106

Strand, Mark 1934- DLB-5

The Strasbourg Oaths 842 .... DLB-148

Stratemeyer, Edward 1862-1930 .... DLB-42

Stratton and Barnard DLB-49

Straub, Peter 1943- Y-84

Strauß, Botho 1944- DLB-124

Strauß, David Friedrich
1808-1874 .... DLB-133

Street, Cecil John Charles (see Rhode, John)

Street, G. S. 1867-1936 .... DLB-135

Street and Smith DLB-49

Streeter, Edward 1891-1976 .... DLB-11

Streeter, Thomas Winthrop
1883-1965 .... DLB-140

Stribling, T. S. 1881-1965 ....DLB-9

Der Stricker circa 1190-circa 1250 .. DLB-138

Strickland, Samuel 1804-1867 ...... DLB-99

Stringer and Townsend DLB-49

Stringer, Arthur 1874-1950 .... DLB-92

Strittmatter, Erwin 1912- DLB-69

Strode, William 1630-1645 .... DLB-126

Strother, David Hunter 1816-1888 ....DLB-3

Strouse, Jean 1945- DLB-111

Stuart, Dabney 1937- DLB-105

Stuart, Dabney, Knots into Webs: Some Autobiographical Sources DLB-105

Stuart, Jesse
1906-1984 ....DLB-9, 48, 102; Y-84

Stuart, Lyle [publishing house] DLB-46

Stubbs, Harry Clement (see Clement, Hal)

Studio DLB-112

The Study of Poetry (1880), by
Matthew Arnold DLB-35

Sturgeon, Theodore
1918-1985 .... DLB-8; Y-85

Sturges, Preston 1898-1959 .... DLB-26

"Style" (1840; revised, 1859), by
Thomas de Quincey [excerpt] DLB-57

"Style" (1888), by Walter Pater DLB-57

Style (1897), by Walter Raleigh
[excerpt] DLB-57

"Style" (1877), by T. H. Wright
[excerpt] DLB-57

"Le Style c'est l'homme" (1892), by
W. H. Mallock DLB-57

Styron, William 1925- DLB-2, 143; Y-80

Suárez, Mario 1925- DLB-82

Such, Peter 1939- DLB-60

Suckling, Sir John 1609-1641? ...DLB-58, 126

Suckow, Ruth 1892-1960 ....DLB-9, 102

Sudermann, Hermann 1857-1928 ...DLB-118

Sue, Eugène 1804-1857 ....DLB-119

Sue, Marie-Joseph (see Sue, Eugène)

Suggs, Simon (see Hooper, Johnson Jones)

Sukenick, Ronald 1932- Y-81

Suknaski, Andrew 1942- DLB-53

Sullivan, Alan 1868-1947 .... DLB-92

Sullivan, C. Gardner 1886-1965 ..... DLB-26

Sullivan, Frank 1892-1976 .... DLB-11

Sulte, Benjamin 1841-1923 .... DLB-99

Sulzberger, Arthur Hays
1891-1968 .... DLB-127

Sulzberger, Arthur Ochs 1926- ... DLB-127

Sulzer, Johann Georg 1720-1779 ..... DLB-97

Sumarokov, Aleksandr Petrovich
1717-1777 .... DLB-150

Summers, Hollis 1916- DLB-6

Sumner, Henry A.
[publishing house] DLB-49

Surtees, Robert Smith 1803-1864 .... DLB-21

A Survey of Poetry Anthologies,
1879-1960 .... DLB-54

Surveys of the Year's Biographies

A Transit of Poets and Others: American
Biography in 1982 ....Y-82

The Year in Literary Biography ...Y-83–Y-94

Survey of the Year's Book Publishing

The Year in Book Publishing Y-86

Survey of the Year's Children's Books

The Year in Children's Books Y-92–Y-94

Surveys of the Year's Drama

The Year in Drama
..................Y-82–Y-85, Y-87–Y-94

The Year in London Theatre Y-92

Surveys of the Year's Fiction

The Year's Work in Fiction:
A Survey Y-82

The Year in Fiction: A Biased View Y-83

The Year in Fiction ... Y-84–Y-86, Y-89, Y-94

The Year in the
Novel Y-87, Y-88, Y-90–Y-93

The Year in Short Stories Y-87

The Year in the
Short Story Y-88, Y-90–Y-93

Survey of the Year's Literary Theory

The Year in Literary Theory Y-92–Y-93

Surveys of the Year's Poetry

The Year's Work in American
Poetry Y-82

The Year in Poetry Y-83–Y-92, Y-94

Sutherland, Efua Theodora
1924- DLB-117

Sutherland, John 1919-1956 ....DLB-68

Sutro, Alfred 1863-1933 ....DLB-10

Swados, Harvey 1920-1972 ....DLB-2

Swain, Charles 1801-1874 ....DLB-32

Swallow Press DLB-46

Swan Sonnenschein Limited DLB-106

Swanberg, W. A. 1907- DLB-103

Swenson, May 1919-1989 ....DLB-5

Swerling, Jo 1897- DLB-44

Swift, Jonathan
1667-1745 .... DLB-39, 95, 101

Swinburne, A. C. 1837-1909 .... DLB-35, 57

Swineshead, Richard floruit
circa 1350 ....DLB-115

Swinnerton, Frank 1884-1982 ....DLB-34

Swisshelm, Jane Grey 1815-1884 .....DLB-43

Swope, Herbert Bayard 1882-1958 ...DLB-25

Swords, T. and J., and Company DLB-49

Swords, Thomas 1763-1843 and
Swords, James ?-1844 ....DLB-73

Sylvester, Josuah
1562 or 1563 - 1618 ....DLB-121

Symonds, Emily Morse (see Paston, George)

Symonds, John Addington
1840-1893 .... DLB-57, 144

Symons, A. J. A. 1900-1941 ....DLB-149

Symons, Arthur
1865-1945 .... DLB-19, 57, 149

Symons, Julian 1912- DLB-87; Y-92

Symons, Scott 1933- DLB-53

A Symposium on *The Columbia History of the Novel* Y-92

Synge, John Millington 1871-1909 ....DLB-10, 19

Synge Summer School: J. M. Synge and the Irish Theater, Rathdrum, County Wiclow, Ireland Y-93

Syrett, Netta 1865-1943 ....DLB-135

T

Taban lo Liyong 1939?- DLB-125

Taché, Joseph-Charles 1820-1894 ....DLB-99

Tafolla, Carmen 1951- DLB-82

Taggard, Genevieve 1894-1948 ......DLB-45

Tagger, Theodor (see Bruckner, Ferdinand)

Tait, J. Selwin, and Sons DLB-49

Tait's Edinburgh Magazine 1832-1861 ....DLB-110

The Takarazaka Revue Company Y-91

Tallent, Elizabeth 1954- DLB-130

Talvj 1797-1870 ....DLB-59, 133

Taradash, Daniel 1913- DLB-44

Tarbell, Ida M. 1857-1944 ....DLB-47

Tardivel, Jules-Paul 1851-1905 ......DLB-99

Targan, Barry 1932- DLB-130

Tarkington, Booth 1869-1946 ....DLB-9, 102

Tashlin, Frank 1913-1972 ....DLB-44

Tate, Allen 1899-1979 .... DLB-4, 45, 63

Tate, James 1943- DLB-5

Tate, Nahum circa 1652-1715 ....DLB-80

Tatian circa 830 ....DLB-148

Tavčar, Ivan 1851-1923 ....DLB-147

Taylor, Bayard 1825-1878 ....DLB-3

Taylor, Bert Leston 1866-1921 ......DLB-25

Taylor, Charles H. 1846-1921 ....DLB-25

Taylor, Edward circa 1642-1729 .....DLB-24

Taylor, Elizabeth 1912-1975 ....DLB-139

Taylor, Henry 1942- DLB-5

Taylor, Sir Henry 1800-1886 ....DLB-32

Taylor, Jeremy circa 1613-1667 .....DLB-151

Taylor, John 1577 or 1578 - 1653 ....DLB-121

Taylor, Mildred D. ?- DLB-52

Taylor, Peter 1917-1994 .... Y-81, Y-94

Taylor, William, and Company DLB-49

Taylor-Made Shakespeare? Or Is "Shall I Die?" the Long-Lost Text of Bottom's Dream? Y-85

Teasdale, Sara 1884-1933 ....DLB-45

The Tea-Table (1725), by Eliza Haywood [excerpt] DLB-39

Telles, Lygia Fagundes 1924- DLB-113

Temple, Sir William 1628-1699 ....DLB-101

Tenn, William 1919- DLB-8

Tennant, Emma 1937- DLB-14

Tenney, Tabitha Gilman 1762-1837 ....DLB-37

Tennyson, Alfred 1809-1892 ....DLB-32

Tennyson, Frederick 1807-1898 .....DLB-32

Terhune, Albert Payson 1872-1942 ... DLB-9

Terry, Megan 1932- DLB-7

Terson, Peter 1932- DLB-13

Tesich, Steve 1943- Y-83

Tessa, Delio 1886-1939 ....DLB-114

Testori, Giovanni 1923-1993 ......DLB-128

Tey, Josephine 1896?-1952 ....DLB-77

Thacher, James 1754-1844 ....DLB-37

Thackeray, William Makepeace 1811-1863 ....DLB-21, 55

Thames and Hudson Limited DLB-112

Thanet, Octave (see French, Alice)

The Theater in Shakespeare's Time DLB-62

The Theatre Guild DLB-7

Thegan and the Astronomer flourished circa 850 ....DLB-148

Thelwall, John 1764-1834 ....DLB-93

Theodulf circa 760-circa 821 ......DLB-148

Theriault, Yves 1915-1983 ....DLB-88

Thério, Adrien 1925- DLB-53

Theroux, Paul 1941- DLB-2

Thibaudeau, Colleen 1925- DLB-88

Thielen, Benedict 1903-1965 ......DLB-102

Thiong'o Ngugi wa (see Ngugi wa Thiong'o)

Third-Generation Minor Poets of the Seventeenth Century DLB-131

Thoma, Ludwig 1867-1921 ....DLB-66

Thoma, Richard 1902- DLB-4

Thomas, Audrey 1935- DLB-60

Thomas, D. M. 1935- DLB-40

Thomas, Dylan 1914-1953 ....DLB-13, 20, 139

Thomas, Edward 1878-1917 .....DLB-19, 98

Thomas, Gwyn 1913-1981 ....DLB-15

Thomas, Isaiah 1750-1831 ....DLB-43, 73

Thomas, Isaiah [publishing house] ...DLB-49

Thomas, John 1900-1932 ....DLB-4

Thomas, Joyce Carol 1938- DLB-33

Thomas, Lorenzo 1944- DLB-41

Thomas, R. S. 1915- DLB-27

Thomasîn von Zerclære circa 1186-circa 1259 ....DLB-138

Thompson, David 1770-1857 ....DLB-99

Thompson, Dorothy 1893-1961 .....DLB-29

Thompson, Francis 1859-1907 ......DLB-19

Thompson, George Selden (see Selden, George)

Thompson, John 1938-1976 ....DLB-60

Thompson, John R. 1823-1873 ....DLB-3, 73

Thompson, Lawrance 1906-1973 ...DLB-103

Thompson, Maurice 1844-1901 ....DLB-71, 74

Thompson, Ruth Plumly 1891-1976 ....DLB-22

Thompson, Thomas Phillips 1843-1933 ....DLB-99

Thompson, William Tappan 1812-1882 ....DLB-3, 11

Thomson, Edward William 1849-1924 ....DLB-92

Thomson, James 1700-1748 ....DLB-95

Thomson, James 1834-1882 ....DLB-35

Thomson, Mortimer 1831-1875 .....DLB-11

Thoreau, Henry David 1817-1862 ....DLB-1

Thorpe, Thomas Bangs 1815-1878 ....DLB-3, 11

Thoughts on Poetry and Its Varieties (1833), by John Stuart Mill DLB-32

Thrale, Hester Lynch (see Piozzi, Hester Lynch [Thrale])

Thümmel, Moritz August von 1738-1817 ....DLB-97

Thurber, James 1894-1961 .... DLB-4, 11, 22, 102

Thurman, Wallace 1902-1934 ....DLB-51

Thwaite, Anthony 1930- DLB-40

Thwaites, Reuben Gold 1853-1913 ....DLB-47

Ticknor, George 1791-1871 ....DLB-1, 59, 140

Ticknor and Fields DLB-49

Ticknor and Fields (revived) DLB-46

Tieck, Ludwig 1773-1853 .... DLB-90

Tietjens, Eunice 1884-1944 .... DLB-54

Tilney, Edmund circa 1536-1610 ... DLB-136

Tilt, Charles [publishing house] DLB-106

Tilton, J. E., and Company DLB-49

Time and Western Man (1927), by Wyndham
Lewis [excerpts] DLB-36

Time-Life Books DLB-46

Times Books DLB-46

Timothy, Peter circa 1725-1782 ..... DLB-43

Timrod, Henry 1828-1867 .... DLB-3

Tinker, Chauncey Brewster
1876-1963 .... DLB-140

Tinsley Brothers DLB-106

Tiptree, James, Jr. 1915-1987 .... DLB-8

Titus, Edward William 1870-1952 ....DLB-4

Toklas, Alice B. 1877-1967 .... DLB-4

Tolkien, J. R. R. 1892-1973 .... DLB-15

Toller, Ernst 1893-1939 .... DLB-124

Tollet, Elizabeth 1694-1754 .... DLB-95

Tolson, Melvin B. 1898-1966 .... DLB-48, 76

Tom Jones (1749), by Henry Fielding
[excerpt] DLB-39

Tomlinson, Charles 1927- DLB-40

Tomlinson, H. M. 1873-1958 ... DLB-36, 100

Tompkins, Abel [publishing house] .. DLB-49

Tompson, Benjamin 1642-1714 ..... DLB-24

Tonks, Rosemary 1932- DLB-14

Toole, John Kennedy 1937-1969 .... Y-81

Toomer, Jean 1894-1967 .... DLB-45, 51

Tor Books DLB-46

Torberg, Friedrich 1908-1979 ...... DLB-85

Torrence, Ridgely 1874-1950 .... DLB-54

Torres-Metzger, Joseph V.
1933- DLB-122

Toth, Susan Allen 1940- Y-86

Tough-Guy Literature DLB-9

Touré, Askia Muhammad 1938- ... DLB-41

Tourgée, Albion W. 1838-1905 ..... DLB-79

Tourneur, Cyril circa 1580-1626 .... DLB-58

Tournier, Michel 1924- DLB-83

Tousey, Frank [publishing house] ... DLB-49

Tower Publications DLB-46

Towne, Benjamin circa 1740-1793 ... DLB-43

Towne, Robert 1936- DLB-44

The Townely Plays
fifteenth and sixteenth
centuries DLB-146

Townshend, Aurelian
by 1583 - circa 1651 .... DLB-121

Tracy, Honor 1913- DLB-15

Traherne, Thomas 1637?-1674 ..... DLB-131

Traill, Catharine Parr 1802-1899 .... DLB-99

Train, Arthur 1875-1945 .... DLB-86

The Transatlantic Publishing
Company DLB-49

Transcendentalists, American DS-5

Translators of the Twelfth Century:
Literary Issues Raised and Impact
Created DLB-115

Traven, B.
1882? or 1890?-1969? DLB-9, 56

Travers, Ben 1886-1980 .... DLB-10

Trediakovsky, Vasilii Kirillovich
1703-1769 .... DLB-150

Trejo, Ernesto 1950- DLB-122

Trelawny, Edward John
1792-1881 .... DLB-110, 116, 144

Tremain, Rose 1943- DLB-14

Tremblay, Michel 1942- DLB-60

Trends in Twentieth-Century
Mass Market Publishing DLB-46

Trent, William P. 1862-1939 .... DLB-47

Trescot, William Henry
1822-1898 .... DLB-30

Trevelyan, Sir George Otto
1838-1928 .... DLB-144

Trevisa, John
circa 1342-circa 1402 .... DLB-146

Trevor, William 1928- DLB-14, 139

Trierer Floyris circa 1170-1180 ...... DLB-138

Trilling, Lionel 1905-1975 ....DLB-28, 63

Trilussa 1871-1950 .... DLB-114

Triolet, Elsa 1896-1970 .... DLB-72

Tripp, John 1927- DLB-40

Trocchi, Alexander 1925- DLB-15

Trollope, Anthony 1815-1882 ....DLB-21, 57

Trollope, Frances 1779-1863 .... DLB-21

Troop, Elizabeth 1931- DLB-14

Trotter, Catharine 1679-1749 .... DLB-84

Trotti, Lamar 1898-1952 .... DLB-44

Trottier, Pierre 1925- DLB-60

Troupe, Quincy Thomas, Jr.
1943- DLB-41

Trow, John F., and Company DLB-49

Truillier-Lacombe, Joseph-Patrice
1807-1863 ....DLB-99

Trumbo, Dalton 1905-1976 ....DLB-26

Trumbull, Benjamin 1735-1820 ......DLB-30

Trumbull, John 1750-1831 ....DLB-31

T. S. Eliot Centennial Y-88

Tucholsky, Kurt 1890-1935 ....DLB-56

Tucker, George 1775-1861 .... DLB-3, 30

Tucker, Nathaniel Beverley
1784-1851 ....DLB-3

Tucker, St. George 1752-1827 ......DLB-37

Tuckerman, Henry Theodore
1813-1871 ....DLB-64

Tunis, John R. 1889-1975 ....DLB-22

Tunstall, Cuthbert 1474-1559 ......DLB-132

Tuohy, Frank 1925- DLB-14, 139

Tupper, Martin F. 1810-1889 ....DLB-32

Turbyfill, Mark 1896- DLB-45

Turco, Lewis 1934- Y-84

Turnbull, Andrew 1921-1970 ......DLB-103

Turnbull, Gael 1928- DLB-40

Turner, Arlin 1909-1980 ....DLB-103

Turner, Charles (Tennyson)
1808-1879 ....DLB-32

Turner, Frederick 1943- DLB-40

Turner, Frederick Jackson
1861-1932 ....DLB-17

Turner, Joseph Addison
1826-1868 ....DLB-79

Turpin, Waters Edward
1910-1968 ....DLB-51

Turrini, Peter 1944- DLB-124

Tutuola, Amos 1920- DLB-125

Twain, Mark (see Clemens,
Samuel Langhorne)

The 'Twenties and Berlin, by
Alex Natan DLB-66

Tyler, Anne 1941- DLB-6, 143; Y-82

Tyler, Moses Coit 1835-1900 .... DLB-47, 64

Tyler, Royall 1757-1826 ....DLB-37

Tylor, Edward Burnett 1832-1917 ....DLB-57

Tyndale, William
circa 1494-1536 ....DLB-132

U

Udall, Nicholas 1504-1556 ....DLB-62

Uhland, Ludwig 1787-1862 ....DLB-90

Uhse, Bodo 1904-1963 . . . . .DLB-69

Ujević, Augustin ("Tin")
 1891-1955 . . . . .DLB-147

Ulibarrí, Sabine R. 1919- DLB-82

Ulica, Jorge 1870-1926 . . . . .DLB-82

Ulizio, B. George 1889-1969 . . . . . . .DLB-140

Ulrich von Liechtenstein
 circa 1200-circa 1275 . . . . .DLB-138

Ulrich von Zatzikhoven
 before 1194-after 1214 . . . . .DLB-138

Unamuno, Miguel de 1864-1936 . . . .DLB-108

Under the Microscope (1872), by
 A. C. Swinburne DLB-35

Unger, Friederike Helene
 1741-1813 . . . . .DLB-94

Ungaretti, Giuseppe 1888-1970 . . . . .DLB-114

United States Book Company DLB-49

Universal Publishing and Distributing
 Corporation DLB-46

The University of Iowa Writers' Workshop
 Golden Jubilee Y-86

The University of South Carolina
 Press Y-94

University of Wales Press DLB-112

"The Unknown Public" (1858), by
 Wilkie Collins [excerpt] DLB-57

Unruh, Fritz von 1885-1970 . . . .DLB-56, 118

Unspeakable Practices II: The Festival of
 Vanguard Narrative at Brown
 University Y-93

Unwin, T. Fisher
 [publishing house] DLB-106

Upchurch, Boyd B. (see Boyd, John)

Updike, John
 1932- DLB-2, 5, 143; Y-80, 82; DS-3

Upton, Bertha 1849-1912 . . . . .DLB-141

Upton, Charles 1948- DLB-16

Upton, Florence K. 1873-1922 . . . . . .DLB-141

Upward, Allen 1863-1926 . . . . .DLB-36

Urista, Alberto Baltazar (see Alurista)

Urzidil, Johannes 1896-1976 . . . . . . .DLB-85

Urquhart, Fred 1912- DLB-139

The Uses of Facsimile Y-90

Usk, Thomas died 1388 . . . . .DLB-146

Uslar Pietri, Arturo 1906- DLB-113

Ustinov, Peter 1921- DLB-13

Uz, Johann Peter 1720-1796 . . . . . . .DLB-97

V

Vac, Bertrand 1914- DLB-88

Vail, Laurence 1891-1968 . . . . DLB-4

Vailland, Roger 1907-1965 . . . . DLB-83

Vajda, Ernest 1887-1954 . . . . DLB-44

Valdés, Gina 1943- DLB-122

Valdez, Luis Miguel 1940- DLB-122

Valduga, Patrizia 1953- DLB-128

Valente, José Angel 1929- DLB-108

Valenzuela, Luisa 1938- DLB-113

Valeri, Diego 1887-1976 . . . . DLB-128

Valgardson, W. D. 1939- DLB-60

Valle, Víctor Manuel 1950- DLB-122

Valle-Inclán, Ramón del
 1866-1936 . . . . DLB-134

Vallejo, Armando 1949- DLB-122

Vallès, Jules 1832-1885 . . . . DLB-123

Vallette, Marguerite Eymery (see Rachilde)

Valverde, José María 1926- DLB-108

Van Allsburg, Chris 1949- DLB-61

Van Anda, Carr 1864-1945 . . . . DLB-25

Van Doren, Mark 1894-1972 . . . . DLB-45

van Druten, John 1901-1957 . . . . DLB-10

Van Duyn, Mona 1921- DLB-5

Van Dyke, Henry 1852-1933 . . . . DLB-71

Van Dyke, Henry 1928- DLB-33

van Itallie, Jean-Claude 1936- DLB-7

Van Rensselaer, Mariana Griswold
 1851-1934 . . . . DLB-47

Van Rensselaer, Mrs. Schuyler (see Van
 Rensselaer, Mariana Griswold)

Van Vechten, Carl 1880-1964 . . . . . DLB-4, 9

van Vogt, A. E. 1912- DLB-8

Vanbrugh, Sir John 1664-1726 . . . . . . DLB-80

Vance, Jack 1916?- DLB-8

Vane, Sutton 1888-1963 . . . . DLB-10

Vanguard Press DLB-46

Vann, Robert L. 1879-1940 . . . . DLB-29

Vargas, Llosa, Mario 1936- DLB-145

Varley, John 1947- Y-81

Varnhagen von Ense, Karl August
 1785-1858 . . . . DLB-90

Varnhagen von Ense, Rahel
 1771-1833 . . . . DLB-90

Vásquez Montalbán, Manuel
 1939- DLB-134

Vassa, Gustavus (see Equiano, Olaudah)

Vassalli, Sebastiano 1941- DLB-128

Vaughan, Henry 1621-1695 . . . . . . .DLB-131

Vaughan, Thomas 1621-1666 . . . . . .DLB-131

Vaux, Thomas, Lord 1509-1556 . . . .DLB-132

Vazov, Ivan 1850-1921 . . . . .DLB-147

Vega, Janine Pommy 1942- DLB-16

Veiller, Anthony 1903-1965 . . . . .DLB-44

Velásquez-Trevino, Gloria
 1949- .DLB-122

Veloz Maggiolo, Marcio 1936- DLB-145

Venegas, Daniel ?-? DLB-82

Vergil, Polydore circa 1470-1555 . . .DLB-132

Veríssimo, Erico 1905-1975 . . . . . . .DLB-145

Verne, Jules 1828-1905 . . . . .DLB-123

Verplanck, Gulian C. 1786-1870 . . . . .DLB-59

Very, Jones 1813-1880 . . . . .DLB-1

Vian, Boris 1920-1959 . . . . .DLB-72

Vickers, Roy 1888?-1965 . . . . .DLB-77

Victoria 1819-1901 . . . . .DLB-55

Victoria Press DLB-106

Vidal, Gore 1925- DLB-6

Viebig, Clara 1860-1952 . . . . .DLB-66

Viereck, George Sylvester
 1884-1962 . . . . .DLB-54

Viereck, Peter 1916- DLB-5

Viets, Roger 1738-1811 . . . . .DLB-99

Viewpoint: Politics and Performance, by
 David Edgar DLB-13

Vigil-Piñon, Evangelina 1949- DLB-122

Vigneault, Gilles 1928- DLB-60

Vigny, Alfred de 1797-1863 . . . . .DLB-119

Vigolo, Giorgio 1894-1983 . . . . .DLB-114

The Viking Press DLB-46

Villanueva, Alma Luz 1944- DLB-122

Villanueva, Tino 1941- DLB-82

Villard, Henry 1835-1900 . . . . .DLB-23

Villard, Oswald Garrison
 1872-1949 . . . . .DLB-25, 91

Villarreal, José Antonio 1924- DLB-82

Villegas de Magnón, Leonor
 1876-1955 . . . . .DLB-122

Villemaire, Yolande 1949- DLB-60

Villena, Luis Antonio de 1951- . . .DLB-134

Villiers de l'Isle-Adam, Jean-Marie
 Mathias Philippe-Auguste, Comte de
 1838-1889 . . . . .DLB-123

Villiers, George, Second Duke
of Buckingham 1628-1687 ...... DLB-80

Vine Press DLB-112

Viorst, Judith ?- DLB-52

Viramontes, Helena María
1954- DLB-122

Vischer, Friedrich Theodor
1807-1887 .... DLB-133

Vivanco, Luis Felipe 1907-1975 .... DLB-108

Viviani, Cesare 1947- DLB-128

Vizetelly and Company DLB-106

Voaden, Herman 1903- DLB-88

Voigt, Ellen Bryant 1943- DLB-120

Vojnović, Ivo 1857-1929 .... DLB-147

Volkoff, Vladimir 1932- DLB-83

Volland, P. F., Company DLB-46

von der Grün, Max 1926- DLB-75

Vonnegut, Kurt
1922- DLB-2, 8; Y-80; DS-3

Voranc, Prežihov 1893-1950 ...... DLB-147

Voß, Johann Heinrich 1751-1826 ... DLB-90

Vroman, Mary Elizabeth
circa 1924-1967 .... DLB-33

W

Wace, Robert ("Maistre")
circa 1100-circa 1175 .... DLB-146

Wackenroder, Wilhelm Heinrich
1773-1798 .... DLB-90

Wackernagel, Wilhelm
1806-1869 .... DLB-133

Waddington, Miriam 1917- DLB-68

Wade, Henry 1887-1969 .... DLB-77

Wagenknecht, Edward 1900- DLB-103

Wagner, Heinrich Leopold
1747-1779 .... DLB-94

Wagner, Henry R. 1862-1957 .... DLB-140

Wagner, Richard 1813-1883 .... DLB-129

Wagoner, David 1926- DLB-5

Wah, Fred 1939- DLB-60

Waiblinger, Wilhelm 1804-1830 .... DLB-90

Wain, John 1925- DLB-15, 27, 139

Wainwright, Jeffrey 1944- DLB-40

Waite, Peirce and Company DLB-49

Wakoski, Diane 1937- DLB-5

Walahfrid Strabo circa 808-849 .... DLB-148

Walck, Henry Z. DLB-46

Walcott, Derek 1930- DLB-117; Y-81

Waldman, Anne 1945- DLB-16

Walker, Alice 1944- DLB-6, 33, 143

Walker, George F. 1947- DLB-60

Walker, Joseph A. 1935- DLB-38

Walker, Margaret 1915- DLB-76

Walker, Ted 1934- DLB-40

Walker and Company DLB-49

Walker, Evans and Cogswell
Company DLB-49

Walker, John Brisben 1847-1931 .... DLB-79

Wallace, Dewitt 1889-1981 and
Lila Acheson Wallace
1889-1984 ....DLB-137

Wallace, Edgar 1875-1932 .... DLB-70

Wallace, Lila Acheson (see Wallace, Dewitt,
and Lila Acheson Wallace)

Wallant, Edward Lewis
1926-1962 ....DLB-2, 28, 143

Waller, Edmund 1606-1687 .... DLB-126

Walpole, Horace 1717-1797 ....DLB-39, 104

Walpole, Hugh 1884-1941 .... DLB-34

Walrond, Eric 1898-1966 .... DLB-51

Walser, Martin 1927- DLB-75, 124

Walser, Robert 1878-1956 .... DLB-66

Walsh, Ernest 1895-1926 ....DLB-4, 45

Walsh, Robert 1784-1859 .... DLB-59

Waltharius circa 825 .... DLB-148

Walters, Henry 1848-1931 .... DLB-140

Walther von der Vogelweide
circa 1170-circa 1230 .... DLB-138

Walton, Izaak 1593-1683 .... DLB-151

Wambaugh, Joseph 1937- DLB-6; Y-83

Waniek, Marilyn Nelson 1946- ...DLB-120

Warburton, William 1698-1779 .... DLB-104

Ward, Aileen 1919- DLB-111

Ward, Artemus (see Browne, Charles Farrar)

Ward, Arthur Henry Sarsfield
(see Rohmer, Sax)

Ward, Douglas Turner 1930- ...DLB-7, 38

Ward, Lynd 1905-1985 .... DLB-22

Ward, Lock and Company DLB-106

Ward, Mrs. Humphry 1851-1920 .... DLB-18

Ward, Nathaniel circa 1578-1652 .... DLB-24

Ward, Theodore 1902-1983 .... DLB-76

Wardle, Ralph 1909-1988 .... DLB-103

Ware, William 1797-1852 .... DLB-1

Warne, Frederick, and
Company [U.S.] DLB-49

Warne, Frederick, and
Company [U.K.] DLB-106

Warner, Charles Dudley
1829-1900 ....DLB-64

Warner, Rex 1905- DLB-15

Warner, Susan Bogert
1819-1885 .... DLB-3, 42

Warner, Sylvia Townsend
1893-1978 .... DLB-34, 139

Warner Books DLB-46

Warr, Bertram 1917-1943 ....DLB-88

Warren, John Byrne Leicester (see De Tabley,
Lord)

Warren, Lella 1899-1982 .... Y-83

Warren, Mercy Otis 1728-1814 ......DLB-31

Warren, Robert Penn
1905-1989 .... DLB-2, 48; Y-80, 89

Die Wartburgkrieg
circa 1230-circa 1280 ....DLB-138

Warton, Joseph 1722-1800 .... DLB-104, 109

Warton, Thomas 1728-1790 ... DLB-104, 109

Washington, George 1732-1799 ......DLB-31

Wassermann, Jakob 1873-1934 ......DLB-66

Wasson, David Atwood 1823-1887 ....DLB-1

Waterhouse, Keith 1929- DLB-13, 15

Waterman, Andrew 1940- DLB-40

Waters, Frank 1902- Y-86

Waters, Michael 1949- DLB-120

Watkins, Tobias 1780-1855 ....DLB-73

Watkins, Vernon 1906-1967 ....DLB-20

Watmough, David 1926- DLB-53

Watson, James Wreford (see Wreford, James)

Watson, Sheila 1909- DLB-60

Watson, Thomas 1545?-1592 ....DLB-132

Watson, Wilfred 1911- DLB-60

Watt, W. J., and Company DLB-46

Watterson, Henry 1840-1921 ....DLB-25

Watts, Alan 1915-1973 ....DLB-16

Watts, Franklin [publishing house] ...DLB-46

Watts, Isaac 1674-1748 ....DLB-95

Waugh, Auberon 1939- DLB-14

Waugh, Evelyn 1903-1966 ....DLB-15

Way and Williams DLB-49

Wayman, Tom 1945- DLB-53

Weatherly, Tom 1942- DLB-41

Weaver, Gordon 1937- DLB-130

Weaver, Robert 1921- DLB-88

Webb, Frank J. ?-? DLB-50

Webb, James Watson 1802-1884 .....DLB-43

Webb, Mary 1881-1927 ....DLB-34

Webb, Phyllis 1927- DLB-53

Webb, Walter Prescott 1888-1963 ...DLB-17

Webbe, William ?-1591 ....DLB-132

Webster, Augusta 1837-1894 ....DLB-35

Webster, Charles L.,
    and Company DLB-49

Webster, John
    1579 or 1580-1634? DLB-58

Webster, Noah
    1758-1843 .... DLB-1, 37, 42, 43, 73

Wedekind, Frank 1864-1918 ....DLB-118

Weeks, Edward Augustus, Jr.
    1898-1989 ....DLB-137

Weems, Mason Locke
    1759-1825 .... DLB-30, 37, 42

Weerth, Georg 1822-1856 ....DLB-129

Weidenfeld and Nicolson DLB-112

Weidman, Jerome 1913- DLB-28

Weigl, Bruce 1949- DLB-120

Weinbaum, Stanley Grauman
    1902-1935 ....DLB-8

Weintraub, Stanley 1929- DLB-111

Weisenborn, Gunther
    1902-1969 ....DLB-69, 124

Weiß, Ernst 1882-1940 ....DLB-81

Weiss, John 1818-1879 ....DLB-1

Weiss, Peter 1916-1982 ....DLB-69, 124

Weiss, Theodore 1916- DLB-5

Weisse, Christian Felix 1726-1804 ...DLB-97

Weitling, Wilhelm 1808-1871 ......DLB-129

Welch, Lew 1926-1971? DLB-16

Weldon, Fay 1931- DLB-14

Wellek, René 1903- DLB-63

Wells, Carolyn 1862-1942 ....DLB-11

Wells, Charles Jeremiah
    circa 1800-1879 ....DLB-32

Wells, Gabriel 1862-1946 ....DLB-140

Wells, H. G. 1866-1946 ....DLB-34, 70

Wells, Robert 1947- DLB-40

Wells-Barnett, Ida B. 1862-1931 ....DLB-23

Welty, Eudora
    1909- DLB-2, 102, 143; Y-87; DS-12

Wendell, Barrett 1855-1921 ....DLB-71

Wentworth, Patricia 1878-1961 .....DLB-77

Werfel, Franz 1890-1945 ....DLB-81, 124

The Werner Company DLB-49

Werner, Zacharias 1768-1823 ....DLB-94

Wersba, Barbara 1932- DLB-52

Wescott, Glenway 1901- DLB-4, 9, 102

Wesker, Arnold 1932- DLB-13

Wesley, Charles 1707-1788 ....DLB-95

Wesley, John 1703-1791 ....DLB-104

Wesley, Richard 1945- DLB-38

Wessels, A., and Company DLB-46

Wessobrunner Gebet
    circa 787-815 ....DLB-148

West, Anthony 1914-1988 ....DLB-15

West, Dorothy 1907- DLB-76

West, Jessamyn 1902-1984 .....DLB-6; Y-84

West, Mae 1892-1980 ....DLB-44

West, Nathanael 1903-1940 ....DLB-4, 9, 28

West, Paul 1930- DLB-14

West, Rebecca 1892-1983 .....DLB-36; Y-83

West and Johnson DLB-49

Western Publishing Company DLB-46

The Westminster Review 1824-1914 ...DLB-110

Wetherald, Agnes Ethelwyn
    1857-1940 ....DLB-99

Wetherell, Elizabeth
    (see Warner, Susan Bogert)

Wetzel, Friedrich Gottlob
    1779-1819 ....DLB-90

Weyman, Stanley J. 1855-1928 .....DLB-141

Wezel, Johann Karl 1747-1819 ......DLB-94

Whalen, Philip 1923- DLB-16

Whalley, George 1915-1983 ....DLB-88

Wharton, Edith
    1862-1937 ....DLB-4, 9, 12, 78

Wharton, William 1920s?- Y-80

What's Really Wrong With Bestseller
    Lists Y-84

Wheatley, Dennis Yates
    1897-1977 ....DLB-77

Wheatley, Phillis
    circa 1754-1784 ....DLB-31, 50

Wheeler, Charles Stearns
    1816-1843 .... DLB-1

Wheeler, Monroe 1900-1988 ....DLB-4

Wheelock, John Hall 1886-1978 .....DLB-45

Wheelwright, John
    circa 1592-1679 ....DLB-24

Wheelwright, J. B. 1897-1940 ....DLB-45

Whetstone, Colonel Pete
    (see Noland, C. F. M.)

Whetstone, George 1550-1587 .....DLB-136

Whicher, Stephen E. 1915-1961 ....DLB-111

Whipple, Edwin Percy
    1819-1886 ....DLB-1, 64

Whitaker, Alexander 1585-1617 .....DLB-24

Whitaker, Daniel K. 1801-1881 ......DLB-73

Whitcher, Frances Miriam
    1814-1852 ....DLB-11

White, Andrew 1579-1656 ....DLB-24

White, Andrew Dickson
    1832-1918 ....DLB-47

White, E. B. 1899-1985 ....DLB-11, 22

White, Edgar B. 1947- DLB-38

White, Ethel Lina 1887-1944 ....DLB-77

White, Henry Kirke 1785-1806 ......DLB-96

White, Horace 1834-1916 ....DLB-23

White, Phyllis Dorothy James
    (see James, P. D.)

White, Richard Grant 1821-1885 ....DLB-64

White, Walter 1893-1955 ....DLB-51

White, William, and Company DLB-49

White, William Allen
    1868-1944 ....DLB-9, 25

White, William Anthony Parker (see Boucher,
    Anthony)

White, William Hale (see Rutherford, Mark)

Whitechurch, Victor L.
    1868-1933 ....DLB-70

Whitehead, Alfred North
    1861-1947 ....DLB-100

Whitehead, James 1936- Y-81

Whitehead, William
    1715-1785 ....DLB-84, 109

Whitfield, James Monroe
    1822-1871 ....DLB-50

Whitgift, John circa 1533-1604 .....DLB-132

Smith, W. H., and Son DLB-106

Whiting, John 1917-1963 ....DLB-13

Whiting, Samuel 1597-1679 ....DLB-24

Whitlock, Brand 1869-1934 ....DLB-12

Whitman, Albert, and Company DLB-46

Whitman, Albery Allson
    1851-1901 ....DLB-50

Whitman, Alden 1913-1990 ....Y-91

Whitman, Sarah Helen (Power)
1803-1878 ....DLB-1

Whitman, Walt 1819-1892 .... DLB-3, 64

Whitman Publishing Company DLB-46

Whitney, Geoffrey
1548 or 1552?-1601 .... DLB-136

Whitney, Isabella
flourished 1566-1573 .... DLB-136

Whitney, John Hay 1904-1982 ..... DLB-127

Whittemore, Reed 1919- DLB-5

Whittier, John Greenleaf 1807-1892 ...DLB-1

Whittlesey House DLB-46

Who Runs American Literature? Y-94

Wideman, John Edgar
1941- DLB-33, 143

Widener, Harry Elkins 1885-1912 ....DLB-140

Wiebe, Rudy 1934- DLB-60

Wiechert, Ernst 1887-1950 .... DLB-56

Wied, Martina 1882-1957 .... DLB-85

Wieland, Christoph Martin
1733-1813 .... DLB-97

Wienbarg, Ludolf 1802-1872 ...... DLB-133

Wieners, John 1934- DLB-16

Wier, Ester 1910- DLB-52

Wiesel, Elie 1928- DLB-83; Y-87

Wiggin, Kate Douglas 1856-1923 ... DLB-42

Wigglesworth, Michael 1631-1705 ... DLB-24

Wilbrandt, Adolf 1837-1911 .... DLB-129

Wilbur, Richard 1921- DLB-5

Wild, Peter 1940- DLB-5

Wilde, Oscar
1854-1900 ....DLB-10, 19, 34, 57, 141

Wilde, Richard Henry
1789-1847 .... DLB-3, 59

Wilde, W. A., Company DLB-49

Wilder, Billy 1906- DLB-26

Wilder, Laura Ingalls 1867-1957 .... DLB-22

Wilder, Thornton 1897-1975 .... DLB-4, 7, 9

Wildgans, Anton 1881-1932 ...... DLB-118

Wiley, Bell Irvin 1906-1980 .... DLB-17

Wiley, John, and Sons DLB-49

Wilhelm, Kate 1928- DLB-8

Wilkes, George 1817-1885 .... DLB-79

Wilkinson, Anne 1910-1961 .... DLB-88

Wilkinson, Sylvia 1940- Y-86

Wilkinson, William Cleaver
1833-1920 .... DLB-71

Willard, L. [publishing house] DLB-49

Willard, Nancy 1936- DLB-5, 52

Willard, Samuel 1640-1707 .... DLB-24

William of Auvergne 1190-1249 .... DLB-115

William of Conches
circa 1090-circa 1154 .... DLB-115

William of Ockham
circa 1285-1347 .... DLB-115

William of Sherwood
1200/1205 - 1266/1271 .... DLB-115

The William Chavrat American Fiction
Collection at the Ohio State University
Libraries Y-92

Williams, A., and Company DLB-49

Williams, Ben Ames 1889-1953 .... DLB-102

Williams, C. K. 1936- DLB-5

Williams, Chancellor 1905- DLB-76

Williams, Charles 1886-1945 ...... DLB-100

Williams, Denis 1923- DLB-117

Williams, Emlyn 1905- DLB-10, 77

Williams, Garth 1912- DLB-22

Williams, George Washington
1849-1891 .... DLB-47

Williams, Heathcote 1941- DLB-13

Williams, Hugo 1942- DLB-40

Williams, Isaac 1802-1865 .... DLB-32

Williams, Joan 1928- DLB-6

Williams, John A. 1925- DLB-2, 33

Williams, John E. 1922- DLB-6

Williams, Jonathan 1929- DLB-5

Williams, Miller 1930- DLB-105

Williams, Raymond 1921- DLB-14

Williams, Roger circa 1603-1683 .... DLB-24

Williams, Samm-Art 1946- DLB-38

Williams, Sherley Anne 1944- DLB-41

Williams, T. Harry 1909-1979 ..... DLB-17

Williams, Tennessee
1911-1983 .... DLB-7; Y-83; DS-4

Williams, Valentine 1883-1946 ..... DLB-77

Williams, William Appleman
1921- DLB-17

Williams, William Carlos
1883-1963 .... DLB-4, 16, 54, 86

Williams, Wirt 1921- DLB-6

Williams Brothers DLB-49

Williamson, Jack 1908- DLB-8

Willingham, Calder Baynard, Jr.
1922- DLB-2, 44

Williram of Ebersberg
circa 1020-1085 .... DLB-148

Willis, Nathaniel Parker
1806-1867 .... DLB-3, 59, 73, 74

Willkomm, Ernst 1810-1886 ....DLB-133

Wilmer, Clive 1945- DLB-40

Wilson, A. N. 1950- DLB-14

Wilson, Angus 1913-1991 ...... DLB-15, 139

Wilson, Arthur 1595-1652 ....DLB-58

Wilson, Augusta Jane Evans
1835-1909 ....DLB-42

Wilson, Colin 1931- DLB-14

Wilson, Edmund 1895-1972 ....DLB-63

Wilson, Ethel 1888-1980 ....DLB-68

Wilson, Harriet E. Adams
1828?-1863? DLB-50

Wilson, Harry Leon 1867-1939 ....DLB-9

Wilson, John 1588-1667 ....DLB-24

Wilson, John 1785-1854 ....DLB-110

Wilson, Lanford 1937- DLB-7

Wilson, Margaret 1882-1973 ....DLB-9

Wilson, Michael 1914-1978 ....DLB-44

Wilson, Mona 1872-1954 ....DLB-149

Wilson, Thomas
1523 or 1524-1581 ....DLB-132

Wilson, Woodrow 1856-1924 ....DLB-47

Wimsatt, William K., Jr.
1907-1975 ....DLB-63

Winchell, Walter 1897-1972 ....DLB-29

Winchester, J. [publishing house] DLB-49

Winckelmann, Johann Joachim
1717-1768 ....DLB-97

Windham, Donald 1920- DLB-6

Wingate, Allan [publishing house] ...DLB-112

Winsloe, Christa 1888-1944 ....DLB-124

Winsor, Justin 1831-1897 ....DLB-47

John C. Winston Company DLB-49

Winters, Yvor 1900-1968 ....DLB-48

Winthrop, John 1588-1649 ...... DLB-24, 30

Winthrop, John, Jr. 1606-1676 ....DLB-24

Wirt, William 1772-1834 ....DLB-37

Wise, John 1652-1725 ....DLB-24

Wiseman, Adele 1928- DLB-88

Wishart and Company DLB-112

Wisner, George 1812-1849 ....DLB-43

Wister, Owen 1860-1938 .... DLB-9, 78

Wither, George 1588-1667 ....DLB-121

Witherspoon, John 1723-1794 . . . . DLB-31

Withrow, William Henry 1839-1908 . . DLB-99

Wittig, Monique 1935- DLB-83

Wodehouse, P. G. 1881-1975 . . . . DLB-34

Wohmann, Gabriele 1932- DLB-75

Woiwode, Larry 1941- DLB-6

Wolcot, John 1738-1819 . . . . DLB-109

Wolcott, Roger 1679-1767 . . . . DLB-24

Wolf, Christa 1929- DLB-75

Wolf, Friedrich 1888-1953 . . . . DLB-124

Wolfe, Gene 1931- DLB-8

Wolfe, Thomas
1900-1938 . . . . . . DLB-9, 102; Y-85; DS-2

Wolff, Helen 1906-1994 . . . . Y-94

Wolff, Tobias 1945- DLB-130

Wolfram von Eschenbach
circa 1170-after 1220 . . . . DLB-138

Wolfram von Eschenbach's *Parzival*:
Prologue and Book 3 . . . . DLB-138

Wollstonecraft, Mary
1759-1797 . . . . DLB-39, 104

Wondratschek, Wolf 1943- DLB-75

Wood, Benjamin 1820-1900 . . . . DLB-23

Wood, Charles 1932- DLB-13

Wood, Mrs. Henry 1814-1887 . . . . . . DLB-18

Wood, Joanna E. 1867-1927 . . . . DLB-92

Wood, Samuel [publishing house] DLB-49

Wood, William ?-? DLB-24

Woodberry, George Edward
1855-1930 . . . . DLB-71, 103

Woodbridge, Benjamin 1622-1684 . . . DLB-24

Woodcock, George 1912- DLB-88

Woodhull, Victoria C. 1838-1927 . . . . DLB-79

Woodmason, Charles circa 1720-? . . . DLB-31

Woodress, Jr., James Leslie
1916- DLB-111

Woodson, Carter G. 1875-1950 . . . . . DLB-17

Woodward, C. Vann 1908- DLB-17

Woolf, David (see Maddow, Ben)

Woolf, Leonard
1880-1969 . . . . DLB-100; DS-10

Woolf, Virginia
1882-1941 . . . . DLB-36, 100; DS-10

Woolf, Virginia, "The New Biography," *New York Herald Tribune*, 30 October 1927
. . . . DLB-149

Woollcott, Alexander 1887-1943 . . . . . DLB-29

Woolman, John 1720-1772 . . . . DLB-31

Woolner, Thomas 1825-1892 . . . . DLB-35

Woolsey, Sarah Chauncy
1835-1905 . . . . DLB-42

Woolson, Constance Fenimore
1840-1894 . . . . DLB-12, 74

Worcester, Joseph Emerson
1784-1865 . . . . DLB-1

Wordsworth, Dorothy
1771-1855 . . . . DLB-107

Wordsworth, Elizabeth
1840-1932 . . . . DLB-98

Wordsworth, William
1770-1850 . . . . DLB-93, 107

The Works of the Rev. John Witherspoon
(1800-1801) [excerpts] DLB-31

A World Chronology of Important Science
Fiction Works (1818-1979) DLB-8

World Publishing Company DLB-46

Worthington, R., and Company DLB-49

Wotton, Sir Henry 1568-1639 . . . . . DLB-121

Wouk, Herman 1915- Y-82

Wreford, James 1915- DLB-88

Wrenn, John Henry 1841-1911 . . . . DLB-140

Wright, C. D. 1949- DLB-120

Wright, Charles 1935- Y-82

Wright, Charles Stevenson 1932- . . . DLB-33

Wright, Frances 1795-1852 . . . . DLB-73

Wright, Harold Bell 1872-1944 . . . . . . DLB-9

Wright, James 1927-1980 . . . . DLB-5

Wright, Jay 1935- DLB-41

Wright, Louis B. 1899-1984 . . . . DLB-17

Wright, Richard
1908-1960 . . . . DLB-76, 102; DS-2

Wright, Richard B. 1937- DLB-53

Wright, Sarah Elizabeth 1928- DLB-33

Writers and Politics: 1871-1918,
by Ronald Gray DLB-66

Writers and their Copyright Holders:
the WATCH project Y-94

Writers' Forum Y-85

Writing for the Theatre, by
Harold Pinter DLB-13

Wroth, Lady Mary 1587-1653 . . . . . DLB-121

Wyatt, Sir Thomas
circa 1503-1542 . . . . DLB-132

Wycherley, William 1641-1715 . . . . . DLB-80

Wyclif, John
circa 1335-31 December 1384 . . DLB-146

Wylie, Elinor 1885-1928 . . . . DLB-9, 45

Wylie, Philip 1902-1971 . . . . DLB-9

Wyllie, John Cook 1908-1968 . . . . . . DLB-140

Y

Yates, Dornford 1885-1960 . . . . DLB-77

Yates, J. Michael 1938- DLB-60

Yates, Richard 1926-1992 . . . DLB-2; Y-81, 92

Yavorov, Peyo 1878-1914 . . . . DLB-147

Yearsley, Ann 1753-1806 . . . . DLB-109

Yeats, William Butler
1865-1939 . . . . DLB-10, 19, 98

Yep, Laurence 1948- DLB-52

Yerby, Frank 1916-1991 . . . . DLB-76

Yezierska, Anzia 1885-1970 . . . . DLB-28

Yolen, Jane 1939- DLB-52

Yonge, Charlotte Mary 1823-1901 . . . DLB-18

The York Cycle
circa 1376-circa 1569 . . . . DLB-146

A Yorkshire Tragedy DLB-58

Yoseloff, Thomas
[publishing house] DLB-46

Young, Al 1939- DLB-33

Young, Edward 1683-1765 . . . . DLB-95

Young, Stark 1881-1963 . . . . DLB-9, 102

Young, Waldeman 1880-1938 . . . . DLB-26

Young, William [publishing house] . . . DLB-49

Yourcenar, Marguerite
1903-1987 . . . . DLB-72; Y-88

"You've Never Had It So Good," Gusted by
"Winds of Change": British Fiction in the
1950s, 1960s, and After DLB-14

Yovkov, Yordan 1880-1937 . . . . DLB-147

Z

Zachariä, Friedrich Wilhelm
1726-1777 . . . . DLB-97

Zamora, Bernice 1938- DLB-82

Zand, Herbert 1923-1970 . . . . DLB-85

Zangwill, Israel 1864-1926 . . . . . . DLB-10, 135

Zanzotto, Andrea 1921- DLB-128

Zapata Olivella, Manuel 1920- DLB-113

Zebra Books DLB-46

Zebrowski, George 1945- DLB-8

Zech, Paul 1881-1946 . . . . DLB-56

Zeidner, Lisa 1955- DLB-120

Zelazny, Roger 1937- DLB-8

Zenger, John Peter 1697-1746 . . . . DLB-24, 43

Zieber, G. B., and Company DLB-49

Zieroth, Dale 1946- DLB-60

Zimmer, Paul 1934- DLB-5

Zindel, Paul 1936- DLB-7, 52

Zola, Emile 1840-1902 .... DLB-123

Zolotow, Charlotte 1915- DLB-52

Zschokke, Heinrich 1771-1848 ...... DLB-94

Zubly, John Joachim 1724-1781 ..... DLB-31

Zu-Bolton II, Ahmos 1936- DLB-41

Zuckmayer, Carl 1896-1977 ....DLB-56, 124

Zukofsky, Louis 1904-1978 ....DLB-5

Župančič, Oton 1878-1949 ....DLB-147

zur Mühlen, Hermynia 1883-1951 ....DLB-56

Zweig, Arnold 1887-1968 ....DLB-66

Zweig, Stefan 1881-1942 .... DLB-81, 118

ISBN 0-8103-5705-4

(Continued from front endsheets)

117 Twentieth-Century Caribbean and Black African Writers, First Series, edited by Bernth Lindfors and Reinhard Sander (1992)

118 Twentieth-Century German Dramatists, 1889-1918, edited by Wolfgang D. Elfe and James Hardin (1992)

119 Nineteenth-Century French Fiction Writers: Romanticism and Realism, 1800-1860, edited by Catharine Savage Brosman (1992)

120 American Poets Since World War II, Third Series, edited by R. S. Gwynn (1992)

121 Seventeenth-Century British Nondramatic Poets, First Series, edited by M. Thomas Hester (1992)

122 Chicano Writers, Second Series, edited by Francisco A. Lomelí and Carl R. Shirley (1992)

123 Nineteenth-Century French Fiction Writers: Naturalism and Beyond, 1860-1900, edited by Catharine Savage Brosman (1992)

124 Twentieth-Century German Dramatists, 1919-1992, edited by Wolfgang D. Elfe and James Hardin (1992)

125 Twentieth-Century Caribbean and Black African Writers, Second Series, edited by Bernth Lindfors and Reinhard Sander (1993)

126 Seventeenth-Century British Nondramatic Poets, Second Series, edited by M. Thomas Hester (1993)

127 American Newspaper Publishers, 1950-1990, edited by Perry J. Ashley (1993)

128 Twentieth-Century Italian Poets, Second Series, edited by Giovanna Wedel De Stasio, Glauco Cambon, and Antonio Illiano (1993)

129 Nineteenth-Century German Writers, 1841-1900, edited by James Hardin and Siegfried Mews (1993)

130 American Short-Story Writers Since World War II, edited by Patrick Meanor (1993)

131 Seventeenth-Century British Nondramatic Poets, Third Series, edited by M. Thomas Hester (1993)

132 Sixteenth-Century British Nondramatic Writers, First Series, edited by David A. Richardson (1993)

133 Nineteenth-Century German Writers to 1840, edited by James Hardin and Siegfried Mews (1993)

134 Twentieth-Century Spanish Poets, Second Series, edited by Jerry Phillips Winfield (1994)

135 British Short-Fiction Writers, 1880-1914: The Realist Tradition, edited by William B. Thesing (1994)

136 Sixteenth-Century British Nondramatic Writers, Second Series, edited by David A. Richardson (1994)

137 American Magazine Journalists, 1900-1960, Second Series, edited by Sam G. Riley (1994)

138 German Writers and Works of the High Middle Ages: 1170-1280, edited by James Hardin and Will Hasty (1994)

139 British Short-Fiction Writers, 1945-1980, edited by Dean Baldwin (1994)

140 American Book-Collectors and Bibliographers, First Series, edited by Joseph Rosenblum (1994)

141 British Children's Writers, 1880-1914, edited by Laura M. Zaidman (1994)

142 Eighteenth-Century British Literary Biographers, edited by Steven Serafin (1994)

143 American Novelists Since World War II, Third Series, edited by James R. Giles and Wanda H. Giles (1994)

144 Nineteenth-Century British Literary Biographers, edited by Steven Serafin (1994)

145 Modern Latin-American Fiction Writers, Second Series, edited by William Luis and Ann González (1994)

146 Old and Middle English Literature, edited by Jeffrey Helterman and Jerome Mitchell (1994)

147 South Slavic Writers Before World War II, edited by Vasa D. Mihailovich (1994)

148 German Writers and Works of the Early Middle Ages: 800-1170, edited by Will Hasty and James Hardin (1994)

149 Late Nineteenth- and Early Twentieth-Century British Literary Biographers, edited by Steven Serafin (1995)

150 Early Modern Russian Writers, Late Seventeenth and Eighteenth Centuries, edited by Marcus C. Levitt (1995)

151 British Prose Writers of the Early Seventeenth Century, edited by Clayton D. Lein (1995)

Documentary Series

1 Sherwood Anderson, Willa Cather, John Dos Passos, Theodore Dreiser, F. Scott Fitzgerald, Ernest Hemingway, Sinclair Lewis, edited by Margaret A. Van Antwerp (1982)

2 James Gould Cozzens, James T. Farrell, William Faulkner, John O'Hara, John Steinbeck, Thomas Wolfe, Richard Wright, edited by Margaret A. Van Antwerp (1982)

3 Saul Bellow, Jack Kerouac, Norman Mailer, Vladimir Nabokov, John Updike, Kurt Vonnegut, edited by Mary Bruccoli (1983)

4 Tennessee Williams, edited by Margaret A. Van Antwerp and Sally Johns (1984)

5 American Transcendentalists, edited by Joel Myerson (1988)

6 Hardboiled Mystery Writers: Raymond Chandler, Dashiell Hammett, Ross Macdonald, edited by Matthew J. Bruccoli and Richard Layman (1989)

7 Modern American Poets: James Dickey, Robert Frost, Marianne Moore, edited by Karen L. Rood (1989)

8 The Black Aesthetic Movement, edited by Jeffrey Louis Decker (1991)

9 American Writers of the Vietnam War: W. D. Ehrhart, Larry Heinemann, Tim O'Brien, Walter McDonald, John M. Del Vecchio, edited by Ronald Baughman (1991)

10 The Bloomsbury Group, edited by Edward L. Bishop (1992)

11 American Proletarian Culture: The Twenties and The Thirties, edited by Jon Christian Suggs (1993)

12 Southern Women Writers: Flannery O'Connor, Katherine Anne Porter, Eudora Welty, edited by Mary Ann Wimsatt and Karen L. Rood (1994)